TRACING THE
RIFLE
VOLUNTEERS

TRACING THE
RIFLE
VOLUNTEERS
1859–1908

A GUIDE FOR MILITARY AND
FAMILY HISTORIANS

RAY WESTLAKE

Pen & Sword
FAMILY HISTORY

First published in Great Britain in 2010 by
Pen & Sword Family History
an imprint of
Pen & Sword Books Ltd
47 Church Street
Barnsley
South Yorkshire
S70 2AS

ISBN 978 1 84884 211 3

A CIP catalogue record for this book is
available from the British Library

Typeset in Ehrhardt
by S L Menzies-Earl

Printed and bound in England
by MPG Books in the UK

Pen & Sword Books Ltd incorporates the imprints of
Pen & Sword Aviation, Pen & Sword Maritime,
Pen & Sword Military, Wharncliffe Local History, Pen & Sword Select,
Pen & Sword Military Classics, Leo Cooper, Remember When,
Seaforth Publishing and Frontline Publishing

For a complete list of Pen & Sword titles please contact
PEN & SWORD BOOKS LIMITED
47 Church Street, Barnsley, South Yorkshire, S70 2AS, England
E-mail: enquiries@pen-and-sword.co.uk
Website: www.pen-and-sword.co.uk

Contents

List of Plates

Introduction

The intention of this work is to put on record the various Rifle Volunteer Corps (RVC) that were created throughout England, Scotland and Wales as a result of the formation in 1859 of the Volunteer Force. Due to the political situation at the time, there were no Volunteer Corps raised in Ireland. Rifle Volunteers were the Infantry of the Volunteer Movement, which also included Mounted Troops (not the Yeomanry, which was a separate force), Artillery, Engineers and, later on, Medical and Army Service Corps units.

Listed under the counties in which they were raised and numbered are the RVC that were accepted by the War Office. Each has the date of its formation, location and, where applicable, the higher formation into which it was placed for administrative purposes – the so-called administrative battalions. Any changes in designation, organization, disbandments or amalgamations have been recorded through to 1908 and transfer to the Territorial Force. In cases where more than one RVC held the same number this has been indicated, eg, 1st (1859–80) or 1st (1880–1908). There were also a small number of formations raised and designated as 'Volunteer Battalions' (VB) and these will be found after the numbered RVC of their county. Cadet units have been dealt with within the RVC to which they were affiliated.

The official formation date of a corps is that on which its offer of service was accepted by the Secretary of State for War. However, in the vast majority of cases these 'letters of acceptance' cannot be traced and here the date of the commission issued to the unit's first officer has been used. These, in most cases, only differ from the acceptance date by a few weeks, or even days.

When a corps becomes part of another its subsequent records will be covered within those of the unit into which is has been 'absorbed', 'merged', 'consolidated' or 'amalgamated'.

The location given ('formed in' or 'raised in') for each corps is that of its headquarters. Recruiting, however, was often carried out in the surrounding areas and detachments of the main corps were also to be found in nearby towns and villages. In cases where a corps consisted of more than one company the location given is again that of its main headquarters. Company locations, if different from those of corps headquarters are, where known, given.

It will be seen that the RVC of several of the smaller counties were to be included in the admin battalions of others. The development of these units will be recorded under their own county until such times that, due to consolidation of their battalion as a new corps, they lose their county number and become a lettered (numbers were sometimes used prior to 1880) company within the new formation. From this point subsequent changes (when known) are noted in the records of the county to which the new corps belongs. An example of this is Radnorshire, whose RVC were included in the 1st Herefordshire Admin Battalion. When this battalion was consolidated as the new 1st Herefordshire RVC in 1880, the 1st and 2nd Radnorshire lost their individual numbers and county reference and from then on were known as 'I' and 'K' Companies of the 1st Herefordshire RVC. Therefore any further changes regarding these companies will be seen under 1st Herefordshire. On occasion, consolidated admin battalions included more than one county name within their titles. For example; in 1880 the Clackmannanshire Admin Battalion, which also included corps from Kinross, became the 1st Clackmannan and Kinross RVC. From here on the post-1880 records of the last-named county will be dealt with in those of the first.

As previously mentioned only RVC recognized by the War Office have been included. In addition to these a number were formed, only to have their offer of service reach no further than the office of the county lord lieutenant. Such units were often in the process of training – even uniformed and badged – but for various reasons did not gain official recognition. These, therefore, are beyond the scope of this book.

Although the primary intention of this book is to provide a checklist of Volunteer Corps, I have, however, included selected references to contemporary events that would have involved, or have been witnessed by, the Volunteer. And, as livings had to be made when not soldiering, I have included (again a selection only) brief details of an area's main sources of employment. For this (outside of the normal scope of a military historian) information I have relied (in the main) on contemporary editions of Cassell's *Gazetteer of Great Britain and Ireland*, town guides, the wonderful *King's England* series by Arthur Mee, *Kelly's Directories* and numerous volumes of *The Buildings of England* and other similar reference works.

Full uniform details, a lifetime's study in their own right, have been omitted from this work. I have, however, noted the colours worn between the years 1880 and 1908 and these appear in the text as, eg, grey/green. When the first colour is anything other than scarlet – grey or green usually – this would apply to both jacket and trousers. In the case of scarlet, however, this would be the jacket colour only. Units wearing scarlet jackets would usually have worn dark blue trousers – Scotland being the exception, where tartan trousers (trews) or kilts were worn. Collars, shoulder-straps, cuffs and piping (the second colour given) were usually different to the rest of the uniform. Therefore: 'grey/green' would indicate an all-grey uniform with green collar, cuffs, piping etc. Scarlet/yellow, on the other hand, would see scarlet jacket with yellow collar, cuffs, etc, worn with dark blue trousers.

Acknowledgements

My sincere thanks to Norman Hurst and Alan Seymour for their help and advice; to Richard Hayes, Ted Molyneux and Alan Seymour for providing photographs from their collections, and to Louis Bannon of Military and Welsh Antiques (Abergavenny and Cardiff) for allowing me to photograph the 'Bulldog' shako badge of the 9th Monmouthshire RVC.

The Rifle Volunteers

Reasons for Formation

It was most probably the Duke of Wellington who was responsible for the formation in 1859 of the Volunteer Force. In a letter to Sir John Burgoyne in 1847 the Duke had made clear his concern regarding this country's national defences. He, at the age of seventy-seven, did not share the general opinion of the government that the United Kingdom was safe from attack. Britain, it was true, had since Waterloo been free from troubles in Europe. And indeed, the several campaigns fought abroad were also far enough away not to render necessary the formation of additional forces to defend these shores. The Duke, however, did not think it sensible to sit back in what he believed was a false sense of security. 'It was time', he said, 'to make provisions for the defence of the country and to take all precautions against invasion. I hope', he went on, 'that the Almighty may protect me from being witness of the tragedy which I cannot persuade my contemporaries to take measures to avert.'

If, as in the days of Napoleon I, home defence was to be supplemented by Volunteers, the Duke's fears were quite understandable. At the time of his letter to Sir John only two units, as far as infantry were concerned, were then in existence. These were the Honourable Artillery Company (later not to be included in the Volunteer Force) and the Royal Victoria Rifles (RVR) who became the 1st Middlesex RVC.

In agreement with the Duke, Barrister and one-time High Sheriff of Radnor, Captain Hans Busk of the RVR later circulated copies of his 1847 letter. Busk's corps had, by 1858, dwindled to just fifty-seven effective men. But, and as a direct result of the action taken, the RVR, by the middle of 1859, would muster no less than 800.

At the same time as Captain Busk was working on behalf of the RVR, others in the country were intent on organizing a Volunteer Force nationwide. A corps had already been sanctioned at Exeter in 1852, and by 1855 the formation of one in Liverpool was well under way. It was not until 1859, however, that the main surge of Volunteers came forward.

Acceptance by the Government

At first the government of the day was not over-keen to see the creation of a part-time army. The idea of 'amateur soldiers' was not appealing, and it was also thought that the establishment of such a system would interfere with the recruiting of the Regular Army. The War Office, however, finally gave way and on 12 May 1859 sanction to form Volunteer Corps throughout the country was given – this authorization being conveyed in a Circular addressed to the lord lieutenants of counties, who were asked to submit any plans they might have.

Formation of Volunteer Corps was to be under the provisions of Act 44, George III, cap. 54, dated 5 June 1804. The main provisions of the 1804 Act were summarized in the 12 May Circular: officers' commissions should be signed by the lord lieutenant; Volunteers could be called out in the case of actual invasion or rebellion; while under arms members of the corps should be subject to military law and while on active service no Volunteer could quit his corps. He could, however, at other times leave after giving fourteen days' notice.

The next Circular concerning the formation of Volunteer Corps was issued on 25 May. Requirements as to standards of drill and discipline were set out, and the establishment of ranges for each corps was advised. It was also suggested in the Circular that Rifle Volunteers should be organized into companies or sub-divisions (half-companies).

The third War Office Circular of 1859 was issued on 13 July and in this the government's requirements regarding arms and training were made clear. Accompanying the Circular was a Memorandum which among other things set out the establishment of each Rifle Corps. A company was to consist of not less than sixty, though not more than one hundred effectives. These were to be officered by one captain, one lieutenant and one ensign. Sub-divisions were to have thirty effectives with one lieutenant and one ensign. Where several companies were raised in the same locality, a battalion could be formed. The requirements here were for eight companies of a total strength of not less than five hundred. In addition to its company officers a battalion could have a lieutenant colonel, a major and the services of an adjutant.

Numbering and Precedence
It was in the Memorandum of 13 July that the subject of precedence was settled. Each arm of the Volunteer Force was to rank more or less along the lines of the Regular Forces. At the time of the Memorandum, RVC (the infantry) were to rank after Artillery Volunteer Corps as these were the only two arms then in existence. Within a short time, however, others were created and the eventual precedence list among the several Volunteer arms read as follows: Light Horse, Artillery, Engineers, Mounted Rifles and Rifles.

The precedence of a corps within its county was indicated by the number allotted to it by the Secretary of State for War. The procedure here was that when the lord lieutenant received an application for the formation of a corps, he would then date it and forward the offer of service on to the War Office. When the Secretary of State for War had satisfied himself that the proposed unit had fulfilled the necessary conditions, he would, according to the date entered on the application by the lord lieutenant, allot the corps its number. The next step was to inform the corps of its acceptance of service by HM the Queen. It is the date of the letter bearing this information that determined an official date of formation. As a rule these dates coincide with the precedence number assigned. On occasion, however, a number was allotted; but due to some special circumstances where reference had to be made to the corps concerned because of some informality in its offer of service, the acceptance date was held up. Very soon after the acceptance of the corps and the assignment of its number, the gazetting of officers was proceeded with. County precedence was settled according to the date on which the first company in the county was formed (see Appendix A).

Higher Organization into Brigades or Battalions
By the beginning of 1860 it was realized by the War Office that due to the unforeseen number of independent companies being formed, some kind of higher organization was necessary. In a Circular issued to lord lieutenants of counties dated 24 March, suggestions for companies to merge, either as consolidated or administrative battalions, were put forward.

A consolidated battalion, the Circular explained, 'applies to a battalion whose constituent companies are drawn from the same town or city.' When such a battalion was formed the corps involved were to lose their individual numbers and continue service either as a numbered or lettered company. It was also laid down that after consolidation the new corps would thereafter be known by the number previously held by its senior company. An example of this procedure can be seen in this work within the Lanarkshire section when at the beginning of 1860 several numbered corps in Glasgow (19th, 23rd, 24th, 28th, 36th and 41st) were consolidated under the title of 19th Lanarkshire RVC.

The administrative battalion in the main catered for corps situated in rural areas. In this case each battalion was designated, eg, 1st Administrative Battalion of Shropshire Rifle Volunteers, and was allotted its own staff and headquarters. The corps included in an admin battalion, unlike those that had consolidated, remained distinct and financially independent units and were permitted to retain their county numbers and titles.

'The object of the formation of an Administrative Battalion', according to a Memorandum dated 4 September 1860, was 'to unite the different corps composing it under one common head, to secure uniformity of drill among them, and afford them the advantage of the instruction and assistance of an adjutant; but it is not intended to interfere with financial arrangements of the separate corps, or with the operation of the respective rules, or to compel them to meet together for battalion drill in ordinary times, except with their own consent.'

In counties where there were insufficient corps to constitute a battalion, these were permitted to join a battalion of one of the neighbouring counties. Admin battalions were also permitted to consolidate if they chose.

Naming and Numbering
Corps were designated, eg, 1st Shropshire Rifle Volunteer Corps, and in the first Regulations published for Volunteers in 1861, special titles in addition to numbers were permitted. The 1861 Regulations also directed that when a corps was disbanded or absorbed into a senior one, its number was to remain vacant.

Closer Links with the Regular Army
By General Regulations and Instructions of 2 July 1873, the United Kingdom was divided into seventy infantry sub-districts. Each was designated as a 'Sub-District Brigade' and to it were allotted for recruiting purposes: two Line battalions (the Regulars), along with the Militia (the Reserves) and Volunteers of a certain area. This was to be the first steps to the closer association of the Volunteers with the Regular Forces.

General Consolidation 1880
Although the proposals of the committee set up in 1878 under the presidency of Viscount Bury (Parliamentary Under-Secretary of State) to look into the organization of the Volunteer Force did not include any material changes in its composition, consolidation of all existing administrative battalions was, however, recommended. It therefore followed that during 1880 this recommendation was carried out and all remaining admin battalions were consolidated. By the practice laid down in 1860, the corps contained within each battalion lost their independent status and became lettered companies of the new large corps. At first each new formation took on the number of its

senior corps, but in counties that had more than one battalion this created a run of numbers with many gaps. By June 1880, however, a general renumbering within each county had commenced and corps were subsequently numbered from 1st on. Only Suffolk, who in 1880 had its RVC organized into two battalions, chose to retain the original numbers (1st and 6th) adopted at the outset. To avoid confusion I have referred to all post-1880 corps by their eventual number.

Further Links with the Regular Army
The Army Reorganizations of 1881 saw the old Sub-Districts formed into Territorial Regiments; better known, perhaps, as 'County Regiments' – Devonshire Regiment, Somerset Light Infantry, Essex Regiment, etc. In then came the former numbered 'Regiments of Foot' as 1st and 2nd battalions, the old Militia following on as 3rd, 4th, etc. The Volunteer Corps, however, who were now to constitute 'Volunteer Battalions' of the new regiments, were to be numbered in a separate sequence. This change in designation, however, was carried out over a period of time with each battalion being notified in General (later Army) Orders. The 1st, 2nd and 3rd Somersetshire RVC would be the first to adopt the new style when, under General Order 261 of October 1882, they became respectively the 1st, 2nd and 3rd Volunteer Battalions Prince Albert's (Somerset Light Infantry). It was by no means all corps that assumed the new 'VB' designations and several, while taking their place in their regiment's Volunteer line-up, chose to retain their RVC titles. These, however, were required to change, eg, from 1st Dumbartonshire Rifle Volunteer Corps to 1st Dumbartonshire Volunteer Rifle Corps in 1891. (See Appendix B).

Volunteer Infantry Brigades
The higher organization of the Volunteer Infantry into brigades commenced in 1888. Nineteen were created under Army Order 314 of July, these to be followed by a further twelve in September (Army Order 408). The number of battalions forming each brigade varied from just three in one case, to seventeen in another. In 1890 (Army Orders 207 and 395) additional brigades were formed and at the same time battalions were distributed on a more even basis. The next change affecting the Volunteer Infantry Brigades occurred in 1906 when under Army Order 130 the total was brought up to forty-four.

War Service
In 1900, and under a Special Army Order dated 2 January, volunteer battalions were called upon to raise companies for active service in South Africa. For each regular battalion serving in the war one company was to be raised from its affiliated Volunteers. These were to consist of 116 all ranks who, in order to surmount the difficulties of the Volunteer Act, had to enlist into the Regular Army for a period of one year or the duration of the war. Such companies were designated, eg, 1st Volunteer Service Company Gordon Highlanders. A separate organization known as the City Imperial Volunteers was also formed within the London area, this taking in the Volunteers from most of Middlesex as well as the capital. As a result, Volunteer Corps, or Volunteer Battalions, as the case may be, received a 'South Africa' battle honour. A date was also included, eg, '1900–02', but this varied according to the period of time the Volunteer contingents had actually served. In the text, if not mentioned, it may be assumed that all Volunteer Corps were represented in South Africa.

Territorial Force 1908
Under the Territorial and Reserve Forces Act of 1907, the Volunteer Force ceased to exist on 31 March 1908. On the following day, 1 April, the Territorial Force (TF) was born and the old Volunteers invited to enlist. The change was not a popular one with the Volunteers as the new system often necessitated the reorganization, and in some cases, disbandment of many of the existing companies. Some infantry battalions were even required to convert to artillery or some other arm of service. The new force was soon established, however, and the majority of battalions were to transfer en bloc. The new TF battalions were, unlike those of the Volunteers, who had their own sequence, numbered on from the Special Reserve.

Cadet Corps
Cadet units, which were to be formed in connection with Volunteer Corps or administrative battalions, were first sanctioned in *Volunteer Regulations* for 1863. Article 279 directed that any cadet corps raised should consist of boys twelve years of age and upwards, these to be officered by gentlemen holding honorary commissions only. There were, however, numerous units formed prior to 1863 – such organizations as the Shrewsbury School Drill Company are known to have existed as early as 1860. Cadet corps were normally organized into companies of not less than thirty boys. These were then affiliated to individual corps or administrative battalions and took precedence with them when on parade.

Recruiting of boys for cadet corps was, in the main, concentrated among the public schools of the day. Youths from all walks of life, however, were involved and many units were to be formed from the junior staff of factories, warehouses and large businesses – the Postal Telegraph Messengers Cadet Corps from the Derby Post Office, for example.

In June 1886 authority was given for the formation of cadet battalions consisting of four companies. These, although linked to a line regiment, were completely independent of any Volunteer Corps.

The contribution made by public schools to the Volunteer Movement is well known. Not only did they raise cadet corps, but some schools such as Eton, Harrow and Rugby also provided Volunteer Corps in their own right. In 1908, and upon the formation of the Territorial Force, all cadet corps formed by schools were invited to join the newly created Officers Training Corps (OTC). The vast majority did so and from then on came under the direct authority of the War Office. At the same time all affiliations to Volunteer Corps (now TF battalions) ceased. The non-school corps, and those schools choosing to remain part of the Territorial Force, were from 1908 recorded in the *Army List* under the heading 'Cadet Companies and Corps'. This section, which appeared immediately after the OTC, was not seen after 1913, by which time all units receiving recognition by the TF had been included once again with their parent unit.

The Rifle Volunteers
by County

ABERDEENSHIRE

From almost the very beginning of the Volunteer Movement the several rifle corps formed within the City of Aberdeen were consolidated into a single battalion. Other corps were to be included in one or other of the county's three administrative battalions, some (in 1876) transferring across the border to the military care of Kincardineshire. With the already consolidated 1st Corps, the merger of the three admin battalions in 1880 reduced the number of Aberdeenshire corps to four. There also existed for a very short period, two numbered (1st and 2nd) sub-divisions; these later to become the 3rd and 4th Corps of the 1860–80 period.

1st (1860) See 2nd Corps (1860–80).

1st (1860–1908) The formation in the early months of 1860 of the several City of Aberdeen companies into the consolidated nine-company-strong 1st Corps saw former 38th Regiment of Foot officer Napier T Christie placed in command as lieutenant colonel commandant. His commission was dated 16 March 1860 and the amalgamation went as follows:

No. 1 Company (late 6th Corps)
No. 2 Company (late 7th Corps)
No. 3 Company (late No. 1 Company, 8th Corps)
No. 4 Company (late No. 2 Company, 8th Corps)
No. 5 Company (late 9th Corps)
No. 6 Company (late 11th Corps)
No. 7 Company (late 13th Corps)
No. 8 Company (late No. 1 Company, 12th Corps)
No. 9 Company (late No. 2 Company, 12th Corps)

A new company was formed on 10 November 1860 and on 4 May 1861, Nos 1 and 2 were merged as No. 1. At the same time the companies from No. 3 down took the next highest number, once again leaving the corps with nine companies numbered 1st to 9th. A new No. 10 was soon raised, but in November 1861, following its refusal to adopt the uniform then being worn by the rest of the battalion, No. 9 was disbanded. No. 10 Company was disbanded in 1862 for the same reason. A new company was formed at Woodside, just outside Aberdeen, in 1870 and on 25 June 1880 the nine companies were lettered 'A' to 'I'.

Became 1st Volunteer Battalion Gordon Highlanders in 1884; 'L' Company was formed in October 1895, 'H' disbanded in 1898, while at the same time Aberdeen University raised a company lettered 'U'. In 1905 'D' and 'I' were amalgamated as 'D', and 'E' and 'L' as 'M'. The battalion maintained a rifle range at Seaton Links just over two miles from Aberdeen.

During the war in South Africa, 128 members of the battalion served alongside the Regulars of the 1st Battalion Gordon Highlanders, the first contingent leaving Aberdeen under the command of Captain J B Buchanan (later mentioned in dispatches) and Lieutenant F J O

Mackinnon on 16 February 1900. Action was seen at Doornkop, near Johannesburg, on 29 May resulting in two men being killed and seven wounded. Both officers were among the latter. There would also be casualties at Leehoek on 11 July, and on 30 September at Komati Poort. Transfer to the Territorial Force in 1908 was as 4th Battalion Gordon Highlanders. Uniform: scarlet/yellow with trews/kilts.

Aberdeen is a fishing port, builder of ships, and supplier of granite to the world, the place itself being built almost entirely from this local material, and known as 'The Granite City'.

2nd (1860–80) Three companies were formed at Tarves on 15 February 1860 with Captain Commandant the Hon Arthur Gordon, CMG of Ellon Castle in command. Originally the 1st Corps, the companies were renumbered as 2nd by July and later joined the 2nd Admin Battalion. There was a reduction to two companies in 1862 and on 11 June 1867 these were divided to form the 2nd Corps, which took headquarters at Methlick, and the 18th, which remained at Tarves. Now at Methlick, the 2nd became 'A' Company of the new 2nd Corps in 1880. On the River Ythan, seventeen miles west-south-west of Peterhead, Methlick's parish church was rebuilt in 1866.

2nd (1880–1908) The 2nd Admin Battalion was formed with headquarters at Tarves in June 1861 and to it were added the 2nd, 5th, 6th, 12th, 13th, 15th, 16th and 18th Corps. Headquarters were transferred to Old Meldrum in 1868, then to Aberdeen in 1877. The battalion was consolidated as the new 2nd Corps in 1880 with seven companies:

'A' Methlick (late 2nd Corps)
'B' Ellon (late 6th Corps)
'C' Newburgh (late 12th Corps)
'D' Turriff (late 13th Corps)
'E' Fyvie (late 15th Corps)
'F' Old Meldrum (late 16th Corps)
'G' Tarves (late 18th Corps)

Designated as 2nd Volunteer Battalion Gordon Highlanders in 1884, headquarters moving to Old Meldrum in 1899, and transferred to the Territorial Force in 1908 as three companies ('D', 'E' and 'F') of 5th Battalion Gordon Highlanders. Uniform: scarlet/yellow with trews.

3rd (1860–80) Formed at Cluny with William Monro commissioned as ensign on 16 April 1860 and shown in the *Army List* as 1st Sub-division until July. As a full company, 3rd Corps joined the 1st Admin Battalion, moved headquarters to Kemnay in 1875, and became 'F' Company of the new 4th Corps in 1880. The parish of Cluny is two miles south of Monymusk, the castle there having been erected between 1840 and 1872. Kemnay, to the north-west of Aberdeen, lies on the River Don and enjoyed much prosperity from the quarrying of granite.

3rd (The Buchan) (1880–1908) The 3rd Admin Battalion was formed with headquarters at Peterhead in January 1862 and to it were added the 5th, 9th, 17th, 20th, 24th, 25th and 26th Corps. In 1868 the additional title of 'The Buchan' was authorized – this the name given to the area of north-east Aberdeenshire extending along the coast from the Ythan to Deveron rivers, a distance of some forty miles. On 23 May 1880 the battalion was consolidated as the new 3rd Corps with headquarters at Old Deer and nine companies:

'A' New Deer (late 5th Corps)
'B' Peterhead (late No. 1 Company, 9th Corps)
'C' St Fergus (late No. 2 Company, 9th Corps)

'D' Old Deer (late No. 1 Company. 17th Corps)
'E' Strichen (late No. 2 Company, 17th Corps)
'F' Longside (late 20th Corps)
'G' Fraserburgh (late 24th Corps)
'H' New Pitsligo (late 25th Corps)
'I' Cruden (late 26th Corps)

Headquarters moved to Peterhead in 1883 and in the same year 'H' Company went from New Pitsligo to Fraserburgh and a new company was formed at Boddam. Designated 3rd (The Buchan) Volunteer Battalion Gordon Highlanders in 1884. Over the next seventeen years numerous changes were made within the battalion's company structure. In 1885 'C' moved to Crimond, changing location yet again to Lonmay in 1888; 'K' went to Peterhead in the same year, and in 1900 'I' was disbanded. 'C' Company was absorbed into 'E' and 'K' became 'C' in 1901. Transfer to the Territorial Force in 1908 was as headquarters and five companies ('A', 'B', 'C', 'G' and 'H') of 5th Battalion Gordon Highlanders. Uniform: green/scarlet, with trews introduced 1883. Scarlet/yellow from 1885.

4th (1860–80) Formed at Alford with Lieutenant James F Leith and Ensign Robert Wilson commissioned on 12 March 1860. The corps was shown in the *Army List* as 2nd Sub-division until July, joined the 1st Admin Battalion, and became 'D' Company of the new 4th Corps in 1880. The village is bounded to the north by the River Don and grew rapidly after the opening of the Vale of Alford Railway in 1859.

4th (1880–1908) The 1st Admin Battalion was formed with headquarters at Inverurie in May 1860 and to it were added the 3rd, 4th, 7th, 8th, 10th, 11th, 14th, 19th, 21st, 22nd and 23rd Corps. Headquarters moved to Aberdeen in 1868 and in 1876, the 8th, 14th, 21st and 23rd Corps were transferred to the 1st Kincardineshire Admin Battalion. Consolidation in April 1880 saw the battalion as the new 4th Corps with seven companies:

'A' Huntly (late 7th Corps)
'B' Kildrummy (late 11th Corps)
'C' Insch (late 19th Corps)
'D' Alford (late 4th Corps)
'E' Inverurie (late 10th Corps)
'F' Kemnay (late 3rd Corps)
'G' Auchmull (late 22nd Corps)

Designated as 4th Volunteer Battalion Gordon Highlanders in 1884, the additional title 'Donside Highland' was granted in 1893, and several new companies were later formed: 'H' at Auchmull in 1897, followed by one each at Kintore and Kildrummy in 1899. Other changes were in 1899, when 'B' Company moved from Kildrummy to Strathdon; in 1903, when 'G' and 'H' went to Bucksburn, and 1906, which saw 'B' and 'C' amalgamated as 'B' at Kildrummy. Volunteers from the battalion saw active service in South Africa during the Boer War, Private J M Meldrum being killed and Lieutenant H Forbes and two privates wounded at Doornkop on 29 May 1900. Another man was wounded at Komati Poort on 30 September and later, two died of disease. Lieutenant Forbes was awarded the Distinguished Service Order (DSO) and Sergeant J R Campbell the medal for Distinguished Conduct. Transfer to the Territorial Force in 1908 was as four companies ('E', 'F', 'G' and 'H') of 6th Battalion Gordon Highlanders. Uniform: green/scarlet, changing to dark green/ light green with trews in 1887, khaki with kilts from 1903.

5th One company formed as 17th Corps at New Deer with Lieutenant William D Fordyce and

Ensign William Johnson holding commissions dated 12 April 1860. Renumbered by July, joined the 2nd Admin Battalion, transferred to 3rd Admin in January 1862, and became 'A' Company of the new 3rd Corps in 1880. (See also 19th Corps). The village and parish of New Deer is situated thirteen miles west of Peterhead.

6th (1859–60) Formed as one company at Aberdeen on 19 November 1859 and joined the new 1st Corps as its No. 1 Company on 16 March 1860.

6th (1860–80) One company formed at Ellon as 18th Corps with Thomas Buchan as captain, Thomas Mair, lieutenant and Alexander Cowie, ensign. All three held commissions dated 18 April 1860. Renumbered 6th by July 1860, joined the 2nd Admin Battalion, and became 'B' Company of the new 2nd Corps in 1880. Ellon village is on the River Ythan to the south-west of Peterhead; its parish church was restored in 1876, the Episcopal church of St Mary of the Rock built six years before that.

7th (1859–60) Formed at Aberdeen on 19 November 1859 and joined the new 1st Corps as its No. 2 Company on 16 March 1860.

7th (1860–80) One company formed at Huntly as 19th Corps with Robert Simpson as captain, William Lawson, lieutenant and Alex McWilliam, ensign. All three held commissions dated 6 March 1860. Renumbered by July 1860, joined the 1st Admin Battalion, and became 'A' Company of the new 4th Corps in 1880. In the north-west of the county, Huntly gave employment in the manufacture of agricultural machinery, bricks and titles. There were two woollen mills and a stocking factory. Gordon School, founded in 1840, is close to Huntly Lodge and was enlarged in 1888.

8th (1859–60) Formed as two companies at Aberdeen on 26 November 1859 and on 16 March 1860 joined the new 1st Corps as its Nos 3 and 4 Companies. The corps was made up of employees from several Aberdeen merchants.

8th (1860–80) Two companies formed as 20th Corps at Echt with Captain Alex F Irvine, the senior company commander, commission on 9 June 1860. Renumbered by July. Joined the 1st Admin Battalion, reduced to one company in 1866, and transferred to the 1st Kincardineshire Admin Battalion in 1876. Became 'F' Company of the new 1st Kincardineshire RVC in 1880. Echt village is in the south-east of the county, twelve miles west of Aberdeen.

9th (1859–60) Formed at Aberdeen on 23 December 1859 and joined the new 1st Corps as its No. 5 Company on 16 March. 1860.

9th (1860–80) Two companies formed as 21st Corps at Peterhead with Captains William Alexander and Thomas John Bremner as company commanders. Both held commissions dated 4 April 1860. Renumbered 9th in July. Joined the 3rd Admin Battalion, absorbed the 24th Corps at St Fergus in September 1875, and became 'B' and 'C' Companies of the new 3rd Corps in 1880. A large seaport with two harbours, the town was once active in the fishing industry. Two large granite-polishing firms also gave employment. The Library in Peter Street was opened in 1892.

10th One company formed as 22nd Corps at Inverurie with James R Allan as lieutenant and James Munro, ensign. Both held commissions dated 20 April 1860. Renumbered in July, joined 1st Admin Battalion, and became 'E' Company of the new 4th Corps in 1880. Situated on the River Don, Inverurie lies sixteen miles north-west of Aberdeen.

11th (1860) Formed at Aberdeen on 13 January 1860 and joined the new 1st Corps as its No. 6 Company on 16 March. 1860. The corps was made up of artisans.

11th (1860–80) Formed as a sub-division at Kildrummy with Lieutenant James Walker and Ensign William Reid holding commissions dated 20 June 1860. Originally designated as 23rd Corps, but renumbered as 11th by July. Joined the 1st Admin Battalion, increased to a full company in 1867, and became 'B' Company of the new 4th Corps in 1880. The parish and village of Kildrummy is in the north-west of the county.

12th (1860) Formed at Aberdeen on 27 January 1860 and joined the new 1st Corps as its Nos 8 and 9 Companies on 16 March 1860.

12th (1860–63) Formed at Old Aberdeen with John Crombie commissioned as ensign on 21 July 1860. Joined the 2nd Admin Battalion and was disbanded in 1863. The town of Old Aberdeen lies about a mile to the north of the main city.

12th (1864–80) Formed at Udny, fourteen miles north of Aberdeen, in June 1864 with Captain John Ramsay, Lieutenant Alex Milne and Ensign William Marr. Joined the 2nd Admin Battalion, moving headquarters south-west to Newmachar at the beginning of 1867, then to the small seaside port of Newburgh in 1877. Became 'C' Company of the new 2nd in 1880.

13th (1860) Formed at Aberdeen on 21 January 1860 and joined the new 1st Corps as its No. 7 Company on 16 March. 1860. The company was recruited mainly from employees of the Scottish North Eastern Railway.

13th (1860–80) One company formed at Turriff with Patrick R Innes as captain, William Cruikshank, lieutenant and James Grieve, ensign. All three held commissions dated 8 August 1860. Joined the 2nd Admin Battalion in 1862 and became 'D' Company of the new 2nd Corps in 1880. Turriff parish, in the north of the county, has the Episcopal church of St Congan which was built in 1862.

14th Formed at Tarland on the western side of the county as a sub-division with Lieutenant Andrew Robertson and Ensign John Grant commissioned on 29 October 1860. Increased to a full company in May 1861. Joined 1st Admin Battalion, transferred to 1st Kincardineshire Admin in 1876, and became 'G' Company of the new 1st Kincardineshire Corps in 1880.

15th One company formed at Fyvie with Captain William C Gordon, Lieutenant James Mackie and Ensign James Wilson commissioned on 1 October 1860. Joined the 2nd Admin Battalion in 1862 and became 'E' Company of the new 2nd Corps in 1880. Fyvie parish lies on the River Ythan in the northern part of the county.

16th One company formed at Old Meldrum with Captain James H Chalmers and Lieutenant James L Manson commissioned on 2 October 1860. Joined the 2nd Admin Battalion in 1862 and became 'F' Company of the new 2nd Corps in 1880. The town is in the north-eastern part of the county and gave employment in the distilling and brewing trades.

17th (1860) See 5th Corps.

17th (1860–80) Two companies formed at Old Deer, west of Peterhead, their company commanders: Captains James Russell and John Ferguson, both being commissioned on 29 October 1860. Joined the 3rd Admin Battalion and became 'D' and 'E' Companies of the new 3rd Corps in 1880.

18th (1860) See 6th Corps (1860–80).

18th (1867–80) On 11 June 1867 the 2nd Corps at Tarves was divided to form the 2nd, which took up headquarters at Methlick, and the 18th Corps, which remained at Tarves. The 18th joined the 2nd Admin Battalion and became 'G Company of the new 2nd Corps in 1880. Tarves village and parish is just over four miles north-east of Old Meldrum.

19th (1860) See 7th Corps (1860–80).

19th (1861) There existed a 19th Corps of one company at New Deer, its officers' commissions being dated 30 March 1861. According to the *London Gazette* of 19 November 1861, this was in fact the 5th Corps (same personnel) and acceptance was subsequently cancelled. On the other hand, General Grierson in *Records of the Scottish Volunteer Force* states that the 19th was amalgamated with the 5th Corps in November 1861.

19th (1867–80) Formed at Insch with Captain Walter D Leslie, Lieutenant Alex Roger and Ensign Jonathan M Grant holding commissions dated 17 December 1867. Joined the 1st Admin Battalion and became 'C' Company of the new 4th Corps in 1880. Twenty-six miles north-west of Aberdeen, Insch gave employment in its numerous slate quarries.

20th (1860) See 8th Corps (1860–80).

20th (1861–80) One company formed at Longside with Captain William Hutchison, Lieutenant Robert Scott and Ensign Alex Smith commissioned on 30 July 1861. Joined the 3rd Admin Battalion and became 'F' Company of the new 3rd Corps in 1880. Six miles west of Peterhead, Longside's several granite quarries employed many.

21st (1860) See 9th Corps (1860–80).

21st (Marquis of Huntly's Highland) (1861–80) One company formed at Aboyne towards the end of 1861 with Captain Alex Davidson and Lieutenant Alex Cochran commissioned on 22 November. Joined the 1st Admin Battalion and in 1871 formed a second company at Ballater. The 21st was transferred to the 1st Kincardineshire Admin Battalion in 1876 and became 'H' and 'I' Companies of the new 1st Kincardineshire RVC in 1880. Aboyne village is on the Dee in the south of the county.

22nd (1860) See 10th Corps.

22nd (1862–80) One company formed at Auchmull in 1862 with Captain John Robertson, Lieutenant Patrick Watt and Ensign James Cooper commissioned on 18 June. Joined the 1st Admin Battalion and became 'G' Company of the new 4th Corps in 1880. Auchmull village is on the railway between Aberdeen and Dyce. There were granite quarries in the neighbourhood.

23rd (1860) See 11th Corps (1860–80).

23rd (1862–80) One company formed at Lumphanan in 1862 with Captain James William Barclay, Lieutenant James Shaw and Ensign John Thompson commissioned on 29 March. Joined the 1st Admin Battalion, moved to Torphins in 1864, and in 1876 transferred to the 1st Kincardineshire Admin Battalion. Became 'K' Company of the new 1st Kincardineshire Corps in 1880. Torphins is just to the north-west of Banchory.

24th (1867–75) One sub-division formed at St Fergus towards the end of 1867 with Lieutenant James Greig and Ensign Alex Walker commissioned on 23 December. Joined the 3rd Admin

Battalion and was absorbed into the 9th Corps in September 1875. A coastal parish, St Fergus is just north of Peterhead.

24th (1875–80) One company formed at Fraserburgh late in 1875 with Captain Andrew Tarras (commissioned 13 November) in command. Joined the 3rd Admin Battalion and became 'G' Company of the new 3rd Corps in 1880. Cassell's *Gazetteer* for 1895 noted that 'The Wine Tower' on a crag overlooking the sea, had a cave under it which 'now serves as a Volunteer armoury and store'. Fraserburgh is at the north-east tip of the county where the Moray Firth meets the North Sea.

25th One company formed at New Pitsligo in 1868 with Captain C H R Lord Clinton (commissioned 14 April) in command. Joined the 3rd Admin Battalion and became 'H' Company of the new 3rd Corps in 1880. Near the village were several granite quarries, its Episcopal church of St John the Evangelist being built in 1871.

26th One company formed at Cruden with Captain James Shepherd (commission 25 September 1872) in command. Joined the 3rd Admin Battalion and became 'I' Company of the new 3rd Corps in 1880. Cruden is a coastal parish eight miles south-east of Peterhead.

ANGLESEY

Anglesey, the island and county in North Wales, is separated from the mainland by the Menai Strait. To the north-west, Holyhead, once the railway had reached there, became the main port for the crossing to Dublin, the town not actually on Anglesey, but on another island – Holy Island. Perhaps Holyhead could be taken as typical of the many towns in the country that in the initial stages of the Volunteer Movement made attempts to form Volunteer companies that for one reason or another did not appear in any *Army List*. The *Swansea and Glamorgan Herald* reported on 25 April 1860 that some eighty-three employees of the Steam Packet Depot of the London and North Western Railway Company, and of the City of Dublin Steam Packet Company, had shown a desire to enrol as volunteer corps. At the same time a 'Mr Rigby' of the New Harbour Works had begun a corps from men in his employ, their arms, uniform and equipment to be provided by him. No services of any corps at Holyhead, however, were accepted. That is until some forty years later when a company raised in 1900 was placed into the 3rd Volunteer Battalion Royal Welsh Fusiliers. Elsewhere on Anglesey three companies were formed and shown in the records, though their existence would be brief.

1st Formed with headquarters on the north coast of Anglesey at Amlwch with Henry B Mitchell as captain on 6 November 1860. He would be joined by John Wynn Paynter, commissioned 20 December, and then by Ensign Benjamin Roose, surgeon Thomas D Griffith MD and chaplain the Revd Robert Hughes – all three not to receive their commissions until 5 April 1861. These would be the only officers to serve with the 1st Anglesey RVC, which was removed from the *Army List* in December 1863. A market town and seaport, Amlwch gave employment at its local tobacco factories, brass foundries and shipbuilding yards. There were also copper mines – in the nineteenth century the area around Amlwch was considered to be one of the most important copper-producing centres of the world – at the Parys mountain close by.

2nd The fishing village and seaport of Aberffraw in the south of Anglesey was the headquarters of the 2nd Corps, which was raised towards the end of 1860 as one company. Recruiting went far from well, however, and the corps was disbanded in March 1862. Captain Owen A F Meyrick, who was commissioned on 5 November 1860, was the only officer appointed. Aberffraw – an ancient stone single-arched bridge takes you to it – is twelve miles south-east of Holyhead.

3rd Recruiting of the 3rd Anglesey RVC went no better than that of the 2nd Corps at Aberffraw on the other side of Anglesey. Menai Bridge was selected as headquarters, the company's appointed commanding officer being Major General, Robert G Hughes, who had recently seen action (1852–53) in Burma. Commissioned as captain in the Volunteer Force on 2 November 1860, he would be the only officer gazetted to the corps, which was disbanded in February 1862. Menai Bridge village is four miles south-west of Beaumaris and gave employment during the nineteenth century in the production of writing slates, memorial tombstones and tablets. Thomas Telford's suspension bridge predates the Volunteers by some thirty-four years; the opening of Stephenson's Britannia Bridge in 1850, however, would have been seen by those that joined the 3rd Corps in 1860. Looking down on both bridges from its ninety-foot tower is the statue of the 1st Marquis of Anglesey, who, as the Earl of Uxbridge, commanded the Cavalry at Waterloo.

ARGYLLSHIRE

In south-west Scotland, Argyllshire covered a vast area which included almost all the isles of the Inner Hebrides. So scattered were the several Argyllshire corps that it would not be until August 1868 than any two or more paraded together – and even then the battalion drill for that year saw three of the companies meet for this purpose in Rothesay across the border in Buteshire. All Argyllshire RVC, with the exception of the 5th, at some time joined the county's 1st Admin Battalion, which was consolidated as 1st Corps in 1880. Although the pre-1880 numbering of the several corps reached fourteen, there were in fact only twelve formed, the 1st and 4th positions never being filled or shown in any *Army List*.

1st (1859–80)
None formed.

1st (Argyllshire Highland) (1880–1908) The 1st Admin Battalion was formed with headquarters at Oban in July 1861, Major Charles Alexander Stewart being appointed as commanding officer with commission dated 9 December 1861. Headquarters were moved to Ardrishaig in 1866, and then to Dunoon in the following year. From 1873 the full title of the battalion was shown as 1st Admin Battalion of Argyllshire Highland Rifle Volunteers, which in part was carried forward upon consolidation as 1st Corps in March 1880. Headquarters remained at Dunoon and there were eight companies:

'A' Inveraray (late 2nd Corps)
'B' Campbeltown (late 3rd Corps)
'C' Campbeltown (late 3rd Corps)
'D' Dunoon (late 7th Corps)
'E' Glendaruel (late 8th Corps)
'F' Ballachulish (late 13th Corps)
'G' Ballachulish (late 13th Corps)
'H' Kilmartin (late 14th Corps)

In December 1882 the headquarters of 'G' Company were transferred from Ballachulish to Southend at the southern portion of Kintyre, about ten miles south of Campbeltown. The 1st Argyllshire RVC had been linked to the Argyll and Sutherland Highlanders in the previous year as one of its volunteer battalions, but it would not be until 1887 that re-designation as 5th Volunteer Battalion took place – notification of the change being made in General Order 181 of 1 December. Some sixty-one members of the battalion served in South Africa with the three Volunteer Service Companies of the Argylls. Corporal W Gillespie, the battalion's only casualty, was killed at Commando Nek on 1 October 1900. As a result of the war, new companies were raised in 1900: 'I' at Carradale, thirteen miles north-east of Campbeltown, and 'K' (Cyclist), which was at Campbeltown itself and recruited from all over the battalion. In the following year the Dunoon Grammar School Cadet Corps was formed and affiliated to the battalion. Around this time 'A' Company is noted as also having detachments at Dalmally and Furness; 'E' at Strachur, Tighnabruaich and Lochgoilhead; 'G' at Kilkenzie and Glenbar; 'H' at Ardrishaig, and 'I' at Tayinloan. At the closing of the Volunteer Force the strength of the battalion was returned as 873 all ranks, its transfer to the Territorial Force in 1908 being as 8th Battalion Argyll and Sutherland Highlanders. Uniform: scarlet/yellow with kilts.

2nd One company formed with headquarters at Inveraray in the early months of 1860 with John McArthur as captain, Henry J B D Smith, lieutenant and John Buchanan, ensign. All three held commissions dated 4 May. Became 'A' Company of the 1st Corps in 1880. The town is situated at the lower end of a small bay where the River Aray enters Loch Fyne and was during the time of the Volunteers well known for its Loch Fyne herring fishery – there were also granite quarries in the area. Inveraray Castle, the seat of the Dukes of Argyll, underwent major restoration during 1879–80.

3rd Formed at Campbeltown, the 3rd Corps comprised two companies with Captains Charles A Stewart and Charles McTaggart appointed as company commanders. Both held commissions dated 16 April 1860. Became 'B' and 'C' Companies of the 1st Corps in 1880. At Campbeltown, on Kintyre, distilleries exported whisky all around the world. Coal and iron were produced, ships were built, and a number were involved in the fishing industry.

4th None formed.

5th One company formed on the Isle of Mull with Farquhar Campbell as captain, William E Oliver, lieutenant and Walter Elliott, ensign. All three held commissions dated 6 December 1860. The corps did not join the 1st Admin Battalion and was disbanded in 1862. The Isle of Mull lies about seven miles west of Oban. Tobermory – established by the British Fishery Society as a station for fishing boats in 1788 – is the only town.

6th It was originally intended to raise two companies with headquarters at Melfort in the early months of 1860. However, at least as far as the officers were concerned, there does not seem to have been the predicted level of interest. In 1864, what constituted the 6th Corps was disbanded. Only three officers appeared in the *Army List*: Captain Richard R Kelly, whose commission was dated 22 April 1860, followed by Lieutenant John D M McGregor and Ensign Malcolm MacQueen on 1 May 1860. Melfort Loch is to the south-west of Oban and took in the parish of Kilninver and Kilmelford.

7th The first officers to appear with the company formed at Dunoon at the beginning of 1860 were Captain John Maclaren and Lieutenant Colin Rae. Both held commissions dated 28 March 1860. Became 'D' Company of the 1st Corps in 1880. The Volunteers at Dunoon, on the west shore of the Firth of Clyde, saw the building of St Mun's Catholic Church in 1863, the United Presbyterian in 1875, and a Free Church in 1876–77. Dunoon Grammar School Cadet Corps was formed in 1901.

8th The original establishment of the 8th Corps was two companies, four officers being appointed all with commissions dated 4 June 1860: Captains Archibald Campbell and John Campbell, Lieutenant John McArthur and Ensign Duncan Buchannan. Headquarters were listed as Cowal, this is the district forming a peninsula between the Firth of Clyde and Loch Fyne, but Glendaruel is given from 1862. It would appear that there was difficulty in enrolling sufficient numbers to maintain the second company – indeed no other officers were ever added to those already mentioned – and subsequently the establishment of the 8th Corps was reduced in 1864. This, in 1880, became 'E' Company of the 1st Corps. Glendaruel is just north of the head of Loch Riddon.

9th Headquarters of the 9th Corps of one company are given as Glenlochy, which is the area that runs between Tyndrum and Dalmally. Formed in the spring of 1860, its first officers all held commissions dated 12 April 1860: Captain Archibald B Macdonald, Lieutenant John Mackay and Ensign Duncan Turner Campbell. Given its close proximity to the neighbouring county, the 9th Corps was attached for drill and administrative purposes to the 3rd Perthshire RVC, and, from 1862, to the 2nd Perthshire Admin Battalion. This unpopular arrangement lasted until 1865 when transfer was made to the 1st Argyllshire Admin. Headquarters appear as Dalmally from 1869, but interest waned and the corps was disbanded in the following year. Dalmally, where the railway did not reach until 1877, lies on the River Orchy about twenty-five miles east of Oban.

10th One company formed with headquarters at Tayvallich, seven miles west of Ardrishaig, by Campbell of Inverneill, who recruited from his employees on the Ross Estate. The officers: Captain James A Campbell, Lieutenant Duncan Campbell, and Ensign James A Campbell, all held commissions dated 4 June 1860. There was also a detachment at Ardrishaig. From the *Army List* it would seem, perhaps, that the Campbell family interest diminished after a very short time. Gradually other names appeared and by 1869, when the 10th Corps was disbanded, only Duncan Campbell, who had been promoted to lieutenant on 29 December 1862, of the original three remained. The Ardrishaig Detachment was absorbed into the 14th Corps at Kilmartin to the north. A seaport at the termination of the Crinan Canal, Ardrishaig on Loch Fyne, was the centre of a brisk shipping and ferry trade. Herring fishing was also important to the town.

11th One company formed at Oban with Captain Sir Angus Campbell Bt and Ensign Robert Corson the first officers appointed. Their commissions were dated 7 July 1860. Donald McCullum was commissioned as captain on 19 October 1863 and shortly after that he would be the only officer listed until the 11th Corps was disbanded. It made its last appearance in the *Army List* for January 1865. A busy seaport and centre for steamer traffic through the Caledonian Canal, Oban was also the terminus (opened in 1880) for the Callander and Oban branch of the Caledonian Railway.

12th One company formed at Bridgend on the Isle of Islay with Captain James Henderson, Lieutenant Charles McNeill and Ensign Charles McAffer commissioned on 7 June 1861. Appointed at the same time were surgeon Angus McIndeor and chaplain the Revd John McGilchrist. The corps was disbanded in 1865. In the parish of Kilarrow and Kilmeny, Bridgend looks out to Loch Indaal.

13th Two companies were formed at Ballachulish with Captains Robert Tennant and Herbert Cornwall and Ensigns William Potts and Robert McIntyre being commissioned on 31 August 1867. For some unknown reason, the required two lieutenants did not appear in the *Army List* for the next two years – Potts and McIntyre being promoted on 1 October 1869, their places as ensigns being taken by Robert Phillips and William Mitchell, whose commissions were signed on the same date. Became 'F' and 'G' Companies of the 1st Corps in 1880. Ballachulish village lies along both shores of Loch Leven, sixteen miles south of Fort William, and extends to Glencoe. The parish church was enlarged in 1880. Slate quarries were established in the area in 1760 and in 1893 some 600 men out of a total population of 1,045 are recorded as being employed in them.

14th The headquarters of the 14th and last corps to be raised in Argyllshire, were at Kilmartin; its first officer, Captain John W Malcolm, being commissioned on 15 January 1868. William J B Martin joined him as lieutenant on 19 February, and William R Malcolm as ensign on 6 December. Absorbed the Ardrishaig Detachment of the 10th Corps in 1869 and became 'H' Company of 1st Argyllshire RVC in 1880. The village is close to Loch Craignish.

AYRSHIRE

The county formed its 1st Admin Battalion at Ayr on 27 August 1860, but with fourteen individual corps under its charge the decision was taken to divide the battalion into two. Subsequently, in March 1873, 1st Admin Battalion became 1st and 2nd, these to provide two new corps in 1880.

1st (1860–80) Formed at Kilmarnock as one company with Captain James Hunter Picken, Lieutenant Robert Railton and Ensign James Bishop Andrews commissioned on 14 January 1860. Transferred from 1st to 2nd Admin Battalion in March 1873; absorbed the 9th Corps, also at Kilmarnock, in 1874, and became 'A' Company of the new 1st Corps in 1880. Walker's 'Kilmarnock' Whisky was already well known, but when Johnnie's son, Alexander, took over in 1859, the business grew to become the largest whisky firm in the world. Opened in 1862, the Corn Exchange at Kilmarnock incorporated a clock tower commemorating Prince Albert. The literary Volunteer would remember, without doubt, the opening of the theatre in 1875; the Public Library at Elmbank, and in 1879, Kay Park in which stands the Burns monument, the poet himself a Volunteer, but of an earlier generation.

1st (1880–1908) In March 1873 the 1st Admin Battalion was divided as 1st and 2nd, the later taking the several corps then in existence in the northern half of the county: 1st, 2nd, 4th, 6th, 7th, 9th and 11th. The 15th and 17th Corps were added later upon formation. Headquarters were placed at Kilmarnock. In June 1880 2nd Admin was consolidated as the new 1st Ayrshire RVC with eight companies:

'A' Kilmarnock (late 1st Corps)
'B' Irvine (late 2nd Corps)
'C' Largs (late 4th Corps)
'D' Beith (late 6th Corps)
'E' Saltcoats (late 7th Corps)
'F' Dalry (late 11th Corps)
'G' Darvel (late 15th Corps)
'H' Galston (late 17th Corps)

Under General Order 181 of December 1887, 1st Ayrshire RVC was re-designated as 1st Volunteer Battalion Royal Scots Fusiliers. Two new companies, one a cyclist, were added at Kilmarnock in 1900, 'C' Company moving to Stewarton and 'H' to Kilmarnock during the same year. The Kilmarnock Academy Cadet Corps was affiliated in 1901 and transfer to the Territorial Force in 1908 was as 4th Battalion Royal Scots Fusiliers. Uniform: scarlet/blue, the trousers changing to trews in 1888.

2nd (1859–80) One company formed at Irvine with Captain John Smith, Lieutenant John Paterson and Ensign Alex Gilmour commissioned on 27 December 1859. Transferred from 1st to 2nd Admin Battalion in March 1873 and became 'B' Company of the new 1st Corps in 1880. Seaport and market town on the north bank of the River of the same name, Irvine lies eleven miles north of Ayr. Its Town Hall was opened in the same year as the 2nd Corps was enrolling its first members, the statue of Lord Justice General Boyle nearby being unveiled eight years after that. Irvine's principal sources of employment were the chemicals, shipbuilding, engineering, coal and iron industries.

2nd (1880–1908) When the 1st Admin Battalion at Ayr was divided in March 1873 it retained the several corps then situated in the southern half of the county: 3rd, 5th, 8th, 10th, 12th, 13th and 14th. The 16th Corps was added upon its formation in December 1873 and in 1880 the battalion was consolidated as the new 2nd Ayrshire RVC with seven companies:

'A' Ayr (late 3rd Corps)
'B' Ayr (late 14th Corps)
'C' Maybole (late 5th Corps)
'D' Girvan (late 10th Corps)
'E' Cumnock (late 12th Corps)
'F' Sorn (late 13th Corps)
'G' Newmilns (late 16th Corps)

In 1883 'H' Company was added at Troon and in the same year 'F' Company moved from Sorn to Catrine. Under General Order 181 of December 1887, 2nd Ayrshire RVC was re-designated as 2nd Volunteer Battalion Royal Scots Fusiliers. A cyclist company ('I') was formed at Ayr in 1900, and transfer to the Territorial Force in 1908 was as 5th Battalion Royal Scots Fusiliers. Uniform: scarlet/blue, the trousers changing to trews in 1898.

3rd Formed at Ayr as one company with Captain H Boyd, Lieutenant Robert Paton and Ensign James Martin commissioned on 19 January 1860. Joined the 1st Admin Battalion and became 'A' Company of the new 2nd Corps in 1880. Robert Burns, in his 'The Twa Brigs o' Ayr', imagined a conversation between Ayr's old and new bridges in which Robert Adam's new construction of 1788 refers to the old fifteenth-century bridge as little more than a footpath. In reply, the old bridge boasts of its long and sturdy service, and that 'I'll be a brig when ye're a shapeless cairn'. Indeed, and as predicted, the new bridge was swept away during flooding and had to be replaced in 1877.

4th Formed as one company at Largs with Captain Hugh Morris Lang, Lieutenant George Elder, Ensign Alexander Blair and surgeon Robert Kirkwood MD commissioned on 27 February 1860. Transferred from 1st to 2nd Admin Battalion in March 1873 and became 'C' Company of the new 1st Corps in 1880. Largs is on the Firth of Clyde twelve miles south-south-west of Greenock.

5th Formed at Maybole as one company with Captain David Browne, Lieutenant William Murray and Ensign Thomas Austin commissioned on 27 February 1860. Also appointed were Robert Girvan MD as surgeon and the Revd John Thomson who became chaplain. Joined the 1st Admin Battalion and became 'C' Company of the new 2nd Corps in 1880. Maybole is eight miles from Ayr, its Town Hall being opened in 1887. Volunteers using the Ayr and Maybole Junction Railway (opened in 1856) would have travelled from a new station after the line was extended on 24 May 1860.

6th Formed as one company at Beith with Captain Hugh Brown, Lieutenant Hugh Crawford and Ensign William Fulton Love commissioned on 15 February 1860. Transferred from 1st to 2nd Admin Battalion in March 1873 and became 'D' Company of the new 1st Corps in 1880. Beith is about eighteen miles south-west of Glasgow, its chief industries during the Volunteer period being flax, cotton, leather, silk dyeing and furniture. Beith station, on the old Glasgow, Barrhead & Kilmarnock Railway, was opened on 26 June 1873.

7th One company formed at Saltcoats (there was also a detachment at Stevenston) with Captain Robert King Barbour, Lieutenant James Baird and Ensign James Anderson commissioned on 28 February 1860. Transferred from 1st to 2nd Admin Battalion in March 1873 and became 'E' Company of the new 1st Corps in 1880. The manufacture of salt employed many until around 1890, the collieries, foundries at Stevenston, and others. The Town Hall opened in 1892, the Volunteer Drill Hall was in Canal Street.

8th Formed at Colmonell as one company with Captain Anthony Thompson, Lieutenant William McCulloch and Ensign Alex D McIlrait commissioned on 25 May1860. Joined the 1st Admin Battalion, the corps later being disbanded and last seen in the *Army List* for May 1878. The coastal village and parish of Colmonell lies on the River Stinchar north of Loch Ryan.

9th Formed at one company at Kilmarnock with Captain J Y Deans, Lieutenant J Wilson and Ensign J McMillan commissioned on 19 May 1860. Also appointed at the same time were the Revd J Symington as chaplain, and John Borland MD, who became surgeon. Transferred from 1st to 2nd Admin Battalion in March 1873 and was absorbed into the 1st Corps, also at Kilmarnock, in 1874.

10th Formed at Girvan as one company with Captain William Brown, Lieutenant John Graham and Ensign John J M Blair commissioned on 27 November 1860. Joined the 1st Admin Battalion and became 'D' Company of the new 2nd Corps in 1880. Fishing was the main industry of Girvan, its harbour being enlarged in 1881. Girvan station, on the Maybole and Girvan Railway, opened on 24 May 1860 followed by a second in October 1877 that served the Girvan and Portpatrick Junction line.

11th Formed at Dalry as one company with Captain William Paton, Lieutenant Andrew B Aitken and Ensign James M McCosh commissioned on 4 December 1860. Appointed at the same time was Archibald Blair as surgeon. Transferred from 1st to 2nd Admin Battalion in March 1873 and became 'F' Company of the new 1st Corps in 1880. On the River Garnock, Dalry lies just under eighteen miles north-north-west of Ayr. The manufacture of woollens and worsteds are noted in the 1890s as being the town's main industries.

12th Formed at Cumnock as one company with Lieutenant William Ettershank and Ensign Andrew White commissioned on 14 January 1861. Appointed at the same time was the Revd James Murray as chaplain and James Lawrence MD, who became surgeon. Joined the 1st Admin Battalion and became 'E' Company of the new 2nd Corps in 1880. At Cumnock, seventeen miles east of Ayr, the parish church was built in 1867 and the station, part of the old Glasgow and South Western line, opened on 1 July 1872. The town's chief employment was in coal and iron.

13th Formed at Sorn as one company with Captain Robert Thompson Pattison, Lieutenant James Barclay and Ensign Andrew Currie commissioned on 18 March 1861. Appointed at the same time was James Ballantine MD as surgeon. Joined the 1st Admin Battalion and became 'F' Company of the new 2nd Corps in 1880. South-east of Kilmarnock, many from the village and parish were employed in local collieries and the production of limestone and iron.

14th Formed at Ayr as a sub-division with Lieutenant David Hunter and Ensign Robert Murray Kay commissioned on 14 April 1862. Joined the 1st Admin Battalion, increased to a full company in 1871, and became 'B' Company of the new 2nd Corps in 1880.

15th Formed at Darvel as one company with Captain Alex Steel, Lieutenant John Wood and Ensign Andrew Cameron commissioned on 24 December 1873. Joined the 2nd Admin Battalion and became 'G' Company of the new 1st Corps in 1880. Nine miles east of Kilmarnock on the River Irvine; the railway (Glasgow and South Western) reached the town in June 1896. The manufacture of muslins, lace and carpets are noted as the main sources of employment in the 1890s.

16th Formed at Newmilns as one company with Captain William Smith commissioned on 24 December 1873. Joined the 1st Admin Battalion and became 'G' Company of the new 2nd Corps in 1880. The town, which employed many in the manufacture of muslin and lace, is twenty-four miles south of Glasgow.

17th Formed at Galston as one company with Captain Robert Anderson commissioned on 10 October 1874. Joined the 2nd Admin Battalion and became 'H' Company of the new 1st Corps in 1880. On the River Irvine, five miles east of Kilmarnock, coal was Galston's main source of employment.

BANFFSHIRE

All corps formed within the county joined its 1st Admin Battalion, which became the new 1st Corps in 1880.

1st (1860) Permission to form a sub-division of rifle volunteers at Macduff on the Moray Firth just to the east of Banff, was granted in 1860. The corps, designated as 1st Banffshire, appeared in the *Army List*, but by May 1862 had disappeared having had no officers appointed.

1st (1862–80) One company formed as the 2nd Corps at Banff, which, with the disappearance of the 1st Corps at Macduff in 1862, was renumbered as 1st. The original officers were: Captain Thomas Adam, Lieutenant Henry A Rannie and Ensign George Cumming, all three holding commissions dated 18 April 1860. Became 'A' Company of the new 1st Corps in 1880. At the mouth of the River Deveron in the north-west of the county, Banff's manufacturers of woollens, leather, bricks, sails and rope employed many. There were also breweries, distilleries, timberyards and an iron foundry. On the Great North Scottish Railway, the station at Banff Harbour was opened in July 1859 while that called Banff and Macduff was closed and replaced by Banff Bridge on 1 July 1872.

1st (1880–1908) The 1st Admin Battalion was formed with headquarters at Keith on 12 August 1861 and in June 1880 was consolidated as the new 1st Corps with six-and-a-half companies:

    'A' Banff (late 1st Corps)
    'B' Aberlour (late 2nd Corps)
    'C' Keith (late 3rd Corps)
    'D' Buckie (late 5th Corps)
    'E' Glenlivet (late 6th Corps)
    'F' Dufftown (late 7th Corps)

The half company was at Glenrinnes (late 7th Corps)

By General Order 12 of 1 February 1884 1st Banffshire RVC became the 6th Volunteer Battalion of the Gordon Highlanders, a new company ('G') being later formed at Aberchirder. Some eighty-five members of the battalion saw active service in South Africa, private D B Stuart being wounded at Rooikopjes on 24 July 1900, and later killed during the action at Lydenburgh on 8 September. Two men were mentioned in Lord Robert's dispatch of 4 September 1901. Transfer to the Territorial Force in 1908 was as four companies ('A' to 'D') of 6th Battalion Gordon Highlanders. Uniform: grey/black, changing to scarlet/yellow with trews in 1891.

2nd (1860–62) See 1st Corps (1862–80).

2nd (1862–80) One company formed as the 3rd Corps at Aberlour with Robert Innes as captain, Charles Grant, lieutenant and William Mackenzie, ensign. All three held commissions dated 29 September 1860, and appointed at the same time was James Gerrard as surgeon. Renumbered as 2nd Corps in 1862 and became 'B' Company of the new 1st Corps in 1880. On the Spey in the western portion of the county, Aberlour looks across the river into Elginshire; its station, on the Great North of Scotland line, was opened on 1 July 1863.

3rd (1860–62) See 2nd Corps (1862–80).

3rd (1862–80) Formed from No. 1 Company of the 4th Corps at Keith in May 1862 with Robert Gordon as captain, James Gordon, lieutenant and George Kynoch, ensign. Absorbed the 4th in 1866 and became 'C' Company of the new 1st Corps in 1880. The Longmore Hall was built at Keith in 1873, and the Turner Memorial Cottage Hospital opened in 1880. Blankets, tweeds, boots, shoes and agricultural implements were manufactured in the area. There were also flour mills, a lime works and distilleries – the town's Strathisla distillery being the oldest in the Highlands. Built mainly to serve the distillers, and opened on 21 February 1862, was the Keith & Dufftown Railway.

4th Two companies formed at Keith, their commanders being Captains Robert Gordon and William Thurburn, both having commissions dated 2 November 1860. Upon the disbandment of the 1st Corps at Macduff in 1862, the 2nd and 3rd were subsequently renumbered as 1st and 2nd respectively. At the same time the two Keith companies of the 4th Corps were divided so as to fill the now-vacant position of 3rd Corps – No. 1 Company became 3rd, No. 2 remaining as 4th with Captain Thurburn in command. In July 1866, due to a fall-off in numbers, the 4th Corps was absorbed into the 3rd.

5th Formed at Buckie as one company with William Hector as captain, John Caldwell, lieutenant, Alexander Macarthur, ensign, and Robert Dugald, who became surgeon. All four held commissions dated 12 March 1863. 'D' Company of the new 1st Corps in 1880. In the north of the county, Buckie had manufacturers of sails, ropes and gas and employed many in the fishing industry. The Great North Scottish Railway served the town, Buckie Station being opened on 1 May 1886.

6th Formed at Glenlivet as one company with John G Smith as captain, Peter G Gordon, lieutenant and Alex Sheed, ensign. All three held commissions dated 19 April 1867. Became 'E' Company of the new 1st Corps in 1880. To the south-west of Dufftown, important to Glenlivet then, as today, was its distillery.

7th Formed at Dufftown as one company and a sub-division with James Petrie commissioned as captain commandant on 1 May 1868. When the 1st Admin Battalion was consolidated as the new

1st Corps in 1880, the 7th Banffshire provided 'F' Company at Dufftown and a half company five miles off at Glenrinnes. A cottage hospital was opened at Dufftown in 1890, the town's chief industry being the distilling of whisky – Glenfiddich Distillery, owned by the Grant family, opened in 1887. The railway came to the town in the form of the Keith and Dufftown Railway, in February 1862. A church was built at Glenrinnes in 1884.

BEDFORDSHIRE

All rifle corps formed were placed into the 1st Admin Battalion, which in 1880 provided the new 1st Corps.

1st (1860–80) Formed as one company at Bedford with former Rifle Brigade officer William Crosbie as captain, Thomas J Jackson, lieutenant and James Howard, ensign. All three held commissions dated 27 February 1860. Griffith F D Evans was appointed as surgeon on 1 March. Increased to two companies in 1878 and became 'A' and 'B' Companies of the new 1st Corps in 1880. Bedford, where John Bunyan did much of his writing, lies on the River Ouse, its Britannia Iron Works being a major employer during the Volunteer period. Not far from Bunyan's statue, a bronze soldier commemorates those that lost their lives in South Africa during the Boer War.

1st (1880–1908) The 1st Admin Battalion was formed in August 1860 with headquarters at Bedford, transferring to Toddington in 1866, then to Woburn in 1870. The battalion was consolidated in 1880 as the new 1st Corps with nine companies:

'A' Bedford (late 1st Corps)
'B' Bedford (late 1st Corps)
'C' Toddington (late 2nd Corps)
'D' Dunstable (late 4th Corps)
'E' Ampthill (late 5th Corps)
'F' Luton (late 6th Corps)
'G' Luton (late 6th Corps)
'H' Shefford (late 7th Corps)
'I' Woburn (late 8th Corps)

Designated 3rd Volunteer Battalion Bedfordshire Regiment in 1887 and by July 1894 company locations were: Bedford (2), Dunstable, Ampthill, Luton (3), Shefford and Biggleswade. The Bedford Modern School Cadet Corps was affiliated in 1900, but was transferred to the 1st Bedfordshire Royal Engineers (Volunteers) in 1904. Transfer to the Territorial Force in 1908 was as four companies of 5th Battalion Bedfordshire Regiment. Uniform: scarlet/yellow, changing to scarlet/white by 1885.

2nd Formed at Toddington with former Bedfordshire Militia officer William C Cooper as captain, John T Green, lieutenant and William F Green, ensign. All three held commissions dated 1 March 1860. Became 'C' Company of the new 1st Corps in 1880. Toddington, set around a large green on a hill above the River Flitt, lies about five miles south-east of Woburn. Toddington Station was opened on 1 December 1904.

3rd None recorded.

4th Formed at Dunstable with Arthur Macnamara as captain, local solicitor William Medland, lieutenant, and William Eames, ensign. All three held commissions dated 24 April 1860. Became

'D' Company of the new 1st Corps in 1880. Five miles east of Luton, and where the ancient Icknield Way crosses the Roman Watling Street, lies Dunstable. Its large printing works employed a good number from the town. Those Volunteers that attended the ancient church of St Peter would have experience disruption when the south aisle was rebuilt in 1871, and again, in 1876, when it was the turn of the north aisle. The old Dunstable Station on the Hertford, Luton & Dunstable Company line, was closed in January 1866 and reopened just to the north.

5th Formed at Ampthill with John H Brooks as captain, Francis J Thynne, lieutenant, Henry Platt, ensign and William Collingwood, who was appointed surgeon. All four held commissions dated 26 April 1860. Captain Brooks had previously held the rank of Major in the Bengal Light Cavalry. Became 'E' Company of the new 1st Corps in 1880. Eight miles from Bedford, the area employed many in its extensive ironworks and large brewery.

6th Formed at Luton with John S Crawley as captain, Edmund W Vyse, lieutenant and Thomas Smith, ensign. All three held commissions dated 16 May 1860. Increased to two companies and became 'F' and 'G' Companies of the new 1st Corps in 1880. In the north transept of St Mary's Church, among some fifteenth- and sixteenth-century brasses, Captain Crawley's family arms appear on a stone shield. Luton's Corn Exchange on Market Hill was opened in 1868, the town, the largest in the county, being well known for its manufacture of straw hats and bonnets.

7th Formed at Biggleswade with Captain Robert Henry Lindsell, Lieutenant Frederick Hogge and Ensign Frederick Gresham holding commissions dated 11 September 1860. Robert Lindsell had previously held the rank of lieutenant colonel in the 28th Regiment of Foot and was present at the battles of Alma, Inkerman and the siege of Sebastopol during the Crimean War. Headquarters moved to Shefford in 1871 and 7th Corps became 'H' Company of the new 1st Corps in 1880. Those Volunteers that attended St Andrew's Church in Biggleswade would have seen the installation of its Venetian mosaic reredos in 1877. In the town, which is ten miles south-east of Bedford, there was a cycle factory and thread lace was made. To the south-west, the River Ivel runs through Shefford, the town's St Francis's Church opening in 1884.

8th Formed at Woburn from workers on the Duke of Bedford's estate with John T Green as captain, William F Green, lieutenant and Henry Russell, ensign. Their commissions were dated 18 September 1860. Also appointed was Benjamin L Hawkins MD as surgeon. Became 'I' Company of the new 1st Corps in 1880. Volunteers would have seen the demolition in 1868 of the ancient church St Mary the Virgin in Bedford Street, its replacement being a former mortuary chapel. Woburn Abbey, the seat of the Dukes of Bedford, is close by.

9th Formed at Bedford from employees of Howard's Britannia Agricultural Implements factory. Ensign William Henry Lester was the first to be commissioned on 16 May 1864, with Lieutenant Charles Johnson following on 24 May and Captain Henry H Green on 6 June. James Howard, one of the directors of the Britannia works, was commissioned as captain on 16 January 1865 and took command. The corps was later disbanded and last seen in the *Army List* for November 1872.

BERKSHIRE

The county provided one Admin Battalion, which included all corps and, in 1873, was consolidated to form the new 1st Corps. Two numbered sub-divisions appeared in the early *Army Lists*, the 1st and 2nd subsequently being numbered as 2nd and 3rd Corps respectively.

1st (1860–73) Formed with headquarters at Reading on 10 September 1859 and soon comprised three companies under the overall command of Major Commandant Robert James Loyd-Lindsay, former lieutenant colonel Scots Fusilier Guards and winner of the Victoria Cross at the Crimea. Loyd-Lindsay later took command of the 1st Admin Battalion, the three 1st Corps companies after that being commanded by Captains Sir Claudius S Paul Hunter, Charles Stephens and William Martin Atkins. The Borough Museum at Reading is in possession of a photograph which shows three officers of the 1st Corps – Loyd-Lindsay, Sir Paul Hunter and William Atkins. Reproduced in Volume 38 of the *Journal for the Society of Army Historical Research*, the photograph inscription refers to the group as 'three officers of the Wantage and Vale of White Horse Companies'. The 1st Corps became 'A', 'B' and 'C' Companies of the new 1st Corps in 1873.

Noted among the main industries of Reading is biscuit making. Oscar Wilde is on record as having visited Huntley & Palmers factory in 1892. He would make another visit to Reading three years later, but for a less enjoyable reason. Indeed, workers from Huntley & Palmers are known to have served in the Volunteers, many, no doubt, taking part in the parade that saw the December 1886 unveiling in Forbury Gardens by Robert Loyd-Lindsay (by then Lord Wantage VC) of the *Maiwand Lion*. Apparently the largest lion statue in the world, this magnificent beast commemorates those of the 66th (Berkshire) Regiment who laid down their lives during the Afghan Campaign of 1879–80.

1st (1873–1908) The 1st Admin Battalion of Berkshire Rifle Volunteers was formed with headquarters at Reading in June 1860. Robert Loyd-Lindsay VC of the 1st Corps took command. When the battalion was consolidated as the new 1st Corps in 1873 the combined strength of the eleven independent corps then in existence totalled thirteen companies. Headquarters remained at Reading and the reorganization went as follows:

'A' Reading (late 1st Corps)
'B' Reading (late 1st Corps)
'C' Reading (late 1st Corps)
'D' Windsor (late 2nd Corps)
'E' Newbury (late 3rd Corps)
'F' Abingdon (late 4th Corps)
'G' Maidenhead (late 5th Corps)
'H' Sandhurst (late 7th Corps)
'I' Faringdon (late 8th Corps)
'K' Wantage (late 9th Corps)
'L' Winkfield (late 10th Corps)
'M' Wallingford (late 11th Corps)
'N' Windsor Great Park (late 12th Corps)

Mention is made, in a work privately produced in 1959 to commemorate the centenary of the 4th Battalion Royal Berkshire Regiment, of an 'O' Company being present at Annual Camp in 1874. According to the book, this company had been formed by the 'cadets of Coopers Hill College' [presumably the Royal Indian Engineering College]. However, there is no record of a cadet company having been formed there and the *Army List* shows no indication that an increase in establishment had taken place. The corps was re-designated 1st Volunteer Battalion Berkshire Regiment in 1882 – the title 'Royal' not being conferred upon that regiment until three years later in 1885. A Mounted Infantry Company was formed in 1886, the total number of companies amounting to fifteen by April 1897.

Some 137 member of the 1st Volunteer Battalion served in the Boer War, the first contingent under Major A F Ewen and Lieutenants R J Clarke and W P Alleyne, being inspected by Queen Victoria at Windsor in the last week of February 1900 before leaving for South Africa. Upon arrival, the first duty given to the Berkshire men was to provide an escort to a convoy going to Bloemfontein. Joined by a second draft under Lieutenant F A Simmonds, the Volunteers, now serving alongside Regulars from their county regiment, were placed under the command of General Sir Ian Hamilton at Pretoria. Action was seen on 2 August, Lord Robert's dispatch of 10 October 1900 noting, 'on approaching Uitval Nek, Hamilton found it strongly held by the enemy, whom he engaged in the front with a portion of Cunningham's brigade, while two companies of the Berkshire Regiment gallantly escaladed the steep cliff overlooking the pass from the east'. The enemy were cleared from the area, the loss to the attackers including Private Lee of the Volunteer Company, who was killed. In the same action Private William House of the 2nd (Regular) Battalion received the Victoria Cross (VC). Guarding lines of communication, escort and garrison duties followed, six of the Volunteers being lost due to disease during this period.

Several cadet corps were formed and affiliated to the battalion – mention has already been made of one possibly existing at Coopers Hill. Those that did appear in the *Army List*, and had officers commissioned to them, were the Wellington College Cadet Corps, formed in 1882; Bradfield College, which appeared in 1884, and a unit raised in the East Berkshire parish of Cookham Dean in 1900 – the latter gone from the *Army List*, however, by July 1902. The last return made by the battalion prior to joining the Territorial Force in 1908 as 4th Battalion Royal Berkshire Regiment, showed a total strength of 1,078 all ranks. Also in 1908, both Wellington and Bradfield Colleges became contingents of the Junior Division OTC. Uniform: scarlet/Lincoln green, changing to scarlet/blue by 1886.

2nd Formed as the 1st Sub-division at Windsor on 27 October 1859 and increased to a full company by the beginning of the following year with Captain the Hon Alexander L M H Ruthven, Lieutenant Samuel Thomas George Evans and Ensign Ramsay Hamilton Couper. All three officers held commissions dated 12 January 1860. Became 'D' Company of the new 1st Corps in 1873. At Windsor in 1881, the Albert Institute was opened with its reading rooms and lecture hall, and on Castle Hill, in Jubilee year, the Volunteers held the ground at the unveiling of Queen Victoria's statue. A great model for them, as far as drill and smartness were concerned, was the several Guards regiments; one of which was always stationed in the town. Headquarters of the company were in Church Lane.

3rd Formed at Newbury as the 2nd Sub-division with Lieutenant Henry Richard Eyre commissioned on 14 December 1859 and Ensign George Charles Cherry on 30 December. Later increased to the strength of a full company and shown as 3rd Corps in the *Army List* for the first time in March 1860. Promoted, Henry Eyre received his captain's commission on 29 May 1860. The Newbury Volunteers became 'E' Company of the new 1st Corps in 1873. Work began on Newbury's Corn Exchange within a year of the formation of the 3rd Corps. The Municipal Buildings near the Town Hall were built between 1876 and 1877, and the District Hospital in 1885. The scene of two Civil War battles, the town lies on the River Kennet – the Kennet and Avon Canal passes through.

4th Formed as one company at Abingdon with Captain Samuel Bowels and Lieutenant John Blandy-Jenkins commissioned on 23 February 1860; Ensign Edward Morland on the following 5 April. Became 'F' Company of the new 1st Corps in 1873. The Volunteers would have seen the Victorian restoration of two of the town's churches: St Helen's in 1873, and St Nicholas's in 1881. Abingdon is six miles south of Oxford.

5th Formed at Maidenhead with Captain Robert Vansittart, Lieutenant Edward Sawyer and Ensign Henry Micklem commissioned on 24 February 1860. Robert Vansittart had previously held the rank of lieutenant colonel in the Coldstream Guards. Became 'G' Company of the new 1st Corps in 1873. On the right bank of the Thames six miles north-west of Windsor, Maidenhead is connected with Taplow and Buckinghamshire on the opposite bank by a seven-arched stone bridge and a viaduct built by the railway. The Town Hall was rebuilt in 1879 and a Technical School opened in 1894.

6th Formed at Wokingham with Lieutenant John Edward Leveson Gower and Ensign William Nelson Suckling commissioned on 14 May 1860. Surgeon James S Barford later joined, but the corps disappeared from the *Army List* in March 1865 having not exceeded the strength of a half company. Wokingham, where the railway reached just four years before the formation of the 6th Corps, is seven miles south-east of Reading, its All Saints' Church being restored in 1880. The progress of the Volunteer Force always being well covered in *The Times*, it would be the owners and founders of the paper (the Walters) who built Bear Wood House, close to Wokingham, in 1865.

7th Formed as half company at Sandhurst with Lieutenant William Walker and Ensign Edward de la Motte commissioned on 25 August 1860. William Walker had previously served as an officer with the 69th (South Lincolnshire) Regiment. Increased to a full company in 1872 and became 'H' Company of the new 1st Corps in 1873. The military college there since 1812, Sandhurst is about five miles south-east of Wokingham.

8th Formed as a half company at Faringdon with Lieutenant Daniel Bennett and Ensign George F Crowdy commissioned on 21 September 1860. George Henry Maskelyne joined as surgeon in March 1861 and about that time the 8th Corps was increased to a full company; the two existing officers being promoted, George James Haines coming in as ensign with commission dated 8 January 1862. Became 'I' Company of the new 1st Corps in 1873. Nine miles north-west of Wantage, Faringdon lies on the slope of a hill overlooking the Thames Valley. The Corn Exchange was built in 1863, the town's trade being noted as bacon, corn, cattle and sheep.

9th Formed as one company at Wantage with Captain Edwin M Atkins, Lieutenant Edward J Hayward and Ensign Perceval Parr commissioned on 24 October 1860. Walter R H Barker became surgeon. Did not join the 1st Admin Battalion until 1863 and became 'K' Company of the new 1st Corps in 1873. A badge of the 9th Corps was illustrated in the *Bulletin* of the Military Historical Society in May 2006, which shows a representation of King Alfred, who is said to have been born in the town. A statue of Alfred was unveiled by the Prince and Princess of Wales in the centre of the market place in 1877. In 1851 Wantage was noted as carrying on a brisk trade in corn and malt, there also being manufacturers of sacking, twine and coarse cloth in the town.

10th Formed as one company with Captain George Dennistoun Scott, Lieutenant V W B Van de Weyer, Thomas Edmund Franklin and Surgeon William Henry Blenkinsopp commissioned on 1 March 1861. Headquarters was first given in the *Army List* as Woodside, the family seat of Captain Scott, but by July, Winkfield is listed. The 10th Corps did not join the 1st Admin Battalion until 1863 and became 'L' Company of the new 1st Corps in 1873. Woodside is about two miles south-east of Windsor, and Winkfield, where St Mary's Church was restored in 1884, is some six miles south-west. At the church, in 1904, was laid to rest Admiral Sir Henry Keppel, who had commanded the Naval Brigade in the Crimea.

11th Formed as one company at Wallingford with Captain Frederick Lawes Austen of Brightwell Park, Tetsworth; Lieutenant George Morrison, Ensign Charles Morrell and surgeon Charles

Albert Barrett commissioned on 13 February 1861. Did not join the 1st Admin Battalion until 1863 and became 'M' Company of the new 1st Corps in 1873. Wallingford is on the right bank of the Thames, the river here being crossed by an ancient bridge of nineteen arches, fifteen miles north-west of Reading. The Great Western Railway station was opened on 2 July 1866 and the town's main trade in 1851 was noted as malt, corn and flour.

12th Formed as a half company in the spring of 1861, headquarters of the 12th Corps are given as Windsor Great Park. The first officer to be enrolled was former major general in the Regular Army, Francis Hugh Seymour, who received his commission as lieutenant on 9 May 1861. He was joined by Ensign William Menzies on 24 May 1861. Became 'N' Company of the new 1st Corps in 1873. Just to the south of Cumberland Lodge in the park is Sir J E Boehm's equestrian statue of Prince Albert. Given by the ladies of England, the memorial is dated 1887–90.

BERWICK-UPON-TWEED

1st Formed at the seaport town of Berwick-upon-Tweed, the company's first officers were: Captain Robert Ramsey jun, Lieutenant Henry L Christison and Ensign Robert Thompson. All three held commissions dated 28 March 1860. In the following November the corps was included in the 1st Northumberland Admin Battalion and in 1880 became 'G' Company of the new 1st Northumberland and Berwick-upon-Tweed RVC. Much of Berwick's employment involved shipping.

BERWICKSHIRE

All rifle corps formed within the county were placed into the 1st Admin Battalion, which was consolidated as the new 1st Corps in 1880.

1st (1859–80) Formed at Duns as one company with the Hon Adolphus F Cathcart as captain, J Cunningham, lieutenant, David Ferguson, ensign and Robert C MacWatt MD as surgeon. All four held commissions dated 16 December 1859. Became 'A' Company of the new 1st Corps in 1880. Duns is to the west of Berwick-upon-Tweed. The railway, the old North British, reached the town in 1849, the station, however, being renamed from Dunse to Duns in May 1883.

1st (1880–1908) The 1st Admin Battalion was formed with headquarters at Duns on 19 November 1863, moving to Coldstream on 1 November 1876. The battalion was consolidated in April 1880 as the new 1st Berwickshire RVC with seven companies:

'A' Duns (late 1st Corps)
'B' Coldstream (late 2nd Corps)
'C' Ayton (late 3rd Corps)
'D' Greenlaw (late 4th Corps)
'E' Lauderdale (late 5th Corps)
'F' Earlston (late 6th Corps)
'G' Chirnside (late 7th Corps)

Became a volunteer battalion (without change in title) of the Royal Scots in 1881, but General Order 61 of May 1887 notified that the corps had been transferred to the King's Own Scottish

Borderers (KOSB). The new designation of 2nd (Berwickshire) Volunteer Battalion was authorized in the following December by General Order 181. Headquarters had moved from Coldstream back to Duns in 1885. On 1 April 1891 'H' Company was formed at Duns, followed by 'I' Company at Ladykirk in May 1900. But the latter was relettered as 'H' upon disbandment of new Duns personnel in 1905. Transfer to the Territorial Force in 1908 was as two companies of the 4th Battalion KOSB. Uniform: all scarlet with grey trousers, changing to scarlet/blue with trews.

2nd Formed at Coldstream as one company with Sir J Majoribanks Bt as captain, Matthew Dysart Hunter, lieutenant, Thomas Hood, ensign and Alexander Brown as surgeon. All four held commissions dated 30 March 1860. Became 'B' Company of the new 1st Corps in 1880. Coldstream, where in 1650 General Monk raised the regiment that would later be known as Coldstream Guards, is on the River Tweed to the north-east of Kelso. The town's station was renamed in 1873; a Volunteer leaving by train on 1 October from Cornhill would return in the evening to Coldstream.

3rd Formed at Ayton as a sub-division on 11 May 1860. Increased to a full company in the following August the officers then being Captain David Poppiewell, Lieutenant David H Somerville and Ensign Joseph Rowat. Became 'C' Company of the new 1st Corps in 1880. At Ayton, just under eight miles from Berwick-upon-Tweed, the Volunteers would have seen the building of the parish church which began in 1864 and was completed in 1866.

4th Formed at Greenlaw as one company with George Warrender as captain, William Broomfield, lieutenant and James Nesbit, ensign. All three held commissions dated 24 February 1860. Also appointed was Robert M Robinson as surgeon. Became 'D' Company of the new 1st Corps in 1880. About seven miles south-west of Duns, Greenlaw lies on the River Blackadder and produced woollens and agricultural implements. The railway, the old Berwickshire line, reached the town in 1863, the station opening on 16 November.

5th Formed at Lauderdale as a sub-division with William Fairholme as lieutenant and Robert Romanes, ensign. Both held commissions dated 10 April 1860. Increased to a full company in March 1864 and became 'E' Company of the new 1st Corps in 1880. Lauderdale is described as an ancient district in the West of Berwickshire. The parish and town of Lauder is on Leader Water, which brought many to the area for trout fishing – no doubt by the Lauder Light Railway, which was opened on 2 July 1901.

6th Formed at Earlston as one company with Alexander Mitchell as captain, James Small, lieutenant and Charles Wilson jun, ensign. All three held commissions dated 5 June 1863. Became 'F' Company of the new 1st Corps in 1880. The Volunteers at Earlston, four miles north-east of Melrose, would have seen the building of the parish church in 1892. The Berwickshire Railway came to the town in 1863, the station opening on 16 November.

7th Formed at Chirnside as a sub-division on 7 July 1863 with Robert N Slight as lieutenant and J T Marshall, ensign. Increased to a full company in August 1868 and became 'G' Company of the new 1st Corps in 1880. In this small village about five miles from Duns, the church was rebuilt in 1878 and paper was manufactured.

BRECKNOCKSHIRE

All corps formed within the county were included in the 1st Admin Battalion, which was consolidated as the new 1st Corps in 1880.

1st (1859–80) Formed at Brecon and comprised two companies by March 1860. In command of No. 1 was former Rifle Brigade officer Captain Henry Gore Lindsay. Became 'A' and 'H' Companies of the new 1st Corps in 1880. The town sits where the rivers Usk and Honddu meet and was for some time the Depot of the 24th Regiment, later South Wales Borderers. A statue of the Duke of Wellington stands in the square outside St Mary's Church. St David's Church, at the west end of the town in the area called Llanfaes, was rebuilt in 1859. Close by is Christ College, where a cadet corps was formed in 1894 and attached to the 1st Volunteer Battalion South Wales Borderers. Also raised in the town (in 1901) was the cadet company at the Intermediate School.

1st (1880–1908) The 1st Admin Battalion was formed on 30 August 1860 with headquarters at Brecon and in March 1880 was consolidated as the new 1st Corps with eight companies:

'A' Brecon (late 1st Corps)
'B' Brynmawr (late 2nd Corps)
'C' Crickhowell (late 3rd Corps)
'D' Hay-on-Wye (late 4th Corps)
'E' Builth Wells (late 5th Corps)
'F' Talgarth (late 6th Corps)
'G' Cefn Coed (late 7th Corps)
'H' Brecon (late 1st Corps)

A Mounted Infantry Company was formed at Glosbury in 1884, this being disbanded in 1898, and in 1894 a new company was raised at Ystradgynlas. In 1894 and 1901 respectively, cadet units were formed and attached to the battalion at Christ College, Brecon and Brecon Intermediate School. The corps was designated 1st Volunteer Battalion South Wales Borderers in 1885 and transfer to the Territorial Force in 1908 was as the Brecknockshire Battalion South Wales Borderers. Uniform: grey/black, changing to scarlet/white in 1884.

2nd Formed at Brynmawr with Captain John Maund, Lieutenant George Phillips Bevan and Ensign Crawshay Bailey commissioned on 13 February 1860. Henry A Butterfield was appointed as surgeon in the following April. Became 'B' Company of the new 1st Corps in 1880. The town, to the south-west of Abergavenny, had extensive ironworks. Its station, on the old Merthyr, Tredegar & Abergavenny Railway, was opened in 1862.

3rd Formed at Crickhowell with Captain Frederick Ximenus Gwynue, Lieutenant John Hotchkis and Ensign Evan Parry commissioned on 25 February 1860. Became 'C' Company of the new 1st Corps in 1880. The town is situated about fourteen miles south-east of Brecon in the valley of the Usk. The area is mostly agricultural.

4th Formed at Hay-on-Wye, the first officer, former Royal Navy officer, Lieutenant Francis T Brown, being commissioned on 7 April 1860. Became 'D' Company of the new 1st Corps in 1880. At Hay, seven miles north-east of Brecon on the outskirts of the Black Mountains, an iron bridge was built across the river in 1864; St Mary's Church was restored three years after that. The Hereford, Hay & Brecon Railway reached the town in 1864, Hay Station opening on 11 July.

5th Formed at Builth Wells with Ensign Trevor G W James, chaplain, the Revd W Williams and Surgeon William P James being commissioned on 4 June 1860. Became 'E' Company of the new 1st Corps in 1880. The railway reached Builth in September 1864, which no doubt brought more to 'take the waters'. The town sits on the River Wye fourteen miles north of Brecon, its ancient bridge of six arches taking you across to Radnorshire.

6th Formed at Talgarth with Lieutenant Edward Williams and Ensign John M Bowes commissioned on 14 February 1861. Became 'F' Company of the new 1st Corps in 1880. Situated at the foot of the Black Mountains, Talgarth's St Gwendoline's Church was restored in 1873, the same year that a chapel was opened in memory of Howell Harris – a native of the town and one of the founders of Welsh Methodism.

7th Formed on 15 June 1878 at Cefn Coed and became 'G' Company of the new 1st Corps in 1880. The tall fifteen-arched railway viaduct of 1865–66, towers above the houses of this small town. Built here in the Volunteer period was St John's Church in 1874, and St Tudor's in 1888.

BUCKINGHAMSHIRE

The county's 1st Admin Battalion became the new 1st Corps in 1875. Two numbered sub-divisions (1st and 3rd) appear in the early *Army Lists*, which subsequently formed the 1st and 2nd Corps respectively. Possibly the half-company raised at Buckingham, the eventual 3rd Corps, filled the 2nd Sub-division slot. However, no such designation appeared in the *Army List*.

1st (1859–75) Formed at Great Marlow as the 1st Sub-division by Mr T Owen Wethered of Marlow and sworn in on 8 December 1859. The first officers: Lieutenant George Henry Vansittart of Bisham Abbey and Ensign T Owen Wethered, were all three commissioned on 16 December. Shown in the *Army List* as 1st Corps for the first time in April 1860 and became part of the new 1st Corps in 1875. The principal sources of employment at Great Marlow are listed in the 1890s as being paper mills, a brewery, the manufacture of chairs and lace making. The town lies on the Thames four miles north-west of Maidenhead. On the Great Western, Great Marlow Station was opened on 28 June 1873.

1st (1875–1908) The 1st Admin Battalion was formed with headquarters at Aylesbury in July 1862. Great Marlow became headquarters in 1872 and in 1875 the battalion was consolidated to form the new 1st Corps which first appeared in the *Army List* for April. There were five companies:

> Great Marlow (late 1st Corps)
> Buckingham (late 3rd Corps)
> Aylesbury (late 4th Corps)
> Slough (late 5th Corps)
> Eton College (late 8th corps)

New companies were later formed at High Wycombe, Buckingham and Wolverton – No. 6 Company at Wolverton was recruited in the main from men employed at the London and North Western Railway Carriage Works; the Volunteers at High Wycombe were from the staff of a local chair manufacturer. In 1876 a cadet corps was also provided by St Paul's College at Stony Stratford; this, however, disappeared from the *Army List* in May 1883. The Eton College personnel were detached to form a new 2nd Corps in 1878. Became a volunteer battalion (without change of title) of the Oxfordshire Light Infantry in 1881, the companies in 1897 being redistributed: two at High Wycombe (still mainly chair-makers), one-and-a-half at Wolverton (LNWR carriage works), half at Buckingham and one each at Marlow, Aylesbury, Slough and Stony Stratford. A ninth company was added in 1900, and transfer to the Territorial Force in 1908 was as The Buckinghamshire Battalion Oxfordshire Light Infantry. Uniform: grey/scarlet.

2nd (1860–72) Formed at High Wycombe as the 3rd Sub-division with Lieutenant Henry H Williams commissioned on 6 March 1860. Shown in the *Army List* as 2nd Corps for the first time in April 1860. The corps, however, was not seen listed after September of the following year. Re-formed, however, as 8th Corps under the command of Lieutenant Colonel W C Pratt of the Royal Bucks Militia, the new officers having commissions dated 22 November 1861. Renumbered as 2nd again from December 1861, but disbanded in 1872. High Wycombe lies on the Wye fifteen miles north-west of Windsor. The making of chairs was an important industry in the town.

2nd (Eton College) (1878–1908) Formed as 8th Corps at Eton College in May 1867 with a cadet corps attached. Commanding Officers' commissions for both units, Captain Samuel Thomas George Evans (8th Corps) and Hon Captain Revd Edmond Warre (cadets), being dated 22 January 1868. Became part of the new 1st Corps in 1875. In June 1878, however, it was decided to removed the Eton College elements and form the companies into an independent corps designated 2nd Buckinghamshire (Eton College) RVC. Designated 4th (Eton College) Volunteer Battalion Oxfordshire Light Infantry in 1887, but reverted to its former title, 2nd (Eton College), in 1902. Establishment was increased from four to five companies in 1900. In 1908 the Eton College Volunteers transferred to the Territorial Force as a contingent of the Junior Division OTC. Uniform: grey/light blue.

3rd Formed at Buckingham as a half-company and shown in the *Army List* for the first time in March 1860. No officers appear until June, however, and then with commissions dated 11 May: Lieutenant the Hon Percy Barrington (afterwards Viscount Barrington) and Ensign Robert A Fitzgerald. Absorbed the 7th Corps at Winslow in 1863 and became part of the new 1st Corps in 1875. On the Ouse, seventeen miles north-west of Aylesbury, the town was an agricultural centre, had several maltings, a brewery and a factory that manufactured artificial manure.

4th Formed on 25 March 1860 at Aylesbury with Captain the Hon Florence G H Irby (afterwards Lord Boston) in command. Became part of the new 1st Corps in 1875. The Corn Exchange on the Market Square was built in 1866, the Library in Temple Street opened in 1880. Users of the railway saw the closing of the original Aylesbury Station (London & Birmingham Line), and its replacement in the High Street on 16 June 1889. In the 1890s a large print works on the edge of town gave employment to many from the area.

5th Formed at Slough on 20 July 1860 under the command of Captain R Bateson-Harvey (afterwards Sir and Member of Parliament) of the Bucks Yeomanry. Became part of the new 1st Corps in 1875. At Slough, just north of Windsor, the Leopold Institute and Public Hall in High Street was built in 1887. Slough Station, opened on the Great Western in 1840, was closed and replaced by a new building just to the west of the old on 8 September 1884.

6th Formed at Newport Pagnell as 7th Corps with Samuel Newman commissioned as ensign on 14 September 1860. Renumbered 6th by January 1861. Disbanded later and last seen in the *Army List* for June 1864. The town is on the south bank of the Ouse.

7th (1860–61) See 6th Corps.

7th (1861–63) Formed at Winslow with Thomas Newman commissioned as ensign on 17 May 1861. Absorbed into the 3rd Corps at Buckingham in 1863. Winslow is just under eleven miles north-west of Aylesbury.

8th Two corps held this number; see 2nd Corps and 2nd Corps (Eton College).

BUTESHIRE

1st Formed with headquarters at Rothesay on the east side of the Isle of Bute, this company joined the 1st Renfrewshire Admin Battalion in 1863 and became 'I' Company of the new 1st Renfrewshire RVC in 1880. The 1st Buteshire had been formed towards the end of 1859, its first officers, Captain Archibald McKirdy, Lieutenant Daniel Macbeth and Ensign Charles Fellows Maclachlan, all holding commissions dated 19 January 1860. The Norman Stewart Institute in Montague Street was opened in July 1885. The group of lavatories at the end of the pier erected in 1899 remain to this day, an attraction of the town. Herring fishing gave employment to many.

CAITHNESS-SHIRE

Too small in numbers to form the county's own admin battalion, from 1864 the several Caithness rifle corps joined that of the neighbouring county of Sutherlandshire.

1st Formed as one company at Thurso with Captain Alexander Henderson, Lieutenant William R Tait and Ensign James Brims all holding commissions dated 10 April 1860. Surgeon J Mill joined in the following month. Became 'G' Company of the new 1st Sutherland Corps in 1880. Thurso Station, opened by the Sutherland and Caithness Railway Company in July 1874, and from where the Volunteers went off to their camps, is the most northerly in Britain.

2nd Formed as one company at Wick with Captain James Horne, Lieutenant John Henry Buik and Ensign Roderick Ross commissioned on 16 February 1861. Became 'H' Company of the new 1st Sutherland Corps in 1880. A busy fishing port, Wick gave employment to hundreds from the town in the gutting and curing of herrings. The Sutherland and Caithness Railway reached the town in 1874, its station being opened on 28 July.

3rd Formed as one company at Halkirk, ten miles south of Thurso, with William Dunbar as captain, George Logan, Lieutenant and Henry Mackay, ensign. Their commissions were all dated 11 April 1861. Became 'I' Company of the new 1st Sutherland Corps in 1880. Flagstones, used to pave streets around the world, were quarried in the area.

4th Formed as one company at Watten with Captain William Innes Patterson, Lieutenant James Patterson and Ensign Donald McKinnon. All three held commissions dated 25 September 1867. Became 'K' Company of the new 1st Sutherland Corps in 1880. Watten is about eight miles north-west of Wick; its railway station was opened by the Sutherland and Caithness Railway Company in July 1874.

CAMBRIDGESHIRE

Two admin battalions existed in Cambridgeshire, the 2nd being formed with headquarters at Cambridge in November 1862 and including the town's 1st and 8th Corps. From November 1863 the 17th Essex RVC was also included. In 1872, however, 2nd Admin was broken up and the 1st Cambridge Corps, together with 17th Essex, were transferred to 1st Admin Battalion. One numbered sub-division was formed, which became the 4th Corps.

1st (1860–80) Steps to raise an RVC in Cambridge were first taken at a meeting held at the Guildhall in May 1859. Subsequently a Rifle and Drill Club was formed and it would be this that, once official recognition had been gained from the government, became the 1st Cambridgeshire RVC of one company. The commissions of its first officers: Captain W P Prest, Lieutenant Frederick Barlow and Ensign Albert Decimus Claydon, were dated 16 January 1860. Francis R Hall joined them as surgeon and Charles H Crosse as chaplain in the following month. On 26 May 1860 the *Cambridge Chronicle* reported that on the previous day Colours had been presented to the 1st Corps by the ladies of Cambridge on Parker's Piece. In May 1862 a second company was added, and to this, Nos 3 and 4 appeared after the 8th Corps, also at Cambridge, was absorbed in 1864. Became 'A' to 'D' Companies of the new 1st Corps in 1880. Brief notes regarding the origins of the 1st Cambridgeshire RVC appear in *The Cambridgeshires 1914–1919*, Major G B Bowes TD pointing out that the officers of the battalion were mostly drawn through two generations from well-known Cambridgeshire families. Large employers such as the Cambridge University Press (which for years provided a full company), the colleges, Post Office, railway and timberyards of Wisbech, all contributed towards the ranks; as did the small-holders of the Fens, together with the clerks, shop assistants and mechanics of local firms.

1st (1880–1908) The 1st Admin Battalion was formed with headquarters at March towards the end of 1860. Captain Frederick D Fryer of the 2nd Corps took command, his commission as Major being dated 7th December 1860. To the battalion were added the 2nd, 4th, 5th, 6th, 7th and 10th Cambridgeshire Corps. The 1st Cambridgeshire, 17th Essex and 1st Huntingdonshire RVC were also included in 1872. The battalion was consolidated as 1st Cambridgeshire RVC with the sub-title 'Cambridge, Essex and Hunts' reflecting its three-county association, in 1880. Headquarters were placed at Cambridge and there were ten companies:

'A', 'B', 'C' and 'D' Cambridge (late 1st Cambridgeshire)
'E' Wisbech (late 2nd Cambridgeshire)
'F' Whittlesea (late 4th Cambridgeshire)
'G' March (late 5th Cambridgeshire)
'H' Ely (late 6th Cambridgeshire)
'I' Saffron Walden (late 17th Essex)
'J' St Neots (late 1st Huntingdonshire)

General Order 181 of December 1887 notified a change in designation to 3rd (Cambridgeshire) Volunteer Battalion Suffolk Regiment. In 1889 the Hunts company ('J') was disbanded. Three cadet corps were affiliated to the 3rd Volunteer Battalion, Leys School in Cambridge forming a company in 1900, followed by the Perse School (also in Cambridge) in 1905. The last formed was by the Cambridge and County School in 1906. On Sunday, 29 March 1908 the Colours presented to the original 1st Corps in May 1860 were committed to the keeping of the vicar and churchwardens of Great St Mary. Two days later the Territorial Force came into being and as the 1st Cambridgeshire RVC stood down, the Cambridgeshire Battalion Suffolk Regiment was born, an unpopular title which was soon changed to the Cambridgeshire Regiment. At the same time Leys and Cambridge and County Schools became contingents of the Junior Division OTC. Uniform: scarlet/blue.

2nd (1860–80) Formed at Wisbech with Captain Frederick D Fryer, Lieutenant Francis Jackson and Ensign Richard Young commissioned on 2 January 1860. Became 'E' Company of the new 1st Corps in 1880. The town gave employment in its breweries, sawmills, rope works, coach-building yard and printing works. When the Peterborough, Wisbeach [sic] & Sutton Bridge Railway came to the area in August 1866, two stations were opened: Wisbeach and, just over two miles south-west of the town, Wisbeach St Mary.

2nd (Cambridge University) (1880–1908) Grateful we must be to Hew Strachan who, in *History of the Cambridge OTC*, did much to simplify the complicated company structure of the Cambridge University Corps. Official approval and acceptance of a corps of Rifle Volunteers raised within Cambridge University was received by the Vice Chancellor in December 1859. An establishment of five companies was sanctioned and on 10 January of the following year the first officers were gazetted to the 3rd Cambridgeshire (Cambridge University) RVC – in command was Major James Baker of the 8th Light Dragoons. Six companies were in existence by March, all formed from members of the university and organized on the following basis:

> No. 1, formed from Gonville and Caius, Clare, Christ's, Corpus Christi, Emmanuel, Queens', Jesus and Sidney Sussex Colleges.
> No. 2, formed from St John's College.
> No. 3, formed from King's, Magdalene, Peterhouse and Trinity Hall Colleges
> Nos 4, 5 and 6, formed from Trinity College.

In 1864 personnel from St Catharine's and Pembroke Colleges were included in No. 1 Company while those from Clare transferred to No. 3. Sidney Sussex was also included in No. 3 the following year, and in November 1867 the six companies were lettered 'A' to 'F' with the following reorganizations:

> 'A' now formed by Pembroke, Corpus Christi, Queens', St Catharine's and Downing
> 'B' by St John's
> 'C' by Clare, Gonville and Caius, Trinity Hall, King's and Sidney Sussex
> 'D' by Jesus, Christ's, Emmanuel and Magdalene
> 'E' and 'F' by Trinity.

The 3rd Corps was renumbered as 2nd (Cambridge University) in 1880 and designated as 4th (Cambridge University) Volunteer Battalion Suffolk Regiment under General Order 181 of December 1887. During 1893–94 the company structure was changed yet again:

> 'A' now from Peterhouse, Pembroke, Queens', Corpus Christi and St Catharine's
> 'B' from St John's
> 'C' from Gonville and Caius
> 'D' from Christ's, Emmanuel, Jesus and Magdalene
> 'E' from Trinity
> 'F' from Clare, Trinity Hall, King's, Sidney Sussex and Selwyn.

St John's became part of 'A' Company in 1896 and at the same time Pembroke became 'B' and Downing part of 'A'. Permission to increase the establishment to eight companies was granted during the early part of 1900, the change requiring the regrouping of the colleges as follows: St John's was removed from 'A' Company to form the new 'G', while at the same time Christ's, Magdalene, Sidney Sussex and Selwyn were taken from 'D' and 'F' to form 'H'. Under Army Order 56 of April 1903 His Majesty the King was graciously pleased to approve the new title of 'The Cambridge University Volunteer Rifle Corps', this being held until transfer to the Senior Division of the OTC in 1908. Uniform: grey/grey, changing to grey/light blue in 1892.

3rd See 2nd Corps (1880–1908).

4th Formed at Whittlesea on the Fens with Lieutenant Edward Loomes and Ensign William Harris Bowker commissioned on 17 January 1860. Known as the 1st Sub-division until March and became 'F' Company of the new 1st Corps in 1880. St Mary's Church at Whittlesea was restored in 1862, the work including the chapel dedicated to Lieutenant General Sir H G Smith GCB, who was born in the town and died in 1860. Many from Whittlesea were employed in the production of bricks – Arthur Mee noted of the town that it was 'flanked by the tall chimneys of brickyards rising in mass formation.'

5th Formed as one company at March with Captain Robert C Catling, Lieutenant Robert Dawbarn jun and Ensign William O Pratt commissioned on 13 June 1860. Became 'G' Company of the new 1st Corps in 1880. In the town, situated on the Nen, much trade in coal, timber and corn was carried out on the river. There was an extensive engineering works and a factory producing agricultural implements. On Sundays, perhaps the Volunteers that attended St Wendreda's Church, with its embattled walls, counted the angels that looked down from the roof – all 200 of them.

6th Formed at Ely with Captain Everard Calthrop, Lieutenant Henry W Marten and Ensign Charles T Harlock commissioned on 11 July 1860. Also attached to the corps were the Revd William E Dickson, MA, as chaplain, and Robert Muriel, who was surgeon. Became 'H' Company of the new 1st Corps in 1880. Dominated by it great octagon-towered cathedral, Ely stands on almost the highest part of the Fenland, bounded to the south by the River Ouse. Close to Ely Porta is Ely Theological College, founded by Bishop Woodford in 1876.

7th Formed as a sub-division at Upwell with Lieutenant William L Ollard and Ensign William Elworthy commissioned on 7 September 1860. Also attached to the corps was John Hemming as surgeon. The corps was increased to a full company in 1864, but over the next years interest began to wane and in consequence the 7th Cambridgeshire RVC was disbanded and last seen in the *Army List* for December 1872. The parish of Upwell is part in Cambridgeshire and part in Norfolk, the River Nen dividing the shires.

8th Formed as one company at Cambridge with Captain George Leapingwell, Lieutenant Charles J Clay and Ensign Josiah Chater commissioned on 6 November 1860. Also attached to the corps were the Revd A V Hadley MA as chaplain, and James Carter as surgeon. Absorbed into the 1st Corps as its Nos 3 and 4 Companies in 1864.

9th Formed as a sub-division at Newmarket with Ashley Patson Cooper as lieutenant and James Neal York, ensign. Both officers held commissions dated 15 January 1861 and in April they were joined by Samuel Gamble, who became surgeon. The corps was shown in the *Army List* for July 1862 as being 'united' with the 1st Suffolk Admin Battalion and in the following month was removed from the Cambridgeshire list having been absorbed into the 20th Suffolk RVC. The town is part in Cambridgeshire and part in Suffolk; All Saints' at the Cambridge end of the High Street was built on the site of an earlier church in 1876–7.

10th Formed at Soham with Richard Cockerton as lieutenant and James Westley, ensign. Both officers held commissions dated 28 January 1862. The corps was later disbanded and not shown in the *Army List* after October 1865. Soham, six miles south-east of Ely, employed many from the town in its extensive orchards.

CARDIGANSHIRE

Due to a series of disbandments and renumberings within the county, details of the 1st, 2nd, 3rd and 4th Cardiganshire RVC can at times prove confusing. Two of the four held different numbers at various times, and one, the last formed, was to hold all four positions throughout its existence. With this in mind the corps are shown by location rather than numerical designation.

Aberystwyth/Talybont A corps raised at Aberystwyth appeared in the *Monthly Army List* for February 1860. Shown as the 1st Sub-division, it was numbered as 1st Corps by the following month, its officers, Lieutenant Griffiths Williams and Ensign Henry Charles Fryer, both holding commissions dated 12 March. In the *List* for June 1861 the 1st Corps is given as being at Talybont, a town some six miles north-east of Aberystwyth. That for January 1864, however, shows it for the last time, its strength never having been above that of a half company.

Aberystwyth also provided the 2nd Corps of the period with Lieutenant W Eardeley Richards and Ensign Thomas Owen Morgan commissioned 12 March 1860. This was included in the 1st Montgomeryshire Admin Battalion in January 1864 and by June of the same year had been renumbered as 1st Corps. In 1866, however, and as a half company only, the Aberystwyth corps was broken up and not shown in the *Army List* after October.

The railway having reached the town in the mid 1860s, a grand hotel was opened, but the visitors stayed away and it was closed down in 1872. The town Library was opened in 1875 and employment for many was in the area's several iron foundries, and from a busy timber trade.

Aberbank Aberbank was the home of the original 3rd Corps. With a strength of just a half company it was soon disbanded and with only one officer appointed, Lieutenant Thomas D Lloyd who held a commission dated 12 March 1860, made its last appearance in the *Army List* for May 1861.

Cardigan When the company at Cardigan was formed its services were accepted as the 4th Cardiganshire RVC. Its officers, Lieutenant D Jenkins and Ensign Thomas Davies; both held commissions dated 8 May 1860. Due, however, to the disappearance of the 3rd Corps at Aberbank in 1861, the company was then renumbered as 3rd. Yet another change appeared in June 1864, the corps now being shown as 2nd and 'united' with the 1st Admin Battalion of Pembrokeshire Rifle Volunteers. The renumbering this time was due to the 2nd Aberystwyth Corps having been re-designated as 1st Corps. The 1st position in the county list had remained vacant since the disbandment in 1866 of the Aberystwyth half company. Subsequently in 1873 the 2nd Corps at Cardigan took the last step up and from May appeared as 1st Corps. Still with the Pembrokeshire Admin Battalion, the 1st Corps at Cardigan became 'F' Company of the new 1st Pembrokeshire RVC in 1880. Situated on the River Teifi, many from the town were employed in the manufacture of tiles, bricks, agricultural implements and woollen garments. Then part of the Whitland & Cardigan Railway Company, Cardigan's station was opened on 1 September 1886.

CARMARTHENSHIRE

All six numbered corps were included in the county's 1st Admin Battalion. Formed in June 1861 with headquarters at Carmarthen, the battalion, however, was broken up in 1875, and the corps then in existence subsequently transferred to the military care of the 1st Pembrokeshire Admin Battalion.

1st Formed at Llandilo with Viscount Emlyn as captain, John Lewis Thomas, lieutenant and Frederick Lloyd Phillips, ensign. All three held commissions dated 28 February 1860. Became 'G' Company of the new 1st Pembrokeshire Corps in 1880. The town rises up from the River Towy and to celebrate the Queen's jubilee the Victoria Jubilee Memorial Hall was opened in 1887. Cassell's for the 1890s notes the town as having a large trade in corn and flour. There was also brewing, tanning, saw and woollen mills. Llandilo's second railway station, Llandilo Bridge, was opened on 24 January 1865.

2nd Formed as one company at Carmarthen with Captain David J B Edwards commissioned on 20 February 1860. Absorbed the 6th Corps, also at Carmarthen, as No. 2 Company in 1872 and became 'H' and 'I' Companies of the new 1st Pembrokeshire Corps in 1880. General Picton, who fell at Waterloo, was a native of Carmarthen, and a monument to his memory now looks down on the town from a hill. Another hero, this time General Nott of Ghuznee, stands in Nott Square. Carmarthen lies on the Towy about twenty-eight miles from Swansea, its main industry during the Volunteer period being the export of timber, slates, marble, lead and tin-plate. Salmon fishing was also important to the town. The Carmarthen and Cardigan Railway Company began on 1 March 1860, the original station closing in 1902 and replaced just to the south by the Great Western on 1 July.

3rd Formed at Llandovery with Captain John Jones, Lieutenant James N Morgan and Ensign David A Price commissioned on 4 May 1860. Later disbanded and last seen in the *Army List* for May 1875. On the River Towy, Llandovery is about eighteen miles from Brecon. The town was an important agricultural centre. Llandovery Station was opened by the Vale of Towy Railway on 1 April 1858.

4th Formed at Llansawel with Sir J W Drummond Bt as captain, A P Jones, late of the 6th Dragoons, lieutenant, and D L Price, ensign. All three officers held commissions dated 29 May 1860. The 4th Corps was disbanded in the latter part of 1869. Llansawel is a small village on the River Cothi nine miles north of Llandilo.

5th Formed at Llanelly with William Henry Nevil as captain, William Roderick, lieutenant and William Bytheway, ensign. All three officers were commissioned on 8 May 1861. Became 'K' Company of the new 1st Pembrokeshire Corps in 1880. The town's St Paul's Church predates the Volunteers by just three years, but All Saints' was built in 1874. The Market Hall was opened in 1888, Custom House built in 1893, and a new Town Hall was completed in 1894. Many from the town were employed in the tin-plate works (the largest in the world at one time), docks, collieries, copper, iron or lead mines.

6th Formed at Carmarthen with John Thirlwall as captain, Owen S Wilson, lieutenant and William de Grouchy Warren, ensign. All three held commissions signed 8 May 1861. Absorbed into the 2nd Corps as its No. 2 Company in 1872.

CARNARVONSHIRE

The 1st Admin Battalion was formed on 2 August 1860 with headquarters at Carnarvon. In 1873 the battalion was broken up and was last seen in the *Army List* for December of that year. The Carnarvonshire corps then joined the 1st Flintshire Admin Battalion.

1st Formed with headquarters at Carnarvon, mostly from men employed at the Pennant Slate Quarry, with G S G D Pennant taking command. His commission was dated 1 March 1860. From the various muster rolls held at the National Library of Wales, it appears that on 14 August 1861, out of a strength of eighty-seven Volunteers, the best part were residents from the parishes of Llanllechid and Llandegai. Headquarters were shown as Penrhyn after 1862. The corps was later disbanded and made its last appearance in the *Army List* for December 1874, never having more than a single lieutenant (John Francis to begin with) appointed to it after Major Pennant had taken command of 1st Admin Battalion in August 1860.

2nd Formed with headquarters at Carnarvon on 1 March 1860 with Hamilton Alder Roberts as lieutenant. Headquarters were shown as Penrhyn after 1862. The vast majority of Volunteers, according to the muster rolls, were residents from the parishes of Llandegai, Llanllechid and Llanddeinioln and were men employed in the Pennant-owned slate quarries. The corps was later disbanded and was last seen in the *Army List* for January 1877.

3rd Formed with headquarters at Carnarvon on 1 March 1860 with Henry Runsey Williams as captain, John Washington Poole, lieutenant and James Wilmot Rees, ensign. Also appointed was William Maughan as surgeon. Muster rolls show that the majority of the corps were residents of the parish of Llanbeblig. Became 'G' and 'H' Companies of the new 1st Flintshire Corps in 1880.

4th Formed with headquarters at Tremadoc on 1 March 1860 with Henry Windus Mathews of Penmorfa as captain, Griffith Humphrey Owen, lieutenant and John Jones Roberts of Ynyscynhaiarn, ensign. Robert Roberts of Ynyscynhaiarn was appointed as surgeon at the same time. Recruits came mostly from the parish of Ynyscynhaiarn. Moved later to Portmadoc and became 'I' Company of the new 1st Flintshire Corps in 1880.

5th (1860–77) Formed with headquarters at Pwllheli on 1 March 1860 with Robert Carreg as captain, Hugh Hunter Hughes, lieutenant and Hugh Pugh, ensign. Also appointed was Thomas H Hughes as surgeon. The corps, which was recruited mainly from the parish of Denio, was disbanded later, making its last appearance in the *Army List* January 1877.

5th (1878–80) Formed at Llanberis on 5 June 1878 and became 'K' Company of the new 1st Flintshire Corps in 1880. About eight miles from Carnarvon, Llanberis parish and village employed many in its slate queries. The church of St Padarn was built in 1886, the much older St Peris's, with its fifteenth-century timber roof, being restored in 1893. The town saw the opening of the Carnarvon & Llanberis Railway on 1 July 1869, and, on 6 April 1896, the Snowdon Mountain Railway, which ran from Llanberis to almost the summit.

6th Formed at Bangor on 3 March 1860 with Pennant Athel Iremonger as captain, John William Hughes, lieutenant and William Pritchard, ensign. Also appointed was Thomas H Hughes as surgeon. Disappeared from the *Army List* in October 1865. Bangor, where many were involved in the slate quarries, lies close to the northern entrance to the Menai Straits, its St Mary's Church in Garth Road being built in 1864.

7th Formed at Conway on 4 April 1860 with James Edwards of Conway as captain, Robert Farrant of Llandudno, lieutenant and Vernon Darbishire who resided at Dwygyfylchi, ensign. The corps, which was recruited mainly from the parishes of Conway, Llandudno and Caerhyn, disappeared from the *Army List* in January 1867.

3rd Volunteer Battalion Royal Welsh Fusiliers Formed on 26 May 1897 by the removal of the eight Carnarvonshire companies then forming part of the 2nd Volunteer Battalion, RWF (see the new 1st Flintshire Corps). Headquarters were placed at Carnarvon, and in 1900 Anglesey, without Volunteers since the disbandment of its last corps in 1863, provided a new company at Holyhead. In the last year of the Volunteer system the strength of the battalion stood at 836 all ranks, its nine companies being located Carnarvon (2), Portmadoc, Penygroes, Llanberis, Conwy, Penmaenmawr, Pwllheli and Holyhead. Transfer to the Territorial Force in 1908 was as headquarters and seven companies of the 6th Battalion Royal Welsh Fusiliers. Uniform: scarlet/blue.

CHESHIRE

Five admin battalions were formed, which in 1880 became the 1st to 5th new corps. The Boer War Memorial in Queen's Park, Victoria Avenue, Crewe, includes the names of fifty men that served with the several Volunteer Service Companies in South Africa.

1st (1859–80) Formed as one company with headquarters at Birkenhead, the first appointed officers being Captain John Cadell, Lieutenant Henry John Ward and Ensign John James Conway. All three held commissions dated 25 August 1859. Joined the 1st Admin Battalion and became 'A' Company of the new 1st Corps in 1880. Looking across the Mersey to Liverpool, Birkenhead set out its tramways in the year after the 1st Corps was raised. William Laird's shipyard, one of the biggest and busiest in the world, employed many from the town.

1st (1880–1908) The 1st Admin Battalion, formed at Birkenhead towards the end of 1860 with Lieutenant Colonel Vincent Ashfield King from the 2nd Corps in command, included the 1st, 2nd, 3rd, 4th, 11th, 14th, 30th, 34th and 35th Cheshire RVC and was consolidated as the new 1st Corps in 1880. Headquarters were placed at Oxton and the battalion's eight companies were located:

'A' Birkenhead (late 1st Corps)
'B' Oxton (late 2nd Corps)
'C' Egremont (late 3rd Corps)
'D' Bebington (late 4th Corps)
'E' Neston (late 11th Corps)
'F' Hooton (late 14th Corps)
'G' Tranmere (late 30th Corps)
'H' Bromborough (late 35th Corps)

General Order 181 of December 1887 directed the change in designation from 1st Cheshire RVC to 1st Volunteer Battalion Cheshire Regiment. New companies were formed at Birkenhead, Liscard and Heswall by 1900 and to answer the call for Volunteers to go out to South Africa, ninety-six from the battalion would see active service, three of that number being killed in action. Called the 'Greys', from the colour of its uniform, the 1st Volunteer Battalion transferred to the Territorial Force in 1908 as 4th Battalion Cheshire Regiment. Uniform: grey/scarlet.

Several cadet units were formed and affiliated to the battalion; the first to appear in the *Army List* being that raised by Wirral College in 1892. Both Mostyn House School at Parkgate and the West Kirby School provided companies the following year, the Wirral College corps, however, was disbanded in 1884 followed by West Kirby in 1900. In 1903 Liscard High School, Wallasey Grammar, and the New Brighton High School all appear in the *Army List* as having formed units. But by April 1904 all three had disappeared having had no officers appointed.

2nd (1859–80) Formed as one company at Oxton with Captain Vincent Ashfield King as captain and William Horner, lieutenant. Both held commissions dated 30 August 1859; Ensign John Usher Cunningham joining them on 20 January 1860. When Captain King was appointed as commanding officer of the 1st Admin Battalion, William Horner replaced him as captain (commission dated 31 December 1860) and to replace him, James Roper came in as lieutenant. About the same time Joseph Godden (commissioned 15 February 1861) became surgeon to the corps. Joined the 1st Admin Battalion and became 'B' Company of the new 1st Corps in 1880. Oxton in north-west Cheshire formed part of the borough of Birkenhead and is noted as being the location of 'many well-built residences occupied by Liverpool merchants'. The railway reached the town in the form of the Lauder Light Railway on 2 July 1901.

2nd (Earl of Chester's) (1880–1908) Chester was the headquarters of the 2nd Admin Battalion, which included the 6th, 7th, 23rd and 24th Corps. Captain Richard Brooke of the 6th Corps was appointed as lieutenant colonel in command with commission dated 30 October 1860. The battalion was consolidated in 1880 as the 2nd Cheshire (Earl of Chester's) RVC with nine companies:

'A' to 'E' Chester (late 6th Corps)
'F' and 'G' Runcorn (late 7th Corps)
'H' Weaverham (late 23rd Corps)
'I' Frodsham (late 24th Corps)

General Order 181 of December 1887 directed the change in designation from 2nd Cheshire RVC to 2nd (Earl of Chester's) Volunteer Battalion Cheshire Regiment. Two new companies were formed in 1900. Just prior to transfer to the Territorial Force in 1908 as headquarters and four companies of 5th Battalion Cheshire Regiment, the returned strength of the 2nd Volunteer Battalion stood at 1,081 all ranks. Uniform: scarlet/buff.

3rd (1859–80) Formed as one company with headquarters at Wallasey with William Chambres as captain, James Harrison, lieutenant and George Edmund Lance, ensign. All three held commissions dated 5 September 1859. These were joined in April 1860 by Surgeon Isaac Byerely. Headquarters moved to Egremont in 1880 and in same year 3rd Cheshire RVC, as part of the 2nd Admin Battalion, became 'C' Company of the new 1st Corps. The early Volunteers would have seen the rebuilding of Wallasey's St Hilary's Church in 1859, it having been destroyed by fire two years earlier. The town is located on a peninsula to the north of Birkenhead which is bounded to the west by the Irish Sea, and to the east by the River Mersey. The small steamboat station of Egremont is in the parish of Wallasey and looks across the Mersey to Liverpool. Wallasey Station was opened when the Seacombe, Hoylake & Deeside Railway reached the town on 2 July 1901.

3rd (1880–1908) Formed towards the end of 1860 with Lieutenant Colonel Thomas W Tatton in command (commissioned 1 November 1860), headquarters of the 3rd Admin Battalion were at first placed at Altrincham and the corps included in it the 12th, 15th, 22nd, 25th, 26th, 28th and 32nd. The battalion moved to Knutsford in 1864 and in 1880 was consolidated as the new 3rd Cheshire RVC with eight companies:

'A' and 'B' Altrincham (late 12th Corps)
'C' Knutsford (late 15th Corps)
'D' Northwich (late No. 1 Company, 22nd Corps)
'E' Winsford (late No. 2 Company, 22nd Corps)
'F' Cheadle (late 26th Corps)
'G' Sale Moor (late 28th Corps)
'H' Lymm (late 32nd Corps)

The 3rd Corps was designated as 3rd Volunteer Battalion Cheshire Regiment in 1887, the change being notified in General Order 181 of December, and at the closing of the Volunteer Force its total strength stood at 736 all ranks. Transfer to the Territorial Force in 1908 was as four companies of the 5th Battalion Cheshire Regiment. Uniform: scarlet/white.

4th (1859–80) Formed as one company at Bebington with Captain Frederick Pembroke Jones, late of the 4th Dragoon Guards, and Ensign William Stock Bower commissioned on 10 September 1859. The position of lieutenant would remain vacant until the spring of 1860 when Ensign Bower was promoted and his place taken by E Wrangham Bird, who was commissioned on 15 May 1860. At the same time a surgeon joined the corps in the form of G T Roper MD. The *Army List* shows an increase to two companies in 1862, all three new officers holding commissions dated 10 March, and in March 1863 headquarters of the 4th Corps are given as Rock Ferry, just a mile or so from Bebington on the Birkenhead road. It would now seem that No. 2 Company was withdrawn and made independent – its officers, as from *Monthly Army List* for April 1863, now being listed under a new formation, the 35th Cheshire RVC at Bromborough. The 4th Corps remains at Rock Ferry until September 1864, but in the *Army List* for the following month there is no mention of a 4th Corps at all. November 1864, on the other hand, shows a new 4th Corps, once again at Bebington and with three completely new officers, Captain John Mayer, Lieutenant John Mathews jun and Ensign Alfred S Walford, all with commissions dated 5 November 1864. As part of the 1st Admin Battalion, the 4th Cheshire became 'D' Company of the new 1st Corps in 1880. On the Mersey, three miles south-east of Birkenhead, there were large brickworks as Bebington. The Volunteer leaving Bebington on the Birkenhead Railway on 1 May 1895 would have returned home to find that the station had been renamed Bebington and New Ferry.

4th (1880–1908) Headquarters of the 4th Admin Battalion were at Stockport and to the several Cheshire corps included (9th, 13th, 17th, 18th, 19th, 20th, 21st, 29th and 31st) were added the 23rd Derbyshire RVC in 1876. Captain Francis D P Astley of the 13th Corps was appointed as lieutenant colonel in command, his commission being dated 5 November 1860. The battalion was consolidated as the new 4th Cheshire RVC in 1880 with thirteen companies:

'A' to 'C' Stalybridge (late 13th Corps)
'D' Stockport (late 17th Corps)
'E' Stockport (late 18th Corps)
'F' Stockport (late 19th Corps)
'G' Stockport (late 20th Corps)
'H' Stockport (late 21st Corps)
'I' Stockport (late 29th Corps)
'K' Hyde (late 31st Corps)
'L', 'M' and 'N' Glossop (late 23rd Derbyshire Corps)

General Order 181 of December 1887 directed the change in designation from 4th Cheshire RVC to 4th Volunteer Battalion Cheshire Regiment and at the close of the Volunteer Movement the last return of the battalion gave a combined strength of 1,066 all ranks. Transfer to the Territorial Force in 1908 was as 6th Battalion Cheshire Regiment. Uniform: scarlet/buff, changing to scarlet/white in 1889.

5th (1859–80) Formed as one company with headquarters at Congleton, the original 5th Corps officers were: Captain Sir Charles Watkin Shakerley Bt of Somerford Park; Lieutenant Francis Henry Randle Wilbraham and Ensign Arthur Isaac Solly. All held commissions dated 15 September 1859 and joining them in February 1860 was Dr Robert Beales MD, who became surgeon. Joined the 5th Admin Battalion and became 'A' and 'B' Companies of the new 5th Corps in 1880. Congleton is situated in the valley of the Dane and gave employment to many in what was described in the 1890s as its main industry, fustian cutting. Fustian a kind of thick, hard-wearing twilled cloth. There were also extensive collieries and stone quarries in the area. The first year of the 5th Corps is also that of the town's St Stephen's Church, its Town Hall in High Street being opened in 1864. Congleton Upper Junction Station on the North Staffordshire line opened on 1 June 1864.

5th (1880–1908) Captain of the 5th Corps, Sir Charles Watkin Shakerley Bt, was commissioned as lieutenant colonel of the 5th Admin Battalion on 15 November 1860. Headquarters were at Congleton and included in the battalion were the 5th, 8th, 16th, 27th, 33rd and 36th Cheshire RVC. When the battalion was consolidated in 1880 it was to include four companies provided by the 36th Cheshire at Crewe. The Crewe corps, however, was disbanded just before the merger and the eventual establishment of the new 5th Cheshire RVC was nine companies:

'A' and 'B' Congleton (late 5th Corps)
'C', 'D', 'E' and 'F' Macclesfield (late 8th Corps)
'G' Sandbach (late 16th Corps)
'H' Wilmslow (late 27th corps)
'I' Nantwich (late 33rd Corps)

By October 1880 the *Army List* indicated a ten-company establishment, the addition being commanded by a former lieutenant of the 27th Wilmslow Corps. General Order 181 of December 1887 directed the change in designation from 5th Cheshire RVC to 5th Volunteer Battalion Cheshire Regiment. The strength of the battalion just prior to transfer to the Territorial Force in 1908 as 7th Battalion Cheshire Regiment was returned as 868 all ranks. Uniform: grey/scarlet.

6th (The Earl of Chester's) Formed as one company with headquarters at Chester, the original officers being: Captain Richard Brooke, who had previously served with the 1st Life Guards; former Honourable East India officer Lieutenant John Ireland Blackburne, both with commissions dated 25 November 1859, and Ensign Francis H Barker, who was not gazetted until 24 February 1860. John D Weaver joined as surgeon to the corps in the following March. Also at Chester was the 10th Cheshire RVC, which in June 1860 joined the 6th Corps as its No. 2 Company. It was a popular corps in the Chester area; the first officer to No. 3 Company was commissioned on 10 August 1860 and to No. 4 on 20 July 1869. In the following year the additional title 'The Earl of Chester's' was authorized and in 1879 yet another company made its way onto the establishment. As part of the 2nd Admin Battalion, 6th Cheshire RVC became 'A' to 'E' Companies of the new 2nd Corps in 1880. The Drill Hall was in Volunteer Street, Chester. There on the right bank of the Dee, Chester would add to its long history when in 1867 a group of Fenians attempted to seize the castle. A year later the massive restoration of the cathedral began under the supervision of Sir Gilbert Scott, and in the year that followed it would be the turn of Holy Trinity Church. Two churches were built, and a Town Hall, Post Office, Library, and a Recreation Ground gifted by the Marquis of Westminster, were all opened during the Volunteer period.

7th Formed as one company with headquarters at Runcorn, the original officers of the 7th Corps were Captain Arthur Brooke, Lieutenant Phillip Whiteway and Ensign John Brundrit. All three held commissions dated 30 November 1859. Henry Wilson joined as surgeon in April 1860, and in the spring of 1866 a second company was added. As part of the 2nd Admin Battalion, 7th Cheshire RVC became 'F' and 'G' Companies of the new 2nd Corps in 1880. Runcorn is on the south side of the Mersey, its prosperity through shipping, according to several sources, being due to the opening of the Duke of Bridgewater's Canal (now the Manchester Ship Canal) in 1773.

8th Formed as one company with headquarters at Macclesfield. The original officers of the 8th Cheshire RVC were Captain Samuel Pearson jun, a former officer with the 1st Dragoon Guards; Lieutenant Charles Edward Proctor and Ensign George Edward Adshead. All three held commissions dated 5 January 1860. John Mayer joined as surgeon to the corps in March 1860. The first officers were commissioned to a second company on 25 April 1860, a third on 5 June 1862 and to a fourth in 1876. As part of the 5th Admin Battalion, 8th Cheshire RVC became 'C' to 'F' Companies of the new 5th Corps in 1880. The magnificent four-columned Town Hall was enlarged in 1870, the County Lunatic Asylum built in 1871 and the Volunteer Drill Hall in 1872. Much of the town's employment was in the silk and cotton trade; there were also coal and slate mines and stone quarries in the area.

9th Formed as one company at Mottram with Captain Alfred K Sidebotton, Lieutenant William Bayley jun, and Henry Algernon West commissioned on 10 February 1860. Edward Sidebottom joined as surgeon to the corps in May 1860. Interest later fell off and the corps, which had been part of the 4th Admin Battalion, made its last appearance in the *Army List* for February 1861. Mottram, in Longden Dale, is about three miles from Glossop.

10th Formed as one company at Chester with Captain Phillip S Humberston, Lieutenant Henry French and Ensign Edward Dixon commissioned on 25 February 1860. Joined the 2nd Admin Battalion and was absorbed into the 6th Corps as its No. 2 Company in June 1860.

11th Formed as one company at Neston with Captain Henry M Edwards, Lieutenant Hugh Craig, Ensign Horatio Lloyd and Surgeon David Russell MD commissioned on 28 February 1860. Joined the 1st Admin Battalion and became 'E' Company of the new 1st Corps in 1880. Neston lies on the south-west side of the peninsula formed by the Dee and the Mersey. There is a church, St Mary and St Helen's, which was rebuilt in 1876 and in the High Street, the Town Hall, which was opened in 1878. Neston Station, on the Birkenhead Railway, was opened on 1 October 1866, the North Wales & Liverpool line reaching the town on 18 May 1896.

12th Formed as one company at Altrincham with Hugh Fleming as captain, Alfred Neild, lieutenant and Stephen Robinson, ensign. All three held commissions dated 1 March 1860, and they were joined in May 1860 by Newcomb Rogers, who became surgeon. Joined the 3rd Admin Battalion, absorbed the 25th Cheshire RVC at Timperley as its No. 2 Company in 1866, and became 'A' and 'B' Companies of the new 3rd Corps in 1880. Sawmills, timberyards and furniture making are listed as the town's main industries. Altrincham is to the west of Stockport.

13th Formed as one company at Dukinfield with Francis Dukinfield P Astley as captain, Charles James Ashton, lieutenant, Thomas B Hall, ensign and Alfred Aspland, surgeon. All four held commissions dated 20 February 1860. This corps was raised by the Astley family and was known unofficially as the 'Astley Rifles'. In November 1860 Captain Astley was appointed as lieutenant colonel in command of the 4th Admin Battalion and at the same time his place was taken in the 13th Corps by Charles Ashton who was promoted captain on 5th November. Ten days later the first officers of No. 2 Company were commissioned and in March 1869, those of No. 3. Headquarters moved to Newton Moor near Hyde in 1863 and then to Stalybridge in 1873. As part of the 4th Admin Battalion, the 13th Cheshire RVC became 'A' to 'C' Companies of the new 4th Corps in 1880. Dukinfield is six miles east of Manchester, its main sources of employment during the Volunteer days being recorded as cotton, engineering, calico printing, hat making and the manufacture of bricks and titles.

14th Formed as one company at Hooton with William Hope Jones as captain, Lancelot Dixon, lieutenant, George Gray Glen, ensign and Alexander R Lingard, surgeon. All four held commissions dated 3 March 1860. Joined the 1st Admin Battalion and became 'F' Company of the new 1st Corps in 1880. Hooton is about seven miles south-south-east of Birkenhead.

15th Formed as one company at Knutsford with John Pennington Legh as captain, David R Davies, lieutenant and Joshua Jackson jun, ensign. All three held commissions dated 5 March 1860. In the following July Edward M Gleeson was appointed as surgeon. Joined the 3rd Admin Battalion and became 'C' Company of the new 3rd Corps in 1880. About eleven miles west-north-west of Macclesfield, Knutsford and its inhabitants feature widely in Elizabeth Cleghorn Gaskell's *Cranford* and other novels. She was buried in the churchyard of the Unitarian Chapel in 1865. The Cheshire Midland Railway station at Knutsford (opened on 12 May 1862) was closed and replaced by one serving the company known as the Cheshire Lines Committee on 1 January 1863.

16th Formed as one company at Sandbach with Edmund J Tipping as captain, Aaron C Howard, lieutenant and Henry S Armitstead, ensign. All three held commissions dated 7 March 1860. Joined the 5th Admin Battalion and became 'G' Company of the new 5th Corps in 1880. Sandbach is about five miles north-east of Crewe, its new Town Hall and Market Place being built in 1889. About this time the chief trade in the town was salt, chemicals and the making of boots and shoes.

17th Formed as one company at Stockport with Henry Coppock as captain, David McClure, lieutenant and John McClure, ensign. All three held commissions dated 10 March 1860, Dr William Rayner MD joining them as surgeon to the corps in August 1860. As part of the 4th Admin Battalion, 17th Cheshire RVC became 'D' Company of the new 4th Corps in 1880. The Volunteers at Stockport would have seen a number of public buildings built. Opened in 1862 was the Mechanics' Institute, the Library in 1875, the Public Baths in 1888 and the Reform Club in 1889. The town's main employment was in cotton, but there were also foundries, machine works and breweries. The 17th Cheshire RVC was the first of six corps to be raised at Stockport.

18th Formed as one company at Stockport with John Thomas Emmerson as captain, William L Eskrigge, lieutenant and Alexander W Thorneley, ensign. All three held commissions dated 12 March 1860 and Dr William H Medd joined them as surgeon in October 1860. Joined the 4th Admin Battalion and became 'E' Company of the new 4th Corps in 1880.

19th Formed as one company at Stockport with Samuel W Wilkinson as captain, George A Ferneley, lieutenant and Henry Smith, ensign. All three held commissions dated 15 March 1860. John T Pearson was appointed surgeon in September 1860. Joined the 4th Admin Battalion and became 'F' Company of the new 4th Corps in 1880.

20th Formed as one company at Stockport with Thomas H Sykes as captain, Godfrey Barnsely, lieutenant and Thomas Dixon Hill, ensign. All three held commissions dated 20 March 1860. Joined the 4th Admin Battalion and became 'G' Company of the new 4th Corps in 1880.

21st Formed as one company at Stockport with Cephas John Howard as captain, Walter Hyde, lieutenant and John Turton, ensign. All three were commissioned on 22 March 1860. Joined the 4th Admin Battalion and became 'H' Company of the new 4th Corps in 1880.

22nd Formed as one company at Northwich with Thomas H Marshall as captain, William S Bradburne, lieutenant and Christopher Cheshire, ensign. All three held commissions dated 26 March 1860. Dr Thomas G Dixon joined them as surgeon to the corps in the following July. Joined the 3rd Admin Battalion, a second company was added at Winsford in 1877, and became 'D' and 'E' Companies of the new 3rd Corps in 1880. Northwich lies at the confluence of the Weaver and Dane and was important for its salt and rock salt mines – likewise Winsford just to the south. Major work had to be carried out at Northwich in 1892 when part of the High Street had to be raised six feet due to it having sunk below the level of the River Weaver.

23rd The first officer to be appointed to the 23rd Corps of one company at Weaverham was Captain John Bolton Littledale, who received his commission on 28 March 1860. He was joined by Lieutenant William Jones and Ensign William C Miller in the following June. As part of the 2nd Admin Battalion, 23rd Cheshire RVC became 'H' Company of the new 2nd Corps in 1880. Weaverham is just to the West of Northwich, its St Mary's Church seeing Victorian restoration in both 1855 and 1877.

24th Formed as one company at Frodsham with Captain Charles H Hitchen, Lieutenant Frederick W Jackson, Ensign Thomas F Linnell and surgeon John Jones commissioned on 30 March 1860. Joined the 2nd Admin Battalion and became 'I' Company of the new 2nd Corps in 1880. Frodsham is on the road from Warrington to Chester and lies close to the Rivers Mersey and Weaver.

25th Formed as one company at Timperley with Captain Alfred Lyon, Lieutenant Ashton M Gardiner and Ensign Robert K Gardiner commissioned on 2 April 1860. A No. 2 Company was later added with officers holding commissions dated 15 October 1860. It would appear from the *Army List* that interest in the 25th Corps waned around 1865, the several vacancies appearing then among the officers not being filled. The corps, which had been part of the 3rd Admin Battalion, made its last appearance in July 1866 and what was left of it absorbed into the 12th Cheshire RVC as its No. 2 Company. Timperley is about nine miles north of Knutsford.

26th Formed as one company at Northenden with Thomas W Tatton as captain, George Peel, lieutenant and Francis Hampton, ensign. All three held commissions dated 4 April 1860. Joined the 3rd Admin Battalion, moved headquarters to Cheadle in 1862, and became 'F' Company of the new 3rd Corps in 1880. Northenden is on the Mersey six miles south of Manchester. Cheadle, where the Literary Institute was opened in 1877, is just to the south-east.

27th Formed as one company at Wilmslow with Captain Edward H Greg, Lieutenant John Railton and Ensign Edwin C Hopps commissioned on 5 April 1860. Joined the 5th Admin Battalion in June 1861 and became 'H' Company of the new 5th Corps in 1880. Wilmslow lies on the River Bollin six miles north-west of Macclesfield.

28th Formed as one company at Sale Moor with Alfred Watkin as captain, John Cunliffe, lieutenant, James Frodsham, ensign and John H Larmuth, who was appointed surgeon. All four held commissions dated 7 April 1860. Joined the 3rd Admin Battalion and became 'G' Company of the new 3rd Corps in 1880. Sale Moor (sometimes written as Salemore) is a locality in Sale where the Bridgewater Canal runs through. The Botanic Gardens were opened in 1860, the Police Station and Court House built in 1881 and the Library in Tatton Road established in 1891.

29th Formed as one company at Stockport with John M Lingard, who had previously served with the 1st Royal Cheshire Militia, as captain, Thomas Steen, lieutenant and John G Graham, ensign. All three held commissions dated 10 April 1860. Joined the 4th Admin Battalion and became 'I' Company of the new 4th Corps in 1880.

30th Formed as one company at Tranmere with Hugh H Nicholson as captain and William Brockie, lieutenant. Both held commissions dated 30 April 1860. They were later joined by Ensign John Mosford, who was gazetted on 20 August 1860. Joined the 1st Admin Battalion and became 'G' Company of the new 1st Corps in 1880. On the Mersey, Tranmere fell within the borough of Birkenhead and opened its Conservative Working Men's Club in 1877.

31st Formed as one company at Hyde with Captain Thomas Mottram, Lieutenant Alfred

Thornely and Ensign Frank Thornely commissioned on 15 August 1860. Thomas C Lear joined them as surgeon to the corps in the following October. Joined the 4th Admin Battalion and became 'K' Company of the new 4th Corps in 1880. Hyde is just under five miles from Stockport, the Volun..... there putting to good use, no doubt, the Mechanics' Institute and Technical School, which was opened in 1861, and the Public Baths which dates from 1887. The Town Hall was built in 1885. The main sources of employment in the town were from cotton, several iron foundries and engineering works.

32nd Formed as one company at Lymm with V Fox as captain, Charles F Bennett, lieutenant, Thomas Draper, ensign and William Brigham, surgeon. All four held commissions dated 10 September 1860. Joined the 3rd Admin Battalion and became 'H' Company of the new 3rd Corps in 1880. Lymm parish and town is just under five miles east of Warrington.

33rd Formed as one company at Nantwich with Captain Samuel C Starkey and Lieutenant John J Garnett commissioned on 5 November 1860. The ensign position was not filled until 1863 when Charles Stuart Brooke was commissioned on 25 August. Joined the 5th Admin Battalion and became 'I' Company of the new 5th Corps in 1880. At Nantwich, where the Grand Union Canal passes through the town via an aqueduct, the manufacture of boots, shoes and clothing gave employment to many.

34th Formed as one company at Upton with Captain William Inman, Lieutenant Thomas Bland Royden and Ensign William Hewitt commissioned on 5 June 1861. Joined the 1st Admin Battalion. Interest in the corps fell off around the middle of 1863, the captain position being vacant for almost a year before disbandment came in October 1864. There are several Uptons in Cheshire, but given its association with the 1st Admin Battalion, that of the 34th Corps is most likely to be the parish and village about four miles west of Birkenhead.

35th Formed at Bromborough from No. 2 Company of the 4th Corps with Captain William Henry Hatcher, Lieutenant John Henry Day and Ensign Charles Alexander Payne commissioned on 25 February 1863. Joined the 1st Admin Battalion and became 'H' Company of the new 1st Corps in 1880. Bromborough is four miles south-east of Birkenhead.

36th Formed as two companies at Crewe with company commanders Captain Francis William Webb commissioned on 20 January 1865 and Captain John N Spencer on 21 January 1865. Joined the 5th Admin Battalion. The 36th Cheshire was always a strong corps; two new companies were formed in the 1870s, but plans for it to join the new 5th Corps in 1880 were cancelled and instead the four Crewe companies were disbanded. Important to the town since it came in 1843 was the London & North Western Railway with its locomotive and carriage works. Some 7,000 were employed according to one source in the 1890s, Cassell's noting about the same time that Crewe 'consists almost entirely of the artisans and officials in the company's service.'

1st Cadet Battalion Cheshire Regiment
Formed with an establishment of four companies at Northenden, the first officer being commissioned on 2 December 1901. The battalion transferred to the Territorial Force in 1908, gaining recognition on 29 June 1910.

CINQUE PORTS

An admin battalion for the Cinque Ports area first appeared in the *Army List* for October 1860. In December 1861 two battalions are listed, three corps from Sussex now included with the 1st. The

2nd Admin Battalion, however, was broken up in 1874, its corps either being absorbed into the 5th Kent RVC, or added to Kent's 4th Admin Battalion. When consolidation came in 1880, 1st Cinque Ports Admin Battalion became the new 1st Cinque Ports RVC. Two numbered sub-divisions (1st and 3rd) existed, which in due course became the 4th and 6th Corps.

1st (1859–80) Formed at Hastings with Captain the Hon George Waldegrave, Lieutenant Vandaleur B Crake and Ensign James Rock jun. All three held commissions dated 17 December 1859 and they were joined by John Savery as surgeon to the corps in September 1860. Joined the 1st Admin Battalion. The corps had been raised out of the Hastings Rifle Club, which, in all but name, was the successor of the old Cinque Ports Volunteers of *c*.1789. Absorbed the 9th Corps at Rye, together with the 16th, 17th and 20th Sussex RVC at Battle, Etchingham and Uckfield respectively in 1876 and became 'A' to 'C' Companies of the new 1st Corps in 1880. A popular seaside resort then, as it is now, Victorian Hastings saw the restoration of All Saints' Church in 1871 and St Clement's, where a cannonball fired into the town by a French ship in 1720 could be seen in the wall of the tower in 1875. A Russian gun taken at Sebastopol could also be seen on the seafront.

1st (1880–1908) The 1st Admin Battalion of Cinque Ports Rifle Volunteers was formed with headquarters at Hastings towards the end of 1860. At first all corps were included, but just the 1st and 9th remained after the formation by December 1861 of the 2nd Admin Battalion. About this time the 16th, 17th and 19th Sussex Corps were also included, followed by 2nd and 4th Sussex in 1863 and the 20th Sussex in 1870. The 19th Sussex, however, was removed in 1868, the 2nd Sussex in 1870 and in 1876 the 16th, 17th and 20th Sussex were absorbed into the 1st Cinque Ports Corps. The Battalion was then consolidated as the new 1st Corps in 1880, the bracketed 'Cinque Ports and Sussex' also forming part of the title. Headquarters were placed at Hastings and the company disposition was as follows:

'A' Hastings (late 1st Cinque Ports)
'B' Battle (late 1st Cinque Ports)
'C' Ticehurst (late 1st Cinque Ports)
'D' Lewes (late 4th Sussex)

Became a volunteer battalion of the Royal Sussex Regiment in 1881, but no change in title was ever conferred. 'E' Company was formed at Rye in 1885, 'F' at Hastings in 1887, 'G' Crowborough and 'H' at Ore in 1890, 'I' Hastings and 'K' Ore in 1900. Eastbourne College provided a cadet corps in 1896. Transfer to the Territorial Force in 1908 was as 5th (Cinque Ports) Battalion Royal Sussex Regiment, the Eastbourne College Cadet Corps at the same time becoming a contingent of the Junior Division, OTC. Uniform: grey/blue, changing to scarlet/blue in 1899.

2nd (1859–60) See 3rd Corps.

2nd (1860–74) Formed at Ramsgate as the 2nd Kent RVC with Captain George Augustus Young, Lieutenant George F Burgess and Ensign Owen F Daniel commissioned on 18 September 1859. Dr James Thomas Hiller was also appointed as surgeon, and later, in March 1860, the Revd George W Sicklemore, vicar of St Lawrence's, Ramsgate, became chaplain to the corps. Ensign Daniel had been a lieutenant in the Royal Navy and had served with the Baltic Fleet during the Crimean War. The trades and professions of those that enrolled into the corps are recorded in Charles Igglesden's book *History of the East Kent Volunteers* and include a brewer, several painters and decorators, a licensed victualler, hotel keeper, labourer, plumber, tailor, baker, an engineer, farmer, several grocers, a carver, guilder and a cabinet maker. The 2nd Kent was re-designated as

2nd Cinque Ports RVC in April 1860. It joined the 1st Admin Battalion, transferring to 2nd Admin by the end of 1861, then was absorbed into the 5th Kent RVC as its 'A' Company in 1874.

3rd The services of a company of rifle volunteers formed from the Rye and Tenterden areas (a half-company each with headquarters at Rye) were accepted on 1 December 1859, its officers, Captain William Mackinnon, Lieutenant Edwin Dawes Saunders, Ensign Francis Bellingham and Surgeon C N Davies, being commissioned on 4 January 1860. The corps was originally numbered as 2nd but due to the transfer of the 2nd Kent RVC to Cinque Ports in April 1860 was restyled as 3rd. Joined the 1st Admin Battalion. The Rye portion of the corps was later to suffer a setback when, due to its commanding officer's lack of interest, it began to break up. Some members were to join the 1st Cinque Ports Artillery Volunteer Corps at Hastings, while those that chose to continue as Riflemen enrolled into the 1st Cinque Ports RVC, also at Hastings. Subsequently, by September 1861, the 3rd Corps appears in the *Army List* as being located at Tenterden, the *List* for the following December showing the corps as having been placed into the 5th Kent Admin Battalion. Became 'G' Company of the new 5th Kent Corps in 1880.

4th Formed at Hythe with Henry Bean Mackeson as lieutenant and James Watts jun as ensign. Both held commissions dated 13 February 1860. Later, the vicar of Hythe, the Revd Brenchley Kingsford, was appointed as chaplain to the corps. The Hythe Volunteers were known as 1st Sub-division until April when numbered as 4th Corps. Henry Mackeson was from the brewing family, who were strong supporters of the Volunteer Movement. One relative had been a member of the old Deal Volunteers of 1804, and others would follow in the footsteps of Henry Mackeson and serve in the Hythe company. James Watts was a member of the legal profession. Joined the 1st Admin Battalion, transferring to 2nd Admin Battalion by the end of 1861, then to 4th Kent Admin Battalion in 1874. Absorbed into the 5th Kent RVC as 'D' Company in the same year. For some time the 4th Corps was allowed to store its weapons at the School of Musketry in Hythe, but the authorities there were not keen on this idea so a room loaned by the London and County Bank in Bank Street was taken into use. There would be yet another move, this time just across the road from the bank to premises owned by Henry Mackeson, which would serve as company headquarters until 1882. Hythe is five miles west of Folkestone. Its St Leonard's Church, where Lionel Lukin, the inventor of the lifeboat is buried in the churchyard, saw two restorations during the Volunteer period. The Royal Military Canal begins just east of Hythe.

5th The 5th Cinque Ports RVC was formed as a result of a meeting held at the Old King's Arms Assemble Rooms in Folkestone. Charles G Percival was appointed to be captain, Angus Mackay Leith as lieutenant and Theodore H N Walsh ensign. All three were gazetted on 30 March 1860. Later the Revd Alfred Gay became chaplain to the corps, Charles E Fitzgerald taking up the post of surgeon. Joined the 1st Admin Battalion, transferring to 2nd Admin Battalion by the end of 1861, then to the 4th Kent Admin Battalion in 1874. Absorbed into the 5th Kent RVC in the same year as its 'F' Company. Once just a small seaside town, the coming of the South Eastern Railway in 1844 and the establishment of the packet service to Boulogne did much towards its Victorian prosperity.

6th Formed at Deal with Julius R Backhouse CB, who had previously served as a colonel in the Bengal Artillery, commissioned as lieutenant on 20 April 1860. He was later joined by Ensign Lamprey Karney and Surgeon Frederick T Hulke, who were both gazetted on 9 May. The Deal corps was known as 3rd Sub-division until April. Joined the 1st Admin Battalion, transferring to 2nd Admin Battalion by the end of 1861. Disbanded later and is last seen in the *Army List* for December 1863. Situated at the southern extremity of the Downs, Deal lies opposite the Goodwin Sands, its inhabitants mostly occupied in maritime traffic.

7th Formed at Margate as one company with Charles James Cox, who resided at Fordwich, as captain, James Standring, a Margate wine merchant and member of the town council as lieutenant, and William Price, who was appointed as ensign. All three officers held commissions dated 22 March 1860 and they were later joined by William Henry Thornton as surgeon. A glance at the first muster roll shows how the occupations of the Volunteers in this, and many other corps, varied. They included a hotel keeper, tobacconist, wine merchant, solicitor's clerk, fruit seller, music seller, someone who made billiard tables, tailors, a ticket collector on the railway, hairdresser, bookseller, several builders, a butcher and a photographer. Private H Chexfield was the Superintendant at the Royal Infirmary. Joined the 1st Admin Battalion, transferring to 2nd Admin Battalion by the end of 1861. Detachments were formed at St Peter's and Birchington in 1866, but these were short-lived and disappeared in 1873. Headquarters of the Margate company were at first placed at the Town Hall, but later moved to the Civil and Military Club in New Inn Yard, and after that to Hawley Street. Absorbed into the 5th Kent RVC as its 'G' Company in 1874. Opened in Margate by the Duke of Connaught on 10 July 1875 was the Deaf and Dumb Asylum, the Margate Volunteers providing a guard of honour on the occasion.

8th Formed at Dover with proprietor of the *Dover Chronicle*, Joseph G Churchward, as captain and local solicitor George Fielding, lieutenant. Both held commissions dated 30 July 1860. Late in 1861 the first ensign to be appointed to the corps was W B Churchward, the son of his commanding officer, and in August of that year the vicar of Trinity Church, the Revd A J Woodhouse, joined as chaplain, and local practitioner Dr W Corke became surgeon. The original headquarters occupied by the 8th Cinque Ports RVC were in Snargate Street on property owned by the Chatham and Dover Railway Company. In 1866 Castle House in Dolphin Lane was taken over, which served the corps until moving to Northampton Street in 1876. Joined the 1st Admin Battalion, transferring to 2nd Admin Battalion by the end of 1861, and was absorbed into the 5th Kent RVC as its 'K' Company in 1874. At Dover the Town Hall was opened in 1883 and the new Promenade Pier on Whitson Monday ten years after that. This was also the year when the Volunteers were among those that provided the guard of honour on the occasion of the Prince of Wales laying the foundation stone of the new Commercial Harbour.

9th When the Rye portion of the 3rd Corps was broken up in 1861 those members wishing to continue as Riflemen were transferred to the 1st Corps at Hasting, the detachment thereafter being known as the Rye Sub-division. At the same time (see *Monthly Army List* for September 1861) a 9th Cinque Ports RVC appears as having been formed at Rye and included in 1st Admin Battalion. According to a booklet published in 1954 entitled The Story of the Rye Volunteers, Rye attended the 'Great Review' at Brighton on 21 April 1862 as 9th Corps. No officers, however, appear in the *Army List* under this heading, which was removed in November 1862. Rye once again appears as providing a 9th Corps in January 1865. This time two officers, Captain John Frewen and Ensign William Henry Crowhurst, are listed with commissions dated 12 December. This new corps was in fact formed by the old Rye elements of 1st Corps. Disbanded yet again in 1876, the personnel returning to the 1st Corps.

10th A 10th Corps at New Romney is shown in the *Army List* for August 1862. No officers were appointed, however, and the corps is not seen after April 1864. In January of the following year, however, the 10th reappears, this time with Lieutenant Henry Stringer and Ensign Henry Cobb both holding commissions dated 22 December 1864. The new sub-division held its first drills sometimes at Lydd or in the neighbouring village of Ruckinge. Headquarters were at the Assembly Rooms, New Romney, and firing ranges were originally on land that became the Littlestone Golf Links; then later at Lydd. Joined the 2nd Admin Battalion, transferring to the 4th Kent Admin

Battalion in 1874 and was absorbed into the 5th Kent RVC as its 'L' Company the same year. At St Nicholas's Church in 1875 a stained-glass window was inserted in memory of the 320 passengers and crew of the *Northfleet*, which was lost off Dungeness, just to the south of New Romney, on 22 January 1873.

CLACKMANNANSHIRE

Two corps were formed within the county and placed into the 1st Stirlingshire Admin Battalion until November 1867 when both joined the newly formed 1st Clackmannanshire Admin. Consolidated in 1880, the battalion formed the new 1st Clackmannan and Kinross RVC.

1st (1860–80) The services of two companies of Rifle Volunteers at Alloa, with Captains Alexander Mitchell and William B Clark in command, were accepted on 2 June 1860 and subsequently designated as 1st Corps. No. 3 Company at Alloa and No. 4 at Dollar were formed in November 1867 and in 1880 1st Corps became 'A' to 'D' Companies of the new 1st Clackmannan and Kinross RVC. Alloa lies on the north bank of the Forth and gave employment to many in its production of wool, glass and iron. In the area were breweries – George Younger the first here in 1764, the Thistle Brewery building still dominates the town – distilleries, sawmills and a large engineering works. The Town Hall was opened in 1887. Six miles north-east of Alloa on the River Devon, Dollar had a bleaching works, collieries, and factories producing brick and tiles.

1st (18⁻⁻ ⁻908) The 1st Admin Battalion of Clackmannanshire Rifle Volunteers was formed with headquarters at Alloa in November 1867 and into it were placed the 1st and 2nd Corps. The 14th Stirlingshire RVC at Alva was added in October 1868, and the 1st Kinross-shire in 1873. The battalion was consolidated in February 1880 as 1st Clackmannan and Kinross RVC with seven companies:

'A' Alloa (late 1st Clackmannanshire)
'B' Sauchie (late 1st Clackmannanshire)
'C' Alloa (late 1st Clackmannanshire)
'D' Dollar (late 1st Clackmannanshire)
'E' Tillicoultry (late 2nd Clackmannanshire)
'F' Alva (late 14th Stirlingshire)
'G' Kinross (late 1st Kinross-shire)

A new section was formed at Clackmannan in 1882 which, in the following year, having increased in number, became 'H' Company. The year 1882 also saw the purchase of the old Alloa Prison, which was enlarged to provide headquarters, a drill hall, offices and an armoury. The battalion also had its own rifle range at Hillend near Alloa, 'G' Company using a 600-yard site at Blairadam. Dollar Institution formed a cadet corps and this was affiliated in 1902. General Order 181 of December 1887 notified re-designation as 7th (Clackmannan and Kinross) Volunteer Battalion Argyll and Sutherland Highlanders, and transfer to the Territorial Force in 1908 was as four companies (three in Clackmannanshire, one in Kinross) of the 7th Battalion Argyll and Sutherland Highlanders. The Dollar Institution Cadets at the same time becoming part of the Junior Division, OTC. Uniform: scarlet/blue with trews.

2nd The services of the 2nd Corps of one company at Tillicoultry were accepted on 10 March 1860 and it will be noted that the 2nd Corps holds an earlier acceptance date to that received by the 1st Corps, and therefore should have carried a higher precedence. The corps was in fact issued the higher number but due to the lord lieutenant being absent, and confusion at his office when the applications to form corps were sent in, the numbering was reversed. The first officers appointed to the 2nd Corps were Captain James Snowdowne, Lieutenant Robert Walker and Ensign John Vicars. Became 'E' Company of the new 1st Clackmannan and Kinross RVC in 1880. Five miles south-east of Alloa, Tillicoultry had numerous collieries. The production of woollen garments also providing employment for the town.

CORNWALL

Two administrative battalions were formed to accommodate the twenty-two individual numbered corps formed within the county. In 1880, these were consolidated to form the new 1st and 2nd Cornwall RVC. One numbered sub-division appeared in the early *Army Lists*, this later being numbered as 10th Corps.

1st (1859–80) Formed at Penzance with George Borlase Tremenhere as captain, Henry Dobree, lieutenant and Thomas Cornish, ensign. All three officers held commissions dated 10 September 1859. Joined the 1st Admin Battalion and became 'A' Company of the new 1st Corps in 1880. A thriving seaport in the Volunteer days, Penzance's main sources of employment were shipping and fishing.

1st (The Duke of Cornwall's) (1880–1908) The 1st Admin Battalion was formed with headquarters at Penzance by May 1860, the additional title of 'The Duke of Cornwall's Rifle Volunteers' was later granted and appears for the first time in the *Army List* for December 1861. Included in the battalion were the several corps from the western portion of the county: 1st, 2nd, 3rd, 7th, 8th (later renumbered as 21st), 11th, 12th, 15th, 17th, 18th and 20th Corps. The battalion was consolidated in 1880 as 1st (The Duke of Cornwall's) RVC with eleven companies:

'A' Penzance (late 1st Corps)
'B' Camborne (late 2nd Corps)
'C' Falmouth (late 3rd Corps)
'D' Helston (late 7th Corps)
'E' Truro (late 11th Corps)
'F' Truro (late 12th Corps)
'G' Hayle (late 15th Corps)
'H' Redruth (late 17th Corps)
'I' Trelowarren (late 18th Corps)
'J' St Just-in-Penwith (late 20th Corps)
'K' Penryn (late 21st Corps)

Headquarters were moved from Penzance to Falmouth in 1881. The corps was designated as 1st Volunteer Battalion Duke of Cornwall's Light Infantry in 1885 and headquarters moved again, this time to Truro, in 1902. Volunteers from the battalion served in South Africa during the Boer War. On 30 May 1901, Captain George Percy Bickford-Smith died at Heilbron from wounds received in action. From Trevarno, he had joined the battalion in 1893, being promoted to captain on 27 June 1900. Two new companies were sanctioned in 1900 and transfer to the Territorial Force in 1908 was as 4th Battalion DCLI. Uniform: grey/scarlet.

2nd (1859–80) Formed at Camborne with John Solomon Bickford as captain, Thomas

Hutchinson, lieutenant and Walter Pike, ensign. All three officers held commissions dated 17 October 1859. Joined the 1st Admin Battalion and became 'B' Company of the new 1st Corps in 1880. Camborne, three miles south-west of Redruth, employed many in its tin mines.

2nd (The Duke of Cornwall's) (1880–1908) The 2nd Admin Battalion was formed with headquarters at Bodmin by May 1860; the additional title of 'The Duke of Cornwall's Rifle Volunteers' was later added and appears for the first time in the *Army List* for December 1861. Included in the battalion were the corps from the eastern portion of the county: 4th, 5th, 6th, 9th, 10th, 13th, 14th, 16th, 19th and 22nd. Consolidated in 1880 as 2nd (The Duke of Cornwall's) with nine companies:

'A' Liskeard (late 4th Corps)
'B' Callington (late 5th Corps)
'C' Launceston (late 6th Corps)
'D' St Austell (late 9th Corps)
'E' Bodmin (late 10th Corps)
'F' Wadebridge (late 13th Corps)
'G' St Columb (late 16th Corps)
'H' Camelford (late 19th Corps)
'I' Saltash (late 22nd Corps)

Designated as 2nd Volunteer Battalion Duke of Cornwall's Light Infantry in 1885 and 'J' Company was added at Bude in 1900. Volunteers served alongside the Regulars of 2nd DCLI in South Africa. Lieutenant Edward G Cowlard, second son of C L Cowlard, Clerk of the Peace for Cornwall, died from enteric fever at Springfontein on 5 March 1901. Educated at Marlborough College, his name can be seen on a memorial in the chapel there. Transfer to the Territorial Force in 1908 was as 5th Battalion DCLI. Uniform: scarlet/white.

3rd Formed at Falmouth with former 2nd Dragoons officer George Reid as captain, Marshall Valentine Bull, late of the 10th Regiment of Foot, lieutenant, and Henry A Sleeman, who had served with the 16th Light Dragoons, ensign. All three officers held commissions dated 28 October 1859. Joined the 1st Admin Battalion and became 'C' Company of the new 1st Corps in 1880. The docks were opened at Falmouth in 1860 – the town's main industries included shipbuilding – and Falmouth Station, on the old Cornwall Line, on 24 August 1863. All Saints' Church in Killigrew Street dates from 1890.

4th Formed at Liskeard with John Samuel Hawker as captain, Christopher Childs, lieutenant and John Sobey, ensign. All three officers held commissions dated 13 December 1859. Joined the 2nd Admin Battalion and became 'A' Company of the new 2nd Corps in 1880. At Liskeard, just under twelve miles from Bodmin, the restoration of St Martin's Church, the second largest in Cornwall, went on over the period 1879–1903. The Town Hall was opened in the same year as the 4th Corps was being formed, as was Liskeard Station. The area around the town was well known for its tin production.

5th Formed at Callington with John Kempthorne as captain and John Peter jun, ensign. Both held commissions dated 3 January 1860. Joined the 2nd Admin Battalion and became 'B' Company of the new 2nd Corps in 1880. Callington is nine miles south-west of Tavistock, the Volunteer attending St Mary's Church there experiencing considerable disruption as a new north aisle was added in 1882.

6th Formed at Launceston with Lieutenant William Day Hanson commissioned on 10 January 1860. Joined the 2nd Admin Battalion and became 'C' Company of the new 2nd Corps in 1880. Eleven miles north-west of Tavistock, Launceston looks down from the side of a steep hill to the River Tamar. An extension of the South Devon & Tavistock Railway to Launceston was opened to the public on 1 July 1865.

7th Formed at Helston with Thomas Phillips Tyacke as captain, Frederick Vivian Hill, lieutenant and George Reid, ensign. All three officers held commissions dated 25 January 1860. Joined the 1st Admin Battalion and became 'D' Company of the new 1st Corps in 1880. Three miles from the sea, Helston lies on the River Cober. Numerous public buildings, including the Godolphin Hall, were built in 1889, the Gwinear Road to Helston Railway having been opened by the Great Western on 9 May 1887. The Volunteer wishing to travel to The Lizard from 17 August 1903 would have done so via the first ever railway-operated bus service.

8th An 8th Corps is shown in the *Army List* as having been formed at Penryn with three officers, Captain William Herbert Mansell, Lieutenant Francis Gilbert Enys and Ensign William Francis Phillpotts, holding commissions dated 2 February 1860. The corps is not shown in October, but reappears again in December only to disappear altogether in January 1861. A new corps at Penryn, this time with different officers, appears at the same time numbered as 21st.

9th Formed at St Austell with Henry Hawkins Tremayne as captain, Edmund Carlyon, lieutenant and John Coode, ensign. All three officers held commissions dated 14 February 1860. Joined the 2nd Admin Battalion and became 'D' Company of the new 2nd Corps in 1880. St Austell is fourteen miles north-east of Truro.

10th Formed at Bodmin on 24 December 1859 and known as the 1st Sub-division until March 1860. Now a full company, its first officers were Captain Francis John Hext, Lieutenant Edmunds G Hamley and Ensign Preston James Wallace. All three held commissions dated 6 March 1860. Joined the 2nd Admin Battalion and became 'E' Company of the new 2nd Corps in 1880. Bodmin was bypassed by the Cornwall Line in 1859, the railway eventually reaching it on 27 May 1887.

11th Formed at Truro with Lieutenant Francis Hearle Cock and Ensign Edwin Parkin commissioned on 13 February 1860. Joined the 1st Admin Battalion and became 'E' Company of the new 1st Corps in 1880. Public Rooms were built 1869–70, and a Post Office completed in 1886. But by far the most important development during the Volunteer period was the demolition, with the exception of the south aisle, of the old parish church of St Mary to make way for the new Truro Cathedral, which was completed in 1880. Cassell's notes that in Truro in the 1890s could be found tin-smelting works, three small potteries, two brush factories, a large flour mill, three sawmills, a tannery, a jam factory and shirt and clothing manufacturers.

12th Formed at Truro with James Henderson as captain, Arthur Willyams, lieutenant and Thomas R Foster, ensign. All three officers held commissions dated 13 February 1860. Joined the 1st Admin Battalion and became 'F' Company of the new 1st Corps in 1880.

13th Formed at Wadebridge with William R Crawford Potter as captain, Richard J M E Symonds, lieutenant and Richard G Pollard, ensign. All three officers held commissions dated 7 April 1860. Joined the 2nd Admin Battalion and became 'F' Company of the new 2nd Corps in 1880. Wadebridge lies on the River Camel, which it crosses via a seventeen-arched medieval bridge, seven miles north-west of Bodmin.

14th Formed at Calstock with Edward Williams as captain, William G Gard, lieutenant and John M Sellers, ensign. All three officers held commissions dated 15 March 1860. Joined the 2nd Admin Battalion, the corps being later disbanded and not shown in the *Army List* after November 1860. The village of Calstock lies on the Tamar, its main industries being tin and copper mining.

15th Formed at Hayle, the first officer to receive a commission being Lieutenant Samuel Hosken on 2 May 1860. Joined the 1st Admin Battalion and became 'G' Company of the new 1st Corps in 1880. Hayle was a busy seaport four miles from St Ives and well known during the Volunteer days for its manufacture of mining machinery. Some of the largest ever pumping machines were made there. The work of the same architect that built Holy Trinity in Sloane Street, London (J D Sedding), St Elwyn's Church at Hayle was completed in 1888.

16th Formed at St Columb with Edward B Willyams as captain, George B Collins, lieutenant and Edward B Whitford, ensign. All three officers held commissions dated 2 April 1860. Joined the 2nd Admin Battalion and became 'G' Company of the new 2nd Corps in 1880. There is a St Columb Major and, about five miles distant, a St Columb Minor. The principal industry in the area was the mining of clay, which brought about the formation of the Cornwall Minerals Railway. A goods line at first, but a later passenger service saw the opening of St Columb Road Station on 20 June 1876.

17th Formed at Redruth with John Haye as captain, William M Grylls, lieutenant and James H Dennis, ensign. All three officers held commissions dated 7 April 1860. Joined the 1st Admin Battalion and became 'H' Company of the new 1st Corps in 1880. Tin was the main source of industry at Redruth, the area said to be the largest producer of the metal in the world. The Mining Exchange was opened in the town in 1880.

18th Formed at Helston with John Tyacke as captain, James P Tyacke, lieutenant and John B Kempthorne, ensign. All three officers held commissions dated 2 June 1860. A glance at the first muster roll of the 18th Corps shows that almost half of the members were farmers. Joined the 1st Admin Battalion towards the end of 1861, headquarters moved to Trelowarren (the seat of the Vyvyans close to Mawgan-in-Meneage) in 1864, and in 1880 the corps became 'I' Company of the new 1st Corps. Helston is twelve miles from Falmouth, its railway station opening on 9 May 1887.

19th Formed at Camelford with Lieutenant William S Rosevear and Ensign William S Hawker, commissioned on 26 July 1860. Joined the 2nd Admin Battalion and became 'H' Company of the new 2nd Corps in 1880. On the River Camel, Camelford is twelve miles north of Bodmin. The old North Cornwall Railway reached Camelford on 14 August 1893.

20th Formed at St Just-in-Penwith with Captain Samuel Borcase, a former major in the Cornwall Rangers Militia, commissioned on 14 August 1860. Joined the 1st Admin Battalion and became 'J' Company of the new 1st Corps in 1880. St Just is seven miles west of Penzance, its church being restored in 1865. The Botallack and other tin mines were in the area.

21st Formed at Penryn with Lieutenant William Lanton and Ensign George A Jenkins commissioned on 1 December 1860. Joined the 1st Admin Battalion and became 'K' Company of the new 1st Corps in 1880. Penryn is two miles south-west of Falmouth, its chief industry being the dressing and polishing of granite. Penryn Station was opened by the old Cornwall Railway Company on 24 August 1863.

22nd Formed at Saltash with Captain Benjamin Snell in command holding a commission dated 23 February 1865. Joined the 2nd Admin Battalion and became 'I' Company of the new 2nd Corps in 1880. Saltash lies on the western bank of the Tamar looking across to Devonshire.

CUMBERLAND

All corps were included in the 1st Admin Battalion, which was consolidated in 1880 to form the new 1st Cumberland RVC.

1st (1860–80) On the Eden, in north-east Cumberland, Carlisle saw the formation on 15 February 1860 of the 1st Corps with Robert Ferguson as captain, William Jackson, lieutenant and Miles MacInnes, ensign. The 2nd Corps at Whitehaven at this time comprised two companies and by June 1860 the second of these, under Captain R S Dixon, an officer formerly with the 9th Light Dragoons (Lancers), was absorbed into the 1st Corps as its No. 2 Company. Became 'A' to 'C' Companies of the new 1st Corps in 1880. The parish church of St Mary (1868) is contemporary with the Volunteers; the much older castle built by William Rufus was used as an armoury and barracks. In 1880, Carlisle's Her Majesty's Theatre became the first in England to be lit by electricity. Chief sources of employment in the 1850s were listed as cotton goods, print and dye works, iron foundries and tanneries.

1st (1880–1908) The 1st Admin Battalion was formed with headquarters at Carlisle in May 1860. Moved to Keswick in 1865 and in 1880 the battalion was consolidated as the new 1st Cumberland RVC, a two-battalion corps with thirteen companies:

'A', 'B' and 'C' Carlisle (late 1st Corps)
'D' Whitehaven (late 2nd Corps)
'E' Keswick (late 3rd Corps)
'F' Brampton (late 4th Corps)
'G' and 'H' Penrith (late 5th Corps)
'I' Alston (late 6th Corps)
'K' Workington (late 7th Corps)
'L' Cockermouth (late 8th Corps)
'M' Egremont (late 10th Corps)
'N' Wigton (late 11th Corps)

General Order 181 of December 1887 notified the change in designation of 1st Cumberland RVC to 1st (Cumberland) Volunteer Battalion Border Regiment. Headquarters were moved back to Carlisle in 1896 and in 1900 the companies at Whitehaven, Workington, Cockermouth, Egremont and Wigton were detached to form the 3rd (Cumberland) Volunteer Battalion. Transfer to the Territorial Force in 1908 was as four companies of the 4th Battalion Border Regiment. Uniform: scarlet/white.

2nd One company formed at the west Cumberland seaport, parish and borough of Whitehaven on 14 February 1860 with Captain Joshua Fletcher in command. The area around the time of the Volunteers provided much employment from its collieries (hematite iron ore being sent worldwide), steel and alabaster works, iron foundries and tannery. A No. 2 company was raised on 2 March 1860 but this, by June 1860, was taken into the 1st Corps as its No. 2 Company. Became 'D' Company of the new 1st Corps in 1880.

3rd Formed at Keswick on 15 February 1860 with Charles H Wade as captain and John J Spedding, lieutenant. John Teather was commissioned as ensign on 10 March. Became 'E' Company of the new 1st Corps in 1880. The public Lecture Hall (1856) predates the Volunteers slightly, but contemporary were the Post Office (1891) and the Mary Hewetson Cottage Hospital, which was built in 1892. Fitz Park was opened in 1887, the town at that time providing much employment in its famous pencil factory. Keswick is near the confluence of the Gretna and Derwent rivers and just a half-mile from the north end of Wordsworth's Derwentwater itself.

4th Brampton, nine miles north-east of Carlisle, was the headquarters of the county's 4th Corps, which was formed on 24 March 1860 with Captain T Charles Thompson in command. Both Lieutenant George L Carrick and Ensign William Dobson were commissioned on the following 4 April. Became 'F' Company of the new 1st Corps in 1880. During the Volunteer period the town gave employment in the manufacture of tweeds and the brewing of ale. The 4th Cumberland RVC was known locally as 'Belted Wills', Mr Phillip Haythornthwaite writing in the *Bulletin* of the Military Historical Society for November 1997 explaining that this name was in reference to Lord William Howard (1563–1640) who lived at Namworth Castle close to Brampton. His lordship had acquired the nickname in a piece written by Sir Walter Scott.

5th Formed at Penrith on 5 March 1860 and sometimes known as the 'Inglewood Rangers', Inglewood Forest, the central plain of north Cumberland extending from Penrith to Carlisle. Captain William Brougham took command; Lieutenant Frederick Cowper jun and Ensign William Wilkinson were also appointed holding commissions dated 24 March. Became 'G' and 'H' Companies of the new 1st Corps in 1880. The Agricultural Hall (1870) and the Public Library and Museum (opened in 1883) are both contemporary with the Volunteer period; the town's several breweries (much of their produce being drunk in the old Two Lions and Gloucester Arms), iron foundries and sawmills giving much employment to the population.

6th In east Cumberland the market town of Alston formed the county's 6th Corps on 2 March 1860 with Theodore Wilson as captain. Lieutenant Joseph Dickinson and Ensign John Friend were also appointed with commissions dated 22 March. Became 'I' Company of the new 1st Corps in 1880. Lead mining provided much employment.

7th Formed at Workington on 12 April 1860 and sometimes known as the 'Solway Marksmen', Solway Firth, that great inlet between England and Scotland extending almost fifty miles inland, Workington almost at its most southerly point. Captain Charles Lamport, Lieutenant Michael Falcon and Ensign Antony Peat were the first officers to be commissioned. Became 'K' Company of the new 1st Corps in 1880. At the mouth of the Derwent, the seaport of Workington provided employment: the Lonsdale Dock being opened in 1868, a breakwater constructed in the harbour in 1873. Other chief industries were the manufacture of steel rails, tin-plate, iron bridges and boilers. There was also a paper mill and brewery. Workington's ancient church of St Michael was almost totally destroyed by fire in 1887.

8th On the confluence of the rivers Derwent and Cocker, Cockermouth in western Cumberland was the headquarters of the 8th Corps. Thomas A Hoskins jun became captain; Thomas Drane, lieutenant and James Hartley, ensign. Formed on 24 March 1860, the 8th Cumberland RVC became 'L' Company of the new 1st Corps in 1880. The Cumberland County Industrial School was opened in 1881. In the town were two woollen factories and four tanneries. The Cockermouth, Keswick & Penrith Railway was opened to passengers on 2 January 1865.

9th Formed at Whitehaven on 21 May 1860 with J Spencer as captain. The corps was not seen in the *Army List* after June 1863.

10th Formed at Egremont on the edge of the Lake District on 3 July 1860 with Captain Henry Jefferson in command. Lieutenant John Stirling and Ensign Henry Baker received their commissions on 20 July. Became 'M' Company of the new 1st Corps in 1880. The Norman church of St Mary dominates the town; the Oddfellows' Hall (1861) and the rooms of the Industrial Cooperative Society (1859) being contemporary with the founding of the Victorian Volunteer movement in Egremont. Iron ore and limestone were quarried in the neighbourhood.

11th Formed at Wigton on 18 July 1860 with Anthony B Were as lieutenant and Thomas O Barwis, ensign. Became 'N' Company of the new 1st Corps in 1880. A drinking fountain constructed of various coloured granite was erected in the market place in 1872. The principal industries in 1887 were the manufacture of cloth, tanning, brewing and the making of spade and shovel handles.

3rd (Cumberland) Volunteer Battalion Border Regiment Formed with headquarters at Workington in 1900 by the withdrawal of the Whitehaven, Workington, Cockermouth, Egremont and Wigton Companies of 1st (Cumberland) Volunteer Battalion Border Regiment. New personnel were also added at Workington, Frizington and Aspatria bringing the new battalion's establishment to eight companies. At St Bees south of Whitehaven, the ancient grammar school formed a cadet corps in 1903. Transfer to the Territorial Force in 1908 was as 5th Battalion Border Regiment, St Bees School becoming a contingent of the Junior Division OTC at the same time. Uniform: scarlet/white.

DENBIGHSHIRE

All corps joined the 1st Admin Battalion, which became the new 1st Corps in 1880.

1st (1860–80) Formed as two companies at Wrexham in the south-east of the county on 30 June 1860 with Captain Sir Watkin W Wynn in command. Became 'A' and 'B' Companies of the new 1st Corps in 1880. Numerous coal mines in the area employed many. Brewing – the first lager brewery in Britain was started here in 1881 – and tanning also went on in and around the town. Its church of St Giles was restored in 1867.

1st (1880–1908) The 1st Admin Battalion of Denbighshire Rifle Volunteers was formed with headquarters at Ruabon on 10 September 1860. The battalion was consolidated in 1880 as the new 1st Denbighshire RVC with eight companies:

'A' and 'B' Wrexham (late 1st Corps)
'C' Ruabon (late 2nd Corps)
'D' Denbigh (late 3rd Corps)
'E' Gresford and Chirk (late 4th and 7th Corps)
'F' Gwersyllt (late 5th Corps)
'G' Ruthin (late 6th Corps)
'H' Llangollen (late 9th Corps)

Soon after consolidation headquarters of the new 1st Corps moved from Ruabon to Wynnstay. General Order 78 of June 1884 notified a change in designation from 1st Denbighshire RVC to 1st Volunteer Battalion Royal Welsh Fusiliers and in the following year headquarters moved yet again, this time to Wrexham. Three new companies were added in 1900 and transfer to the Territorial Force in 1908 was as 4th (Denbighshire) Battalion Royal Welsh Fusiliers. Uniform: scarlet/blue.

2nd Ruabon, in the south-east of the county and with the Dee forming a boundary to the parish on the south, provided headquarters of the 2nd Corps. Its first officers, Lieutenant Richard C

Roberts and Ensign John Jones, were gazetted on 12 April 1860. Richard Blackwood-Price, formerly a lieutenant colonel in the Royal Artillery, was commissioned as captain on 7 May. Became 'C' Company of the new 1st Corps in 1880. Many of the area were employed in coal mining and at Ruabon's iron, brick and terracotta works.

3rd Formed at Denbigh in the Vale of Clwyd on 21 July 1860 with Captain Townshend Mainwaring in command. His junior officers, Lieutenant Thomas Evans and Ensign M Owen, were both commissioned on 11 December. Became 'D' Company of the new 1st Corps in 1880. Many from the town were employed in the manufacture of boots and shoes, and there were quarries for slate and lime. St Mary's Church was built in 1874, the Denbigh, Ruthin & Corwen Railway opened on 1 March 1862. The Volunteer Drill Hall was at 9 Love Lane, Denbigh.

4th Three miles north-east of Wrexham, Gresford raised the 4th Corps; its first officer, Lieutenant Bevis Heywood Thelwall, being commissioned on 10 September 1860. Became part of 'E' Company of the new 1st Corps in 1880. Coal mines and brickworks gave employment.

5th Formed at Gwersyllt three miles north-west of Wrexham, with Lieutenant Colin Napier commissioned on 10 September 1860. Became 'F' Company of the new 1st Corps in 1880. The church of Holy Trinity (1850) predates the Volunteers by ten years. Much of the population were employed in local ironworks and coal mines. The railway came to the town in 1886, the Wrexham, Mold & Connah's Quay line opening Gwersyllt Station on 1 May of that year.

6th On the right bank of the Clwyd, Ruthin provided the 6th Corps with William Cornwallis West commissioned as captain, Robert George Johnson, lieutenant and Llewellyn Adams as ensign on 20 February 1861. Became 'G' Company of the new 1st Corps in 1880. The railway (the old Denbigh, Ruthin & Corwen line) reached the town in March 1862, the Town Hall built the year after, and St Peter's Church restored in 1885. Mainly agricultural, the area also had a brick and terracotta works.

7th Formed at Chirk with Lieutenant John Edmunds and Ensign Edwin Bellyse both holding commissions dated 24 August 1861. Became part of 'E' Company of the new 1st Corps in 1880. The Ellesmere Canal crosses the Ceiriog here via an aqueduct. Chirk Station on the old Glynn Valley Tramroad was opened on 15 March 1891. Employment was in coal, lime and the manufacture of paper.

8th On the Conway in the west of the county, Llanrwst provided the 8th Corps; its first officers, Captain Henry R Sandbach, Lieutenant John Blackwall and Ensign R R Griffith, all being commissioned on 19 October 1861. The corps was later disbanded and appeared for the last time in the *Army List* for January 1865. The town was once notable for the manufacture of harps. Brewing and tanning also gave employment.

9th (1861) A 9th Corps is shown in the *Army List* for June 1861 as having been formed at Wrexham, but this disappeared in the following October having had no officers appointed to it.

9th (1868–80) No doubt many of those employed by the local flannel and slate manufacturers at Llangollen joined the 9th Corps, its officers, Captain Marcell Convan, Lieutenant Edward H Parry and Ensign John Williams, being commissioned on 6 June 1868. Became 'H' Company of the new 1st Corps in 1880. The North Wales Baptist College, founded at Llangollen in 1862, moved from the town to Bangor in 1892.

DERBYSHIRE

Three admin battalions were formed by the county, the 2nd being broken up in 1869 with its corps absorbed into 3rd Admin. The 2nd Admin, which included the 2nd, 8th and 10th Corps, had been formed with headquarters at Sudbury in June 1860, moving to Ashbourne in 1864. In 1880, 1st and 3rd Admin Battalions were consolidated to form the new 1st and 2nd Corps. Situated on the Derwent, just a few miles above where the river joins the Trent, Derby contributed five of the corps raised. Two of the town's churches, St Alkmund (1846) and St Michael's (1858) would have been relatively new buildings when the Volunteers got started in 1859. The Market Hall was opened in 1866, the Royal Drill Hall in 1869, the Corporation Art Gallery in 1883 and the Grand Theatre in 1886. Paper, silk, cotton and sawmills gave employment, as did several iron foundries, tanneries and the Derby porcelain factory. In the 1890s, the Midland Railway was known to have employed upwards of 10,000 men at Derby.

1st (1859–80) Formed at Derby with Captain Charles Edmund Newton and Lieutenant William Turpie commissioned on 23 July 1859. Joined the 1st Admin Battalion and became 'A' Company of the new 1st Corps in 1880.

1st (1880–1908) The 1st Admin Battalion was formed with headquarters at Derby on 10 July 1860 and consolidated as the new 1st Corps with twelve companies in 1880:

'A' Derby (late 1st Corps)
'B' Derby (late 4th Corps)
'C' and 'D' Derby (late 5th Corps)
'E' Butterley (late No. 1 Company, 12th Corps)
'F' Condor Park (late No. 2 Company, 12th Corps)
'G' Belper (late 13th Corps)
'H' and 'I' Derby (late 15th Corps)
'K' Derby (late (19th Corps)
'L' Long Eaton (late 20th Corps)
'M' Long Eaton (late 20th Corps and part of 13th)

A cadet corps was formed and affiliated to the 1st Admin Battalion in 1870. It disappears from the *Army List* in 1881, returns again in 1883, and by 1895 is shown as being formed by Derby School. Another cadet corps was formed and affiliated at Trent College in 1886, but this was disbanded towards the end of 1889. Repton School provided a company in December 1900, followed by a unit raised by the Derby General Post Office called the Postal Telegraph Messengers Cadet Corps, in 1905. The 1st Derbyshire was re-designated as 1st Volunteer Battalion Sherwood Foresters under General Order 39 of April 1887 and transferred to the Territorial Force in 1908 as 5th Battalion Sherwood Foresters. Both Derby and Repton Schools at the same time joined the OTC. Uniform: scarlet/white.

2nd (1859–69) In north Derbyshire, the 2nd Corps at Sudbury had its first officers gazetted on 6 December 1859. One company became two in February 1860; the corps joined the 2nd Admin Battalion, and was disbanded in 1869. At All Saints' Church there are numerous memorials to the Vernon family, the Rt Hon George J W Lord Vernon of Sudbury Hall being made Captain Commandant of the 2nd Derbyshire RVC in February 1860.

2nd (1880–1908) The 3rd Admin Battalion was formed in June 1860 with headquarters at Bakewell and absorbed the remaining two corps of the 2nd Admin Battalion in 1869. The battalion was consolidated in 1880 as the new 2nd Corps with ten companies:

'A' Chesterfield (late 3rd Corps)
'B' Chapel-en-le-Frith (late 7th Corps)
'C' Ashbourne (late 8th Corps)
'D' Bakewell (late 9th Corps)
'E' Wirksworth (late 10th Corps)
'F' Matlock (late 11th Corps)
'G' Clay Cross (late 17th Corps)
'H' Whaley Bridge (late 18th Corps)
'I' Hartington (late 21st Corps)
'K' Staveley (late 22nd Corps)

Under General Order 39 of April 1887 2nd Derbyshire RVC was re-designated as 2nd Volunteer Battalion Sherwood Foresters. Headquarters moved from Bakewell to Chesterfield in 1898 and in 1900 three new companies (two at Chesterfield, one Buxton) were formed. Transfer to the Territorial Force in 1908 was as 6th Battalion Sherwood Foresters. Uniform: scarlet/blue, changing to scarlet/white in 1886.

3rd Formed at Chesterfield with John Hallewell as captain, James B White, lieutenant and John Sanders Clarke, ensign. All three officers held commissions dated 7 January 1860. Joined the 3rd Admin Battalion and became 'A' Company of the new 2nd Corps in 1880. The industries of the town included tanning, iron and brass founding and the manufacture of engines and agricultural implements.

4th Formed at Derby with Nathaniel Charles Curzon commissioned as captain on 31 December 1859. Joined the 1st Admin Battalion and became 'B' Company of the new 1st Corps in 1880.

5th Formed at Derby with William Henry Cox as captain, Alexander James Henley, lieutenant and Alexander Buchanan, ensign. All three officers held commissions dated 18 January 1860. Joined the 1st Admin Battalion and became 'C' and 'D' Companies of the new 1st Corps in 1880.

6th Formed on the Wye at Buxton with Captain Francis Westby Bagshawe, Lieutenant M O Bright and Ensign William Barker commissioned on 16 February 1860. Joined the 3rd Admin Battalion, but disbanded later and last seen in the *Army List* for December 1861.

7th Formed at Chapel-en-le-Frith with Arthur Neild as captain, Norman Bennett, lieutenant and Andrew Welsh, ensign. All three officers held commissions dated 1 February 1860. Joined the 3rd Admin Battalion and became 'B' Company of the new 2nd Corps in 1880. The chief industries of the town were paper and wadding making, and there was also a brewery. The railway reached the town in the form of the Stockport, Disley & Whaley Bridge line in June 1863.

8th On the River Henmore, Ashbourne formed the 8th Corps with Charles Okeover as captain, Andrew George Corbet, lieutenant and Edward Alfred Dyke, ensign. All three officers held commissions dated 1 February 1860. Joined the 2nd Admin Battalion, transferring to the 3rd Admin in 1869, and became 'C' Company of the new 2nd Corps in 1880. Ashbourne Station, on the old Staffordshire Railway, was closed in August 1899 and a new one opened just to the north-east of the original. At Compton, a suburb of the town, there was a large stay factory.

9th Formed at Bakewell with Lord George H Cavendish as captain, William Pole Thornhill, lieutenant and Robert W M Nesfield, ensign. All three officers held commissions dated 28

February 1860. Joined the 3rd Admin Battalion and became 'D' Company of the new 2nd Corps in 1880. The Town Hall was opened in 1890 and there were works that turned and polished the marble quarried in the area. The railway came to the town in 1862, its station being opened on 1 August 1862.

10th Formed at Wirksworth with Albert Frederick Hurt as captain, Henry W Walthall, lieutenant and William P Huddersty, ensign. All three officers held commissions dated 10 March 1860. Joined the 2nd Admin Battalion, transferring to 3rd Admin in 1869, and became 'E' Company of the new 2nd Corps in 1880. Wirksworth Station, on the old Midland Railway, was opened on 1 October 1867, the Town Hall in 1871. Lead mines and local quarries gave employment to the area.

11th Formed at Matlock with Sir Joseph Paxton as captain, Samuel Prince, lieutenant and Robert Chadwick, ensign. All three officers held commissions dated 17 March 1860. Joined the 3rd Admin Battalion and became 'F' Company of the new 2nd Corps in 1880. Matlock lies on the Derwent, its All Saints' Church dating from 1884. The Market Hall and Assembly Rooms in the Matlock Bridge part of the parish were built in 1867. Paper, cotton and corn mills, a bleach works and stone quarries provided employment to the town.

12th Formed as one company at Butterley with William Jessop as captain, John G N Alleyne, lieutenant and John T Featherstone, ensign. All three officers held commissions dated 3 April 1860. Joined the 1st Admin Battalion; a new company was added later at Condor Park, and became 'E' and 'F' Companies of the new 1st Corps in 1880. At Butterley, ten miles south-east of Derby, there were numerous coal mines, blast furnaces, foundries, a boiler works, and cannon and shot were produced for the Woolwich Arsenal. Butterley Station, on the old Midland Railway, was opened on 1 May 1875.

13th Formed at Belper with Alfred W Holmes as captain, William Statham, lieutenant and Charles W Wilkinson, ensign. All three officers held commissions dated 14 March 1860. Joined the 1st Admin Battalion and became 'G' and part of 'M' Companies of the new 1st Corps in 1880. Belper lies on the River Derwent seven miles north of Derby. Cotton yarn, hosiery and gloves have been noted as the staple industries of the town, the first cotton mill being established by the Strutt family in 1776. The Hon Arthur Strutt was commissioned as lieutenant in the 13th Corps in May 1865. At Belper, the old North Midland Railway station of 1840 was closed on 10 March 1878 and a new one opened just to the north.

14th None recorded.

15th Formed at Derby with Robert E Wilmot as captain and T E Cox, ensign. Both held commissions dated 7 July 1860. Joined the 1st Admin Battalion and became 'H' and 'I' Companies of the new 1st Corps in 1880.

16th Formed at Ilkeston with Meynell H M Mundy as captain, Edwin Whitehouse, lieutenant and Philip Potter, ensign. All three held commissions dated 7 September 1860. Joined the 1st Admin Battalion and disappeared from the *Army List* in August 1863. The town lies close to the Erewash Canal where there were ironworks and brickfields.

17th Formed at Clay Cross with Gladwin Turbutt as captain, William Milnes, lieutenant and William Clayton, ensign. All three held commissions dated 26 January 1861. Joined the 3rd Admin Battalion and became 'G' Company of the new 2nd Corps in 1880. The parish and town are south of Chesterfield and employed many at its several coal pits and ironworks.

18th Formed as one company at Whaley Bridge with Edward Hall as captain, James H Williamson, lieutenant and George W Higinbotham, ensign. All three held commissions dated 16 March 1866. Joined the 3rd Admin Battalion and became 'H' Company of the new 2nd Corps in 1880. The village is three miles west of Chapel-en-le-Frith on the Peak Forest Canal and River Goyt. The Mechanics' Institute was built there in 1876.

19th (Elvaston) Headquarters of the 19th Corps were at Derby, but most of the recruiting took place in the parish of Elvaston on the River Derwent five miles to the south-east. The first officers of the company were Captain Viscount C A S Peersham, Lieutenant Henry H Bemrose and Ensign Edwin Pratt. All three held commissions dated 23 April 1868. Joined the 1st Admin Battalion and became 'K' Company of the new 1st Corps in 1880.

20th (Trent) Formed at Long Eaton, seven miles south-east of Derby, with James Bembridge as captain, William H Sweet, lieutenant, Robert Hogwood, ensign. All three held commissions dated 31 July 1871 and appointed at the same time were Surgeon John Ewart and chaplain, the Revd Frederick Atkinson. Joined the 1st Admin Battalion and became 'L' and 'M' Companies of the new 1st Corps in 1880. At Long Eaton, a new railway station was opened in July 1863. Much work went on at St Lawrence's Church in 1868, Trent College being opened there in the same year. A large railway carriage works employed many from the area.

21st Formed at Hartington on 25 May 1872. Joined the 3rd Admin Battalion and became 'I' Company of the new 2nd Corps in 1880. The village of Hartington in the west of the county is situated just over nine miles south-west of Bakewell. On the old London and North Western Railway, Hartington Station was opened on 4 August 1899.

22nd Formed at Staveley with Josiah Court as captain and Francis A Turner, lieutenant. Both held commissions dated 23 September 1874. Joined the 3rd Admin Battalion and became 'K' Company of the new 2nd Corps in 1880. The village lies just under five miles from Chester, its St John's Church being restored there in 1865. Many were employed in the several coal pits in the area; there was also a long-established brush manufacturer, as well as another firm that made spades and shovels.

23rd Formed at Glossop with Captain Commandant William Sidebottom commissioned on 22 January 1876. Joined the 4th Admin Battalion of the neighbouring county of Cheshire, whose headquarters were just over nine miles away at Stockport. Became 'L' to 'N' Companies of the new 4th Cheshire RVC in 1880. The Library and Public Hall at Glossop date from 1887; Woods Hospital in Howard Park from the same year. Cotton was produced in Glossop; there were also paper mills and a calico-printing works in the area.

DEVONSHIRE

A 1st Admin Battalion containing the 2nd, 3rd and 16th Corps first appeared in the *Army List* for June 1860. In the issue for September, however, there is no mention of a 1st Admin Battalion but instead, four are now listed and numbered as 2nd, 3rd, 4th and 5th. The corps previously shown with the 1st are now forming the 3rd Admin Battalion. By April, however, the four are now shown as 1st, 2nd, 3rd and 4th and it would be these that in 1880 provided four new corps numbered 2nd, 3rd, 4th and 5th.

1st (Exeter and South Devon) The 1st Devonshire RVC is the senior Volunteer unit in the United Kingdom, it being the first to be officially recognized by the government. It was in January

1852 that Superintendant of the Exminster Lunatic Asylum, Dr John Bucknill of Exeter (through Earl Fortescue, the Lord Lieutenant of Devonshire), submitted a proposal to the Secretary of State (Sir George Grey) that a corps of Volunteer Riflemen be formed in South Devon for the defence of the coast. Subsequently the services of the Exeter and South Devon Rifle Corps were accepted under the Volunteer Act of 1804. The officers' commissions were signed by Queen Victoria on 4 January 1853. When the Volunteer Force got under way proper in 1859, the corps received the title 1st Devonshire (Exeter and South Devon). It absorbed the 24th Corps at Budleigh Salterton in 1860 and later comprised eleven companies after personnel were added at Exmouth, Crediton, Dawlish and Teignmouth (possibly the missing numbers 7th, 12th and 15th were intended for these locations). Exeter School formed an affiliated cadet corps in 1897. Under General Order 114 of 1885, 1st Devonshire was re-designated as 1st (Exeter and South Devon) Volunteer Battalion Devonshire Regiment and transfer to the Territorial Force in 1908 was as part of the 4th Battalion Devonshire Regiment. Exeter School Cadet Corps at the same time became part of the OTC. Uniform: green/black.

In Northernhay Gardens, Exeter there is a small Renaissance pillar commemorating the formation of the 1st Devonshire RVC. The memorial, by local sculptor Harry Hems, erected in 1895, includes plaques recording the names of the first officers to receive commissions, the committee that was responsible for the formation of the corps, and a list of places from where the recruits were drawn – 'Exeter, Cullompton, Tiverton, Bovey Tracey, Exmouth, Honiton, Brixham, Torquay, Totnes'.

2nd (1859–80) Formed as one company at the market town, naval base and seaport of Plymouth with Captain Charles Duperrier commissioned on 7 December 1859. No. 2 Company was formed in February 1860. Joined the 2nd Admin Battalion, absorbed the 16th Corps of two companies at Stonehouse in 1874, increased by a further two companies in 1868, and became 'A' to 'F' Companies of the new 2nd Corps in 1880. The cathedral dedicated to St Mary and St Boniface would have been barely a year old when the Volunteers first appeared on the streets of Plymouth. The Guildhall in Royal Parade was built 1870–74; the Royal Naval Barracks in Saltash Road started in 1879; the Post Office in Guildhall Square came in 1884. In the area, several firms involved in the manufacture of chemicals, soap, starch, biscuits and candles gave employment, and down one of Plymouth's cobbled streets, close to the harbour, is the Black Friars Distillery, where gin has been made since 1793.

2nd (1880–1908) The 2nd Admin Battalion was formed with headquarters at Plymouth in 1860 and to it were added the 2nd, 3rd, 16th and 22nd Corps. The battalion was consolidated in 1880 as the 2nd (Prince of Wales's) Corps with eleven companies:

'A' to 'F' Plymouth (late 2nd Corps)
'G' to 'I' Devonport (late 3rd Corps)
'K' and 'L' Tavistock (late 22nd Corps)

Designated 2nd (Prince of Wales's) Volunteer Battalion Devonshire Regiment under General Order 114 of 1885 and increased to twelve companies in 1900. Reduced to eight, however, in 1905. The former 3rd Corps cadet unit disappeared from the *Army List* in 1885, but Kelly College at Tavistock provided a company in 1894 and in 1906 the *Army List* indicates that the Postal Telegraph Messengers of Plymouth had been formed. This, though, disappeared in July 1907. The Plymouth and Mannamead College Cadet Corps transferred from the 2nd Devonshire RGA (Vols) in 1907. Transfer to the Territorial Force in 1908 was as part of 5th (Prince of Wales's) Battalion Devonshire Regiment. The cadets at Kelly College and Plymouth and Mannamead College at the same time joined the OTC. Uniform: green/scarlet.

3rd (1859–80) Formed as one company at Devonport with Captain John Beer and Lieutenant William Clark commissioned on 7 December 1859. No. 2 Company was formed on 1 March 1860. Joined the 2nd Admin Battalion. A cadet corps was formed and attached in 1874 and a third company added by 1871. Became 'G' to 'I' Companies of the new 2nd Corps in 1880. Two miles from Plymouth, Devonport is the home of the Royal Dockyard, which gives employment to many from the town. The Royal Albert Hospital in Marlborough Street was opened in 1861 and soldiers garrisoned in the town were quartered at the Raglan and Granby Barracks.

3rd (1880–1908) The 1st Admin Battalion was formed with headquarters at Exeter in 1860 and to it were added the 5th, 8th, 11th, 13th, 14th, 20th, 25th and 27th Corps. The battalion was consolidated as the new 3rd Corps in 1880 with seven companies:

'A' Cullompton (late 5th Corps)
'B' Buckerell (late 8th Corps)
'C' Bampton (late 11th Corps)
'D' Honiton (late 13th Corps)
'E' Tiverton (late 14th Corps)
'F' Ottery St Mary (late 25th Corps)
'G' Colyton (late 27th Corps)

The corps was designated 3rd Volunteer Battalion Devonshire Regiment under General Order 114 of November 1885. That same year a new company ('H') was added at Sidmouth, followed in 1900 by 'I' at Axminster. Cadet corps were formed and affiliated at All Hallows School in Honiton and at Blundell's School, Tiverton in 1900. Transfer to the Territorial Force in 1908 was as part of 4th Battalion Devonshire Regiment, both All Hallows and Blundell's Schools at the same time joining the OTC. Uniform: grey/green.

4th (1860–72) Formed at the market town and seaport of Ilfracombe with Captain Nathan Vye, Lieutenant William Broderick and Ensign Henry Camp commissioned on 3 March 1860. Joined the 3rd Admin Battalion, disappearing from the *Army List* in December 1872. The Market Hall in Market Street and the Town Hall in High Street both date from 1862; the Tyrell Cottage Hospital was established in 1868, Ilfracombe Station in July 1874.

4th (1880–1908) The 3rd Admin Battalion was formed with headquarters at Barnstaple in 1860 and to it were added the 4th, 6th, 18th, 21st and 28th Corps. The battalion was consolidated in 1880 as the new 4th Corps with seven companies:

'A' and 'B' Barnstaple (late 6th Corps)
'C' Hatherleigh (late 18th Corps)
'D' Okehampton (late 18th Corps)
'E' Bideford (late 21st Corps)
'F' Torrington (late 21st Corps)
'G' South Molton (late 28th Corps)

Designated as 4th Volunteer Battalion Devonshire Regiment under General Order 114 of November 1885; an additional two companies, one each at Buckfastleigh and Torquay, were sanctioned in 1886. The United Services College Cadet Corps at Westward Ho! was formed and attached in 1900 but, having moved to Harpenden in 1904, its affiliation was transferred to the 2nd Volunteer Battalion Bedfordshire Regiment. Transfer to the Territorial Force in 1908 was as 6th Battalion Devonshire Regiment. Uniform: scarlet/white.

5th (1860–80) Formed at Upper Culm Vale with Captain John W Walrond, Lieutenant R Collins and Ensign J G Sydenham commissioned on 22 March 1860. Joined the 1st Admin Battalion, headquarters moving to Cullompton twelve miles north-east of Exeter in 1862, and became 'A' Company of the new 3rd Corps in 1880. At Cullompton, several paper and flour mills gave employment. Cullompton Station, on the old Bristol & Exeter line, was opened in December 1867.

5th (1880–1908) The 4th Admin Battalion was formed with headquarters at Totnes in 1860 and to it were added the 9th, 10th, 17th, 23rd, 26th and 28th Corps. Headquarters moved to Newton Abbot in 1865. A cadet corps was formed and affiliated to the battalion in 1871, but this was not shown in the *Army List* after 1875. Consolidation in 1880 was as the new 5th Corps with six companies:

'A' Ashburton (late 9th Corps)
'B' Newton Abbot (late 10th Corps)
'C' Totnes (late 17th Corps)
'D' Chudleigh (late 23rd Corps)
'E' Kingsbridge (late 26th Corps)
'F' Torquay (late 26th Corps)

Designated as 5th (The Hay Tor) Volunteer Battalion Devonshire Regiment under General Order 114 of November 1885 and transferred to the Territorial Force in 1908 as part of 5th Battalion Devonshire Regiment. Uniform: Scarlet/green, changing to scarlet/white in 1895.

6th Formed at Barnstaple with Captain Robert Wyllie, Lieutenant Edward B Savile and Ensign John May Miller holding commissions dated 23 February 1860. Joined the 3rd Admin Battalion and became 'A' and 'B' Companies of the new 4th Corps in 1880. Situated on the River Taw, Barnstable made lace, gloves and had several tanneries, flour mills and potteries. Throughout much of the 6th Corps's existence its members would have seen first-hand Gilbert Scott's restoration at St Peter and St Paul's church, between High Street and Bouthport Street, which began in 1866 and went on right into the 1880s.

7th None recorded.

8th Formed at Buckerell, on the River Otter with Captain William Porter, Lieutenant the Hon Colin Lindsey and Ensign George Newman commissioned on 8 February 1860. Joined the 1st Admin Battalion and became 'B' Company of the new 3rd Corps in 1880. Buckerell is just over two miles west of Honiton.

9th Formed as one company at Ashburton on the River Yeo with Captain Thomas Eales Rogers, Lieutenant Robert Coard Tucker and Ensign William Richard Coulton commissioned on 23 February 1860. Joined the 4th Admin Battalion and became 'A' Company of the new 5th Corps in 1880. At Ashburton, on the old Exeter and Plymouth road, there were breweries, corn mills and a silicate paint factory, which employed many from the area. Ashburton Station was opened in May 1872.

10th Formed at Newton Abbot with Captain G H S Yates, Lieutenant Francis Young and Ensign Cyrus W Croft commissioned on 27 March 1860. Joined the 4th Admin Battalion and became 'B' Company of the new 5th Corps in 1880. At Newton Abbot the Great Western Railway had carriage-building workshops; there was a large tannery, an iron foundry, breweries and sawmills.

11th Formed at Bampton with Captain Glyn Grylls and Lieutenant Charles S M Phillips holding commissions dated 28 February 1860. Joined the 1st Admin Battalion and became 'C' Company of the new 3rd Corps in 1880. Bampton lies on the River Bathern seven miles north of Tiverton.

12th None recorded.

13th Formed at Honiton with Captain Horace V Mules, Lieutenant John H Jerrard and Ensign J R Rogers commissioned on 20 February 1860. Joined the 1st Admin Battalion and became 'D' Company of the new 3rd Corps in 1880. Honiton had an iron foundry, saw and flour mills. Titles, bricks and brown pottery were also made in the town. Lloyds bank at the corner of new street, with its polished granite columns, was built *c*.1870. All Hallows School, which formed a cadet corps affiliated to the 3rd Volunteer Battalion Devonshire Regiment in 1900, moved from Honiton to Rousdon in 1938, a schoolroom (All Hallows Chapel by St Paul's Church) remains in the town as a museum.

14th Formed at Tiverton with Captain John H Amory, Lieutenant F Dunsford and Ensign George Mackenzie commissioned on 1 March 1860. Joined the 1st Admin Battalion and became 'E' Company of the new 3rd Corps in 1880. The Town Hall was built in 1864; the Drill Hall and Armoury, with a house next door for the Sergeant Instructor, in 1884. In the town were breweries, flour mills, a factory making lace, which, in 1898, is said to have employed more than 1,000.

15th None recorded.

16th Formed at Stonehouse, close to Plymouth, with Captain Viscount Valletort, Lieutenant Richard M Dunn and Ensign Richard R Rodd commissioned on 29 February 1860. Joined the 2nd Admin Battalion and was absorbed into the 2nd Corps in 1874. The town's St George's Church was completed in 1879, the Grand Theatre ten years later. At the harbour, in the days of the Volunteers, many Stonehouse vessels were employed in the coal and timber trade.

17th William Ruston took command of the 17th Corps formed at Totnes on the west bank of the River Dart on 3 March 1860. Joined the 4th Admin Battalion and became 'C' Company of the new 5th Corps on 1880. Cider was made at Totnes.

18th Lieutenant Lewis P Madden and Ensign Chomeley Morris, both commissioned on 1 March 1860, were the first officers gazetted to the 18th Corps, which was formed at the market town of Hatherleigh in North Devon. Joined the 3rd Admin Battalion and became 'C' and 'D' Companies of the new 4th Corps in 1880. In the same year as the 18th Corps was being formed, a monument was erected at Hatherleigh Moor (close by the town) in memory of Crimean War hero and resident of the parish Lieutenant Colonel Morris CB.

19th Formed at Okehampton, but disappeared from the *Army List* in February 1861 having had two officers appointed – Lieutenant William Hunt Holly and Ensign Richard Hodges. Both held commissions dated 3 March 1860.

20th Formed at Broadhembury, just over five miles north-west of Honiton, with Edward Drew of Hembury Grange as lieutenant, and William B Henderson, ensign. Both held commissions dated 3 March 1860. Joined the 1st Admin Battalion and was disbanded in 1875. At St Andrew's Church there are several memorials to members of the Drewe family, Albert C R Drewe being gazetted lieutenant to the 20th Corps on 13 March 1865. In the village the Drewe Arms can be found still.

21st Formed at the market town and seaport of Bideford with Captain T G Harding, Lieutenant R Reynolds and Ensign W R Keats commissioned on 6 March 1860. Joined the 3rd Admin Battalion and became 'E' and 'F' Companies of the new 4th Corps in 1880. At Bideford, where Henry Williamson based his story of *Tarka the Otter*, cuffs and collars were made. There was also a large foundry, potteries and tanneries.

22nd Formed at Tavistock, fifteen miles north of Plymouth, on 5 March 1860 with E B Gould appointed as captain. Joined the 2nd Admin Battalion and became 'K' and 'L' Companies of the new 2nd Corps in 1880. Kelly College, on a hill overlooking Dartmoor, was founded in 1867, a cadet corps being formed there in 1894 and affiliated to the 2nd Volunteer Battalion Devonshire Regiment. The Town Hall, close to the Pannier Market, was completed in 1860. Cassell's *Gazetteer* for 1898 notes that rooms at The New Hall, built on the site of an old abbey, were then being used 'as an armoury by the Volunteers'. The Public Swimming Baths at Trelawny Road were built in 1883, Drake's statue (a native of the town) being erected the same year. Copper mining was Tavistock's main industry

23rd Formed at Chudleigh, ten miles south-west of Exeter, with Lieutenant G A Ferreira and Ensign Charles Archibald Langley commissioned on 27 March 1860. Joined the 4th Admin Battalion and became 'D' Company of the new 5th Corps in 1880.

24th Formed at Budleigh Salterton with Captain Frederick Blandy, Lieutenant George Peters Neave and Ensign Francis Richard Hole commissioned on 28 March 1860. Absorbed into the 1st Corps the same year.

25th Formed at Ottery St Mary, Surgeon Charles William Whittry being the first officer listed with a commission dated 2 March 1860. Joined the 1st Admin Battalion and became 'F' Company of the new 3rd Corps in 1880. Much of the town was destroyed by a fire in 1866 resulting in some 500 being made homeless.

26th Formed at Kingsbridge with Lieutenant H Square (commission dated 5 July 1860) the first officer appointed. Joined the 4th Admin Battalion and became 'E' and 'F' Companies of the new 5th Corps in 1880. The railway reached Kingsbridge in the form of the Kingsbridge & Salcombe line in December 1893.

27th Formed at Colyton, just over four miles south-west of Axminster, with Lieutenant James John H Cottle commissioned on 7 December 1860. Joined the 1st Admin Battalion and became 'G' Company of the new 3rd Corps in 1880. The trade of the town was mostly agricultural. Paper was made there, and a tannery still exists. The station, from which the Volunteers went to camp, was opened in 1868.

28th (1861–65) Formed at Lynton, east of Ilfracombe, with Robert Roe commissioned as lieutenant on 13 April 1861. Joined the 3rd Admin Battalion in 1863 and disbanded 1865.

28th (1868–75) Formed at South Brent, on the Avon seven miles west of Totnes, with Captain James Westhead commissioned on 14 October 1868. Joined the 4th Admin Battalion and disbanded 1875. Many from the town were employed in the leather industry.

28th (1876–80) Formed at South Molton, twelve miles south-east of Barnstaple, with Captain William H Brewer commissioned on 8 March 1876. Joined the 3rd Admin Battalion and became 'G' Company of the new 4th Corps in 1880. South Molton Station was opened in November 1873, the former Corn Exchange converted as the Post Office in 1888.

DORSETSHIRE

All corps joined the county's 1st Admin Battalion, which formed the new 1st Corps in 1880.

1st (1859–80) Formed at Bridport, eighteen miles west of Dorchester with Lieutenant Henry Saunders Edwards commissioned on 22 August 1859. Became 'A' Company of the new 1st Corps in 1880. The corps was formed just as Bridport's St Mary's Church was being restored (1859–60), St Andrew's, in St Andrew's Road, being built at the same time. The manufacture of fishing nets, sailcloth and twines provided much employment in the area.

1st (1880–1908) The 1st Admin Battalion was formed with headquarters at Dorchester on 9 May 1860 and consolidated as the new 1st Corps in 1880 with eleven companies:

'A' Bridport (late 1st Corps)
'B' Wareham (late 2nd Corps)
'C' Dorchester (late 3rd Corps)
'D' Poole (late 4th Corps)
'E' Weymouth (late 5th Corps)
'F' Wimborne (late 6th Corps)
'G' Sherborne (late 7th Corps)
'H' Blandford (late 8th Corps)
'I' Shaftesbury (late 9th Corps)
'K' Stalbridge (late 10th Corps)
'L' Gillingham (late 11th Corps)

Re-designated as 1st Volunteer Battalion Dorsetshire Regiment under General Order 181 of December 1887. A service company from the battalion served with the 2nd Dorsetshire Regiment in South Africa and saw action at Alleman's Nek on 11 June 1900: 'I was much pleased with their action,' noted General Buller in his dispatch of 19 June. The general also said of Captain H L Kitson, who commanded the Volunteers, 'He has proved himself thoroughly capable of taking any position his rank requires.' The Sherborne School Cadet Corps was affiliated in 1888 and the County School Cadet Corps at Dorchester in 1893. The latter, however, was removed from the *Army List* in January 1897. Transfer to the Territorial Force in 1908 was as 4th Battalion Dorsetshire Regiment, Sherborne School at the same time joining the OTC. Uniform: green/scarlet.

2nd Formed at Wareham, seventeen miles south-east of Dorchester, with Oliver William Farrer as captain, William Charles Lacey, lieutenant and Charles James Radclyfle, ensign. All three officers held commissions dated 28 January 1860. Became 'B' Company of the new 1st Corps in 1880. A large brewery gave employment to the town. The new railway station on the Northport side of Wareham was opened in April 1887.

3rd Formed at Dorchester with Edward Leigh Kindersley as captain, Thomas Coombs, lieutenant and Robert Devenish, ensign. All three held commissions dated 14 February 1860. Became 'C' Company of the new 1st Corps in 1880. The Corn Exchange was built in 1867, Holy Trinity Church in High West Street opened in 1876, the County Museum in 1883. The Barracks (now the Dorset Military Museum) was built 1876–77 and at the Post Office (1904–05) in South Street can be seen a War Memorial inscription designed by Thomas Hardy in 1920. Work on the writer's home at Max Gate in Alington Avenue began in 1885. The Eldridge Pope Brewery in Weymouth Avenue, which dates from 1880, gave employment to many from the town.

4th Formed at Poole with Captain William Parr, Lieutenant Thomas Cox and Ensign George B Aldridge commissioned on 13 February 1860. Became 'D' Company of the new 1st Corps in 1880. The Library and School of Art was extended in 1889 and 1891. Shipbuilding yards and firms manufacturing netting, sailcloth and other fittings for vessels employed many form the area. At the Haven Hotel, by the entrance to Poole Harbour in October 1898, Guglielmo Marconi set up one of the world's earliest radio stations.

5th Formed at the Georgian seaside resort of Weymouth with Lieutenant George Poulter Welsford and Ensign John Thresher commissioned on 14 May 1860. Became 'E' Company of the new 1st Corps in 1880. The Royal Victoria Jubilee Hall in St Thomas Street was built in 1887 (the Volunteers taking part in the celebrations throughout the town that year), the Royal Hotel ten years later. Portland stone was exported from Weymouth; employment was also provided in the manufacture of bricks, titles and maritime equipment. Weymouth Town railway station was just three years old when the 5th Corps was formed, the station at the Quay, from where steam packets crossed to the Channel Islands, opened in 1889.

6th Formed at Wimborne, six miles north of Poole, with Captain St John Coventry, Lieutenant Thomas Rawlings and Ensign Edward Robinson commissioned on 14 March 1860. Became 'F' Company of the new 1st Corps in 1880.

7th Formed at Sherborne, six miles east of Yeovil, with Captain John Frederick Falwasser, Lieutenant John George Bergman and Ensign John Young Melmoth commissioned on 29 March 1860. Became 'G' Company of the new 1st Corps in 1880. Sherborne Station, on the old London & South Western line, was opened in May 1860, the Yeatman Memorial Hospital in Yeatman Lane completed in 1866. Sherborne School formed a cadet corps in 1888. Long associated with Sherborne, the Digby family of Sherborne Castle have numerous monuments in the town, the Revd Richard H W Digby being made chaplain to the 7th Corps in 1868.

8th Formed at Blandford, sixteen miles north-east of Dorchester, with George P Mansel as captain, Robert C Farquharson, lieutenant and Francis T John, ensign. All three officers held commissions dated 29 February 1860. Became 'H' Company of the new 1st Corps in 1880. A cottage hospital was opened in 1889, the Volunteers no doubt enjoying a drink at the Badger Inn, which was opened in the same year.

9th Formed at Shaftesbury on the Wiltshire border with Thomas B Bower, who had previously served with the 73rd Regiment of Foot, as captain, William E Barridge, lieutenant and William R H Bennett, ensign. All three officers held commissions dated 10 March 1860. Became 'I' Company of the new 1st Corps in 1880. The Crown Inn would have sold its first ale to the Volunteers in 1862, St James's Church, at the bottom end of town, was built 1866–67, the Westminster Memorial Cottage Hospital in Park Road opened in March 1874.

10th (Blackmoor Vale) Formed at Sturminster Newton on the banks of the Stour with Lieutenant Montague Williams and Ensign Henry C Dashwood commissioned on 10 July 1860. Absorbed the 12th Corps at Stalbridge towards the end of 1876. Headquarters had moved to Stalbridge by April of the following year and at the same time 'Blackmoor Vale' was added to title. Blackmoor Vale is the valley of the River Cale and is situated on the borders of Somerset and Dorset extending south-east from Wincanton. Became 'K' Company of the new 1st Corps in 1880.

11th Formed at Gillingham, on the Stour where it joins the Lidden, with Lieutenant Robert S Freame commissioned on 7 July 1860. Became 'L' Company of the new 1st Corps in 1880. At

Gillingham bricks, tiles, rope and twine were made. Beer was brewed there, the Wyke Brewery still to be seen just a mile west of the town. The Vicarage was built in 1883, home, possibly, to the Revd George Glover, who became chaplain to the 11th Corps in 1877.

12th Formed at Stalbridge, close to the Somerset border, with Lieutenant John R Lyon and Ensign Henry W Langton commissioned on 7 July 1860. Absorbed into the 10th Corps towards the end of 1876. The railway reached Stalbridge in the form of the Dorset Central line in August 1863.

DUMBARTONSHIRE

All corps raised within the county joined the 1st Admin Battalion, which was consolidated as the new 1st Corps in 1880. Badges of the Dumbartonshire Rifle Volunteers featured an elephant with a castle on its back. This device was taken from the arms of the county, the elephant being chosen, it is said, because its shape resembled that of the massive Dumbarton Rock, which towers over the Firth of Clyde.

1st (1860–80) One company formed at Row with Alex H Denistoun as captain, Colin D Wilson, lieutenant and James Honeyman, ensign. All three held commissions dated 18 February 1860. Absorbed the 8th Corps at Gareloch in June 1865; headquarters moving to Helensburgh, two miles away, in January 1873, and became 'A' Company of the new 1st Corps in 1880. The railway had arrived at Helensburgh in 1858, but it would not be until 1894 that the West Highland line would have brought the Row Volunteers down to headquarters.

1st (1880–1908) The 1st Admin Battalion was formed with headquarters at Balloch on 7 May 1860 and was consolidated as the new 1st Corps in 1880. Headquarters were placed at Helensburgh and there were twelve companies:

'A' Helensburgh (late 1st Corps)
'B' Cardross (late 7th Corps)
'C' Dumbarton (late 6th Corps)
'D' Bonhill (late 3rd Corps)
'E' Jamestown (late 4th Corps)
'F' Alexandria (late 5th Corps)
'G' Clydebank (late 14th Corps)
'H' Maryhill (late 2nd Corps)
'I' Milngavie (late 13th Corps)
'K' Kirkintilloch (late 10th Corps)
'L' Cumbernauld (late 11th Corps)
'M' Luss (late 9th Corps)

Became a volunteer battalion of the Argyll and Sutherland Highlanders (without change of title) in 1881. 'M' Company at Luss was disbanded in January 1882, but replaced the following month at Renton. The disbandment of the Luss Company had been as a result of the direct defiance by the corps to change its uniform to that then in use by the whole battalion (see 9th Corps). 'L' Company was absorbed into 'K' as a detachment in 1884 and at the same time a new 'L' was formed at Yorker. A Mounted Infantry Company lettered 'O' was added at Maryhill in 1900, then in the same year 'Q' (Cyclist) was raised at Dumbarton. Some ninety-eight members of the battalion were sent out to join the Regulars of 1st Battalion Argyll and Sutherland Highlanders during the war in South Africa. Of those who lost their lives, the names of Sergeant J C Morrison,

Corporal W L L Fitzwilliams, Lance Corporal T Stevenson, Privates M Donnelly, R M Duncan, W Kelly and D W Moore, appear on the war memorial outside the Municipal Buildings in Garshake Road, Dumbarton. The 1st Dumbartonshire RVC transferred to the Territorial Force in 1908 as 9th Battalion Argyll and Sutherland Highlanders. Uniform: green/scarlet, changing to scarlet/yellow with trews in 1887.

2nd One company formed at East Kilpatrick with Captain Archibald Campbell Colquhoun, Lieutenant John Leckie Ewing and Ensign Hugh Kirkwood commissioned on 8 February 1860. Headquarters moved to Maryhill in 1868, the strength increasing by a half-company at the same time. Became 'H' Company of the new 1st Corps in 1880. Limestone and coal were quarried and mined at East Kilpatrick, just under six miles north-west of Glasgow.

3rd One company formed at Bonhill with Captain Mathew Gray, Lieutenant Thomas Logan Stillie and Ensign Edward McIntyre commissioned on 8 February 1860. Became 'D' Company of the new 1st Corps in 1880. An iron suspension bridge crossed the River Leven at Bonhill just under four miles north of Dumbarton. Cassell's for 1883 notes that some 4,000 were employed at the 'Turkey red dye, calico printing and bleaching works'.

4th One company formed at Jamestown with Captain Archibald Orb Ewing and Ensign Thomas Roxburgh commissioned on 8 February 1860. Became 'E' Company of the new 1st Corps in 1880. Jamestown lies on the left bank of the Leven about four miles north of Dumbarton, its church being built in 1869.

5th One company formed at Alexandria with Captain Mathew Clark commissioned on 8 February 1860. Became 'F' Company of the new 1st Corps in1880. An iron suspension bridge crossed the Leven at Alexandria which takes you to Bonhill and the 3rd Dumbartonshire RVC. Here too were bleaching, dying and calico-printing works. Before the days of the Volunteer were over, perhaps some of them went to work at the Argyll Motor Works, which was opened in 1906.

6th One company formed at Dumbarton with John Macausland as captain, William Paterson, lieutenant and William Graham, ensign. All three officers held commissions dated 8 February 1860. Increased to one-and-a-half companies in 1878 and became 'C' Company of the new 1st Corps in 1880. Market town and seaport on the Clyde and Leven sixteen miles north-west of Glasgow, in the 1890s Dumbarton was one of the chief centres for the construction of iron and steel steamers, William Denny and Brothers probably the most famous.

7th The services of one company were accepted at Cardross on 11 November 1859, the officers' commissions: Captain Tucker Geils, Lieutenant John William Burnes and Ensign David MacBrayne, being dated 15 March 1860. Became 'B' Company of the new 1st Corps in 1880. Cardross village is on the Firth of Clyde about four miles north-west of Dumbarton.

8th One sub-division formed at Gareloch with Lieutenant John Cabbell and Ensign Robert Bennett Browne commissioned on 16 February 1860. Increased to a full company in 1863. General Grierson in *Records of the Scottish Volunteers* states that the 8th was absorbed into the 1st Corps at Row on 24 June 1865. The corps, however, remained in the *Army List* with all three of its officers until 1869. Gare Loch sits at the opening of the Firth of Clyde.

9th One sub-division formed at Luss with Lieutenant Montagu J Martin and Alex Macniven being commissioned on 8 February 1860. Increased to a full company on 28 August 1868 and became 'M' Company of the new 1st Corps in 1880. The village of Luss is on the west side of Loch Lomond.

To enlarge upon the disbandment of 'M' Company in January 1882 (see 1st Corps), it would seem that for some time the commanding officer of the new 1st Dumbartonshire RVC, Henry Currie, was far from satisfied with the conduct of the Luss Volunteers. As a kilted company wearing blue bonnets, it was the colonel's opinion that they spoilt the appearance on parade of the rest of the battalion, who were dressed in helmets and green uniforms. On 25 August 1881 a Royal Review at Edinburgh attended by Queen Victoria was to include the 1st Dumbarton. Colonel Currie, who did not wish 'M' Company to attend, issued orders directing that it was 'to stay at home' and subsequently the battalion left for Edinburgh without Luss. After taking up their positions in the parade, members of the Dumbarton RVC were astonished to see 'M' Company, not only there, but marching with another battalion.

10th One company formed at Kirkintilloch with John M Gartshore as captain, Alex Brown Armour, lieutenant and Thomas Brown, ensign. All three officers held commissions dated 5 March 1860. Increased to one-and-a-half companies in 1874 and became 'K' Company of the new 1st Corps in 1880. The town is eight miles north-east of Glasgow and employed many in its chemical works and iron foundries.

11th One company formed at Cumbernauld with James Mackenzie as captain, Thomas Watson, lieutenant and David Coutts, ensign. All three held commissions dated 13 June 1860. Became 'L' Company of the new 1st Corps in 1880. To the north-east of Glasgow, Cumbernauld village is on the Forth and Clyde Canal, its population in the days of the Volunteers being mostly employed in the production of coal, limestone and iron.

12th One sub-division formed at Tarbert with a detachment at Arrochar on 7 March 1861, the original officers being Lieutenant Thomas Shedden and Ensign James McMurrich. The corps was disbanded in 1869. The communities at Tarbert and Arrochar shared the same station, but the West Highland line would not reach the area until August 1894.

13th The services of one company were accepted at Milngavie on 9 August 1867; its original officers, Captain Hugh Kirkwood, Lieutenant Alex Ross, Ensign John Granger, Surgeon Peter F Robertson MD, and Chaplain the Revd Robert Bell were all commissioned on 23 August. Became 'I' Company of the new 1st Corps in 1880. The parish, part in Dumbarton, part in Stirling, and town had bleaching and dyeing businesses, a print works and large paper mill. Opened in August 1863, the Glasgow & Milngavie Junction Railway served the area.

14th The services of one company at Clydebank were accepted on 18 May 1875, its first officers, Captain James R Thomson and Sub Lieutenant Robert Carswell, being commissioned on 23 June 1875. Became 'G' Company of the new 1st Corps in 1880. Just under six miles from Glasgow, most of the population of Clydebank were employed in the numerous shipbuilding yards. John Brown & Co. came to Clydebank in 1899, the company launching the Cunard liner *Lusitania* in 1906.

DUMFRIESSHIRE

All corps formed within the county joined the 1st Admin Battalion, which became the new 1st Corps in 1880.

1st (1860–80) Formed as one company at Dumfries with Patrick Dudgeon as captain, James Sloan, lieutenant and Henry Gordon, ensign. All three officers held commissions dated 25 February 1860. Increased to two companies in 1872 and became 'A' and 'B' Companies of the new

1st Corps in 1880. Born in Dumfries, and a Volunteer of the 1790s, was Scotland's national poet, Robert Burns. The County Hall was opened in 1863, Greyfriars Church completed in 1867, the Episcopal Church of St John the year after that. In 1875 a suspension bridge was opened connecting Dumfries with Maxwelltown just across the River Nith. Tweeds, hosiery, clogs, baskets, iron implements, leather and carriages were all manufactured in the area.

1st (1880–1908) The 1st Admin Battalion was formed with headquarters at Dumfries on 4 January 1862 and consolidated in April 1880 as the new 1st Corps with ten companies:

'A' and 'B' Dumfries (late 1st Corps)
'C' Thornhill (late 2nd Corps)
'D' Sanquhar (late 3rd Corps)
'E' Penpont (late 4th Corps)
'F' Annan (late 5th Corps)
'G' Moffat (late 6th Corps)
'H' Langholm (late 7th Corps)
'I' Lockerbie (late 8th Corps)
'K' Lochmaben (late 9th Corps)

Became a volunteer battalion (without change of title) of the Royal Scots Fusiliers in 1881, but transferred to King's Own Scottish Borderers with title 3rd (Dumfries) Volunteer Battalion in 1887. The change was notified in General Order 181 of December. In March 1885 'E' Company was absorbed into 'C' as a section and at the same time a new 'E' was formed at Ecclefechan. 'K' Company moved to Canonbie in December 1888. Transfer to the Territorial Force in 1908 was as headquarters and four companies of the 5th (Dumfries and Galloway) Battalion KOSB. Uniform: scarlet/yellow, changing to scarlet/blue with trews in 1888.

2nd Formed as one company at Thornhill with William Maxwell as captain, Thomas Dickson, lieutenant and William Smith, ensign. All three held commissions dated 6 March 1860. Became 'C' Company of the new 1st Corps in 1880. Fourteen miles north-west of Dumfries, the area's employment was mainly agricultural.

3rd Formed as one company at Sanquhar with James Kennedy as captain, Hamilton D B Hystop, lieutenant and William Otto Macqueen, ensign. All three held commissions dated 28 February 1860. Became 'D' Company of the new 1st Corps in 1880. Sanquhar coalfield gave much employment to the area, as well as several brick and tile works.

4th Formed as one company at Penpont, two miles south-west of Thornhill, with John G Clark as captain, Robert Kennedy, lieutenant and George Dalziel, ensign. All three held commissions dated 29 February 1860. Became 'E' Company of the new 1st Corps in 1880. The church at Penpont was restored in 1872.

5th Formed as one company at the seaport of Annan with Frederick McConnell as captain, William Dobbie, lieutenant and William Roxburgh, ensign. All three held commissions dated 14 June 1860. Became 'F' Company of the new 1st Corps in 1880. Among the industries in the area were cotton manufacturers, a distillery, tannery, sawmills and shipbuilding yards. The railway had reached the town in 1848, but in August 1870 the Solway Junction passenger line was brought through the town, just to the south of which was built the then-longest viaduct in the world.

6th Formed as one company at Moffat with George G H Johnstone as captain, Thomas Welsh, lieutenant and Walter Johnstone, ensign. All three officers held commissions dated 20 June 1860.

Became 1880 'G' Company of the new 1st Corps in 1880. The parish church was built 1885–87, the United Presbyterian 1863–64. Beechgrove Recreation Ground was opened in 1870.

7th Formed as one company at Langholm with Captain William E Malcolm commissioned on 1 June 1860. Became 'H' Company of the new 1st Corps in 1880. Fifteen miles north-east of Annan, Langholm's tweeds production industry gave employment to many. There were also distilleries. Work on a new hospital began in the early 1890s.

8th Formed as one company at Lockerbie with Osmond de H Stewart as captain, Thomas Stobart, lieutenant and William Wallace, ensign. All three officers held commissions dated 20 June 1860. Became 'I' Company of the new 1st Corps in 1880. In the town, the Free Church was built in 1872, the United Presbyterian rebuilt three years later. The Town Hall dates from 1891.

9th Formed as one company at Lochmaben, eight miles north-east of Dumfries, with John Johnstone as captain, James Watt, lieutenant and James Johnstone, ensign. All three officers held commissions dated 18 February 1861. Became 'K' Company of the new 1st Corps in 1880. A new Town Hall was built in 1878, a statue of Robert Bruce being erected in front of the building in 1879.

DURHAM

The county formed four admin battalions, which were consolidated in 1880 to form four new corps numbered 1st, 2nd, 4th and 5th. All pre-1880 corps were included, save for the 3rd, which was of sufficient strength to remain independent.

1st (1860–80) Formed as two companies at Stockton-on-Tees with Captains Robert Thompson and John James Wilson commissioned on 27 February 1860. Joined the 2nd Admin Battalion, transferred to 4th Admin in 1862, and became 'A' to 'C' Companies of the new 1st Corps in 1880. At Stockton the Freemasons' Hall was erected in 1875, the Free Public Library in 1877 and Roper Park, on the south side of town, opened by the Duke and Duchess of York in 1893. The railway employed many at Stockton; there were also shipbuilding yards, iron and brass foundries, brick yards and several firms making maritime equipment.

1st (1880–1908) The 4th Admin Battalion of Durham Rifle Volunteers was formed on 1 February 1862 with headquarters at Stockton-on-Tees and included the 1st, 15th, 16th and 19th Corps. The 21st Yorkshire (North Riding) RVC was added in 1877. The battalion was consolidated as the new 1st Corps in 1880 with eight companies:

'A' to 'C' Stockton-on-Tees (late 1st Corps)
'D' and 'E' Darlington (late 15th Corps)
'F' Castle Eden (late 16th Corps)
'G' and 'H' Middlesbrough (late 21st Yorkshire North Riding Corps)

General Order 181 of December 1887 directed a change in designation to 1st Volunteer Battalion Durham Light Infantry. Four new companies were added; 'I' Stockton, 'K' Darlington, 'L' Middlesbrough and 'M' (Cyclist) Stockton in 1900, and transfer to the Territorial Force in 1908 was as 5th Battalion Durham Light Infantry. Uniform: scarlet/white.

2nd Durham's 2nd Admin Battalion was formed with headquarters at Bishop Auckland in December 1860 and to it were added the 1st, 4th, 12th, 15th, 16th, 17th, 18th, 19th, 20th and 21st

Corps. In February 1862, the 1st, 15th, 16th and 19th were transferred to the 4th Admin Battalion, 2nd Admin being consolidated in 1880 as the new 2nd Corps with six companies:

'A' Bishop Auckland (late No. 1 Company 4th Corps)
'B' Coundon (late No. 2 Company 4th Corps)
'C' Darlington (late No. 3 Company 4th Corps)
'D' Middleton-in-Teesdale (late 12th Corps)
'E' Stanhope (late 20th Corps)
'F' Barnard Castle (late 21st Corps)

In 1883 'C' Company was moved to Woodland. 'G' and 'H' Companies were added at Spennymore in 1886, then under General Order 181 of December 1887, 2nd Corps became 2nd Volunteer Battalion Durham Light Infantry. 'D' Company was disbanded in 1899 and a new 'D' formed at Crook the same year. 'I' (Cyclist) Company at Bishop Auckland, 'K' and 'L' at Consett were added in 1900, 'C' moving yet again, this time to Shildon, in 1903. Transfer to the Territorial Force in 1908 was as 6th Battalion Durham Light Infantry. Uniform: green/scarlet.

3rd (The Sunderland) The 3rd Corps was formed at Sunderland on 6 March 1860 and included six companies by 1862 with Major Lord Adolphus Vane Tempest in command. The subtitle 'The Sunderland' was authorized in 1867. The corps became 3rd (Sunderland) Volunteer Battalion Durham Light Infantry in 1887, the change being notified in General Order 181 of December. A new company was added in 1900 and transfer to the Territorial Force in 1908 was as 7th Battalion Durham Light Infantry. The great port at Sunderland on the Wear and the coal trade employed many, as did several works manufacturing anchors and chain cable. Cassell's *Gazetteer* for 1898 notes that the corn market was then held on Saturdays at the Garrison Drill Hall. Uniform: scarlet/blue, changing to scarlet/white in 1884.

4th (1860–80) Formed as one company at Bishop Auckland with Captain William Trotter commissioned on 24 May 1860. Joined the 2nd Admin Battalion. No. 2 Company was soon added at Coundon, two miles south-east of Bishop Auckland, followed in 1865 by No. 3 at Shildon. The latter, however, moved to Darlington in 1872. Became 'A' to 'C' Companies of the new 2nd Corps in 1880. At Bishop Auckland many earned their living in the numerous collieries. St James's Church at Coundon was opened in 1872, the population there also employed in the several coal pits close to the village. Shildon too had numerous collieries, as well as an ironworks.

4th (1880–1908) The 1st Admin Battalion was formed with headquarters at Durham in October 1860 and to it were added the 7th, 10th, 11th, 13th and 14th Corps. Headquarters were moved to Chester-le-Street in 1862 and the battalion was consolidated in 1880 as the new 4th Corps with ten companies:

'A' to 'C' Durham (late 7th Corps)
'D' Beamish (late 10th Corps)
'E' Chester-le-Street (late 11th Corps)
'F' Birtley (late No. 1 Company, 13th Corps)
'G' Washington (late No. 2 Company, 13th Corps)
'H', 'I' and 'K' Felling (late 14th Corps)

Under General Order 181 of December 1887 4th Durham RVC was re-designated as 4th Volunteer Battalion Durham Light Infantry. Headquarters moved to Durham in 1890, 'K' Company being disbanded in 1892 with a new 'K' added at Stanley. 'H' and 'I' Companies were amalgamated as 'H' in 1896, the 'I' position being taken up by a new company raised at Sacriston. 'H' Company transferred to the 5th Volunteer Battalion DLI as its 'L' Company in 1897 and at the same time a new 'H' was formed at Houghton-le-Spring. 'L' (Cyclist) Company was added at Stanley in 1900 and transfer to the Territorial Force in 1908 was as 8th Battalion Durham Light Infantry. 'C' Company, however, joined the OTC as part of the Durham University contingent. Uniform: green/scarlet.

5th The 3rd Admin Battalion of Durham Rifle Volunteers was formed with headquarters at Gateshead in May 1861 and to it were added the 6th, 8th and 9th Corps. The battalion was consolidated as the new 5th Corps in 1880 with eight companies:

'A' to 'C' Gateshead (late 8th Corps)
'D' to 'F' South Shields (late 6th Corps)
'G' Blaydon Burn (late No. 1 Company, 9th Corps)
'H' Winlaton (late No. 2 Company, 9th Corps)

The corps was designated as 5th Volunteer Battalion Durham Light Infantry by General Order 181 of December 1887. Two new companies had been added by 1887 and the battalion was subsequently reorganized as follows:

'A' to 'D' Companies at Gateshead
'E' to 'G' Companies South Shields
'H' Company Blaydon
'I' and 'K' Companies Winlaton

In 1897 'H' Company of the 4th Volunteer Battalion DLI at Felling was transferred to the 5th Volunteer Battalion as its 'L' Company. 'M' (Cyclist) Company was formed at Blaydon in 1900 and transfer to the Territorial Force in 1908 was as 9th Battalion. Uniform: scarlet/dark green.

6th (1860–63) Formed as one company at South Shields, on the south bank of the Tyne, with Captain John Williamson, Lieutenant Charles W Anderson and Ensign Cuthbert Young commissioned on 20 March 1860. Joined the 3rd Admin Battalion. Converted to artillery in December 1863 and was absorbed into the 3rd Durham AVC.

6th (1867–80) Formed at Tyne Docks, South Shields, under the command of Captain George Russell, whose commission was dated 8 August 1867. Joined the 3rd Admin Battalion and became 'D' to 'F' Companies of the new 5th Corps in 1880. The Missions to Seamen Church and Institute in Commercial Road was completed in 1885 replacing the old Tyne Mission.

7th Formed at Durham with Captain John Fogg Elliott and Lieutenant James Monks commissioned on 24 March 1860. Joined the 1st Admin Battalion and became 'A' to 'C' Companies of the new 4th Corps in 1880. The Durham Miners' Association Hall was opened in New Road in 1875. Iron foundries and carpet manufacturers gave employment to a number in the town.

8th Formed as two companies at Gateshead with Captain George H L Hawkes and Captain Stephen W Hawkes as company commanders. Both officers held commissions dated 14 March 1860. Joined the 3rd Admin Battalion, later added a third company, and became 'A' to 'C' Companies of the new 5th Corps in 1880. The Town Hall was opened in 1870, Public Library in 1884. Cassell's *Gazetteer* for 1896 notes that the principal locomotive works of the North Eastern Railway Company were located at Gateshead. Employment was also given at the shipbuilding yards and several ironworks producing anchors and chain cables.

9th Formed as one company at Blaydon, five miles west of Gateshead, with Captain J Cowen commissioned on 3 May 1860. Joined the 3rd Admin Battalion. Headquarters moved to Blaydon Burn suburb in 1862, No. 2 Company being formed at Winlaton in 1864. Became 'G' and 'H' Companies of the new 5th Corps in 1880. At Blaydon; sanitary pipes, fire bricks and bottles were manufactured; sawmills, collieries and iron foundries also gave employment, and large firms at Winlaton manufactured ironwork for shipbuilding.

10th Formed at Beamish with Captain John Joicey, Lieutenant Nathaniel Clark and Ensign George Bolton commissioned on 12 May 1860. Joined the 1st Admin Battalion and became 'D' Company of the new 4th Corps in 1880. Beamish is six miles south-west of Gateshead, its St Andrew's Church being built in 1876.

11th Formed at Chester-le-Street with Captain Patrick S Reid, Lieutenant Thomas H Murray and Ensign Robert F Gibson commissioned on 5 June 1860. Joined the 1st Admin Battalion and became 'E' Company of the new 4th Corps in 1880. Five miles north of Durham, the area employed many in its numerous collieries and ironworks. Much of the 11th Corps was recruited from the Pelton Colliery.

12th Formed as one company at Middleton-in-Teesdale with Captain Robert W Bainbridge, Lieutenant John Elliott and Ensign John Sherlock commissioned on 14 July 1860. The corps was formed mainly from employees of the London Lead Company. Joined the 2nd Admin Battalion and became 'D' Company of the new 2nd Corps in 1880. Just as the 12th Corps was reorganizing as 'D' Company, its members would have seen first-hand the town's church of St Mary the Virgin being rebuilt on the site of its ancient predecessor. Situated on the north bank of the Tees, the men from Middleton worked the several lead mines surrounding the town.

13th Formed as one company at Birtley with Captain Edward M Perkins, Lieutenant Augustus H Hunt and Ensign Isaac L Bell commissioned on 17 August 1860. Joined the 1st Admin Battalion. No. 2 Company was later formed at Washington. Became 'F' and 'G' Companies of the new 4th Corps in 1880. Birtley, five miles south-east of Gateshead, had coal pits and ironworks, as did Washington – Sir Thomas Bell was the great iron master there – just to the east.

14th Formed as one company at Felling with Captain William W Pattison, Lieutenant John Foster and Ensign John M Redmayne commissioned on 31 October 1860. Joined the 1st Admin Battalion, increased later to three companies, and became 'H', 'I' and 'K' Companies of the new 4th Corps in 1880. Felling, just over a mile south-east of Gateshead, employed many from the village at a colliery close by the railway station.

15th Formed at Darlington with Captain George J Sairfield commissioned on 6 October 1860. Joined the 2nd Admin Battalion, transferred to the 4th in 1862, and became 'D' and 'E' Companies of the new 1st Corps in 1880. Several of the town's churches were either built or restored during the Volunteer period. The Cattle Market was established in 1878, the Edward Pease Library built in 1885, the Corn Exchange completed in 1888. The railway, of course, gave employment, locomotives being made in the town from 1824.

16th Formed as one company at Castle Eden with Captain Robert C Bewicke, Lieutenant Robert Wilson and Ensign C H Johnstone commissioned on 14 December 1860. Joined the 2nd Admin Battalion, transferred to the 4th in 1862, and became 'F' Company of the new 1st Corps in 1880. Just under ten miles from Durham, the village of Castle Eden mined coal, made bricks, tiles, ropes, and brewed beer.

17th Formed as one company at Wolsingham with Captain Thomas H Bates, Lieutenant John P Dolphin and Ensign William Nicholson commissioned on 24 November 1860. Joined the 2nd Admin Battalion and disbanded in 1866. On the Wear and well known for its fine black-spotted marble, Wolsingham made shovels, had several sawmills, lead mines, and manufactured steel.

18th Formed as one company at Shotley Bridge with Captain Jonathan B Richardson, Lieutenant Thomas Richardson and Ensign Charles Janson commissioned on 1 December 1860. Joined the 2nd Admin Battalion and disbanded in July 1865. On the Derwent, fourteen miles north-west of Durham, Shotley Bridge once made swords and knife blades; the establishment later of paper mills providing greater employment. The railway, in the form of the old North Eastern line, came to Shotley Bridge in 1867.

19th Formed as one company at Hartlepool with Captain George William Jaffrey, Lieutenant Peter Barr and Ensign Archibald Wilson commissioned on 26 January 1861. Joined the 2nd Admin Battalion, transferred to the 4th in 1862, and was disbanded in November 1872. Built in the time of the Volunteers were the Borough Hall and Market Buildings in 1866 and St Andrew's Church, which was completed in 1886. The collieries close by; the docks, which exported much of the coal; shipbuilding yards, engine and boiler works, employed many from the area.

20th Formed as one company at Stanhope with Captain John Joseph Roddam, Lieutenant Richard Cordner and Ensign William Christopher Arnison commissioned on 19 February 1861. Joined the 2nd Admin Battalion and became 'E' Company of the new 2nd Corps in 1880. A Savings Bank, which also included a reading room, library and lecture hall, was opened five years after the 20th Corps was formed. The old Frosterley & Stanhope line reached the town in 1862, the station being closed in 1895 and a new one opened just to the south-west when the railway was extended to Wearhead.

21st Formed at Startforth as the 7th Yorkshire (North Riding) RVC on 29 February 1860 and attached to the 4th Durham Admin Battalion in November 1863. In the following month, however, 7th Yorks (North Riding) moved to Barnard Castle, was placed into the 2nd Durham Admin Battalion and at the same time retitled 21st Durham RVC. Became 'F' Company of the new 2nd Corps in 1880. A stone bridge across the Tees connects Startforth with Barnard Castle. Another of wood replaced one destroyed in a great river flood that took place in 1881. At Barnard Castle the Mechanics' Institution and the Bowes Museum were opened between 1869 and 1875, and the North Eastern County School in 1886.

EDINBURGH

1st (The Queen's City of Edinburgh Rifle Volunteer Brigade) From the very beginning it was decided to group all companies of rifle Volunteers raised within the City of Edinburgh into one regiment to be known as the 1st City of Edinburgh RVC. Lieutenant Colonel Commandant the Rt Hon James Lord Moncreiff, whose commission was dated 31 August 1859, took command, and by the end of 1860 the regiment consisted of twenty-two companies divided into two battalions. All companies were numbered, and in addition held sub-titles which served to indicate the trade or profession of its members:

No. 1 (Advocates), formed 31 August 1859
No. 2 (1st Citizens), formed 31 August 1859
No. 3 (Writers to the Signet), formed 31 August 1859

No. 4 (Edinburgh University), formed 31 August 1859
No. 5 (Solicitors before the Supreme Court), formed 31 August 1859
No. 6 (Accountants), formed 31 August 1859
No. 7 (Bankers), formed 31 August 1859
No. 8 (1st Artisans), formed 31 August 1859
No. 9 (2nd Artisans), formed 31 August 1859
No. 10 (Civil Service), formed 7 October 1859
No. 11 (3rd Artisans), formed 7 December 1859
No. 12 (Freemasons), formed 7 December 1859
No. 13 (4th Artisans), formed 7 December 1859
No. 14 (2nd Citizens), formed 8 December 1859
No. 15 (1st Merchants), formed 21 December 1859
No. 16 (Total Abstainers), formed 29 February 1860
No. 17 (2nd Merchants), formed 11 May 1860
No. 18 (High Constables), formed 25 May 1860
No. 19 (5th Artisans), formed 8 November 1860
1st (Highland), formed 31 August 1859
2nd (Highland), formed 18 May 1860
3rd (Highland), formed 23 July 1860

Additional information regarding the several companies appears in Lieutenant General Sir James Moncrieff Grierson's book *Records of the Scottish Volunteer Force 1859–1908*. It appears that the 1st to 6th Companies were all self-supporting companies, ie, the members paid for their own uniforms, equipment and arms, and paid a fixed amount annually towards general expenses. In the case of No. 7 (Bankers) Company, formed from clerks and other employees, the several banks concerned contributed towards costs, while the men of the Artisan companies paid for their uniforms by instalments – the expenses of the companies being defrayed by public subscription. Interest in the Freemasons Company (No. 12) soon fell off and had, by 1861, almost ceased to exist. A Miss Catherine Sinclair, however, came forward with funds and as a result No. 12 was reorganized and recruited mainly from the Water of Leith District. While on the subject of Freemasonry, it is of interest to note that Rifle Lodge No. 405 was formed from within the brigade on 7 May 1860. Messrs Cowen & Co., and Messrs C Lawson & Sons paid the expenses of forty members from No. 15 (1st Merchants). Tailoring firms provided members of their staff and expenses for No. 19 (5th Artisans), but after 1873 this company was recruited from all trades. The Highland companies came from members of the Highland Society of Edinburgh.

The title '1st Queen's City of Edinburgh Rifle Volunteer Brigade' was conferred in 1865, and on 23 February 1867 the 1st Corps absorbed the 2nd at Messrs W D Young's Ironworks, Fountainbridge, at the west end of the city, as its 4th, 5th and 6th (Highland) Companies. Formed on 27 December 1867 was the 7th (Highland) Company, recruits for this being, in the main, natives of Caithness now living in Edinburgh. Nos 1 and 3 Companies were disbanded in 1868. A No. 20 Company was added on 19 March 1869, and at the same time the regiment was divided into two battalions: 1st Battalion, comprising Nos 2, 4, 5, 6, 7, 10, 18 and 1st to 7th Highland Companies; 2nd Battalion made up of Nos 8, 9, 11, 12, 13, 14, 15, 16, 17, 19 and 20. Three years later, in 1872, premises in Forrest Road, Edinburgh were taken over as headquarters. The brigade provided two volunteer battalions of the Royal Scots in 1881 and was designated the Queen's Rifle Volunteer Brigade Royal Scots in 1888. Further company reorganization at the same time saw the brigade divided, this time into three battalions and with the companies lettered:

1st Battalion
'A' (late No. 2)
'B' (late No. 5)
'C' (late No. 6)
'D' (late No. 7)
'E' (late No. 10)
'F' (late No. 18)
'G' (late 1st Highland)
'H' (late 2nd Highland)
'I' (late 3rd Highland).

2nd Battalion
'A' (late No. 8)
'B' (late No. 9)
'C' (late No. 11)
'D' (late No. 12)
'E' (late No. 13)
'F' (late No. 14)
'G' (late No. 15)
'H' (late No. 16).

3rd Battalion
'A' (late No. 4)
'B' (late No. 17)
'C' (late No. 19)
'D' (late No. 20)
'E' (late 4th Highland)
'F' (late 5th Highland)
'G' (late 6th Highland)
'H' (late 7th Highland).

A new company ('I') was added to the 3rd Battalion four miles south-west of Edinburgh at Colinton and a cyclist company attached to brigade headquarters in 1900. In the same year the Mounted Infantry detachment formed in 1886 was increased from one to three sections. A complete new kilted battalion of eight companies, designated as The Highland Battalion, was formed in 1900, but this was detached to form the 9th (Highlanders) Volunteer Battalion of the Royal Scots in the following year (see below). A cadet corps was formed and attached to the brigade by Merchiston Castle School in 1886, followed by another at George Watson's Boys' College in 1905. Transfer to the Territorial Force in 1908 was as 4th and 5th Battalions Royal Scots. 'A' Company of the 3rd Battalion, the old No. 4 (Edinburgh University) Company, joined the Senior Division of the OTC as part of the Edinburgh University Contingent; Merchiston Castle and George Watson's both provided contingents of the Junior Division. Uniform: grey/grey.

2nd (1862–67) Contrary to the practice whereas the several Rifle Volunteer companies so far raised in Edinburgh had been placed into the 1st Corps, on 3 May 1862 the company of Highlanders raised at Messrs W D Young's Ironworks at Fountainbridge was numbered separately as 2nd Corps. William D Young himself took command, his lieutenant being John Macdonald, Alexander Maclagan his ensign. On 23 February 1867, however, two more companies were formed and at the same time the whole 2nd Corps was taken into the 1st as its 4th, 5th and 6th (Highland) Companies.

2nd (1880–1908) As previously mentioned, No. 16 Company of the Queen's City of Edinburgh Rifle Volunteer Brigade (see 1st Corps) was formed entirely from total abstainers. These Volunteers were all men who had 'signed the pledge' of total abstinence and were members of the British Temperance League. In 1867 it was decided by John Hope, the founder of No. 16 Company, that a complete corps of total abstainers should be raised in Edinburgh and in consequence, on 27 May 1867, two companies with John Hope in command were formed and designated as 3rd Corps. Hope had in fact drawn his recruits mainly from the ranks of No. 16 Company, his new corps soon becoming known locally as 'John Hope's Water Rats'. New companies (all total abstainers) were added in 1868 and 1872, a sixth joining the corps in 1877. The 3rd Corps was renumbered as 2nd in 1880, then designated 4th Volunteer Battalion Royal Scots in 1888. 'G' Company was formed at Portobello, 'H' at the Church of Scotland Teachers Training College in 1900. The British League Cadet Corps comprising four companies of boys (John Hope in command) had been affiliated to No. 16 Company since 1861 and this association continued with the 3rd (later 2nd) until 1892 when the corps disappeared from the *Army List*. Transfer to the Territorial Force in 1908 was as 6th Battalion Royal Scots. Uniform: scarlet/blue, trews from 1888.

3rd See 2nd Corps (1880–1908).

9th (Highlanders) Volunteer Battalion Royal Scots In 1900 eight kilted companies were formed in Edinburgh and called the Highland Battalion of the Queen's Rifle Volunteer Brigade, James Ferguson being given command, his commission dated 24 July. Formation of such a battalion had been in hand almost since 1875 when the old 1st to 7th (Highland) Companies had been ordered to discontinue their Highland dress for that being worn by the rest of the brigade, therefore losing their individual character. Further individuality came in 1901 when the Highlanders were detached and re-designated as 9th (Highlanders) Volunteer Battalion of the Royal Scots. Headquarters were at 7 Wemyss Place and transfer to the Territorial force in 1908 as 9th Battalion Royal Scots. Uniform: scarlet/blue with kilts.

ELGINSHIRE

All nine of the numbered corps formed within the county joined its 1st Admin Battalion, which was consolidated as the new 1st Corps in 1880.

1st (1860–80) Formed at Forres, its services being accepted as one company on 11 January 1860, with Sir Alexander P Gordon Cumming as captain, Felix Calvers Mackenzie, lieutenant and Robert Davidson, ensign. All three officers held commissions dated 30 January 1860. Became 'A' and 'H' Companies of the new 1st Corps in 1880. At Forres, twelve miles west of Elgin, repairs were being carried out at the parish church as the 1st Corps was being formed in 1860. Woollens, boots, shoes, carriages and chemicals were made in the area.

1st (1880–1908) The 1st Admin Battalion of Elgin Rifle Volunteers was formed with headquarters at Elgin on 4 May 1860 and consolidated in March 1880 as the new 1st Corps with ten-and-a-half companies located:

'A' Forres (late 1st Corps)
'B' Elgin (late 2nd Corps)
'C' Elgin (late 3rd Corps)
'D' Rothes (late 4th Corps)

'E' Fochabers (late 5th Corps)
'F' Carrbridge (late 6th Corps)
'G' Urquhart (late 7th Corps) with a half-company at Pluscarden
'H' Forres (late 1st Corps)
'I' Garmouth (late 8th Corps)
'K' G............n (late 9th Corps)

The new 1st Corps was linked with the Seaforth Highlanders in 1881 and in December 1887 designated as its 3rd (Morayshire) Volunteer Battalion – Morayshire an alternative name for Elginshire. In the same year the headquarters of 'F' Company were moved from Carrbridge to Abernethy. Ten years later the half-company at Pluscarden was increased to form 'L' Company; its headquarters, however, moved to Alves in 1904. 'G' Company transferred from Urquhart to Lhanbryde in the following year. A total of two officers (Captain C Ernest Johnston and Lieutenant W C Reid) and 145 other ranks from the battalion served alongside the Regulars of the 2nd Battalion Seaforth Highlanders in South Africa. One man, Corporal John Dow, received a commission while serving at the front, but on 20 December 1901 was killed in action at Hake Banagher. By 1905 'D' Company had added a detachment at Archiestown and 'K' one at Cromdale. Battalion headquarters were located at Cowper Park, Elgin and transfer to the Territorial Force in 1908 was as 6th Battalion Seaforth Highlanders. Uniform: scarlet/blue, changing to scarlet/yellow with trews (later kilts) in 1886.

2nd Moves to form a rifle corps at Elgin were first made in June 1859, then again in the following December when the master tradesmen of the city resolved at a meeting to form two companies. The firs... ...ese companies, its services accepted on 31 January 1860, subsequently became the 2nd Corps, its membership being open to all citizens. Joshua Johnson became captain; Alexander Cameron lieutenant and James Jamerson ensign – all three holding commissions dated 24 February 1860. Became 'B' Company of the new 1st Corps in 1880. Elgin lies on the banks of the River Lossie. Elgin sandstone was quarried and well known throughout the world; the manufacture of woollens, tweeds, plaiding and leather also employed many.

3rd We have seen above how two companies were raised at Elgin. The second of these, having its services accepted on 20 February 1860, was made up from artisans of the town and as 3rd Elgin RVC became 'C' Company of the new 1st Corps in 1880. The first officers to be commissioned (6 March 1860) were Captain William Culbard, Lieutenant Hugh Squire and Ensign Charles Cumming.

4th Formed as one company at Rothes with John Grant as captain, John Gardner, lieutenant and Peter Dean, ensign. All three officers held commissions dated 28 May 1860. Became 'D' Company of the new 1st Corps in 1880. Eleven miles south-east of Elgin, Rothes had three distilleries.

5th Formed as one company at Fochabers with John Barclay as captain, James Wallace, lieutenant and Alexander Mitchell, ensign. All three officers held commissions dated 10 April 1861. Became 'E' Company of the new 1st Corps in 1880. Perhaps the Volunteers of Fochabers patronized George Baxter's grocery shop, his son later to make his name from his 'Royal Game' and other soups.

6th Formed as one company at Carrbridge with Donald Menzies as captain, Alister McGregor, lieutenant and Donald McBean, ensign. All three officers held commissions dated 26 August 1861. Became 'F' Company of the new 1st Corps in 1880. Carr Bridge [sic] Station, on the Highland line, was opened in July 1892.

7th (Duff) Formed as one company at Lhanbryde with Alexander Lawson as captain, William Proctor, lieutenant and David Cruickshank, ensign. All three officers held commissions dated 15 April 1863. Headquarters moved to Urquhart later in the same year and a half-company was raised at Pluscarden about the same time. The additional title 'Duff' (the company wore a band of Duff tartan around their shakos) was also held by the 7th Elgin, which became 'G' Company of the new 1st Corps in 1880. Lhanbryde is just over three miles from Elgin.

8th Formed as one company at Garmouth with John Mitchell as captain, William H Thompson, lieutenant and Kenneth M Black, ensign. All three officers held commissions dated 2 December 1867. Became 'I' Company of the new 1st Corps in 1880. Garmouth is on the west bank of the River Spey to the north of Fochabers. The railway (Great North of Scotland line) reached Garmouth in 1884.

9th Formed as one company at Grantown on 9 January 1871 and became 'K' Company of the new 1st Corps in 1880. Queen Victoria and Prince Albert wrote of the 'excellent golf course' at Grantown and no doubt enjoyed the whisky that was distilled there. Two stations served the area. Both opened in 1863, one, to the west of the town was opened by the Inverness & Perth Junction line, the other, across the Spey to the east, by the Strathspey Railway.

ESSEX

Essex had three admin battalions, of which the 2nd, formed with headquarters at Plaistow in June 1860 with the 5th, 8th and 9th Corps, was broken up in 1866. The 1st and 3rd provided the new 2nd and 1st Corps respectively in 1880. Two sub-divisions, both numbered as 1st, appeared in the *Army Lists* and these can be seen under 6th and 10th Corps.

1st (1860–80) Formed at Romford with Captain Alfred Hamilton commissioned on 16 February 1860. Joined the 1st Admin Battalion, transferring to 3rd Admin Battalion in 1861, and became 'A' and 'B' Companies of the new 1st Corps in 1880. Agriculture was the chief occupation in Romford, but Messrs Ind and Coope's brewery employed many from the town.

1st (1880–1908) The 3rd Admin Battalion was formed with headquarters at Ilford in July 1861 and to it were added the 1st, 2nd, 3rd, 7th, 15th, 18th, 19th, 21st and 24th Corps. Consolidation in 1880 was as the new 1st Corps with eight companies:

'A' and 'B' Romford (late 1st Corps)
'C' Ilford (late No. 1 Company, 2nd Corps)
'D' Barking (late No. 2 Company, 2nd corps)
'E' Walthamstow (late No. 3 Company, 2nd Corps)
'F' Brentwood (late 3rd Corps)
'G' Chipping Ongar (late 18th Corps)
'H' Hornchurch (late 15th Corps)

Re-designated as 1st Volunteer Battalion Essex Regiment by General Order 14 of February 1883. Headquarters moved to Brentwood in 1890; two new companies were added in 1896, followed by four more in 1900. Several cadet units have been associated with the battalion: Ongar Grammar School in 1865, then a company raised at Forest School, Walthamstow in May 1883. Chigwell School raised a company in 1900 and three years later a unit at Loughton and Buckhurst Hill appeared. Transfer to the Territorial Force in 1908 was as 4th Battalion Essex Regiment. Forest and Chigwell Schools became contingents of the OTC. Uniform: green/green.

2nd (1859–80) Formed as one company at Ilford with Captain John Coope Davis commissioned on 12 August 1859. Joined the 1st Admin Battalion, transferring to 3rd Admin Battalion in 1861. New companies were later added at Barking and Walthamstow, the three becoming 'C' to 'E' Companies of the new 1st Corps in 1880. Almost London, Ilford lies on the River Roding just eight miles from St Paul's. At Barking, even closer to the capital, was the great North London Sewage works; and at Walthamstow, where St Saviour's Church was built in 1874 and St Stephen's in 1878, there were 'superior middle-class villas inhabited by well-to-do artisans'.

2nd (1880–1908) The 1st Admin Battalion was formed with headquarters at Colchester in June 1860 and to it were added the 4th, 6th, 10th, 11th, 12th, 13th, 14th, 16th, 20th and 23rd Corps. The 1st, 2nd, 3rd and 7th also formed part of the battalion, but these corps transferred to the 3rd Admin Battalion in 1861. Headquarters moved to Chelmsford in February 1862, but transferred to Braintree upon consolidation as the new 2nd Corps in 1880. There were eight companies:

> 'A' and 'B' Chelmsford (late 4th Corps)
> 'C' and 'D' Colchester (late 6th Corps)
> 'E' Witham (late 10th Corps)
> 'F' Braintree (late 12th Corps)
> 'G' Maldon (late 23rd Corps)
> 'H' Walton-on-the-Naze (late 23rd Corps)

Designated as 2nd Volunteer Battalion Essex Regiment under General Order 14 of February 1883 and in 1895 headquarters moved yet again, this time back to Colchester. Two new companies were added in 1900. A cadet corps was formed and affiliated to the 1st Admin Battalion in 1872, but this disappeared from the *Army List* in October 1880. Felstead School Cadet Corps was affiliated in 1883 and in 1904 the King Edward VI School Cadet Corps was formed at Chelmsford. Transfer to the Territorial Force in 1908 was as 5th Battalion Essex Regiment. Uniform: green/green

3rd (1859–80) Formed at Brentwood with Captain Octavius Edward Coope commissioned on 12 October 1859. Joined the 1st Admin Battalion, transferring to 3rd Admin Battalion in 1861. Absorbed the 21st Corps, also at Brentwood, in 1872 and became 'F' Company of the new 1st Corps in 1880. Brentwood's church of St Thomas the Martyr was opened in 1883. The chief industries of the town were brewing and brick making. A large number of the corps were recruited from a factory that made agricultural tools owned by William Burges and Sir K G Key.

3rd (1880–1908) Formed at Plaistow as 5th Corps comprising four companies with all officers holding commissions dated 30 January 1860. Much of the corps was recruited from the Royal Victoria Dock, its commanding officer being docks manager, Charles Cooper. Included in the 2nd Admin Battalion until 1866, renumbered as 3rd Corps in 1880, then designated 3rd Volunteer Battalion Essex Regiment in 1883. Headquarters moved to West Ham two years later. The battalion reached an establishment of thirteen companies in 1900 and a cadet corps was formed and affiliated in 1907. Transfer to the Territorial Force in 1908 was as 6th Battalion Essex Regiment. Uniform: green/green, changing to scarlet/white in 1895.

4th (1859–80) Formed at Chelmsford with Captain William M Tufnell, Lieutenant John Henry Bringhurst and Ensign Josiah Alfred Hardcastle commissioned on 8 November 1859. Joined the 1st Admin Battalion and became 'A' and 'B' Companies of the new 2nd Corps in 1880. Cassell's *Gazetteer* for 1895 noted that Chelmsford's corn market was the most extensive in the country. Other chief industries were electrical engineering, agricultural implement making, iron founding, tanning and brewing. Marconi opened the world's first radio factory in Hall Street, Chelmsford in 1899.

4th (1880–1908) Formed at Silvertown as 9th Corps on 1 February 1860 and included in the 2nd Admin Battalion until 1866. Renumbered 4th in 1880 and designated 4th Volunteer Battalion Essex Regiment in 1883. Headquarters moved to Leyton in 1900 and in that same year the battalion's establishment was increased to eleven companies. Transfer to the Territorial Force in 1908 was as 7th Battalion Essex Regiment. Just four miles from London's St Paul's Cathedral, Silvertown's church of St Mark was opened in 1863. The town takes its name from the india-rubber works founded by the firm of Silver. Sugar was refilled there; chemicals and soap were also manufactured. Uniform: green/green, changing to scarlet/white in 1902.

5th See 3rd Corps (1880–1908).

6th Formed at Colchester on 8 September 1859 and known as the 1st Sub-division until December. The officers, Captain Sir Claude W C de Crespigny, Lieutenant J Fitzsimmons Bishop and Ensign Henry Egerton Green, then holding commissions dated 20 December 1859. Joined the 1st Admin Battalion and became 'C' and 'D' Companies of the new 2nd Corps in 1880. On the south bank of the Colne, the town's oyster fishery gave employment, as did firms manufacturing clothing, boots and shoes.

7th Formed at Rochford with Lieutenant Arthur Tawke commissioned on 8 March 1860. Joined the 1st Admin Battalion, transferring to 3rd Admin Battalion in 1861. The company disappeared from the *Army List* in February 1877. At Rochford, four miles south-east of Southend-on-Sea, the restoration of St Andrew's Church was completed in 1862, the Corn Exchange being built in 1866.

8th Formed as four companies at Stratford with all officers holding commissions dated 6 March 1860. The corps was recruited from staff of the Eastern Counties Railway, which had reached the town in 1840. Joined the 2nd Admin Battalion in 1864 and disbanded in the following year.

9th See 4th Corps (1880–1908).

10th Formed at Witham on 30 December 1859 and known as 1st Sub-division until March 1860. Joined the 1st Admin Battalion and became 'E' Company of the new 2nd Corps in 1880. Situated fourteen miles south-west of Colchester, the town's Public Hall was built in 1894.

11th Formed at Dunmow, eleven miles north-west of Chelmsford, with Lieutenant John Mayon Wilson commissioned on 21 March 1860. Joined the 1st Admin Battalion and was disbanded on 14 August 1863.

12th Formed at Braintree with Lieutenant Basil Sparrow and Ensign George Courtauld jun commissioned on 6 March 1860. Joined the 1st Admin Battalion and became 'F' Company of the new 2nd Corps in 1880. Situated on the River Blackwater, Braintree employed many in its corn mills and breweries. The railway, in the form of the Great Eastern line, reached Braintree in 1869.

13th (Stour Valley) Formed at Dedham with former 42nd Royal Highland Regiment officer, Lieutenant Augustus Paterson and Ensign Edward M Alderson commissioned on 8 March 1860. Joined the 1st Admin Battalion and disappeared from the *Army List* in December 1870.

14th Formed at Manningtree, just under nine miles from Colchester, with Lieutenant Barnard W Cocker, a former lieutenant colonel in the 38th Regiment of Foot, and Ensign Thomas W Nunn commissioned on 17 May 1860. Joined the 1st Admin Battalion and disappeared from the *Army List* in June 1862.

15th Formed at Hornchurch, two miles south-east of Romford, with Captain Peter E Bearblock,

Lieutenant William Mashiter and Ensign Richard Denby commissioned on 11 June 1860. Joined the 3rd Admin Battalion and became 'H' Company of the new 1st Corps in 1880. The main offices of the South Essex Waterworks were to be found at Hornchurch in the 1890s, as well as a factory making bicycles. The London, Tilbury & Southend Railway opened its Hornchurch Station in May 1885.

16th Formed at Great Bentley, eight miles south-east of Colchester, with Lieutenant James Hardy and Ensign Joseph G Watson commissioned on 10 September 1860. Joined the 1st Admin Battalion and was disbanded in 1875.

17th Formed at Saffron Walden with Captain the Hon Charles C Neville, Lieutenant Henry Byng and Ensign Douglas Lane commissioned on 23 October 1860. Included in the 2nd Admin Battalion of Cambridgeshire Rifle Volunteers from November 1863. This battalion was broken up in 1872 and its corps, including 17th Essex, were then transferred to the 1st Cambridgeshire Admin Battalion. Upon consolidation of that battalion in 1880, 17th Essex became 'I' Company of the new 1st Cambridgeshire RVC. Fifteen miles from Cambridge, two heroes of the Crimea, both sons of Lord Braybrooke, are remembered at St Mary's Church, Saffron Walden: Captain the Hon H A Neville, who was killed at Inkerman, and the Hon G Neville, mortally wounded at Balaclava.

18th Formed at Chipping Ongar with Captain Phillip J Budworth, Lieutenant Phillip H Meyer and Ensign Frederick A S Fane commissioned on 4 December 1860. Joined the 3rd Admin Battalion and became 'G' Company of the new 1st Corps in 1880. Chipping Ongar is on the River Roding eleven miles from Chelmsford. A Volunteer Drill Hall was built there in 1873, a south aisle added to St Martin's Church in 1884 and, attached to the Congregational Chapel is Dr Livingstone's room, in which the explorer lived as a student. Budworth Hall was erected as a memorial to Captain Budworth.

19th Formed at Epping with Lieutenant Sir William B Smyth Bt and Ensign Loftus W Arkwright commissioned on 22 September 1860. Joined the 3rd Admin Battalion and disappeared from the *Army List* in November 1872. Epping Town Hall was built three years after the 19th Corps was formed. The corps took possession of a new drill hall in 1873. The town's St Martin's Church was restored in 1884.

20th Formed at Haverhill with Lieutenant Ellys Anderson Stephens Walton and Ensign Henry Wyld Jackson commissioned on 27 December 1860. Joined the 1st Admin Battalion and was disbanded in 1871. At Haverhill, the rebuilding of St Mary's Church had only been completed two years prior to the formation of the 20th Corps, the red brick Town Hall being built in 1883 and the Corn Exchange in 1889. About the same time, notes Cassell's *Gazetteer*, the town had a large factory employing some 3,000 in the manufacture of clothing and mats. There were also firms producing silk, boots, shoes and bricks.

21st Formed at Brentwood with Captain Sir Kingsmill G Key Bt commissioned on 24 September 1860. Joined the 3rd Admin Battalion and was absorbed into the 3rd Corps in 1872. At Brentwood, ten miles from Chelmsford, the chief industries were brewing and brick making.

22nd Formed at Waltham Abbey with Captain William Leask and Lieutenant Edward S Bulmer commissioned on 27 November 1860. Placed into the 2nd Hertfordshire Admin Battalion in 1862, absorbed part of the 11th Hertfordshire RVC at Cheshunt in November 1870, and became 'H' Company of the new 1st Hertfordshire Corps in 1880. Cassell's *Gazetteer* for 1898 notes that on the banks of the Lea was a large Government establishment for refining saltpetre and for the manufacture of gunpowder, new works having been erected in 1890 about a half-mile from the town for the making of cordite. Percussion caps were also made. Much of the 22nd Corps was recruited from the Royal Gunpowder Mills.

23rd Formed at Maldon with Captain James A Hamilton, late of the 41st Regiment of Foot, Lieutenant Edward H Bentall and Ensign Sampson Hanbury commissioned on 13 November 1860. Joined the 1st Admin Battalion and became 'G' and 'H' Companies of the new 2nd Corps in 1880. The town's two main churches, All Saints' and St Mary's, saw their Victorian restoration during the time that the 23rd Corps existed. A river port, Maldon gave employment in the shipping trade and its oyster fisheries. At some time between 1878 and 1880 a second company was formed to the north-east at the seaside resort of Walton-on-the-Naze. Here, in 1884, a lifeboat called *Honourable Artillery Company* was presented to the Royal National Lifeboat Institution by the Dramatic Club of the HAC.

24th Formed as two companies at Woodford with Captain George Noble commissioned on 10 April 1861. Joined the 3rd Admin Battalion and was disbanded in 1872.

FIFESHIRE

All rifle corps formed within the county were placed into the 1st Admin Battalion, which became the new 1st Corps in 1880.

1st (1860–80) The services of two companies at Dunfermline were accepted on 25 February 1860 with Erskine Beveridge and Kenneth Mathieson as company commanders. Became 'A' and 'B' Companies of the new 1st Corps in 1880. Listed among the sources of employment about the time of the Volunteers was the manufacture of table linen, brass utensils, machinery, soap, terracotta articles and rope. There were also bleach works, corn mills and breweries in the area.

1st (1880–1908) The 1st Admin Battalion of Fifeshire Rifle Volunteers was formed with headquarters at St Andrews on 21 September 1860. All Fifeshire corps were included, the 1st Kinross being part of the battalion between 1861 and 1873. Consolidated as the new 1st Corps in 1880 with twelve companies:

'A' and 'B' Dunfermline (late 1st Corps)
'C' and 'D' Cupar (late 2nd Corps)
'E' East Anstruther (late 3rd Corps)
'F' Colinsburgh (late 4th Corps)
'G' St Andrews (late 5th Corps)
'H' Leslie (late No. 1 Company, 6th Corps)
'I' Falkland (late No. 2 Company, 6th Corps)
'K' Kirkcaldy (late 7th Corps)
'L' Lochgelly (late 8th corps)
'M' Newburgh (late 9th Corps)

Re-designated as 6th (Fifeshire) Volunteer Battalion Black Watch under General Order 181 of December 1887. In March 1900 both 'C' and 'D' Companies moved to Kirkcaldy, 'K' at the same time going to Cupar. A cyclist company ('O') was added at Dunfermline in January 1901, and in 1906 'F' was moved to Leven. Transfer to the Territorial Force in 1908 was as 7th Battalion Black Watch. Uniform: scarlet/blue.

2nd Formed as two companies at Cupar, thirteen miles south of Dundee, on 6 March 1860 with David Gillespie and George Hogarth as company commanders. Became 'C' and 'D' companies of the new 1st Corps in 1880. On the Eden, Cupar provided employment in brewing and the manufacture of linen, flax, leather and cloth. Part of the St Andrews University Press was located in the town.

3rd Formed as one company at Kilconquhar on 25 April 1860 with Sir Thomas Erskine Bt as captain, James Clark, lieutenant and John Key, ensign. Moved headquarters to East Anstruther in 1861 and became 'E' Company of the new 1st Corps in 1880. In south-east Fifeshire, coal and limestone were worked at Kilconquhar. There were fisheries at East Anstruther, about four miles to the east.

4th Formed as one company at Colinsburgh on 20 April 1860 with David Briggs as captain, Walter Davidson, lieutenant and William R Ketchen, ensign. Became 'F' Company of the new 1st Corps in 1880.

5th Formed as one company at St Andrews on 23 April 1860 with Walter T Hilton as captain, Sir Charles M Ochierlonie, lieutenant and Thomas Hodge, ensign. Became 'G' Company of the new 1st Corps in 1880. The 'Rifle Volunteers Hall' was also used by the town for entertainments and public meetings. Golf – the Royal and Ancient Club being established at St Andrews in 1754 – was, as today, important to the town.

6th Formed as one company at Strathleven on 25 August 1860 with Lieutenant Charles Anderson the first officer to be gazetted. Headquarters moved to Leslie in 1872 and at same time a new company was added at Falkland. Lieutenant General Sir James Moncrieff Grierson notes that the latter was not recognized until 1880. Became 'H' and 'I' Companies of the new 1st Corps in 1880. At Leslie, on the River Leven, many were employed in flax spinning, bleaching and the manufacture of paper. At Falkland, to the north, there were linen industries and breweries.

7th Formed as one company at Kirkcaldy on 23 April 1860 with James F Bremner as captain, Robert R Landale, lieutenant and James Shepherd, ensign. Became 'K' Company of the new 1st Corps in 1880. The Corn Exchange was built in the same year that the 7th Corps was formed; the Swan Memorial Hall, commemorating a formed provost, was completed in 1895. Work began on the Adam Smith and Beveridge Halls and Library in the following year. Linoleum was manufactured at Kirkcaldy, the docks giving employment to many in shipbuilding and other jobs connected with sea trade.

8th Formed as one company at Auchterderran, five miles south-west of Kirkcaldy, on 20 April 1860 with Roger S Aytoun as captain, Andrew Landale, lieutenant and Thomas Goodall, ensign. Headquarters were moved to Lochgelly in 1862 and became 'L' Company of the new 1st Corps in 1880. Iron, coal and limestone were worked in the area around Auchterderran. At Lochgelly, where a large Drill Hall was built for the Volunteers in 1892, collieries and ironworks gave employment.

9th Formed as one sub-division at Newburgh, just over eight miles from Perth, on 28 July 1860 with Peter H Paterson as lieutenant and A Walker Russell, ensign. Increased to a full company on 2 June 1862 and became 'M' Company of the new 1st Corps in 1880. The Public Library was opened the year after the formation of the 9th Corps.

FLINTSHIRE

All Flintshire corps joined the 1st Admin Battalion, which formed the new 1st Corps in 1880.

1st (1860–80) Formed at Mold, six miles south of Flint, on 27 March 1860 with John S Banks as captain, Thomas T Kelly, lieutenant and George Bellis, ensign. Became 'A' Company of the new 1st Corps in 1880. In the area were lead mines, tin-plate works, a nail-making factory and a company making fire bricks. The Volunteer Drill Hall was in High Street, Mold.

1st (1880–1908) The 1st Admin Battalion of Flintshire Rifle Volunteers was formed with headquarters at Rhyl in August 1860. Headquarters moved to Holywell in 1863, but moved back to Rhyl in 1874. In 1874 the then 1st to 5th Carnarvonshire Corps were added, thus bringing about the dual title upon consolidation in 1880 – 1st Flintshire and Carnarvonshire RVC. There were ten companies:

'A' Mold (late 1st Flintshire Corps)
'B' Hawarden (late 2nd Flintshire)
'C' Rhyl (late 3rd Flintshire)
'D' Holywell (late 4th Flintshire)
'E' Flint (late 5th Flintshire)
'F' Caergwle (late 6th Flintshire)
'G' and 'H' Carnarvon (late 3rd Carnarvon)
'I' Portmadoc (late 4th Carnarvon)
'K' Llanberis (late 5th Carnarvon)

Under General Order 78 of June 1884 the corps was re-designated as 2nd Volunteer Battalion Royal Welsh Fusiliers, the establishment of which by 1896 had reached sixteen companies. On 26 May 1897, however, this was reduced to eight when the Carnarvonshire personnel were withdrawn to form the new 3rd Volunteer Battalion, RWF. That same year headquarters of 2nd Volunteer Battalion, now exclusively in Flintshire, moved to Hawarden. Three years later an additional three companies were sanctioned then, in 1904, a reduction was made to ten. Transfer to the Territorial Force in 1908 was as headquarters and seven companies of the 5th Battalion Royal Welsh Fusiliers. Uniform: scarlet/green, changing to scarlet/blue in 1888.

2nd Formed at Hawarden, six miles west of Chester, on 1 June 1860 with Gregory Burnett as captain, Edward Thompson, lieutenant and William Henry Gladstone, ensign. Became 'B' Company of the new 1st Corps in 1880. A fountain was erected at the village cross in 1889 to commemorate the Golden Wedding of several-times Prime Minister W E Gladstone and his wife (heiress to Hawarden Castle, Catherine Glynn), who were married at Hawarden. Their son (see above) was an officer in the 2nd Corps.

3rd A 3rd Corps with headquarters at Rhyl first appeared in the *Army List* for May 1860 with Herbert W W Wynn as captain, Thomas Sleight, lieutenant and John Frankland Fishwick, ensign. Became 'C' Company of the new 1st Corps in 1880. A popular seaside resort still, in 1891 its Pavilion was erected at the entrance to the pier.

4th Formed at Holywell, fifteen miles north-west of Chester, on 29 June 1860 with Rudolph W B Viscount Feilding as captain, Alexander Cope, lieutenant and Charles Crockford, ensign. Became 'D' Company of the new 1st Corps in 1880. The several industries in and around the town included lead mining, copper and iron production. There were also paper mills, cement works, collieries and lime quarries.

5th Formed at Flint on 3 February 1863 with William Henry Porritt as captain and Isaac Taylor, ensign. Became 'E' Company of the new 1st Corps in 1880. The manufacture of chemical products was important to the town; employment was also available at the area's several copper works, paper mills and brick-making establishments. St David's Church was opened in 1872, St Thomas's two years after that.

6th Formed at Caergwle, five miles north-west of Wrexham, on 27 November 1872 and became 'F' Company of the new 1st Corps in 1880. The 1893 edition of Cassell's *Gazetteer of Great Britain and Ireland* notes that Caergwle is important for its manufacture of spades and shovels. Caergwle Station, opened in 1866 as part of the Wrexham, Mold & Connah's Quay Railway, was renamed Hope Village in January 1899.

FORFARSHIRE

Two admin battalions were formed to include those corps raised outside of Dundee. The 1st took in the eastern half of the county, while the 2nd, headquarters at Forfar, covered the west. In 1874, however, 2nd Admin was broken up and what remained of its corps were placed into the 1st. This, in 1880, became the new 2nd Corps. Towards the end of 1876 those corps still remaining in the 1st Admin (with the exception of the 8th) were permitted to include their headquarters location as part of the official titles. The change was first seen in the *Army List* for January 1877.

1st (Dundee) The 1st Corps of the county was formed as the result of a public meeting held in Dundee on 20 May 1859, its service being accepted in the following November with Sir John Ogilvy Bt in command. Five companies were authorized, followed by two more in February 1860 and another in April. Re-designation as 1st (Dundee) Volunteer Battalion Black Watch was notified in General Order 181 of December 1887, the sub-title changing, however, to (City of Dundee) in February 1889. Formed and attached in 1879 was a company of cadets, but this was later disbanded and last seen in the *Army List* for September 1888. Two new companies (one a cyclist) were added in 1900 and another cadet corps, that raised at Morgan Academy, was affiliated in the same year. Battalion headquarters and drill hall were in the Albany Quarters, Bell Street, Dundee and its rifle range just over seven miles off at Monifieth Links. Transfer to the Territorial Force in 1908 was as 4th Battalion Black Watch. Uniform: scarlet/blue.

During the Volunteer period several new churches were built in the city: St Mark's in 1869; Rosebank Church, 1872; St Enoch's, 1873, St Mathew's, 1875 and Chepington Church in 1881. The Town Hall was completed in 1876, the Technical Institution founded in 1888. As a thriving seaport, Dundee employed many in its dockyards. Flax, carpets, sails, rope and, of course, marmalade, were all made in Dundee.

2nd (Forfar) (1859–80) Formed as one company at Forfar on 15 November 1859 with William Gray as captain, George Lyon, lieutenant and David Crighton, ensign. A second company was added on 10 January 1861. Joined the 2nd Admin Battalion, transferring to the 1st in 1874, and became 'A' and 'B' Companies of the new 2nd Corps in 1880. The manufacture of linen gave employment, as well as several bleach fields and ironworks.

2nd (Angus) (1880–1908) The 1st Admin Battalion was formed with headquarters at Montrose in May 1861 and included the 3rd, 5th, 7th and 13th Corps. Headquarters moved to Friockheim by Arbroath in 1874 and in same year the 2nd Admin Battalion was broken up and its corps transferred to 1st Admin Battalion. The battalion then became known as 1st Admin

Battalion of Forfarshire or Angus Rifle Volunteers which, in 1880, was consolidated as the new 2nd Corps with fourteen companies:

'A' and 'B' Forfar (late 2nd Corps)
'C' to 'F' Arbroath (late 3rd Corps)
'G' and 'H' Montrose (late 5th Corps)
'I' and 'K' Brechin (late 7th Corps)
'L' Newtyle (late 8th Corps)
'M' Glamis (late 9th Corps)
'N' Kirriemuir (late 12th Corps)
'O' Friockheim (late 13th Corps)

The new corps at first also included 'Forfarshire or Angus' in its title, but this was changed to 'Angus' in 1883. Next came the re-designation in 1887 as 2nd (Angus) Volunteer Battalion Black Watch, that same year seeing headquarters moved to Arbroath. In 1894 the company structure of the battalion underwent a number of changes beginning with the disbandment of 'F' and the amalgamation of 'L' and 'M' as 'K'. Further reorganizations saw 'G' designated as 'F', 'H' as 'G', 'I' as 'H', the original 'K' as 'I', 'N' as 'L' and 'O' as 'M'. A cadet corps formed at the Chapel Works in Montrose was affiliated in 1907 and transfer to the Territorial Force in 1908 was as six companies of 5th Battalion Black Watch. Uniform: scarlet/blue, trews from 1882.

3rd (Arbroath) (1859–80) Formed as one company at Arbroath on 15 November 1859 with James Anderson Dickson as captain, David Salmond, lieutenant and Charles W Corsar, ensign. The 4th Corps, also at Arbroath and with James Muir as captain, John A Anderson, lieutenant and David Corsar, ensign, being absorbed as No. 2 Company in May 1860. Two new companies were raised in 1864. Joined the 1st Admin Battalion, increased to four companies in 1864, and became 'C' to 'F' Companies of the new 2nd Corps in 1880. Linen, sailcloth, flax, chemicals, tar and asphalt were manufactured at Arbroath. Fisheries, engineering and shipbuilding also provided employment.

3rd (Dundee Highland) (1880–1908) One company formed at Dundee as 10th Corps on 10 April 1860 with Edward Guild as captain, J Cunningham Kilgour, lieutenant and Hugh Ballingail, ensign. A second company was added on 29 June 1867. Amalgamated with the 14th Corps, also at Dundee, in September 1868, the new formation comprising six companies under the title 10th Forfarshire (Dundee Highland) RVC with Lieutenant Colonel David Guthrie of Carlogie in command. Renumbered in March 1880 as 3rd (Dundee Highland), then designated as 3rd (Dundee Highland) Volunteer Battalion Black Watch under General Order 181 of December 1887. Increased to eight companies in 1900 and transferred to the Territorial Force in 1908 as two companies of 5th Battalion Black Watch. Headquarters of the battalion and its drill hall were at Albany Quarters, Bell Street, Dundee, its musketry being carried out at the Barry Links government range. Uniform: scarlet/blue, trews from 1882.

4th See 3rd Corps (1859–80).

5th (Montrose) Formed as one company at Montrose on 15 November 1859 with Thomas Renny Tailyour as captain, Robert Smart, lieutenant and Andrew Greig, ensign. Joined the 1st Admin Battalion. A second company was added on 10 April 1860, the two becoming 'G' and 'H' Companies of the new 2nd Corps in 1880. The North British Railway opened a station at Montrose in May 1883.

6th None recorded.

7th (Brechin) Formed as one company at Brechin on 26 March 1860 with David Gutterie as captain, James Loudon Gordon, lieutenant and George Alexander Scott, ensign. Joined the 1st Admin Battalion. A second company was added on 18 April 1865, the two becoming 'I' and 'K' Companies of the new 2nd Corps in 1880. At Brechin, on the Esk five miles west of Montrose, firms made paper, flax, linen and sailcloth. Breweries and distilleries provided employment.

8th (Wharncliffe) Formed as one company at Newtyle on 4 April 1860 with Robert Thomas as captain, David Waddel, lieutenant and Alexander Black, ensign. Joined the 2nd Admin Battalion, transferring to the 1st Admin Battalion in 1874, and became 'L' Company of the new 2nd Corps in 1880. The old Newtyle & Dundee Railway closed its station at Newtyle in August 1868 and was replaced by a new one on the Caledonian line.

9th (Glamis) Formed at Glamis on 8 May 1860 with the Hon Claude B Lyon as captain, John Barry, lieutenant and John Hood, ensign. Joined the 2nd Admin Battalion, transferring to the 1st in 1874, and became 'M' Company of the new 2nd Corps in 1880. Glamis is eleven miles from Dundee.

10th See 3rd (Dundee Highland) Corps.

11th Formed as a sub-division at Tannadice on 8 October 1860 with James R Haig as lieutenant and David B Ogilvy, ensign. Increased to a full company on 29 September 1867, joined the 2nd Admin Battalion and was disbanded in 1869. Tannadice is on the South Esk four miles north of Forfar; its railway station, on the old Caledonian line, opened in January 1895.

12th (Kirriemuir) Formed as one company at Kirriemuir on 17 September 1860 with the Earl of Airlie as captain, James Brodie, lieutenant and Robert Forrest, ensign. Joined the 2nd Admin Battalion, transferring to 1st in 1874, and became 'N' Company of the new 2nd Corps in 1880. Just under nine miles north-west of Forfar, the town's main industry was linen weaving.

13th (Friockheim) Formed as one company at Friockheim on 4 June 1861 with Thomas M'P B Gardyne as captain, Alexander R Laing as lieutenant and Hector Young, ensign. Joined the 1st Admin Battalion and became 'O' Company of the new 2nd Corps in 1880. At Friockheim, just under seven miles from Arbroath, there were bleach fields and several manufacturers of textile materials.

14th Formed as one company at Dundee on 14 June 1861 with John Zuill Kay as captain, John Keay, lieutenant and James Stuart, ensign. A second company was added on 29 June 1867, the two amalgamated with the 10th Corps in September 1868.

15th Formed as one company at Cortachy with Captain Peter M Geekie commissioned on 16 August 1865. Joined the 2nd Admin Battalion, but was disbanded in 1872.

GALLOWAY

The Galloway RVC Galloway is the district of south-west Scotland comprising the counties of Wigtownshire and Kircudbrightshire. The RVC formed within these areas were on 30 June 1860 grouped together under the title of The Galloway Admin Battalion of Rifle Volunteers. In command was Lieutenant Colonel William K Laurie, his adjutant being William Munro, who had previously served with the 79th Regiment of Foot. In 1880 the battalion was consolidated as the Galloway RVC with headquarters at Newton Stewart and eight companies:

'A' Kirkcudbright (late 1st Kirkcudbright Corps)
'B' Castle Douglas (late 2nd Kirkcudbright Corps)
'C' Stranraer (late 2nd Wigtown Corps)
'D' Newton Stewart (late 3rd Wigtown Corps)
'E' New Galloway (late 3rd Kirkcudbright Corps)
'F' Maxwelltown (late 5th Kirkcudbright Corps)
'G' Maxwelltown (late 5th Kirkcudbright Corps)
'H' Dalbeattie (late 6th Kirkcudbright Corps)

Joined the Royal Scots as one of its volunteer battalions (without change in title) in 1881, but transferred to the King's Own Scottish Borderers in 1899. Again, no change in designation was assumed. Headquarters moved to Castle Douglas in 1885, then to Maxwelltown in 1904. Some ninety-five Volunteers from the corps served in South Africa during the Boer War, Colour Sergeant R Grierson, Lance Corporal J McMillan and Private R Dixon were all three mentioned for gallantry at the capture of Commandant Wolmarans and thirty of his men near Damhoek on 10 August 1901. Transfer to the Territorial Force in 1908 was as four companies of 5th KOSB and one company 5th Royal Scots Fusiliers. Uniform: grey/scarlet.

GLAMORGANSHIRE

Of the twenty numbered corps formed within the county all but the 3rd were included in one or other of its two admin battalions. These provided the new 1st and 2nd Corps in 1880.

1st (1859–80) Formed as one company at Margam on 12 October 1859 with Christopher R Mansel Talbot as captain, Theodore Mansel Talbot, lieutenant and William Llewellyn, ensign. Joined the 1st Admin Battalion, increased to two companies in March 1861, and became 'A' and 'B' Companies of the new 1st Corps in 1880. Several collieries gave employment to the area. In the town, St Mary's Church saw its Victorian restoration in 1873.

1st (1880–1908) The 1st Admin Battalion was formed with headquarters at Margam in March 1861 and to it were added the 1st, 4th, 5th, 6th, 7th, 9th, 11th, 15th, 17th and 18th Corps. The battalion was consolidated in March 1880 to form the new 1st Corps with twelve companies:

'A' and 'B' Margam (late 1st Corps)
'C' to 'E' Swansea (late 4th Corps)
'F' and 'G' Taibach (late 7th Corps)
'H' Cwm Avon (late 9th Corps)
'I' Bridgend (late 11th Corps)
'K' and 'L' Neath (late 15th Corps)
'M' Cowbridge (late 18th Corps)

Designated as 2nd (Glamorgan) Volunteer Battalion Welsh Regiment under General Order 181 of December 1887. The sub-title was not, however, shown in the *Army List* after December 1888. Headquarters moved to Bridgend in 1896 and even greater reorganizations in 1905 saw the three Swansea Companies ('C', 'D' and 'E') transferred to the 3rd Corps. At the same time, personnel from around the Cardiff area then serving with the 3rd Volunteer Battalion Welsh Regiment were absorbed. This was to bring 2nd Volunteer Battalion's establishment up to fourteen companies, headquarters at the same time changing to Cardiff. Volunteers from the battalion saw active service in South Africa. Frank P J Charles, who was commissioned as lieutenant in January 1901, was badly wounded near Germiston on 11 March 1902 and subsequently died back at Netley Hospital on 4 July. In 1908 much of the battalion was converted to 2nd Welsh Brigade RFA. Some members joined the Glamorgan Battery RHA and others the 7th Battalion Welsh Regiment. Uniform: scarlet/blue, changing to scarlet/white.

2nd (1859–80) Formed as one company at Dowlais on 12 October 1859 with George Thomas Clark as captain, William Menelaus, lieutenant and George Martin, ensign. Joined the 2nd Admin Battalion, increased to two companies in December 1861, and became 'A' and 'B' Companies of the new 2nd Corps in 1880. Close to Merthyr Tydfil, the Dowlais Iron Company is said to have employed close to 10,000 in its production of iron, tin bars, rails and other articles of steel in the 1890s.

2nd (1880–1908) The 2nd Admin Battalion was formed with headquarters at Dowlais, near Merthyr Tydfil, in March 1861 and included the 2nd, 8th, 10th, 12th, 13th, 14th, 16th, 19th and 20th Corps. Headquarters moved to Cardiff in 1872 and consolidation in 1880 saw 2nd Admin consolidated as the new 2nd Corps with twenty-two companies:

'A' and 'B' Dowlais (late 2nd Corps)
'C' to 'E' Mountain Ash (late 8th Corps)
'F' and 'G' Cardiff (late 10th Corps)
'H', 'I','K' and 'L' Merthyr Tydfil (late 12th Corps)
'M' and 'N' Taff's Well (late 13th Corps)
'O' and 'P' Aberdare (late 14th Corps)
'Q' to 'U' Cardiff (late 16th Corps)
'V' Pontypridd (late 19th Corps)
'W' Hirwain (late 20th Corps)

Under General Order 181 of December 1887 the 2nd Corps was re-designated as 3rd (Glamorgan) Volunteer Battalion Welsh Regiment, the sub-title, however, was removed from the *Army List* in March 1891. An increase in establishment to twenty-four companies took place in 1900, but this was reduced to fifteen upon transfer of personnel from around the Cardiff area to the 2nd Volunteer Battalion Welsh Regiment in 1905. Headquarters at the same time moved to Pontypridd. A cadet corps was formed and affiliated to the battalion at Cardiff in 1889, but this was not shown in the *Army List* after August 1892. Transfer to the Territorial Force in 1908 was as 5th Battalion Welsh Regiment. Uniform: scarlet/blue, changing to scarlet/white.

3rd Formed at Swansea on 12 October 1859 and soon comprised four companies under the command of Major Lewis Llewellyn Dillwyn. Later increased to six companies and became a volunteer battalion (without change in title) of the Welsh Regiment in 1881. Increased from six to nine companies in 1900 and then twelve as the Swansea personnel of 2nd Volunteer Battalion Welsh Regiment were transferred in 1905. The 3rd Corps provided the 6th Battalion Welsh Regiment upon transfer to the Territorial Force in 1908. Uniform: scarlet/green, changing to scarlet/white.

4th Formed as one company at Swansea on 12 October 1859 with Henry Hussey Vivian as captain, Iltyd Thomas, lieutenant and Edward Strick, ensign. Comprised four companies by January 1861 (later reduced to three), attached to the 3rd Corps for the period 1872–73, then included in the 1st Admin Battalion. Became 'C' to 'E' Companies of the new 1st Corps in 1880.

5th Formed at Penllergaer with Captain John Dillwyn Llewelyn in command (his commission dated 12 October 1859), and formed part of the 1st Admin Battalion for the period 1861 to 1864 when attached to the 3rd Corps. Disbanded 1873. Penllergaer is a small hamlet to the east of Llanelli. Both tin and coal were produced in the area.

6th Formed as one company at Swansea on 10 December 1859 with Pascoe St Leger Grenfell as captain, A Riversdale Grenfell, lieutenant and Henry Tregoning Nancarrow, ensign. Joined the 1st Admin Battalion and was disbanded in 1872.

7th Formed as one company at Taibach on 3 January 1860 with Arthur Pendarves Vivian as captain and John Richards Homfray, lieutenant. Joined the 1st Admin Battalion, increased to two companies on 29 June 1861, and became 'F' and 'G' Companies of the new 1st Corps in 1880. Taibach village, close to Margam, had extensive copper mines.

8th Formed as one company at Aberdare on 14 December 1859 with Henry Austin Bruce as captain, Thomas Powell, lieutenant and Richard Partridge, ensign. Joined the 2nd Admin Battalion, increased to two companies in January 1861, a third being added later. Headquarters moved to Mountain Ash in 1876 and became 'C' to 'E' Companies of the new 2nd Corps in 1880. At Aberdare in 1859 the parish church of St John the Baptist was nearing the completion of its Victorian restoration, the town employing many in a large brickworks. At Mountain Ash, just four miles down the old Taff Vale Railway from Aberdare, St Margaret's Church was built in 1862, the Town Hall in 1864, and many were employed in the area's many collieries.

9th Formed as one company at Baglan on 17 February 1860 with Griffith Llewellyn as captain, William Price Struve, lieutenant and George Young, ensign. Joined the 1st Admin Battalion, headquarters moved to Cwm Avon in 1861, and became 'H' Company of the new 1st Corps in 1880. Baglan, which lies at the mouth of the Neath, gave employment to many in its collieries and fireclay works. At Cwm Avon there were extensive copper, iron and tin works, the Copper Miners' Company being the main employer.

10th Formed at Cardiff as one company on 13 January 1860 with Richard Bassett as captain, Frederick Ridge Greenhill, lieutenant and Charles Henry Williams, ensign. A second company had been raised by the following month. Joined the 2nd Admin Battalion and became 'F' and 'G' Companies of the new 2nd Corps in 1880.

11th Formed as one company at Bridgend, just under eighteen miles west of Cardiff, on 14 February 1860 with John Cole Nicholl as captain, James Brogen, lieutenant and Henry Randall, ensign. Joined the 1st Admin Battalion and became 'I' Company of the new 1st Corps in 1880. Bridgend during the Volunteer period provided work in its steam joinery works, brewery, agricultural implement factory, tannery, iron and brass foundries.

12th Formed as one company at Merthyr Tydfil on 7 February 1860 with James Ward Russell as captain (he would command the corps for the next twenty-five years); Robert Jones, lieutenant, and Richard B Collins, ensign. Joined the 2nd Admin Battalion, increased to four companies in 1875, and became 'H', 'I', 'K' and 'L' Companies of the new 2nd Corps in 1880. Cassell's *Gazetteer* for 1895 notes that nearly all the inhabitants of Merthyr Tydfil were employed in coal mining and the manufacture of iron and steel. Indeed, a tower in flames made to look like a furnace featured on a shako plate worn by the 12th Corps.

13th One company raised at Llandaff, three miles north-west of Cardiff, by local tin-plate merchant Thomas William Booker, who became captain with commission dated 7 February 1860. His two other officers were Lieutenant Evan William David and Ensign John Partridge Booker. Joseph Lewis MD acted as surgeon. Bryn Owen in an article published by the Military Historical Society notes how the men drilled in Llandaff Fields. On the march the corps had the services of the Melingryffydd Works Band whom, notes Bryn Owen, 'the gallant captain had persuaded to enlist en masse.' The 13th Corps joined the 2nd Admin Battalion in September 1860. Headquarters moved to Taff's Well, some four miles up the valley, in 1876 and in 1880 the 13th Corps became 'M' and 'N' Companies of the new 2nd Corps. At Llandaff, the Working Men's Club and Institute was opened in 1867, the Cathedral School in 1880.

14th Formed as one company at Aberdare on 14 February 1860 with Thomas Bowes Powell as captain, Thomas Davies, lieutenant and Frederick Davies, ensign. Joined the 2nd Admin Battalion, later increased to two companies, and became 'O' and 'P' Companies of the new 2nd Corps in 1880.

15th Formed as one company at Neath on 14 February 1860 with John Henry Rowland as captain, William Griffith Jones, lieutenant and Phillip Henry Rowland, ensign. Joined the 1st Admin Battalion, later increased to two companies, and became 'K' and 'L' Companies of the new 1st Corps in 1880. The Church of St Thomas was restored in 1874; Gwyn Hall, where the council assembles, opened in 1888. The town employed many at its tin-plate works, collieries, iron and brass foundries.

16th (Bute) Formed as one company at Cardiff on 18 January 1860 with Charles Williams David as captain, Clement Waldron, lieutenant and Jeremiah Box Stockdale, ensign. Joined the 2nd Admin Battalion. Many members of this corps were employed at the Bute Docks and in 1869 'Bute' was added to the title. Increased to two companies in April 1865, three in July 1869 and four in March 1875. Became 'Q' to 'U' Companies of the new 2nd Corps in 1880.

17th Formed as one company at Cadoxton on 2 June 1860 with Evan Evans as captain, David Bevan, lieutenant and James Kerr, ensign. Joined the 1st Admin Battalion and was disbanded in 1873. Coal, iron and copper were mined at Cadoxton. The old Barry Railway opened its Biglis Junction Station in December 1888, renaming it Cadoxton in June 1890.

18th Formed as one company at Cowbridge, to the south-west of Cardiff, on 25 June 1860 with Robert Boteler, late of the Royal Engineers, as captain, Frederick C A Royds, lieutenant and Samuel J Hornsby, ensign. Joined the 1st Admin Battalion and became 'M' Company of the new 1st Corps in 1880. The old Taff Vale Railway opened its first station at Cowbridge in September 1865.

19th Formed as one company at Newbridge (Pontypridd) on 23 May 1861 with Robert Thomas as captain, William Williams, lieutenant and Joseph Henry Mayor, ensign. Joined the 2nd Admin Battalion and became 'V' Company of the new 2nd Corps in 1880. The church of St Catherine was opened in 1868, the Library in 1890, Town Hall in 1893. Both coal and iron production gave employment to the town, which changed its name from Newbridge to Pontypridd around 1866.

20th Formed at Hirwain, four miles north-west of Aberdare, on 11 September 1878 and joined the 2nd Admin Battalion. Became 'W' Company of the new 2nd Corps in 1880.

GLOUCESTERSHIRE

All Gloucestershire rifle corps, with the exception of the 1st, joined the 1st Admin Battalion, which in 1880 formed the new 2nd Corps. There also existed a 2nd Admin Battalion, which had its headquarters at Cheltenham and included the 7th, 10th, 13th and 14th Corps, but this disappeared from the *Army List* in January 1864. The corps was then placed with the 1st Admin Battalion. A 1st Sub-division existed for a short while, which upon reaching the strength of a full company was then numbered as 8th Corps.

1st (City of Bristol) Lieutenant Colonel Robert Bush, late of the 96th Foot, was commissioned as commanding officer of the 1st Corps on 13 September 1859. The battalion comprised ten companies by June 1860 and was permitted to include 'City of Bristol' as part of its official title. Under General Order 63 of May 1883 1st Gloucestershire was re-designated as 1st (City of Bristol) Volunteer Battalion Gloucestershire Regiment. The Bristol Grammar School Cadet Corps was affiliated in 1900. An eleventh company was authorized in 1902 and transfer to the Territorial Force in 1908 was as 4th Battalion Gloucestershire Regiment. Bristol Grammar School at the same time became a contingent of the OTC. Uniform: green/green.

2nd (1859–80) Formed as one company at Gloucester Dock with Captain William Vernon Guise, Lieutenant John Jones and Ensign Theodore Aylmer Preston, late of the 43rd Regiment of Foot. All three held commissions dated 21 October 1859. They were later joined by John Peydell Wilson, who became surgeon to the corps. Became 'A' Company of the new 2nd Corps in 1880.

2nd (1880–1908) The 1st Admin Battalion was formed with headquarters at Gloucester in 1860 and consolidated in 1880 as the new 2nd Corps with ten companies:

'A' Gloucester Dock (late 2nd Corps)
'B' Gloucester (late 3rd Corps)
'C' Stroud (late 5th Corps)
'D' Cirencester (late 9th Corps)
'E' Cheltenham (late 10th Corps)
'F' Dursley (late 11th Corps)
'G' Coleford (late late 12th Corps)
'H' Newnham (late 12th Corps)
'I' Stow-on-the-Wold (late 15th Corps)
'K' Chipping Campden (late 16th Corps)

Re-designation as 2nd Volunteer Battalion Gloucestershire Regiment was notified in General Order 63 of 1883. A cadet corps is shown as affiliated to the 1st Admin Battalion in 1867 and in 1883 this same unit is given as being formed by Cheltenham College. The college transferred its affiliation to the 1st Gloucestershire Engineer Volunteers in 1889, but returned to the 2nd Volunteer Battalion in 1904. Gloucester County School at Hempstead provided a company of cadets in 1889, as did Cirencester in 1896. Both, however, were disbanded, in 1891 and 1897 respectively. Transfer to the Territorial Force in 1908 was as 5th Battalion Gloucestershire Regiment. Cheltenham College at the same time became a contingent of the OTC. Uniform: green/scarlet.

3rd Formed as one company at Gloucester Dock with Captain Thomas De Winton, late of the Royal Artillery, Lieutenant Henry Dowling and Ensign Richard T Smith. All three held commissions dated 21 October 1859. James P Heane was appointed surgeon to the corps in the following May. Became 'B' Company of the new 2nd Corps in 1880.

4th Formed at Stroud with Captain Henry Daniel Cholmeley, Lieutenant William Antony Freston and Ensign John Tuppen Woodwright. All three officers held commissions dated 5 September 1859. Disappeared from the *Army List* in August 1861.

5th Formed at Stroud with Captain J Watts Haliwell, Lieutenant Sebastian Stewart Dickinson and Ensign Sidney Biddle. All three held commissions dated 6 September. Absorbed the 6th Corps, also at Stroud, in 1865 and became 'C' Company of the new 2nd Corps in 1880. All along the River Frome cloth mills and factories appeared, Cassell's *Gazetteer* for 1898 noting that the broadcloth produced by 'several thousand persons at Stroud is celebrated all over the world'. Another large business employing as many made items for the clothing trade.

6th Formed at Stroud, the first officers gazetted to the 6th Corps were Captain John Dutton Hunt, a local mill owner, and Ensign Arthur Twisden Playne. Both held commissions dated 7 September 1859. The Revd Edward Cornford was later appointed as chaplain to the corps and Robert Blagden, its surgeon. The establishment was completed in December when J Tuppen Wollwright joined the other officers. Interest in the corps, however, began to fall off about 1863. Captain Hunt transferred to the 1st Gloucestershire Light Horse Volunteers in May 1865 and with Ensign Playne the only officer remaining, in that same year what remained of the 6th Corps was absorbed into the 5th.

7th Formed at Cheltenham, the first officer to be gazetted was Captain Robert Dwarris Gibney, who was commissioned on 20 September 1859. He was joined in the following October by Lieutenant Henry Bromby and Ensign William Martin, then by William Dalton, who was appointed as surgeon to the corps in February 1860. Joined the 2nd Admin Battalion, then to 1st Admin by January 1864. Disbanded in September 1864. Sheltered to the north and east by the Cotswolds, Cheltenham is seven miles north-east of Gloucester.

8th Formed at Tewkesbury as a half company with Lieutenant James Primatt Sargeaunt and Ensign George Howard Banaster holding commissions dated 6 December. Simon S Bowen MD was appointed as surgeon to the corps. Known as the 1st Sub-division until March 1860, James Sargeaunt was promoted captain to a full company on 7 November. Disbanded in 1877. On the Worcestershire border ten miles north of Gloucester and bounded by the Severn, Tewkesbury Abbey's five-year restoration began in 1874. The old Birmingham and Gloucester Railway station at Tewkesbury was replaced by a new one in May 1864.

9th Formed at Cirencester with Captain Alex Bathurst, former 6th Dragoon Guards officer; Lieutenant John Davis Sherston, and Ensign William Tombs Dewe holding commissions dated 13 February 1860. Edward Cripps was appointed surgeon. Became 'D' Company of the new 2nd Corps in 1880. Cirencester is sixteen miles south-east of Gloucester. A second station at Cirencester was opened by the old Midland & South Western Junction Railway in December 1883.

10th Formed at Cheltenham with Captain Herbert W Wood, who had previously served as lieutenant colonel in the 4th Madras Native Infantry; Lieutenant Shapland Swiny, late captain in the Royal Dublin City Militia, and Ensign Stanhope T Speer. All three held commissions dated 1 March 1860. Augustus Eves was appointed as surgeon. Joined the 2nd Admin Battalion, then transferring to 1st Admin by January 1864, and became 'E' Company of the new 2nd Corps in 1880. Within a few years of architect John Middleton coming to Cheltenham in 1860, no less than five churches were built by him in the town. His work also included the Delancey Hospital in Charlton Lane. The Public Library was opened in Clarence Street in 1887, the art gallery being added in 1899, and the museum in 1907.

11th Formed at Dursley with John Vizard as captain, Edward Bloxsome, lieutenant and William Cornock. ensign. All three held commissions dated 9 March 1860. William J Hill was later appointed as surgeon. Became 'F' Company of the new 2nd Corps in 1880. At Dursley, fifteen miles south-west of Gloucester, there were rope works, breweries and a tannery.

12th Formed with headquarters given as the Forest of Dean, the 12th Gloucester RVC's original officers were Captain Sir Martin H C Boevey Bt, Lieutenant John H Dighton and Ensign Sir James Campbell Bt. All three held commissions dated 21 April 1860. Became 'G' and 'H' Companies of the new 2nd Corps in 1880. The Forest of Dean is a district between the Severn and Wye some twenty miles long and about ten miles wide. The mining of coal and production of tin employed many from the area.

13th Formed as one company at Cheltenham with Captain Edmund P Morphy, late of the Monaghan Militia, Ensign Edward J Gregory, and Robert Wollaston MD, who was appointed as surgeon. All three held commissions dated 23 March 1860. Lieutenant Thomas Swain, who was gazetted on 27 April 1860, made up the establishment. Joined the 2nd Admin Battalion, then to 1st Admin by January 1864. Disbanded in 1874.

14th Formed as one company at Cheltenham, the first officer to be commissioned (3 July 1860) being Captain Sir Alex Ramsay. Lieutenant Hugh Kennedy, ensign William Gardner and surgeon Thomas J Cottle made up the establishment on 8th August. Joined the 2nd Admin Battalion, then transferring to 1st Admin by January 1864, and disbanded in September 1864.

15th Formed as a sub-division at Stow-on-the-Wold with Lieutenant Cecil C V N Pole commissioned on 3 December 1860. Francis E B Witts joined him as ensign on 12 December. The 15th Corps remained as a sub-division until brought up to a full company in December 1868. Became 'I' Company of the new 2nd Corps in 1880. The railway reached Stow in the form of the Burton-on-the-Water line in March 1862.

16th Formed at Moreton-in-the-Marsh, the first officer to be commissioned (23 November 1860) being Captain Sir John M Steele Bt. He was joined by Lieutenant Thomas Commeline and Ensign William H Baker in the following December. The Revd Charles E Kennaway was appointed as chaplain to the corps and Leonard K Yelf MD its surgeon. Headquarters moved to Chipping Campden in 1862 and became 'K' Company of the new 2nd Corps in 1880. Moreton-in-the-March is just to the south-east of the location of the new headquarters, which is itself to the south-east of Evesham.

3rd Volunteer Battalion Gloucestershire Regiment Eight companies formed with headquarters at Bristol on 24 July 1900. Transfer to the Territorial Force in 1908 was as 6th Battalion Gloucestershire Regiment. Uniform: khaki/scarlet.

HADDINGTONSHIRE

All corps formed within the county joined the 1st Admin Battalion, which was consolidated to form the new 1st Corps in 1880.

1st (1860–80) Formed at Haddington, the company's first officers were Captain Alex Kinloch, Lieutenant George Gaukroger and Ensign Robert Richardson. All three held commissions dated 19 January 1860. Became 'A' Company of the new 1st Corps in 1880. The Knox Memorial

Institute was built at Haddington in 1878–80. Several small businesses in the town provided employment in the manufacture of woollen goods, agricultural implements and sacking.

1st (1880–1908) With Sir George Warrender Bt (late captain, 92nd Foot and Coldstream Guards) of Lochend and Bruntsfield in command, the 1st Admin Battalion was formed with headquarters at Haddington on 19 August 1860. The battalion was consolidated as the new 1st Corps in April 1880 with six companies:

'A' Haddington (late 1st Corps)
'B' Company Haddington (late 3rd Corps)
'C' Aberlady (late 4th Corps)
'D' East Linton (late 5th Corps)
'E' West Barns (late 6th Corps)
'F' North Berwick (late 7th Corps)

Shortly after consolidation 'E' Company was absorbed into 'D', a new 'E', together with a section at Prestonpans, being added at Tranent in 1881. In 1888, under General Order 144 of April, the 1st Corps was re-designated as 7th Volunteer Battalion Royal Scots. 'C' Company was absorbed into 'A' in 1906 and at the same time the Prestonpans section was increased to a full company and lettered 'C'. North Berwick High School Cadet Corps was formed and affiliated to the battalion in 1901 and the Haddington Cadet Corps in 1906. Transfer to the Territorial Force in 1908 was as four companies of 8th Battalion Royal Scots. Uniform: green/scarlet, changing to khaki with trews in 1904.

2nd Formed as one company at Gifford with Captain John Charles Hay, Lieutenant Peter Burn Swinton and Ensign Robert Hope Bogue. All held commissions dated 20 January 1860. The corps, which was disbanded in 1874, was mainly formed from agricultural workers on the Lord Tweeddale Estate.

3rd Formed as one company at Haddington with Captain David Roughead, Lieutenant David Shirriff and Ensign William James Dods. All three held commissions dated 21 January 1860. The 3rd Haddingtonshire, which became 'B' Company of the new 1st Corps in 1880, was mainly formed from mechanics and artisans.

4th Formed at Aberlady, about five miles north-west of Haddington, the company's first officers were Captain Thomas Maitland Rodney, Lieutenant Francis C Burnet and Ensign William Findlayson. All three held commissions dated 17 March 1860. The 4th Haddingtonshire, which became 'C' Company of the new 1st Corps in 1880, was formed mainly from employees on the Lord Wemyss Estate.

5th Formed at East Linton as one company with Captain Sir Thomas B Hepburn Bt, Lieutenant Alexander Scott and Ensign William Mason. All three held commissions dated 7 April 1860. Became 'D' Company of the new 1st Corps in 1880. East Linton's Volunteer Drill Hall was built in 1875, the property also being used for public meetings and entertainments. East Linton village is about five miles east of Haddington on the road to Dunbar.

6th Formed as one sub-division at Dunglass with Lieutenant Charles Scott and Ensign John Johnston both holding commissions dated 27 August 1861. Headquarters moved to West Barns near Dunbar on the road from Haddington in 1873, the 6th becoming 'E' Company of the new 1st Corps in 1880.

7th Formed as one company at North Berwick with Captain Allen Dalzell, late of the 27th Foot, and Lieutenant John R Whitecross commissioned on 21 July 1868. Walter B Blaikie made up the establishment in the following December. Became 'F' Company of the new 1st Corps in 1880. Cassell's *Gazetteer* for 1897 notes that North Berwick's chief trade was the export of potatoes.

HAMPSHIRE

With the exception of the 2nd, 3rd, 10th, 14th and 19th, the several rifle corps then in existence within the county of Hampshire were, in December 1860, divided up into three admin battalions. In January 1865 a 4th Admin was formed and the *Army List* for that month shows it to contain the above corps. During 1868 the 3rd Admin at Fareham (formed 1860 with 7th, 8th, 12th, 17th, 20th, 21st and 22nd Corps) was broken up and its corps dispersed among the 1st and 2nd Battalions. These, together with the 4th, were consolidated in 1880 to form the new 1st, 2nd and 3rd Corps, a 4th later being formed out of the 2nd.

1st (1859–80) Formed at Winchester on 18 October 1859 with Captain Thomas Faunce, late of the 13th Regiment of Foot, and Lieutenant Charles Simeon, who had served with the 75th Foot. Joined the 1st Admin Battalion and became 'A' and 'B' Companies of the new 1st Corps in 1880. Just over a year after the 1st Corps was formed, Christ Church in Church Road was built. The Guildhall came in 1871–73 and an old barracks, known as the King's House, was partially destroyed by fire in 1894. In Hyde Street the Hyde Brewery, which employed many in Winchester, can still be seen.

1st (1880–1908) The 1st Admin Battalion was formed with Headquarters at Winchester in December 1860 and was consolidated in 1880 as the new 1st Corps with ten companies:

'A' and 'B' Winchester (late 1st Corps)
'C' Botley (late 8th Corps)
'D' Romsey (late 11th Corps)
'E' Andover (late 13th Corps)
'F' Hartley Wintney (late 15th Corps)
'G' Alresford (late 16th Corps)
'H' Alton (late 21st Corps)
'I' Winchester (late 24th Corps)
'K' Basingstoke (late 25th Corps)

Changes made after consolidation were in 1884, when 'L' Company was added at St Mary's College, Winchester; in 1889, when 'M' Company was raised from the Aldershot section of 'H', and in 1892, when another company was formed at Stockbridge. The latter, according to C T Atkinson's *Regimental History of the Hampshire Regiment* (Vol. 1), became an ASC (Volunteers) company in 1903. The total establishment by 1900 stood at eighteen companies. There was also a cadet corps affiliated at Winchester College since 1870. The 1st Hampshire was re-designated as 1st Volunteer Battalion Hampshire Regiment under General Order 91 of 1885 and transfer to the Territorial Force in 1908 was as 4th Battalion Hampshire Regiment. The Winchester College company, together with the cadet corps, became a contingent of the OTC. Uniform: scarlet/black, changing to scarlet/white in 1882.

2nd (1859–80) Formed at Southampton with Thomas Willis Fleming commissioned as captain on 24 February 1860. Joined the 4th Admin Battalion and became 'A' to 'D' Companies of the new 2nd Corps in 1880. At Southampton the Cunard offices were opened in 1899 and still remain in the town, as does the South Western House, the once South Western Hotel of the London and South Western Railway, which was completed in 1872.

2nd (1880–1908) The 4th Admin Battalion was formed in January 1865, moving headquarters from Lyndhurst to Southampton in 1872. Consolidated in 1880 as the new 2nd Corps with nine companies:

'A' to 'D' Southampton (late 2nd Corps)
'E' Lymington (late 3rd Corps)
'F' Christchurch (late 10th Corps)
'G' Lyndhurst (late 14th Corps)
'H' and 'I' Bournemouth (late 19th Corps)

By 1883 the establishment of the 2nd Corps had reached twelve companies, but in 1885 this was reduced to eight when part of the corps was detached to form the new 4th Hampshire RVC. According to the regimental history of the Royal Hampshire Regiment, the companies removed were those from the Bournemouth, Christchurch, Lymington and Ringwood. This would suggest that one of the Bournemouth companies ('H' or 'I') had been lost and its place taken by another at Ringwood. Also in 1885 the corps took the title of 2nd Volunteer Battalion Hampshire Regiment. Another new company was raised in 1900 and transfer to the Territorial Force in 1908 was as 5th Battalion Hampshire Regiment. Uniform: scarlet/yellow, changing later to scarlet/white.

3rd (1859–80) Formed at Lymington on 30 December 1859 under the command of former 12th Dragoons officer Captain Richard H Smith Barry. Joined the 4th Admin Battalion and became 'E' Company of the new 2nd Corps in 1880. Lymington, at the mouth of the River Lymington, is just under twelve miles south-west of Southampton.

3rd (1880–1908) The 2nd Admin Battalion was formed with headquarters at Portsmouth in December 1860 and consolidated as the new 3rd Corps in 1880 with eleven companies:

'A' to 'E' Portsmouth (late 5th Corps)
'F' and 'G' Gosport (late 6th Corps)
'H' Havant (late 4th Corps)
'I' Petersfield (late 12th Corps)
'K' Fareham (late 7th Corps)
'L' Porchester (late 23rd Corps)

A new company was added in 1884, and in 1897 a cadet corps was formed and affiliated by Portsmouth Grammar School. In 1900 an additional six companies were raised, followed in 1905 by another cadet corps at Churcher's College, near Petersfield. The 3rd Corps had been re-designated as 3rd Volunteer Battalion Hampshire Regiment by General Order 91 of September 1885. In 1893 HRH the Duke of Connaught was made Hon Colonel and from that year the title of the battalion became 3rd (The Duke of Connaught's Own) Volunteer Battalion. Transfer to the Territorial Force in 1908 was as 6th Battalion Hampshire Regiment. Portsmouth Grammar School and Churcher's College at the same time became contingents of the OTC. Uniform: scarlet/yellow, changing later to scarlet/white.

4th (1859–80) Formed at Havant, just under seven miles north-east of Portsmouth, on 3

February 1860 and joined the 2nd Admin Battalion. The first officer to be commissioned into the corps was Captain Edward Davison. Became 'H' Company of the new 3rd Corps in 1880. Volunteers from the town would have seen the opening of the Town Hall in 1870, the restoration of the old St Faith's Church in 1875 and the completion of the Recreation Ground in 1889. Cassell, in the 1890s, noted that parchment was made at Havant.

4th (1885–1908) We have seen how in April 1885 the Bournemouth, Christchurch, Lymington and Ringwood companies of the new 2nd Corps were detached so as to form a new 4th Corps of six companies. Headquarters were place at Bournemouth and shortly after formation the title of the corps was changed to 4th Volunteer Battalion Hampshire Regiment. Bournemouth raised a new company in 1891, followed by another at Fordingbridge in 1895. Three more companies were added: Bournemouth again, and one of Mounted Infantry in 1900, which became known as the 'New Forest Scouts'. Bournemouth School Cadet Corps was formed and affiliated in 1903 and a company at Lymington in 1905. Transfer to the Territorial Force in 1908 was as 7th Battalion Hampshire Regiment. Bournemouth School at the same time became a contingent of the OTC. Uniform: scarlet/white.

An interesting badge (a stirrup) is associated with the 4th Corps and its successors. It is said that King Rufus used the device in the New Forest in a way that any dog too big to fit through it would have the three middle claws of its front paws removed so as to prevent it running fast enough to chase deer.

5th (The Portsmouth Rifle Volunteer Corps) Formed at Portsmouth with Captain Commandant George P Vallaney, late of the Indian Army, commissioned on 16 March 1860. Joined the 2nd Admin Battalion and became 'A' to 'E' Companies of the new 3rd Corps in 1880. The Portsmouth Grammar School, which formed a cadet corps in 1897, moved into a new building in 1878. No doubt many from the town were occupied in the construction of the numerous forts and gun positions that appeared as a result of the threatened invasion from France in 1860. And there was the building of the several Victorian barracks: Victoria and Clarence, between Alexander Road and Pembroke Road (*c*.1880); HMS *Victory* Barracks in Queen Street, Portsea (1899–1903).

6th Formed at Gosport on 9 March 1860 and joined the 2nd Admin Battalion. The first officer to be commissioned was Captain William Yates Peel. Became 'F' and 'G' Companies of the new 3rd Corps in 1880. The Barracks at Gosport were completed in 1859, a Soldiers' Home in 1884 and the Thorngate Memorial Hall, built in memory of local merchant William Thorngate, opened in 1885. 'Seamen's' biscuits were made in the town for the Royal Navy.

7th Formed at Fareham on 14 May 1860, the first officer to be commissioned being Lieutenant William Kelsall. Joined the 3rd Admin Battalion, transferred to the 2nd in 1868, and became 'K' Company of the new 3rd Corps in 1880. A seaport nine miles north-west of Portsmouth, Fareham produced bricks known as 'Fareham Reds'. The corps was also recruited from the neighbouring villages of Wymering and Porchester.

8th Formed as two companies at Botley with Captain Commandant Robert Richardson in command on 14 May 1860. Headquarters were being shown as Bitterne, on the Southampton road to the west, by July. Joined the 3rd Admin Battalion, transferring to 1st Admin Battalion in 1868, and became 'C' Company of the new 1st Corps in 1880. Bitterne is two miles north-east of Southampton, the Southampton & Notley Railway opening Bittern Road Station there in March 1866.

9th None recorded.

10th Formed at Christchurch with Captain James H H Earl of Malmesbury commissioned on 9 March 1860. Joined the 4th Admin Battalion and became 'F' Company of the new 2nd Corps in 1880. The Town Hall at Christchurch was being completed just as the townspeople were contemplating the formation of a volunteer corps. The chief industry, notes Cassell's in the 1890s, was the manufacture of watch and clock fuse chains, though many of the inhabitants were employed in salmon fishing and the hosiery trade. The Ringwood, Christchurch & Bournemouth Railway opened Christchurch Station in November 1862.

11th Formed at Romsey, seven miles south-west of Southampton, on 24 March 1860 with Captain Thomas W Henderson, Lieutenant Alexander Stead and Ensign George Allsop. Joined the 1st Admin Battalion and became 'D' Company of the new 1st Corps in 1880. The Corn Exchange (now Barclay's Bank) was opened in 1864, a bronze statue to Viscount Palmerston being erected in the market place in 1867. Cassell's notes that in the 1890s there were in the area breweries, corn mills, ironworks a paper mill and jam maker. The Berthon Boatbuilding Company employed many.

12th Formed at Petersfield on 28 April 1860 with Captain Edward H Chawner, Lieutenant Sir W W Knighton and Ensign George Haw Seward. Joined the 3rd Admin Battalion, transferred to 2nd Admin in 1868, and became 'I' Company of the new 3rd Corps in 1880. Six years after the formation of the 12th Corps the Corn Exchange was opened facing The Square and High Street. At the north end of College Street, Churcher's College formed a cadet corps in 1905.

13th Formed at Andover, its services accepted on 13 May 1860, the first appointed officers of the corps were: Captain W W Humphrey, lieutenant Allan B Heath and Ensign Phillip H Poore. Joined the 1st Admin Battalion and became 'E' Company of the new 1st Corps in 1880. At Andover in 1876 a new cottage hospital was built in fine red brick. The town gave much employment in its brewery and ironworks.

14th Formed at Lyndhurst on 16 June 1860 with Captain Alexander H L Popham, Lieutenant William C D Esdale and Ensign Walter Williams. Joined the 4th Admin Battalion and became 'G' Company of the new 2nd Corps in 1880. In the middle of the New Forest, Lyndhurst is eight miles from Southampton, its St Michael's Church being built over the period 1858–70.

15th Formed at Yateley, five miles from Farnborough, the services of the 15th Corps were accepted on 30 May 1860 with Lieutenant George Mason, late of the 4th Foot, and Ensign Frederick G Stapleton. Joined the 1st Admin Battalion, moved headquarters to Hartley Wintney in 1870 and became 'F' Company of the new 1st Corps in 1880. At Hartley Wintney the Church of St John Evangelist was being completed as the 15th Corps moved to the town, its Victoria Hall being built in 1898.

16th Formed at Alresford, just under seven miles north-east of Winchester, the services of the 16th Corps were accepted on 14 June 1860. Lieutenant Francis J P Mar and Ensign William Gatty were the first officers to be commissioned. Joined the 1st Admin Battalion and became 'G' Company of the new 1st Corps in 1880. Alresford Station, on the old Mid Hampshire line, was opened in October 1865.

17th Formed at Titchfield, six miles north-west of Gosport, on 29 August 1860 with Lieutenant George Wingate and Ensign Frederick Bradshaw. Joined the 3rd Admin Battalion, transferred to the 2nd in 1868, and was disbanded in 1874.

18th Formed at Basingstoke, the services of the 18th Corps were accepted on 31 July 1860 with Captain Thomas Harvey and Lieutenant Chaloner W Chute appointed as its first officers. Joined the 1st Admin Battalion, but was disbanded in 1864. Just over fourteen miles south-west of Reading, Basingstoke was the centre of an agricultural district. Breweries, foundries and several large clothing factories gave employment during the Volunteer period. One in New Street, then later, London Street, was the premises where a local draper, Thomas Burberry, first made garments from a waterproofed material which he called 'gabardine'.

19th Formed at Bournemouth on 18 August 1860 and joined the 4th Admin Battalion. Lieutenant Charles A King and Ensign Henry Ledgard were the first officers to be commissioned. Became 'H' and 'I' Companies of the new 2nd Corps in 1880. The Town Hall in St Stephen's Road was opened in the same year.

20th Formed at Wickham, twelve miles north-west of Portsmouth, on 27 July 1860 with Lieutenant Henry Carter and Ensign Charles B Smith the first officers appointed. Joined the 3rd Admin Battalion, transferred to the 2nd in 1868, and was disbanded in 1874. The Wickham Brewery can still be seen opposite Chesapeake Mill (built from timbers of a captured American ship by that name) at the bottom of Bridge Street.

21st Formed at Alton, eleven miles from Basingstoke, the services of the 21st Corps were accepted on 10 August 1860. The company's first officers were Lieutenant Cecil Rivers and Ensign James B Coulthard. Joined the 3rd Admin Battalion, transferring to 1st Admin Battalion in 1868, and became 'H' Company of the new 1st Corps in 1880. The Volunteers would have seen the restoration of the ancient St Lawrence's Church in 1867 and the opening of All Saints', Winchester Road, in 1874. In the town were two breweries, a paper factory and an iron foundry.

22nd Formed at Bishops Waltham, just over nine miles south-east of Winchester, on 13 September 1860 with Lieutenant Butterworth P Shearer and Ensign Walter Clark. Joined the 3rd Admin Battalion and disbanded in 1865.

23rd Formed at Cosham on 29 November 1860 and joined the 2nd Admin Battalion with Lieutenant Edward Goble and Ensign Henry Monk the first officers to be commissioned. Headquarters moved to Porchester in 1869 and became 'L' Company of the new 3rd Corps in 1880. Cosham is four miles north of Portsmouth, Porchester just over seven to the north-west.

24th Formed from the senior members and staff at Winchester College on 21 December 1874 with J C Moore as lieutenant and Charles D Collier, sub-lieutenant. Joined the 1st Admin Battalion and became 'I' Company of the new 1st Corps in 1880.

25th Formed at Basingstoke with Lieutenant Gerald R Fitzgerald and Surgeon Charles F Webb the first to be commissioned, on 9 June 1875. Joined the 1st Admin Battalion and became 'K' Company of the new 1st Corps in 1880.

HAVERFORDWEST

1st Raised in the Borough of Haverfordwest, Pembrokeshire, as one company in the last weeks of 1859; the first officer, Captain Xavier de Castanos R Peel, received his commission on 4 February 1860. Gazetted on 15 February were Lieutenant Richard Carrow and Ensign John Harvey jun, who were joined in the following March by Edward Picton Phillips, who became surgeon to the corps. Joined the 1st Pembrokeshire Admin Battalion in 1862. A second company was added in

August 1861, a third in 1863 and in 1880 1st Haverfordwest RVC provided 'B', 'C' and 'D' Companies of the new 1st Pembrokeshire RVC. Prior to 1885 Haverfordwest was an independent parliamentary borough with its own lord lieutenant. St Martin's Church was restored there in 1869, St Thomas's enlarged in 1881, and a Masonic Hall built in 1872. Employment was mainly agricultural, the area also having a paper mill and brewery.

HEREFORDSHIRE

All corps formed within the county joined the 1st Admin Battalion, which was consolidated as the new 1st Corps in 1880.

1st (1860–80) Formed as one company at Hereford on 10 April 1860. Robert Feildon, who had served previously as a lieutenant colonel in the 44th Regiment of Foot, took command. Became 'A' Company of the new 1st Corps in 1880. St Paul's, in Church Road, was opened in 1865, St James's in Green Street in 1869, Holy Trinity in 1883. The city then, as now, was strongly associated with the making of cider, Bulmers still employing many.

1st (1880–1908) The 1st Admin Battalion of Herefordshire Rifle Volunteers was formed with headquarters at Hereford on 20 February 1861. From 1864 the 1st, 2nd and 3rd Radnorshire RVC were shown in the *Army List* as part of the battalion, which was consolidated as the new 1st Corps in 1880 with ten-and-a-half companies:

'A' Hereford (late 1st Corps)
'B' Ross-on-Wye (late No. 1 Company, 2nd Corps)
'C' Ledbury (late 3rd Corps)
'D' Bromyard (late 4th Corps)
'E' Ross-on-Wye (late No. 2 Company, 2nd Corps)
'F' Leominster (late 6th Corps)
'G' Kington (late 7th Corps)
'H' Hereford (late 8th Corps)
'I' Presteigne (late 1st Radnorshire Corps)
'K' Rhayader (late 2nd Radnorshire Corps)
The half-company was located at Hereford

Became a volunteer battalion (without change of title) of the King's Shropshire Light Infantry in 1881 and in the same year the two Ross companies ('B' and 'E') were merged as 'B'. A new 'E' Company was formed at Weobley in 1889. Also in 1889 a Bearer Company was formed at Hereford to serve the Welsh Border Infantry Brigade. This company, as no authorization had been received to increase the establishment of the battalion, formed part of 'A' Company. In 1905 several further changes in organization took place: 'L' Company was added at Hereford from members of the Cyclist Section created there in 1888, and 'M' was formed at Ruardean. An amalgamation between 'I' and 'G' Companies took place and the Bearer Company was constituted as a separate unit designated Welsh Border Brigade Company RAMC (Vols.). In 1902 the Hereford Cathedral School applied to the War Office to form a cadet corps, which was affiliated to the 1st Herefordshire RVC on 28 March 1903. Transfer to the Territorial Force in 1908 was as the Herefordshire Battalion King's (Shropshire Light Infantry); this was changed after a few months, however, to the Herefordshire Regiment. Hereford Cathedral School at the same time became a contingent of the OTC. Uniform: scarlet/black.

2nd Formed as one company at Ross-on-Wye on 27 March 1860 with Captain Kingsmill M Power, who had previously served as a captain in the 16th Dragoons; Lieutenant Nathaniel K Cobins and Ensign Francis W Herbert. Became 'B' and 'E' Companies of the new 1st Corps in 1880. In the High Street, the Corn Exchange came two years after the Volunteers first marched through the town, St Mary's Church was restored in 1878. In and near the town were machine works, a brewery, boot factory and flour mills.

3rd Formed as one company at Ledbury on 27 March 1860, the Earl Somers taking command with Lieutenant Thomas Heywood, late of the 16th Dragoons, and former 79th Regiment of Foot officer Ensign James M Aynesley as his junior officers. Became 'C' Company of the new 1st Corps in 1880. In 1894 a clock tower was erected in the town in memory of Elizabeth Barrett Browning (1809–61) and a new cottage hospital opened in 1892. Limestone was quarried in the area and, of course, the production of cider gave employment to many.

4th Formed as one company at Bromyard on 15 May 1860 with Captain Charles E Hopton, a former officer of the 23rd (Royal Welsh Fusiliers) Regiment of Foot, Lieutenant Thomas S Uphill and Ensign James P Eckley as its first officers. Became 'D' Company of the new 1st Corps in 1880. Seventeen miles west of Worcester, the area around Bromyard was mainly agricultural. There was, however, a firm in the 1890s making spade and shovel handles. The railway, in the form of the Worcester, Bromyard & Leominster line, reached the town in October 1877.

5th Formed at South Archenfield with Captain Edward O Partridge in command on 15 May 1860. Was later disbanded and disappeared from the *Army List* in January 1873.

6th Formed as one company at Leominster with Captain the Rt Hon Robert D Rodney Lord Rodney in command on 4 May 1860. Became 'F' Company of the new 1st Corps in 1880. The town is hirteen miles north of Hereford. Work on the restoration of the priory church of St Peter and St Paul was carried on from 1866 to 1891. The Corn Exchange dates from the year before the Volunteers first enrolled, the library from 1893. Cider is produced, and there were brickfields.

7th Formed as one company at Kington on 18 May 1860 with Captain John Coke, Lieutenant John G R War and Ensign Anthony Temple. Became 'G' Company of the new 1st Corps in 1880. At Kington the main employment source was agricultural. Nails were also manufactured.

8th Formed as one company at Hereford on 27 September 1860 with Captain Richard Arkwright, Lieutenant Richard Clarkson and Ensign James Phillips. The corps was made up entirely from members of a lodge of Oddfellows. Became 'H' Company of the new 1st Corps in 1880.

HERTFORDSHIRE

The several rifle corps formed within the county were placed into one or other of two admin battalions, the 1st taking in the corps from the western half of Hertfordshire, the 2nd incorporating those in the east. In 1880 the seniority of the old 1st Corps (2nd Admin Battalion) was recognized, and the eventual reorganization resulted in the 1st Admin Battalion numbered as the new 2nd Corps, while the 2nd Admin became 1st.

1st (1859–80) Formed as one company at Hertford on 22 November 1859 and joined the 2nd Admin Battalion. The Rt Hon Earl Cowper took command, his junior officers being Lieutenant William Robert Baker and Ensign the Hon Henry Frederick Cowper. A second company was added on 26 October 1860, the two to form 'A' and 'B' Companies of the new 1st Corps in 1880.

J D Sainsbury in his book *Hertfordshire Soldiers* tells how the 1st Corps had came about as the result of a meeting held by members of the Hertford Rifle Club on 25 October 1859. In 1859 Hertford's Corn Exchange and Public Hall were completed. Local farms gave much employment; there were also iron foundries, breweries, malthouses, brickfields and limekilns. The town is well known, of course, for its paper making, John Tate establishing the first paper mill in Britain at Sele Mill in 1494.

1st (1880–1908) The 2nd Admin Battalion was formed with headquarters at Hertford in October 1860, the 22nd Essex RVC at Waltham Abbey being added to the Hertfordshire corps in 1862. The battalion was consolidated as the new 1st Corps in 1880 with eight companies:

'A' and 'B' Hertford (late 1st Corps)
'C' Bishop's Stortford (late 6th Corps)
'D' Ware (late 9th Corps)
'E' Royston (late 10th Corps)
'F' Welwyn (late No. 1 Company, 14th Corps)
'G' Hitchin (late No. 2 Company, 14th Corps)
'H' Waltham Abbey and Cheshunt (late 22nd Essex Corps)

Re-designated as 1st (Hertfordshire) Volunteer Battalion Bedfordshire Regiment under General Order 181 of 1887. A new company ('I') was added at Hoddesdon in 1900. Three cadet corps were affiliated to the battalion: Haileybury College in 1886, Bishop's Stortford Grammar School and Hertford Grammar School in 1906. Transfer to the Territorial Force in 1908 was as part of the Hertfordshire Regiment, although a portion of the battalion went to form a nucleus of the 1st and 2nd Hertfordshire Batteries Royal Field Artillery. All three cadet corps at the same time became contingents of the OTC. Uniform: grey/scarlet, changing to scarlet/white in 1887.

2nd (1860–80) Formed as one company at Watford on 5 January 1860 with Lieutenant the Hon Reginald A Capel and Ensign Charles F Humbert. Joined the 1st Admin Battalion and became 'A' Company of the new 2nd Corps in 1880. At Watford, noted Cassell's, there were corn mills, a steam laundry, several malt kilns, three extensive breweries (Benskin's was one) and an iron foundry. A new railway station was opened in Watford High Street in October 1862.

2nd (1880–1908) The 1st Admin Battalion was formed with headquarters at Little Gaddesden in October 1860 and was consolidated as the new 2nd Corps in 1880 with five companies:

'A' Watford (late 2nd Corps)
'B' St Albans (late 3rd Corps)
'C' Ashridge (late 4th Corps)
'D' Hemel Hempstead and Redbourn (late 5th Corps)
'E' Great Berkhamsted and Tring (late 7th Corps)

Headquarters remained at Little Gaddesden, but later moved to Hemel Hempstead. In 1883 a new company ('F') was added at Tring, then, under General Order 181 of December 1887, the 2nd Corps was re-designated as 2nd (Hertfordshire) Volunteer Battalion Bedfordshire Regiment. 'G' Company was added at Watford in 1892 and cadet corps formed and affiliated to the battalion at Berkhamsted School and St Albans School in 1891 and 1903 respectively. Another cadet corps, the United Services College, joined the battalion in May 1904 having moved its location from Westward Ho! to Harpenden. Yet another move, this time to Windsor in 1907, saw the company transferred to the 1st London RE (Vols). Transfer to the Territorial Force in 1908 was as part of the Hertfordshire Regiment, the cadet corps at the same time becoming contingents of the OTC. Uniform: grey/green, changing to grey/grey around 1887.

3rd Formed as one company at St Albans on 5 March 1860 with Lieutenant William T K Church and Ensign William H Evans. Joined the 1st Admin Battalion and became 'B' Company of the new 2nd Corps in 1880. At St Albans, the Midland Railway station was opened in 1866, the Public Library and Reading Room in Victoria Street in 1880. Perhaps Arthur Melbourne-Cooper photographed the Volunteers of the 1890s; or even earlier, his father, who had a studio in Osborne Street. Arthur, who is credited with having begun the film industry in Britain, produced an appeal on behalf of the Bryant & May company for donations to supply matches to the troops then serving in South Africa in the Boer War. The town gave employment in its breweries, boot factory and brush works.

4th Formed as one company at Ashridge on 1 March 1860 with Captain William P Cust and Lieutenant William Paxton. Joined the 1st Admin Battalion and became 'C' Company of the new 2nd Corps in 1880. Ashridge Park near Berkhamsted was the seat of the Cust family –Adelbert Wellington Browlow Cust, Earl Brownlow, later commanded the 4th Corps and after that the 2nd (Hertfordshire) Volunteer Battalion Bedfordshire Regiment.

5th Formed as one company at Hemel Hempstead on 10 March 1860 with Captain Robert Eden in command, John Day as lieutenant and Henry Balderson, ensign. Joined the 1st Admin Battalion and became 'D' Company of the new 2nd Corps in 1880. As the 5th Corps was being raised, work was still going on at the large site (began in 1851, completed 1868) that become the Town Hall, Corn Exchange and Literary Institute. A Working Men's Club was opened in 1874, the recreation ground in 1878. At Hemel Hempstead there were large paper mills, iron foundries and breweries.

6th Formed as one company at Bishop's Stortford on 20 March 1860 with Captain John A Houblon in command, Thomas H Holyn as lieutenant and Frederick W Nash, ensign. Joined the 2nd Admin Battalion and became 'C' Company of the new 1st Corps in 1880. At Bishop's Stortford, twelve miles north-east of Hertford, the ancient church of St Michael saw restoration both in 1869 and 1886. The town's chief sources of employment were brewing and the production of bricks and sacking. There was also a coach works, foundry and limekilns.

7th Formed as one company at Great Berkhamsted on 13 March 1860 and joined the 1st Admin Battalion. A former commander in the Royal Navy, Arthur Tower, took command, his junior officers being Lieutenant H Pearse and Ensign John H Salter. Absorbed the 8th Corps, five miles south-east at Tring, on 1 May 1866 and became 'E' Company of the new 2nd Corps in 1880. The early Volunteers would have seen the completion of the Town Hall in 1860. Cassell's noted that in the 1890s there was a brisk trade in coals, malt, timber and brushes. There were also manufacturers of straw plait and articles of carved and turned wood.

8th Formed as one company at Tring on 20 April 1860 with Lieutenant Richard Bright and Ensign Arthur H Jenney. Joined the 1st Admin Battalion and was absorbed into the 7th Corps on 1 May 1866. The main industries at Tring were canvas weaving, straw plaiting and brewing.

9th Formed as one company at Ware on 13 June 1860 with William Parker as captain, Charles Cass, lieutenant and James Cullyer, ensign. Joined the 2nd Admin Battalion and became 'D' Company of the new 1st Corps in 1880. At Ware, two miles east of Hertford, brewing and brick making gave employment.

10th Formed as one company at Royston and Baldock on 25 June 1860 with Joseph Simpson as captain, John Phillips, lieutenant and Henry Perkins, ensign. Joined the 2nd Admin Battalion and became 'E' Company of the new 1st Corps in 1880. At Baldock, where the company had a detachment, trade was carried on in malting, brewing and the manufacture of straw plait.

11th Formed as one company at Cheshunt on 25 August 1860 with Francis G Goodliffe as captain, Livingston War, lieutenant and John M Levick, ensign. Joined the 2nd Admin Battalion and disbanded 22 November 1870 with part of the corps being absorbed into the 22nd Essex RVC. At Cheshunt there were large nurseries, market gardens and brickfields.

12th Formed at Hitchin, close to the border with Bedfordshire, on 15 September 1860 with Frederick P D Radcliffe as captain, George E Hughes, lieutenant and Charles Times, ensign. There was also a sub-division at Stevenage. Joined the 2nd Admin Battalion and disbanded on 27 February 1867.

13th Formed at Watton-on-Stone on 8 September 1864 and joined the 2nd Admin Battalion. Disbanded on 28 July 1868, Lieutenant Russell H Barrington and Ensign Herbert B Hodges being the only officers commissioned.

14th Formed as one company at Welwyn on 13 September 1876 and joined the 2nd Admin Battalion. No. 2 Company formed at Hitchin in 1877 and became 'F' and 'G' Companies of the new 1st Corps in 1880.

HUNTINGDON

1st Only one numbered corps was raised within the county. Formed at Huntingdon on 18 April 1860, and from 1872 included in the 1st Admin Battalion of Cambridgeshire Rifle Volunteers. The first officers to be appointed to the corps, which became 'J' Company of the new 1st Cambridgeshire RVC in 1880, were Captain the Hon Octavius Duncombe, late of the 1st Life Guards, Lieutenant John M Heathcote jun and Ensign William V Theed. From Cromwell's birthplace, the corps moved to St Neots, nine miles south-west on the east bank of the Ouse in 1876, where the Working Men's Club opened in 1881 and a museum in 1887. A large paper mill, several breweries, flour mills and engineering works gave employment.

4th (Hunts) Volunteer Battalion, Bedfordshire Regiment Formed on 4 December 1900. Six companies were authorized, the recruiting for these being carried out in the main from around Huntingdon, St Ives, Fletton and St Neots. Transfer to the Territorial Force in 1908 saw the personnel from these areas form four companies of the 5th Battalion Bedfordshire Regiment. Uniform: khaki.

INVERNESS-SHIRE

All rifle corps formed within the county were included in the 1st Admin Battalion, which became the new 1st Corps in 1880.

1st (1859–80) Formed at Inverness on 18 November 1859 as a result of a meeting held on the previous 21 May; officers elected were Captain Colin Lyon Mackenzie, Lieutenant Donald Angus Nicol and Henry C McAndrew. Became 'A' Company of the new 1st Corps in 1880. The headquarters of the Highland Railway were at Inverness, the town also forming the eastern terminus of the Caledonian Canal. St Andrew's Cathedral was consecrated in 1869, the Town Hall built in 1882; and certainly the Volunteers would have taken part in the unveiling ceremony ten years later of the white stone monument to those officers and men of the Cameron Highlanders who fell in the Egyptian campaign. There was shipbuilding at Inverness, also brewing and distilling. Cassell's notes that in the 1890s the shopkeeping business of the town was extensive.

1st (Inverness Highland) (1880–1908)

The 1st Admin Battalion of Inverness-shire Rifle Volunteers was formed with headquarters at Inverness on 18 June 1860 and from 1864 included 'Inverness Highland' as part of its title. The battalion was consolidated in 1880 as the new 1st Corps with ten companies:

'A' Inverness (late 1st Corps)
'B' Inverness (late 3rd Corps)
'C' Inverness (late 4th Corps)
'D' Inverness (late 5th Corps)
'E' Fort William (late 2nd Corps)
'F' Kingussie (late 6th Corps)
'G' Beauly (late 7th Corps)
'H' Portree (late 8th Corps)
'I' Ardersier (late 9th Corps)
'K' Roy Bridge (late 10th Corps)

Became a volunteer battalion of the Seaforth Highlanders in 1881, transferring to the Cameron Highlanders in 1883 with the title 1st (Inverness Highland) Volunteer Battalion authorized under General Order 181 of December 1887. In September 1903 the headquarters of 'K' Company moved to Fort Augustus with a section at Drumnadrochit. Transfer to the Territorial Force in 1908 was as 4th Battalion Cameron Highlanders. Uniform: Elcho grey/green with kilts, changing to scarlet/buff with kilts in 1880, then to scarlet/blue with kilts in 1883.

2nd Formed at Fort William on 9 April 1860 and became 'E' Company of the new 1st Corps in 1880. The first officers to be commissioned were Captain Donald Cameron, Lieutenant Andrew Frazer and Ensign Ronald McGregor. Fort William itself was dismantled and sold by the government in 1860, the site passing into the hands of the West Highland Railway, which employed many from the town, in 1892. Two distilleries are noted as important employers during the 1890s: the Nevis and Ben Nevis producing a then famous whisky called 'Long John'.

3rd Formed at Inverness from among the several merchants in the town on 26 March 1860 with George Grant McKay as captain, Robert Grant, lieutenant and Ensign John McEwen, ensign. Became 'B' Company of the new 1st Corps in 1880.

4th Formed at Inverness on 3 May 1860 with Charles F Mackintosh as captain, William Fraser, lieutenant and Alexander Matheson, ensign. Became 'C' Company of the new 1st Corps in 1880.

5th Formed at Inverness on 16 July 1860 with John Mackenzie as captain, Fountain Walker, lieutenant and James Anderson, ensign. Became 'D' Company of the new 1st Corps in 1880.

6th Formed at Kingussie on 3rd June 1861 with A F Macpherson as captain, Robert Macpherson, lieutenant and Lachlan Macpherson, ensign. Became 'F' Company of the new 1st Corps in 1880. The Highland Railway came to Kingussie, twenty-eight miles from Inverness, two years after the formation of the 6th Corps.

7th Formed at Beauly on 1 July 1861 with the Hon Simon Fraser, Master of Lovat as captain, Alex Fraser, lieutenant (Beaufort Castle near Beauly then the seat of the Frasers of Lovat) and

Donald D Mackenzie, ensign. Became 'G' Company of the new 1st Corps in 1880. At Beauly, ten miles west of Inverness, in 1891, the railway viaduct crossing the river from which the town takes its name was destroyed by floods.

8th Formed as one company at Portree on 20 July 1867 with George H Rainy as captain, Alex Martin, lieutenant and Alex Macdonald, ensign. An additional half-company was added on 7 February 1868. Became 'H' Company of the new 1st Corps in 1880. The village and seaport of Portree on the Isle of Skye produced tweeds, plaids, yarns and carpets.

9th Formed at Campbeltown, Ardersier on 12 November 1867 with James Rose as captain, John Corbet, lieutenant and Percival R Munroe, ensign. Became 'I' Company of the new 1st Corps in 1880. Campbeltown lies on the Moray Firth just under two miles north-west of Fort George. The main employment there was fishing.

10th Formed at Roy Bridge on 11 February 1869 with Alex Mackintosh as captain, G Gillespie, lieutenant and Donald Macdonell, ensign. Became 'K' Company of the new 1st Corps in 1880. The West Highland Railway's Roy Bridge Station was opened in August 1894.

ISLE OF MAN

1st (1860–70) Formed at Castletown with Patrick T Cunningham commissioned as lieutenant on 29 September 1860. The Revd Edward Ferrier was appointed as chaplain at the same time. Headquarters moved to Ballasalla, just under three miles north-east of Castletown, in 1867. On 10 March 1870 the War Office issued an order directing the disbandment of the 1st Isle of Man RVC with effect from 14 July 1870.

1st (1880–1908) Formed as 2nd Corps at Douglas with Captain J S G Taubman in command on 29 September 1860. Renumbered as 1st in 1880 and designated 7th (Isle of Man) Volunteer Battalion King's (Liverpool Regiment) under Army Order 81 of March 1888. The battalion was not included in the Territorial Force and instead continued service as 7th VB King's from 1908 under the Volunteer system. Uniform: scarlet/blue. In *A Military History of the Isle of Man* B E Sargeaunt notes that on 28 June 1873 the corps paraded 'at the Drill Shed on the Lake (Douglas)' prior to leaving by rail to form a Guard of Honour to His Excellency the Lieutenant Governor of the Isle of Man on the occasion of the first railway line being opened on the island from Douglas to Peel. Also recorded is the opening of a new rifle range at Howe Farm, Douglas Head on 10 August 1895. Prior to this the corps had, between 1884 and 1894, used a range at Langness. A new drill hall in Peel Road, Douglas was opened in June 1896.

2nd See 1st Corps (1880–1908).

3rd Formed at Ramsey on 29 September 1860 with George Hall as captain, Edward Yates, lieutenant and John C Goldsmith, ensign. The corps was later disbanded and appeared for the last time in the *Army List* for June 1869. St Olave's Church at Ramsey was opened in the year after the formation of the 3rd Corps.

4th Formed at Crosby to the north-west of Douglas on 24 April 1866 with Captain Thomas K Clucas in command. Disappeared from the *Army List* in December 1870, the War Office having directed disbandment on the previous 10 March.

ISLE OF WIGHT

All rifle corps formed were included in the 1st Admin Battalion, which became the new 1st Corps in 1880. Two numbered sub-divisions appeared in the *Army List*, which were later numbered as 4th and 5th Corps.

1st (1860–80) Formed as one company at Ryde on 25 January 1860 with Sir John Lees as captain, Charles Cavendish Clifford, lieutenant and Francis Newman, ensign. Absorbed the 3rd Corps, also at Ryde, as No. 2 Company in 1864 and became 'A' and 'B' Companies of the new 1st Corps in 1880. The railway came to Ryde in 1864, a tramway opened at the same time was built to take passengers from the station, along the pier to the pier-head. All Saints' Church in Queen's Road was built in 1870.

1st (1880–1908) The 1st Admin Battalion of Isle of Wight Rifle Volunteers was formed with headquarters at Newport on 5 July 1860 and consolidated in 1880 as the new 1st Corps with eight companies:

'A' and 'B' Ryde (late 1st Corps)
'C' and 'D' Newport (late 2nd Corps)
'E' Nunwell (late 4th Corps)
'F' and 'G' Ventnor (late 5th Corps)
'H' Cowes (late 7th Corps)

Re-designated as 5th (Isle of Wight 'Princess Beatrice's') Volunteer Battalion Hampshire Regiment under General Order 91 of September 1885. Princess Beatrice being the wife of HRH Prince Henry of Battenberg, the battalion's first Hon Colonel. In 1900 a cyclist company was added at Newport and transfer to the Territorial Force in 1908 was as 8th Battalion Hampshire Regiment. Uniform: green/green.

2nd Formed as one company at Newport on 14 January 1860 with Sir John Simeon as captain, Arthur H Estcourt, lieutenant and John Tooke, ensign. Increased to two companies in 1874 and became 'C' and 'D' Companies of the new 1st Corps in 1880. Cassell's *Gazetteer* for 1897 notes that the Volunteer Drill Hall was also used for 'dramatic entertainments'. Newport Station was opened in June 1862.

3rd Formed as one company at Ryde on 25 January 1860 with John B W Fleming as captain, George Rendall, lieutenant and Ernest Edwards, ensign. Absorbed into the 1st Corps in 1864.

4th Formed at Nunwell on 16 February 1860 with Sir Henry Oglander as lieutenant and Augustus F Leeds as ensign. Known as the 1st Sub-division until July when increased to a full company, the two officers being promoted to captain and lieutenant, and Francis W Popham joining them as ensign. Became 'E' Company of the new 1st Corps in 1880. Nunwell Park was the seat of the Oglander family.

5th Formed at Ventnor on 25 February 1860 with Albert J Hambrough as lieutenant and Charles F Fisher as ensign. Known as the 2nd Sub-division until October when increased to a full company – the officers were promoted to captain and lieutenant, William M Judd joining them as ensign. Increased to two companies sometime in 1879 and became 'F' and 'G' Companies of the new 1st Corps in 1880. At Ventnor, on the south-east coast of the island, the Police Station was opened in the first year of the Volunteers, the Town Hall in 1878, the Albert Hall in Victoria Street in 1887. The Railway reached the town in September 1866.

6th Formed at Sandown on 31 March 1860 with Henry Farnell as captain and Sir George Lowther, late of the 69th Regiment of Foot, lieutenant. The 6th Corps was last seen in the *Army List* for March 1862.

7th Formed as one company at Cowes on 27 April 1860 with William S Graham, late of the 2nd Bengal European Light Cavalry, as captain, John R Mann, lieutenant and James B Bird, ensign. Became 'H' Company of the new 1st Corps in 1880. Much restoration went on during the Volunteer period at the town's several churches: Holy Trinity in 1862; St Mary's, 1867 and St James's in 1868 and 1870. As a seaport, many were employed in shipping and shipbuilding.

8th Formed at Freshwater on 6 July 1860 with Benjamin T Cotton as lieutenant and William C Plumley as ensign. The corps disappeared from the *Army List* in February 1869.

KENT

The county formed five Admin battalions, the 1st, 2nd 4th and 5th later to provide the new 3rd, 1st, 2nd and 5th Corps respectively. The 3rd Admin Battalion, which was formed with headquarters at Maidstone in August 1860 and included the 1st, 9th, 12th, 15th, 19th, 20th, 22nd, 31st, 38th and 39th Corps, was broken up in 1874. There were two numbered sub-divisions: for 1st, see 13th Corps, 2nd, see 14th Corps.

1st (1859–77) Formed as two companies at Maidstone on 25 August 1859 with Captain Commandant Edward Scott in command. Joined the 3rd Admin Battalion, transferred to 2nd Admin in 1874, and became 'A' and 'B' Companies of the new 1st Corps in 1877. Many in Maidstone were employed in the production of paper – leading mill owners, John Hollingworth and R J Balston were members of the 1st Kent Corps.

1st (1877–1908) The 2nd Admin Battalion of Kent Rifle Volunteers was formed with headquarters at Tunbridge Wells on 3 July 1860, moving to Penshurst in 1863, Sevenoaks in 1867 and Tonbridge in 1871. The battalion was consolidated in 1877 as the new 1st Corps with eight companies:

> 'A' and 'B' Maidstone (late 1st Corps)
> 'C' Tonbridge (late 14th Corps)
> 'D' Tunbridge Wells (late 17th Corps)
> 'E' Penshurst (late 23rd Corps)
> 'F' Leeds Castle (late 31st Corps)
> 'G' Sevenoaks (late 33rd Corps)
> 'H' Westerham (late 35th Corps)

Under General Order 14 of February 1883 the 1st Corps was re-designated as 1st Volunteer Battalion Queen's Own (Royal West Kent Regiment). The establishment was increased to eleven companies in 1900. Several cadet corps were formed and affiliated to the battalion: Skinner's School at Tunbridge Wells in 1901, a company at Westerham in 1904 and Maidstone Grammar School in 1906. Transfer to the Territorial Force in 1908 was as parts of both the 4th and 5th Battalions Queen's Own. Skinner's and Maidstone Schools at the same time joined the OTC. Uniform: green/green, changing to scarlet/blue in 1893.

2nd (1859–60) See 2nd Cinque Ports Corps.

2nd (East Kent) (1880–1908) The 4th Admin Battalion of Kent Rifle Volunteers was formed with headquarters at Canterbury in August 1860 and included the 5th, 6th, 16th, 24th, 29th and 36th Corps. In April 1874 the 2nd, 7th and 8th Cinque Ports RVC joined the Kent corps of 4th Admin and together they were amalgamated as the new 5th Kent (East Kent) RVC. The 5th Kent remained as part of the 4th Admin Battalion, which now also included the 4th, 5th and 10th Cinque Ports Corps. By the end of 1874, however, the Cinque Ports companies had been absorbed into the 5th Kent. This bringing its establishment up to ten companies: 'A' Ramsgate, 'B' and 'C' Canterbury, 'D' Hythe, 'E' Sittingbourne, 'F' Folkestone, 'G' Margate, 'H' Ashford, 'I' Wingham, 'K' Dover and 'L' New Romney.

Charles Igglesden notes in his book *History of the East Kent Volunteers* how 'A' (Ramsgate) Company were disadvantaged in not having a drill hall or headquarters. They met for some years in Ellington Park, or St George's Hall, but at the time of writing his book (1899) he notes that drills were being carried out at the Sergeant Instructor's house in Cavendish Street, and at Chatham House. Permission had been given in 1877 to raise a detachment at Minster, but with just nine men enrolling the project was closed down within the year.

Both 'B' and 'C' Companies at Canterbury drilled under the Corn Exchange until 1887 when they got the use of the Agricultural Hall. The armoury was at first in an old disused public house in Burgate Street called The Volunteer; later, though, the weapons were kept an Northgate Street, in yet another old pub – The Old City Arms. The Hythe Company used premises in Bank Street as headquarters until taking over an old chapel in Great Conduit Street in 1882. The Folkestone contingent was disbanded in 1878 and the 2nd Corps would be without an 'F' Company for the remainder of its existence.

In September 1880 the 5th Corps was renumbered as 2nd and in 1883, under General Order 63 of May, was designated as 1st Volunteer Battalion Buffs (East Kent Regiment). The year 1888 saw 'H' Company at Ashford moving into a new drill hall in Tufton Street, then in 1893, 'I' Company was transferred to Lydd. The headquarters of 'D' Company moved from Hythe to Folkestone in 1896, and those of the battalion from Canterbury to Dover in 1901. Additional personnel were raised at Westgate-on-Sea, Herne Bay, Birchington, Broadstairs, Canterbury and Dover during the war in South Africa, which brought the establishment of the battalion up to sixteen companies, two being cyclist formations. A reduction, however, to twelve was made in 1905, these in 1907 being listed as Ramsgate, Canterbury (2), Birchington, Folkestone, Sittingbourne, Herne Bay, Margate, Ashford, Wingham, Dover and Lydd. Transfer to the Territorial Force in 1908 was as 4th Battalion Buffs. Uniform: green/scarlet.

Associated with the battalion were several cadet corps, the first of which was formed at Dane Hill School, Margate in 1889. This company was disbanded, however, in 1897. The Chatham House College Company was formed at Ramsgate in 1891 and in 1908 became part of the OTC. Also affiliated, and to join the OTC in 1908, were the South Eastern College Cadets at Ramsgate (formed in 1898 and re-designated St Lawrence College in 1907); Dover College Cadet Corps (formed 1901); St Edmund's School, Canterbury and Sir Roger Manwood's School in Sandwich (both formed 1903). Other cadet units associated with the 1st Volunteer Battalion were at Margate College (formed 1892 and disbanded 1901) and New College Schools Herne Bay (see 4th Volunteer Battalion Queen's Own Royal West Kent Regiment below).

3rd (1859–80) Formed as one company at Lee on 7 November 1859 with Henry Burrard Farneil as captain, Henry D Drury, lieutenant and William H L Barnet, ensign. Joined the 1st Admin Battalion and increased to two companies in February 1864. Became 'A' and 'B' Companies of the new 3rd Corps in 1880. Just six miles south-east of St Paul's Cathedral, Lee is situated on the south side of Greenwich Park. Cassell's for 1895 noted that the suburb consisted of for the most part of villas belonging to City merchants and men of business.

3rd (West Kent) (1880–1908) The 1st Admin Battalion was formed with headquarters at Blackheath on 12 June 1860 and consolidated in 1880 as the 3rd Kent (West Kent) RVC with eleven companies:

> 'A' and 'B' Lee (late 3rd Corps)
> 'C' and 'D' Dartford (late 12th Corps)
> 'E' Greenwich (late 13th Corps)
> 'F' Bromley (late 18th Corps)
> 'G' and 'H' Blackheath (late 25th Corps)
> 'I' Deptford (late 27th Corps)
> 'K' Charlton (late 28th Corps)
> 'L' Deptford (late 34th Corps)

General Order 14 of February 1883 directed re-designation to 2nd Volunteer Battalion Queen's Own (Royal West Kent Regiment). By 1900 the strength of the battalion stood at thirteen companies and in that year the Proprietary School in Blackheath and Quernmore School at Bromley were affiliated. Transfer to the Territorial Force in 1908 was as part of the 20th Battalion London Regiment. Quernmore School at the same time became part of the OTC. Uniform: green/black. Mr J W Reddyhoff, writing in the *Bulletin* of the Military Historical Society in November 1987, noted that the West Kent Volunteer Freemason Lodge No. 2041 was formed from within the battalion on 14 March 1884.

4th (1859–80) Formed as one company at Woolwich on 21 December 1859 with George E Thorold as captain, William Henry Carter, lieutenant and John Mathew Butler, ensign. Formed part of the 1st Admin Battalion until 1870 when attached to the 26th Corps. Became part of the new 4th Corps in 1880.

4th (Royal Arsenal) (1880–1908) The 26th Kent RVC with headquarters at the Royal Arsenal in Woolwich first appears in the *Army List* for April 1860 and is shown as a two-battalion corps. The first officers' commissions were dated 25 February; that of the commanding officer, Colonel Alex T Tulloh of the Royal Artillery, 29 February. It was at first intended to number the 2nd Battalion as 30th Corps, but this arrangement never appeared in any *Army List*. By August 1860 the corps comprised sixteen companies and had obtained permission to include 'Royal Arsenal' as part of its official title. In July 1864 the corps was divided. The 1st Battalion became 21st Corps, which was to fill the gap in the county's list left by the disbandment of the Lewisham RVC in 1861, while the 2nd Battalion remained with the number 26th. Both units retained 'Royal Arsenal' as part of their title, and from January 1865 the 26th Corps is shown as having its headquarters at the Royal Gun Factory Office, Woolwich.

The 21st and 26th were once again united when in 1870 they were merged under the title of 26th Kent (Royal Arsenal) RVC. The 4th Corps, also at Woolwich, was absorbed in 1880, the whole at the same time being renumbered as 4th Kent (Royal Arsenal) RVC with an establishment of ten companies. The new 4th Corps was designated as 3rd Volunteer Battalion Queen's Own (Royal West Kent Regiment) in 1883 and transfer to the Territorial Force in 1908 was as part of the 20th Battalion London Regiment. Uniform: green/scarlet, changing to scarlet/blue in 1893.

5th (1859–74) Formed as one company at Canterbury on 1 December 1859 with Edward Plummer as captain, Henry George Austin, lieutenant and H T Sankey, ensign. Soon to join them were C Holttum as surgeon, and the Dean of Canterbury, Dr Henry Alford, who became chaplain to the corps. Canterbury was to raise two companies as it was the wish of some in the city to separate the Volunteers by class. The 5th Corps was to be made up of professional and tradesmen, the 6th from the working classes. A glance at the muster roll of the 5th Corps will show that both Captain Plumber and Ensign Sankey were solicitors, while Lieutenant Austin was the surveyor to the Dean and Chapter of Canterbury. Among the other ranks we find included victuallers, a brewer, chemists, tailors, a hotel proprietor, jeweller, boot maker, butcher, gardener, printer, schoolmaster, cabinetmaker, tobacconist, watchmaker, builders and a baker. Joined the 4th Admin Battalion and became part of the new 5th (East Kent) Corps in 1874. The Canterbury Library and Museum was opened in 1899, St Edmund's School at St Thomas's Hill, Canterbury forming a cadet corps in 1903.

5th (1874–80) See 2nd Corps (1880–1908).

5th (The Weald of Kent) (1880–1908) The 5th Admin Battalion was formed with headquarters at Cranbrook in May 1861 and as well as several Kent corps also included the 3rd Cinque Ports and 17th Sussex. The latter was transferred to 1st Cinque Ports Admin Battalion by November 1861. The additional title 'The Weald of Kent' was added in 1877. The battalion was consolidated in 1880 as the new 5th Corps with seven companies:

'A' Cranbrook (late 37th Corps)
'B' Hawkhurst (late 38th Corps)
'C' Staplehurst (late 40th Corps)
'D' Lamberhurst (late 41st Corps)
'E' Brenchley (late 42nd Corps)
'F' Rolvenden (late 43rd Corps)
'G' Tenterden (late 3rd Cinque Ports Corps)

Under General Order 63 of May 1883 the 5th Corps was re-designated as 2nd (The Weald of Kent) Volunteer Battalion the Buffs (East Kent Regiment). The Cranbrook Grammar School Cadet Corps was formed in February 1900 and until the following December, when it transferred to the 2nd Volunteer Battalion, was attached to the 1st Cadet Battalion of the Buffs. Transfer to the Territorial Force in 1908 was as 5th Battalion Buffs. Cranbrook Grammar School at the same time became part of the OTC. Uniform: green/green.

6th Formed as one company at Canterbury with Captain George Austin, Lieutenant Allen Fielding, who was the city's Town Clark, and Ensign James Delmar jun. All three held commissions dated 6 December 1859. As previously mentioned in the notes referring to the 5th Corps of 1859–74, it was the intention in Canterbury to divide the several classes in the city by placing the Volunteers into two separate companies. We have seen how the 5th Corps was to include professional and tradesmen, whereas the 6th was to be made up of the 'working classes'. But inspection of the muster roll of the corps shows more or less similar descriptions of occupation – shoe maker, engineer, upholsterer, artist, stonemasons, jeweller, tailors, etc. Obviously these were the men working for those that saw themselves suitable for the 5th. And the nicknames given locally to each corps seem also to have been based on class distinction – the 'Fighting 5th', and the 'Drunken 6th', possibly saying it all. Joined the 4th Admin Battalion and became part of the new 5th (East Kent) Corps in 1874.

7th Formed as one company at Kidbrooke on 21 December 1859 with Simon F Jackson (late captain and adjutant, East Kent Militia) as captain, Frederick Morris, lieutenant and Richard J Walmesley, ensign. Joined the 1st Admin Battalion and was disbanded in January 1869. Kidbrooke is just a half-mile south of Greenwich.

8th Formed as one company at Sydenham on 22 December 1859 with John Scott Russell as captain, J Hiscutt Crossman, lieutenant and William Morphew, ensign. Joined the 1st Admin Battalion, disappearing from the *Army List* in April 1871. The Crystal Palace was opened five years before the 8th Corps was formed, the great fire there being seen by many from the area.

9th Formed as one company at Chatham on 31 December 1859 with George Robinson Brock as captain, Charles Isaacs, lieutenant and James Grover, ensign. Joined the 3rd Admin Battalion, but removed from the *Army List* in December 1872. Several thousand were employed at Chatham's large docks, the Soldiers' Institute being opened within months of the Volunteers' first parade.

10th None recorded.

11th Formed as one company at Farnborough on 24 January 1860 with Montague Lubbock as captain, Edward Osmond Berens, lieutenant and William Darwin, ensign. Joined the 2nd Admin Battalion and was disbanded in November 1862. Farnborough is a village in north-west Kent four miles from Bromley.

12th Formed as one company at Dartford on 23 February 1860 with Thomas Hern Fleet as captain, Charles Edward Rashleigh, lieutenant and Thomas Butler, ensign. Joined the 3rd Admin Battalion, transferred to the 1st Admin in 1874, and became 'C' and 'D' Companies of the new 3rd Corps in 1880. The chief industries of Dartford were the manufacture of steam engines – the engineer Richard Trevethick is buried at Holy Trinity – and the making of gunpowder. The first English paper mill was established at the town.

13th Formed at Greenwich on 11 November 1859 and known as the 1st Sub-division until February 1860. John Robert Harris became captain, William Bristow, lieutenant and Thomas William Marchant, ensign. Joined the 1st Admin Battalion and formed 'E' Company of the new 3rd Corps in 1880. At Greenwich the former infirmary at the Royal Naval College was, in 1870, taken over by the Seaman's Hospital Society, while at Greenwich Marches, the Metropolitan Gas Company had extensive works. Other employers made chemicals and soap.

14th Formed at Tonbridge on 2 December 1859 and known as the 2nd Sub-division until March 1860. The Rt Hon Charles Stewart, Viscount Hardinge was appointed as lieutenant and Henry Dorlen Streatfeild as ensign. Viscount Hardinge had previously served as a major with the Kent Militia Artillery. Joined the 2nd Admin Battalion and became 'C' Company of the new 1st Corps in 1877. Seated in a valley on the banks of the Medway, Tonbridge produced gunpowder and brewed beer.

15th Formed as one company at Sutton Valence, six miles south-east of Maidstone, on 15 February 1860 with Sir Edmund Filner Bt, late of the Grenadier Guards, as captain, David Arthur Monro, lieutenant and Thomas Balston, ensign. Muster rolls of the corps show that almost half of the 15th Corps were farmers and agricultural workers from, as well as Sutton Valence, East Sutton, Headcorn and Linton. Joined the 3rd Admin Battalion and disbanded in 1873.

16th Headquarters of the 16th Corps were at Sittingbourne. The company, however, was also recruited from among the neighbouring villages of Milton, Greenstreet, Rainham and Tynham. The first appointed officers were Captain John Dixon Dyke, who had previously served with the Madras Army, local banker Lieutenant William Frederick Baring and Ensign William Whitehead Gascoyne, who owned land in the area. All held commissions dated 15 February 1860. In the early years of the 16th Kent RVC drills took place at the Corn Exchange in Sittingbourne, at the Dover

Castle Inn at Greenstreet and at a barn belonging to a Mr Paxman at Rainham. Eventually headquarters were set up at the Town Hall and a range opened in 1862 at the Motley Hill Butts, Rainham. Joined the 4th Admin Battalion and became part of the new 5th (East Kent) Corps in 1874. The Town Hall at Sittingbourne was less than a year old when the 16th Corps first began to drill, the Library opening in 1888, the Masonic Hall the year after. In the 1890s, more than 6,000 from the area were employed in the manufacture of bricks and cement.

17th Formed as one company at Tunbridge Wells on 29 March 1860 with Cuthbert J Fisher as captain, John S Wigg, lieutenant and Charles R F Lutwidge, ensign. Joined the 2nd Admin Battalion and became 'D' Company of the new 1st Corps in 1877. For visitors to 'drink the waters', the Pump Room at the south end of the Pantiles was built in 1877. The Skinners' Company Middle School was opened in the town ten years later.

18th Formed as three companies at Bromley on 26 March 1860 with Captain Commandant Clement Satterthwaite in command. Joined the 1st Admin Battalion, was later reduced in size and became 'F' Company of the new 3rd Corps in 1880.

19th Formed as two companies at Rochester on 23 February 1860 with Captain Henry Bowen, who had previously served with the Scots Fusiliers Guards, and Captain Henry Savage in command. Joined the 3rd Admin Battalion and was removed from the *Army List* in January 1874.

20th Formed as a sub-division at Northfleet on 11 April 1860 with Bedford W Kenyon as lieutenant and George Turner, ensign. Joined the 3rd Admin Battalion and disbanded in 1868. At Northfleet, two miles west of Gravesend, the Portland Cement Works employed many from the area.

21st (1860–61) Formed as a sub-division at Lewisham on 25 February 1860 with Thomas W Parker as Lientenant and Stephen J Newman as ensign. Joined the 1st Admin Battalion and disbanded in October 1861.

21st (1864–70) See 4th (1880–1908).

22nd Formed as one company at Sheerness on 30 March 1860 with Richard Conryn as captain, Robert Chapman, lieutenant and Caleb Selby, ensign. Joined the 3rd Admin Battalion and disbanded in November 1870. In the 1890s, the dockyard at Sheerness is on record as giving employment to between 1,500 and 2,000 artisans and mechanics.

23rd Formed as one company at Penshurst on 28 February 1860 with Captain William Wells, who had served previously with the 1st Life Guards, Lieutenant Edward O Streathfield, late of the 47th Regiment of Foot, and Ensign Richard D Turner. Joined the 2nd Admin Battalion and became 'E' Company of the new 1st Corps in 1877. At the confluence of the Eden and Medway, Penshurst is about six miles north-west of Tunbridge Wells.

24th Formed as one company at Ash, just under three miles west of Sandwich, with Frederick M Godden as captain, William Gillow, lieutenant and Thomas T Collett, ensign. All three held commissions dated 29 February 1860. The 24th joined the 4th Admin Battalion and although it flourished for a time, began to reduced in strength as interest diminished. There were just fifty-eight on the muster roll in 1865, this dwindling steadily over the coming years until disbandment was ordered in 1869.

25th Formed as one company at Blackheath on 18 February 1860, with former 55th Madras

Native Infantry colonel John Blaxland as captain, William P J Rogers, lieutenant and William G Barnes, ensign. Joined the 1st Admin Battalion, increased to two companies in 1877, and became 'G' and 'H' Companies of the new 3rd Corps in 1880.

26th See 4th Corps (1880–1908).

27th Formed as one company at Deptford on 28 February 1860 with Edward Wilkinson as captain, William Benjamin Pembroke, lieutenant and Charles Stubbins, ensign. The corps was recruited mainly from the dockyards. Joined the 1st Admin Battalion and became 'I' Company of the new 3rd Corps in 1880. At the London suburb of Deptford many were employed in engineering, the building of river barges and the production of galvanized iron. The London Electric Supply Company also employed many from the area.

28th Formed as one company at Charlton on 18 February 1860 with ex-Royal Marines colonel George W Congden in command. His junior officers were Lieutenant George H Graham and Ensign William Carlyl. Joined the 1st Admin Battalion and became 'K' Company of the new 3rd Corps in 1880.

29th Formed as one company at Ashford with Stephen P Groves, late of the 1st Dragoon Guards, as captain, William Pomfret Burra, lieutenant; John Furley, a local solicitor, as ensign, and Henry Maund, who was appointed as surgeon. All four held commissions dated 15 March 1860. The first enrolment of the 29th Kent RVC took place on 15 March and shown on the muster roll are a number of varied trades and professions. The list includes a gas manager, paperhanger, several tailors, carpenters, bank clerks and mechanics, an inn keeper, footman, Sergeant J H Bailey, who was an auctioneer, and Private James Harris, who ran a sweet shop. The first drills of the corps were held in the yard of the railway station. The armoury was originally in the basement of the Assembly Rooms, later moving to premises in Elwick Road opposite the entrance to the cattle market. The Volunteers even had their own social club in rooms behind the offices of the *Kentish Express* in Park Street. In 1860 attempts were made to set up a sub-division at the nearby village of Wye, but this was short-lived. Wye in fact provided a number of recruits to the main company – students enrolling when the South Eastern Agricultural College was opened there. A glance at a Kent local paper around October 1861 would reveal the sad event on 12 October which saw the accidental death of Sergeant Instructor Whorley from a rifle bullet to the head. The event took place at the Warren range. Joined the 4th Admin Battalion and became 'H' Company of the new 5th (East Kent) Corps in 1874. At Ashford a factory making agricultural implements provided many with jobs. The South Eastern Railway Company's locomotive and carriage works were employing some 1,300 in the 1890s.

30th This number was intended for No. 2 Company of the 26th Corps, but was never used.

31st Formed as one company at Leeds Castle on 23 March 1860 with Charles Wykeham Martin as captain, Baldwin Francis Duppa, lieutenant and George Blackett, ensign. Joined the 3rd Admin Battalion, transferring to 2nd Admin Battalion in 1874, and became 'F' Company of the new 1st Corps in 1877.

32nd Formed as one company at Eltham on 22 March 1860 with Frederick George Saunders as captain, Robert Courage, lieutenant and Thomas Jackson, ensign. Joined the 1st Admin Battalion and disbanded in 1876. The old South Eastern Railway opened Eltham Station in 1866.

33rd Formed as one company at Sevenoaks on 23 March 1860 with Multon Lambarde as captain, Nelson Bycroft, lieutenant and the Earl of Brecknock, ensign. Joined the 2nd Admin Battalion and became 'G' Company of the new 1st Corps in 1877. At the west end of the north aisle of St Nicholas's Church can be seen monuments to Captain Lambarde and his family.

34th Formed as one company at Deptford on 23 March 1860 with former member of the Canadian Volunteers, H E Montgomerie as captain, James Batten, lieutenant and Edward Callow, ensign. Joined the 1st Admin Battalion and became 'L' Company of the new 3rd Corps in 1880.

35th Formed as a sub-division at Westerham on 7 March 1860 with John Board as lieutenant and Charles R Thomson, ensign. Joined the 2nd Admin Battalion and was made up to a full company on 5 March 1861. Became 'H' Company of the new 1st Corps in 1877. Westerham Station was opened by the South Eastern & Chatham Railway in July 1881 and, as part of the Jubilee celebrations of 1887, the drinking fountain in the market place.

36th Formed as one company with headquarters at Wingham, six miles east of Canterbury, the first officers appointed were: Captain N H D'Aeth, Lieutenant J Bridges Plumtre, who was from Goodstone, and Ensign Charles John Plumtre, who came from Fredville. All three held commissions dated 18 May 1860. Joining them later were the Revd William Hales as chaplain, and Dr Frederick H Sankey, who was appointed as surgeon. A glance at the first muster roll taken by the 36th Corps shows that recruits joined from the neighbouring villages of Littleborne, Nonnington, Goodnestone and Inkham, as well as Wingham. Also shown are the numerous trades and professions followed by the Volunteers – an innkeeper, several bakers, builders and shoemakers; Private George Reakes, who was a veterinary surgeon at Littleborne; painters, a saddler, Private George Holloway, who laid bricks at Nonnington, a groom, gamekeeper, and two related engine drivers, Thomas and George Pegden, who lived at Wingham. Joined the 4th Admin Battalion and became 'I' Company of the new 5th (East Kent) Corps in 1874.

37th Formed at Cranbrook on 6 June 1860 and soon comprised six companies with Major John Bell in command. In the *London Gazette* dated 5 April 1861 it was noted that the 37th was to divide and its companies formed into separate and independent corps, these to be grouped together as an administrative battalion. The battalion, which was numbered as 5th, was formed in the following month and the corps created from the 37th were: 37th, 38th, 40th, 41st, 42nd, 43rd and 44th. The 37th, which remained at Cranbrook, became 'A' Company of the new 5th Corps in 1880. Cranbrook, on the Crane in mid-Kent, is six miles south of Staplehurst. The Cranbrook & Paddock Wood Railway opened its station there in September 1893.

38th (1860) Formed at Sheerness on 30 May 1860 and joined the 3rd Admin Battalion. Disbanded in October of the same year.

38th (1861–80) Formed with headquarters at Hawkhurst as part of the 37th Corps. Detached in April 1861 as 38th Corps and at the same time placed into the 5th Admin Battalion. Disbanded in 1872, but re-formed again in May 1877. Became 'B' Company of the new 5th Corps in 1880. At Hawkhurst in 1886, Babies' Castle, one of Dr Barnardo's institutions, was opened, and the old Cranbrook & Paddock Wood Railway's station in September 1893.

39th Formed as one company at West Malling on 26 June 1860 with Maximilian H Dalison as captain, Frederick Devon, lieutenant and Henry D Wildes as ensign. Joined the 2nd Admin Battalion, transferring to 3rd Admin Battalion in May 1861. Was later disbanded and disappeared from the *Army List* in August 1874. Malling Station, on the old Sevenoaks, Maidstone & Tonbridge Railway, opened in the same year.

40th Formed at Staplehurst as part of the 37th Corps. Detached in April 1861 as 40th Corps and at the same time placed into the 5th Admin Battalion. The officers were Captain Thomas S Usborne, Lieutenant Henry Hoar jun and Ensign Thomas H Cole. Became 'C' Company of the new 5th Corps in 1880. Nine miles south of Maidstone, Staplehurst's All Saints' Church underwent its second Victorian restoration in 1876.

41st Formed at Goudhurst, four miles north-west of Cranbrook, as part of the 37th Corps. Detached in April 1861 as 41st Corps and at the same time placed into the 5th Admin Battalion. The officers were Captain Samuel T Newington, Lieutenant H F S Marriott and Ensign George Hinds. Headquarters moved to Lamberhurst, just to the south-east, in 1874 and became 'D' Company of the new 5th Corps in 1880. Opened in 1892, Goudhurst (first called Hope Mill) Station on the Cranbrook & Paddock Wood line served both Goudhurst and Lamberhurst.

42nd Formed at Brenchley, seven miles north-east of Tunbridge Wells, as part of the 37th Corps. Detached in April 1861 as 42nd Corps, with Captain John M Hooker in command, and at the same time placed into the 5th Admin Battalion. Absorbed the 44th Corps at Lamberhurst in May 1863 and became 'E' Company of the new 5th Corps in 1880.

43rd Formed at Rolvenden as part of the 37th Corps. Detached in April 1861 as 43rd Corps, with Lieutenant Thomas Ayerst in command, and at the same time placed into the 5th Admin Battalion. Became 'F' Company of the new 5th Corps in 1880. Rolvenden is fifteen miles south-west of Ashford, its railway station (opened by the Rother Valley line in 1900) was called Tenterden until 1903.

44th Formed at Lamberhurst as part of the 37th Corps. Detached in April 1861 as 44th Corps, with Lieutenant Arthur C Ramsden in command, and at the same time placed into the 5th Admin Battalion. Absorbed into the 42nd Corps in May 1863.

45th Formed as one company at Rochester on 4 July 1861 with Jesse Thomas as captain, Charles Ross Foord, lieutenant and John William Death, ensign. Joined the 3rd Admin Battalion, transferring to 2nd Admin in 1874. Disbanded in 1876.

4th Volunteer Battalion Queen's Own (Royal West Kent Regiment) Formed with headquarters at Chatham on 27 April 1900 with nine companies. Borden School Cadet Corps was attached in 1903, but removed from *Army List* in November 1906. The officers, however, now appear under New College Schools (affiliated to 1st VB Buffs) at Herne Bay. Uniform: scarlet/blue.

1st Cadet Battalion the Buffs (East Kent Regiment) Formed on 24 October 1894 with four companies at St George's Hall, Ramsgate. Headquarters moved to Margate in 1903. Disbanded in June 1907. Uniform: green/scarlet.

KINCARDINESHIRE

All rifle corps formed within the county joined the 1st Admin Battalion, which provided the new 1st Corps in 1880. A 1st Sub-division with officers holding commissions dated 31 January 1860 appeared in the *Army List*. This, however, had disappeared by August 1861.

1st (1860–70) Formed as one company at Fetteresso on 10 January 1860 with T Fraser Duff as captain, J Black, lieutenant and John Milne, ensign. Headquarters moved to Stonehaven in 1867 and disbanded in October 1870. The small coastal village of Fetteresso is just to the west of Stonehaven.

1st (Deeside Highland) (1880–1908) The 1st Admin Battalion of Kincardineshire Rifle Volunteers was formed with headquarters at Stonehaven on 14 May 1861; William McInroy, late of the 91st and 69th Regiments of Foot, taking command. Headquarters transferred to Banchory on 23 February 1876 and in the same year the 8th, 14th, 21st and 23rd Aberdeenshire RVC were also included. By the end of 1876 'Deeside Highland' formed part of the battalion title. When the battalion was consolidated in 1880 the title then assumed was 1st Kincardineshire and Aberdeenshire (Deeside Highland) RVC. There were ten companies:

'A' Banchory (late 2nd Kincardine)
'B' Laurencekirk (late 5th Kincardine)
'C' Portlethen (late 6th Kincardine)
'D' Durris (late 7th Kincardine)
'E' Maryculter (late 8th Kincardine)
'F' Echt (late 8th Aberdeen)
'G' Tarland (late 14th Aberdeen)
'H' Aboyne (late No. 1 Company, 21st Aberdeen)
'I' Ballater (late No. 2 Company, 21st Aberdeen)
'K' Torphins (late 23rd Aberdeen)

In 1883 a series of company mergers and changes in location began when on 28 November 'K' Company was amalgamated with 'A' and a new 'K' formed at Stonehaven. 'G' and 'H' were merged in May 1885, battalion headquarters moved to Aberdeen in May 1886 and in 1887 and 1891 respectively 'E' Company moved to Peterculter and 'F' to Skene. The corps was re-designated 5th (Deeside Highland) Volunteer Battalion Gordon Highlanders on 17 January 1884 and headquarters moved back to Banchory in July 1894. Some seventy-eight members from the battalion saw active service in South Africa, one man being wounded at Komati Poort on 30 September 1900, and two at Rooikopjes on 24 July. Private P Stuart was killed on 8 September at Lydenburg. Transfer to the Territorial Force in 1908 was as 7th Battalion Gordon Highlanders. Uniform: green/green with kilts.

2nd Formed as one company at Banchory on 28 January 1860 with Patrick Davidson as captain, William Black Fergusson, lieutenant and John Gordon, ensign. Became 'A' Company of the new 1st Corps in 1880. Banchory is on the River Dee seventeen miles south-west of Aberdeen.

3rd Formed as a sub-division at Laurencekirk in February 1860 with Alfred H W Farrell in command. Increased to a full company on 23 May 1860 and absorbed into the 5th Corps in 1873. At Laurencekirk in 1866, St Laurence Hall was opened as a public meeting place. Cassell's notes that the town was famous for making snuffboxes.

4th Formed as a sub-division at Fettercairn on 13 March 1860 with William McInvoy as lieutenant and David Durie, ensign. Absorbed into the 5th Corps in 1871. In the year after the formation of the 4th Corps, Queen Victoria visited the village.

5th Formed as one company at Auchinblae on 9 June 1860 with James C Burnett as captain, Alexander Taylor, lieutenant and George Smart, ensign. Absorbed the 4th Corps to the south-west at Fettercairn in 1871 and 3rd Corps at Laurencekirk on the Stonehaven road in 1873. Headquarters moved to Laurencekirk in 1878 and became 'B' Company of the new 1st Corps in 1880.

6th Formed as one company at Netherley on 7 May 1860 with Horatio Ross as captain, Robert

Walker, lieutenant and George J Walker, ensign. Headquarters moved to Portlethen, on the coast to the north-east, in May 1869 and became 'C' Company of the new 1st Corps in 1880. Netherley is six miles north-west of Stonehaven. The inhabitants of Portlethen were mainly engaged in fishing.

7th Formed as one company at Durris on 13 February 1861 with James Thompson Mackenzie as captain, David Morrice, lieutenant and Robert Salmon, ensign. Became 'D' Company of the new 1st Corps in 1880. Durris is on the Dee to the east of Banchory.

8th Formed at Maryculter and Peterculter on 21 October 1869 and became 'E' Company of the new 1st Corps in 1880. At Peterculter, in the 1890s, the Culter Mills Paper Company employed some 350 from the area. Maryculter is just across the Dee to the west.

KINROSS-SHIRE

1st Formed as a sub-division at Kinross on the west side of Loch Leven on 31 October 1860 with William P Adam as lieutenant and Henry Maitland, ensign. Raised to the strength of a full company on 1 May 1861, the 1st Corps was in June of the same year included in the 1st Admin Battalion of Fifeshire Rifle Volunteers. In 1873, however, the company transferred to Clackmannanshire and that county's 1st Admin. Consolidated in 1880, that battalion became the 1st Clackmannan and Kinross RVC, the 1st Kinross forming 'G' Company. The railway reached Kinross in June 1860.

KIRKCUDBRIGHTSHIRE

All rifle corps formed within the county were included in the Galloway Admin Battalion.

1st Formed as one company at Kirkcudbright on 2 March 1860 with William K Laurie as captain and George Hamilton, ensign. Became 'A' Company of the Galloway RVC in 1880. An old sixteenth-century building in the town was converted into a Fire Station, Volunteer Drill Hall and Armoury.

2nd Formed as one company at Castle Douglas on 2 March 1860 with J Mackie as captain, John Bell, lieutenant and William John Renny, ensign. Became 'B' Company of the Galloway RVC in 1880. Cassell's in the 1890s noted that Castle Douglas was the chief business centre in the whole of the Galloway area. There were manufacturers of iron, leather, farm implements and mineral water. The town was served by two railway stations: Castle Douglas, opened by the old Castle Douglas & Dumfries Railway in November 1859, and the Kirkcudbright Company's Castle Douglas St Andrew Street in March 1864.

3rd Formed as one company at New Galloway, fourteen miles north-west of Castle Douglas, on 28 March 1860 with Wellwood Maxwell as captain, James Carruthers, lieutenant and Peter Daizel, ensign. Became 'E' Company of the Galloway RVC in 1880. The Portpatrick Railway Company opened New Galloway Station in March 1861.

4th Formed as a sub-division at Gatehouse on 19 May 1860 with Frederick Bainsforth Hannay as lieutenant and David James Ewart, ensign. Disbanded in 1866. On the River Fleet, Gatehouse is nine miles north-west of Kirkcudbright.

5th Formed as one company at Maxwelltown on 1 June 1860 with James B A McKinnel as captain, Francis S Allen, lieutenant and James G Starke, ensign. Increased to one-and-a-half companies in 1865, then to two in 1880. Became 'F' and 'G' Companies of the Galloway RVC in 1880. Maxwelltown, on the right bank of the Nith opposite Dumfries, had sawmills, a dye works, and a factory making hosiery.

6th Formed as one company at Dalbeattie on 24 July 1868 with W Platt as captain, James Grieve, lieutenant and Robert Burnie, ensign. Became 'H' Company of the Galloway RVC in 1880. There were several large granite quarries in the Dalbeattie area.

LANARKSHIRE

The last rifle corps to be raised and numbered in Lanarkshire was that formed at Leadhills in 1875. This company received the title 107th and as such held the highest number of any Volunteer corps in the land. The county was to provide the usual administrative battalions for its smaller corps. Of the seven created only one, the 3rd, was still in existence in 1880, the others all having been subject to consolidation before the reorganizations of that year. As a result the Lanarkshire rifle corps before 1880 stood at nine corps of at least battalion strength. The consolidation of the 3rd Admin in 1880 made this ten.

1st (Glasgow 1st Western) (1859–60) General Grierson in *Records of the Scottish Volunteer Force* notes that the first meeting of this corps for drill was held in the playground of the Glasgow Academy in Elmbank Street, Glasgow on 27 July 1859. Its services as one company were offered on the following 5 August and accepted on 24 September. Sir Archibald Islay Campbell Bt of Garscube became captain, Charles Hutchison Smith, lieutenant and Ruthven Campbell Todd, ensign. Became No. 1 Company of the new 1st Corps on 28 February 1860. An entirely self-supporting corps, all expenses were paid by its members.

1st (1860–1908) Sir Archibald Islay Campbell Bt of the original 1st Corps was gazetted as lieutenant colonel in command of the new 1st Lanarkshire RVC with effect of 6 March 1860, this having been formed by the amalgamation of the following Glasgow corps: 1st, 2nd, 9th, 11th, 15th, 17th, 18th, 33rd, 39th, 50th, 53rd, 63rd, 72nd, 76th, 77th and 79th, a total of sixteen companies that in June 1860 were formed into two battalions of eight each:

1st Battalion
No. 1 Company (late 1st Corps)
No. 2 Company (late 9th Corps)
No. 3 Company (late 11th Corps)
No. 4 Company (late 15th Corps)
No. 5 Company (late 17th Corps)
No. 6 Company (late 33rd Corps)
No. 7 Company (late 39th Corps)
No. 8 Company (late 79th Corps)

2nd Battalion
No. 9 Company (late 2nd Corps)
No. 10 Company (late 18h Corps)
No, 11 Company (late 50th Corps)
No. 12 Company (late 53rd Corps)

No. 13 Company (late 63rd Corps)
No. 14 Company (late 72nd Corps)
No. 15 Company (late 76th Corps)
No. 16 Company (late 77th Corps)

In 1863 No. 11 Company was disbanded and in the same year No. 14 was absorbed into No. 15. In 1864 No. 7 was absorbed by No. 3 and the remaining companies were lettered: 'A' to 'G', for the 1st Battalion, 'K' to 'Q' for the 2nd. The latter only numbered six companies, the letter 'O' not being used. There was a reduction in strength in 1870, 'K', the old University Company, being absorbed into 'Q', which had originated as the old 77th Corps and in part made up from university members. A new 'K' and an 'O' Company were added in 1878, but the former was relettered as 'I', and another 'K' formed in 1881. 'H' Company was formed and added in 1881, the 1st Corps then becoming (without change of title) a volunteer battalion of the Cameronians (Scottish Rifles). Transfer to the Territorial Force in 1908 was as 5th Battalion Cameronians, 'K' Company (the university company) at the same time became a contingent of the Senior Division OTC. The corps carried out its first drills on the Burnbank ground in Great Western Road, building there in 1866–67 a drill hall at the cost of £1250. Later, new headquarters were built at 261 West Princes Street, the cost this time being £16,000. Associated with the 1st Corps since its formation in 1902 was the High School Glasgow Cadet Corps, which, in 1908, became a contingent of the Junior Division OTC. Uniform: grey/blue.

2nd (University of Glasgow) (1859–60) The services of the 2nd Corps were accepted on 24 September 1859, the company being raised by professors, graduates and students at Glasgow University. Became No. 9 Company of the new 1st Corps on 28 February 1860.

2nd (1880–1908) The 1st Admin Battalion (shown in the *Army List* as 3rd until March 1861) was formed with headquarters at Hamilton on 8 May 1860 and consolidated in November 1873 as 16th Corps. There were ten companies:

'A' Hamilton (late 16th Corps)
'B' Hamilton (late 52nd Corps)
'C' Uddingston (late 42nd Corps)
'D' Strathaven (late 106th Corps)
'E' Bothwell (late 56th Corps)
'F' and 'G' Wishaw (late 57th Corps)
'H' Motherwell (late 102nd Corps)
'I' Blantyre (late 44th and 103rd Corps)
'K' Motherwell (newly formed)

Renumbered as 2nd in 1880 and designated 2nd Volunteer Battalion Cameronians (Scottish Rifles) by General Order 181 of December 1887. In 1892 'D' Company was absorbed into 'K' (with headquarters at Strathaven) and at the same time a new 'D' formed at Larkhall. 'L' (Cyclist) Company was added at Hamilton in 1899. In 1904 the headquarters of 'K' Company were transferred to Motherwell and transfer to the Territorial Force in 1908 was as 6th Battalion Cameronians. Uniform: scarlet/blue.

3rd (Glasgow 1st Southern) (1859–60) One company formed in Glasgow south of the Clyde, its services accepted on 9 September 1859, with David Dreghorn as captain, William Cochran, lieutenant and William Mactear, ensign. Became part of the new 3rd Corps in August 1860.

3rd (1860–1908) Formed on 8 August 1860 as a battalion of seven companies from the following Glasgow corps: 3rd, 10th, 14th, 22nd, 54th, 82nd and 87th. By December 1860 a new company had been added at the Etna Foundry. Headquarters on record are: No. 58 Hope Street, Glasgow, changing to Victoria Road. In 1877 the establishment was raised to twelve companies, then again to thirteen when a cyclist company was formed in 1902. The corps became a volunteer battalion of the Cameronians (Scottish Rifles) (without change in title) in 1881 and transferred to the Territorial Force in 1908 was as 7th Cameronians. Uniform: scarlet/blue.

4th (Glasgow 1st Northern) (1859) Formed in Glasgow, its services accepted on 10 October 1859, and became 'A' Company of the new 4th Corps in December 1859.

4th (Glasgow 1st Northern) (1859–1908) Formed on 12 December 1859 by the amalgamation of the 4th, 6th, 7th, 8th, 12th and 13th Corp,s which became lettered companies ('A' to 'F'). Lieutenant Colonel John Tennant was in command with commission dated 23 December 1859. The establishment was increased in July 1861 when the 60th, 61st and 93rd Corps were absorbed as 'G', 'H' and 'I' Companies. These were Highland kilted companies and when the 105th (Glasgow Highlanders) Corps was formed in 1868 some 187 men were transferred. Having lost their Highland character, what remained of the three companies adopted tunics and trews. The corps was re-designated as 4th Volunteer Battalion Cameronians (Scottish Rifles) by General Order 181 of December 1887. Headquarters were at 149 Cathedral Street, Glasgow and a rifle range was used at Flemington. Transfer to the Territorial Force in 1908 was as 8th Battalion Cameronians. The Kelvinside Academy Cadet Corps, which had been formed and attached in September 1893, at the same time became a contingent of the OTC. Uniform: scarlet/green.

5th (1st Eastern) (1859–60) Formed in Glasgow, its services accepted on 24 September 1859, with John Anderson as captain, John Wilson, lieutenant and J Alex Wilson, ensign. Joined the 7th Admin Battalion and became part of the new 5th Corps in November 1860.

5th (1860–73) The 7th Admin Battalion was formed with headquarters in Glasgow in September 1860 and to it were added the 5th, 21st, 34th, 35th, 58th, 59th, 64th, 65th, 66th and 90th Corps. Consolidated as the new 5th Corps in November 1860, its establishment being set at twelve companies. There was, however, a reduction to ten in 1864 and from then on the 5th Corps suffered a steady decline in its numbers. Subsequently, in 1873, what remained was absorbed into the 31st Corps.

5th (1880–1908) In the *Army List* for February 1860 the following Glasgow rifle corps are shown as having amalgamated under the title of 19th Lanarkshire (Glasgow 2nd Northern): 19th, 23rd, 24th, 28th, 36th and 41st. By September 1860 the several corps (51st, 67th, 74th, 80th, 81st and 83rd) that until then constituted the 5th Admin Battalion were absorbed, as were the 85th, 89th and 91st by the end of the year. The new 19th Corps, under the command of Lieutenant Colonel Commandant John Middleton, now comprised fifteen companies which were divided into two battalions. In 1864, however, the establishment was reduced to a single battalion of twelve companies. The 19th was renumbered as 5th in June 1880 then designated as 1st Volunteer Battalion Highland Light Infantry by General Order 181 of 1887. The first headquarters of the corps were at 179 West George Street, Glasgow, its drill hall being in Parliamentary Road. In July 1874, however, new headquarters premises were taken over at 13 Renfrew Street, then again, in July 1879, at Ark Lane, Dennistoun. The next move was on 25 December 1879 when, as a result of a great storm, in which the Ark Lane premises were blown down, the corps moved to Crown Halls, 98 Sauchiehall Street. These premises were rented until 1885 when a new headquarters and drill hall were purchased at 24 Hill Street, Garnethill. Transfer to the Territorial Force in 1908 was as 5th Battalion Highland Light Infantry. At the same time the Glasgow Academy Cadet Corps, which had been formed and affiliated to the battalion in 1902, joined the OTC. Uniform: scarlet/buff, changing to scarlet/yellow with trews in 1883, changing to scarlet/buff with trews in 1903.

6th (1859) Formed in Glasgow, its services accepted on 10 October 1859, and became 'B' Company of the new 4th Corps in December 1859.

6th (1880–1908) The corps included in the 6th Admin Battalion of Lanarkshire Rifle Volunteers (25th, 26th, 27th, 40th, 68th, 69th, 70th and 71st) were all formed from Clyde shipbuilding and engineering yards. The battalion was first seen in the *Army List* for July 1860 and in that for April 1861 was shown as having consolidated as the new 25th Corps with headquarters at Kelvinhaugh Road, Glasgow. There were eight companies:

'A' (late 26th Corps)
'B' (late 68th Corps)
'C' (late 71st Corps)
'D' (late 40th Corps)
'E' (late 70th Corps)
'F' (late 27th Corps)
'G' (late 69th Corps)
'H' (late 25th Corps)

The 25th Corps was renumbered as 6th in June 1880, two new companies being added in 1882, and designated as 2nd Volunteer Battalion Highland Light Infantry by General Order 181 of December 1887. Some fifty-seven Volunteers served in South Africa with the Regulars of the Highland Light Infantry, Sergeant W Black being accidentally drowned in the Orange River, and Private R A McGilvray dying of disease. Headquarters now at Yorkhill Street, Overnewtown, Glasgow, the battalion transferred to the Territorial Force in 1908 as 6th Battalion Highland Light Infantry. The Govan High School Cadet Corps, which had been formed and affiliated to the battalion in 1901, was eventually accepted by the OTC in 1911. Uniform: scarlet/black, changing to scarlet/blue in 1904, changing to khaki with kilts in 1906.

7th (1859) Formed in Glasgow, its service accepted on 10 October 1859, and became 'C' Company of the new 4th Corps in December 1859.

7th (1880–97) The 4th Admin Battalion was formed with headquarters at Airdrie on 14 May 1862 and to it were added the 29th, 32nd, 43rd, 48th, 95th, 97th, 98th, 99th, 100th, 101st and 104th Corps. The first commanding officer of the battalion was former 2nd Dragoons officer Major W W Hozier. On 19 September 1873 the battalion was consolidated as the new 29th Corps, which comprised twelve companies:

'A' Coatbridge (late 29th Corps)
'B' Airdrie (late 32nd Corps and No. 1 Company of 48th)
'C' Shotts (late 43rd Corps)
'D' Airdrie (late No. 2 Company of 48th Corps)
'E' Baillieston (late 95th Corps)
'F' Coatbridge (late 97th Corps)
'G' Greengairs (late 98th Corps)

'H' Clarkston (late 99th Corps)
'I' Calderbank (late 100th Corps)
'K' Newarthill (late 101st Corps)
'L' Bellshill (late 104th Corps)
'M' Harthill and Benhar (late 100th Corps)

In 1875 'E' and 'F' Companies were amalgamated 'E' at Coatbridge and a new 'F' formed at Chryston. Two years later the corps was reduced to eight companies and reorganized as follows:

'A' Coatbridge
'B' Airdrie
'C' Shotts (formed by 'C' and 'M' Companies)
'D' Airdrie (formed by 'D' and 'L' Companies)
'E' Coatbridge
'F' Cheyston
'G' Caldecruix (formed by 'G' and 'H' Companies)
'H' Newarthill (formed by 'I' and 'K' Companies.

The 29th Corps was renumbered 7th in 1880 and designated 5th Volunteer Battalion Cameronians (Scottish Rifles) in 1887. On 1 April 1897 the battalion was disbanded as a result of severe criticism regarding discipline by the officer commanding the 26th Regimental District. Uniform: scarlet/yellow.

8th (1859) Formed in Glasgow, its services accepted on 10 October 1859, and became 'D' Company of the new 4th Corps in December 1859.

8th (The Blythswood Rifles) (1880–1908) The 2nd Admin Battalion (shown in the *Army List* as 4th until March 1861) was formed with headquarters in Glasgow on 4 July 1860 and included in it were the 30th, 31st, 38th, 45th, 46th, 47th, 75th, 84th, 86th, 88th and 96th Corps. Consolidated on 10 May 1865 as the new 31st Corps with headquarters in North John Street, Glasgow, and in June 1869 received the additional title of 'The Blythswood Rifles' in honour of the commanding officer, Archibald Campbell Campbell (afterwards Lord Blythswood). Absorbed the 5th Corps in 1873 and added a further two companies in 1877. The 31st was renumbered as 8th Corps in 1880 and designated 3rd (The Blythswood) Volunteer Battalion Highland Light Infantry by General Order 181 of December 1887. Of the Volunteers from the battalion who served in South Africa, Sergeant J Cooper died of wounds and Private A Dobie of disease. Private H Pearson was wounded at Vecht Kop. In 1902 a new headquarters and drill hall were built at 69 Main Street, Bridgeton at a cost of £12,000. Musketry was carried out at Gilbertfield near Cambuslang. Transfer to the Territorial Force in 1908 was as 7th Battalion, Highland Light Infantry. Uniform: scarlet/blue, changing to scarlet/yellow with trews in 1886.

9th (Bankers) (1859–60) Services accepted on 10 October 1859 and formed from members of the Glasgow banking profession. The banks, with the exception of the City of Glasgow and the Clydesdale, subscribed and paid for the armament and equipment for a number of members. Became No. 2 Company of the new 1st Corps on 28th February 1860.

9th (1880–1908) The 3rd Admin Battalion (shown in the *Army List* as 8th until March 1861) was formed with headquarters at Lanark in December 1860 and to it were added the 37th, 55th, 62nd, 73rd, 94th and 107th Corps. Consolidated in 1880 as the new 9th Corps with six companies:

'A' Lesmahagow (late 37th Corps)

'B' Lanark (late 55th Corps)
'C' Biggar (late 62nd Corps)
'D' Carluke (late 73rd Corps)
'E' Douglas (late 94th Corps)
'F' Leadhills (late 107th Corps)

Became a volunteer battalion of the Highland Light Infantry (without change in title) in 1881. 'E' Company moved to Forth in 1894, 'F' to Law in 1901. Transfer to the Territorial Force in 1908 was as 8th Battalion Highland Light Infantry. Uniform: scarlet/blue, changing to scarlet/yellow with trews in 1883, changing to scarlet/buff with trews in 1904.

10th (Glasgow 2nd Southern) (1859–60) One company formed in Glasgow south of the Clyde, its services accepted on 19 October 1859, with William Smith Dixon as captain, Charles O'Neill, lieutenant and J Loudon, ensign. Became part of the new 3rd Corps in August 1860.

10th (Glasgow Highland) (1880–1908) The origins of the 10th Corps begin with a meeting held by the numerous Highlanders then resident in Glasgow on 24 April 1868. Some 800 men showed an interest in forming a corps and subsequently the services of the 105th (Glasgow Highland) RVC of twelve companies were accepted on 21 July 1868. Francis Robertson-Reid, late of the Royal Renfrew Militia, took command, and headquarters were established at 97 Union Street, Glasgow. Although recruited in general from all over Glasgow, 'C' Company was made up by residents of the Partick area, 'E' from Crosshill, 'F' by natives of Islay and 'G' by exiles from Argyllshire. The 105th made its first appearance at the laying of the new Glasgow University building foundation stone by HRH the Prince of Wales on 8 October 1868. In June 1880 the 105th was renumbered as 10th and designated 5th (Glasgow Highland) Volunteer Battalion Highland Light Infantry by General Order 181 of December 1887. A cyclist company was added in 1900. Blairlodge School Cadet Corps, which had been affiliated to the battalion on 1891, was disbanded in 1904. General Grierson in *Records of the Scottish Volunteer Force* notes that in the latter years of the battalion's history, 'A' Company was recruited from Highland residents of Springburn, 'B' from Whiteinch, 'C' from Partick, 'E' from Queen's Park, 'M' from Hillhead and 'F', as always, from natives of Islay. The last headquarters and drill hall were at 81 Greendyke Street, Glasgow, the rifle range being at Patterton. Transfer to the Territorial Force in 1908 was as 9th Battalion Highland Light Infantry. Uniform: scarlet/blue with kilts.

11th (Glasgow 2nd Western) Formed in Glasgow, its services accepted on 4 November 1859, with Captain C H Smith in command. Became No. 3 Company of the new 1st Corps on 28 February 1860.

12th (North Eastern) Formed in Glasgow, its services accepted on 5 December 1859, from employees of Tennant's Wellpark Brewery. Became 'E' Company of the new 4th Corps in the same month.

13th Formed in the St Rollox district of Glasgow, its services accepted on 5 December 1859, and became 'F' Company of the new 4th Corps in the same month.

14th (South Western) One company formed in Glasgow, its services accepted on 5 December 1859, with George Guttridge Gunniss as captain, Thomas Reid Kerr, lieutenant and Robert Maclean Blake, ensign. Became part of the new 3rd Corps in August 1860.

15th (Procurators') Formed in Glasgow, its services accepted on 5 December 1859, after a meeting held in the Faculty Hall on the previous 23 September by members of the legal profession. A sum of £150 was given by the Faculty towards expenses. Became No. 4 Company of the new 1st Corps on 28 February 1860.

16th (1860–73) One company formed at Hamilton, its services accepted on 24 February 1860, with Samuel Simpson as captain, John Austine, lieutenant and Dr Henry Muirhead, ensign. Joined the 1st Admin Battalion and became 'A' Company of the new 16th Corps in 1873. One of the most important mining towns in Scotland, Hamilton is located ten miles south-east of Glasgow near the junction of the Clyde and Avon rivers.

16th (1873–80) See 2nd Corps (1880–1908).

17th (Stockbrokers and Accountants) Formed in Glasgow from men employed in the several stockbrokers and accountants offices, its service accepted on 5 December 1859. Became No. 5 Company of the new 1st Corps on 28 February 1860. The Stock Exchange and the Institute of Accountants and Actuaries contributed a total of £250 to the initial running of the corps.

18th Formed in Glasgow, its services accepted on 5 December 1859, from employees of Messrs Wylie & Lochhead, a Glasgow firm of furnishers and undertakers. Robert Downie Wylie became captain, John Wylie, lieutenant and William Lochhead, ensign. Became No. 10 Company of the new 1st Corps on 28 February 1860. Wylie & Lochhead contributed £80 to corps funds; an additional £4 per man was borne either by the members themselves, or via outside subscriptions.

19th (Glasgow 2nd Northern) (1859–60) Formed as one company recruited from employees of the Western and Clyde Engineering Works, its services accepted on 5 December 1859. Became part of the new 19th Corps in February 1860.

19th (Glasgow 2nd Northern) (1860–80) See 5th Corps (1880–1908).

20th This number was intended for a company raised by the western shipbuilding yards which was never, in fact, formed.

21st (Parkhead Artisans) Formed in the Parkhead district of Glasgow, its services accepted on 5 December 1859, with John Boag as captain, John Robertson, lieutenant and William Robertson, ensign. Joined the 7th Admin Battalion and became part of the new 5th Corps in November 1860.

22nd Formed in Glasgow, its services accepted on 5 December 1859, from employees of Messrs Cogan's Spinning factory. The company's first officers were Captain Robert O Cogan, Lieutenant Ebenezer Mackinlay and Ensign Donald McDonald. Became part of the new 3rd Corps in August 1860.

23rd (Warehousemen) Formed in Glasgow from employees in drapery firms, its services accepted on 5 December 1859. Became part of the new 19th Corps in February 1860.

24th (North Western) Formed in the Cowcaddens district of Glasgow, its services accepted on 6 December 1859. Became part of the new 19th Corps in February 1860.

25th (1859–61) Formed in Glasgow from employees of Messrs Barclay, Curle & Co., its services accepted on 14 December 1859, with John Ritchie Miller as captain, Donald Anderson, lieutenant and William E Jevons, ensign. Joined the 6th Admin Battalion and became 'H' Company of the new 25th Corps in April 1861.

25th (1861–80) See 6th Corps (1880–1908).

26th Formed in Glasgow from employees of Messrs R Napier & Sons at Govan, its services accepted on 14 December 1859. The first officers of the corps were: John David Napier, Captain, J McIntyre, lieutenant and John Downall, ensign. Joined the 6th Admin Battalion and became 'A' Company of the new 25th Corps in April 1861.

27th Formed in Glasgow from employees of Messrs R Napier & Sons Engineering Department, its services accepted on 14 December 1859. Captain Thomas Small, Lieutenant Archibald D MacConnell and Ensign J Hooken were the first officers. Joined the 6th Admin Battalion and became 'F' Company of the new 25th Corps in April 1861.

28th (Railway) Formed in Glasgow from employees of the Edinburgh and Glasgow Railway Company, its services accepted on 22 December 1859. Became part of the new 19th Corps in February 1860.

29th (1860–73) Formed as one company at Coatbridge, its services accepted on 13 February 1860, with Thomas Jackson as captain, George Pollock, lieutenant and John Maxwell, ensign. Joined the 4th Admin Battalion and became 'A' Company of the new 29th Corps in September 1873. Cassell's notes that Coatbridge, on the Monkland Canal just under ten miles east of Glasgow, was in the 1890s the principal seat of the iron trade in Scotland. Railway wagons and boilers were manufactured.

29th (1873–80) See 7th Corps (1880–97).

30th (1st Central) Formed in the East Central district of Glasgow, its services accepted on 28 December, with Alexander Crum Ewing as captain, Dugald Maclie, lieutenant and Allan McNaughton, ensign. Joined the 2nd Admin Battalion and was disbanded in 1865.

31st (1859–65) Formed in Glasgow from workers in the leather trade, its services accepted on 21 December 1859, with J McIntosh as captain, William Eglin, lieutenant and J McGregor, ensign. Joined the 2nd Admin Battalion and became part of the new 31st Corps in May 1865.

31st (The Blythswood Rifles) (1865–80) See 8th Corps (1880–1908).

32nd Formed at Summerlee, its services accepted on 10 January 1860, from employees of Messrs Neilson's Ironworks. Captain John Neilson, Lieutenant J Lang and Ensign J Muir were the first officers. Joined the 4th Admin Battalion and became part of 'B' Company of the new 29th Corps in September 1873. At Summerlee, close to Coatbridge, many were employed in ironworks.

33rd (Partick) Formed in the Partick Division of Glasgow, its services being accepted on 22 December 1859. The 33rd was a self supporting company, each member finding his own uniform and equipment and paying a £2/2/0 annual subscription. Became No. 6 Company of the new 1st Corps on 28 February 1860.

34th (1st Rifle Rangers) Formed in Glasgow, its services accepted on 27 December 1859, with John Clark Crawford as captain, Thomas Russell, lieutenant and John McFarlane Wilson, ensign. Joined the 7th Admin Battalion and became part of the new 5th Corps in November 1860.

35th (2nd Rifle Rangers)
Formed in Glasgow, its services accepted on 27 December 1859, with Captain John Kerr Clark and Ensign John Russell jun the first officers to be commissioned. Joined the 7th Admin Battalion and became part of the new 5th Corps in November 1860.

36th Formed in Glasgow from employees of Messrs Edington & Co.'s Phoenix Ironworks at Port Dundas, its services being accepted on 28 December 1859. Became part of the new 19th Corps in February 1860.

37th Formed at Lesmahagow, its services accepted on 3 February 1860, with J Thomas Brown as captain, Hugh Mossman jun, lieutenant and John B Greenshields, ensign. Joined the 3rd Admin Battalion and became 'A' Company of the new 9th Corps in 1880. Lesmahagow is six miles southwest of Lanark. Lesmahagow Station, on the old Caledonian line, was opened as Brocketsbrae in December 1866 and renamed in June 1869.

38th (Rifle Rangers) Formed in the Central district of Glasgow from men employed as mechanics, its services being accepted on 29 December 1859. The first officers to be commissioned were William Bowstead as captain, and Alexander Smith jun, ensign. Joined the 2nd Admin Battalion and became part of the new 31st Corps in May 1865.

39th Formed in Glasgow, its services accepted on 29 December 1859, from employees of shipping companies. Became No. 7 Company of the new 1st Corps on 28 February 1860.

40th Formed in Glasgow from various small shipyards, its services accepted on 29 December 1859, with William Rigby as captain, J Wellington Whitehall, lieutenant and John Parry, ensign. Joined the 6th Admin Battalion and became 'D' Company of the new 25th Corps in April 1861.

41st (North Western Artisans) Formed in Glasgow mainly from stonemasons, its services being accepted on 31 December 1859. Became part of the new 19th Corps in February 1860.

42nd Formed as one company at Uddingston, its services accepted on 31 January 1860, with J Wilkie as captain, John Gray, lieutenant and T Scott, ensign. Joined the 1st Admin Battalion and became 'C' Company of the new 16th Corps in 1873. Uddingston is four miles north-west of Hamilton.

43rd Formed at Gartsherrie from employees of W Bird & Co.'s Ironworks, its services accepted on 10 January 1860, with John Alexander as captain, John Campbell, lieutenant and Daniel C Warnock, ensign. Joined the 4th Admin Battalion and moved headquarters to Shotts in 1872. Became 'C' Company of the new 29th Corps in September 1873. Shotts Station, on the old Caledonian line, was opened in July 1869.

44th Formed as one company at Blantyre, its services accepted on 6 February 1860, from employees of Messrs Henry Monteith & Co. The first officers were: Captain J Reid, Lieutenant J Hutton Watkins and Ensign Robert Valentine Reid jun. Joined the 1st Admin Battalion and became part of 'I' Company of the new 16th Corps in 1873. Blantyre is three miles north-west of Hamilton.

45th Formed in Glasgow from members of the grocery trade, its services accepted on 10 January 1860, with John Gowland as captain, John Forbes, lieutenant and John McCulloch, ensign. Joined the 2nd Admin Battalion and became part of the new 31st Corps in May 1865.

46th Formed in Glasgow from members of the grocery trade, its services accepted on 10 January 1860, with Archibald Henderson as captain, J Cooper Webster, lieutenant and Mathew Johnston, ensign. Joined the 2nd Admin Battalion and became part of the new 31st Corps in May 1865.

47th Formed in Glasgow from members of the grocery trade, its services accepted on 10 January 1860, with John Mowat as captain, William Smith, lieutenant and J Oswald Munro, ensign. Joined the 2nd Admin Battalion and became part of the new 31st Corps in May 1865.

48th Formed at Airdrie, its services accepted on 11 February 1860, with J Kidd as captain, John Rankin, lieutenant and Robert Addie, ensign. Joined the 4th Admin Battalion. Comprised two companies; No. 1 became part of 'B' Company, No. 2 part of 'D' Company of the new 29th Corps in September 1873. Cassell's notes that in the 1890s there were over forty collieries, several ironstone mines and various blast furnaces in the Airdrie area.

49th Formed at Lambhill, two miles from Glasgow, on 3 May 1860 and disbanded in 1862.

50th (1st Press Corps) Formed in Glasgow, its services accepted on 10 January 1860, from newspaper employees and pressmen and became No. 11 Company of the new 1st Corps on 28 February 1860.

51st (2nd Press Corps) Formed in Glasgow from employees of various newspapers' offices, its services accepted on 11 January 1860, with Robert Buchanan as captain, John Crawford, lieutenant and Frederick J C Dietrichsen, ensign. Joined the 5th Admin Battalion and became part of the new 19th Corps in September 1860.

52nd Formed as one company at Hamilton, its services accepted on 24 February 1860, and joined the 1st Admin Battalion. The corps was made up of artisans with J Nisbet as captain, William Forrest jun, lieutenant and Edward P Dykes, ensign. Became 'B' Company of the new 16th Corps in 1873.

53rd Formed in Glasgow, its services accepted on 30 January 1860, from employees of J & W Campbell Ltd. Mr J W Campbell contributed £200 towards the running of the corps, which became No. 12 Company of the new 1st Corps on 28 February 1860. Sir Henry Campbell-Bannerman, who became Prime Minister in December 1905, served as a lieutenant, and then, until 1867, a captain in this company. When new uniforms were required in 1862, Campbell-Bannerman contributed £50 towards the cost of re-clothing the men.

54th One company formed in Glasgow, its services accepted on 30 January 1860, with Thomas Steel as captain, William Morier, lieutenant and Peter Fulton, ensign. Members were all total abstainers. Became part of the new 3rd Corps in August 1860.

55th Formed at Lanark, its services being accepted on 23 February 1860, with William Bertram as captain, Edward Gilroy, lieutenant and David Stodart, ensign. Joined the 3rd Admin Battalion and became 'B' Company of the new 9th Corps in 1880.

56th Formed as one company at Bothwell, its services accepted on 23 February 1860, with Alex Turner as captain, Joshua Bain, lieutenant and David Lockhart, ensign. Joined the 1st Admin Battalion and became 'E' Company of the new 16th Corps in 1873. Bothwell is eight miles south-east of Glasgow.

57th Formed as one company at Wishaw, its services accepted on 7 March 1860, with John M Mackenzie as captain, J Glass, lieutenant and J Steel, ensign. Joined the 1st Admin Battalion. Increased to two companies in 1872 and became 'F' and 'G' Companies of the new 16th Corps in 1873. At Wishaw, fifteen miles south-west of Glasgow, the ironworks and distillery gave employment to many from the area.

58th (Eastern Artisans) Formed in Glasgow, its services accepted on 10 February 1860, with J Thomason as captain, Hugh Colquhoun, lieutenant and Robert McCullum, ensign. Joined the 7th Admin Battalion and became part of the new 5th Corps in November 1860.

59th (Eastern Artisans) Formed in Glasgow, its services accepted on 21 February 1860, from the overspill of the 58th Corps. Captain John J Alston, Lieutenant John Bankier and Ensign Patrick Robertson were the first officers. Joined the 7th Admin Battalion and became part of the new 5th Corps in November 1860.

60th (Glasgow 1st Highland) Formed in Glasgow, its services accepted on 18 February 1860, from Highlanders resident in the city. Captain Duncan Macfarlan, Lieutenant Donald Campbell and Ensign William Whyte were the first officers. Became 'G' Company of the new 4th Corps in July 1861.

61st (Glasgow 2nd Highland) Formed in Glasgow, its services accepted on 18 February 1860, from Highlanders resident in the city. Captain Hugh Reid, Lieutenant George M Kerr and Ensign Malcolm C McGregor were the first officers. Became 'H' Company of the new 4th Corps in July 1861.

62nd Formed at Biggar, its services being accepted on 22 February 1860, with A D R W B Cochrane as captain, Robert Paterson, lieutenant and William Handyside, ensign. Joined the 3rd Admin Battalion. Disbanded by the end of 1860, but re-formed in 1863. Became 'C' Company of the new 9th Corps in 1880. The railway came to Biggar, the old Symington, Biggar & Broughton line, in November 1860.

63rd Formed in Glasgow, its services accepted on 15 February 1860, from employees in the baking, grain and provision trades. The various firms contributed a total of £450 towards expenses. Captain John Ure, Lieutenant J Sinclair and Ensign David Watt were the first officers. Became No. 13 Company of the new 1st Corps in March 1860.

64th (1st Rutherglen) Formed at Rutherglen, its services being accepted on 18 February 1860, with J Farie as captain, John Matheson, lieutenant and John Campbell Matheson, ensign. Joined the 7th Admin Battalion and became part of the new 5th Corps in November 1860. Many at Rutherglen were employed at the town's dye works, paper mill and numerous collieries. The Town Hall was opened in the year after formation of the 64th Corps.

65th (2nd Rutherglen) Formed at Rutherglen, its services being accepted on 18 February 1860, with J R Reid as captain, John Fleming, lieutenant and William Laurie Dunn, ensign. Joined the 7th Admin Battalion and became part of the new 5th Corps in November 1860.

66th (Eastern Rifle Rangers) Formed in Glasgow, its services accepted on 17 February 1860, with J T Henderson as captain, John Patterson, lieutenant and Duncan Stewart, ensign. Joined the 7th Admin Battalion and became part of the new 5th Corps in November 1860.

67th Formed in Glasgow from employees of Messrs D Laidlaw & Sons of the Alliance Foundry, its services accepted on 17 February 1860, with Robert Laidlaw as captain, Thomas Kennedy, lieutenant and Peter T Ramsay, ensign. Joined the 5th Admin Battalion and became part of the new 19th Corps in September 1860.

68th Formed in Glasgow from employees of Messrs Neilson & Co.'s Locomotive Works, its services accepted on 17 February 1860, with Walter M Neilson as captain, Henry Martini, lieutenant and Henry L Graham, ensign. Joined the 6th Admin Battalion and became 'B' Company of the new 25th Corps in April 1861.

69th Formed in Glasgow from employees of Messrs J & G Thomson, its services accepted on 17 February 1860, with George Thomson as captain, John McKendrick, lieutenant and John Grant, ensign. Joined the 6th Admin Battalion and became 'G' Company of the new 25th Corps in April 1861.

70th Formed in Glasgow from employees of A & J Inglis and Todd and Macgregor's, its service accepted on 17 February 1860, with William Tod as captain, William H Inglis, lieutenant and William Mackay, ensign. Joined the 6th Admin Battalion and became 'E' Company of the new 25th Corps in April 1861.

71st Formed in Glasgow from employees at Lancefield Forge and the Anderston Foundry, its services accepted on 17 February 1860, with J Murdoch as captain, William L E McLean, lieutenant and J C Bunten, ensign. Joined the 6th Admin Battalion and became 'C' Company of the new 25th Corps in April 1861.

72nd (Fine Arts) Formed by Glasgow jewellers, silversmiths, engravers, watch and clockmakers. The services of the 72nd Corps were accepted on 23 February 1860 with John J Muirhead as captain, John Mossman, lieutenant and Neil McPhail, ensign. Became No. 14 Company of the new 1st Corps in March 1860.

73rd Formed at Carluke, its services accepted on 12 March 1860, with Thomas Matthews as captain, Andrew Crusoe Selkirk, lieutenant and William S Kerr, ensign. Joined the 3rd Admin Battalion and became 'D' Company of the new 9th Corps in 1880. Carluke is just over nineteen miles south-east of Glasgow.

74th (Grenadiers) Formed in Glasgow, its services accepted on 29 February 1860, with Thomas C Orr as captain, William Cumming, lieutenant and Alex Sword, ensign. Members of the corps were required to be not less than five-feet-nine inches in height. Joined the 5th Admin Battalion and became part of the new 19th Corps in September 1860.

75th Formed in Glasgow from members of the leather trade, its services accepted on 29 February 1860, with J Wilson as captain, Henry Herzfield, lieutenant and J Sandlands, ensign. Joined the 2nd Admin Battalion and became part of the new 31st Corps in May 1865.

76th (Port Dundas) Formed in Glasgow, its services accepted on 26 March 1860, from men working in the wharves, stores, distilleries, sawmills and sugar works at Port Dundas. Became No. 15 Company of the new 1st Corps in April 1860.

77th (City Rifle Guard, or 2nd University) Formed in Glasgow, its services accepted on 8 March 1860, and for a few months had existed as a drill class at Glasgow University. Some members came from this source, but in the main recruits were of the mercantile community. Drills were held in College Green, headquarters were in the college and the first captain, William Thompson, was a professor. Became No. 16 Company of the new 1st Corps in April 1860.

78th It was at a meeting held in Glasgow in February 1860 that several of the survivors of the old Glasgow Light Horse of 1796, the Volunteers of 1803 and the Sharpshooters of 1819 resolved that they should form themselves into a veteran rifle corps to be known as the 'Glasgow Old Guard'. The official acceptance date of the corps was 3 April 1860, the government numbering the veterans as 78th Lanarkshire – the Glasgow Museum and Art Gallery is in possession of a framed Muster Roll of the Old Guard, on which 100 names are recorded. The *Glasgow Gazette* of 10 March 1860 reported that the average age of the corps was sixty-three years. Walter Buchanan, Glasgow's MP since 1857, became captain, George Crawford, lieutenant and John Gilmour, ensign. General Grierson in *Records of the Scottish Volunteer Force* notes, 'It does not appear that the members ever appeared in uniform or did any drill, but they set an example to the younger generation which was of much value to the cause of Volunteering.' A subsequent report by the Assistant Inspector of Volunteers, however, led to the government informing the 78th of its dissatisfaction as to the way the corps was being run. As a result, the Glasgow Old Guard was disbanded in November 1860.

79th (Glasgow 3rd Western) Formed in Glasgow, its services accepted on 29 March 1860, and became No. 8 Company of the new 1st Corps in April 1860.

80th Formed in Glasgow from employees of Messrs Magazine & Co. Ironworks at Windmill Croft, its services accepted on 29 March 1860, with Robert McGavin as captain, John A S McGavin, lieutenant and George Quigley, ensign. Joined the 5th Admin Battalion and became part of the new 19th Corps in September 1860.

81st (Northern Artisans) Formed in Glasgow mainly from employees of Law & Co.'s Ironworks at Port Dundas, its services accepted on 2 April 1860, with Graham Gilmour, late of the Royal London Militia, as captain, John Kennedy, lieutenant and William Grant, ensign. Joined the 5th Admin Battalion and became part of the new 19th Corps in September 1860.

82nd One company formed in Glasgow, its services were accepted on 11 April 1860, from total abstainers and men of the artisan class. Became part of the new 3rd Corps in August 1860.

83rd (Northern Artisans) Formed in Glasgow mainly from joiners, its services accepted on 24 April 1860. Joined the 5th Admin Battalion and became part of the new 19th Corps in September 1860.

84th Formed in Glasgow from members of the grain and provisions trades, its services accepted on 24 April 1860, with John Arthur jun as captain, Andrew Ballantyne, lieutenant and James Thompson, ensign. Joined the 2nd Admin Battalion and became part of the new 31st Corps in May 1865.

85th (2nd North Eastern) Formed in Glasgow from ironworkers of the North Eastern and St Rollox districts, its services accepted on 7 May 1860. Became part of the new 19th Corps by the end of 1860.

86th Formed in Glasgow from members of the tailoring trade, its services being accepted on 7 May 1860, with Mungo P Weir as captain, James Fraser, lieutenant and Thomas D Humphreys, ensign. Joined the 2nd Admin Battalion and became part of the new 31st Corps in May 1865.

87th The services of one company formed by employees of Messrs Ingles & Wakefields at Busby just outside Glasgow were accepted on 18 May 1860. Became part of the new 3rd Corps in August 1860.

88th Formed in Glasgow, its services being accepted on 9 May 1860, with William Robertson as captain, William McWhinnie, lieutenant and Alex Sheridan Knowles, ensign. Joined the 2nd Admin Battalion in October 1861 and disbanded in 1864. Members of the corps were all butchers.

89th (Manufacturers) Formed in Glasgow from employees in textile firms, its services accepted on 9 May 1860. Became part of the new 19th Corps by the end of 1860.

90th Formed in the Whitevale district of Glasgow, its services being accepted on 24 May 1860. Joined the 7th Admin Battalion and became part of the new 5th Corps in November 1860.

91st (3rd Abstainers) Formed in Glasgow mainly from total abstainers living in the Whitevale district, its services accepted on 24 May 1860. Became part of the new 19th Corps by the end of 1860.

92nd This number was intended for a company at Uddingston, but its services were not accepted.

93rd (Glasgow Highland Rangers) Formed in Glasgow, its services accepted on 8 August 1860, from Highlanders resident in the city with James Dewar as captain, Malcolm C McGregor, lieutenant and John R Irvine, ensign. Became 'I' Company of the new 4th Corps in July 1861.

94th Formed at Douglas, its services accepted on 21 September 1860, with Thomas R Scott as captain, James Gillespie, lieutenant and Archibald D Scott, ensign. Joined the 3rd Admin Battalion and became 'E' Company of the new 9th Corps in 1880. Douglas is just under eleven miles south-west of Lanark, its first station being opened in April 1864. Douglas West opened in 1895. Both were on the old Caledonian Railway.

95th Formed at Baillieston, its services being accepted on 16 October 1860, with James Wiseman as captain, George Pollock, lieutenant and James Hunter, ensign. Joined the 4th Admin Battalion and became 'E' Company of the new 29th Corps in September 1873. Baillieston lies on the old Caledonian Railway between Glasgow and Airdrie, most of its population being employed in the area's vast coal mines.

96th Formed as one company in Glasgow, its services being accepted on 29 November 1860, with Captain David Marshall Lang in command. Later increased to two companies, joined the 2nd Admin Battalion and became part of the new 31st Corps in May 1865.

97th (1861–63) Formed at Glasgow on 30 July 1861 and soon comprised four companies. Also known as the 'Glasgow Guards', the 97th was absorbed into 1st Lanarkshire Engineer Volunteer Corps in 1863.

97th (1865–73) Formed at Woodhead, its service being accepted on 11 January 1865, with Captain John Hendre in command. Joined the 4th Admin Battalion, headquarters were later transferred to Coatbridge, and became 'F' Company of the new 29th Corps in September 1873.

98th Formed at Gartness from employees of the Calderbank Iron Works and the Chapelhall Iron and Steel Works, its services being accepted on 12 May 1865 with William Hawksworth as captain. Joined the 4th Admin Battalion, moved to Wattstown in 1869, and became 'G' Company (with headquarters at Greengairs, near Gartness) of the new 29th Corps in September 1873. Gartness, on the North Calder, is just south-east of Airdrie, Wattstown three miles north-east.

99th Formed at Clarkston, its services accepted on 27 July 1865, with William Towers-Clark as captain. Joined the 4th Admin Battalion, moved to Caldercruix, Airdrie in 1866, and became 'H' Company of the new 29th Corps in September 1873.

100th Formed at Calderbank, its services accepted on 8 July 1865, with Francis Murray as captain. Joined the 4th Admin Battalion, moved to Caldercruix in 1866, and became 'I' and 'M' Companies of the new 29th Corps in September 1873.

101st Formed at Newarthill, its services accepted on 7 June 1866, with Thomas Johnston as captain, John Ferguson, lieutenant and J Boag, ensign. Joined the 4th Admin Battalion and became 'K' Company of the new 29th Corps in September 1873. Newarthill is on the Edinburgh road, just under three miles north-east of Motherwell.

102nd Formed as one company at Motherwell, its services accepted on 14 February 1867, with Robert Jack as captain, Thomas Whitelaw, lieutenant and John Topping, ensign. Joined the 1st Admin Battalion and became 'H' Company of the new 16th Corps in 1873. On the Caledonian line, a new station replaced that of the old Wishaw & Coltness Railway in July 1885.

103rd Formed as one company at East Kilbride, its services accepted on 6 June 1867, with Robert E Stuart Harington, late of the Rifle Brigade, in command. Joined the 1st Admin Battalion and became part of 'I' Company of the new 16th Corps in 1873. On the Renfrewshire border, seven miles from Glasgow, the area around East Kilbride mined iron, coal and was well known for its potters' clay.

104th Formed at Mossend, Holytown, Bellshill from employees of Messrs Neilson's Mossend Works, its services accepted on 18 April 1868 with Walter Neilson as captain, Robert Hogg, lieutenant and Hugh Neilson, ensign. Joined the 4th Admin Battalion and became 'L' Company of the new 29th Corps in September 1873.

105th (Glasgow Highland) See 10th Corps (1880–1908).

106th Formed as one company at Strathaven, its services accepted in October 1873, and joined the 1st Admin Battalion. Became 'D' Company of the new 16th Corps in the same year. Fifteen miles south-east of Glasgow, the local trade of Strathaven was mainly in cheese and grain. Silk, cotton and hosiery goods were also manufactured.

107th Formed at Leadhills in May 1875 and joined the 3rd Admin Battalion. Became 'F' Company of the new 9th Corps in 1880. The area was well known for its production of lead.

LANCASHIRE

The last rifle corps to be raised and numbered in Lancashire was that formed at Flixton in 1872. This company received the title of 91st Corps and as such held the second highest number allotted to any Volunteer unit in the land. The county was to provide the usual administrative battalions for its smaller corps. Of the nine created, three were to be consolidated before the general reorganizations of 1880. The remaining six, together with the larger corps, were in that year to form twenty-one. A 22nd followed in 1882. Sub-divisions numbered 1st, 2nd and 3rd existed and these can be seen under 13th and 38th Corps (1st), 14th Corps of 1859–61 (2nd) and 14th Corps of 1880–1908 (3rd).

1st (1859–61) Formed as three companies at Liverpool with Captain Commandant Nathanial G P Bousfield in command. A Liverpool cotton merchant, Bousfield's commission was dated 11 June 1859 and as such was the first in the land to be issued under the new Volunteer system. His company commanders were J Burnside Taylor and George Hunter Robertson. Joined the 1st Admin Battalion and became part of the new 1st Corps in December 1861.

1st (1861–1908) The 1st Admin Battalion was formed with headquarters in Liverpool in May 1860 and to it were added the 1st, 22nd, 38th, 45th, 66th and 69th Corps. When the battalion was consolidated as the new 1st Corps of eight companies in December 1861, also included in the merger was the 14th Corps at Edge Hill. The 74th Corps in Liverpool was absorbed in 1862. Re-designation as 1st Volunteer Battalion King's (Liverpool Regiment) was notified in Army Order 81 of March 1888, the establishment of the corps being ten companies. Two more were sanctioned in 1883, another in 1900, and a cadet corps formed in April 1865 was disbanded in 1884. Transfer to the Territorial Force in 1908 was as 5th Battalion King's. Uniform: green/black.

2nd (1859–80) Formed at Blackburn on 4 October 1859. Absorbed the 3rd Corps, also at Blackburn, in February 1860, this bringing the establishment of the corps up to four companies under Captains Thomas Lund, John Gerald Potter, William Harrison and Arthur Ingram Robinson. Joined the 8th Admin Battalion and became 'A' to 'H' Companies of the new 2nd Corps in 1880. In this large manufacturing town, much of Blackburn's trade was in cotton.

2nd (1880–1908) The 8th Admin Battalion was formed with headquarters at Blackburn in March 1864 and included the 2nd, 62nd and 81st Corps. The new 2nd Corps was formed upon consolidation in 1880 with ten companies:

'A' to 'F' Blackburn (late 2nd Corps)
'G' and 'H' Over Darwen (late 2nd Corps)
'J' and 'K' Clitheroe (late 62nd Corps)

Re-designated as 1st Volunteer Battalion East Lancashire Regiment in June 1889 and transferred to the Territorial Force in 1908 as 4th Battalion. Stonyhurst College Cadet Corps, which was formed and affiliated in January 1901, at the same time joined the OTC. Uniform: scarlet/white.

3rd (1859–60) Formed at Blackburn on 4 October 1859 and absorbed into the 2nd Corps in February 1860.

3rd (1880–1908) Burnley was the headquarters of the 3rd Admin Battalion, which was formed in September 1860 and included the 4th, 7th, 17th, 29th, 36th, 57th, 84th, 87th, 88th and 90th Corps. Headquarters were transferred to Rossendale in 1862, to Accrington in 1865, and back to Burnley in 1874. The battalion was consolidated in 1880 as the new 3rd Corps with twelve companies:

'A' to 'D' Burnley (late 17th Corps)
'E' Padiham (late 84th Corps)
'F' to 'H' Accrington (late 7th Corps)
'J' Haslingden (late 88th Corps)
'K' Ramsbottom (late 57th Corps)
'L' Stacksteads (late 4th Corps)
'M' Lytham (late 29th Corps)

Re-designation as 2nd Volunteer Battalion East Lancashire Regiment was notified by Army Order 263 of June 1889. Volunteers from the battalion served with the Regulars of the East Lancashire Regiment in South Africa during the Boer War. Lieutenant Percy S Parker, who had joined the battalion in January 1898, died of enteric at Heilbron on 1 February 1902. Transfer to the Territorial Force in 1908 was as 5th Battalion East Lancashire Regiment. Uniform: scarlet/black.

4th (1859–80) The 4th Corps was formed as one company, the *Army List* giving its location as Rossendale, which is a parish and borough incorporating the towns of Bacup, Haslington and Rawtenstall. The first to receive a commission was James Munn as captain on 4 July 1859, he being followed by Servetus Aitken as lieutenant (22 August 1859), and Samuel Hal, a solicitor from Bacup, who was promoted ensign from sergeant major on 12 April 1860. James Munn, who resided at Fern Hill, Stacksteads, was the eldest son of cotton manufacturer Robert Munn and was drowned when his yacht overturned at Lytham Regatta in July 1871. There is a memorial to him in Trinity Churchyard, Tunstead, Stacksteads. The 4th Corps joined the 3rd Admin Battalion and became 'L' Company of the new 3rd Corps in 1880.

4th (1880–1908) The 4th Admin Battalion was formed with headquarters at Eccles in October 1860 and included the 21st, 46th, 55th, 60th, 67th, 76th and 91st Corps. Headquarters moved to Manchester in 1862, Wigan by the beginning of 1877, and back to Manchester in 1879. The battalion was consolidated in 1880 as the new 4th Corps with thirteen companies:

'A' to 'E' Wigan (late 21st Corps)
'F' Swinton (late No. 1 Company, 46th Corps)
'G' Eccles (late No. 2 Company, 46th Corps)
'H' Leigh (late 55th Corps)
'J' Atherton (late 60th Corps)
'K' Worsley (late 67th Corps)
'L' and 'M' Farnworth (late 76th Corps)
'N' Flixton (late 91st Corps)

The Farnworth Companies ('L' and 'M') were transferred to the 14th Corps in 1883. Re-designated as 1st Volunteer Battalion Manchester Regiment in 1888. Volunteers from the battalion went to South Africa, the first draft going out under Lieutenant H C Darlington and seeing service in Natal and the Transvaal. Action was seen at Reint Vlei and Belfast, in which two men were killed. Two further drafts followed the first. An additional company was sanctioned in 1900 and transfer to the Territorial Force in 1908 was as 5th Battalion Manchester Regiment. Uniform: green/scarlet.

5th (1859–62) Formed as two companies at Liverpool on 19 August 1859 with Adam Stuart Gladstone and Robert John Tinley as captains; Charles Edward Crosbie and Jacob Willink, lieutenants, Samuel Sandbach Parker and Richard George Bushby, ensigns. It would seem that not all were satisfied with how recruiting for the 5th Corps was being carried out. On record is a meeting held by Adam Gladstone at the Liverpool Sessions House on 20 May 1859 in which one R J Tilney (and others) smashed the ballot-boxes. Joined the 2nd Admin Battalion and became part of the new 5th Corps in 1862.

5th (Liverpool Rifle Volunteer Brigade) (1862–1908) The 2nd Admin Battalion was formed with headquarters at Liverpool in May 1860 and to it were added the 5th, 14th, 19th, 39th, 63rd, 64th, 68th, 71st and 86th. The 81st was included for a few months in 1861, but was then transferred to 8th Admin Battalion. In March 1862 the battalion was consolidated as the new 5th Corps with the additional title of 'The Liverpool Rifle Volunteer Brigade', at the same time adding additional companies by absorbing the 32nd and 79th Corps. With an establishment of ten companies the 5th Corps was re-designated as 2nd Volunteer Battalion King's (Liverpool Regiment) in 1888. The battalion sent three drafts out to South Africa, the first seeing action at Laing's Nek and Belfast. Among the casualties was Lieutenant William Henry Kenyon, who died of enteric at No. 4 Stationary Hospital, Newcastle. Back home, a memorial in his memory was placed in Sefton Park Presbyterian Church by all ranks of the 2nd Volunteer Battalion. Transfer to the Territorial Force in 1908 was as 6th Battalion King's (Liverpool Regiment). Uniform: green/scarlet.

6th (1st Manchester) Formed as twelve companies in Manchester on 25 August 1859, the Viscount Grey de Wilton being appointed as Lieutenant Colonel Commandant on 19 February 1860. A number of large Manchester firms such as Messrs J P and E Westhead and Messrs J and N Phillips provided whole companies. No. 12 Company (headquarters in Eccles) was absorbed into the 46th Corps at Swinton in October 1860, the 43rd at Fallowfield being absorbed in 1861.

The 6th Corps for many years occupied headquarters at Wolstenholm's Court, Market Street, Manchester and afterwards at 3 Stretford Road, Hulme. Designation as 2nd Volunteer Battalion Manchester Regiment was notified in Army Order 409 of 1888. A new company was sanctioned in 189°, followed by two more in 1900. Transfer to the Territorial Force in 1908 was as 6th Battalion Manchester Regiment, 'N' Company, however, which had been formed at Manchester University, became part of the Senior Division OTC. Uniform: scarlet/yellow.

7th (1859–80) Formed as one company at Accrington on 20 September 1859 with John Hargreaves jun as captain, William Halstead Dewhirst, lieutenant and William Bullough, ensign. Joined the 3rd Admin Battalion and absorbed the 36th Corps, also at Accrington, in 1861. Increased to two companies in 1867, three in 1874, and became 'F' to 'H' Companies of the new 3rd Corps in 1880. Cotton mills were the main employer during the time of the Volunteers; there were also collieries, breweries and quarries in the area.

7th (1880–1908) The 7th Admin Battalion was formed with headquarters at Ashton-under-Lyne in November 1863 and included the 23rd and 31st Corps. Consolidated as the new 7th Corps in 1880 with twelve companies: 'A' to 'F' at Ashton-under-Lyne (late 23rd Corps) and 'G' to 'M', which were formed by the 31st at Oldham. The letter 'I' was not used. In 1882 the establishment was reduced when the Oldham companies were withdrawn to form a new corps numbered as 22nd. The remainder were designated as 3rd Volunteer Battalion Manchester Regiment in 1888. Three additional companies were sanctioned in 1900 and transfer to the Territorial Force in 1908 was as 9th Battalion Manchester Regiment. Uniform: scarlet/green, changing to scarlet/white in 1885.

8th Acceptance of the services of a corps of riflemen at Bury was received on 8 August 1859, the commissions of Captain John Hutchinson, Lieutenant William Hardman and Ensign Oliver Ormerod Walker being signed on 22 August. T H Hathurst wrote in *A History and Some Records of the Volunteer Movement in Bury* how the 8th Corps embraced members of every branch of local society, 'There were gentry and the manufacturers, men of large families and men with no family at all, skilled workmen of high standing in their calling, clerks and labourers.' In February 1860 a second company was raised and in July a third and fourth, both at Heywood, and another at Radcliffe in December 1863. T H Hathurst records that within a few days of the Radcliffe men being drafted into the battalion the corps was formed into six companies – he later notes these as being located as Nos 1 and 2 (Bury), Nos 3 and 4 (Heywood) and Nos 5 and 6 (Bury). A corps of very high standard, the 8th Lancashire was described by a Liverpool paper in 1869 as 'amongst the best drilled men in the county'. The corps was re-designated as 1st Volunteer Battalion Lancashire Fusiliers under General Order 14 of 1883 and in the same year two more companies were added. The Bury Grammar School Cadet Corps was formed and affiliated in 1892. Transfer to the Territorial Force in 1908 was as 5th Battalion Lancashire Fusiliers. Bury Grammar School at the same time joined the OTC. Uniform: scarlet/blue, changing to scarlet/white by 1886.

9th (1859–80) Formed as one company at Warrington on 16 September 1859 with J Fenton Greenland as captain, John Richard Pickmere jun, lieutenant and Sylvanus Reynolds, ensign. Joined the 9th Admin Battalion in 1865 and by 1880 comprised six companies, which provided 'A' to 'F' Companies of the new 9th Corps. During the Volunteer period Warrington employed many in its foundries, breweries, chemical and ironworks. Glass products were made, as well as soap and borax.

9th (1880–1908) The 9th Admin Battalion was formed with headquarters at Warrington on 16 September 1865 and included the 9th and 49th Corps. These were merged as 9th Corps in 1880, the combined strength of seven companies being located: 'A' to 'F' at Warrington (late 9th Corps) and 'G' at Newton-le-Willows (late 49th). The new 9th Corps was designated 1st Volunteer Battalion South Lancashire Regiment in 1886. During 1900–03 additional personnel were sanctioned bringing the establishment of the battalion up to eleven companies. Transfer to the Territorial Force in 1908 was as 4th Battalion South Lancashire Regiment. Uniform: scarlet/green, changing to scarlet/white in 1890.

10th (1859–76) Formed at Lancaster on 20 September 1859. Joined the 5th Admin Battalion in 1862 and became 'A' and 'B' Companies of the new 10th Corps in 1876. At Lancaster in 1859, the Roman Catholic Church of St Peter was opened, the Storey Institute and Art Gallery in 1891. Many in the town were employed in the manufacture of furniture, linoleum and railway plant.

10th (1876–1908) The 5th Admin Battalion was formed with headquarters at Ulverston in April 1861 and to it were added the 10th, 37A, 37B, 37C, 52nd, 53rd, 65th and 75th Corps. Consolidated as the new 10th Corps in 1876 with nine companies:

'A' and 'B' Lancaster (late 10th Corps)
'C' and 'D' Ulverston (late 37A Corps)
'E' and 'F' Barrow (late 37B Corps)
'G' Hawkshead (late 37C Corps)
'H' Rossall (late 65th Corps)
'J' Grange (newly formed)

The newly formed 'J' Company also included a detachment at Cartmel which had been formed by former members of the old 53rd Corps. The 10th Corps was re-designated as 1st Volunteer Battalion King's Own (Royal Lancaster Regiment) in 1883. 'K' and 'L' Companies were added at Dalton in 1887, 'L' moving to Millom in 1889. The Rossall Company was disbanded in 1890, its cadet corps at the same time being transferred to 1st Lancashire Engineer Volunteers. In 1900, the battalion was divided so as to form a new 2nd Volunteer Battalion, the 1st remaining at Ulverston with 'A' and 'B' Companies at Ulverston; 'C' and 'D' at Barrow; 'E', Hawkshead; 'F', Barrow; 'G' Dalton and 'H' Millom. Transfer to the Territorial Force in 1908 was as 4th Battalion King's Own. Uniform: scarlet/blue.

11th (Preston) (1859–80) Formed at Preston on 4 October 1859, and in February 1860 absorbed two other Preston corps, the 12th and 30th, bringing the establishment to three companies – the Hon Newsham Pedder, late of the 3rd Royal Lancashire Militia, William Henry Goodair and George Eastham were captains. Joined the 6th Admin Battalion and in 1865 'Preston' was authorized to be included in the title. In 1866 the 44th Corps at Longton was also absorbed into the 11th, as was the 61st at Chorley in November 1868. Now of eight companies, in 1880 the 11th Corps became 'A' to 'E' and 'G', 'H' and 'J' Companies of the new 11th Corps. At Preston there were several iron foundries, biscuit bakeries, engine and steam boiler works.

11th (1880–1908) The 6th Admin Battalion was formed with headquarters at Preston in September 1861 and included the 11th, 44th, 59th and 61st Corps. Consolidated in 1880 as the new 11th Corps with nine companies:

'A' to 'E' Preston (late 11th Corps)
'F' Leyland (late 59th Corps)
'G', 'H' and 'J' Chorley (late 11th Corps)

The corps was re-designated as 1st Volunteer Battalion Loyal North Lancashire Regiment under General Order 14 of February 1883. Two new companies were sanctioned in 1900 and transfer to the Territorial Force in 1908 was as 4th Battalion Loyal North Lancashire Regiment. Uniform: scarlet/white.

12th (1859–60) Formed at Preston on 7 October 1859 and absorbed into the 11th Corps in February 1860.

12th (1880–1908) Formed at Rochdale on 24 February 1860 as 24th Corps, its first officers being Captain Joseph Fenton, Lieutenant Henry Fishwick and Ensign Theodore R Phillippi. Three new companies were added in 1861, a fifth in 1868, sixth in 1869 and a seventh in 1875. Renumbered 12th in 1880 and designated as 2nd Volunteer Battalion Lancashire Fusiliers under General Order 14 of February 1883. Transfer to the Territorial Force in 1908 was as 6th Battalion Lancashire Fusiliers. Uniform: scarlet/blue, changing to scarlet/white by 1886. Rochdale's Volunteers would have seen the restoration of St Chad's Church in 1885 and the opening of the Public Baths in 1868, Town Hall in 1871 (its tower destroyed by fire in 1883), Library in 1884, and the Technical School in Nelson Street (1893).

13th The 13th at Southport first appeared in the *Army List* for October 1859 as the 1st Sub-division. In that for the following December the corps is shown as a full company, its officers, Captain William McInroy, Lieutenant George Bretherton and Ensign John A Robinson, holding commissions dated 6 December. Now of two companies, was amalgamated with 54th Corps at Ormskirk in 1880. Later increased to six (four at Southport, two, Ormskirk), and designated 3rd Volunteer Battalion King's (Liverpool Regiment) in 1888. Two more companies were sanctioned in 1899, the personnel being found out of the Mounted Infantry and Cyclist sections. The battalion was disbanded in 1908. Uniform: scarlet/blue.

14th (1859–61) Formed at Edge Hill on 10 November 1859 and known as the 2nd Sub-division until December. Soon comprised two companies, both company commanders, Tyndal Bright and John Brady, holding commissions dated 16 February 1860. Joined the 2nd Admin Battalion and became part of the new 1st Corps in December 1861.

14th (1880–1908) Formed at Bolton on 2nd December 1859 and known as the 3rd Sub-division until numbered as 27th in February 1860 – by now four companies with Major William Gray in command. Increased to six companies in 1861, eight in 1863. Amalgamated with the 82nd Corps at Hindley in 1876, renumbered as 14th in 1880, and designated 2nd Volunteer Battalion Loyal North Lancashire Regiment in 1883. In the same year 'L' and 'M' (Farnworth) Companies of the 4th Corps were transferred to the battalion. Two new companies were sanctioned in 1900 and transfer to the Territorial Force in 1908 was as 5th Battalion Loyal North Lancashire Regiment. Uniform: scarlet/green, changing to scarlet/white in 1883.

15th Formed as four companies at Liverpool on 10 January 1860, a 5th being added in the following November. An interesting article by Mr Dennis Reeves regarding the origins of No. 5 Company appeared in the *Bulletin* of the Military Historical Society for May 2003. In the early days of the Volunteer Movement it was found that members of the press and allied trades, because of their anti-social working hours, were restricted from joining the Volunteers. The answer was to raise a corps composed entirely of such workers, the first steps towards this end being in the form of an advertisement which appeared in the *Liverpool Daily Post* for 28 September 1860 headed 'Liverpool Press Corps of Volunteers'. The item had called for men interested to come forward and enrol at a meeting to be held on the following day. At that meeting, records Dennis Reeves, Mr William Henry Peat, Proprietor of the *Liverpool Daily Times* was elected as chairman with his editor, Mr William Maitland, as one of his Honorary Secretaries. Subsequently a 'No. 1 Press

Company' was enrolled consisting of those employed in newspaper management, printing shop owners and booksellers – there were in this company, 'no working class newspaper printers' (Reeves). The company was sworn in at the Lyceum drill hall at Bold Street on 6 October 1860 and carried out drills at the Seel Street Police Station. The 15th Corps was re-designated 4th Volunteer Battalion King's (Liverpool Regiment) by General Order 81 of March 1888 and transfer to the Territorial Force in 1908 was as 7th Battalion King's (Liverpool Regiment). Uniform: scarlet/blue.

16th (3rd Manchester) Eight companies under the command of Major John Snowdon Henry formed in Manchester as the 40th Lancashire (3rd Manchester) RVC on 29 February 1860. Renumbered as 16th in 1880 and designated 4th Volunteer Battalion Manchester Regiment in 1888, the headquarters at this time being in Burlington Street, Manchester and the strength twelve companies. Transfer to the Territorial Force in 1908 was as 7th Battalion Manchester Regiment. Uniform: scarlet/green, changing to scarlet/white in 1888.

17th (1860–80) Formed as two companies at Burnley on 16 January 1860 with Captains John Dugdale and Henry Moore the first company commanders. Joined the 3rd Admin Battalion, increased to three companies in 1866, four in 1868, and became 'A' to 'D' Companies of the new 3rd Corps in 1880. The chief industry of Burnley during the time of the Volunteers was cotton spinning and weaving. There were also in the area foundries, machine works, quarrying and coal mining.

17th (1880–1908) Formed as the 56th Corps of four companies at Salford on 5 March 1860 with Major George A Hill taking command as of 20 July 1860. Renumbered 17th in 1880 (by now eight companies) and joined the Manchester Regiment as one of its volunteer battalions (without change in title) in 1881. Transferred to the Lancashire Fusiliers as 3rd Volunteer Battalion in March 1886. The Salford Cadet Corps was formed and affiliated to the battalion in 1888, but disbanded in 1891. Some 117 Volunteers served in South Africa, Private A Brown being awarded the Royal Humane Society's First Class Bronze Medal for saving Private A Rogers of the King's Own from drowning in the Buffalo River. Transfer to the Territorial Force in 1908 was as 7th and 8th Battalions Lancashire Fusiliers. Uniform: scarlet/blue, changing to scarlet/white by 1886.

18th (Liverpool Irish) Formed as the 64th Corps at Liverpool on 25 April 1860 with Captain James G Plunket in command. Joined the 2nd Admin Battalion, increased to two companies in June 1860, later four, then six in September 1863. 'Liverpool Irish' was included in the title from 1864. Headquarters about this time are shown in the *Army List* as 9 Everton Crescent, Liverpool, moving later to 206 Netherfield Road North. Renumbered as 18th Corps in 1880 and designated 5th (Irish) Volunteer Battalion King's (Liverpool Regiment) in 1888. In 1900 the battalion was increased to eight companies, but in 1905 one of these was disbanded and replaced by a cyclist company. Transfer to the Territorial Force in 1908 was as 8th Battalion King's. Uniform: green/scarlet, changing to green/green in 1904.

19th (1860–62) Much can be understood regarding the two-year existence of this corps thanks to an article by Mr Dennis Reeves published in the *Bulletin* of the Military Historical Society for February 1972. As a result of a meeting held at the George Hotel, Liverpool by some influential Scots then resident in the city, a resolution was passed that a Scottish corps should be raised; the suggested title being the 'Black Watch Scottish Volunteer Rifles'. Sufficient numbers came forward to form a No. 1 (Lowland) Company, followed quickly by No. 2 (Highland). Temporary headquarters were found in the Liverpool and London Chambers in Dale Street, but soon a house was rented in Great George Square, which served as a combined headquarters and storehouse.

Acceptance by the government came on 10 January 1860, the title allowed in no way reflecting the Scottish origins and simply shown in the *Army List* as 19th Lancashire RVC. A strong corps now of three companies, the company commanders:Captains James Maxwell, G A Mackenzie and James M Dowie, were all sworn in at Seel Street police station within a few days. The 19th Corps was placed into the 2nd Admin and as such were included in the consolidation of that battalion as 5th Corps in 1862; Dennis Reeves noting that the old 19th had now become its 'B' (Scottish) Company.

19th (Liverpool Press Guard) (1880–1908) Formed in Liverpool in January 1861 as the 80th Corps from employees of the newspaper and printing trades – the 2 March edition of the *Illustrated London News* included a full-page engraving showing the corps being sworn in at St George's Hall. The additional title 'Liverpool Press Guard' was added in 1862. For details of the events that led up to the formation of the 80th Corps we must turn to an article published in the *Bulletin* of the Military Historical Society in May 2003 in which Dennis Reeves records how a number of pressmen met in the library of St George's Hall to discuss the formation of a corps. At this time there was already a 'Press' Company in Liverpool but, as the cost of uniform and equipment was in the main beyond the reach of the average print worker, this was confined to the management and press owners. The meeting included Mr George McCorquodale, a printer of 38 Castle Street, who was subsequently to become the Lieutenant Colonel of the 80th Corps. The 80th, its services accepted on 10 January 1861, at first comprised five companies; three more were approved on 19 January. Lieutenant Colonel McCorquodale was a resident of Newton-le-Willows, where men from his printing works had enrolled in the 73rd Lancashire RVC. On 31 March 1863, this corps was incorporated into the 80th as its No. 9 Company. McCorquodale's eldest son Hugh took command. Renumbered 19th in 1880 and designated 6th Volunteer Battalion King's (Liverpool Regiment) in 1888. A cyclist company was added in 1902, but by 1907 one company had been disbanded. Transfer to the Territorial Force in 1908 was as 9th Battalion King's (Liverpool Regiment). Uniform: scarlet/blue.

As a follow-up to Dennis Reeves's article both Garry Gibbs and W Y Carman provided illustrations showing how the Liverpool Press Guard took the latter part of their title seriously. In both we see Grenadier Guard-style scarlet jackets and bearskin headdress, grenade badges, even the buttons on the tunic are arranged as in the senior guards regiment. One item, however, is possibly unique: an early button showing an old printing press.

20th (2nd Manchester) The 33rd Lancashire RVC of four companies formed at Ardwick 28 January 1860. A fifth was soon added and in 1863 the 78th Corps, another Ardwick corps, was absorbed. In 1864 the 28th Corps, known as '2nd Manchester' and with a large number of Irish within its ranks, was also absorbed, the sub-title now taken into use by the 33rd. The overall strength of the corps now stood at fourteen companies. Renumbered 20th in 1880 and designated 5th (Ardwick) Volunteer Battalion, Manchester Regiment in 1888. A cadet corps was formed and affiliated in the same year. An additional company was sanctioned in 1900 and transfer to the Territorial Force in 1908 was as 8th Battalion Manchester Regiment. Uniform: green/scarlet. Mr J W Reddyhoff, writing in the *Bulletin* of the Military Historical Society in November 1997, notes that the East Lancashire Centurion Freemason Lodge No. 2322 was formed from within the battalion on 23 July 1889.

21st (1860–80) Formed as two companies at Wigan on 20 January 1860, its company commanders being Captains Nathaniel Eckersley and Egerton Leigh Wright. Joined the 4th Admin Battalion in 1869. The establishment was increased to five companies during the 1870s, and in 1880 became 'A' to 'E' Companies of the new 4th Corps. Among the several buildings put up in Wigan during the Volunteer period – Borough Courts in 1866, the Arcade, 1872, Library in 1878 – was the Volunteer Drill Hall, which was opened in 1884. In and around the town, cotton mills provided employment, as well as works manufacturing railway wagons, nails, screws and bolts.

21st (1880–1908) Formed in 1880 by the amalgamation of the 47th Corps, raised as five companies at St Helens on 29 February 1860 (Major Commandant David Gambler in command), and the 48th, which was formed as one company at Prescot under Captain Walter Wren Driffield on 15 March 1860. The combined establishment of six companies was later increased to eight. Designated 2nd Volunteer Battalion South Lancashire Regiment in 1886 and transferred to the Territorial Force in 1908 as 5th Battalion South Lancashire Regiment. Uniform: green/scarlet.

22nd (1860–63) Formed as two companies in Liverpool on 30 January 1860 with Captain Commandant Edward Brailsford Bright in command. The corps was included in the 1st Admin Battalion until December 1861, disappearing from the *Army List* in 1863.

22nd (1882–1908) Formed at Oldham on 29 July 1882 by the withdrawal of the Oldham companies from the 7th Corps, the establishment by the end of the year rising to eight companies. Designated 6th Volunteer Battalion Manchester Regiment in 1888; two additional companies were sanctioned in 1900, and transfer to the Territorial Force in 1908 was as 10th Battalion Manchester Regiment. Uniform: scarlet/green, changing to scarlet/white in 1890.

23rd Formed as two companies at Ashton-under-Lyne on 7 February 1860 with Captains John Lees and Ely Andrew in command. Joined the 7th Admin Battalion, the establishment steadily rising to six companies, and became 'A' to 'F' Companies of the new 7th Corps in 1880. Much of Ashton's employment was in collieries and iron foundries.

24th See 12th Corps (1880–1908).

25th Formed in Liverpool on 9 January 1860 with Alexander McNeil as captain, Charles Lee Campbell, lieutenant and Robert Horsfall, ensign. Absorbed into the 8th Lancashire Artillery Volunteers in April 1864. The corps was recruited in the main from the Mersey Ironworks.

26th Formed as three companies at Haigh on 9 February 1860 with John Thompson as Captain Commandant. Disbanded in April 1864. On the Leeds and Liverpool Canal north-east of Wigan, the town had collieries and breweries.

27th See 14th Corps (1880–1908).

28th (2nd Manchester) Formed at Manchester on 21 February 1860, much of the corps was made up of Irishmen living in the area. Absorbed the 70th Corps at Droylesden in 1862, and in 1864 was itself absorbed into the 33rd Corps.

29th Formed as one company at Lytham on 28 January 1860 with George J Lennock as captain, Thomas Fair, lieutenant and William Elsworth Stevenson, ensign. Joined the 3rd Admin Battalion in 1864 and became 'M' Company of the new 3rd Corps in 1880. Lytham lies on the north shore of the estuary of the Ribble. Opened in the town were a cottage hospital in 1871 and the Institute and Lower Gardens Recreation Ground in 1872.

30th Formed at the Preston suburb of Fishwick on 16 January 1860 and absorbed into 11th Corps by the following month.

31st Formed as one company at Oldham on 1 February 1860 with John George Blackburne as captain, Hilton Greaves, lieutenant and William Blackburne, ensign. Joined the 7th Admin Battalion, the establishment steadily rising to six companies, and became 'G', 'H', 'J' and 'K', 'L' and 'M' Companies of the new 7th Corps in 1880. Many in and around Oldham worked in the collieries. The manufacture of gas meters and hats was also important to the town.

32nd (Victoria Rifles) Formed as one company at Liverpool on 28 January 1860 with William Walker as captain, George Henry Garratt, lieutenant and Frederick Allender, ensign. Absorbed into the new 5th Corps in March 1862.

33rd (2nd Manchester) See 20th Corps (1880–1908).

34th None recorded.

35th None recorded.

36th Formed as one company at Accrington on 7 January 1860 with Robert Ellis Green as captain, Walter Watson, lieutenant and John Bullough, ensign. Joined the 3rd Admin Battalion and was absorbed into the 7th Corps in 1861.

37th (North Lonsdale) The 37th Lancashire RVC was formed with the additional title 'North Lonsdale' as a direct result, notes Mr Howard Ripley in an article published in the *Bulletin* of the Military Historical Society in November 1994, of a meeting held at the Assembly Room in Ulverston on 1 December 1859. Here, William Gale, the senior Deputy Lieutenant for Lonsdale North, proposed the formation of a corps drawn from the Ulverston, Dalton, Hawkshead, Broughton, Cartmel and Barrow areas. Official acceptance received, the first commissions were dated 29 February 1860. Although the early *Army Lists* suggest that the towns previously mentioned were to be organized as separate corps, the eventual outcome was to be a single battalion of four companies and two sub-divisions numbered as 37th and with C C Spencer, the Marquis of Hartington as major in command as of 12 July. In April 1861, however, the *London Gazette* announced that the 37th Lancashire was to divide as five individual corps, the 37A, 37B, 37C, 52nd and 53rd. See under those numbers for further information.

37A Formed at Ulverston on 28 February 1860 as a company of the 37th Corps with Captain William George Ainslie in command. Separated as 37A in April 1861 and placed into the 5th Admin Battalion. Became 'C' and 'D' Companies of the new 10th Corps in 1876.

37B Formed at Barrow-in-Furness on 28 February 1860 as a company of the 37th Corps with Captain James Ramsden in command. Separated as 37B in April 1861 and placed into the 5th Admin Battalion. Absorbed the 52nd Corps at Dalton in 1870 and became 'E' and 'F' Companies of the new 10th Corps in 1876. Shipbuilding was the town's main industry. There is a statue to Sir James Ramsden in the town.

37C Formed at Hawkshead on 28 February 1860 as a company of the 37th Corps with Captain William Alcock Beck in command. Separated as 37C in April 1861 and placed into the 5th Admin Battalion. Became 'G' Company of the new 10th Corps in 1876.

38th Formed in the Fairfield area of Liverpool on 20 January 1860 and known as the 1st Sub-division until March. Lieutenant George Frederick Martin was the first officer commissioned. Joined the 1st Admin Battalion and became part of the new 1st Corps in December 1861.

39th An article by Mr D Reeves published in the *Bulletin* of the Military Historical Society in

Bandsmen, 1st Clackmannanshire RVC *c.*1867–74. Dark grey doublets with scarlet collars, cuffs and piping are worn with Murray tartan trews out of compliment to Lord-Lieutenant of Clackmannanshire, Lord Mansfield. The caps are also dark grey and have a red, white and green diced band.

Captain Henry H Williams of the 19th Middlesex RVC, who won the Earl Dudley prize at Wimbledon in 1862. The uniform here is bluish-grey with scarlet collar, cuffs, piping and cap band. At this time officers' rank was indicated by the elaborate decoration of the cuffs. Clearly seen is the corps number '19', but it was not unusual for rifle volunteer corps to display their county precedence ranking on insignia.

Officers' silver pouch-belt ornament and pouch badge of the 1st Volunteer Battalion, Manchester Regiment. A feature of the uniform worn by rifle regiments was the purely decorative belt worn across the chest from the right shoulder, to which was attached, at the rear, a small pouch. These were usually enhanced with whistles attached to chains and fine regimental ornaments at the front, the pouch itself also having some form of badge. Here we see displayed the Sphinx with Egypt below, one of the many battle honours held by the Manchester Regiment. Although, in this case it seems to have gone unnoticed, Rifle Volunteer Corps were not permitted the use of battle honours won by their Regular counterparts.

Shooting team, 3rd London RVC seen here with the Napier Challenge Cup. Scarlet jackets are worn with blue trousers, the collars and cuffs being buff. Crossed rifles Marksman badges are clearly seen on the lower left arm. Note also the man standing, his elaborate shoulder wings indicating that he is a drummer. (Photo courtesy of Richard Hayes)

Hy. Walker

37 West St.
Gateshead.

A photographer's address on a photograph can do much to indentify the unit of the subject shown. Here we have Gateshead, which leads to Durham. The insignia now, which clearly shows the numeral '5' and a light infantry bugle horn collar badge. Surely the 5th Durham RVC which, in 1881 had become a volunteer battalion of the Durham Light Infantry. (Photo courtesy of Richard Hayes)

W C Atkinson of the 1st Durham RVC, winner of the Queen's Prize in 1874. (Photo courtesy of Richard Hayes)

GOSHAWK. Photographer   HARROW

This young rifleman from Harrow School (18th Middlesex RVC) wears on his left arm a horizontal rifle with two four-pointed stars above. The photo dates to around the 1860s, the badge at this time given in *Volunteer Regulations* as an award to a Volunteer that had obtained seven points or more on a range extending to 900 yards. Once more the photographer and badges do much to aid identification – crossed arrows a play on Harrow perhaps. (Photo courtesy of Richard Hayes)

HER MAJESTY'S
REVIEW AT WINDSOR.

ON Saturday next, the 20th of June, 1868, to enable those Officers of the Post Office who are Volunteers to attend the Review, Letters will be delivered in London as follows, viz.:—

At 7.30 a.m.	At 4.10 p.m.
„ 9.30 „	„ 6.10 „
„ 12.10 p.m.	„ 7.30 „
„ 2.10 „	

On the same day Letters will be collected from the Receiving Offices and Pillar Boxes

At 4. 0 a.m.			At 4. 0 a.m.	
„ 8.30 „			„ 8.30 „	
„ 11. 0 „	In the		„ 10.45 „	
„ 1. 0 p.m.	Eastern		„ 12.45 p.m.	In the
„ 3. 0 „	Central and		„ 2.45 „	other
„ 4. 0 „	Western		„ 4.45 „	Districts.
„ 5. 0 „	Central		„ 5.30 „	
„ 5.30 „	Districts.		„ 6. 0 „	
„ 6. 0 „			„ 9. 0 „	
„ 9. 0 „				

By Command of the Postmaster General.

[401]   Printed by W. P. Griffith, 5, Langley Street, Long Acre, W.C.

Notice amending postal collections and deliveries so that the Volunteers could attend a Review in 1868. How did the Victorians manage with just seven deliveries each day? – and a Saturday at that.

Private of the 7th Middlesex (London Scottish) RVC around 1882. In view of the many clans represented by the men of the corps no existing tartan was chosen. Instead a colour called Elcho grey was settled upon for the whole uniform, not so much a grey, but more of a reddish-brown mix devised by the commanding officer Lord Elcho.

Members of the Ambulance Section 1st Volunteer Battalion Buffs (East Kent Regiment). In this first aid demonstration we see how a rifle could be used as a temporary splint. Note also, on two of the men, circular arm badges with the intertwined letters 'SB' (Stretcher Bearer) which indicate that wearer had been issued a certificate of proficiency in ambulance work. (Photo courtesy Alan Seymour)

1st Volunteer Battalion Royal Berkshire Regiment. The leather ammunition bandolier indicates that the wearer is a member of the battalion's Mounted Infantry company. Both the Dragon cap and collar badges are those of the Royal Berkshires and represent the service of that regiment's 1st Battalion (the old 49th Foot) during the China War of 1840–42. (Photo courtesy of Alan Seymour)

Rugby School Cadet Corps. The school cadet corps was affiliated to the 2nd Volunteer Battalion Royal Warwickshire Regiment until its transfer to the OTC in 1908. The uniform worn is scarlet with blue collar and cuffs. In the centre of the helmet plate can be seen the Antelope badge of the Royal Warwicks, while the collar shows the Bear and Ragged Staff device of the Earl of Warwick. This badge was taken into use by the regiment in 1881. The school arms are worn on the left arm and indicate that the wearer was a member of the corps shooting team on the occasion of it winning the Ashburton Shield in 1894.

Private, 4th Volunteer Battalion East Surrey Regiment. Here we have a good example of the stars awarded to Volunteers as an indication that they had been passed as 'Efficient' in rifle drill and practice for a five-year period. One star for every five years, here then we see a Volunteer of at least thirty years' experience.

These Cyclists of the 26th Middlesex RVC show how the rifle was carried on the machine. Here too, in the corporal second from the front, we see a clear example of the shoulder letters and numbers used to identify corps – in this case 26 over Mx. His collar badge is a cycle wheel and the two flags above his chevrons indicate that he is an instructor in signalling. (Photo courtesy of Alan Seymour)

It is always nice to have a named and dated photograph. Here we see Alan Blackburn of the '1st Highland Company'. Once again our photographer's name helps, Edinburgh in this case taking us straight to the Queen's Edinburgh Rifle Volunteer Brigade which had four Highland companies. To the Army List now where we find that Alan Blackburn was commissioned as second lieutenant on 4 May 1889, then as lieutenant on 19 December 1891. (Photo courtesy of Alan Seymour)

Certificate of Service issued to Volunteers at the close of the Volunteer Force on 31 March 1908.

CERTIFICATE
OF
SERVICE

This is to Certify

that *Sergeant John Stott*
served in *2nd V.B. Lancashire Fusiliers* from
the *Twenty second* day of *June* 1884
till the *Thirty first* day of *March* 1908
having served continuously for
Twenty years *two hundred & eighty four* days.

Corps in which service was given

2nd Volunteer Battalion
Lancashire Fusiliers.

Charles J. Burnett LT-GENERAL.
COMMANDING-IN-CHIEF, WESTERN COMMAND.

Campaigns and Medals

Charles J. Burnett LT-GENERAL *Medal*
COMMANDING-IN-CHIEF, WESTERN COMMAND.

Andrew Reid & Compy., Ltd., Grey Street, Newcastle-on-Tyne.

A better study of the Volunteer being used for practice by the stretcher bearers in the earlier photograph. Here we have, from Folkestone, Corporal A R Ames with one of the many prizes he was awarded for rifle shooting.
(Photo courtesy of Alan Seymour)

This unnamed private of the 7th Volunteer Battalion Argyll and Sutherland Highlanders ('A' and 'C' Companies were at Alloa) wears on his right sleeve a diamond-shaped badge (lozenge) indicating that he had been returned as efficient in rifle and other drills. Several corps chose not to wear this distinction, the reasoning being that as all in their ranks were well trained, their efficiency should be taken for granted.

PRESENTATION OF COLOURS TO THE ST. GEORGE'S VOLUNTEERS.

The Volunteers, a feature of almost every edition of the *Illustrated London News*, this issue from the 1860s show the Victorian St George's (11th Middlesex RVC) receiving the Colours of the old St George's Volunteers of 1778 in the grounds of the Duke of York's Royal Military School at Chelsea. Lord Elcho addresses the Colour Party while the mounted CO of the 11th, Colonel the Hon C H Lindsay, looks on.

Detail from a supplement entitled 'The Volunteers in 1887' published by *The Graphic* on 9 July 1887. Here the artist (F Dadd) has included a member of the Naval Volunteers (far left), a Mounted Rifleman (centre) and a representative from an Engineer Volunteer Corps (far right).

ORDERS OF THE DAY,

FOR THE VOLUNTEER REVIEW,
TO BE HELD

IN PONTYPOOL PARK,

ON THE 5th OF SEPTEMBER, 1864.

No. 1.—All volunteers to be on the ground at 1 o'clock, p.m., entering the Park through the Pontymoile Gate, and will pass through the Deer Park and second Gate.

No. 2.—Corps will on their arrival in the inner Park, rendezvous on flags placed for their Battalions as follows:—

ARTILLERY,—*RED*.
1st ADMINISTRATIVE BATTALION,—*WHITE*.
2nd   ,,   ,,   *BLUE*.
2nd PONTYPOOL CORPS,—*RED & WHITE*.

No. 3.—Each Corps will have Inspection Returns made out in triplicate.

No. 4.—The Battalions will be told off and formed on their parades at 1.30, p.m.

No. 5.—Each Volunteer will be provided with 15 Rounds of Blank Ammunition—the Artillery 15 Rounds per Gun.

No. 6.—At 2.15 the Advance will sound, when the several Battalions will take up their respective positions in Brigade, in line of contiguous columns at quarter distance, in Review Order; Artillery on the Right, 1st Administrative Battalion, 2nd Administrative Battalion; 2nd Pontypool Corps on the left. The Bands will be massed thirty paces in the rear of the centre of the Line. The Brigade will await the arrival of the Lord Lieutenant.

No. 7.—The Lord Lieutenant having been saluted, the Brigade will receive its orders from the Assistant Inspector, and march past in open or quarter distance Column, each Battalion being played past by one of its own Bands, who will be careful to take up the time correctly from the Battalion preceding.

No. 8.—At the termination of the Review, the attention of Officers commanding is called to *Art.* 108, *Vol. Regs.* All Volunteers whose Rifles may be loaded must be marched to the reverse flank where their Rifles must be discharged.

No. 9.—Officers commanding Corps are requested not to allow any Volunteer to fall in with the Battalion, who is not, in point of proficiency in drill, fit to do so. Recruits and those above mentioned must fall in on the reverse flank, with an interval of a few paces, and will be inspected either before or after the Review.

BY ORDER,

T. WICKHAM,
Adjutant 1st. Administrative Battalion,
Abergavenny, August 31st, 1864.   *Mon. Rifle Volunteers.*

J. Hiley Morgan, Abergavenny.

'Orders of the Day' for review of Monmouthshire Volunteers at Pontypool Park on 5 September 1864. (Courtesy of Louis Bannon)

Headdress badge of the Tower Hamlets Rifles featuring the White Tower from the Tower of London.

Headdress badge of the 9th Monmouthshire RVC featuring the head of a bulldog.

Colonel Lachlan Mackinnon, appointed commanding officer of the 1st Volunteer Battalion Gordon Highlanders on 10 December 1904, retired 2 November 1906. The colonel wears the Volunteer Officers' Decoration which was instituted in July 1892 for the purpose of rewarding 'efficient and capable' officers who had completed twenty years' service. The award is in silver and gold, suspended from a green ribbon.

1st Northamptonshire RVC. Volunteer corps can often be identified by lettering on the shoulder straps. Sometimes numbers and an abbreviated form of the county name were used: eg 2 over Mx (2nd Middlesex), or as seen in this photograph, 1 over V over NORTHAMPTON in full. The uniform is grey; collar, piping and shoulder identification, scarlet. 'H' and 'I' Companies were at Peterborough.

I ꜰꜱᵗ VOLUNTEER BATT ⁿ.
NORTHUMBERLAND FUSILIERS,
PRIVATE, ON "SENTRY GO".

The caption on this cigarette card clearly identifies the subject. The uniform worn is grey with scarlet collar, shoulder straps, piping, cuffs, Austrian knot cuff-ornament, piping and trouser stripe. The helmet, also grey, is of the 'Home Service' pattern introduced into the British Army in 1878.

PRIVATE — 5th DUMBARTON R.V. 1860 — PRIVATE 6th DUMBARTON R.V. 1861–1864 — SERJEANT 1st A.B. DUMBARTON R.V. 1864–1874 — PRIVATE 1874–1882 — LIEUTENANT 1882–1887 — COLOUR-SERJEANT Review Order 1887–1908
1ST DUMBARTON V.R.C.

Here, in one of Lieutenant General Sir James Moncrieff Grierson's magnificent colour plates, we see the course of uniform changes that affected the Dumbartonshire Rifle Volunteers. On the left, the slate-grey jackets and trousers of the early companies; the sergeant, third from left, wearing the green with scarlet facings introduced to the 1st Administrative Battalion in 1864. Next to him a private of the battalion shows the change of headdress from shako to busby in 1874, the officer to his left having the helmet introduced to the 1st Dumbartonshire RVC in November 1881. The next change would come in 1887 (far right) when the scarlet doublet, yellow facings, glengarry cap and Sutherland pattern trews of the Argyll and Sutherland Highlanders were authorized for wear.

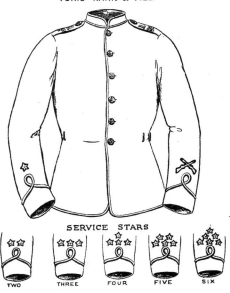

Three illustrations taken from the 1891 edition of *1st London Rifle Volunteer Corps Brigade Rules*. Right: how the numerous Efficiency Stars should be correctly worn on the tunic. Below: front and back diagrams showing the equipment carried in marching order.

SERVICE STARS

TWO	THREE	FOUR	FIVE	SIX

MARCHING ORDER—N.C.O.'s & MEN.

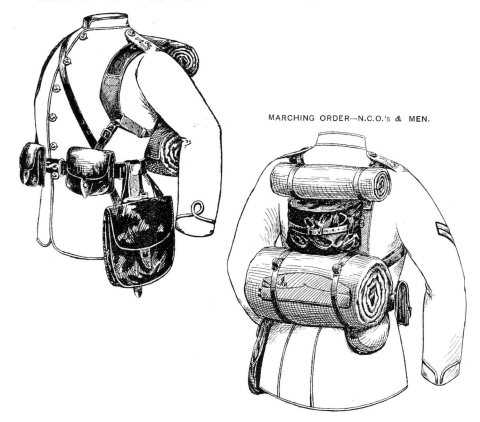

MARCHING ORDER—N.C.O.'s & MEN.

Drill Hall, 'H' Company 4th Volunteer Battalion South Wales Borderers.

L D Greenhalgh, 4th
Volunteer Battalion
Manchester Regiment. The
badges worn on Mr
Greenhalgh's left arm, and
medals on his right breast,
are awards for good
shooting. The five stars on
the right sleeve indicate at
least twenty-five years
service in the Volunteer
Force, twenty years of that
being recognised by the
award of the Volunteer Long
Service Medal (instituted in
1894) seen here on the right.
To its left, the Queen's
medal for service in South
Africa during the Boer War.
(Photo courtesy of Richard Hayes)

Postcard published by W & A K Johnston, Ltd of Edinburgh showing Lieutenant Colonel James Clark of the 9th (Highlanders) Volunteer Battalion Royal Scots. Seen also is a corporal in full marching order, a cap badge and the battalion's headquarters at 7 Wemyss Place, Edinburgh.

Two postcards from a set of six published by the 13th Middlesex (Queen's) RVC, one showing a cyclist of 'T' (Cyclist) Company, the other a member of 'S' (Mounted Infantry) Company.

Comic postcard published by C Modena & Co. By artist Alf Hilton, the card is one from a set of six entitled 'Volunteering'.

Secure Arms.   Shoulder Arms.   Order Arms.   Port Arms.   Present Arms.

A plate from *Rifle Volunteers: How To Organize and Drill Them* by Hans Busk (1815–82). Published in 1859, the book predates any official publication on the subject (the first *Volunteer Regulations* were published in January 1861), this illustration showing from left to right the 'Secure Arms', 'Shoulder Arms', 'Order Arms', 'Port Arms' and 'Present Arms' positions.

Important to the Volunteer were the regular shooting competitions held at such places as Wimbledon and Bisley. Here we see a typical group of Riflemen ready for a session on the ranges.

Note the mixed and informal order of dress – some men in civilian clothing, above, shows Volunteers firing at Wimbledon *c.*1863, while the photographer responsible for the 1873 image below seems to have caught three members of the Westminster Rifles napping during a break in the firing. (Photos courtesy of Ted Molyneux)

February 1974 records how on 16 November 1859 a meeting was held at the Liverpool Institute to discuss the possibilities of forming a corps of Welsh Riflemen in the town. At a second meeting held at the Common Hall on 25 November, a committee was formed to take care of recruitment and fund raising. A uniform of grey with red facings was proposed. The services of the corps as the 39th Lancashire RVC of one company were eventually accepted by the War Office, its appointed officers: Captain William James Griffith, Lieutenant William Henry Lloyd and Ensign Benjamin Gibson, being gazetted on 9 February 1860. Drills soon began at the Welsh School in Russell Street and an additional sub-division was later formed at Everton. The corps maintained its own storehouse at 37 Russell Street and undertook musketry at the Hightown (Altcar) range. Joined the 2nd Admin Battalion and in March 1862 became No. 5 (Welsh) Company of the new 5th Corps.

40th (3rd Manchester) See 16th Corps (1880–1908).

41st Formed as one company at Liverpool on 16 February 1860 with Richard Patchett as captain, John Tyson, lieutenant and Hugh McMonagle, ensign. Disappeared from the *Army List* in February 1864.

42nd Formed as one company at Childwall on 3 March 1860 with Samuel R Graves as captain, Harold Cunningham, lieutenant and Henry C Lucy, ensign. Disbanded in 1870. Childwall is just under five miles east of Liverpool.

43rd Formed at Fallowfield on 11 February 1860 and absorbed into 6th Corps the following year.

44th Formed as one company at Longton on 2 March 1860 with William Naylor as captain, John McKean, lieutenant and Henry Hunt, ensign. Joined the 6th Admin Battalion and absorbed into the 11th Corps in 1866. At Longton, five miles south-west of Preston, many were employed in brewing and malting.

45th Formed in Liverpool on 27 February 1860 with Percy C Dove as captain and Thomas H Bowen, ensign. Joined the 1st Admin Battalion and became part of the new 1st Corps in December 1861.

46th Formed as one company at Swinton on 24 February 1860 with J Bowers as captain, Jonathan Dorking, lieutenant and Thomas Beckton, ensign. Joined the 4th Admin Battalion and at the same time absorbed No. 12 (Eccles) Company of the 6th Corps. Became 'F' and 'G' Companies of the new 4th Corps in 1880. Volunteers in 1869 would have seen the building, on an ancient site of St Peter's Church. At Swinton, four miles north-west of Manchester, many were employed in the manufacture of cotton and bricks.

47th See 21st Corps (1880–1908).

48th See 21st Corps (1880–1908).

49th Formed at Newton-le-Willows on 3 March 1860 with J Hornby Burley as captain, Julius Caesar J Bailey, lieutenant, and Robert Stephenson, ensign. Joined the 9th Admin Battalion in 1865 and became 'G' Company of the new 9th Corps in 1880. As Newton, five miles east of St Helens, a large foundry employed some 750 and a print works more than 500. There were also paper mills, glass works and collieries.

50th None recorded.

51st Formed as one company at Liverpool on 3 March 1860 with Captain George M Corryde Bentley in command. Absorbed the 72nd Corps at Old Swan in 1862 and disappeared from the *Army List* in August 1866.

52nd Formed at Dalton on 28 February 1860 as part of the 37th Corps. Separated as 52nd in April 1861 and placed into the 5th Admin Battalion. Absorbed into 37B Lancashire RVC in 1870.

53rd Formed at Cartmel on 28 February 1860 as part of the 37th Corps. Separated as 53rd in April 1861 and placed into the 5th Admin Battalion. Disbanded in 1875.

54th Formed as one company at Ormskirk on 15 March 1860 with Richard Welsby as captain, J H Pye, lieutenant and Henry Barton Wareing, ensign. Now of two companies, was absorbed into the 13th Corps in 1880.

55th Formed as a sub-division at Leigh on 3 March 1860 with George Edward Jee as lieutenant and Henry Kirkpatrick, ensign. Increased to a full company in June, joined the 4th Admin Battalion in October 1861, and became 'H' Company of the new 4th Corps in 1880. Seven miles south-east of Wigan, Leigh's principal industries were coal mining, cotton mills, brewing and the manufacture of agricultural implements.

56th See 17th Corps (1880–1908).

57th Formed as one company at Ramsbottom on 26 March 1860 with Thomas Greig Stork as captain, James Wild, lieutenant and William Grant McLean, ensign. Joined the 3rd Admin Battalion late in 1861 and became 'K' Company of the new 3rd Corps in 1880. Fourteen miles north of Manchester, the town had iron and brass foundries, machine shops, printing and spinning works.

58th None recorded.

59th Formed as a sub-division at Leyland on 29 February 1860 with J C Morrell as lieutenant and Thomas H Morrell, ensign. Increased to a full company in September 1861, joined the 6th Admin Battalion, and became 'F' Company of the new 11th Corps in 1880. Five miles south of Preston, Leyland is noted in Cassell's *Gazetteer* for 1895 as a centre for the manufacture of india-rubber and gold thread.

60th Formed as one company at Atherton on 6 March 1860 with J P Fletcher as captain, John D Selby, lieutenant and Ralph Fletcher jun, ensign. Joined the 4th Admin Battalion in October 1861 and became 'J' Company of the new 4th Corps in 1880. Thirteen miles south-west of Manchester, Atherton's people were principally employed in cotton mills, collieries and ironworks.

61st Formed as two companies at Chorley on 6 March 1860 with Richard Smethurst and George H Lightoller as captains. Joined the 6th Admin Battalion and was absorbed into the 11th Corps in November 1868. The early Volunteers of the 61st Corps would have seen the restoration work carried out at St Lawrence's Church during 1860–61. On the Leeds and Liverpool Canal, Chorley gave employment to many in its cotton mills, iron foundries, railway wagon works and breweries.

62nd Formed as one company at Clitheroe on 27 March 1860 with William Garnet as captain, Frederick S Leach, lieutenant and Felix W Grimshaw, ensign. Joined the 8th Admin Battalion; a second company was added in December 1873, and became 'J' and 'K' Companies of the new 2nd Corps in 1880. At Clitheroe there were cotton and print works, paper mills, foundries and breweries. There was also a cement works and lime quarries in the area.

63rd Formed at Toxteth Park on 9 April 1860 with Isaac Simm as Captain and James Nuttall, lieutenant. Joined the 2nd Admin Battalion and became part of the new 5th Corps in 1862.

64th See 18th Corps (1880–1908).

65th Formed at Rossall School, Fleetwood, on 27 April 1860 with John H Croad as captain, Arthur D Gill, lieutenant and Edward V Forshall, ensign. An entry in *The Times* dated 16 June 1860 reports the swearing-in of the first members of the 65th. The corps was formed by masters and senior boys of Rossall School and the paper noted that this was the first instance of a large public school enrolling under the provisions of the Volunteer Act. The 65th joined the 5th Admin Battalion in 1863 and in 1873 a cadet corps was formed by the junior boys. Became 'H' Company of the new 10th Corps in 1876.

66th Formed in Liverpool on 25 April 1860 with Captain Joseph Mayer in command. Joined the 1st Admin Battalion and became part of the new 1st Corps in December 1861.

67th Formed as one company at Worsley on 7 May 1860 with Nathaniel Topp as captain, John N K Grover, lieutenant and Peter Ramsbotham jun, ensign. Joined the 4th Admin Battalion and became 'K' Company of the new 4th Corps in 1880. The town, seven miles from Manchester, is on the Bridgewater Canal. On the London & North Western Railway, Worsley Station was opened in September 1864.

68th Formed at Liverpool on 31 May 1860 with Captain William G Bradley in command. Joined the 2nd Admin Battalion and became part of the new 5th Corps in 1862.

69th Formed in Liverpool on 31 May 1860 with Henry Tristian as captain, Charles V Macarthy, lieutenant and John Archer, ensign. Joined the 1st Admin Battalion and became part of the new 1st Corps in December 1861.

70th Formed at Droylesden on 5 May 1860 and absorbed into the 28th Corps in 1862.

71st (Liverpool Highland) Dennis Reeves in an article published by the Military Historical Society in February 1972 notes that the 71st Corps was formed in Liverpool mainly from ex-members of No. 2 Company of the 19th (Liverpool Scottish Rifles). The first officer, Captain John Scott's commission was dated 24 May 1860. This one company corps, which was also known as the 'Liverpool Highland', joined the 2nd Admin Battalion and in January 1862 was increased to two companies when the Scottish element of the 79th Corps was absorbed. The 71st was not included when the 2nd Admin Battalion was consolidated as 5th Corps in March 1862, choosing instead to remain independent. Declining numbers, however, saw the corps disbanded in June 1863.

72nd Formed as one company at Old Swan, Liverpool on 8 June 1860 with Charles A J McBride as captain, Richard S Harding, lieutenant and Thomas Varty, ensign. Absorbed into the 51st Corps in 1862.

73rd Formed at Newton on 8 June 1860 from workers at McCorquodale's Print Works. Absorbed into the 80th Corps as its No. 9 Company on 31 March 1863. A number of the McCorquodale family were officers in the corps.

74th Formed in Liverpool on 2 July 1860 and absorbed into the new 1st Corps in 1862.

75th Formed at Broughton-in-Furness on 28 August 1860 but was removed from the *Army List* in February of the following year. The corps returns in April 1861, however, and is now shown as part of the 5th Admin Battalion. The 75th was eventually disbanded in 1875.

76th Formed as one company at Farnworth on 3 July 1860 with Alfred Barnes as captain, Alfred Topp, lieutenant and Thomas Kershaw, ensign. Joined the 4th Admin Battalion, increased to two companies in 1877, and became 'L' and 'M' Companies of the new 4th Corps in 1880. On the road from Bolton to Manchester, Farnworth gave employment in its paper mills, iron foundries, cotton mills, collieries and brickworks.

77th Formed as one company at Widnes on 1 October 1860 with John Knight as captain, James Hallows, lieutenant and Reginald Young, ensign. Disappeared from the *Army List* in August 1863. At Widnes there were iron foundries, chemical and locomotive works.

78th (4th Manchester) Dennis Reeves, in an article published by the Military Historical Society in February 1977, records how on 15 October 1859 a letter appeared in the *Manchester Guardian* suggesting the formation of a local Scottish Volunteer Rifle Corps. In consequence, the first members to enrol met for their first drill at the large hall above 37 Corporation Street on Saturday 10 December 1859. Known unofficially as the 'Manchester Scottish', this corps by now comprising two companies, subsequently joined a new unit at Alnwick titled 78th Lancashire (4th Manchester) RVC. Acceptance of its services being notified in the *Manchester Guardian* on 25 September 1860, headquarters of the 78th were placed at 4 Kennedy Street. With a strength of six companies the corps was incorporated into the 33rd Corps in 1863.

79th Formed as three companies in Liverpool on 16 February 1861, the company commanders being James Cuthbert, John Rogers and Robert Lamont. Absorbed into the new 5th Corps in March 1862.

80th See 19th Corps (1880–1908)

81st Formed as a sub-division at Withnell on 20 February 1861 with John A Parke as lieutenant and George Hoult, ensign. Included in 2nd Admin Battalion for a short time, but attached to the 2nd Corps by the end of 1861. Increased to a full company in March 1863 and joined the 8th Admin Battalion in July 1864. Headquarters were transferred to Wheelton in the same year, and in 1876 the corps was disbanded. Withnell is five miles south-west of Blackburn and had cotton, paper and bleaching mills. Wheelton, just to the south-west of Withnell, had similar industries.

82nd Formed as one company at Hindley, just under three miles from Wigan, on 14 June 1861 with John Johnson as captain, J B Latham, lieutenant and Thomas Southwark, ensign. Amalgamated with the 27th Corps as 27th in 1876. The town employed many in its coal mines, ironworks and cotton mills.

83rd Formed as one company at Knowsley on 11 February 1861 with Captain H R Whistler in command. Disappeared from the *Army List* in December 1872. North-west of Prescot, the town of Knowsley erected a memorial in memory of the 14th Earl of Derby (died 1869) in 1871, Knowsley Hall being the seat of the Stanleys since the reign of Richard II.

84th Formed as one company at Padiham on 18 February 1861 with James Dugdale jun as captain, Edward Sutcliffe, lieutenant and J Bury Haworth, ensign. Joined the 3rd Admin Battalion and became 'E' Company of the new 3rd Corps in 1880. On the Calder, three miles from Burnley on the road to Clitheroe, Padiham's main employer was the cotton trade. Its station was opened by the old Lancashire & Yorkshire Railway in October 1877.

85th None recorded.

86th It was at a meeting held at Liverpool's Custom House on 23 November 1860 that a decision was taken to form a corps of riflemen from within the Civil Service. Known at first as the 'Civil Service Rifle Corps', but by most as the 'Customs Corps', the two companies sanctioned by the War Office were given the title of 86th Lancashire RVC. Captain Commandant Jeremiah C Johnstone received a commission dated 18 May 1861. Joined the 2nd Admin Battalion and became part of the new 5th Corps in 1862.

87th Formed at Nelson on 7 February 1862. Joined the 3rd Admin Battalion, but disappeared from the *Army List* in June 1865.

88th Formed as one company at Haslingden on 27 February 1863 with George William L Schofield as captain, Abraham Haworth, lieutenant and J T Stott, ensign. Joined the 3rd Admin Battalion and became 'J' Company of the new 3rd Corps in 1880. Seven miles from Blackburn, two of the town's churches were built during the Volunteer period: St Stephen's in 1867 and St John the Evangelist in 1886. Cotton mills were the main employers; there were also collieries, ironworks and quarries in the area.

89th None recorded.

90th Formed at Fleetwood on 3 June 1868. Joined the 3rd Admin Battalion and was disbanded in 1870.

91st Formed as one company at Flixton on 14 August 1872 with Adam Stott as captain. Joined the 4th Admin Battalion and became 'N' Company of the new 4th Corps in 1880. Flixton is seven miles from Manchester; Cassell's *Gazetteer* for 1895 noting that 'in the town is a Volunteer Drill Hall, which is also used for public assembles, and is capable of accommodating 500 persons.'

2nd Volunteer Battalion King's Own (Royal Lancaster Regiment) Formed from the 1st Volunteer Battalion in 1900. Headquarters were placed at Lancaster and there were six companies located: 'A' to 'D' in Lancaster; 'E' Morecambe and 'F' Grange. Transfer to the Territorial Force in 1908 was as 5th Battalion King's Own. Uniform: scarlet/blue.

8th (Scottish) Volunteer Battalion King's (Liverpool Regiment) Mr David A Rutter writing in the *Bulletin* of the Military Historical Society in May 1978, noted that the idea of a Scottish Volunteer Corps in Liverpool was suggested in a letter signed 'G Forbes Milne', which appeared in the press on 27 January 1900. Lord Balfour subsequently headed the committee formed to see this through – permission to raise the proposed unit coming from the War Office on 30 April 1900. Enrolment in the 8th (Scottish) Volunteer Battalion King's (Liverpool Regiment) began in the following November, Major C Forbes-Bell becoming commanding officer (commission dated 10 October), Captain J C Robertson, late of the West India Regiment his Adjutant. Eight companies were sanctioned, but it would seem that just four were in existence by the end of the year. In 1902 Lieutenant John Watson and twenty-one other ranks sailed for South Africa, where they were to serve alongside of the 1st Battalion Gordon Highlanders. Also from the battalion, but serving with the Imperial Yeomanry, was Lieutenant John Anderson Bingham, who died from wounds received at De Hook on 11 February 1902. At home, the strength of the battalion had grown to the required eight companies and a new drill hall had been opened at 7 Fraser Street. Transfer to the Territorial Force in 1908 was as 10th (Scottish) Battalion, King's (Liverpool Regiment). Uniform: khaki/scarlet.

1st Cadet Battalion King's (Liverpool Regiment) Formed in January 1890 with headquarters at the Gordon Institute in Stanley Road, Liverpool. Amalgamated with 2nd Cadet Battalion King's in 1904. Uniform: scarlet /blue.

2nd Cadet Battalion King's (Liverpool Regiment) Formed in 1902 and amalgamated with the 1st Cadet Battalion King's in 1904.

1st Cadet Battalion Manchester Regiment Formed in February 1889 with A P Ledward as Hon Major. Headquarters were at Tongue Street, Manchester and the uniform worn was scarlet/white.

LEICESTERSHIRE

All corps formed within the county joined the 1st Admin Battalion, which in 1880 provided the new 1st Corps.

1st (1859–80) Formed as one company at Leicester with Captain Mansfield Turner commissioned on 31 August 1859. Ensign Samuel Harris was gazetted on the following 5 September, then Lieutenant Alfred Donisthorpe on 1 March 1860. Became 'A' Company of the new 1st Corps in 1880. Opened in Leicester in 1877 was the Opera House, the Public Baths in 1879, Post Office in 1887 and Prince of Wales's Theatre three years after that. The main industries of the town noted in the 1890s were the manufacture of boots, shoes, elastic webbing, hats and cigars.

1st (1880–1908) The 1st Admin Battalion of Leicestershire Rifle Volunteers was formed with headquarters at Leicester in July 1860 and consolidated as the new 1st Corps with eleven companies in 1880:

> 'A' Leicester (late 1st Corps)
> 'B' Belvoir (late 2nd Corps)
> 'C' Melton Mowbray (late 3rd Corps)
> 'D' and 'E' Leicester (late 4th Corps)
> 'F' and 'G' Leicester (late 5th Corps)
> 'H' Loughborough (late 6th Corps)
> 'J' Ashby de la Zouch (late 8th Corps)
> 'K' Leicester (late 9th Corps)
> 'L' Hinckley (late 10th Corps)

A new company was raised at Market Harborough in 1882 and in the following year General Order 14 of February directed that the 1st Corps was to be re-designated as 1st Volunteer Battalion Leicestershire Regiment. Further increases in establishment saw new companies added, two at Leicester and one each at Wigston and Mountsorrel in 1900. Volunteers from the battalion served in South Africa alongside the Regulars of the Leicestershire Regiment and saw action at Laing's Nek, Belfont and in the operations around Lydenberg. General Buller noted in his dispatches the effective handling by the Volunteers of the Boers in the Crocodile Valley on 4 September 1900. Casualties numbered four killed and four wounded. Transfer to the Territorial Force in 1908 was as 4th Battalion (formed by the Leicester and Wigston personnel) and 5th Battalion (formed by the remainder less the Belvoir Company, which was disbanded) of the Leicestershire Regiment. Uniform: scarlet/white.

2nd Formed as one company at Belvoir with William Earle Welby as captain, George Gordon, lieutenant and George Gillett, ensign. All three held commissions dated 13 February 1860. Became 'B' Company of the new 1st Corps in 1880. Belvoir, in the Vale of Belvoir and close to the

Grantham Canal, is seven miles south-west of Grantham. Its castle, the seat of the Duke of Rutland, looks down on the area from the south side of the valley.

3rd Formed as one company at Melton Mowbray on 2 March 1860 with Edward H M Clarke as captain, George Marriott, lieutenant, Frederick J Oldham, ensign and Nathanial Whitchurch, who was appointed as surgeon. Became 'C' Company of the new 1st Corps in 1880. The town is just over thirteen miles north-east of Leicester, its pork pies as well known to the Volunteer as they are to us today.

4th Formed as one company at Leicester with George Henry Hodges commissioned as captain on 4 March 1860. He was later joined by Lieutenant George Bankart and Ensign Thomas Wood Cox, who were both gazetted on 9th April. Increased to two companies in November 1863 and became 'D' and 'E' Companies of the new 1st Corps in 1880. Much restoration work was done on Leicester's churches during the time of the Volunteers: St Mary's, originally the castle chapel, in 1861; St Martin's got a new spire in 1867; All Saints' was an almost three-year job during 1875–77; St Nicholas's in 1876 and again in 1889. After drill, or perhaps work in one of Leicester's many boot and shoe factories, a thirsty rifleman could get a drink at the Blue Boar Inn in Highcross Street, where Richard III passed the night before the battle of Bosworth.

5th Formed as one company at Leicester with Robert Brewin as captain, Joshua T Wordsworth, lieutenant and Charles S Smith, ensign. All three officers held commissions dated 3 March 1860. Increased to two companies in 1879 and became 'F' and 'G' Companies of the new 1st Corps in 1880.

6th Formed as one company at Loughborough with Edward Warner commissioned as captain on 7 July 1860. He was later joined by Lieutenant John H Eddowes, Ensign Isaac B Dobell and Surgeon William G Palmer, all three being gazetted on 1st August 1860. Became 'H' Company of the new 1st Corps in 1880. Loughborough made locomotives for the railway and bells for the church. 'Great Paul', now in St Paul's Cathedral and the largest bell in Britain, was cast at Taylor's, Loughborough in 1881.

7th Formed as a sub-division at Lutterworth with Theophilus J Levett commissioned as lieutenant on 6 October 1860. He was later joined by Ensign Arthur W Arkwright (gazetted 18 October) and Charles Bond MD, who was appointed surgeon to the corps in November 1860. During the next five years sufficient recruits had enrolled and in consequence 7th Leicestershire became a full company in 1866. Interest later diminished, however, and the corps was disbanded in 1873. Lutterworth is about eight miles north-east of Rugby and sits on the slope of a hill descending down to the River Swift. St Mary's Church, with its lofty tower, was restored there in 1869; Lutterworth Station, on the old Great Central Railway, thirty years after that.

8th Formed as one company at Ashby de la Zouch with Alexander Hadden as captain, Henry E Smith, lieutenant and Thomas Fisher, ensign. All three were commissioned on 16 September 1860. The Revd John Denton looked after the men's spiritual welfare, as chaplain, while surgeon Percy Dicken saw to their medical needs. Became 'J' Company of the new 1st Corps in 1880. At Ashby de la Zouch, sixteen miles north-west of Leicester, there were many coal mines, the Moira Colliery being one of the biggest. St Helen's Church saw restoration in 1880, Holy Trinity in 1885. The Volunteer wishing to relieve his rheumatism would no doubt have been a regular visitor to the Ivanhoe Baths, whose mineral waters were considered to be most beneficial. Ashby de la Zouch, the setting, of course, in Walter Scott's *Ivanhoe* for the great tournament in which Richard the Lionheart fights with Ivanhoe and Robin Hood takes the honours in the archery.

9th Formed as one company at Leicester with George Clarke Bellairs as captain, Edgar Franklin Cooper, lieutenant and Thomas Edmund Paget, ensign. All three held commissions dated 24 December 1860. Became 'K' Company of the new 1st Corps in 1880.

10th Formed as one company at Hinckley with William Brookes as captain, James H Ward, lieutenant and John C D D Cotman, ensign. All three held commissions dated 27 November 1860. Became 'L' Company of the new 1st Corps in 1880. Hinckley is twelve miles south-west of Leicester. The Volunteer attending St Mary's Church would have seen the restoration that went on there in 1875 and for some years after that; and in Station Road enjoyed the Free Library, which was opened in 1888. Work for him could have been connected with the production of Hinckley's famous coarse cotton stockings, or perhaps in one or other of the many boot and shoe factories that gave employment in and around the town.

LINCOLNSHIRE

The county formed three admin battalions, of which the 3rd was later broken up. It had been formed at Boston on 6 July 1860 and included the 4th, 13th, 14th, 16th and 17th Corps. The 1st and 2nd were to provide the new 1st and 2nd Corps in 1880. There also existed a 1st Sub-division, see 2nd Corps (1859–80) and 12th Corps.

1st (1859–80) Formed at Lincoln on 26 October 1859 with Weston C Amcotts in command and joined the 1st Admin Battalion. A report in the 18 January 1861 issue of the *Illustrated London News* refers to an event that took place on the previous 29 December which saw 'three companies' of the 1st Lincolnshire RVC form up on the iced-over River Witham wearing skates and in perfect order skated off several miles downriver. Became 'A', 'B' and 'C' Companies of the new 1st Corps in 1880. Ian Becket in *Riflemen Form* notes that three of Lincoln's largest employers – Clayton, Shuttleworth & Co. at Stamp End Iron Works; Ruston, Proctor & Co., of the Sheaf Iron Works, and Robey & Co. of the Perseverance Iron Works – encourage their employees to join by offering to supply uniforms at a repayment of 1s 6d weekly. Both Joseph Shuttleworth and Nathaniel Clayton became officers, and looking from the front like a castle, the Rifle Drill Hall was presented by Joseph Ruston and opened in the 1890.

1st (1880–1908) Formed with headquarters at Lincoln on 15 May 1860, the 1st Admin Battalion included the 1st, 2nd, 6th, 7th, 9th, 11th, 12th, 19th and 20th Corps. The battalion was consolidated as the new 1st Corps in 1880 with eleven companies:

'A', 'B','C' Lincoln (late 1st Corps)
'D' Louth (late 2nd Corps)
'E' Great Grimsby (late 6th Corps)
'F' Spilsby (late 7th Corps)
'G' Horncastle (late 9th Corps)
'H' Alford (late 11th Corps)
'I' Barton (late 12th Corps)
'J' Gainsborough (late 19th Corps)
'K' Market Rasen (late 20th Corps)

The headquarters of 'K' Company had moved to Frodingham by 1881. General Order 63 of May 1882 directed a change in designation to 1st Volunteer Battalion Lincolnshire Regiment. In June 1900 the establishment of the battalion was reduced to seven companies: 'A' to 'D' at Lincoln; 'E' and 'F.' Gainsborough, 'G' Horncastle, the remainder of the strength going to form the 3rd Volunteer Battalion Lincolnshire Regiment. Lincoln Grammar School Cadet Corps was formed and affiliated in 1903. Transfer to the Territorial Force in 1908 saw the Lincoln and Horncastle Companies as part of the 4th Battalion Lincolnshire Regiment while the Gainsborough personnel joined the 5th. Uniform: scarlet/yellow, changing to scarlet/white by 1885.

2nd (1859–80) Formed at Louth on 21 November 1859 with William Henry Smyth as captain, William Chaplain, lieutenant and William Thomas Kime, ensign. Known as the 1st Sub-division until January 1860, joined the 1st Admin Battalion, and became 'D' Company of the new 1st Corps in 1880. On the River Lud, to the north-east of Lincoln, Louth's Market Hall was opened in 1867, its St James's Church restored in 1868. Iron foundries, breweries and a rope-making works gave employment.

2nd (1880–1908) Formed with headquarters at Grantham on 21 May 1860, the 2nd Admin Battalion included the 3rd, 5th, 8th, 15th and 18th Corps; the 4th, 13th, 16th and 17th being added upon the break-up of 3rd Admin in 1862. The battalion was consolidated as the new 2nd Corps in 1880 with eight companies:

'A', 'B' Grantham (late 3rd Corps)
'C' Boston (late 4th Corps)
'D' Stamford late 5th Corps)
'E' Sleaford (late 8th Corps)
'F' Spalding (late 13th Corps)
'G' Gosberton (late 17th Corps)
'H' Billingborough (late 18th Corps)

Re-designation as 2nd Volunteer Battalion Lincolnshire Regiment was notified in General Order 63 of 1883. King's School, Grantham Cadet Corps was formed and affiliated in 1904. Transfer to the Territorial Force in 1908 was as part of 4th Battalion Lincolnshire Regiment. King's School at the same time became part of the OTC. Uniform: scarlet/blue.

3rd Formed as two companies at Grantham on 28 February 1860 with William Earle Welby and Charles J B Parker as company commanders. Joined the 2nd Admin Battalion and became 'A' and 'B' Companies of the new 2nd Corps in 1880. The Victorian restoration of St Wulfram's church spanned the years 1866 to 1870. A hospital was opened on the Manthorpe Road in 1875; the theatre burnt down in 1888. There were paper mills in the town, tanneries and a business manufacturing carriages.

4th Formed as one company at Boston on 9 February 1860 with Frederick L Hopkins as captain, Thomas Wright, lieutenant and William Gee, ensign. Joined the 3rd Admin Battalion, transferring to 2nd in 1862, and became 'C' Company of the new 2nd Corps in 1880. In Boston, agricultural implements and rope were made; there was also brewing, tanning, brickfields and a deep-sea fishing company.

5th Formed as one company at Stamford on 14 February 1860 with Richard Cautley, late of the Bengal Army, as captain, Robert N Newcomb, lieutenant and J Phillips jun, ensign. Joined the 2nd Admin Battalion and became 'D' Company of the new 2nd Corps in 1880. Just under thirteen miles north-west of Peterborough, Stamford had a large works building carts and road wagons.

6th Formed as one company at Great Grimsby on 20 March 1860 with William H Daubney as captain, Peter K Seddon, lieutenant and Richard J Nainby, ensign. Joined the 1st Admin Battalion and became 'E' Company of the new 1st Corps in 1880. At Grimsby during the Volunteer period the Custom House was opened in 1873, Church of St John the Devine in Albion Street in 1892, and the Prince of Wales's Theatre in 1886. A bronze statue of Prince Albert was unveiled in front of the Royal Hotel in 1879.

7th Formed as one company at Spilsby on 17 March 1860 with Henry Hollway as captain, Harwood Makinder, lieutenant and John W Preston, ensign. Joined the 1st Admin Battalion and became 'F' Company of the new 1st Corps in 1880. The railway came to the town when the Spilsby & Firsby line was opened in May 1868.

8th Formed as one company at Sleaford on 23 February 1860 with A Wilson as captain, Henry Peacock, lieutenant and Bruce Tomlinson, ensign. Joined the 2nd Admin Battalion and became 'E' Company of the new 2nd Corps in 1880. Sleaford is eighteen miles south of Lincoln.

9th Formed as one company at Horncastle on 22 March 1860 with Henry F Conington as captain, Richard Clitherow, lieutenant and Robert Jalland, ensign. Joined the 1st Admin Battalion and became 'G' Company of the new 1st Corps in 1880. Horncastle is twenty-one miles east of Lincoln.

10th None recorded.

11th Formed as one company at Alford on 23 February 1860 with John Samuel Lister as captain, Augustus Laurent, lieutenant and John Higgins jun, ensign. Joined the 1st Admin Battalion and became 'H' Company of the new 1st Corps in 1880. The Church of St Wilfrid underwent much restoration in 1869, people from the town being mainly employed in the making of bricks, rope and iron.

12th Formed at Barton-on-Humber on 12 January 1860, with George Charles Uppleby as lieutenant and John Stephenson, ensign, and known as the 1st Sub-division until March. Joined the 1st Admin Battalion and became 'I' Company of the new 1st Corps in 1880. At Barton, six miles south-west of Hull, there were rope, brick and title manufacturers.

13th Formed as one company at Spalding on 28 February 1860 with T Hilliam as captain, F T Selby, lieutenant and Ashley Maples, ensign. Joined the 3rd Admin Battalion, transferring to the 2nd in 1862, and became 'F' Company of the new 2nd Corps in 1880. Much work involving Spalding's churches went on during the Volunteer period: St Mary and St Nicholas, restored in 1865; St John's opened in 1873; St Peter's in 1875; the Catholic church in Henrietta Street, built in 1876 then enlarged in 1879.

14th Formed at Swineshead, seven miles south-west of Boston, on 6 March 1860 with John Cooper jun as lieutenant and Frederick H Bate, ensign. Joined the 3rd Admin Battalion and disbanded in 1861.

15th Formed as one company at Bourne on 23 April 1860 with J Compton Lawrence as captain, Edward Hardwicke, lieutenant and John Thomas Pawlett, ensign. Joined the 2nd Admin Battalion and disbanded in 1873.

16th Formed at Holbeach on 20 March 1860 with William S Clark as lieutenant. Joined the 3rd Admin Battalion, transferring to the 2nd in 1862. Disbanded later and last seen in the *Army List* for November 1871. Holbeach is just under eight miles from Spalding.

17th Formed as one company at Donington on 17 March 1860 with Richard G Calthrop as captain, John Holland, lieutenant and George Casswell, ensign. Joined the 3rd Admin Battalion, transferring to the 2nd Admin in 1862. Moved to Gosberton, just to the south-east, in 1876 and became 'G' Company of the new 2nd Corps in 1880. Both Donington Road and Gosberton stations were opened by the Great Northern & Great Eastern Joint Railway in March 1882.

18th Formed as one company at Folkingham on 13 March 1860 with Henry Smith as captain, William Emerson Chapman, lieutenant and William Cragg, ensign. Joined the 2nd Admin Battalion, moved three miles east at Billingborough in 1872, and became 'H' Company of the new 2nd Corps in 1880. Folkingham is twelve miles south-east of Grantham.

19th Formed as one company at Gainsborough on 10 July 1860 with John E Saunders as captain, Francis Gamble jun, lieutenant and Thomas H Oldman, ensign. Joined the 1st Admin Battalion and became 'J' Company of the new 1st Corps in 1880. At Gainsborough, fifteen miles north-west of Lincoln, Holy Trinity Church was enlarged in 1864, St John's opened in 1882, the Town Hall and Market Place ten years after that.

20th Formed at Market Rasen on 16 July 1860 with John Brown as lieutenant and William Goodson, ensign. Joined the 1st Admin Battalion and became 'K' Company of the new 1st Corps in 1880. To the north-east of Lincoln, brewing gave employment at Market Rasen.

3rd Volunteer Battalion Lincolnshire Regiment Formed with headquarters at Grimsby in June 1900 by the withdrawal from 1st Volunteer Battalion of its Louth, Grimsby, Spilsby, Alford, Barton and Frodingham companies. The King Edward VI Grammar School Cadet Corps at Louth was formed and affiliated in 1905, followed by Grimsby Municipal College Cadet Corps in 1906. Transfer to the Territorial Force in 1908 was as part of 5th Battalion Lincolnshire Regiment. Both King Edward VI and Grimsby Schools at the same time joined the OTC. Uniform: scarlet/white.

LINLITHGOWSHIRE

All rifle corps in the county joined the 1st Admin Battalion, which in 1880 became the new 1st Corps.

1st (1860–80) Formed as one company at Linlithgow with Robert H J Stewart as captain, Thomas Chalmers, lieutenant and Adam Dawson jun, ensign. All three held commissions dated 19 March 1860. Became 'A' Company of the new 1st Corps in 1880. The town sits on the Avon about eight miles east of Falkirk. At St Michael's Church, where James IV had a vision warning him against his journey to England, restoration went on in 1894–95, and before that a new Free church was opened in 1874. The Victoria and Jubilee Town Hall replaced a former building in 1888.

1st (1880–1908) The 1st Admin Battalion of Linlithgowshire Rifle Volunteers was formed with headquarters at Linlithgow towards the end of 1862. Captain Robert H J Stewart from the 1st Corps was appointed as Major in command and gazetted on 21 October 1862. Consolidation in March 1880 was as the new 1st Corps with seven companies:

'A' Linlithgow (late 1st Corps)
'B' Bo'ness (late 2nd Corps)
'C' Torphichen (late 3rd Corps)

'D' Bathgate (late 4th Corps)
'E' Uphall (late 5th Corps)
'F' Addiewell (late half company of 6th Corps)
'G' West Calder (late 6th Corps)

In 1881 the headquarters of 'C' Company moved to Armadale and in 1888, under General Order 144 of April, the 1st Linlithgowshire RVC was re-designated as 8th Volunteer Battalion Royal Scots. 'H' Company was added at South Queensferry and 'I' at Kirkliston in 1900 and 'F' Company moved to Fauldhouse the same year. 'H' Company was disbanded in 1906 and at same time 'I' was relettered as 'H'. The battalion, which returned a strength of 740 all ranks in 1907, transferred to the Territorial Force in 1908 as the 10th Battalion Royal Scots. Uniform: green/scarlet.

2nd Formed as one company at Bo'ness, the original officers, Captain William Wilson, Lieutenant Patrick Turnbull and Ensign John Begg, all commissioned on 19 March 1860. In the following May they were joined by William Murray, who became surgeon to the corps. Increased to one-and-a-half companies in 1866 and became 'B' Company of the new 1st Corps in 1880. Bo'ness, or to give the place its full name, Borrowstounness, is a seaport on the Firth of Forth. It produced coal, iron, bricks, salt and soap and there were shipbuilding yards, malthouses and distilleries.

3rd Formed as one company at Bathgate with Andrew Gillon as captain, William McKininlay, lieutenant and David Simpson, ensign. All three held commissions dated 25 April 1860 and joining them in May was James Longmuir, who became surgeon. Headquarters moved to Torphichen in 1864 and became 'C' Company of the new 1st Corps in 1880. Seventeen miles south-west of Edinburgh, Bathgate produced coal, iron, lime and paraffin as well as carrying on a large trade in corn and cattle. Torphichen is about a mile north of Bathgate and also had a brick and tile works, and paper mill.

4th Formed as one company at Bathgate mainly from employees of Young's Chemical Works. James Young jun became captain, Alex C Kirk his lieutenant and Alex Birnie, ensign. All three held commissions dated 9 August 1862. Became 'D' Company of the new 1st Corps in 1880. A major employer in the area, James Young had invented paraffin, extended his works out to nearby Addiewell and became the world's first oil tycoon.

5th Formed as one company at Uphall on 28 January 1870 and became 'E' Company of the new 1st Corps in 1880. Uphall, eleven miles west of Edinburgh on the road that runs to Glasgow, had several shale works which gave employment to many from the area. Uphall Station, on the old North British line, was opened in August 1865.

6th Formed at West Calder as one company and a sub-division with Captain John Calderwood in command. His commission was dated 17 April 1878, those of his four junior officers, 1 May 1878. Became 'F' and 'G' Companies of the new 1st Corps in 1880, 'G' being found by the sub-division. West Calder is just under sixteen miles south-west of Edinburgh, its church being built in 1880. The area gave employment in the production of coal, iron, shale and limestone.

LONDON

1st (City of London Rifle Volunteer Brigade) Formed as a result of an inaugural meeting convened by the Lord Mayor held on 23 July 1859; Richards, in *His Majesty's Territorial Army*, noting that within a week some 1,200 had enrolled. The first officers' commissions were dated 14 December 1859, by which time recruiting had reached in excess of 1,800 – the men forming two battalions each of eight companies. HRH Field Marshal the Duke of Cambridge became honorary colonel, George Montagu Hicks, a former officer on the 41st Regiment of Foot and Governor of Whitecross Street Prison, commanding officer. The corps occupied several headquarters: 17 Finsbury Place South, EC2; later 48 Finsbury Pavement, EC2, and after that, 130 Bunhill Row, EC1. Absorbed the 12th Tower Hamlets RVC at Stoke Newington in 1870 and became a volunteer battalion (without change of title) of the King's Royal Rifle Corps in 1881. After the Boer War the strength of the brigade fell off resulting in a reduction in establishment, first to ten, then to eight companies – in the last year of the Volunteer Force (1907) a strength of just 489 out of an establishment of 928 was returned. Transfer to the Territorial Force in 1908 was as 5th Battalion London Regiment. Uniform: green/green.

The first mention of a cadet corps having been formed within the brigade was in the *Army List* for May 1877. There was, however, a unit formed as early as 1860, which according to one source had a strength of 400 boys. Included in the *c*.1860 cadet unit were boys from the Merchant Taylors, City of London, University College and King's College School, and in 1900 these school corps are shown in the *Army List* by name for the first time. By 1902 the schools, together with the 1877 unit, appear under the heading of 1st City of London Cadet Corps with a total establishment of five companies. Became part of the OTC in 1908.

2nd Formed 16 May 1860 from employees of the newspaper and printing trade – much of the corps was made up of workers at the *Daily Mail* and the printing firms of Messrs Eyre and Spottiswoode and Messrs Harmsworth – George A Spottiswoode and William Spottiswoode being among the first officers to be commissioned. With headquarters at Little New Street, the 2nd London was known unofficially as 'The Printers' Battalion'. Absorbed 48th Middlesex RVC in 1872, making an overall strength of nine companies, and joined the King's Royal Rifle Corps (without change in title) as one of its volunteer battalions in 1881. In 1887 the memorial stone to a new headquarters at 57a Farringdon Road was laid. At headquarters, the memorial bearing the names of the six to lose their lives in South Africa is surrounded by that commemorating the sacrifice made in 1914–1918. The City of London School Cadet Corps became affiliated in 1905 and Transfer to the Territorial Force in 1908 was as 6th Battalion London Regiment. The City of London School at the same time joined the OTC. Uniform: green/scarlet.

3rd (City of) Recruiting began late in 1860 – a number, notes Richardson, coming forward from the ranks of the old Temple Bar and St Paul's Association Volunteers, which had been formed in 1798 – and the first officers' commissions were dated 8 March 1861. Sir William de Bathe was appointed as commanding officer. Twelve companies were soon established, the majority of the men being of the 'Artisan' class, which led to the unofficial title of the 'Working Men's Brigade'. Headquarters were at 26 Great Tower Street, moving later to 38 New Broad Street, then to 79 Farringdon Street, EC4 and finally to 24 Sun Street, Finsbury. Became a volunteer battalion of the King's Royal Rifle Corps (without change in title) in 1881, the additional title of '(City of)' being shown in the *Army List* by 1904. Transfer to the Territorial Force in 1908 was as 7th Battalion London Regiment. Uniform: scarlet/buff.

4th (1861–65) Formed as eight companies on 2 October 1861 with Lieutenant Colonel William Henry Sykes in command. Headquarters were at 8 Union Court, Broad Street, EC. Later reduced to six companies and disappeared from the *Army List* in April 1865.

4th (1900–05) Two companies formed on 18 May 1900 from ex-members of the Grocers' Company Schools in Clapton, North East London. With the 1st London RVC provided a volunteer battalion of the King's Royal Rifle Corps. The 4th Corps was disbanded in 1905, Major General Sir Frederick Maurice noting in his *History of the London Rifle Brigade* that 'the numbers having fell off, what remained of the 4th London was absorbed into 'E' company of 1st London'. Uniform: green/scarlet.

5th In February 1973 Bryn Owen, writing in the *Bulletin* of the Military Historical Society, recalled how he had found in the *Swansea Herald* for 21 November 1860 a report giving details of a meeting held at the Freemasons Tavern by influential Welshmen in the City of London. Its purpose, to discuss the possibility of raising a Welsh Corps in the capital. Mr Owen later found a second reference to the corps in the form of a brief entry dated 2 February 1861 published in *The Star of Gwent* which told how the 'London Welsh Rifles' had attended their first drill in the Floral Hall adjoining the Covent Garden Theatre. The corps apparently numbered 150 at this time and additional parades were also being held at the London residence of Sir Watkyn Williams Wynn. There is no doubt that at this point the London Welsh Corps was uniformed and badged, Mr Owen illustrating with his article a splendid silver device bearing the title 'London Welsh Rifle Corps' with a rampant dragon centrepiece.

Later, in May 1996, Mr Howard Ripley placed an item in the MHS *Bulletin* which more or less tidied up the mystery of the London Welsh. The *Volunteer Service Gazette* in May 1861, he states, reported that drills were being held at the Ward School in Aldersgate by a 'London Welsh Rifle Corps'. Nothing, however, appeared in the *Army List* regarding this formation, but in January 1862 (the *Gazette* again) notice was given that the services of the '5th (Welsh) London Rifle Volunteers' had been accepted.

In the following month the 5th did indeed appear in the *Army List* (the heading made no mention of the word 'Welsh', however) indicating that the corps was to be of two companies. Headquarters was given as 160 Aldersgate Street, but the expected six officers were not listed. This was to be the case right up until 1863 when in May, all reference to a 5th London RVC disappeared.

MERIONETHSHIRE

1st (1859–64) Formed at Bala as one company in 1859 with Henry Thomas Richardson, late 4th Dragoon Guards, as captain, William Baskerville Glegg, lieutenant and Hugh Owen Jones, ensign. All three held commissions dated 11 November. Disbanded in March 1864.

1st (1864–72) At the same time as the original 1st Corps was disbanded, the 2nd Merionethshire Corps, which had been raised at Dolgellau on 15 May 1860, was renumbered as 1st and included in the 1st Admin Battalion of Montgomeryshire Rifle Volunteers. The Dolgellau company, however, was also disbanded and last seen in the *Army List* for February 1872. Three officers were appointed: Captain John Vaughan, Lieutenant Griffith Williams and Ensign Francis Hallowes jun. Welsh Gold was produced at Dolgellau, the last two mines being closed down in 2007.

2nd See 1st Corps (1864–72).

3rd Formed at Corwen on 15 September 1860. Festiniog became the headquarters in 1861 and in February 1864 the company disappeared from the *Army List* having had three officers appointed:

Captain John Casson, Lieutenant Walter H Blacden and Ensign William Davies. Drawn to Corwen, twelve miles north-east of Bala, were tourists attracted by excellent fishing and the area's connection with Owen Glendower.

5th Volunteer Battalion South Wales Borderers After the disbandment in 1872 of the 1st Merionethshire RVC at Dolgellau, the county would not be represented within the Volunteer Force until 1897 and the formation that year of the 5th Volunteer Battalion South Wales Borderers – four of the battalion's six companies being recruited in Montgomeryshire, while two were found at: 'E' (Aberdovey) and 'F' (Towyn), both in Merionethshire. It would seem that sometime before March 1900, 'E' (Aberdovey) Company was either disbanded or merged into 'F' (Towyn). The 1909 edition of the *Territorial Yearbook* noted that 'E' Company had been formed at Aberystwyth University College on 17 March 1900. Transfer to the Territorial Force in 1908 was as 7th Battalion Royal Welsh Fusiliers. Uniform: scarlet/white.

MIDDLESEX

Like the counties of Kent, Essex and Surrey, Middlesex also recruited its volunteer corps throughout the greater London area. Previous to 1880 fifty numbered corps were raised and to administer those of insufficient strength, seven admin battalions were formed. Of the seven, only two, the 2nd and 7th, survived up to 1880 and the reorganizations of that year. The 6th was absorbed into the 2nd and the remaining four were broken up, their corps being made independent. The 1st Admin Battalion was formed in August 1860 and had its headquarters at Tyndale Place, Islington. The corps included were the 4th and 7th, the battalion being removed from the *Army List* in March 1861 upon their amalgamation. The 3rd Battalion – its headquarters were never recorded – was formed in August 1860 with the 39th and 40th Corps and was broken up in April 1861. Also to disappear in that month was the 4th Battalion, headquarters at Cardington Street in Euston, formed August 1860 with 20th, 29th and 37th Corps. The 5th Battalion, which was also formed in August 1860, had its headquarters at Custom House and included the 26th and 42nd Middlesex RVC. In 1880 the remaining two battalions and the surviving independent corps were organized into twenty-five new corps, the 2nd and 7th Admin Battalion providing the 3rd and 8th. Afterwards, a 26th and 27th Corps were formed.

1st (Victoria) Upon the general disbandment of Volunteers in 1814 the Duke of Cumberland's Sharpshooter, which had been formed in 1803, was permitted to continue service – although not formally recognized as a military body, but as a rifle club. In 1835 permission was granted to style the club as the Royal Victoria Rifle Club and in 1853 sanction to form a volunteer corps was given. As the Victoria Volunteer Rifle Corps, whose first officers' commissions were dated 4 January 1853, the club subsequently, in 1859, became the 1st Middlesex RVC. The additional title 'Victoria' was added by March 1860. Headquarters were at Kilburn, but a move was made to Marlborough Place, off Hamilton Terrace, St John's Wood in 1867. Became a volunteer battalion of the King's Royal Rifle Corps (without change in title) in 1881. Headquarters moved to 56 Davies Street, Westminster in 1892, and in the same year an amalgamation took place on 1 June with the 6th Middlesex (St George's) RVC. The new title adopted being 1st Middlesex (Victoria and St George's). Transfer to the Territorial Force in 1908 saw the 1st Middlesex amalgamated with the 19th Middlesex to form the 9th Battalion London Regiment. Uniform: green/black, changing to green/scarlet in 1892. A cadet corps with headquarters in Marlborough Place was formed towards the end of 1866, but this was later disbanded and was last seen in the *Army List* for January 1898. Mr J W Reddyhoff, writing in the *Bulletin* of the Military Historical Society in November 1997, notes that the Victoria Rifles Freemason Lodge No. 1124 (later No. 822) was formed from within the corps on 4 June 1860.

2nd (South Middlesex) Formed with headquarters at Beaufort House, Waltham Green on 14 October 1859. Raised by Viscount Ranelagh, the 2nd Corps included among its first officers: Evan Macpherson, late major in the 68th Regiment of Foot; the Hon W E Fitzmaurice, major, 2nd Life Guards; F H Atherely, of the Rifle Brigade and long time MP for the Isle of Wight; John Walrond Clark of the 10th Dragoons, and Charles Smyth Vereker, who had served as lieutenant colonel in the Limerick Artillery Militia. Among the junior officers were: Lord Ashley and the Hon Robert Bourke, afterwards Earl of Mayo and Governor General of India. Recruitment went well and within a few months the strength of the corps, one of the largest in the country, stood at sixteen companies. By the end of March 1860 some 1,261 members had subscribed twenty-one shillings each on being enrolled. In addition every man paid the cost of his uniform and equipment, besides an annual regimental subscription of twenty-one shillings.

As founder of the 2nd Middlesex Viscount Ranelagh's crest of a dexter arm embowed in armour and grasping a dart was used on the later uniforms as a collar badge. His Lordship was to command the corps until his death in November 1885. Became a volunteer battalion (without change in title) of the King's Royal Rifle Corps in 1881 and in 1902, the tenancy at Beaufort House having come to an end, moved to new headquarters at Fulham House, 7 High Street, Fulham. This historic property had once been owned by Sir Ralph Warren, Lord Mayor of London in 1536 and 1543, and later the Cromwell family. A fine gateway was purported to have been built by Inigo Jones, and the Officers' Mess possessed a number of carvings by Grinling Gibbons.

The strength of the 2nd Middlesex eventually fell to twelve companies, the headquarters of these, in addition to Fulham, being found at Chelsea, Chiswick, Hammersmith, Kensington, Brompton, Knightsbridge and Acton. The headquarters of 'K' Company were at the War Office. A cadet corps was formed in 1865, but this was removed from the *Army List* in 1880. St Paul's School at West Kensington formed a cadet corps in 1890 – B L Montgomery, the future field marshal, becoming a pupil of the Army Class in 1902. In 1908 some 300 officers and other ranks of the 2nd Middlesex provided a nucleus for the 10th Battalion Middlesex Regiment. However, the 10th was regarded as a new unit and no connection with any previous volunteer corps was permitted. Consequently, the battle honour 'South Africa 1900–02' gained by the Volunteers from the 2nd Middlesex while serving as part of the City Imperial Volunteers was not carried forward. St Paul's School, in 1908, became part of the OTC. Uniform: grey/scarlet.

In the *Bulletin* of the Military Historical Society for August 1993, a button was offered for identification, which bore the inscription 'Volunteer Corps of Old Blues'. In the centre was a representation of the head and shoulders of King Edward VI. Subsequent research by Mr Howard Ripley (MHS May 1996) discovered an item published in the *Volunteer Service Gazette* for 30 June 1860 indicating that a volunteer corps had been raised from former pupils of Christ's Hospital School in the City of London. In a latter edition, however, it was announced that as insufficient numbers had come forward from the 'Old Blues' those already enrolled should be merged into Viscount Ranelagh's 2nd Middlesex. Another item published in the *Bulletin* (November 1997) deals with Freemasonry in the Volunteer Force and in this Mr J W Reddyhoff notes that South Middlesex Lodge No. 1160 (later No. 858) was formed from within the 2nd Corps on 12 February 1861.

3rd (Hampstead) (1859–80) E T Evans, in his book *Records of the Third Middlesex Rifle Volunteers*, records how in about June 1859 three residents of Hampstead (Messrs Jay, Bennett, and another) met a number of Highgate residents at the Spaniards Inn to consider the formation of a volunteer corps; but through lack of interest, nothing more was done until Monday 4 July when another meeting took place at the residence of J Gurney Hoare Esq. of The Hill, Hampstead Heath. Subsequently the 3rd Middlesex RVC was formed with a strength of sixty, the first drills taking place at the Holly Bush Assembly Rooms and the Infant School in Well Road. The first officers, John R MacInnes, Basil Field and George Holford, were gazetted on 6 December 1859. In May 1860 rifle practice began at Child's Hill. During 1860 the corps used the Christ Church School for drill, Evans mentioning a 'Kilburn' contingent that used the St Mary's School in that area for a short time. Permission was obtained to increase the establishment to two companies in September 1860.

The corps joined the 2nd Admin Battalion of Middlesex Rifle Volunteers on 28 November 1860 and in 1862 permission was received to include 'Hampstead' in the title. New headquarters in Well Walk were taken over on Tuesday 16 December 1862. The building was a former chapel and before that, the old Hampstead pump-room. These premises, and the house next door, were used until notice to quit was received at the end of 1881. Not having the required enrolled strength, the corps was reduced to one company and a sub-division in July 1864. A room was taken for drill purposes at Hendon for Volunteers formed there in July 1866, but lack of interest in the area saw the detachment soon disbanded. The Hampstead Athletic Club, which met at Well Walk, was formed from within the corps in 1878. In March 1880 the 2nd Admin Battalion was consolidated as 3rd Middlesex RVC, the 3rd Corps becoming its 'A' and 'B' Companies.

3rd (1880–1908) The 2nd Admin Battalion of Middlesex Rifle Volunteers was formed on 28 November 1860 and consisted then of the 3rd, 13th and 14th Corps. Battalion headquarters were at Southwood Lane, Highgate. Drills took place at Albany Street Barracks. Absorbed the 6th Admin Battalion containing the 12th, 33rd and 41st Corps on 17 January 1862. An Orderly Room was established at 96 Farringdon Street, London, EC at the end of March 1864. Battalion headquarters moved to Crouch End, Hornsey in October 1870 and in 1880 consolidation took place as 3rd Corps with nine companies:

'A', 'B' Hampstead (late 3rd Corps)
'C' Barnet (late 12th Corps)
'D' Hornsey (late 13th Corps)
'E', F' Highgate (late 14th Corps)
'G' Tottenham (late 33rd Corps)
'H', 'I' Enfield Lock (late 41st Corps)

A new company ('K') was added at Enfield Town in September 1881. Sanction to form a drill station attached to 'A' and 'B' (Hampstead) Companies at Hendon was obtained from the War Office in 1884, the first drill taking place at the Assembly Rooms, the Burroughs in the beginning of February 1885. In the same year, 'D' (Hornsey) Company began recruiting in Southgate, Wood Green and Finsbury Park. The new Southgate detachment carrying out drills in the Village Hall. 'E' and 'F' (Highgate) Companies also recruited at North Finchley. The corps was designated 1st Volunteer Battalion Middlesex Regiment in 1898. Highgate School Cadet Corps was affiliated in 1883 but, with no officers appointed, was removed from the *Army List* by the end of 1884. The school appears again, however, in 1892. As a result of the war in South Africa permission was received to increase the battalion's establishment by three companies, the total establishment by the end of 1900 being now: Hampstead and Barnet, one company each; Hornsey four, Highgate two, Tottenham three and Enfield two. Transfer to the Territorial Force in 1908 was as 7th Battalion Middlesex Regiment. Highgate School at the same time became part of the Junior

Division, OTC. Uniform: grey/scarlet, changing later to grey/grey, then scarlet/white in 1898, scarlet/yellow in 1902.

4th (West London) Formed as one company at Islington with Alfred Alexander as captain, Edward Russell Cummins, lieutenant and John William Docwra, ensign. All three held commissions dated 15 October 1859. Joined the 1st Admin Battalion and absorbed the 5th and 6th Corps in June 1860, the 8th in August 1860. This bringing the establishment up to four companies with Major Charles R C Baron Truro in command. Amalgamated with the 7th Corps in 1861, 'West London' being added to the title in 1864. Headquarters moved from 1 Tyndale Place to Swallow Street, Piccadilly and became a volunteer battalion (without change in title) of King's Royal Rifle Corps in 1881. Headquarters to Adam and Eve Mews off Kensington High Street in 1885 having been situated in the West End of London since 1864. Designated 4th (Kensington) in 1905 and transfer to the Territorial Force in 1908 was as 13th Battalion London Regiment. Uniform: grey/scarlet.

Members of the corps served with the City Imperial Volunteers in South Africa; a memorial to all those from Islington that died in that conflict was erected by the people of the borough at Highbury Fields opposite Highbury Station in July 1905.

5th (1859–60) Formed as one company at Islington with James Childs commissioned as captain on 27 December 1859. Absorbed into the 4th Corps in June 1860.

5th (West Middlesex) (1880–1908) Formed as 9th Corps with headquarters at Lord's Cricket Ground, St John's Wood on 14 October 1859. There were six companies at first, rising to eight in April 1860, the Rt Hon Granville Augustus William, Baron Radstock taking command as lieutenant colonel commandant. Renumbered as 5th in 1880. Became a volunteer battalion (without change in title) of the Royal Fusiliers in the following year, but transferred in 1883 to the King's Royal Rifle Corps. Headquarters moved to 29 Park Road, Regents Park. Absorbed the 9th Corps at Harrow in 1899, bringing with it the Harrow School Cadet Corps. The latter was to become the 27th Corps on 1 April 1902 and serving as such until disbandment in January 1906. The personnel then returned to the 5th Corps as a cadet company. Transfer to the Territorial Force in 1908 was as 9th Battalion Middlesex Regiment, the cadet corps at the same time joining the OTC. Uniform: grey/scarlet, changing to green/scarlet in 1891.

6th (1859–60) Formed as one company at Islington in November 1859 and absorbed into the 4th Corps in June 1860.

6th (St George's) (1880–92) Formed in the Parish of St George's, Westminster – headquarters have included 2 Boyle Street, Old Burlington Street and 8 Mill Street off Regent Street – as the 11th Middlesex (St George's) RVC on 14 January 1860. With four companies the Hon Charles Hugh Lindsay of the Grenadier Guards was appointed as major commandant, his company commanders being G M Ives (Coldstream Guards), Sir J E Harrington Bt, J C Knox and George H Elliott. The last two both former officers with the 2nd Dragoon Guards. The companies were recruited from the Bond Street, Grosvenor Square, Hanover Square and Belgravia areas. The corps was renumbered as 6th in 1880 and became a volunteer battalion (without change in title) of the King's Royal Rifle Corps in the following year. Amalgamated with 1st Middlesex RVC on 1 June 1892. Uniform: green/black, changing to green/scarlet in 1886.

7th (1859–61) Formed as one company at Islington with Alfred J Ebsworth commissioned as captain on 26 November 1859. John Reynolds jun became his lieutenant, J Poole Wagstaff his ensign. Joined the 1st Admin Battalion and amalgamated with the 4th Corps in 1861.

7th (London Scottish) (1880–1908) The services of a rifle corps composed of Scotsmen living in the London area were accepted by the War Office on 2 November 1859. The corps consisted of six companies and was designated as the 15th Middlesex (London Scottish) RVC, Lord Elcho (afterwards Earl of Wemyss) being appointed as lieutenant colonel in command. Headquarters were established at 8 Adelphi Terrace, Westminster and the six companies were located:

No. 1 (Highland), 10 Pall Mall, East
No. 2 (City), The Oriental Bank
No. 3 (Northern), Rosemary Hall, Islington
No. 4 (Central), Scottish Corporation House, Crane Court
No. 5 (Southern), 68 Jermyn Street
No. 6 (Western), Chesterfield House, West London.

Members of the corps paid an entrance fee of £1 (abolished in 1862) and were required to provide their own uniforms and equipment. General Grierson in *Records of the Scottish Volunteer Force* notes that of the 600 men originally enrolled: 340 were artisans who paid no entrance fee and only a five shillings per year subscription, and of these only fifty provided their own uniforms, the rest being equipped from a central fund.

In 1861 No. 2 Company became No. 7, and a new No. 2, together with a No. 8, were raised. No. 3 Company was absorbed into the rest in 1865 and the following year company numbers were replaced by letters. This required the following reorganization:

'A' Company (formed by No. 1)
'B' Company (newly formed)
'C' Company (from No. 4)
'D' Company (from No. 5)
'E' Company (from No. 2 and No. 6)
'F' Company (from No. 7)
'G' Company (left vacant)
'H' Company (from No. 8)

The 15th was renumbered as 7th in September 1880 and in the following year a new 'G' Company was formed. At the same time the corps became a volunteer battalion (without change in title) of the Rifle Brigade. Additions in 1884 were 'I' and 'K' Companies. Some 218 Volunteers from the corps saw active service in South Africa, the first contingent under Lieutenant B C Green joining the City Imperial Volunteers in December 1899. Four men were mentioned in dispatches, two receiving the Distinguished Conduct Medal. Another detachment served with the 2nd Battalion Gordon Highlanders, one man, Sergeant W F Budgett, and ten men were wounded when a shell burst immediately above the Volunteers on 8 September 1901 near Lydenburgh. Transfer to the Territorial Force in 1908 was as 14th Battalion London Regiment, headquarters having moved to Adam Street in 1873, then 1 Adam Street, Adelphi, then James Street, Buckingham Gate in 1886. Uniform: grey/blue. Mr J W Reddyhoff, writing in the *Bulletin* of the Military Historical Society in November 1997, noted that the London Scottish Rifle Freemason Lodge No. 2310 was formed from within the corps on 18 April 1889.

8th (1859–60) Formed as one company at Islington in November 1859 and absorbed into the 4th Corps in August 1860.

8th (South West Middlesex) (1880–1908) The 7th Admin Battalion was formed with headquarters at Whitton Park, Hounslow in April 1861 and included the 16th, 24th, 30th, 43rd, 44th and 45th Corps. Included 'South West Middlesex' in its title and was consolidated in 1880 as the new 8th Corps with eight companies:

'A', 'B', 'C', 'D' Hounslow (late 16th Corps)
'E' Uxbridge (late 24th Corps)
'F' Ealing (late 30th Corps)
'G' Sunbury (late 43rd Corps)
'H' Staines (late 44th Corps)

Re-designated as 2nd Volunteer Battalion Middlesex Regiment in 1887. The Ealing Schools Cadet Corps was formed and affiliated in 1901. An increase in establishment to ten companies was authorized in 1900, but this was reduced back to eight four years later. Transfer to the Territorial Force in 1908 was as 8th Battalion Middlesex Regiment. Uniform: grey/grey, changing to scarlet/white by 1896. Mr J W Reddyhoff, writing in the *Bulletin* of the Military Historical Society in November 1997, noted that the Gostling Murray Freemason Lodge No. 1871 was formed from within the battalion on 3 August 1880.

9th (1859–80) See 5th Corps (1880–1908).

9th (1880–1908) The first officers of the 18th Corps, formed at Harrow as one company, were John Charles Templer, captain; Edward Francis Elliott, lieutenant and Duncan Mackenzie, ensign. All three held commissions dated 30 December 1859. Also appointed were Thomas Bridgewater MD as surgeon and the Revd F W Farrar, who became chaplain. Much of the corps was recruited from the staff and senior boys of Harrow School, which, in 1870, provided a cadet corps. Renumbered as 9th Corps in 1880 and became a volunteer battalion (without change of title) of the Royal Fusiliers the following year. Transferred to King's Royal Rifle Corps under General Order 99 of July 1883. Now four companies, the 9th amalgamated with the 5th Corps (as 5th) in 1899. Uniform: green/green.

10th (1859–60) It was intended to raise a 10th Corps with headquarters at St Marylebone and this is recorded in the *Army List* for the first time in November 1859. No officers were gazetted, however, and the corps was removed in February 1860.

10th (1880–1908) The 19th Middlesex RVC was formed at Bloomsbury of three companies on 13 December 1859 from members of the Working Men's College in Great Ormond Street, Holborn. The commanding officer was Thomas Hughes, the author of *Tom Brown's Schooldays*, which led to the corps often being referred to as 'Tom Brown's Corps'. The 19th later comprised ten companies, of which three were supplied by the college, others by the St John's Institute in Cleveland Street, the Price Belmont Works at Battersea, the Working Men's College in Paddington Green and the Westminster parishes of St Luke and St. Anne's. Headquarters later moved to 33 Fitzroy Square.

Renumbered 10th in 1880 and became a volunteer battalion (without change in title) of the King's Royal Rifle Corps in 1881. General Order 99 of July 1883, however, directed a transfer to the Royal Fusiliers and re-designation as 1st Volunteer Battalion. An eleventh company was added in 1900 and transfer to the Territorial Force in 1908 was as 1st Battalion London Regiment. Uniform: scarlet/blue.

11th (St George's) (1860–80) See 6th Corps (1880–92).

11th (Railway) (1880–1908) On 13 December 1859 the 20th Corps of three companies was formed with headquarters at Euston Square mainly from men employed by the London and North Western Railway Company. Thomas Edward Bigge, who had previously served with the 23rd Royal Welsh Fusiliers, was appointed captain commandant in command. The corps was included in the 4th Admin Battalion until May 1861 and in 1880 renumbered as 11th. Joined the King's Royal Rifle Corps (without change in title) as one of its volunteer battalions in 1881, transferring to the Middlesex Regiment in 1882 and then the Royal Fusiliers as its 3rd Volunteer Battalion in 1890. Additional personnel were sanctioned in 1900/01 bringing the establishment from eight to thirteen companies. After the war in South Africa, however, a reduction was made to eleven. The battalion occupied several headquarters in the Euston area, was at 5 Albany Street, Regent's Park, then from Edward Street, off Hampstead Road, transferred to the Territorial Force in 1908 as 3rd Battalion London Regiment. Uniform: grey/scarlet, changing later to scarlet/blue.

12th (1859–80) E T Evans, in his book *Records of the Third Middlesex Rifle Volunteers* , notes that the 12th Middlesex RVC was brought into existence through the exertions of Mr Wilbraham Taylor of Hadley Hurst, a gentleman usher to the Queen who had organized a meeting at the Town Hall, Barnet to consider the question of raising a Volunteer Corps in the Barnet and Hadley areas on 6 July 1859. Pending the official acceptance of the services of the corps, a number of men were enrolled at Hadley Hurst and drills commenced at the Militia Barracks, Barnet. Notification of the Queen's acceptance was read on parade on 15 October 1859, the first commissions being granted on 20 October 1859, to Captain Wilbraham Taylor, Lieutenant Charles Addington Hanbury.

The headdress worn by the 12th Middlesex was of a style called 'Garibaldi', this leading to the corps's nickname 'the Garibaldians'. A rifle range was taken into use at Moat Mount, Highwood Hill in 1860 and the 12th joined the 6th Admin Battalion of Middlesex Rifle Volunteers in 1860. With other corps of 6th Admin, the 12th joined the county's 2nd Admin Battalion on 17th January 1862. A cadet corps was formed at Brunswick House School, but this was disbanded after two years. A new range on ground owned by Mr Henry Hyde of the Manor House, Monken Hadley was opened on 21 March 1863. In the same year a house in High Street, Barnet was taken into use as an armoury, and a combined armoury, drill-shed and headquarters was set up in High Street, Barnet in 1871. Became 'C' Company of the new 3rd Middlesex in 1880.

12th (Civil Service) (1880–1908) From the very beginning of the Volunteer Movement it had been intended to merge all units raised by government departments into one corps. In the early months there had been formed the 21st, 27th, 31st and 34th Corps, all of which were manned by civil servants, and it would be these that in June 1860 were merged as the 21st Middlesex (Civil Service) RVC with former Scots Guards officer Lieutenant Colonel William C Viscount Bury in command. Headquarters were placed at Somerset House and the several companies, eight in all, were organized:

'A' (Audit Office), late No. 1 Company, 21st Corps
'B' (Post Office), late No. 2 Company, 21st Corps
'C' (Post Office), late No. 3 Company, 21st Corps
'D' (Inland Revenue), late No. 1 Company, 27th Corps)
'E' (Inland Revenue), late No. 2 Company, 27th Corps
'F' (Whitehall), late No. 1 Company, 31st Corps
'G' (Whitehall), late No. 2 Company, 31st Corps
'H' (Admiralty) late 34th Corps

It should be noted that the two Post Office companies, made up as they were from senior staff, were in no way connected with the 49th Middlesex RVC, later to become the Post Office Rifles, which comprised the lower grades of postal workers.

In July 1866 an additional company ('K') was raised by the clerks and senior members of the Bank of England and at the same time 'F' (Whitehall) and 'G' (Whitehall) Companies were amalgamated as 'G'. The 21st Corps was renumbered as 12th in 1880 and became a volunteer battalion (without change in title) of the King's Royal Rifle Corps in the following year. A change in designation did occur, however, in May 1898 when the corps became styled as The Prince of Wales's Own 12th Middlesex (Civil Service) RVC, HRH having been honorary colonel since its formation. Two new companies, 'F' and 'I' (Cyclist) were raised from employees of the London County Council in 1900 and a cadet corps was formed and affiliated in 1903. Transfer to the Territorial Force in 1908 was as 15th Battalion London Regiment. Uniform: grey/blue.

There exists the *Blue Book*, which was first published in 1899 with the purpose of providing 'useful information' to members – the battalion's 'Standing Orders', in fact. Details included are of the annual nine-day camp at Old Deer Park, Richmond, notes on the rifle range at Runnymede in Surrey, and the regimental tailor, who was Hobson and Son of 1/2 Great Lexington Street, London

13th (1859–80) Formed as a result of a meeting held at Crouch Hall, Crouch End on the evening of Friday 10 June 1859. Application to form a corps was subsequently submitted, notification that its services had been accepted as 13th Middlesex RVC being received on 2 November 1859 – Joseph H Warner was appointed as captain, J Bird, lieutenant and John Martineau Fletcher, ensign. Establishment was fixed at one company. Headquarters were in Hornsey. Joined the 2nd Admin Battalion on 22 November 1860. The corps used a range belonging to the 12th Middlesex RVC at Highwood Hill and another at Hornsey Wood House. A range at Tottenham was taken in 1862. E T Evans notes the death from small-pox in 1865 of Sergeant Henry St John Walton, a window in his memory being erected in Hornsey Church. Thirty recruits were enrolled at Southgate in 1866, but plans to set up a company or sub-division at Wood Green were dropped in 1869. At the a general meeting of the corps held on 26 April 1870 it was announced that a lease had been taken out on premises in Crouch End for use as headquarters. Evans records a general fall-off in numbers; the year 1872 seeing a reduction from seventy to sixty-four, of which the majority were resident in Southgate. Upon the consolidation of 2nd Admin Battalion in 1880, the 13th became 'D' Company of the new 3rd Corps.

13th (Queen's) (1880–1908) The post-1880 13th Corps was originally numbered as the 22nd Middlesex (Queen's) at Pimlico, having been formed in January 1860 from several companies raised earlier; a standing order of the time stating that 'On 13 January 1860, the Queen's Rifle Volunteers amalgamated with the several companies raised in the parishes of St John's, St Margaret's, St Mary's Strand, St Paul's Covent Garden, St James, St-Martin-in-the-Fields, St Anne's John Street, St Clement Danes and with the King's College. Also included in the corps were a number of men who had enrolled into a corps formed at Messrs J Broadwood & Sons Ltd of Horseferry Road, Westminster. The first officers' commissions were dated 25 February 1860. The corps comprised fifteen companies, divided into two battalions, under the command of Lieutenant Colonel Commandant the Earl Grosvenor. Headquarters were given as Westminster from March 1860. The corps was renumbered as 13th in 1880 and became a volunteer battalion (without change in title) of the King's Royal Rifle Corps in 1881. By 1900 the establishment had reached sixteen companies, which were organized and named as follows:

'A', 'B', 'C', 'D' Pimlico Division
'E', 'F' St John's Division

'G' St Margaret's Division
'H' St James's Division
'I', 'K' St Martin's Division
'L' Schoolbread's Company
'M' St Clement Dane's Division
'O' Royal Welsh
'R' Greater Westminster
'S' Mounted Infantry
'T' Cyclists

A cadet corps was formed in 1900. Headquarters are noted as 106 Buckingham Palace Road and after that, James Street, Westminster. Transfer to the Territorial Force in 1908 was as 16th Battalion London Regiment. Uniform: grey/scarlet. Mr J W Reddyhoff, writing in the *Bulletin* of the Military Historical Society in November 1997, noted that the Queen's Westminster Freemason Lodge No. 2021 was formed from within the battalion on 14 November 1883.

14th (1860–80) E T Evans records in his book *Records of the Third Middlesex Rifle Volunteers* that the origins of the 14th Corps lay in a private meeting held to discuss the possibilities of forming a Volunteer Rifle Corps in Highgate and is vicinity at the home of William H Bodkin (afterwards Sir William Bodkin) on 24 May 1859. A subsequent meeting was held at the Swain's Lane cricket field on 21 June 1859. First drills later took place at Swain's Lane. The services of the Highgate Volunteers were accepted in the autumn of 1859, the War Office allotting the title 14th Middlesex RVC with an establishment of one company. Officers' commissions were dated 2 November 1859. Headquarters were established at Southwood Lane, Highgate in a building belonging to the governors of Highgate School. An additional company was authorized on 16 February 1860 – Captain Commandant Josiah Wilkinson in command – and a third in June 1860. Although the latter was never formed. Rifle practice was now taking place at Hornsey Wood House and drills, not only in Highgate, but in Gray's Inn Hall or Gardens, and frequently at Albany Street Barracks. The corps became part of 2nd Admin Battalion on 28 November 1860. Evans notes how in 1860 efforts were made to form companies at Kentish Town and Finchley without success. There were, however, always many members of the 14th that were resident in those areas. A cadet corps was formed and affiliated to the corps at Christ College, Finchley in 1864, its commanding officer being appointed on 5 December – but this was disbanded towards the end of 1867. Headquarters, at the end of 1870 were moved to Hornsey, but were back again at Highgate in 1879. The new location, Northfield Hall, was taken over on 6 January. Establishment was reduced to one company on 23 September 1874, but a new second company was authorized before the end of 1876, its first officer not, however, being commissioned until 10 January 1878. Became 'E' and 'F' Companies of the new 3rd Corps in 1880.

14th (Inns of Court) (1880–1908) Formed as 23rd Corps at Lincoln's Inn, London from members of the legal profession on 15 February 1860 with six companies under the command of Lieutenant Colonel Commandant William B Brewster, late of the Rifle Brigade. Renumbered as 14th in 1880 and became a volunteer battalion (without change in title) of the Rifle Brigade in 1881. The St Peter's College Cadet Corps, Westminster was affiliated in 1902 and shown as Westminster School from May 1904. It was the intention to transfer the 14th to the Territorial Force in 1908 as the 27th Battalion of the London Regiment, but the members were not happy with this decision and chose to continue service as the Inns of Court OTC. Uniform: grey/scarlet.

15th (London Scottish) (1859–80) See 7th Corps (1880–1908).

15th (The Customs and Docks) (1880–1908)   Formed as the 26th Corps with headquarters at Custom House, London on 9 February 1860 and recruited from Customs Officers in the London Docks – four companies under the command of Major Commandant Ralph William Grey. Joined the 5th Admin Battalion and amalgamated with 9th Tower Hamlets RVC in 1864 under the title 26th (The Customs and Docks). Absorbed the 42nd Corps, also a dockland formation, in 1866, and the 8th Tower Hamlets in 1868. Now with thirteen companies, was renumbered 15th in 1880 and became a volunteer battalion (without change of title) of the Rifle Brigade in 1881. By 1891 the establishment had been reduced to eight companies and transfer to the Territorial Force in 1908 was as part of 17th Battalion London Regiment. Uniform: green/scarlet.

16th (1860–80)   Formed as two companies at Hounslow on 6 January 1860 with Charles Edward Murray as captain commandant. Joined the 7th Admin Battalion, increased to four companies by 1863, and became 'A' to 'D' Companies of the new 8th Corps in 1880. Both St Paul's (1874) and St Stephen's (1877) churches at Hounslow were built during the time of the Volunteers. Gunpowder was made at Hounslow, a large explosion taking place at the works in 1874.

16th (London Irish) (1880–1908)   The 28th Corps of eight companies was raised as a result of a meeting arranged by Mr G T Dempsey, an Irishman resident in London, at his rooms in Essex Street, Strand in the latter weeks of 1859. Headquarters were placed at Burlington House and the first officers' commissions were dated 28 February 1860. It is of interest to note that out of the nineteen officers recorded in the *Army List* for December 1860, no less than five held tiles: the Marquis of Donegal (lieutenant colonel), Lord Otho A Fitzgerald (captain), Lord Ashley (captain), Lord Francis N Conynhham (lieutenant) and the Earl of Belmore (ensign). Headquarters were transferred to York Buildings, Adelphi in 1866, Leicester Square in 1869, King William Street in 1873 and Duke Street, Charing Cross in 1897. The 28th was renumbered as 16th in 1880 and became a volunteer battalion (without change of title) of the Rifle Brigade in 1881. Transfer to the Territorial Force in 1908 was as 18th Battalion London Regiment. Uniform: green/light green. Mr J W Reddyhoff writing in the *Bulletin* of the Military Historical Society in November 1997 notes that the London Irish Rifles Freemason Lodge No. 2312 was formed from within the battalion on 24 May 1899.

17th (North Middlesex)   Formed as the 29th Corps of five companies at St Pancras on 1 March 1860, Lieutenant Colonel Viscount Enfield taking command. A good number of recruits for this corps were provided by men from Lord Elcho's proposed corps, the 'Euston Road Rifles'. Included in the 4th Admin Battalion for period August-December 1860 and in 1861 moved headquarters to Regent's Park. Included 'North Middlesex' in the title from 1864 and moved once again, this time to High Street Camden Town, during the same year. Renumbered 17th in 1880 and became a volunteer battalion (without change in title) of the Middlesex Regiment in 1881. Transfer to the Territorial Force in 1908 was as 19th Battalion London Regiment. Uniform: green/black, changing to green/green in 1904.

18th (1859–80)   See 9th Corps (1880–1908).

18th (1880–1908)   A little over five years after the first railway passengers had boarded their trains below the ironwork of Matthew Digby Wyatt's roof at Paddington Station, a short distance to the north in the Vestry Hall, the committee set up to establish a corps of riflemen in Paddington had agreed to present the plans gathered so far to the War Office.

Another meeting on record indicates that as of 10 January 1860, no sanction had yet been received from the War Office; but nonetheless, recruiting had gone well and within a few days sufficient numbers had come forward to man a full company. By 29 February, the date of the first officer's commission, a second had been raised and in March a captain commandant had been appointed in the form of Major General David Downing (late of the Indian Army) who, on the 7th, attended a levee of Volunteer Officers given by Queen Victoria at St James's Palace. By this time the Paddington Volunteers, their motto 'arm for peace', had been ranked as 36th in the County of Middlesex.

A third company well under way, the 36th Middlesex held its first parade and march around the borough on 8 May, 1860. A band made up of Metropolitan Railway workers and musicians from the Working Men's College at Paddington Green led the way. Weeks later, at the first Volunteer Review held in Hyde Park, Nos 1 and 2 Companies took the field and earned much praise for their smartness and soldierly appearance from those present.

Well on the way to four companies now, a cadet corps had also been formed, along with a drum and bugle band. Situated in the grounds of St Mary's Church next to Paddington Green, the Vestry Hall provided headquarters, while across the Harrow Road at the Hermitage Street Fire Station, drills were carried out and weapons stored. The corps also had the use of two riding schools – Pearce's in Westbourne Grove and Gapp's in Gloucester Terrace.

In 1865 the 36th Middlesex provided the Guard of Honour when HRH the Prince of Wales laid the foundation stone of the Paddington Infirmary (later Paddington General Hospital) adjacent to the Workhouse in the Harrow Road near Lock Bridge. Four years later, as the Vestry Hall began to grow into the Town Hall, temporary headquarters had to be found in rooms above the King and Queen public house in Harrow Road. A location within view of the next move, which took the 36th across Paddington Green to Greville House, once the premises of the Working Men's College, and even before that the home of Emma Hart, the future Lady Hamilton and friend of Lord Nelson.

A gradual increase in establishment seems to have taken place over the first ten years of the corps's existence. Mention of a No. 7 Company at Kensal Green made up mainly from employees of the Metropolitan Railway is noted in 1870 and in 1872, 'H' Company (presumably letters have replaced numbers by now) is on record as having held a dinner on 10 September. The 36th was renumbered as 18th in 1880 and in the following year became a volunteer battalion (without change in title) of the Rifle Brigade.

The premises at Paddington Green became more and more crowded as the battalion grew – transport and ambulance sections had been added to the still growing number of companies, and the band was restricted to practising in the hallways – so in 1895 property was acquired at 207–209 Harrow Road which occupied enough land to permit the building of a drill hall and rifle range. On the evening of 31 March 1896, the 18th were marched out of Paddington Green for the last time. Making their way past St Mary's Church, Sarah Siddons in her white Carrara not yet looking on, and into the Harrow Road, where the parade took the battalion past the old Vestry Hall (now Town Hall); Paddington Green Police Station (later made famous in the film *The Blue Lamp*); Porteus Road, where the local Artillery Volunteers met and drilled; over the bridge that crossed the Grand Junction Canal and took the road down to where it skirted the Great Western; past the Red Lion public house to headquarters. The journey today would be in the most part within the shadow of the great Westway Flyover. Transfer to the Territorial Force in 1908 was as 10th Battalion London Regiment. Uniform: green/black.

Mr J W Reddyhoff, writing in the *Bulletin* of the Military Historical Society in November 1997, notes that the Paddington Rifles Freemason Lodge No. 2807 was formed from within the battalion in 1900.

19th (1859–80) See 10th Corps (1880–1908).

19th (St Giles and St George's Bloomsbury) (1880–1908) Four companies formed as 37th Corps with headquarters at the Local Board of Works, Holborn on 31 March 1860 with Major John W Jeakes in command. Joined the 4th Admin Battalion in August 1860, but was made independent in May of the following year. Headquarters moved in 1861 to the Foundling Hospital in Guildford Street, WC1. Comprised eight companies by 1866. The additional title 'St Giles and St George's, Bloomsbury' was added in 1869 and in 1880 the corps was renumbered as 19th. Became a volunteer battalion (without change in title) of the Rifle Brigade in 1881. Headquarters moved to Chenies Street, Bedford Square, WC1 in 1887 and transfer to the Territorial Force in 1908 saw the 19th Middlesex amalgamated with 1st Middlesex to form the 9th Battalion London Regiment. Uniform: green/green. Mr J W Reddyhoff, writing in the *Bulletin* of the Military Historical Society in November 1997, noted that the Bloomsbury Rifles Freemason Lodge No. 2362 was formed from within the battalion on 1 May 1890.

20th (1859–80) See 11th Corps (1880–1908).

20th (Artists) (1880–1908) Formed as three companies with headquarters at Burlington House, London on 25 May 1860 with the painter Henry W Phillips as captain commandant. Numbered as 38th, the corps was recruited from painters, sculptors, musicians, architects, actors and other members of artistic occupations. A private in the corps was Queen's Medallist and Engraver to the Signet J W Wyon, who was responsible for designing the Artists Rifles badge, an apt device which included the heads of Mars, the god of war, and Minerva, the goddess of the arts. Later increased to four, then six companies. Headquarters moved to the Arts Club, Hanover Square in 1869, 'Artists' being included in the title from 1877. Renumbered 20th in 1880 and as eight companies with headquarters at in Fitzroy Square became a volunteer battalion (without change in title) of the Rifle Brigade in 1881. A move was later made to Duke's Road. The University College School Cadet Corps was affiliated in 1904 and transfer to the Territorial Force in 1908 was as 28th Battalion London Regiment, University College School at the same time joining the OTC. Uniform: grey/grey.

21st (1860) Three companies formed with headquarters at Somerset House, London on 2 January 1860 from staff of the Audit Office and Post Office. The three company commanders were Captains Francis Alfred Hawker, Nicholas H Harrington and John L de Plat Taylor. Became 'A', 'B' and 'C' Companies of the new 21st Corps in June 1860.

21st (Civil Service) (1860–80) See 12th Corps (1880–1908).

21st (The Finsbury Rifle Volunteer Corps) (1880–1908) Formed as the 39th Corps of eight companies at Clerkenwell on 6 March 1860, Thomas H Colvill, late of the 74th Regiment of Foot, and at the time Governor of Coldbathfields Prison, being appointed as lieutenant colonel in command. Included in the 3rd Admin Battalion until 1861 and 'The Finsbury RVC' was added to the title in 1862. Increased to ten companies in the 1870s, renumbered 21st in 1880. Became a volunteer battalion (without change in title) of the Rifle Brigade in 1881, transferring to the King's Royal Rifle Corps in 1883. Two new companies were authorized in 1900 and from headquarters in Penton Street, Pentonville, transferred to the Territorial Force in 1908 as 11th Battalion London Regiment. Uniform: green/scarlet.

22nd (Queen's) (1860–80) See 13th Corps (1880–1908).

22nd (Central London Rifle Rangers) (1880–1908) From members of the legal profession, formed as the 40th Corps of eight companies at Gray's Inn, London on 30 April 1860 and included in the 3rd Admin Battalion until 1861 when made independent. In that year Lieutenant Colonel Alfred P F C Somerset, late of the 13th Regiment of Foot, took command, 'Central London Rifle Rangers' was added to title and the 35th Corps at Enfield was absorbed. Renumbered 22nd in 1880, became a volunteer battalion (without change in title) of the Royal Fusiliers in 1881, and transferred to the King's Royal Rifle Corps in the following year. Mayall College Cadet Corps at Herne Hill was affiliated in 1891, but removed from the *Army List* in 1899. Volunteers from the corps saw active service in South Africa during the Boer War. Lieutenant W Brian L Alt, who had been first commissioned into the 22nd on 2 June 1894 – his father, W J Alt, had commanded the corps since 1881 – was killed at Diamond Hill on 12 June 1900 while serving with the City Imperial Volunteers. He would be the only officer of the CIV to lose his life. Also from the 22nd Middlesex RVC was Charles Gwyn Trivet Bromfield, who died from wounds received in action near Boshof on 16 February 1902. From the ranks, he had risen to captain in the 87th Company, Imperial Yeomanry. Transfer to the Territorial Force in 1908 was as 12th Battalion London Regiment. Uniform: green/scarlet.

23rd (Inns of Court) (1860–80) See 14th Corps (1880–1908).

23rd (1880–1908) It was in January 1861 that the War Office accepted the services of a corps of Volunteer Riflemen raised within the City and Westminster areas of London. Number 5 Victoria Street, just a short walk down from Westminster Abbey, was its first headquarters; Sir John Villiers Shelley (MP for Westminster), its first Commanding Officer and 46 its allotted number within the fast-growing order of battle of Middlesex RVC. Such was the enthusiasm that when the corps, in June 1861, moved just around the corner to new headquarters at 31 Great Smith Street – across the road from the building was the first free public library in London, which had been opened four years earlier – eight companies (four in the City, four in Westminster) had been formed. The rank and file, according to one source, were drawn almost entirely from 'the respectable working classes', while the officers were men 'of good social position'. VC hero of the Crimea Lieutenant Colonel Sir Charles Russell was appointed as first honorary colonel in 1877 and he was succeeded six years later by Lord Wolseley.

During the next three years the 46th Middlesex RVC was to be subject to two changes in designation: firstly as 23rd Middlesex (this to comply with the general 1880 renumbering of Volunteer Corps throughout the country), then in 1883 as 2nd Volunteer Battalion Royal Fusiliers. The corps had been allotted as one of that regiment's four volunteer battalions two years previous. In 1899 a new headquarters was built just around the corner from Great Smith Street at 9 Tufton Street. The move to Tufton Street coincided of course with the commencement of the war in South Africa, the battalion sending out a total of four officers and more than 150 other ranks to serve alongside the 2nd Royal Fusiliers. Nine of that number were either killed or died while on active service. Transfer to the Territorial Force in 1908 was as 2nd Battalion London Regiment. Uniform: scarlet/blue.

24th (1860–80) Formed as two companies at Uxbridge on 22 February 1860 with Lieutenant William Edward Hilliard and Ensign John F W de Salis the first officers to receive commissions. Joined the 7th Admin Battalion, reduced to one company in 1873, and became 'E' Company of the new 8th Corps in 1880.

24th (1880–1908) The formation of a Rifle Corps at the General Post Office in London was sanctioned by the War Office on 13 February 1868. Designated as 49th Middlesex, it was to consist of seven companies each recruited from the minor staff of the several London postal districts and departments – the senior members had enrolled separately and had, since 1860, formed part of the 21st Corps at Somerset House. With headquarters at the General Post Office, London, the seven companies were recruited:

'A', from EC District
'B', Inland Office
'C', Newspaper and Money-Order Offices
'D',WC District
'E', E, SW and S Districts
'F', N and NW Districts
'G', E and SE   Districts

In June 1869 a new 'H' Company provided by SW District was formed, this being followed in July 1870 by 'I' Company from the Telegraph Branch. By the end of 1876 sufficient numbers had been enrolled by the E and SE Districts to increase the establishment by one company and subsequently, from January 1877, 'G' Company was recruited from E District only while the SE men provided the new 'K'. The 49th was renumbered as 24th in 1880 and in the following year became a volunteer battalion (without change of title) of the Rifle Brigade.

On 18th July 1882 the War Office approved a scheme for the formation by the 24th Middlesex RVC of an Army Post Office Corps (APOC). The idea being that this would undertake all postal duties connected with an army on active service overseas. The APOC would be placed on the Army Reserve and consist of two officers and 100 men, all recruited from the 24th. It followed that on 8 August 1882, London postal workers embarked to join the expeditionary force then in Egypt.

In 1883 the telegraph company 'I' was recruited up to 200 and subsequently divided as two divisions, 'A' and 'B', and shown in the *Army List* as 'Field Telegraph Companies' (FTC). The formation of the FTC had been authorized to run along the same lines as the APOC, the FTC to consist of fifty rank and file. In 1889 both the APOC and FTC were constituted as companies of the 24th, the former becoming 'M' Company, while the telegraph personnel formed 'L'. Additional companies were raised by the 24th during the Boer War, the battalion supplying regular drafts for the front line. At the General Post Office in Aldersgate Street, opposite Gresham Street, a bronze tablet was erected to commemorate those that lost their lives. Transfer to the Territorial Force in 1908 was as 8th Battalion London Regiment. Uniform: grey/blue, changing to green/blue in 1887. Unique among the Volunteer and later Territorial Forces was the battle honour 'Egypt 1882,' which had been gained by the work of the 24th Corps during that campaign. Although 'South Africa 1899–1902' was soon to appear below the name of the regiment in the *Army List* it would not be until 1908 that the honour gained in Egypt was recognized.

25th (1860) The February 1860 *Army List* indicates that a 25th Corps was to be formed at St Martin-in-the-Fields, London. No officers were gazetted, however, and the corps was removed in March 1860.

25th (Bank of England) (1875–1907) In July 1866 the clerks and senior staff of the Bank of England formed a company of Rifle Volunteers which became part of the 21st Middlesex (Civil Service) RVC. On 1 December 1875 a new company was formed, this time by the porters and messengers of the bank. The new company with Captain Samuel O Gray, Lieutenant Walter J Coe and Ensign John H Green, was designated as 50th (Bank of England), being renumbered 25th in 1880. The corps was disbanded in 1907. green/green.

26th (1860–64) See 15th Corps (1880–1908).

26th (Cyclist) (1888–1908) Notification of the acceptance of a corps of Cyclists in Middlesex was received on 11 February 1888. The new formation was to rank after the 25th (Bank of England) Corps and to be made up of three troops lettered: 'A', 'B' and 'C – this would be the first battalion in the history of the British Army to be completely dedicated to a cyclist role. The cyclists functioned as scouts, signallers, pulled Colt machine guns into action attached to specially designed carriages and even, according to one source writing in the *Volunteer Gazette* , practised laying their machines down in the road so as to hinder oncoming enemy cavalry. The battalion's first headquarters was at Ashley Place where, seven years after formation of the corps, the first red bricks of John Francis Bentley's Westminster Cathedral would be set in place. By the end of 1888, however, a move had been made to Hare Court, this time in the City and within a few yards of the Temple Church and Fleet Street. Further moves would be made: first to 2 Queen's Road, West Chelsea (1890); 69 Lillie Road, West Brompton (1899) and Horseferry Road, Westminster (1904). Upon formation, the 26th Corps was allotted to the King's Royal Rifle Corps as one of its volunteer battalions. It transferred to the Rifle Brigade in 1889 and became the 25th London Regiment in 1908. Uniform: grey/scarlet.

27th (1860) Two companies formed with headquarters at Somerset House, London on 10 February 1860 from the staff of the Inland Revenue office. William Ennis, who had previously served with the 11th Dragoons, was made captain commandant in command. Became 'D' and 'E' Companies of the new 21st Corps in June 1860.

27th (Harrow School) (1902–1906) On 1 April 1902 the cadet corps formed at Harrow School and hitherto attached to the 5th Middlesex RVC became a corps in its own right. Designated as 27th Middlesex, the new corps was allotted to the King's Royal Rifle Corps as one of its volunteer battalions. The 27th appeared as such for the last time in the *Army List* for April 1906, being disbanded officially with effect from the previous 31 January, the personnel returning to the 5th Corps as a cadet company. Uniform: described as neutral tint with dark-blue facing.

28th (London Irish) See 16th Corps (1880–1908).

29th See 17th Corps.

30th Formed as one company at Ealing on 29 February 1860 with Captain John Fitz Maurice, KH, late colonel in the Rifle Brigade, in command. Joined the 7th Admin Battalion and became 'F' Company of the new 8th Corps in 1880. The Victorian rebuilding of Ealing's St Mary's Church took place between 1866 and 1872.

31st Two companies formed with headquarters at Whitehall, London on 25 February 1860 from the management and staff of various Government offices. The first officers to be commissioned were Captain Thomas Taylor, Lieutenant Richard Mills and Ensign Frederick William Kirby. Became 'F' and 'G' Companies of the new 21st Corps in June 1860.

32nd Two companies formed with headquarters in Seymour Place, St Marylebone with Captain Commandant the Hon Thomas Charles Bruce being commissioned on 14 February 1860. On 27 October 1860 the *Illustrated London News* published a short item regarding the 32nd, or as they became known the 'Six-foot Volunteer Guards': 'The 32nd Middlesex Rifle Corps, known to the public as the "Six-foot Volunteer Guards", was established last February, with a view to meet the requirements of men whose stature ... rendered their appearance in the ranks of ordinary-sized corps somewhat awkward. More than one hundred and fifty gentlemen of the required standard, including several military officers and six-footers from other corps, have been enrolled.'

The corps carried on their drills at either St George's Barracks or Hungerford Hall. The military artist Lady Butler (1864–1933) mentions in her autobiography how 'I stuffed my sketch books with British Volunteers ... there was a very short-lived corps called the Six-foot Guards!' The 32nd Middlesex was disbanded in 1868.

33rd A meeting for the purpose of forming a corps of Rifle Volunteers in the Tottenham area was held by the churchwardens of the parish at the Lecture Hall, Tottenham on Wednesday 28 December 1859. E T Evans in his history of the 3rd Middlesex RVC, notes that during the meeting 'a gentleman of the Quaker persuasion, who spoke against the movement, occasioning some uproar, but the meeting refused to hear him.' Some sixty enrolled and these were soon drilling at the National Schoolroom, Marsh Lane, Tottenham. On 16 February, the services of the Tottenham Volunteers were accepted, the War Office allotting the title 33rd Middlesex RVC and an establishment of one company – George Goss to be captain; Edward B L Hill, lieutenant and William A Hall, ensign. Recruits were also found in neighbouring Edmonton. An armoury was set up at Northumberland Park, rifle practice took place at Tottenham Marches and Enfield Lock. A cadet corps of one company was formed in September 1860 consisting of fifty-eight pupils from Bruce Castle School and twenty-two others. Joined the 6th Admin Battalion in 1860, transferring to 2nd Admin in January 1862. Evans records that the novelist Anthony Trollope delivered a lecture at the Lecture Hall on 8 April 1864 in aid of funds for the corps. One of the officers, Captain William A Hall, died in October 1867, a tablet in his honour being erected in the parish church. Became 'G' Company of the new 3rd Corps RVC in 1880.

34th Formed as one company at the Admiralty, London on 22 February 1860 with William Willis as captain, Charles John Cox, lieutenant and Thomas Bell Gripper, ensign. Became 'H' Company of the new 21st Corps in June 1860.

35th Formed as one company at Enfield with captain A P F C Somerset commissioned on 20 April 1860. Joined the 6th Admin Battalion and was absorbed into the 40th Corps in April 1861.

36th See 18th Corps (1880–1908).

37th (St Giles and St George's) See 19th Corps (1880–1908).

38th (Artists) See 20th Corps (1880–1908).

39th (The Finsbury Rifle Volunteer Corps) See 21st Corps (1880–1908).

40th (Central London Rifle Rangers) See 22nd Corps (1880–1908).

41st Three companies formed at Enfield Lock, their services being accepted on 11 June 1860. Gordon S Munro, Charles Sendey and William C Barnes were appointed as captains. Members were principally employees in the Royal Small Arms Factory. Joined the 6th Admin Battalion, transferring to the 2nd Admin Battalion in January 1862. E T Evans, in his history of the 3rd Middlesex RVC, notes that 'as a special favour the officers were permitted to carry gilt-mounted swords, presumably because the corps was raised at the Royal Small Arms Factory, and for the like reason the royal arms were borne upon the officers' pouches'. Evans also notes that a member of the corps, Bugle Major Kennedy, had served in the 17th Lancers as trumpeter and had taken part in the Light Brigade charge at Balaclava. Establishment reached six companies in 1868, reducing to four in July 1872, three on 17 June 1873, two in 1874. Evans remarks that the fall-off in numbers was due to the introduction of machinery in the factory to replace hand labour. Became 'H' and 'I' Companies of the new 3rd Corps in 1880.

42nd Formed as one company at St Catherine's Docks, London with Thomas W Collet as captain, Thomas Crundwell, lieutenant and Rupert Flindt, ensign. All three held commissions dated 19 June 1860. Joined the 5th Admin Battalion and was absorbed into the 26th Corps by 1866.

43rd Formed as one company at Hampton on 25 September 1860 with Captain Clement R Archer, late of the 4th Dragoon Guards, in command. Joined the 7th Admin Battalion, absorbed the 45th Corps at Sunbury in 1863 and moved headquarters to Sunbury in 1870. Became 'G' Company of the new 8th Corps in 1880.

44th Formed as one company at Staines with James Paine as captain, Edmund G Phillips, lieutenant and Christopher C Horne, ensign. All three held commissions dated 7 December 1860. Joined the 7th Admin Battalion and became 'H' Company of the new 8th Corps in 1880. At Staines there were factories producing linoleum and mustard. 'H' Company headquarters were in Thames Street.

45th Formed as a sub-division at Sunbury on 20 December 1860 with Lieutenant William Anthony Mitchison in command. Joined the 7th Admin Battalion and was absorbed into the 43rd Corps in 1863. The old East London Waterworks Company employed many at Sunbury.

46th See 23rd (1880–1908).

47th Formed as one company at Stanmore on 13 January 1862 with John H Hulbert as captain, Charles D E Fortnum, lieutenant and Charles E Blackwell, ensign. Also appointed was the Revd L J Bernays as chaplain. Disbanded in 1865.

48th (or 'Havelock's) Formed on 27 February 1862, the corps had been raised by cartoonist George Cruikshank who had previously been involved with the 24th Surrey RVC across the Thames at Southwark. Like the 24th, the 48th Middlesex consisted entirely of members of the Temperance League. It also held the title 'or Havelock's' in memory of hero of India and noted member of the Temperance Movement, General Sir Henry Havelock (1795–1857). A strong corps, it soon numbered eight companies; Cruikshank was appointed lieutenant colonel in command. Headquarters were at 48 Mornington Place, St Pancras, then later at 6 Cook's Court, Serle Street, Lincoln's Inn Fields. Cruikshank's biographer (professor William Bates) recalls how the great age of the artist became a concern of his officers, who in 1868 made their feeling known to the War Office. The government, however, supported the seventy-six-year-old commander and subsequently issued an order cashiering the fourteen officers that had signed the document. But great damage had been done and Cruikshank's resignation soon followed. 'Havelock's' was removed from the title about November 1870. Interest in the corps steadily waned and the 48th made its last appearance in the *Army List* for January 1872. The corps having merged with the 2nd London.

49th See 24th Corps (1880–1908).

50th See 25th Corps (1875–1907).

1st Cadet Battalion Royal Fusiliers Formed with headquarters at St Pancras on 8 May 1901. Moved to Pond Street, Hampstead in 1904. Uniform: scarlet/blue.

MIDLOTHIAN

All rifle corps formed within the county, except the 1st and 4th, joined the 1st Admin Battalion, which in 1880 became the new 2nd Corps.

1st (Leith) General Grierson, in *Records of the Scottish Volunteer Force*, records that on 6 August 1859 the services of 153 'gentlemen of Leith' were offered to form two companies. The men were to pay all their own expenses and provide their own arms. The services of two more companies, artisans this time, were later offered – the men here being required to pay thirty shillings each, the rest of their expenses to be covered by public subscription. All four companies were accepted and the first officers received their commissions on 6 December 1859 – the commanding officer was Major Henry Hawker Arnaud, late of the Honourable East India Company. A No. 5 Company was added on 28 May 1860, No. 6 on 24 September 1860, No. 7 on 18 March 1861 and No. 8 on 28 May 1861. All were recruited in Leith. In 1863 No. 9 Company was added when the 4th Corps at Corstorphine was absorbed, and in 1866 and 1868 increases in establishment brought the strength of the corps up to twelve companies. The 1st Corps was re-designation as 5th Volunteer Battalion Royal Scots under General Order 144 of 1888, two companies being struck off in the same year. A cyclist company was added in 1900, but in the following year there was another reduction, this time to ten companies.

Some 196 Volunteers from the battalion saw active service in South Africa, two men dying of disease, two being wounded. Captain R Wemyss Campbell and Corporal T H Greig were mentioned in Lord Robert's dispatch of 4 September 1901; Corporal Greig was also to receive the Distinguished Conduct Medal; Private J G Lochart (promoted to corporal for gallantry at Balmoral on 5 April 1902) in Lord Kitchener's Dispatches of 1 June 1902. At a cost of £3,000, drill hall and headquarters premises were built in Stead's Place, Leith, but were burnt down in 1900 and replaced by a new property in Delmeny Street in 1902. Transfer to the Territorial Force in 1908 was as 7th Battalion Royal Scots. Uniform: scarlet/black, changing to scarlet/blue with trews in 1890.

The Volunteers would have seen the building and opening of the Corn Exchange in 1862, the Albert Dock in 1869, new Sailors' Home in 1883–84 and the Edinburgh Dock in 1881. A busy seaport, Leith provided employment in shipbuilding, brewing, distilling, engineering and at a large chemical works.

2nd (1860–80) Formed as two companies at Dalkeith on 22 May 1860, the company commanders being D E Brewer and William Mushet. The establishment was increased to three companies in 1864, then to four in 1867. Became 'A' to 'D' Companies of the new 1st Corps in 1880. Just under seven miles from Edinburgh, Dalkeith in the 1890s employed many in the production of iron, brushes and carpets.

2nd (Midlothian and Peebles) (1880–1908) The 1st Admin Battalion of Midlothian Rifle Volunteers was formed with headquarters at Dalkeith on 22 January 1862, the 1st, 2nd and 3rd Peeblesshire RVC also being included from 1863. Headquarters transferred to Penicuik in 1875 and in April 1880 the battalion was consolidated as the new 2nd Corps with eleven companies:

'A' to 'D' Dalkeith (late 2nd Midlothian)
'E' Penicuik (late No. 1 Company, 3rd Midlothian)
'F' Valleyfield (late No. 2 Company, 3rd Midlothian
'G' Musselburgh (late 5th Midlothian)
'H' Loanhead (late 6th Midlothian)
'I' and 'K' Peebles (late 1st Peeblesshire)
'L' Innerleithen (late 3rd Peeblesshire)

Re-designation as 6th Volunteer Battalion Royal Scots was directed by General Order 144 of April 1888. 'D' Company moved to Bonnyrigg in 1895 and battalion headquarters to Peebles in

February 1907. Transfer to the Territorial Force in 1908 was as four companies of 8th Battalion Royal Scots. Uniform: scarlet/black, changing to scarlet/blue with trews in 1888.

3rd The services of the 3rd Corps of three companies – No. 1 Penicuik, No. 2 Valleyfield and No. 3 Roslin – were accepted on 22 May 1860. The latter, however, was disbanded in 1864, the company commanders for Nos 1 and 2 Companies being James Clark and John Cowan. Became 'E' and 'F' Companies of the new 2nd Corps in 1880. The area in and around all three companies was involved in printing and the production of paper, the main mill being at Valleyfield, which, in about 1800, notes Cassell's *Gazetteer*, was taken over by the government for the reception of 5,000 French prisoners of war. Some 300 died in captivity and in 1860 a monument in their memory was erected near the spot. The first ceremonial duty of the 3rd Midlothian RVC, perhaps?

4th Formed as one company at Corstorphine on 26 November 1860 with William Macfie as captain, John Macnai, lieutenant and Thomas Bonnar Scott, ensign. Absorbed into the 1st Corps as its No. 9 Company in 1863. The village of Corstorphine is three miles west of Edinburgh.

5th Formed as one company at Musselburgh on 19 April 1861 with William Stuart as captain, George Laurie, lieutenant and Robert Stirling, ensign. Became 'G' Company of the new 2nd Corps in 1880. Just over five miles from Edinburgh, Musselburgh lies on the east side of the mouth of the Esk, Fisherrow close by being where the main fishing population were located. In the area around the town others were employed in the manufacture of nets, twine and paper.

6th Formed as one company at Loanhead on 28 April 1876 and became 'H' Company of the new 2nd Corps in 1880. Five miles from Edinburgh, many from the town were employed in mines and paper mills.

MONMOUTHSHIRE

Two administrative battalions were formed within the county, which provided the new 1st and 3rd Corps.

1st (1859–80) Formed as one company at Chepstow with John Lewis Baldwin as captain, James Evans, lieutenant and James Proctor Carruthers, ensign. All three held commissions dated 9 September 1859. Joined the 1st Admin Battalion and provided 'A' Company of the new 1st Corps in 1880. At Chepstow, two bridges take you across the Wye and into England.

1st (1880–1908) The 1st Admin Battalion was formed with headquarters at Newport in August 1860 and included the 1st, 3rd, 4th, 10th and 11th Corps. The battalion was consolidated as the new 1st Corps in 1880 with seven companies:

'A' at Chepstow (late 1st Corps)
'B' Newport (late 3rd Corps)
'C' Newport (late 3rd Corps)
'D' Pontymister (late 3rd Corps)
'E' Pontymister (late 3rd Corps)
'F' Tredegar (late 11th Corps)
'G' Bassaleg (newly formed)

Re-designated 2nd Volunteer Battalion South Wales Borderers in 1885. By 1900 the establishment of the battalion stood at eleven companies – Chepstow, Newport (4), Tredegar, Pontymister, Blackwood, Rogerstone, Rhymney and Caerleon – which in 1908 transferred to the Territorial Force as 1st Battalion, Monmouthshire Regiment. Uniform: green/black. A tablet unveiled by the Rt Hon Lord Tredegar on 29 October 1904, now in Newport's Civic Centre, records the names of twenty-seven men from the town that saw active service in South Africa.

2nd Formed as one company at Pontypool towards the end of 1859 and shown as 3rd Corps until April 1860, when renumbered as 2nd. Colonel Thomas Mitchell, in *History of the Volunteer Movement in Monmouthshire*, notes of the 2nd Corps that its headquarters were at 'Pontypool Works'. To the company were commissioned three officers on 31 December 1859: Captain Richard Brown Roden, Lieutenant Richard Bailey Hawkins and Ensign Henry Tothill. During the later months of 1859 companies were formed near to Pontypool, which, towards the end of 1860, were drawn into the 2nd Corps to form a battalion of six companies. Captain Roden was then gazetted as lieutenant colonel on 8 December 1860 and the companies were located: No. 1 (Pontypool), No. 2 (Ebbw Vale), No. 3 (Abersychan), No. 4 (Ebbw Vale, No. 5 (Sirhowy) and No. 6 (Abercarn). Headquarters about this time were transferred to Bank Chambers, Pontypool, where the Post Office now stands. Absorbed the 11th Corps in May 1861 and the companies were later lettered 'A' to 'F'.

The Abercarn Company was removed from the records after 1866, but Regimental Orders dated 14 May 1868 make mention of a six-company establishment carrying out drills at Cwmbran. G A Brett, in his 1933 history of the 2nd Monmouthshire Regiment, suggests that a new company was formed in 1867 in the district between Pontypool and Cwmbran – references, he notes, were made in later years to a company described variously at Panteg, Upper Pontnewydd and Cwmbran.

In 1877 'G' Company was added at Garndiffaith, with 'H' following in 1884 at Victoria. This, records G A Bret, necessitated the reorganization of the 2nd Corps as 'A' Company (Pontypool), 'B' (Abersychan), 'C' and 'D' (Ebbw Vale), 'E' (Garndiffaith) 'F' (Sirhowy), 'G' (Panteg) and 'H' (Victoria). Re-designated 3rd Volunteer Battalion South Wales Borderers in 1885. Yet further changes in company organization took place in 1897 when 'A' was to be found at Pontypool; 'B', Abersychan; 'C', Upper Pontnewydd; 'D' and 'E', Ebbw Vales; 'F', Sirhowy; 'G', Abersychan and 'H', Abertillery. This would remain the order of battle of the battalion until 1900 when 'C' Company was located at Cwmbran and 'E' at Newbridge – the move from Ebbw Vale was in December 1898. Two new companies were added in 1900, 'I' at Abercarn and 'K' (Cyclist), Ebbw Vale. In 1903 the Ebbw Vale Iron and Coal Company presented a building for use as a drill hall for the Abercarn Company.

Although, noted G A Bret, the whole of the battalion expressed their willingness to proceed overseas, at first just one sergeant, one corporal and seventeen men were permitted to join the 2nd Battalion South Wales Borderers in South Africa. The contingent under Sergeant A Search left Pontypool on 26 January 1900. Subsequently, action was seen at the Zand River crossing on 10 May. A second draft landed at Cape Town on 16 April, 1901, and a third went out in April 1902. There would be just one casualty throughout the campaign, Sergeant Rosser. Francis dying of enteric. There is a memorial plate to him at St Cadoc's Church, Trevethin which also includes the battalion motto '*Gwell Angau na Garth*' (Rather death than disgrace). On 20 December 1902 a new headquarters building in Osborne Road, Pontypool was opened by Honorary Colonel J C Hanbury. Transfer to the Territorial Force in 1908 was as 2nd Battalion Monmouthshire Regiment. Uniform: scarlet/grass green, changing to scarlet/white in 1885.

We have seen how in 1859 Richard Brown Roden had become commanding officer of the 2nd Monmouthshire RVC. He remained at the head of the corps for the next twenty-eight years, his command only to be terminated at his tragic death ('assassinated' records Bret) in Corsica in 1887. Buried at Usk on 16 April, a memorial to him can be seen in St Mary's Church.

3rd (1860–80) Formed 11 February 1860 with headquarters at Newport and was, until April 1860, shown in the *Army List* as 2nd Corps. The corps had been formed as a result of several meetings held in Newport, the first of which took place at the Town Hall on 26 May 1859. The first company formed in Newport was under the command of the Captain the Hon Frederick Courtenay Morgan; Sir George F Radzivil Walker taking No. 2, also in Newport. Before the end of the year No. 3 Company had been raised at Pontymister, about six miles north-west of Newport, No. 4, also at Pontymister, following in 1868. Joined the 1st Admin Battalion in August 1860 and provided 'B', 'C', 'D' and 'E' of the new 1st Corps in 1880. An item in the *Bristol Daily Post* for Thursday 20 February 1862, which reported on a recent inspection, referred to the 3rd Corps as the 'Newport Knickerbockers' – a popular name in and around Newport which alluded to the style of trousers worn. Volunteers were present at the opening in 1906 of Newport's Transporter Bridge. Crossing the Usk, it is one of only two such bridges in the country.

3rd (1880–1908) The 2nd Admin Battalion was formed with headquarters at Pontypool in September 1860 and to it were added the 4th, 5th, 6th, 7th, 8th and 9th Corps. The battalion was consolidated as the new 3rd Corps in 1880, its eight companies being found at:

'A' Blaenavon (late 4th Corps)
'B' Pontypool (late 5th Corps)
'C' Monmouth (6th Corps)
'D' Newport (7th Corps)
'E' Newport (7th Corps)
'F' Newport (7th Corps)
'G' Usk (8th Corps)
'H' Abergavenny (9th Corps)

Re-designated as 4th Volunteer Battalion South Wales Borderers in 1885. The establishment was increased to ten companies in 1900 and in 1904 a cadet corps was raised and affiliated to the battalion at Monmouth Grammar School. Headquarters moved from Pontypool to Newport in 1901 and in 1908 transfer to the Territorial Force was as 3rd Battalion Monmouthshire Regiment. Uniform: green/black, changing to scarlet/white in 1887, scarlet/green before 1908. At Newport Civic Centre the names of forty members of the 4th Volunteer Battalion that saw active service in South Africa are recorded on a tablet unveiled by the Rt Hon Lord Tredegar on 29 October 1904.

4th (1860–64) The *Volunteer Service Gazette* mentions the existence of a Tredegar company in December 1859; the officers' commissions of the 4th Corps, however, were not issued until 17 February 1860, Captain Samuel George Homfray, Lieutenant Nathaniel Coates and Ensign Richard Waters being joined by Thomas G Anthony as surgeon in the following month. Joined the 1st Admin Battalion and was last seen in the *Army List* for March 1864.

4th (1866–80) Formed at Blaenavon towards the end of 1866 from part of the 5th Corps and placed with the 2nd Admin Battalion. Captain Richard J P Steel took command. Became 'A' Company of the new 3rd Corps in 1880. Iron and coal is what Blaenavon was known for in the days of the Volunteer, and iron and coal is what it is known for today – if only as heritage sites and museums.

5th Formed at Pontypool and at first known as the 'Hanbury' Company, it being formed from the Hanbury Tinplate Works. There was also a sub-division at Blaenavon (raised in October 1859 and recruited from the ironworks), which in 1866 was withdrawn and made independent as 4th Corps.

The original 5th Corps officers, all commissioned on 11 February 1860, were: Captain Henry Charles Bird, Lieutenant Richard James Pye Steel and Ensign Charles Conway. David Lawrence was appointed as surgeon. Joined the 2nd Admin Battalion and provided 'B' Company of the new 3rd Corps in 1880.

6th Formed at Monmouth with James P King as captain, Alfred Evans, lieutenant and Egerton Isaacson, ensign. All three held commissions dated 29 February 1860. Also appointed was Thomas Prosser as surgeon. Included in 2nd Admin Battalion and provided 'C' Company of the new 3rd Corps in 1880. Headquarters of the 6th Corps were in Monnow Street.

7th Formed as one company at Newport with Robert J Cathcart as captain, John Phillpotts, lieutenant and John Henry Wilmett, ensign. All three held commissions dated 1 March 1860. Also appointed was William Williams Morgan as surgeon. Known as the 'Borough Corps', the 7th comprised four companies by the end of 1860, but was reduced to three in 1863. Early records of this corps show that its membership was made up of tradesmen, clerks, craftsmen and professional men. More than half of the corps were involved with Newport's shipping industry – shipbuilders, shipping agents and brokers. Included in the 2nd Admin Battalion and provided 'D', 'E' and 'F' Companies of the new 3rd Corps in 1880.

8th Formed at Usk with the Hon James F C Butler as captain, William H Nicholl, lieutenant and W F Greatwood, ensign. All three held commissions dated 14 June 1860. Also appointed was Surgeon Alexander J Shepard. Included in 2nd Admin Battalion and provided 'G' Company of the new 3rd Corps in 1880. Outside the Town Hall in New Market Street a memorial remembers those Volunteers from the area that served in South Africa during the Boer War.

9th Formed at Abergavenny with James C Hill as captain, Cornelius Lloyd, lieutenant and Richard B Gabb, ensign. All three held commissions dated 11 August 1860. Also appointed was surgeon Robert Smythe. Included in 2nd Admin Battalion and provided 'H' Company of the new 3rd Corps in 1880. In 1926 Colonel W D Steel, in writing a short forward to the war history of the 3rd Battalion Monmouthshire Regiment, recalled how 'In July 1879 I joined the Abergavenny Company as a subaltern to my father, who then commanded the 9th (Abergavenny Corps). At that time the whole Battalion [2nd Admin] was clothed in Rifle Green, but, as each Corps or Company provided its own cloth, the shades varied to some extent and there were other slight discrepancies. The Abergavenny Company for instance wore a small bull-dog's head in bronze on their shakos and were known as the "Bulldogs", a nickname due to a special breed of dog peculiar to the town.' The town sits where the rivers Gavenny and Usk meet; its breweries, malthouses, engineworks and iron foundries employed many.

10th Formed 19 November 1860 at Risca from men employed at the Risca Colliery Company, their commanding officer being Captain Thomas Phillpotts jun, who was colliery manager at the time. Also appointed were David Morris as lieutenant and Charles A Harrison, ensign. Joined the 1st Admin Battalion. In the Risca colliery disaster of 1861, a number of Volunteers are known to have been included among the 100 dead. Disbanded in 1875. Risca is just over six miles north-west of Newport.

11th (1860–61) At the beginning of 1861 an 11th Corps appears in the *Army List*. No location is given and a single officer, Lieutenant John Bladon jun, is listed, with commission dated 21 November 1860. This remains the case until May 1861 when the 11th Corps disappears and Lieutenant Bladon appears with the 2nd Corps at Pontypool.

11th (1878–80) Formed 12 October 1878 at Tredegar. Included in 1st Admin Battalion and provided 'F' Company of the new 1st Corps in 1880.

MONTGOMERYSHIRE

All rifle corps raised within the county were placed into the 1st Admin Battalion, formed with headquarters at Welshpool in March 1861. Headquarters were transferred to Newtown in 1864, then back to Welshpool in 1870. The 2nd (later 1st) Cardigan RVC and the 1st Merionethshire RVC were also included in the battalion between 1864 and 1866. In 1873 the battalion was broken up, its remaining corps then transferred to the 1st Shropshire Admin Battalion.

1st Formed as one company at Newtown with John Pryce Drew as captain, Richard Edward Jones, lieutenant and David Lloyd, ensign. All three held commissions dated 19 February 1860. Also appointed was Richard Jones as surgeon. There would be a steady fall-off in numbers after 1870 resulting in disbandment in 1872. Much of Newtown's prosperity came from the manufacture of flannel.

2nd Formed as one company at Welshpool with former 90th Regiment of Foot officer Charles Vaughan Pugh as captain, Robert Devereux Harrison, lieutenant, Peter Arthur Beck, ensign and Edward T D Harrison, who was appointed as surgeon. All four held commissions dated 26 March 1860. Disbanded in 1876. Welshpool's St Mary's Church was greatly restored in 1871. The town's employment was largely agricultural.

3rd Formed at Welshpool with Jasper W Johns as captain, Benjamin Piercey, lieutenant and Thomas Savin, ensign. All three held commissions dated 14 August 1860. Also appointed was John P Wilding as surgeon. Comprised two companies by May 1861, but disbanded in 1872.

4th (1861–64) Formed as a sub-division at Machynlleth with Francis Johnson Ford as lieutenant and Thomas Ellis, ensign. Both held commissions dated 10 January 1861. The corps also included the Revd John Evans as chaplain and David Pugh Evans, who became surgeon. Disbanded in March 1864. There were lead mines and slate quarries in the area.

4th (1864–76) Formed as a sub-division at Llanidloes and first numbered as 5th Corps. The first officers were Lieutenant Charles Thomas Woosnam and Ensign Evan Powell, both with commissions dated 2 March 1816. Also appointed were John P Morgan as chaplain and William A P Dickin, who became surgeon. Renumbered as 4th in 1864 and disbanded 1876. The town is on the Severn about eleven miles from Newtown.

5th See 4th Corps (1864–76).

5th Volunteer Battalion South Wales Borderers Formed with headquarters at Newtown on 1 April 1897 with Major E Pryce-Jones in command. The original establishment was four companies, two more being added later – one according to the *Territorial Yearbook* for 1909, being raised by Aberystwyth University College on 17 March 1900. Transferred to the Territorial Force in 1908 as headquarters and four companies of 7th Battalion Royal Welsh Fusiliers. The University personnel became part of the OTC. Uniform: scarlet/white.

NAIRNSHIRE

1st Formed as one company at Nairn with Augustus Clarke as captain, Archibald Campbell, lieutenant and James Macpherson, ensign. All three held commissions dated 14 April 1860. Captain Clarke left the corps during the summer of 1861; his place was never filled and subsequently, in 1862, 1st Nairn RVC was disbanded. On the Moray Firth, Nairn lies about fifteen miles north-east of Inverness.

NEWCASTLE-UPON-TYNE

1st Formation of the 1st Newcastle-upon-Tyne RVC began in 1859 when the Newcastle Rifle Club decided to form a corps. By the end of the year sufficient members had been enrolled to form a battalion of nine companies. The first officers were gazetted on 22 February 1860, Sir John Fife becoming commanding officer, Robert Robey Redmayne his second-in-command. The nine companies were made up from all sections of the Newcastle community, each named to indicate the origins of their members, eg, 'Quaysiders' 'Oddfellows' or 'Temperance'. There was even a kilted company recruited from Scotsmen resident in the city and one, known as 'Guards', which required its members to be not less than six foot in height. Others came from the Hampton factory, two from Robert Stephenson's locomotive works, another was found at the Elswick Ordnance factory. The battalion had increased to thirteen companies by 1861, but this establishment was later reduced to eight. Designation as 3rd Volunteer Battalion Northumberland Fusiliers was notified in General Order 14 of February 1883 and two new companies were added (one from Durham University) in 1900. Transfer to the Territorial Force in 1908 was as 6th Battalion Northumberland Fusiliers. The University Company at the same time became a contingent of the Senior Division, OTC. Uniform: scarlet/black, changing to scarlet/white in 1886.

NORFOLK

Three admin battalions were formed (two numbered as 1st) which later provided the new 2nd, 3rd and 4th Corps. Six numbered sub-divisions appeared in the early *Army Lists*: for 1st see 6th Corps; 2nd, see 7th Corps; 3rd, see 8th Corps; 4th, see 9th Corps; 5th, see 10th Corps and 6th, see 11th Corps.

1st (1859–60) Formed at Norwich on 31 August 1859 and became part of the new 1st Corps by February 1860.

1st (City of Norwich) (1860–1908) In the *Army List* for February 1860 the 1st, 2nd and 3rd Norfolk RVC are shown as having been amalgamated under the title of 1st (City of Norwich) RVC. The new formation comprised six companies under the command of Major Commandant John Davy Brett, who had previously served with the 7th Dragoons. Designated 1st Volunteer Battalion Norfolk Regiment in 1883. A cadet corps was formed in 1893, but this was absorbed into the 1st Cadet Battalion Norfolk Regiment in 1895. Transfer to the Territorial Force in 1908 was as part of the 4th Battalion Norfolk Regiment. Uniform: scarlet/white.

During the Volunteer period the Corn Exchange was completed in 1861, the Post Office in 1875 and the Agricultural Hall opened in 1882 by the Prince of Wales. Among the products manufactured in the city were clothing, wire netting, iron fencing and gates. Colman's English Mustard was made here since the early nineteenth century.

2nd (1859–60) Formed at Norwich on 15 September 1859 and became part of the new 1st Corps by February 1860.

2nd (Great Yarmouth) (1860–80) Formed as the 4th Corps at Great Yarmouth on 3 September 1859 and soon comprised four companies under the command of Major J H Orde. Renumbered as 2nd by September 1860. Towards the end of 1877 joined the 1st Admin Battalion and became 'A', 'B', 'C' and 'D' Companies of the new 2nd Corps in March 1880. The fishing industry was one of Great Yarmouth's main sources of employment.

2nd (1880–1908) The 1st Admin Battalion was formed with headquarters at Great Yarmouth towards the end of 1876 and included the 2nd Norfolk RVC with the 4th, 14th and 17th Suffolk – this was the second admin battalion to hold this number, the original having been consolidated as 3rd Corps in 1872. The new 1st Admin was consolidated as the new 2nd Corps in March 1880 with nine companies:

'A', 'B', 'C', 'D' Great Yarmouth (late 2nd Norfolk Corps)
'E' Gorleston (newly formed)
'F' Bungay (late 4th Suffolk)
'G' Beccles (late 14th Suffolk)
'H', 'I' Lowestoft (late 17th Suffolk)

Re-designated as 2nd Volunteer Battalion Norfolk Regiment under General Order 79 of June 1883, a tenth company being added in 1885. Transfer to the Territorial Force in 1908 was as part of 5th Battalion Norfolk Regiment. Uniform: scarlet/white.

3rd (1859–60) Formed at Norwich on 2 September 1859 and became part of the new 1st Corps by February 1860.

3rd (1872–1908) On 4 April 1861 the original 1st Admin Battalion was formed with headquarters at Fakenham and to it were added the 5th, 6th, 10th, 11th, 12th, 13th, 15th, 16th, 17th, 19th, 23rd and 24th Corps. Headquarters transferred to Norwich in 1862, then to East Dereham in 1866. On 3rd July 1872 the battalion was consolidated as the new 3rd Corps of ten companies. General Order 79 of June 1883 notified re-designation as 3rd Volunteer Battalion Norfolk Regiment. A cadet corps was formed by the 5th Corps at King's Lynn in 1867 and this appears with headquarters at East Dereham from 1883, but is shown once again at King's Lynn from 1885. The company finally disappeared from the *Army List* in February 1888. Another cadet corps was formed at the Norfolk County School at North Elmham in 1888, but this too was disbanded and last seen in 1893. Next came Gresham's School at Holt in 1902. Transfer to the Territorial Force in 1908 was as part of 5th Battalion Norfolk Regiment. Gresham's at the same time joined the OTC. Uniform: scarlet/white.

4th (1859–60) See 2nd Corps (1860–80).

4th (1872–1908) The 2nd Admin Battalion was formed with headquarters at Norwich on 25 March 1861 and to it were added the 7th, 8th, 9th, 14th, 18th, 20th, 21st and 22nd Corps. The 16th and 23rd joined in 1863, but these were transferred to 1st Admin in 1864. Consolidated in 1872 as the new 4th with six companies and designated 4th Volunteer Battalion Norfolk Regiment in 1883. Harleston, Diss, Loddon, Stalham, Blofield and Attleborough were the company locations in 1899, four more being added in 1900. Transfer to the Territorial Force in 1908 was as part of 4th Battalion Norfolk Regiment. Uniform: grey/grey, changing to scarlet/white in 1888.

5th Formed as one company at King's Lynn on 5 September 1859 with William Swatman Bt as captain, Francis Joseph Cresswell, lieutenant and Somerville Arthur Gurney, ensign. Joined the

1st Admin Battalion in 1863, a cadet corps being formed and affiliated in 1867. Became part of the new 3rd Corps in 1872. Situated on the Ouse, the docks at King's Lynn were opened in 1869, and the old Lynn & Dereham Railway station (opened in 1846) replaced with a new one in August 1871.

6th Formed at Aylsham on 23 September 1859 and known as 1st Sub-division until March. 1860. The first officers to receive commissions were Lientenant Henry Scott and Ensign Harold Augustus Ernuin. Joined the 1st Admin Battalion and became part of the new 3rd Corps in 1872. Aylsham is twelve miles north-west of Norwich.

7th Formed at Harleston on 30 September 1859 and known as the 2nd Sub-division until March 1860. The first officers to be commissioned were Captain Charles Mortlock, Lieutenant William T W Wood and Benjamin Charles Chaston. Joined the 2nd Admin Battalion and Became part of the new 4th Corps in 1872. Harleston is south of Norwich on the road from Diss to Great Yarmouth.

8th Formed at Diss on 7 October 1859 and known as the 3rd Sub-division until March 1860. The first officers to receive commissions were Lieutenant George Edward Frere and Ensign Thomas William Salmon. Joined the 2nd Admin Battalion and became part of the new 4th Corps in 1872. At Diss, on the River Waverly nineteen miles south-west of Norwich, there was a brewery and a factory making matting.

9th Formed at Loddon on 8 October 1859 and known as the 4th Sub-division until March 1860. The first officers to be commissioned were Lieutenant Thomas William B Proctor Beauchamp and Ensign Richard Henry Gilbert. Joined the 2nd Admin Battalion and became part of the new 4th Corps in 1872. At Loddon, seven miles north-west of Beccles, the Town Hall was opened in 1870.

10th Formed at Fakenham on 20 October 1859 and known as the 5th Sub-division until March 1860. The first officers to be commissioned were Lieutenant Sir Willoughby Jones Bt and Ensign Robert Nicholas Hammond. Joined the 1st Admin Battalion and disbanded in 1866. Fakenham, to the north-east of King's Lynn, is on the road to Cromer.

11th Formed at Holkham on 21 October 1859 and known as the 6th Sub-division until March 1860. The first to be commissioned were Lieutenant James Holloway and Ensign Charles Horatio Day Blyth. Joined the 1st Admin Battalion and became part of the new 3rd Corps in 1872. The village is just to the west of Wells-next-the-Sea.

12th Formed with headquarters given in the *Army List* as Eynesford, on 26 April 1860, but shown as Reepham, twelve miles north-west of Norwich, by the end of 1860. The first to be commissioned were John McMahon Wilder as lieutenant and Francis S Bircham as ensign. Joined the 1st Admin Battalion and became part of the new 3rd Corps in 1872. The old East Norfolk Railway reached Reepham in May 1881.

13th Formed at Cromer on 16 April 1860 with the Rt Hon Edward Vernon Lord Suffield as lieutenant and Thomas Cremer, ensign. Joined the 1st Admin Battalion and was disbanded in 1866. Cromer is twenty miles north of Norwich.

14th Formed at Stalham on 18 April 1860 with Henry A Cubitt, late of the 63rd Regiment of Foot, as lieutenant and Randall Burroughs as ensign. Joined the 2nd Admin Battalion and became part of the new 4th Corps in 1872. Stalham is sixteen miles north-west of Great Yarmouth.

15th Formed at East Dereham on 27 April 1860 with William R Freeman as lieutenant and

Simpson Backhouse, ensign. Joined the 1st Admin Battalion and became part of the new 3rd Corps in 1872. At East Dereham, sixteen miles north-west of Norwich, there were iron foundries, breweries, a factory making shoes and a coachworks.

Extracts from the diary of the Revd Benjamin J Armstrong, who was vicar of East Dereham from 1850 to 1888, were published by Harrap in 1949. Revd Armstrong mentions how, on 6 June 1859, he attended a public meeting at the Corn Hall in which he spoke urging people to form a Dereham Rifle Corps. The propose corps having formed, drills were being held at the Corn Hall by 7 May, when Revd Armstrong noted some thirty Volunteers wearing grey uniform, the ranks containing a 'fat old banker of seventy, and next to him, perhaps, a slim youth of seventeen'.

Benjamin Armstrong was appointed chaplain to the 15th Corps on 19 July 1868, his diary going on to reveal a number of interesting incidents. On the way to camp at Hunstanton Park in June 1868, 'Near Wells the van took fire, and, as it contained the ammunition, considerable excitement was felt till it was extinguished.' Gradually the several corps belonging to the 1st Admin Battalion changed their uniforms from grey to scarlet, Revd Armstrong noting that on 25 July 1877 although 'two-thirds' of the battalion had done so, the 15th had yet to comply. On 8 September 1878, however: 'In the afternoon I preached to the local Company of Volunteers, who appeared in their scarlet uniform and black helmets ....'

16th Formed at Swaffham on 12 June 1860 with William A T Amhurst as captain, Antony Hammond, lieutenant and Andrew Margam, ensign. Joined the 2nd Admin Battalion in 1863, transferring to the 1st in the following year, and became part of the new 3rd Corps in 1872. The town is twelve miles west of East Dereham.

17th Formed at Snettisham, on the coast road to Hunstanton, on 4 September 1860 with William C T Campbell as captain, John de C Hamilton, lieutenant and Charles W Preedy, ensign. Joined the 1st Admin Battalion in 1863, moving headquarters to Heacham, just to the north along the old Lynn & Hunstanton line, in 1867. Became part of the new 3rd Corps in 1872. Both Snettisham and Heacham Stations were opened in October 1862.

18th Formed at Blofield on 16 August 1860 with William H Jary as lieutenant and Edward Gilbert, ensign. Joined the 2nd Admin Battalion and became part of the new 4th Corps in 1872. At Blofield, seven miles east of Norwich, St Andrew's Church was restored in 1878.

19th Formed at Holt on 1 March 1861 with George Barker as lieutenant and George Wilkinson, ensign. Joined the 1st Admin Battalion and became part of the new 3rd Corps in 1872. Holt is a mile inland on the road from Fakenham to Cromer.

20th Formed at Attleborough on 6 October 1860 with Sir R T Buxton Bt as captain, Thomas Beevor, lieutenant and A J E B Smyth, ensign. Joined the 2nd Admin Battalion and became part of the new 4th Corps in 1872. Attleborough is sixteen miles south-west of Norwich.

21st Formed at Wymondham on 11 October 1860 with Edmund H W Bellairs as captain, George Forrester, lieutenant and Edmund Larke, ensign. Joined the 2nd Admin Battalion and became part of the new 4th Corps in 1872. Just under ten miles south-west of Norwich, the town had a large brewery, sawmills, and a brush factory.

22nd Formed at Thetford on 13 December 1860 with Thomas Thornhill jun as lieutenant and Alexander H Baring, ensign. Joined the 2nd Admin Battalion and became part of the new 4th Corps in 1872. Two venues for social gathering were built during the Volunteer days: the Mechanics' Institute in 1887 and the Odd Fellows' Hall in 1891. The town gave employment in its breweries, brick and lime kilns, chemical works and extensive iron foundry. Thetford Bridge Station was opened when the Thetford & Watton Railway reached the town in November 1875.

23rd Formed at Downham Market on 23 February 1861 with William Bagge as lieutenant and Thomas Lancelot Reed, ensign. Joined the 2nd Admin Battalion, transferring to the 1st in 1864, and became part of the new 3rd Corps in 1872. The town is eleven miles south-west of King's Lynn.

24th Formed at North Walsham on 13 November 1862 with J Duff, late of the 23rd Royal Welsh Fusiliers as captain, Martin J Shepheard, Lientenant and John Shepheard, ensign. Joined the 1st Admin Battalion and became part of the new 3rd Corps in 1872. The town, fourteen miles north of Norwich, employed many in a factory manufacturing agricultural implements.

1st Cadet Battalion Norfolk Regiment Formed with headquarters at the Drill Hall, Theatre Street, Norwich as four companies on 23 January 1895. Location is given later given as St Peter's Hall, Norwich, and by 1898 as Britannia Barracks. The battalion was last seen in the *Army List* for March 1900. Uniform: scarlet/white.

NORTHAMPTONSHIRE

All rifle corps formed within the county joined the 1st Admin Battalion, which became the new 1st Corps in 1880. A 1st Sub-division was shown in *Army List* for March 1860 with headquarters at Overstone, but this was removed the following month.

1st (1859–80) Formed at Althorp on 29 August 1859 from tenants of Earl Spencer's estate. The earl took command, with John Beasley jun as his lieutenant. Became 'A' Company of the new 1st Corps in 1880. Althorp Park Station, on the old London & North Western Railway, was opened in December 1881.

1st (1880–1908) The 1st Admin Battalion was formed with headquarters at Northampton on 8 August 1860 and consolidated in 1880 as the new 1st Corps with thirteen companies:

'A' Althorp (late 1st Corps)
'B' Towcester (late 2nd Corps)
'C' to 'G' Northampton (late 3rd Corps)
'H' and 'I' Peterborough (late 6th Corps)
'K' and 'L' Wellingborough (late 7th Corps)
'M' Daventry (late 8th Corps)
'N' Kettering (late 9th Corps)

Re-designated as 1st Volunteer Battalion Northamptonshire Regiment under General Order 181 of December 1887. Three new companies were added in 1900. Wellingborough Grammar School Cadet Corps was formed and affiliated in 1900, Oundle School Cadet Corps in 1902. Transfer to the Territorial Force in 1908 was as 4th Battalion Northamptonshire Regiment. Two of the Peterborough companies, however, were converted to artillery, under the title of Northamptonshire Battery RFA, and as supply and transport troops, the East Midland Brigade Company ASC. Wellingborough and Oundle Schools became contingents of the Junior Division, OTC. Uniform: grey/scarlet.

2nd Formed at Towcester on 19 October 1859 with the Rt Hon George William Fermor, Earl of

Pomfret, in command; his lieutenant being John Wardlaw, who had previously served with the King's Own Militia. Became 'B' Company of the new 1st Corps in 1880. Eight miles south-west of Northampton, Towcester, like many other towns in the area, employed a number in the manufacture of boots and shoes. Towcester Station was opened in May 1866.

3rd A 3rd Corps appeared in the *Army List* for March 1860, but this disappeared in the following April having had no officers or location allotted to it. This position in the county list was to remain vacant until 1872 when, upon the amalgamation of the two Northampton corps (4th and 5th) as 3rd of five companies, the space was filled. The new 3rd Corps became 'C' to 'G' Companies of the new 1st Corps in 1880. Northampton, then, as now, the largest manufacturer of shoes and boots in the country, several factories supplying the latter to the army. There were also a number of large breweries.

4th Formed as one company at Northampton, its members were described as 'professional men and tradesmen', on 15 February 1860 with William Alexander Barr as captain, William Griffiths Hollis, lieutenant, and George Norman Welton, ensign. Increased to two companies in December 1861, then to three in March 1865. Amalgamated with the 5th Corps in 1872 and renumbered as 3rd.

5th Formed as one company by the Northampton firm Messrs Isaac, Campbell & Co. on 3 March 1860 with Samuel Isaac as captain, Saul Isaac, lieutenant and Michael L Levey, ensign. Increased to three companies by the end of 1861, amalgamated with the 4th Corps in 1872, and renumbered as 3rd Corps.

6th Formed at Peterborough on 3 March 1860 with the Hon George W Fitzwilliam as captain, Leonard Deacon, lieutenant, and John Beecroft, ensign. Became 'H' and 'I' Companies of the new 1st Corps in 1880. As well as boots and shoes, agricultural implements were made at Peterborough.

7th Formed at Wellingborough on 20 September 1860 with Henry M Stockdale as captain, local solicitor George H Burnham, lieutenant, and William C Trotman, ensign. Became 'K' and 'L' Companies of the new 1st Corps in 1880. The Corn Exchange in the market square was opened in 1861, the town's main employment being in the production of boots and shoes.

8th Formed at Daventry on 23 November 1860 with Rainald Knightley as captain, Edmund C Borton, lieutenant and Thomas Willoughby, ensign. Became 'M' Company of the new 1st Corps in 1880. The town, twelve miles north-west of Northampton, gave employment to many in its several shoe and boot factories. Daventry Station, on the old London & North Western Railway, was opened in March 1888.

9th Formed at Kettering on 22 April 1867 with Frederick M Eden as captain, John G Willows, lieutenant and J W Dryland, ensign. Became 'N' Company of the new 1st Corps in 1880. At Kettering, seven miles north of Wellingborough, a hospital for infectious diseases was opened in 1886, the Working Men's Club in 1887 and the Victoria Hall in 1889. Boots and shoes were manufactured in the town.

NORTHUMBERLAND

Two admin battalions were formed, of which the 2nd was broken up in 1865. The 1st went on to provide the new 1st Corps in 1880. The 2nd had been formed with headquarters at Tynemouth in August 1861 and included the 1st, 8th and 9th Corps. Headquarters moved to Walker in 1863.

1st (1859–62) Formed at Tynemouth on 16 August 1859 and absorbed the 2nd Corps, also at Tynemouth, in February 1860. The corps, which included companies at Walker and Cramlington, was raised by coal owner Edward Potter and divided as 1st, 8th and 9th Northumberland RVC in August 1861 and at the same time placed into the newly formed 2nd Admin Battalion. Of the three, the 1st Corps was disbanded in October 1862.

1st (1880–1908) The 1st Admin Battalion was formed with headquarters at Alnwick in November 1860 and into it were placed the 2nd, 3rd, 4th, 5th, 6th, 7th, 10th, 11th and 12th Corps. The 1st Berwick-upon-Tweed was also included. Consolidated as the 1st Northumberland and Berwick-upon-Tweed RVC with ten companies in 1880:

'A' Hexham (late 2nd Corps)
'B' Morpeth (late 3rd Corps)
'C' Belford (late 4th Corps)
'D' Alnwick (late 5th Corps)
'E' Bellingham (late 6th Corps)
'F' Allendale (late 7th Corps)
'G' Berwick-upon-Tweed (late 1st Berwick-upon-Tweed)
'H' Lowick (late 10th Corps)
'I' Corbridge (late 11th Corps)
'K' Haltwhistle (late 12th Corps)

Under General Order 14 of February 1883 the 1st Corps was re-designated as 1st Volunteer Battalion Northumberland Fusiliers. In 1885 the Lowick Company was disbanded and in its place a new 'K' was formed at Newburn. Nine years later the personnel of this company were transferred to the 2nd Volunteer Battalion and at the same time replaced by a new 'H' at Prudhoe. Headquarters moved to Hexham in 1891 and two new companies were added in 1900. By this time certain reorganizations had taken place within the battalion resulting in the company locations being arranged as: Hexham (2), Belford, Alnwick, Bellingham, Haydon Bridge, Prudhoe, Corbridge, Haltwhistle and Morpeth (2). The two Hexham companies ('A' and 'B') were merged as 'A' in 1903, a replacement 'B' being found by the transfer of No. 7 Company of the 2nd Northumberland Royal Garrison Artillery Volunteers at Ashington. Transfer to the Territorial Force in 1908 was as 4th Battalion Northumberland Fusiliers, the Alnwick personnel providing the nucleus of the 7th Battalion. Uniform: grey/scarlet.

2nd (1860) Formed at Tynemouth on 4 January 1860 and absorbed into the 1st Corps in the following month.

2nd (1860–80) Formed at Hexham on 10 March 1860 with John M Ridley as captain, Richard J Gibson, lieutenant and William B Ridley, ensign. Joined the 1st Admin Battalion and became 'A' Company of the new 1st Corps in 1880. Once known for its manufacture of gloves and other leather items, Hexham is nineteen miles west of Newcastle-upon-Tyne.

2nd (1880–1908) Formed at Walker as three companies of the 1st Corps and made independent as 8th Corps in August 1861. Placed into the newly formed 2nd Admin Battalion and renumbered as 2nd Corps in 1880. Designated 2nd Volunteer Battalion Northumberland Fusiliers in 1883, the corps by then consisted of six companies, all at Walker, lettered 'A' to 'F'. In 1894 the Newburn Company of the 1st Volunteer Battalion was transferred to the 2nd as 'G'. The following year 'H' was formed at Wallsend and in 1900 additional personnel raised saw the battalion's companies rearranged as follows: Walker (4), Newburn (2), Wallsend (2) and Gosforth (2).

Transfer to the Territorial Force in 1908 was as 5th Battalion Northumberland Fusiliers. Uniform: scarlet/green.

3rd Formed at Morpeth on 12 March 1860 with George Brummell as captain, Charles Septimus Swan, lieutenant and William Jobling, ensign. Joined the 1st Admin Battalion and became 'B' Company of the new 1st Corps in 1880. Breweries, brick and tile manufacturers gave employment to the area, Morpeth's new Town Hall being built 1869–70.

4th Formed at Wooler on 23 April 1860 with the Earl of Tankerville as captain in command. Joined the 1st Admin Battalion, moved to Belford in 1861, and became 'C' Company of the new 1st Corps in 1880. At Wooler, where its Mechanics' Institute was opened in 1889, Cassell's notes that in the 1890s the town's population were chiefly employed in agriculture and sheep-herding. Wooler Station, on the old North Eastern Railway, was opened in September 1887.

5th Formed at Alnwick on 27 March 1860 with Walter J Browne, a former major general of the Bombay Army, as captain and John Atkinson Wilson, lieutenant. Joined the 1st Admin Battalion and became 'D' Company of the new 1st Corps in 1880. At Alnwick in 1863, the Church of St Mary and St Michael, with its many references to that keen supporter of the Volunteer Movement, the Percy family, was restored. In the town there were tobacco and snuff factories. Alnwick Station, on the North Eastern line, was replaced by a new one just to the north in September 1887.

6th Formed at Tynedale on 23 April 1860 with William H Charlton as captain, Edward C Charlton, lieutenant and Francis Charlton, ensign. Joined the 1st Admin Battalion and became 'E' Company of the new 1st Corps in 1880. Although the 6th Corps headquarters location is given in the *Army List* through to 1880, the records accompanying the overall reorganizations of that year show 'E' Company as being at Bellingham. This town and parish is situated of the North Tyne, sixteen miles south-west of Hexham.

7th Formed at Allendale on 11 September 1860 with Thomas Sopwith as captain, Joseph Coats, lieutenant and George Armison, ensign. Joined the 1st Admin Battalion and became 'F' Company of the new 1st Corps in 1880. Allendale, ten miles south-west of Hexham, was lit by electricity in 1889. The Hexham & Allendale Railway reached Allendale in 1869, Catton Road Station (renamed Allendale in May 1898) being opened on 1st March.

8th See 2nd Corps (1880–1908).

9th Formed at Cramlington from one company of the 1st Corps in August 1861. Joined the 2nd Admin Battalion and disbanded in December 1864. Collieries provided the main employed at Cramlington, just over six miles south-east of Morpeth.

10th Formed at Lowick on 20 December 1861 with the Earl of Durham as captain, Henry Gregson, lieutenant and Thomas Hunt, ensign. Joined the 1st Admin Battalion and became 'H' Company of the new 1st Corps in 1880. The Lowick Volunteers attending the town's St Peter's Church would have seen the restoration that went on there during 1869.

11th Formed at Lee St John on 25 April 1868 with Richard Gibson as captain, John P Walton, lieutenant and James Mewburn, ensign. Joined the 1st Admin Battalion and moved to Corbridge in 1876. Became 'I' Company of the new 1st Corps in 1880. Almost within the shadow of Hadrian's Wall, the parish of Lee St John lies just to the north of Hexham; Corbridge, three miles or so along the old Newcastle & Carlisle Railway.

12th Formed at Haltwhistle on 3 July 1878. Joined the 1st Admin Battalion and became 'K' Company of the new 1st Corps in 1880. Haltwhistle is on the north bank on the Tyne to the west of Hexham and employed many in its collieries and brickworks.

NOTTINGHAMSHIRE

All rifle corps formed within the county, other than the 1st, joined the 1st Admin Battalion, which provided the new 2nd Corps in 1880.

1st (Robin Hood) In the *Army List* for October 1859, five separate companies of unnumbered Rifle Volunteers are shown as having been formed at Nottingham. In that for December the five now appear as having been amalgamated under the title of The Robin Hood RVC, the officers' commissions being dated 15 November 1859. By March 1860 the corps had been designated as the 1st Nottinghamshire (Robin Hood) RVC and comprised nine companies, a former Rifle Brigade officer, Robert Crawford, being appointed as Lieutenant Colonel Commandant. Became a volunteer battalion (without change in title) of the Sherwood Foresters in 1881 and as such contributed Volunteers for the war in South Africa, the first contingent under Captain Turner sailing in February 1900. Richards, in *His Majesty's Territorial Army*, notes, 'During their presence at the seat of war they were in three pitched battles and no less than twenty-five engagements, and under fire on twenty-eight occasions.' Sergeant Hickinbottom was mentioned in dispatches and awarded the Distinguished Conduct Medal.

By 1881 the Robin Hoods comprised ten companies, an eleventh was added in 1895, a twelfth, a year later, and in 1900/01 a further six brought the establishment up to eighteen companies. These were then divided equally into two battalions. A cadet corps was also formed at this time by Nottingham High School. Transfer to the Territorial Force in 1908 was as 7th Battalion Sherwood Foresters, Nottingham High School Cadet Corps at the same time becoming part of the OTC. Uniform: green/black.

Jesse Boot opened his first chemist shop (Boots) in Nottingham in 1877. The cyclists of the town, and indeed, the battalion, would all have known of the premises in Raleigh Street that began to make 'Raleigh' bicycles towards the end of the 1890s. Nottingham, of course, would be best known for its production of lace.

2nd (1860–80) Formed as one company at East Retford on 3 March 1860 with Charles S Burnaby as captain, T Wagstaff, lieutenant and John Smith, ensign. Became 'A' Company of the new 2nd Corps in 1880. At East Retford there were iron and brass foundries and an india-rubber works.

2nd (1880–1908) The 1st Admin Battalion was formed at Newark in May 1861, headquarters being transferred to East Retford in 1865. The battalion was consolidated in 1880 as the new 2nd Corps with eight companies:

'A' East Retford (late 2nd Corps)
'B', 'C' Newark (late 3rd Corps)
'D' Mansfield (late 4th Corps)
'E' Thorney Wood Chase (late 5th Corps)
'F' Collingham (late 6th Corps)
'G' Worksop (late 7th Corps)
'H' Southwell (late 8th Corps)

In 1887, under General Order 39 of April, the 2nd Corps was re-designated as 4th (Nottinghamshire) Volunteer Battalion Sherwood Foresters, headquarters transferring to Newark in 1890. Two cadet corps were associated with the battalion: Worksop College in 1900 and the Queen Elizabeth School at Mansfield in 1906. Transfer to the Territorial Force in 1908 was as 8th Battalion Sherwood Foresters, both Worksop College and Queen Elizabeth School at the same time joining the OTC. Uniform: scarlet/green.

3rd Formed as one company at Newark on 3 March 1860 with Sir Henry Bromley Bt as captain, William Newton, lieutenant and James H Betts, ensign. Increased to two companies in March 1863 and became 'B' and 'C' Companies of the new 2nd Corps in 1880. At Newark in 1883, the Gilstrap Free Library was opened in Castle Gate, and the Fire Station in 1890. There were numerous iron and brass foundries in the area, the manufacture of plaster also being important to the town.

4th Formed as one company at Mansfield on 9 March 1860 with James Salmond as captain, J Paget as lieutenant and Charles Seely jun, ensign. Became 'D' Company of the new 2nd Corps in 1880. Restoration work was carried out at Mansfield's St Peter's Church throughout 1874–91, while on the railway a new station was opened when the old Midland line was extended to Shirebrook in March 1872. Employment in and around the town was mostly from the manufacture of boots and shoes. There were also large iron foundries and engine works.

5th Formed as one company on 9 March 1860 with Mansfield Parkyns as captain, Charles Storer, lieutenant and William L Hoskinson, ensign. Headquarters are given as Thorney Wood Chase, the southern division of Sherwood Forest. Became 'E' Company of the new 2nd Corps in 1880.

6th Formed as one company at Collingham on 9 March 1860 with Thomas S Wooley as captain, William L Dominichetti, lieutenant and John Broadbent, ensign. Became 'F' Company of the new 2nd Corps in 1880. Probably among the finest records of service within the Volunteer Force is that of the Wooleys; a member of that family commanding the 6th Corps (and later 'F' Company) for just two years short of a half century. Divided into North and South Collingham, the villages are just under six miles north-east of Newark.

7th Formed as one company at Worksop on 28 April 1860 with James Mason, late of the 94th Regiment of Foot as captain, Henry S Hodding, lieutenant and Frederick M Buy, ensign. Became 'G' Company of the new 2nd Corps in 1880. At Worksop there were iron and brass foundries, sawmills, and a chemical works.

8th Formed as one company at Southwell on 7 July 1860 with John H Becher as captain, Thomas Elliott, lieutenant and Harrington O'Shore, ensign. Became 'H' Company of the new 2nd Corps in 1880. Southwell is seven miles west of Newark. On the old Midland Railway, its station was renamed Rolleston Junction four months after the formation of the 8th Corps.

ORKNEY AND SHETLAND

1st Formed as a sub-division at Lerwick on 24 April 1860 with Lieutenant Robert Bell and Ensign Arthur J Hay. Joined the 1st Admin Battalion of Sutherland Rifle Volunteers in 1864, increased to a full company in August 1866, and became 'F' Company of the new 1st Sutherland Corps in 1880. Disbanded in 184. On the east coast of Mainland, Shetland, Lerwick's County Buildings were opened in 1872, its Town Hall in 1883.

7th Volunteer Battalion Gordon Highlanders Since the disbandment of 'F' Company,

1st Sutherland RVC at Lerwick in 1884 there were no Volunteers on the Shetlands until 1900 when three new companies – 'A' and 'B' at Lerwick, 'C' at Scalloway – were raised as 7th VB Gordon Highlanders. Their captain commandant was Alexander Moffatt, whose commission was dated 19 December 1900. Both the Lerwick companies used a range at Ness of Sound, the Scalloway Volunteers took musketry at Asta. Transfer to the Territorial Force in 1908 was as The Shetland Companies Gordon Highlanders. Uniform: khaki. Both Lerwick and, just under seven miles south-west, Scalloway, rely on fishing as their main industry.

OXFORDSHIRE

All corps, other than the 1st, joined the 1st Admin Battalion, which became the new 2nd Corps in 1875.

1st (Oxford University) On 8 August 1859 three companies of Rifle Volunteers were formed within Oxford University. A fourth followed on 16 December. In the *Army List* for February 1860 all four companies are shown as having been amalgamated under the title of 1st University of Oxford RVC. Fifth and sixth Companies were added in March 1860 with, in command, the Hon Robert C H Spencer, late of the Royal Artillery. In 1887, under General Order 181 of December, the corps was re-designated as 1st (Oxford University) Volunteer Battalion Oxfordshire Light Infantry. Magdalen College School Cadet Corps was formed and affiliated in May 1873, but this disbanded late in 1884. Another unit known as the Oxford Military College Cadet Corps was formed in July 1885, but again, this was to be removed from the *Army List* in January 1898. Transfer to the Territorial Force in 1908 was as the Oxford University Contingent Senior Division OTC. Uniform: scarlet/dark blue.

2nd (1860–75) Formed at Oxford on 4 February 1860 with Henry Atkins Bowyer, late of the 14th Dragoons, as captain, John Parsons jun, lieutenant and Thomas Mallam, ensign. Became part of the new 2nd Corps in July 1875. Much building work went on in Oxford during the time of the Volunteers: the new Town Hall and Municipal Buildings in St Aldate's Street, the Corn Exchange between George Street and Gloucester Green, Probate Court, Post Office and numerous college buildings.

2nd (1875–1908) The 1st Admin Battalion was formed with headquarters at Oxford in May 1860 and consolidated as the new 2nd Corps of six companies on 8 July 1875, a seventh being added at Chipping Norton in 1876. The title of 2nd Volunteer Battalion Oxfordshire Light Infantry was assumed under General Order 181 of December 1887. Two new companies were formed in 1900, and transfer to the Territorial Force in 1908 was as 4th Battalion Oxfordshire Light Infantry. Uniform: scarlet/white.

3rd Formed as one company at Banbury on 13 February 1860 with John Edmund Severne, late of the 16th Dragoons, as captain, Timothy Edward Cobb, lieutenant and John Potts, ensign. A second company was raised from workers at the Britannia Works (where agricultural implements were manufactured) in May 1860. Became part of the new 2nd Corps in July 1875. At Banbury, sacking, rope, bricks, titles and, of course, cakes were manufactured.

4th Formed at Henley-on-Thames on 13 March 1860 with Thomas F Maitland as lieutenant and Arthur D'O Brooks, ensign. Became part of the new 2nd Corps in July 1875. Cassell's notes that malting, brewing and a large trade in corn, flour and timber gave employment to the area.

5th Formed at Woodstock on 26 May 1860 with Charles E Thornhill as captain, William E Taunton, lieutenant and James Clinch, ensign. Part of the company was detached to form the 9th Corps in October 1861, headquarters of 5th Corps then changing to Witney. Disbanded in December 1864. Witney, eleven miles from Oxford, made gloves and, for centuries, blankets.

6th Formed at Deddington on 25 April 1860 with Samuel Field as lieutenant and C D Faulkner, ensign. Became part of the new 2nd Corps in July 1875. On the Cherwell, Deddington is six miles south of Banbury.

7th Formed at Bicester on 12 May 1860 with William W M Dewar as lieutenant and C J Bullock Marsham, ensign. Disbanded in 1870. The town is ten miles north-east of Oxford, its main business, notes Cassell's, being the many cattle markets held there.

8th Formed at Thame on 27 November 1860 with Phillip T H Wykenham as lieutenant and Duncan G Robinson, ensign. Became part of the new 2nd Corps in July 1875. On the border of Buckinghamshie, ten miles south-west of Aylesbury, Thame Town Hall stands on the site of the old Market Hall which was demolished in 1887. Thame station was opened when the old Wycombe Railway reached the town in 1862.

9th Formed from part of the 5th Corps in October 1861 with headquarters at Woodstock with Captain Charles E Thornhill in command. Became part of the new 2nd Corps in July 1875. About ten miles north-west of Oxford, Woodstock was for many years well known for its glove making.

PEEBLESHIRE

All corps formed within the county joined the 1st Midlothian Admin Battalion in 1863, which became the new 2nd Midlothian RVC in 1880.

1st Formed as one company at Peebles on 31 August 1860 with Robert Hay as captain, James W Murray, lieutenant and John Gracie, ensign. Increased to two companies in 1873 and became 'I' and 'K' Companies of the new 2nd Midlothian RVC in 1880. The manufacture of woollen garments – there were five mills in the town in the 1890s – seems to have been the main Victorian source of employment at Peebles.

2nd Formed as one company at Broughton on 31 August 1860 with James Tweedie as captain, John Tweedie, lieutenant and John Pretsell, ensign. Disbanded late in 1873. Broughton is to the south-west of Peebles, the railway reaching the town in the form of the old Symington, Biggar and Broughton Company in the same year that the 2nd Corps was being formed.

3rd Formed as one company at Innerleithen on 31 August 1860 with Charles Tennant as captain, George W Muir, lieutenant and Robert Gill, ensign. Became 'L' Company of the new 2nd Midlothian RVC in 1880. Innerleithen is just over six miles east of Peebles.

4th Formed at West Linton, just over ten miles north-west of Peebles, on 16 October 1860 with Charles Alexander as captain, James Thomas, lieutenant and William Sanderson, ensign. Disbanded in 1862.

PEMBROKESHIRE

All rifle corps formed within the county, with the exception of Haverfordwest, joined the 1st

Admin Battalion, which was consolidated as the new 1st Corps in 1880. The Haverfordwest Volunteers were not listed as a Pembrokeshire numbered corps, but appeared separately.

1st (1859–80) Formed as one company at Milford Haven on 23 June 1859 with Captain the Hon Robert Fulke Greville in command. Became 'A' Company of the new 1st Corps in 1880. A large seaport, the 'finest in Christendom' according to Lord Nelson, Milford Haven had numerous shipyards giving employment and a large fishing industry.

1st (1880–1908) The 1st Admin Battalion of Pembrokeshire Rifle Volunteers was formed with headquarters at Haverfordwest in June 1861. The 1st Haverfordwest RVC was added in 1862, 2nd Cardiganshire in 1864, 1st, 2nd, 3rd and 5th Carmarthenshire in 1875. The battalion was consolidated in 1880 as the new 1st Corps with ten companies:

'A' Milford Haven (late 1st Pembroke Corps)
'B' to 'D' Haverfordwest (late 1st Haverfordwest Corps)
'E' Pembroke (late 3rd Pembroke Corps)
'F' Cardigan (late 1st Cardigan Corps)
'G' Llandilo (late 1st Carmarthen Corps)
'H' and 'I' Carmarthen (late 2nd Carmarthen Corps)
'K' Llanelly (late 5th Carmarthen Corps)

Designated 1st (Pembrokeshire) Volunteer Battalion Welsh Regiment under General Order 181 of December 1887 and transfer to the Territorial Force in 1908 was as two companies of 4th Battalion Welsh Regiment. Uniform; scarlet/dark blue, changing after 1897 to scarlet/white.

2nd Formed as one company at Pembroke Dock on 26 September 1860 with Edgecumbe Chevallier as captain, Alister A McAlpin, lieutenant and Allen Long, ensign. Converted to 2nd Pembrokeshire Artillery Volunteers in April 1864.

3rd Formed as one company at Pembroke on 26 September 1860 with Edmund S Stanley as captain, Nicholas A Roch, lieutenant and Henry J Adams, ensign. Became 'E' Company of the new 1st Corps in 1880. Two of Pembroke's churches, St Mary's in 1883, and St Michael's in 1887, were restored in the time of the Volunteers. The Town Hall and Assembly Rooms were opened six years after formation of the 3rd Corps.

4th Formed at New Milford on 2 July 1861 with Thomas Thompson Jackson as lieutenant and John McMurtrie, ensign. Disbanded in 1863. New Milford, on the north shore of Milford Haven, was the terminus of the South Wales Railway and port for steamers crossing to Ireland.

PERTHSHIRE

Two admin battalions were formed, which in 1880 provided the new 1st and 2nd Corps.

1st (1859–80) Formed as one company at Perth on 13 December 1859 with George Moncrieff as captain, William Duncan, lieutenant and Thomas Watson Greig, ensign. Absorbed the 2nd Corps, also at Perth, as No. 2 Company in June 1860, joined the 1st Admin Battalion, and became 'A' and 'B' Companies of the new 1st Corps in 1880. Cassell's notes Perth's principal Victorian industries as being the manufacture of inks, linen, and gauge glasses. There was also a large dye works.

1st (1880–1908) The 1st Admin Battalion was formed with headquarters at Perth on 20

November 1860 and included the 1st, 5th, 6th, 7th, 8th, 9th, 11th, 12th, 13th, 14th, 15th, 16th, 17th, 18th, 19th and 21st Corps. Of these, the 5th, 7th, 9th, 13th and 14th Corps were transferred to 2nd Admin in 1869 and the Glenalmond College Cadet Corps was formed and affiliated to the battalion in 1875. Consolidated in 1880 as the new 1st Corps with seven companies:

'A' and 'B' Perth (late 1st Corps)
'C' Dunblane (late 6th Corps)
'D' Crieff (late 8th Corps)
'E' Doune (late 11th Corps)
'F' Auchterarder (late 15th Corps)
'G' Perth (late 18th Corps)

A new company ('H') was added at Bridge of Allan in March 1885 and by General Order 181 of December 1887 the 1st Corps was re-designated as 4th (Perthshire) Volunteer Battalion Black Watch. Volunteers from the battalion served with the Regulars of the Black Watch in South Africa during the Boer War, Sergeant J R Deas and Private J Chalmers, both from Perth, being killed in action. Three new companies were added at Perth in 1900. 'I' Company was disbanded in 1902, as were 'K' and 'L' in 1905. Battalion headquarters were at Tay Street, Perth and transfer to the Territorial Force in 1908 was as 6th Battalion Black Watch. Glenalmond College at the same time joined the OTC. Uniform: grey/scarlet, changing to scarlet/blue with trews in 1883 and kilts from 1905.

2nd (Perthshire Highland) (1859–60) Formed as one company at Perth on 13 December 1859 with John Dickson as captain, Robert Walker, lieutenant and Frank Sandeman, ensign. Absorbed into the 1st Corps as its No. 2 Company in June 1860.

2nd (1880–1908) The 2nd Admin Battalion was formed with headquarters at Taymouth on 12 November 1861 and included the 3rd and 10th Corps. The 9th Argyllshire RVC was added in 1862, but transferred to 1st Argyllshire Admin in 1865. In 1869 the 5th, 7th, 9th, 13th, 14th and 20th Corps were added, battalion headquarters in the same year transferring to Birnam. 'Perthshire Highland' was added to the title in 1873, and in 1880 2nd Admin was consolidated as the new 1st Corps of eight companies:

'A' Aberfeldy (late 3rd Corps)
'B' Killin (late 4th Corps)
'C' Blairgowrie (late 5th Corps)
'D' Coupar Angus (late 7th Corps)
'E' Alyth (late 9th Corps)
'F' St Martin's (late 13th Corps)
'G' Birnam (late 14th Corps)
'H' Pitlochry (late 20th Corps)

'B' Company also had detachments at Crainlarich, Lochearnhead and Kenmore. The new 2nd Corps was re-designated as 5th (Perthshire Highland) Volunteer Battalion Black Watch under General Order 181 of December 1887. The headquarters of 'F' Company were moved to New Scone in 1899; two new companies, 'I' (Blairgowrie) and 'K' (Birnam), being added in the same year. 'I', however, was disbanded in 1904, followed by 'K' in 1905. Transfer to the Territorial Force in 1908 was as 8th Battalion Black Watch, this title being soon changed, however, to Highland Cyclist Battalion. Uniform: grey/scarlet. Some companies wore kilts, others trews, but all changed to kilts in 1883.

3rd (Breadalbane) Four companies of Rifle Volunteers were raised by the Marquis of Breadalbane and designated as 3rd Perthshire (Breadalbane) RVC, the officers' commissions (the marquis was major commandant in command) being dated 29 February 1860. Headquarters were at Taymouth Castle and the four companies were located: No. 1 at Kenmore, No. 2 Aberfeldy, No. 3 Killin, No. 4 Strathfillan. Joined the 2nd Admin Battalion in 1861. Nos 1 and 4 Companies were disbanded and No. 3 was made independent as 4th Corps in 1869. The remaining No. 2 Company became 'A' Company of the new 2nd Corps in 1880. The four companies were located more or less in a line beginning with Aberfeldy, where General Wade's five-arched bridge crosses the Tay; then running south-west to Kenmore, Taymouth Castle close by, along the northern edge of Loch Tay down to Killin, where the Lochay and Dochart meet, then on into the parish of Strathfillan.

4th Formed at Killin in 1869 from No. 3 Company of the 3rd Corps. Became 'B' Company of the new 2nd Corps in 1880. Killin was well known for its manufacture of tweeds, the railway reaching the village in 1870.

5th Formed as one company at Blairgowrie on 16 March 1860 with John L Campbell as captain, William S Soutar, lieutenant and Richard Penkeith, ensign. Joined the 1st Admin Battalion, transferring to 2nd Admin in 1869, and became 'C' Company of the new 2nd Corps in 1880. Blairgowrie lies on the Ericht to the north-west of Coupar Angus. Flax, linen, jute, malt and beer were produced in the town, which saw the coming of the railway five years before the formation of the 5th Corps.

6th Formed at Dunblane as one company, its services accepted on 13 December 1859, with John Graham as captain, William Mitchell, lieutenant and Lawrence Pullar, ensign. Joined the 1st Admin Battalion and became 'C' Company of the new 1st Corps in 1880. At Dunblane, where much Victorian restoration work was carried out at its cathedral, woollen mills provided employment for many in the town.

7th Formed as one company at Coupar Angus on 5 May 1860 with Mungo Murray as captain, David Bultar, lieutenant and Stewart T M Hood, ensign. Joined the 1st Admin Battalion, transferring to 2nd Admin in 1869, and became 'D' Company of the new 2nd Corps in 1880. At Coupar Angus, to the north-east of Perth, the rebuilding of its church was just being completed as the 7th Corps was being formed. The manufacture of coarse linen and leather provided employment.

8th Formed as one company at Crieff on 5 May 1860 with James Maxton as captain, John Gibson, lieutenant and Alexander Graham, ensign. Joined the 1st Admin Battalion and absorbed the 19th Corps, also at Crieff, in 1878. Became 'D' Company of the new 1st Corps in 1880. Crieff is eighteen miles west of Perth, its parish church being built in 1881.

9th Formed as one company at Alyth on 26 May 1860 with James W Ogilvy as captain, George G Ramsay, lieutenant and William Japp, ensign. Joined the 1st Admin Battalion, transferring to 2nd Admin in 1869, and became 'E' Company of the new 2nd Corps in 1880. Just to the north-east of Blairgowrie, Alyth had linen mills and a factory producing woollen clothing. The railway, in the form of the old Caledonian line, reached the town within a year of the 9th Corps being formed.

10th Formed as one company at Strathtay on 19 May 1860 with J Stewart Robinson as captain and W Roper Craigie, lieutenant. Joined the 2nd Admin Battalion and was disbanded in 1873. Strathtay is described by Bartholomew's *Survey Gazetteer* as a hamlet four-and-a-half-miles north-east of Aberfeldy.

11th Formed as one company at Doune on 26 May 1860 with John Campbell as captain, James MacFarlane, lieutenant and Alexander Mitchell, ensign. Joined the 1st Admin Battalion and became 'E' Company of the new 1st Corps in 1880. Pride of place among the possessions of pistol and sporran collectors would be items made at Doune. Doune, its castle being mentioned in Scott's *Waverley* and more recently the location of *Monty Python and the Holy Grail*, is to the north-west of Stirling.

12th Formed as one company at Callander on 26 May 1860 with John H Skinner as captain, Dougal MacGregor, lieutenant and James C Hands, ensign. Joined the 1st Admin Battalion and disbanded in 1861. Callander, at the foot of the Trossachs and the scene of Scott's *Lady of the Lake*, is sixteen miles north-west of Stirling. Its station, Callander Dreadnought, was opened by the Callander & Oban Railway Company in June 1870.

13th Formed as one company at St Martin's on 22 August 1860 with William M MacDonald as captain, Robert P Wylie, lieutenant and James MacFarlane, ensign. Joined the 1st Admin Battalion, transferring to 2nd Admin in 1869, and became 'F' Company of the new 2nd Corps in 1880. The parish and village is on the Tay just under six miles north-east of Perth.

14th Formed as one company at Birnam on 10 November 1860 with Captain William W Cargill in command. Joined the 1st Admin Battalion, transferring to 2nd Admin in 1869 and became 'G' Company of the new 2nd Corps in 1880. On the Tay, Birnam is just to the south-east of Dunkeld. Beatrix Potter (1866–1943) spent her childhood holidays at Birnam and it was from there that she wrote the original version of what became *The Tale of Peter Rabbit*. She no doubt arrived via Birnam and Dunkeld Station, on the old Scottish Midland Junction Railway, which was opened just four years prior to the formation of the 14th Corps.

15th Formed as one company at Auchterarder on 4 December 1860 with Francis Grove as captain, George Halley, lieutenant and James Smitton, ensign. Joined the 1st Admin Battalion and became 'F' Company of the new 1st Corps in 1880. Auchterarder is just under fourteen miles south-west of Perth.

16th Formed as one company at Stanley on 22 January 1861 with Samuel Howard as captain, John Wildeman Buttle, lieutenant and James Cuthbertson, ensign. Joined the 1st Admin Battalion and disbanded in 1863. The village, six miles north of Perth, lies on the Tay and grew from the several cotton mills established in 1785.

17th (1861) A 17th Corps appears as having been raised at Comrie in the *Army List* for February 1861, but this disappears by the following May, having had no officers appointed.

17th (1863) Formed as a sub-division at Bridge of Earn in April 1863. Included in the 1st Admin Battalion and disbanded in the following June, having had no officers appointed.

18th (Highland) Formed as one company at Perth on 8 May 1863 with Archibald Reis as captain and John McLean, ensign. Joined the 1st Admin Battalion and became 'G' Company of the new 1st Corps in 1880.

19th (Highland) Formed as one company at Crieff, its services accepted on 7 December 1868, and joined the 1st Admin Battalion. Absorbed into the 8th Corps in 1878.

20th Formed at Pitlochry on 27 May 1869 with Donald Fisher as captain, David Ferguson lieutenant and Adam Menzies, ensign. Joined the 2nd Admin Battalion and became 'H' Company of the new 2nd Corps in 1880. To the north of Perth, and the geographical centre of Scotland,

Pitlochry employed many in its production of Highland tweeds, plaids and whisky.

21st Formed at Comrie in July 1875. Joined the 1st Admin Battalion and was disbanded in March 1876. Cassell's notes of Comrie, just over six miles west of Crieff, that the place was subject to frequent earthquakes and severe shocks.

RADNORSHIRE

From 1864 all Radnorshire rifle corps were included in the 1st Herefordshire Admin Battalion, which in 1880 became the new 1st Herefordshire RVC.

1st Formed as one company at Presteigne on 8 March 1860 with Robert B R Mynors as captain, James Beavan, lieutenant and Henry M Jones, ensign. Became 'I' Company of the new 1st Herefordshire RVC in 1880. Presteigne lies on the west bank of the Lugg, the river here forming the border with Wales and England. Opened in 1865 was the Market Hall, and a good trade in timber and brewing employed many.

2nd (1860–78) Formed as one company at Knighton on 25 April 1860 with Richard Green as captain, Richard D Green, lieutenant and John Weyman, ensign. Disbanded in 1878. Knighton is just under six miles from Presteigne. Close to Knighton runs the Shrewsbury to Swansea railway line, which crosses the Teme valley by the thirteen-arched Knucklas Viaduct, built in 1863.

2nd (1878–80) Formed as one company at Rhayader on 11 September 1878 and became 'K' Company of the new 1st Herefordshire RVC in 1880. The Volunteers attending Rhayader St Clement's Church would have seen the rebuilding of its west tower in 1887. The old tannery, which employed a good number from the town, can now be seen relocated at the Welsh Folk Museum, St Fagan's.

3rd Formed as one company at New Radnor on 6 August 1860 with Thomas B Mynors as captain, Thomas S Duggan, lieutenant and Henry O Brown, ensign. Disbanded and last seen in the *Army List* for August 1872. In the town stands a tall monument to the mid-Victorian Chancellor of the Exchequer Sir George Cornewall Lewis, who lived at close-by Harpton Court and died in 1863.

RENFREWSHIRE

The county formed three admin battalions, which provided the new 1st, 2nd and 3rd Corps in 1880.

1st (1859–80) Formed as one company at Greenock on 10 September 1859 and absorbed the 2nd, 13th and 18th Corps as Nos 2, 3 and 4 Companies in February 1860. Major David Macduff Latham, late of the Royal Renfrew Militia, took command. Joined the 1st Admin Battalion and became 'A' to 'D' Companies of the new 1st Corps in 1880. On the south bank of the Clyde, Greenock's chief industries were shipbuilding, marine and general engineering. In the 1890s, notes Cassell's, there were about a dozen large sugar refineries giving employment to several thousand.

1st (1880–1908) The 1st Admin Battalion was formed with headquarters at Greenock on 1 August 1860 and included the 1st, 5th, 10th, 11th and 22nd Corps. The 1st Buteshire was added in 1863 and in 1880 the battalion was consolidated as the new 1st Corps with nine companies:

'A', 'B', 'C' and 'D' Greenock (late 1st Corps)
'E' Port Glasgow (late 5th Corps)
'F' and 'G' Greenock (late 10th Corps)
'H' Gourock (late 22nd Corps)
'I' Rothesay (late 1st Bute Corps)

Under General Order 181 of December 1887 the 1st Corps was re-designated as 1st (Renfrewshire) Volunteer Battalion Argyll and Sutherland Highlanders. A cyclist company was added in 1900, 'I' Company was disbanded in 1906. Headquarters of the battalion were at 37 Newton Street, Greenock and transfer to the Territorial Force in 1908 was as 5th Battalion Argyll and Sutherland Highlanders. Uniform: grey/scarlet, changing to scarlet/yellow with trews in 1889. Kilts were worn after 1899.

2nd (1859–60) Formed at Greenock on 10 September 1859 and absorbed into the 1st Corps as its No. 2 Company in February 1860.

2nd (1880–1908) The 2nd Admin Battalion was formed with headquarters at Paisley on 2 June 1860 and to it were added the 3rd, 6th, 9th, 14th, 15th, 17th, 20th and 24th Corps. Consolidated in 1880 as the new 2nd Corps with eight companies:

'A' Paisley (late 3rd Corps)
'B' Paisley (late 6th Corps)
'C' Johnstone (late 9th Corps)
'D' Paisley (late 14th Corps)
'E' Kilbarchan (late 15th Corps)
'F' Lochwinnoch (late 17th Corps)
'G' Renfrew (late 20th Corps)
'H' Paisley (late 24th Corps)

A new company ('I') was added at Paisley in 1884 and the corps was re-designated as 2nd (Renfrewshire) Volunteer Battalion Argyll and Sutherland Highlanders under General Order 181 of December 1887. 'K' (Cyclist) Company was formed at Paisley in 1900, 'E' was disbanded and 'F' moved to Elderslie with detachments at Howwood, Kilbarchan and Lochwinnoch in 1903. Battalion headquarters were in High Street, Paisley, its rifle range at Foxbar on the Gleniffder Hills. Transfer to the Territorial Force in 1908 was as five companies of 6th Battalion Argyll and Sutherland Highlanders. Uniform: scarlet/blue, changing to scarlet/yellow with trews in 1898. Kilts were worn after 1903.

3rd (1859–80) Formed as one company at Paisley on 22 September 1859 with Captain Alex Fullerton in command. Joined the 2nd Admin Battalion and became 'A' Company of the new 2nd Corps in 1880. The Town Hall was built in 1882, the Sheriff's Court House in 1885 and Queen Victoria visited the town in 1888. Fabric manufacture was Paisley's main source of employment, but some of its inhabitants, no doubt, paid the rent from wages received from Robinson's – manufacturers of 'Golden Shred' marmalade in the town since 1864.

3rd (1880–1908) The 3rd Admin Battalion was formed with headquarters at Barrhead on 4 August 1860 and to it were added the 4th, 7th, 8th, 16th, 19th, 21st, 23rd and 25th Corps. Consolidated in 1880 as the new 3rd Corps with eight companies:

'A' Pollockshaws (late 4th Corps)
'B' Barrhead (late 7th Corps)
'C' Neilston (late 8th Corps)
'D' Thornliebank (late 16th Corps)
'E' Hurlet (late 19th Corps)
'F' Barrhead (late 21st Corps)
'G' Cathcart (late 23rd Corps)
'H' Thornliebank (late 25th Corps)

In 1881 3rd Corps headquarters moved from Barrhead to Pollockshaws, 'E' Company going to Newton Mearns in the same year. Re-designation as 3rd (Renfrewshire) Volunteer Battalion Argyll and Sutherland Highlanders was notified in General Order 181 of 1887 and two new companies, 'I' and 'K' (Cyclist), were added at Barrhead in 1900. 'I', however, was disbanded in 1903. Forty-six Volunteers from the battalion served in South Africa during the Boer War, Private J Campbell being killed at Rustenburg on 1st October 1900 and Private C Clanachan at Kaal Spruit on 14th March 1902. Private G Williams was mortally wounded at Driekuil on 3 April 1902. Transfer to the Territorial Force in 1908 was as three companies of 6th Battalion Argyll and Sutherland Highlanders. Uniform: scarlet/blue, changing to scarlet/yellow with trews in 1889.

4th Formed as one company at Pollockshaws on 22 September 1859 with Robert Gillies Lowndes as captain, James Tassie, lieutenant and John Petrie, ensign. Joined the 3rd Admin Battalion and became 'A' Company of the new 3rd Corps in 1880. Just under three miles from Glasgow, the town's main source of employment was weaving. There were also iron foundries, bleach works and paper mills.

5th Formed as one company at Port Glasgow on 15 November 1859 with James Anderson as captain, John Burkmyre, lieutenant and James Dunbar, ensign. Joined the 1st Admin Battalion and became 'E' Company of the new 1st Corps in 1880. An important seaport on the south bank of the Clyde, twenty miles north-west of Glasgow, the town employed many in its numerous shipbuilding yards. The Moffat Library in King Street was opened in 1887.

6th Formed as one company at Paisley on 23 November 1859 with William MacKean as captain, Stewart Clark, lieutenant and Archibald Coats, ensign. Joined the 2nd Admin Battalion and became 'B' Company of the new 2nd Corps in 1880.

7th Formed as one company at Barrhead on 15 February 1860 with John Graham as captain, James Cunningham, lieutenant and Francis Heys, ensign. Joined the 3rd Admin Battalion and became 'B' Company of the new 3rd Corps in 1880. Barrhead is on the River Levan seven miles south-west of Glasgow, its chief industries during the Volunteer period being cotton spinning, fabric printing and dying. There were also iron foundries and machine shops.

8th Formed as one company at Neilston on 6 March 1860 with Alex Graham as captain, Matthew Anderson, lieutenant and Malcolm C Thompson, ensign. Joined the 3rd Admin Battalion and became 'C' Company of the new 3rd Corps in 1880. On the Leven nine miles south-west of Glasgow, the town had extensive bleach works and print shops.

9th Formed as one company at Johnstone on 6 February 1860 with John Stirling Napier as captain, John Salmond, lieutenant and John Starke, ensign. Joined the 2nd Admin Battalion and became 'C' Company of the new 2nd Corps in 1880. Just under four miles from Paisley, Johnstone had cotton mills and collieries.

10th (The Greenock Highlanders) Formed as one company from Highlanders resident in Greenock on 3 February 1860 with James Johnston Grieve as captain, Daniel MacLean lieutenant and John Rennie, ensign. Joined the 1st Admin Battalion and absorbed the 11th Corps, also at Greenock, as No. 2 Company in 1863. At the same time 'The Greenock Highlanders' was added to the title. Became 'F' and 'G' Companies of the new 1st Corps in 1880.

11th Formed as one company from Highlanders resident in Greenock on 3 February 1860 with Colin Campbell as captain, Thomas Ballantyne, lieutenant and Allan Weir, ensign. Joined the 1st Admin Battalion and was absorbed into the 10th Corps as its No. 2 Company in 1863.

12th Formed as one company at Greenock on 3 February 1860 with James Steel as captain, Dugard Ferguson, lieutenant and Donald Macfarlane, ensign. Disbanded by the end of the year.

13th Formed at Greenock on 24 January 1860 and absorbed into the 1st Corps as its No. 3 Company in the following month.

14th Formed as one company at Paisley on 8 February 1860 with William Carlisle as captain, Stewart Clark, lieutenant and Robert Peacock, ensign. Joined the 2nd Admin Battalion and became 'D' Company of the new 2nd Corps in 1880.

15th Formed as one company at Kilbarchan on 20 January 1860 with Charles Cairns as captain, Alex Kirkland, lieutenant and John Stevenson, ensign. Joined the 2nd Admin Battalion and became 'E' Company of the new 2nd Corps in 1880. Five miles from Paisley, Kilbarchan manufactured shawls, mined coal and produced iron. The railway, in the form of the old Glasgow & South Western line, did not reach the town until 1905.

16th Formed as one company at Thornliebank on 15 February 1860 with Alexander Crum as captain, his son, Alexander Crum jun, lieutenant and Thomas Colledge, ensign Joined the 3rd Admin Battalion and became 'D' Company of the new 3rd Corps in 1880. Four miles south-west of Glasgow, the town, notes Cassell's, owes its existence to the cotton works established there in the latter part of the eighteenth century.

17th Formed as one company at Lochwinnoch on 20 January 1860 with Henry Lee Harkey as captain, John Harkey, lieutenant and John McNab, ensign. Joined the 2nd Admin Battalion and became 'F' Company of the new 2nd Corps in 1880. A small town situated on the left bank of the Calder, Lochwinnoch manufactured chairs, carried on silk weaving and printing, and had a large steam laundry.

18th Formed at Greenock on 6 February 1860 and absorbed into the 1st Corps as its No. 4 Company in the same month.

19th Formed as one company at Hurlet on 6 March 1860 with Robert King as captain, James Coats, lieutenant and Dugard Dove, ensign. Joined the 3rd Admin Battalion and became 'E' Company of the new 3rd Corps in 1880. A small village on the Leven, three miles south-east of Paisley, Hurlet lay in the centre of coal and iron fields. There was also a large chemical works.

20th Formed as one company at Renfrew on 1 March 1860 with James M Henderson as captain, Robert Gallacher, lieutenant and Robert Robin, ensign. Joined the 2nd Admin Battalion and became 'G' Company of the new 2nd Corps in 1880. The parish church was built in 1862, the town giving employment to many in its extensive engineering and shipyards. In 1895, Babcock and Wilcox built the largest boiler-making works in the world at Renfrew.

21st Formed as one company at Barrhead on 12 March 1860 with Henry Heys as captain, John Drennan, lieutenant and John H McNab, ensign. Joined the 3rd Admin Battalion and became 'F' Company of the new 3rd Corps in 1880.

22nd Formed as one company at Gourock on 6 April 1860 with Duncan Danoch as captain, his son, Duncan Danoch jun, as lieutenant and John Munsie, ensign. Joined the 1st Admin Battalion and became 'H' Company of the new 1st Corps in 1880. The town is two miles north-west of Greenock, the Caledonian Railway reaching there in June 1889.

23rd Formed as one company at Cathcart on 6 April 1860 with Robert Cooper as captain, Malcolm McCallum, lieutenant and James Graham, ensign. Joined the 3rd Admin Battalion and became 'G' Company of the new 3rd Corps in 1880. Cathcart is in Western Renfrewshire three miles south of Glasgow.

24th Formed as one company at Paisley on 10 April 1860 with Andrew Brown as captain, John Reid, lieutenant and Thomas Graham, ensign. Joined the 2nd Admin Battalion and became 'H' Company of the new 2nd Corps in 1880.

25th Formed as one company at Thornliebank on 15 May 1862 with Allan Graham as captain, Walter Ewing Crum, lieutenant and John Crum, ensign. Joined the 3rd Admin Battalion and became 'H' Company of the new 3rd Corps in 1880.

ROSS-SHIRE

All corps joined the 1st Admin Battalion, which in 1880 became the new 1st Corps.

1st (1860–80) Formed as one company at Invergordon on 15th February 1860 with Robert Bruce E MacLeod as captain, David Monro, lieutenant and Kenneth Murray, ensign. Moved to Tain in 1869 and became 'A' Company of the new 1st Corps in 1880. Invergordon is thirteen miles north-east of Dingwall on the Cromarty Firth; its castle, burnt down in 1801, was rebuilt in 1873–74. On the old Inverness & Perth Junction Railway, Invergordon Station was opened in 1863, the line extending up to Tain in the following year.

1st (Ross Highland) (1880–1908) The 1st Admin Battalion was formed with headquarters at Dingwall on 30 September 1861 and consolidated in 1880 as the 1st (Ross Highland) RVC of nine companies:

'A' Tain (late 1st Corps)
'B' Dingwall (late 2nd Corps)
'C' Fortrose (late 3rd Corps)
'D' Munlochy (late 4th Corps)
'E' Ullapool (late 5th Corps)
'F' Invergordon (late 6th Corps)
'G' Evanton (late 7th Corps)
'H' Moy (late 8th Corps)
'I' Gairloch (late 9th Corps)

Designated 1st (Ross Highland) Volunteer Battalion Seaforth Highlanders by General Order 181 of 1887. In the same year 'G' Company moved to Dingwall (with a detachment at Alness) and 'H' to Fairburn near Moy on the Brahan estate. Transfer to the Territorial Fore in 1908 was as 4th

Battalion Seaforth Highlanders. Uniform: scarlet/blue with trews (kilts replaced trews gradually after 1880), changing to scarlet/yellow with kilts in 1888, scarlet/buff in 1903.

2nd Formed as one company at Dingwall on 15 February 1860 with Keith Stewart Mackenzie as captain, Alex Stewart Mackenzie, lieutenant and Edward Hay M Matherson, ensign. Became 'B' Company of the new 1st Corps in 1880. Opened in 1863, the old Inverness & Ross-shire Railway station welcomed Victorian tourists on their way to points further north.

3rd Formed as one company at Avoch on 17 February 1860 with Sir J R Mackenzie as captain, Alex George Mackenzie, lieutenant and Roderick G Mackenzie, ensign. Moved to Fortrose, a mile from Avoch, in 1876 and became 'C' Company of the new 1st Corps in 1880. Both Avoch and Fortrose are on Black Isle, Moray Firth and were served by the old Highland Railway, which reached the area in 1894.

4th One company formed at Knockbain, its services accepted on 22 March 1860, with James Wardlaw as captain, James Fowler Mackenzie, lieutenant and James Cameron, ensign. Moved to Munlochy, in the parish of Knockbain, in 1876 and became 'D' Company of the new 1st Corps in 1880.Knockbain is on the Beauly Firth five miles north-west of Inverness.

5th (1861–64) Formed at Alness on 20 May 1861 with Andrew Munro as captain, David Forsyth, lieutenant and Alexander Maclean, ensign. Disbanded in September 1864. Alness is to the north-east of Dingwall.

5th (1865–80) Formed at Ullapool on 24 May 1865 with Duncan H C R Davidson as captain, Alexander R MacDonald, lieutenant and Duncan Menzies, ensign. Became 'E' Company of the new 1st Corps in 1880. On the north shore of Loch Broom, important to the area was herring-fishing.

6th Formed as a sub-division at Alness on 21 May 1861 with Frederick Walton as lieutenant and Norman Walker, ensign. Increased to a full company and headquarters moved to Invergordon, just to the east, in 1871. Became 'F' Company of the new 1st Corps in 1880. The old Inverness & Aberdeen Junction Railway reached both Alness and Invergordon in 1863, both areas employing many in their distilleries.

7th Formed as one company at Evanton on 12 May 1866 with Charles Munro as captain, David Forsyth, lieutenant and James Forbes, ensign. Became 'G' Company of the new 1st Corps in 1880. Evanton is on the Cromarty Firth to the north-east of Dingwall.

8th Formed as one company at Moy, near Dingwall, on 11 August 1866 with Hector Munro as captain, Andrew Blake, lieutenant and George McLennan, ensign. Became 'H' Company of the new 1st Corps in 1880. The corps was recruited from workers on the Braham estate.

9th Formed as one company at Gairloch on 23 February 1867 with Sir Kenneth S Mackenzie as captain, Alex Burgess, lieutenant and Munro MacRae, ensign. Became 'I' Company of the new 1st Corps in 1880. Gairloch is in Western Ross-shire.

ROXBURGHSHIRE

All corps joined the 1st Admin Battalion, which became the new 1st Corps in 1880.

1st (1859–80) One company sworn in at Jedburgh on 15 September 1859 with William Scott as captain and the Hon Hallyburton Campbell, lieutenant. There was also a detachment at

Denholm, but this was absorbed into the 4th Corps as its No. 2 Company in 1863. Became 'A' Company of the new 1st Corps in 1880. At Jedburgh, ten miles north-east of Hawick, the parish church was built during the years 1873 to 1875. The manufacture of tweeds, blankets and hosiery gave employment to many in the town.

1st (The Border) (1880–1908) The 1st Admin Battalion (also called 'The Border Rifles' from 1868) was formed with headquarters at Melrose on 9 November 1861. The 1st and 2nd Selkirkshire RVC were added in 1862, headquarters transferred to Newtown St Boswells on 30 June 1878, and the battalion was consolidated as 1st Roxburgh and Selkirk (The Border) RVC in April 1880. There were nine companies:

'A' Jedburgh (late 1st Roxburgh Corps)
'B' Kelso (late 2nd Roxburgh Corps)
'C' Melrose (late 3rd Roxburgh Corps)
'D' and 'E' Hawick (late 4th Roxburgh Corps)
'F' and 'G' Galashiels (late 1st Selkirk Corps)
'H' and 'I' Selkirk (late 2nd Selkirk Corps)

Became one of the volunteer battalions allotted to the Royal Scots Fusiliers in 1881, but General Order 61 of May 1887 notified a transferred (without change in title) to the King's Own Scottish Borderers. At the same time, 'H' Company moved to Galashiels. A new company ('K') was added at Hawick in 1892, followed by 'L' and 'M', also at Hawick, in 1901. The latter two, however, were disbanded in 1903. Battalion headquarters were transferred to Melrose, 'L' (Cyclist) Company was formed at Newcastleton, and Kelso High School Cadet Corps was affiliated in 1901. Transfer to the Territorial Force in 1908 was as six companies of 4th Battalion King's Own Scottish Borderers. Uniform: grey/grey.

2nd The first public meeting to form a company at Kelso took place on 27 May 1859, but its services were not accepted until March 1860. The first enrolled Volunteers were sworn in on 26 March, and the officers: Sir G H S Douglas, late of the 34th Regiment of Foot, as captain, James Johnstone, lieutenant and John Munro, ensign, gazetted on 29 March. Became 'B' Company of the new 1st Corps in 1880. Cassell's, in the 1890s, notes that the chief industries of the town were coach building, agricultural machinery, cabinet and upholstery works.

3rd The first-enrolled Volunteers for this company at Melrose were sworn in on 15 June 1860, the officers being: Captain Thomas Tod, Lieutenant Thomas A R Carre and Ensign James Curle. Became 'C' Company of the new 1st Corps in 1880. Opened in 1872, the Waverley Hydropathic Establishment stands on Skirmish Hill, the site of a Border fight in 1526.

4th The first public meeting held with a view to forming a company at Hawick took place on 8 December 1859, its offer of service being accepted on 11 June 1860. The appointed officers were John S Chisholme as captain, William S Watson, lieutenant and William Dickson, ensign. Members, noted General Grierson, paid for their own uniforms and equipment and gave an annual subscription of ten shillings. Absorbed the Denholm Detachment of the 1st Corps as No. 2 Company on 1 December 1863 and became 'D' and 'E' Companies of the new 1st Corps in 1880. At Hawick, the Exchange was opened in 1865; new Municipal Buildings built 1885–87 and the Post Office in 1892. The old Wilton Lodge Estate was formed into a public park in 1890. Employment in the area was provided by numerous clothing manufactures, sawmills and quarries.

5th Formed as one company at Hawick on 15 January 1861 with George Wilson as captain, George Hardy Frazer, lieutenant and Robert Frazer Watson, ensign. Disbanded in 1867.

SELKIRKSHIRE

1st Known unofficially as the 'Gala Forest Rifles', the 1st Selkirkshire RVC was formed on 27 March 1860 with Hugh Scott as captain, William Clack, formerly a captain in the Royal Navy, lieutenant and Adam L Cochrane, ensign. The originally establishment of the corps, which had its headquarters at Galashiels, was one company, but this increased to two in 1870. In 1880 the 1st Admin Battalion of Roxburghshire Rifle Volunteers, with which the 1st Selkirk had been united since 1862, was consolidated as 1st Roxburgh and Selkirk RVC. The Galashiels Volunteers formed 'F' and 'G' Companies of the new battalion. During the first twenty years of the existence of the 1st Corps, several building were opened that possibly would not have passed without ceremony: the Town Hall and Corn Exchange, both in 1860; a library in 1873, and in 1874, a new headquarters for the corps known as the Volunteers Hall. In the town, which lies on both sides of the Gala extending to within a short distance of its confluence with the Tweed, twenty-two woollen factories were noted in the area around 1890. There was also a yard where skins were tanned and dressed, which was said to be the largest in Scotland.

2nd 'Selkirk' means 'the church in the forest' and it was in this royal burgh that the 2nd Selkirkshire RVC was formed as one company on 15 June 1860 with Charles S Plummer as captain, Alexander Pringle, lieutenant and William Brown, ensign. The forest referred to is the Royal Forest of Ettrick, giving rise to the unofficial title of 'Ettrick Forest Rifles'. A second company was authorized on 1st November 1879. Like the 1st Corps, the 2nd also joined the Roxburghshire Admin Battalion in 1862, and in 1880 became part of the new 1st Roxburgh and Selkirk Corps, in this case providing 'H' and 'I' Companies.

SHROPSHIRE

Two admin battalions were formed, which in 1880 provided the new 1st and 2nd Corps. There was also a 1st Sub-division, which became the 7th Corps.

1st (1859–80) Formed as one company at Shrewsbury on 14 December 1859 with Thomas Cholmondeley as captain, William Harley Bailey, lieutenant and Charles Chandler, ensign. Joined the 1st Admin Battalion and became 'A' Company of the new 1st Corps in 1880. The town gave employment in its breweries, iron foundry, tannery, timberyards, sawmills and glass-staining works.

1st (1880–1908) The 1st Admin Battalion was formed with headquarters at Shrewsbury in July 1860 and to it were added the 1st, 4th, 5th, 6th, 10th, 11th, 14th, 16th and 17th Corps. The 2nd and 4th Montgomeryshire RVC were also included between 1873 and 1876. The battalion was consolidated in 1880 as the new 1st Corps with eight companies:

'A' Shrewsbury (late 1st Corps)
'B' Shrewsbury (late 17th Corps)
'C' Condover (late 5th Corps)
'D' Ironbridge (late 6th Corps)
'E' Shifnal (late 14th Corps)
'F' Bridgnorth (late 4th Corps)
'G' Ludlow (late 10th Corps)
'H' Cleobury Mortimer (late 11th Corps)

Re-designated as 1st Volunteer Battalion King's (Shropshire Light Infantry) by General Order 181 of December 1887. The Shrewsbury School Cadet Corps and the Bridgnorth Cadet Corps were formed and affiliated in 1900, the Shrewsbury Town Cadet Corps in 1906. Transfer to the Territorial Force in 1908 was as part of 4th Battalion King's (Shropshire Light Infantry), the Shrewsbury School Cadets at the same time joining the OTC. Uniform: scarlet/white, changing to scarlet/blue in 1898.

2nd (1860–80) Formed as one company at Market Drayton on 15 February 1860 with Alfred Hill, late of the 68th Regiment of Foot, as captain, William Manly Wilkinson, lieutenant and George Gordon Warren, ensign. The latter had once served with the Royal Flint Militia. Joined the 2nd Admin Battalion and became 'A' Company of the new 2nd Corps in 1880. The town was an important agricultural centre with ironworks and factories producing tools to work the land. Market Drayton Station was opened by the old Nantwich & Market Drayton Railway in October 1863.

2nd (1880–1908) The 2nd Admin Battalion was formed with headquarters at Shrewsbury in July 1860 and to it were added the 2nd, 3rd, 7th, 8th, 12th, 13th, 15th and 18th Corps. The battalion was consolidated in 1880 as the new 2nd Corps with seven companies:

'A' Market Drayton (late 2nd Corps)
'B' Whitchurch (late 3rd Corps)
'C' Wellington (late 7th Corps)
'D' Hodnet (late 8th Corps)
'E' \ ... late 12th Corps)
'F' Oswestry (late 15th Corps)
'G' Newport (late 18th Corps)

Corps headquarters were transferred to Newport shortly after consolidation. 'H' Company was added at Ellesmere in 1885 and in 1887, under General Order 181 of December, 2nd Shropshire RVC became 2nd Volunteer Battalion King's (Shropshire Light Infantry). Ellesmere College Cadet Corps was formed and affiliated in 1900 and transfer to the Territorial Force in 1908 was as part of 4th Battalion King's (Shropshire Light Infantry). Ellesmere College at the same time joined the OTC. Uniform: grey/black.

3rd Formed as one company at Whitchurch on 13 February 1860 with Clement Delves Hill as captain, William Lee Brookes, lieutenant and Charles Clay, ensign. Joined the 2nd Admin Battalion and became 'B' Company of the new 2nd Corps in 1880. The town is twelve miles north-west of Market Drayton.

4th Formed as one company at Bridgnorth on 13 February 1860 with John Charles Lloyd as captain, Hubert Smith, lieutenant and William Bache, ensign. Joined the 1st Admin Battalion and became 'F' Company of the new 1st Corps in 1880. Bridgnorth's church of St Leonard was being rebuilt as the 4th Corps was being raised in 1860. The town's main source of employment was the manufacture of carpets and brewing.

5th Formed as one company at Condover on 5 March 1860 with William J Hope Edwards as captain, George Downward, lieutenant and William James Hughes, ensign. Joined the 1st Admin Battalion and became 'C' Company of the new 1st Corps in 1880. The village is just under five miles south of Shrewsbury.

6th Formed as one company at Much Wenlock on 29 February 1860 with William Layton Lowndes as captain, Roger Charles Blackeway, lieutenant and William R Anstice, ensign. Joined the 1st Admin Battalion, moving headquarters to Ironbridge in 1863, and became 'D' Company of the new 1st Corps in 1880. The production of iron gave employment to many in Ironbridge; there were also brick and title works.

7th Formed at Wellington on 17 September 1859 and known as the 1st Sub-division until February 1860, its appointed officers being Captain Thomas Campbell Eyton, the Hon Robert Charles Herbert, lieutenant and William Anslow, ensign. Joined the 2nd Admin Battalion and became 'C' Company of the new 2nd Corps in 1880. The 7th Corps Drill Hall was in King Street. Agricultural implements and machinery were manufactured in the town.

8th Formed as one company at Hodnet on 2 March 1860 with Algernon C H Percy of Hodnet Hall as captain, Walter Minor, lieutenant and William Powell, ensign. Joined the 2nd Admin Battalion and became 'D' Company of the new 2nd Corps in 1880. Hodnet is five miles south-west of Market Drayton, the railway (Wellington & Drayton line) reaching the town in October 1867.

9th Formed as one company at Shrewsbury on 2 March 1860 with William Field as captain, William Patchett, lieutenant and Arthur J Peece, ensign. Converted to artillery and re-designated as 1st Shropshire AVC in July 1860.

10th Formed as one company at Ludlow on 2 March 1860 with Sir C H R Broughton as captain, Rodney Anderson, lieutenant and John Kilvert, ensign. Joined the 1st Admin Battalion and became 'G' Company of the new 1st Corps in 1880. St Laurence's Church at Ludlow was being restored as the 10th Corps was being raised in 1860; St John's at the other end of town was opened in 1881.

11th Formed as one company at Cleobury Mortimer on 4 May 1860 with Charles W Wicksted as captain, Adam P Trow, lieutenant and Charles C Purton, ensign. Joined the 1st Admin Battalion and became 'H' Company of the new 1st Corps in 1880. The town is on the Ludlow road to the west of the Wyre Forest.

12th Formed at Wem on 3 May 1860 with John N C Vaughan as lieutenant and John E Eversall, ensign. Joined the 2nd Admin Battalion and became 'E' Company of the new 2nd Corps in 1880. Wem is ten miles north of Shrewsbury.

13th Formed as one company at Ellesmere on 2 June 1860 with Richard G Jebb as captain, the Hon Abelbert Cust, lieutenant and Salisbury Mainwaring, ensign. Joined the 2nd Admin Battalion and was disbanded in 1879. The town takes its name from the lake on which it situated, the railway (the old Oswestry, Ellesmere & Whitchurch) reaching there in May 1863.

14th Formed as on company at Shifnal on 21 April 1860 with Henry Corbett, late of the Shropshire Militia, as captain, Daniel Jones, lieutenant and John Meire, ensign. Joined the 1st Admin Battalion and became 'E' Company of the new 1st Corps in 1880. At Shifnal, ten miles north of Bridgnorth, the Market Hall was opened in 1868.

15th Formed at Oswestry on 28 April 1860 with John Hamer as lieutenant and George H Williams, ensign. Joined the 2nd Admin Battalion and became 'F' Company of the new 2nd Corps in 1880. At Oswestry, eighteen miles north-west of Shrewsbury, new Municipal Buildings were opened to replace the old Town Hall in 1893. There were iron and brass foundries in the area, but many were employed at the engine and carriage works belonging to the Cambrian Railway Company.

16th Formed at Munslow, ten miles north of Ludlow, on 24 May 1860 with C O C Pemberton as lieutenant and T Wetherhead, ensign. Joined the 1st Admin Battalion and was disbanded in 1863.

17th Formed as one company at Shrewsbury on 8 January 1861 with William Salt as captain, William Patchett, lieutenant and Thomas C Townshend, ensign. Joined the 1st Admin Battalion and became 'B' Company of the new 1st Corps in 1880.

18th Formed as one company at Newport on 17 January 1862 with Thomas F Boughey as captain, Edward Hodges, lieutenant and John Holland jun, ensign. Joined the 2nd Admin Battalion and became 'G' Company of the new 2nd Corps in 1880. The town is eight miles north-east of Wellington on the border of Staffordshire and employed a number in the manufacture of agricultural implements and machinery.

SOMERSETSHIRE

Three admin battalions were formed which provided the new 1st, 2nd and 3rd Corps in 1880. There was also a 1st Sub-division, which became the 7th Corps.

1st (1859–80) Formed as one company at Bath on 20 October 1859 with John Randle Ford, late of the 95th Regiment of Foot, as captain, Thomas Frederick Inman, lieutenant and Henry Batchelor Inman, ensign. Joined the 1st Admin Battalion and became 'A' Company of the new 1st Corps in 1880. Old Bath, on a bend in the Avon; New Bath, looks down from the hills.

1st (1880–1908) The 1st Admin Battalion was formed with headquarters at Bath in August 1860 and to it were added the 1st, 2nd, 7th, 14th, 17th, 18th and 22nd Corps. Consolidated in 1880 as the new 1st Corps with seven companies:

'A' Bath (late 1st Corps)
'B' Bathwick (late 2nd Corps)
'C' Keynsham (late 7th Corps)
'D' Warleigh Manor (late 14th Corps)
'E' Lyncombe (late 17th Corps)
'F' Walcot (late 18th Corps)
'G' Kilmersdon (late 22nd Corps)

Under General Order 261 of October 1882 the 1st Corps became 1st Volunteer Battalion Somerset Light Infantry making it the first in the land to take on the title of its parent regiment. A new company was added in 1885, followed by two more in 1900. Three school cadet corps were associated with the battalion: Bath College, becoming affiliated in March 1900; King Edward's School in Bath, in the same year; Monkton Combe School joining in 1904. Transfer to the Territorial Force in 1908 was as parts of both the 4th and 5th Battalions Somerset Light Infantry. Bath College, King Edward's and Monkton Combe at the same time joined the OTC. Uniform: scarlet/black, changing to scarlet/blue in 1884.

2nd (1859–80) Formed as one company at Bathwick on 21 October 1859 with Edmund Francis Ansley as captain, Henry Holland Burne, lieutenant and William Attfield, ensign. Joined the 1st Admin Battalion and became 'B' Company of the new 1st Corps in 1880. Bathwick is part of the Borough of Bath.

2nd (1880–1908) The 2nd Admin Battalion was formed with headquarters at Taunton in August 1860 and included the 3rd, 5th, 8th, 9th, 11th, 12th, 16th, 20th, 21st, 26th and 28th Corps. Consolidated in 1880 as the new 2nd Corps with twelve companies:

'A' and 'B' Taunton (late 3rd Corps)
'C' Wellington (late 8th Corps)
'D' Williton (late 9th Corps)
'E' Wiveliscombe (late 12th Corps)
'F' Yeovil (late 16th Corps)
'G' Crewkerne (late 20th Corps)
'H' Langport (late 21st Corps)
'I' Bridgwater (late 5th Corps)
'K' and 'L' Bridgwater (late 26th Corps)
'M' South Petherton (late 28th Corps)

Re-designated as 2nd Volunteer Battalion Somerset Light Infantry under General Order 261 of October 1882. A new company was added in 1900 and in 1901 and 1903 respectively both the County School at Wellington and King's College in Taunton provided affiliated cadet corps. Transfer to the Territorial Force in 1908 was as parts of both 4th and 5th Battalions Somerset Light Infantry. County School and King's College at the same time joined the OTC. Uniform: grey/black.

3rd (1859–80) Formed as one company at Taunton on 22 October 1859 with William Ayshford Sanford as captain, Arthur Allen, lieutenant and Richard Easton, ensign. Joined the 2nd Admin Battalion and became 'A' and 'B' Companies of the new 2nd Corps in 1880. The great tower at St Mary Magdalene's church was being rebuilt (1858–62) as the first members of the 3rd Corps enrolled. Factories producing silk, collars and cuffs, gloves and boxes gave employment to many from the area.

3rd (1880–1908) The 3rd Admin Battalion was formed with headquarters at Wells in August 1860 and included the 4th, 6th, 10th, 13th, 15th, 19th, 23rd, 24th, 25th and 27th Corps. Consolidated in 1880 as the new 3rd Corps with nine companies:

'A' Burnham (late 4th Corps)
'B' Weston-super-Mare (late 6th Corps)
'C' Wells (late 10th Corps)
'D' Frome (late 13th Corps)
'E' Shepton Mallet (late 15th Corps)
'F' Glastonbury (late 19th Corps)
'G' Castle Cary (late 23rd Corps)
'H' Keinton (late 25th Corps)
'I' Langford (late 27th Corps)

Headquarters moved to Weston-super-Mare in 1882 and by General Order 261 of October 1882 re-designation took place as 3rd Volunteer Battalion Somerset Light Infantry. Transfer to the Territorial Force in 1908 was as parts of both 4th and 5th Battalions Somerset Light Infantry. Uniform: grey/black.

4th Formed as one company at Burnham on 12 January 1860 with Benjamin Tuthill Allen as captain, Joshua Allen, lieutenant and Charles James Brody Mais, ensign. Joined the 3rd Admin

Battalion and became 'A' Company of the new 3rd Corps in 1880. Burnham is on the Bristol Channel, just under eight miles from Bridgwater, the railway having reached the town little under two years prior to the formation of the 4th Corps.

5th Formed as one company at Bridgwater on 14 January 1860 with Gabriel Stone Poole as captain, Charles Robert Bate, lieutenant and William John Ford, ensign. Joined the 2nd Admin Battalion and became 'I' Company of the new 2nd Corps in 1880. Cassell's notes the chief industries of the town as brewing, malting, foundry work and the manufacture of oil cake.

6th Formed as one company at Weston-super-Mare on 11 February 1860 with James Adeane Law as captain, Samuel Edward Baker, lieutenant and Charles Whitting, ensign. Joined the 3rd Admin Battalion and became 'B' Company of the new 3rd Corps in 1880. Looking across to the coast of Wales, a new seafront was completed in 1887.

7th Formed at Keynsham on 25 February 1860 and known as the 1st Sub-division until April; the first appointed officers of the 7th Somerset RVC were Captain James Ireland C Ireland, Lieutenant Charles John Simmons and Ensign Harford Lyne. The corps was recruited mainly from farmers and farm workers. Joined the 1st Admin Battalion and became 'C' Company of the new 1st Corps in 1880. The town, where electric light was introduced in 1890 and the Avon divides Somerset from Gloucestershire, is just under five miles south-east of Bristol.

8th Formed as one company at Wellington, seven miles south-west of Taunton, on 28 February 1860 with William Burridge as captain, William Thomas, lieutenant and F S Bridget, ensign. Joined the 2nd Admin Battalion and became 'C' Company of the new 2nd Corps in 1880. Company headquarters were in South Street.

9th Formed at Williton, on the road from Taunton to Minehead, on 22 February 1860 with John Halliday as lieutenant and John Blommart, ensign. Joined the 2nd Admin Battalion and became D' Company of the new 2nd Corps in 1880. Williton Station was opened by the old West Somerset Railway in March 1862.

10th Formed as one company at Wells on 14 February 1860 with Edwin Lovell as captain, William J Slade Foster, lieutenant and William Chester Berrymen, ensign. Joined the 3rd Admin Battalion and became 'C' Company of the new 3rd Corps in 1880. At the foot of the Mendip Hills, Wells employed a good number in its manufacture of brushes and paper. The Volunteer would not have failed to see, in 1873, the massive repair and restoration to the west front of Wells Cathedral.

11th Formed at Stogursey on 21 February 1860 with George Fownes Luttrell as lieutenant and Robert Guy Evered, ensign. Joined the 2nd Admin Battalion, moved headquarters just to the south at Nether Stowey on the Bridgwater road in 1868, and was disbanded in 1873.

12th Formed as one company at Wiveliscombe, eleven miles west of Taunton, on 29 February 1860 with Henry George Moysey as captain, Richard Bere, lieutenant and Benjamin Boucher, ensign. Joined the 2nd Admin Battalion and became 'E' Company of the new 2nd Corps in 1880. There were extensive slate quarries in the area. Wiveliscombe Station was opened by the Devon & Somerset Railway in June 1871.

13th Formed as one company at Frome on 9 March 1860 with James W D T Wickham as captain, Francis P Devenish, lieutenant and John Sinkins, ensign. Joined the 3rd Admin Battalion and became 'D' Company of the new 3rd Corps in 1880. Frome is twelve miles south of Bath. Recruits were also drawn from the neighbouring villages of Nunney and Berkley.

14th Formed as one company at Warleigh Manor, three miles east of Bath, on 5 March 1860 with Edward Sawyer as captain, William Sanderson, lieutenant and Henry Mills Skrine, ensign. Joined the 1st Admin Battalion and became 'D' Company of the new 1st Corps in 1880.

15th Formed as one company at Shepton Mallet on 24 March 1860 with Henry Ernst as captain, Henry T Wickham, lieutenant and Samuel Craddock, ensign. Joined the 3rd Admin Battalion and became 'E' Company of the new 3rd Corps in 1880. Brewing and the manufacture of cloth were the main sources of employment at Shepton Mallet, five miles south-east of Wells.

16th Formed as one company at Yeovil on 4 April 1860 with Thomas Messiter as captain, Robert Donne, lieutenant and Henry S Watts, ensign. Joined the 2nd Admin Battalion and became 'F' Company of the new 2nd Corps in 1880. At Yeovil, the Public Baths were opened in 1884, the Victoria Temperance Hall, in 1887, and the Constitutional Club in 1889. In the area there were breweries and brickfields.

17th Formed as one company at Lyncombe on 2 March 1860 with William V Hewitt as captain, George J Robertson, lieutenant and John S Falkner, ensign. Joined the 1st Admin Battalion and became 'E' Company of the new 1st Corps in 1880. A south suburb of Bath, Lyncombe's St Mark's Church was restored in 1881.

18th Formed as one company at Walcot, close to Bath, on 3 March 1860 with B H Holme, late of the 88th Regiment of Foot, as captain, Arthur W Weston, lieutenant and Robert Allen Cook, ensign. Joined the 1st Admin Battalion and became 'F' Company of the new 1st Corps in 1880.

19th Formed as one company at Glastonbury on 17 March 1860 with Arthur W A Hood, a former captain in the Royal Navy, as captain, William G L Lovell, lieutenant and Walter T Swayne, ensign. Joined the 3rd Admin Battalion and became 'F' Company of the new 3rd Corps in 1880. The Volunteer leaving Glastonbury Station in July 1886 would have returned to find it renamed as Glastonbury and Street.

20th Formed as one company at Crewkerne on 25 April 1860 with William Mathews as captain, John J Tidcombe, lieutenant and James H Jolliffe, ensign. Joined the 2nd Admin Battalion and became 'G' Company of the new 2nd Corps in 1880. Crewkerne is eight miles east of Chard, the railway reaching the town within weeks of the formation of the 20th Corps.

21st Formed as one company at Langport on 12 April 1860 with Richard T Combe as captain, John Louch, lieutenant and Walter Bagshot, ensign. Joined the 2nd Admin Battalion and became 'H' Company of the new 2nd Corps in 1880. A new station, Langport East, was opened in October 1906, which required the old Bristol & Exeter Railway's Langport to be renamed as Langport West.

22nd Formed as one company at Temple Cloud, ten miles south of Bristol, on 10 September 1860 with William B Nash as captain, Wallington Coates, lieutenant and Jacob F Y Mogg, ensign. Joined the 1st Admin Battalion, moving headquarters to Kilmersdon in 1869, and became 'G' Company of the new 1st Corps in 1880. Kilmersdon village is just under six miles north-west of Frome.

23rd Formed as one company at Wincanton on 30 June 1860 with William S W Sandford as captain, Thomas E Rogers, lieutenant and Herbert Messiter, ensign. Joined the 3rd Admin Battalion, moving headquarters to Castle Cary in 1863, and became 'G' Company of the new 3rd Corps in 1880. The Town Hall at Wincanton was destroyed by fire in 1877 and rebuilt in the following year. The railway reached the town in November 1861.

24th Formed as one company at Somerton on 20 July 1860 with Francis H Dickinson as captain, George Tuson, lieutenant and William Fraser, ensign. The corps also recruited from the neighbouring villages of Kingweston, Kingdon and Long Sutton Joined the 3rd Admin Battalion and was disbanded in 1871. In the 1890s, Somerton had a factory making shirtcollars.

25th Formed as one company at Baltonsborough on 14 January 1861 with Ebenezer Chaffey as captain, Reginald Dickinson, lieutenant and Robert Culling, ensign. Joined the 3rd Admin Battalion, moving headquarters just to the south-east at Keinton in 1870, and became 'H' Company of the new 3rd Corps in 1880. Baltonsborough is four miles south-east of Glastonbury.

26th Formed as one company at Bridgwater on 5 February 1861 with Henry Bridge as captain, John Woodland, lieutenant and Joseph B Clarke, ensign. Joined the 2nd Admin Battalion and became 'K' and 'L Companies of the new 2nd Corps in 1880.

27th Formed as one company at Wrington on 23 July 1861 with Nathaniel John Newnham jun, late of the Bombay Army, as captain, Charles Edwards, lieutenant and Oliver Coathupe, ensign. Joined the 3rd Admin Battalion, moving headquarters to Langford, just to the south-east, in 1866, and became 'I' Company of the new 3rd Corps in 1880. Wrington is south-west of Bristol off the road to Weston-super-Mare.

28th Formed as one company at South Petherton, five miles north of Crewkerne, on 4 November 1876 with Malachi L Blake as captain, Henry W Tuller, lieutenant and Robert McMillan, sub-lieutenant. Joined the 2nd Admin Battalion and became 'M' Company of the new 2nd Corps in 1880.

STAFFORDSHIRE

Five admin battalions were formed, which became the 1st to 5th new Corps in 1880. There was also a 1st Sub-division, which became the 14th Corps.

1st (1859–80) Formed at Handsworth on 15 August 1859 with Henry Elwell as captain, Sir Francis Edward Scott Bt, lieutenant and Richard L H Mile, ensign. Joined the 3rd Admin Battalion and became 'A' and 'B' Companies of the new 1st Corps in 1880. On a hill looking down on the town, St Mary's Church was restored and partly rebuilt in 1877. The offices of the Local Board were opened in Soho Street in 1879 and Handsworth's London & North Western Railway station in April 1889.

1st (1880–1908) Handsworth was the headquarters of the 3rd Admin Battalion, formed in July 1860 and containing the 1st, 15th, 17th, 18th, 20th, 27th, 31st and 35th Corps. The battalion was consolidated in 1880 as the new 1st Corps with eight companies:

'A' and 'B' Handsworth (late 1st Corps)
'C' Brierley Hill (late 15th Corps)
'D' Kingswinford (late 18th Corps)
'E' West Bromwich (late 20th Corps)
'F' Seisdon (late No. 2 Company, 27th Corps)
'G' Patshull (late No. 1 Company, 27th Corps)
'H' Smethwick (late 31st Corps)

Under General Order 63 of May 1883 the 1st Corps was re-designated as 1st Volunteer Battalion

South Staffordshire Regiment, the headquarters of 'D' Company later transferring to Wordsley. 'I' Company was formed at Smethwick and 'K' at West Bromwich in 1900, followed by 'L' (Cyclist) at Handsworth in 1901. 'G' was later disbanded and at the same time a battalion reorganization resulted in the following company locations: Handsworth (3), Brierley Hill (2), West Bromwich (2), Sutton Coldfield and Smethwick (2). Transfer to the Territorial Force in 1908 saw the bulk of the battalion converted to engineers and formed into the 1st North Midland Field Company, RE. Some of the Handsworth personnel, however, remained as infantry and became part of the 5th Battalion South Staffordshire Regiment. The Handsworth Grammar School Cadets, which had been affiliated since 1907, at the same time joined the OTC. Uniform: scarlet/white.

2nd (1859–80) Formed at Longton on 30 September 1859 with William Kenwright Harvey as captain, Edward Clarke, lieutenant and William Goddard, ensign. Joined the 1st Admin Battalion and became 'A' Company of the new 2nd Corps in 1880. The town, three miles south-east of Stoke-upon-Trent, had potteries, collieries, ironworks; opened its Town Hall in 1863, Public Baths in 1881, Queen's Theatre in 1888 and Library in 1892.

2nd (The Staffordshire Rangers) (1880–1908) Stoke-upon-Trent was the headquarters of the 1st Admin Battalion, formed in May 1860 and including the 2nd, 3rd, 6th, 9th, 10th, 13th, 16th, 28th, 36th, 37th, 38th and 40th Corps. The battalion was consolidated in 1880 as the new 1st Corps, 'The Staffordshire Rangers' being soon permitted as part of the official title. There were eleven companies:

'A' Longton (late 2nd Corps)
'B' Hanley (late 3rd Corps)
'C' Burslem (late 6th Corps)
'D' Tunstall (late 9th Corps)
'E' Stoke-upon-Trent (late 10th Corps)
'F' Kidsgrove (late 13th Corps)
'G' and 'H' Newcastle-under-Lyne (late 16th Corps)
'J' Leek (late 28th Corps)
'K' Hanley (late 36th Corps)
'L' Stone (late 40th Corps)

Re-designation as 1st Volunteer Battalion North Staffordshire Regiment was notified in General Order 14 of February 1883. The cadet corps at Stoke-upon-Trent (see 10th Corps) was removed from the *Army List* in 1884 and battalion establishment reached fourteen companies by 1900, but was later reduced to thirteen. Transfer to the Territorial Force in 1908 was as 5th Battalion North Staffordshire Regiment. Uniform: scarlet/blue, changing to scarlet/white by 1886.

3rd (1859–80) Formed at Hanley on 27 September 1859 with Thomas C Brown Westhead as captain, Septimus Bourne, lieutenant and John Dimmock, ensign. Joined the 1st Admin Battalion and became 'B' Company of the new 2nd Corps in 1880. Hanley, north of Stoke-upon-Trent, is a potteries town, its station, on the old North Staffordshire Railway, opened in July 1864.

3rd (1880–1908) Walsall was the headquarters of the 5th Admin Battalion, formed in November 1860 and including the 4th, 14th, 22nd, 33rd and 34th Corps. The battalion was consolidated in 1880 as the new 3rd Corps with six companies:

'A' and 'B' Walsall (late 4th Corps)

'C' Bloxwich (late 14th Corps)
'D' Brownhills (late 22nd Corps)
'E' Cannock (late 33rd Corps)
'F' Wednesbury (late 34th Corps)

Re-designated as 2nd Volunteer Battalion South Staffordshire Regiment under General Order 63 of May 1883. A new company was later added at Walsall, but this was soon disbanded. In 1884 another company was formed at Walsall, together with one at Wednesbury; 'E' Company at the same time moving to Brownhills. 'D' Company at Brownhills was disbanded before 1901, but re-formed later at Walsall. 'I' was added at Walsall in 1901. Also in 1901, Queen Mary's School at Walsall provided a cadet corps and transfer to the Territorial Force in 1908 was as part of 5th Battalion South Staffordshire Regiment. Queen Mary's School at the same time joined the OTC. Uniform: scarlet/white.

4th (1859–80) Formed at Walsall on 4 November 1859 with Charles Frederick Darwall as captain, John W Newman, lieutenant and Frederick Furhman Clarke, ensign. Joined 5th Admin Battalion and became 'A' and 'B' Companies of the new 3rd Corps in 1880. Among the items manufactured at Walsall were bridles, saddles, bits and most other things connected with horses and carriages.

4th (1880–1908) Included in the 4th Admin Battalion, formed with headquarters at Wolverhampton in May 1860, was the 5th, 11th, 12th, 23rd, 26th, 29th, 30th and 32nd Corps. The battalion was consolidated in 1880 as the new 4th Corps with twelve companies:

'A', 'B' and 'C' Wolverhampton (late Nos 1, 2 and 3 Companies, 5th Corps)
'D' Willenhall (late No. 4 Company, 5th Corps)
'E' Tipton (late 11th Corps)
'F' Sedgley (late 29th Corps)
'G' and 'H' Bilston (late 12th Corps)
'I' Wolverhampton (late 23rd Corps)
'K' and 'L' Wolverhampton (late 32nd Corps)
'M' Tettenhall (late 30th Corps)

Re-designation as 3rd Volunteer Battalion South Staffordshire Regiment was notified by General Order 63 of May 1883. 'N' (Cyclist) Company was added at Wolverhampton in 1900, 'H' Company moved to Darlaston in the same year, and transfer to the Territorial Force in 1908 was as 6th Battalion South Staffordshire Regiment. Uniform: scarlet/blue. Mr J W Reddyhoff writing in the *Bulletin* of the Military Historical Society in November 1997 notes that the Freemason's Tudor Lodge of Rifle Volunteers No. 1838 was formed from within the battalion on 16 July 1879.

5th (1859–80) Formed at Wolverhampton on 26 December 1859 with former Coldstream Guards officer George Augustus Vernol as captain, Frederick Walton, lieutenant and Henry Underhill, ensign. Joined the 4th Admin Battalion and absorbed the 26th Corps at Willenhall as No. 4 Company in 1874. Became 'A' to 'D' Companies of the new 4th Corps in 1880.

5th (1880–1908) The corps included in the 2nd Admin Battalion, formed with headquarters at Lichfield in July 1860, were the 7th, 8th, 19th, 21st, 24th, 25th and 39th. The battalion was consolidated in 1880 as the new 5th Corps with eight companies:

'A' Burton-upon-Trent (late 7th Corps)
'B' Burton-upon-Trent (late 8th Corps)

'C' Tamworth (late 19th Corps)
'D' Rugeley (late 21st Corps)
'E' Lichfield (late 24th Corps)
'F' and 'G' Stafford (late 25th Corps)
'H' Burton-upon-Trent (late 39th Corps)

Re-designation as 2nd Volunteer Battalion North Staffordshire Regiment was notified in General Order 14 of February 1883, headquarters transferring to Burton-upon-Trent in 1884. A new company was added at Uttoxeter in 1900, Denstone College Cadet Corps affiliated in the same year. In the north aisle of Lichfield Cathedral on 1st August 1903, a window was dedicated by the Bishop of Lichfield to those Staffordshire Volunteers that fell in South Africa. Transfer to the Territorial Force in 1908 was as 6th Battalion North Staffordshire Regiment, Denstone College joining the OTC at the same time. Uniform: scarlet/blue.

6th Formed at Burslem, twenty miles north-east of Stafford, on 28 December 1859 with Richard Edwards as captain, Gilbert Elliott, lieutenant and William Baker, ensign. Joined the 1st Admin Battalion and became 'C' Company of the new 2nd Corps in 1880. The main trade of the town was its potteries; an Institute commemorating Josiah Wedgwood, who was born in the town, was opened in Queen Street 1869.

7th Formed at Burton-upon-Trent on 10 February 1860 with George Tenant, one of the brewery family, as captain, Henry Warde, lieutenant and Richard Radcliff, ensign. Joined the 2nd Admin Battalion and became 'A' Company of the new 5th Corps in 1880. At Burton, in the 1890s, it is said that the breweries employed more than 7,000 people.

8th Formed at Burton-upon-Trent on 10 February 1860 with Abram Bass, of the brewing family, as captain, John Gretton jun, lieutenant and John Anderson, ensign. Joined the 2nd Admin Battalion and became 'B' Company of the new 5th Corps in 1880.

9th Formed at Tunstall on 4 January 1860 with William Adam jun, as captain, John Nash Peake, lieutenant and William Simms Ball, ensign. Joined the 1st Admin Battalion and became 'D' Company of the new 2nd Corps in 1880. Tunstall's red-brick Town Hall was built in 1885, the Victorian Institute, with its school of art, library and lecture rooms, in 1889. The potteries, ironworks and collieries in the area gave employment to many.

10th Formed at Stoke-upon-Trent on 19 January 1860 with M Daintry Hollins as captain, Edward Copland, lieutenant and Edward Adams, ensign. Joined the 1st Admin Battalion and became 'E' Company of the new 2nd Corps in 1880. A cadet corps was formed in 1875. Stoke's Free Library and Museum was opened in London Road in 1878, and in the centre of the town, in 1883, the red-brick Market Hall. The manufacture of earthenware was important to the town, a statue of Josiah Wedgwood being erected facing the railway station in 1863.

11th Formed at Tipton, just to the north of Dudley, on 11 January 1860 with William Barrows jun, as captain, William Hall, lieutenant and George Homfray, ensign. Joined the 4th Admin Battalion and became 'E' Company of the new 4th Corps in 1880. At Tipton many great furnaces produced heavy ironwork for the railways, steam boilers, large chains and anchors. There were also cement and brickworks.

12th Formed at Bilston on 26 January 1860 with John Nock Bagnall as captain, Benjamin Whitehouse, lieutenant and T Waterhouse, ensign. Joined the 4th Admin Battalion and became

'G' and 'H' Companies of the new 4th Corps in 1880. At Bilston, just under three miles south-east of Wolverhampton, iron, coal and stone were produced from its mines and quarries and all forms of metal items manufactured in its factories.

13th Formed at Kidsgrove on 26 February 1860 with William S Williamson as captain, Edward Williamson, lieutenant and Thomas Brindley, ensign. Joined the 1st Admin Battalion and became 'F' Company of the new 2nd Corps in 1880. Six miles from Stoke-upon-Trent, Kidsgrove had large collieries and ironworks.

14th Formed at Bloxwich, three miles north-west of Walsall, on 10 December 1859 and known as the 1st Sub-division until March 1860. The first two officers were Lieutenant George Strongitarm and Ensign Edward Jenks Stanley. Joined the 5th Admin Battalion and became 'C' Company of the new 3rd Corps in 1880. All Saints' Church at Bloxwich was almost entirely rebuilt in 1877.

15th Formed at Brierley Hill on 1 August 1860 with Frederick Smith as captain, Henry O Firmstond, lieutenant and Joseph B Cochrane, ensign. Joined the 3rd Admin Battalion and became 'C' Company of the new 1st Corps in 1880. At Brierley Hill there were factories making anchor chains, nails and glass bottles.

16th Formed at Newcastle-under-Lyme on 24 February 1860 with J Knight as captain, William Henry Dutton, lieutenant and John Smith Mayer, ensign. Joined the 1st Admin Battalion and became 'G' and 'H' Companies of the new 2nd Corps in 1880. The Town Hall was enlarged about the same year as the 16th Corps was being raised, the Smithfield Cattle Market in Friars' Street established in 1871. The old barracks, which was taken over by the Volunteers, has been described as a quadrangular imposing building in modern Italian style. Clothing for the army was made at the Enderley Mills.

17th Formed at Seisdon on 21 February 1860 with George Pudsey Aston as captain, Frederick Turton Sparrow, lieutenant and William Aston, ensign. Joined the 3rd Admin Battalion and was absorbed into the 27th Corps as its No. 2 Company in 1873. Seisdon is just under seven miles south-west of Wolverhampton.

18th Formed at Kingswinford on 21 February 1860 with Benjamin St John Mathews as captain, John Barrows, lieutenant and J Pearson, ensign. Joined the 3rd Admin Battalion and became 'D' Company of the new 1st Corps in 1880. Three miles west of Dudley, Kingswinford had collieries and ironworks.

19th Formed at Tamworth on 21 February 1860 with Francis Willington as captain, Robert Whately Nevil, lieutenant and John Webster Mayou, ensign. Joined the 2nd Admin Battalion and became 'C' Company of the new 5th Corps in 1880. A large clothing factory employed many at Tamworth in the 1890s.

20th Formed at West Bromwich on 25 February 1860 with Thomas Bagnall jun as captain, Henry Williams, lieutenant and Edwin Hooper, ensign. Joined the 3rd Admin Battalion and became 'E' Company of the new 1st Corps in 1880. The numerous public buildings erected during the Volunteer period include the Library, in 1874, and Town Hall, which was opened in 1875.

21st Mr P G Smith, in an item published in the *Bulletin* of the Military Historical Society in February 1981, tells how the proposed tile of the eventual 21st Corps was the 'Rugeley Rangers' – 'Come join the Rugeley Rangers', so said a verse written by a local draper that appeared in the press. An alternative name, but not one the Rugeley Volunteers delighted in, was 'The Poisoners'.

That then-notorious poisoner William Palmer having been a doctor in Rugeley. Sanction to form the corps came on 18 February 1860, Captain Newton John Lane's commission being dated 23 February, those for Lieutenant Josiah Spode and Ensign Robert Landor being signed on the day after. The headmaster of Rugeley Grammar School, the Revd Edward R Pitman, was made acting chaplain. The Rugeley company joined the 2nd Admin Battalion and in 1880 became 'D' Company of the new 5th Corps.

22nd Formed at Brownhills on 24 February 1860 with John Harrison as captain, William Bealy Harrison, lieutenant and Robert Nelson Boyd, ensign. Joined the 5th Admin Battalion and became 'D' Company of the new 3rd Corps in 1880. There were extensive coal mines at Brownhills, six miles west of Lichfield.

23rd Formed at Wolverhampton on 1 March 1860 with A Clement Foster Gough as captain, George Singleton Tudor, lieutenant and Thomas Ironmonger, ensign. Joined the 4th Admin Battalion and became 'I' Company of the new 4th Corps in 1880. The town employed many in the production of locks, keys, locomotive tubing, guns, bicycles, toys and kitchen furniture.

24th Formed at Lichfield on 6 March 1860 with William Biddulph Parke, late of the 60th King's Royal Rifle Corps, as captain, Charles J Mott, lieutenant and John St V Jervis, ensign. Joined the 2nd Admin Battalion and became 'E' Company of the new 5th Corps in 1880. A contingent from 'E' Company, under Captain W R Coleridge Roberts, formed a Guard of Honour at the laying-up of the old Colours of the 38th Regiment at Lichfield Cathedral on 1st August 1903.

25th Formed at Stafford on 6 March 1860 with Viscount Sandon of Sandon Hall, Stafford as captain, Robert William Hand, lieutenant and John Lea, ensign. Joined the 2nd Admin Battalion and became 'F' and 'G' Companies of the new 5th Corps in 1880. The Volunteer in Stafford would have seen the opening of Borough Hall in 1877, the second Victorian restoration of St Mary's Church during 1877–79, and the completion of the new County council Building in Martin Street in 1895. The manufacture of ladies' boots and shoes, notes Cassell's, was the town's largest source of employment.

26th Formed at Willenhall on 27 February 1860 with Ralph Dickenson Gouch as captain and William Deakin, lieutenant. Joined the 4th Admin Battalion and was absorbed into the 5th Corps as its No. 4 Company in 1874. Three miles east of Wolverhampton on the road to Walsall, Willenhall was noted for its production of door locks, padlocks, bolts, latches, keys and hinges.

27th Formed as one company at Patshull on 7 March 1860 with William Walter Earl of Dartmouth taking command. Joined the 3rd Admin Battalion and absorbed the 17th Corps at Seisdon as No. 2 Company in 1873. Became 'F' and 'G' Companies of the new 1st Corps in 1880. At St Mary's Church, Patshull, a north aisle was added in 1874. The town is on the border of Shropshire, nine miles north-west of Wolverhampton.

28th Formed at Leek on 26 April 1860 with William B Badnall as captain, John Russell, lieutenant and Charles H Halcombe, ensign. Joined the 1st Admin Battalion in May 1861 and became 'J' Company of the new 2nd Corps in 1880. The Nicholson Institute, built in 1884, had a fine Library, Art Gallery and Museum. Many in the town were employed in the manufacture of silk.

29th Formed at Sedgley on 9 April 1860 with Henry B Whitehouse as captain, Edward J Gibbs, lieutenant and Daniel G Ward, ensign. Joined the 4th Admin Battalion and became 'F' Company of the new 4th Corps in 1880. At Sedgley, just to the south of Wolverhampton, nails, rivets, chains, locks and safes were made.

30th Formed at Tettenhall on 30 March 1860 with Edward P Stubbs as captain, James Prior, lieutenant and Thomas Evans, ensign. Joined the 4th Admin Battalion and became 'M' Company of the new 4th Corps in 1880. The Wolverhampton Waterworks were in the town.

31st Formed at Smethwick on 19 April 1860 with Sampson Hanbury as captain, Ralph Docker, lieutenant and George Stevens, ensign. Joined the 3rd Admin Battalion and became 'H' Company of the new 1st Corps in 1880. Cassell's notes that in the 1890s, 'The glass, chemical and lighthouse works' employed upwards of 2,000 people, with a machine works providing jobs for 2,000 more.

32nd Formed at Wolverhampton on 19 April 1860 with Henry Loveridge as captain, William H Tudor, lieutenant and Alfred Young, ensign. Joined the 4th Admin Battalion and became 'K' and 'L' Companies of the new 4th Corps in 1880.

33rd Formed at Cannock on 14 July 1860 with Joseph S Mosely as captain, Bernard Gilpin, lieutenant and George Lee, ensign. Joined the 5th Admin Battalion and became 'E' Company of the new 3rd Corps in 1880. The mining of coal and the manufacture of bricks, titles and paving material employed many from the town.

34th Formed at Wednesbury on 11 May 1860 with Thomas Russell as captain, John Hunt Thursfield, lieutenant and George Gaddick Whitehouse, ensign. Joined the 5th Admin Battalion and became 'F' Company of the new 3rd Corps in 1880. All manner of ironwork was produced in the area including rails, boiler plates and carriage axles for the railways.

35th Formed at Kinver, four miles from Stourbridge, on 3 July 1860 with Offley F D Wakeman as captain, Robert Woodward jun, lieutenant and Joseph L Stenson, ensign. Joined the 3rd Admin Battalion and was disbanded in 1864.

36th Formed at Hanley on 18 June 1860 with Edward J Ridgway as captain and Clement Wedgwood, lieutenant. Joined the 1st Admin Battalion and became 'K' Company of the new 2nd Corps in 1880.

37th Formed at Cheadle on 30 August 1860 with John W Phillips as captain, John Adamthwaite, lieutenant and Charles J Biagg, ensign. Joined the 1st Admin Battalion, disappearing from the *Army List* in November 1872. Most of the inhabitants of Cheadle found employment in its collieries.

38th Formed at Eccleshall on 17 September 1860 with Robert Hargreaves as captain, Basil Fitzherbert, lieutenant and Thomas Robinson, ensign. Joined the 1st Admin Battalion and disbanded in 1869. The town is seven miles north-west of Stafford.

39th Formed at Burton-upon-Trent on 27 September 1860 with member of the brewing family, William H Worthington as captain, Josiah T Poyser, lieutenant and William Drewery, ensign. Joined the 2nd Admin Battalion and became 'H' Company of the new 5th Corps in 1880.

40th Formed at Stone on 1 December 1860 with Basil T Fitzherbert as captain. Joined the 1st Admin Battalion and became 'L' Company of the new 2nd Corps in 1880. Seven miles north of Stafford, Stone is close to the Trent and Mersey Canal, which runs through the town parallel with its High Street. Perhaps the Volunteers of the 40th Corps took part in the opening of the new chancel and organ chamber erected at St Michael's Church in 1887. The additions to the church being in memory of Captain Viscount St Vincent, who was mortally wounded at Abu Klea, Sudan, in 1885.

STIRLINGSHIRE

All but the 10th and 14th Corps joined 1st Admin Battalion, which became the new 1st Corps in 1880.

1st (1859–80) One company formed at Stirling on 14 October 1859 with Robert Graham Moir as captain, Robert Sconce, lieutenant and Alexander Wilson jun, ensign. Became 'A' Company of the new 1st Corps in 1880. The 1st Corps was also known as the 'Citizens' Corps. Opposite the County Court House in Viewfield Place, the Volunteers saw the unveiling in 1887 of a fountain in honour of Queen Victoria's Jubilee. Carpets, tartans, tweeds and shawls were made in the town, as well as two businesses producing iron bedsteads and carriages.

1st (1880–1908) The 1st Stirlingshire Admin Battalion was formed with headquarters at Stirling on 9 June 1860. Both the 1st and 2nd Clackmannanshire Corps were also included in 1862, but in 1867 these were removed and transferred to their own county administration. The battalion was consolidated in March 1880 as the new 1st Corps with ten companies:

'A' Stirling (late 1st Corps)
'B' Stirling (late 2nd Corps)
'C' Falkirk (late 3rd Corps)
'D' Lennox Mill (late 7th Corps)
'E' Lennoxtown (late 4th Corps)
'F' Stirling (late 11th Corps)
'G' Denny, (late 6th Corps)
'H' Bannockburn (late 9th Corps)
'I' Carron (late 12th Corps)
'K' Kilsyth (late 13th Corps)

Shortly after amalgamation the headquarters of 'D' Company moved from Lennox Mill to Falkirk and in 1887 1st Stirlingshire RVC was re-designated as 4th (Stirlingshire) Volunteer Battalion Argyll and Sutherland Highlanders. Some fifty-seven members of the battalion served in South Africa alongside of the Regulars of the Argyll and Sutherland Highlanders. Lieutenant J Hunter, who had been commissioned in 1898, died at Heilbron on 30 June 1900 of enteric fever. In 1904 the headquarters of 'H' and 'I' Companies moved to Stenhousemuir in 1904, 'F' transferring to Falkirk in 1906. In 1908 transfer to the Territorial Force was as four companies of 7th Battalion Argyll and Sutherland Highlanders. Uniform: green/scarlet with trews, changing to green/green with trews in 1882, then scarlet/yellow with trews in 1886.

2nd One company formed at Stirling from artisans on 3 February 1860 with Francis Mackison as captain, William Mackison, lieutenant and George Christie, ensign. Became 'B' Company of the new 1st Corps in 1880.

3rd One company formed at Falkirk on 27 March 1860 with John Archibald S Nicolson as captain, Alexander Nimmo, lieutenant and James Aitken, ensign. Became 'C' Company of the new 1st Corps in 1880. Five years before the Volunteers held their first parade, a statue of the Duke of Wellington was unveiled in the High Street. The Town Hall was opened in 1878, a Science and Art School the same year, and the Dollar Library ten years after that. Collieries, title and fire-brickworks, a brewery and distillery, gave employment to the area.

4th One company formed at Lennoxtown on 6 March 1860 with William Peareth as captain,

Charles M King, lieutenant and William Reid, ensign. Became 'E' Company of the new 1st Corps in 1880. The main industries of Lennoxtown, notes Cassell's, were printing, bleaching, coal mining and the quarrying of limestone.

5th One company formed at Balfron on 1 May 1860 with Alexander G Speirs as captain, Andrew G Jeffrey, lieutenant and John B Buchanan, ensign. The 5th Corps was not seen in the *Army List* after September 1877. Balfron village, on the River Endrick twelve miles north-east of Dumbarton, was founded as a cotton manufacturing centre in 1781 and in the 1890s had a large factory employing many from the area.

6th One company formed at Denny on 11 April 1860 with James Laing as captain, James Cousland, lieutenant and Robert S Gray, ensign. Became 'G' Company of the new 1st Corps in 1880. Denny is on the River Carron to the south of Stirling, its collieries, ironworks, paper mills and chemical works employed many from the town.

7th Headquarters of the 7th Corps of one company were given in the *Army List* as Lennox Mill, its three officers: Captain Gordon Wilson, Lieutenant Thomas Wilson and Ensign James Purdon, all holding commissions dated 1 May 1860. Became 'D' Company of the new 1st Corps in 1880.

8th One sub-division formed at Strathblane on 25 May 1860 with John Coubrough as lieutenant and Archibald Mcindoe Graham, ensign. Disbanded in 1863. The village, eight miles north of Glasgow, takes its name from the vale of the River Blane and had a large calico-printing works.

9th One company formed at Bannockburn on 21 May 1860 with Alexander Wilson as captain, John Fisken Halket, lieutenant and George Watson, ensign. Became 'H' Company of the new 1st Corps in 1880. Here, where Robert the Bruce fought Edward II in June 1314, the town in the Volunteer days was a busy manufacturing centre turning out woollens, tweeds, tartans, carpets and leather.

10th (Highland) One company formed at Stirling on 10 November 1860 with Allan Anderson as lieutenant and Andrew Hutton jun, ensign. Disbanded in February 1864.

11th One company formed at Stirling on 6 December 1860 with George D Mercer as captain, Neil Cochrane, lieutenant and David D Syme, ensign. Became 'F' Company of the new 1st Corps in 1880.

12th One company formed at Carron on 10 February 1862 with John Bell Sherriff as captain, John Campbell, lieutenant and Robert Adam, ensign. Became 'I' Company of the new 1st Corps in 1880. Two miles north-west of Falkirk, Carron takes its name from the river on which it stands. Once carronades and shot were made there, but by the time of the Volunteers, it was the manufacture of stoves, grates, drainpipes and boilers that gave employment. Carron Station was opened by the old Strathspey Railway in July 1863.

13th One company formed at Kilsyth on 19 July 1866 with Alexander Brown as captain, John Walker, lieutenant and William White, ensign. Became 'K' Company of the new 1st Corps in 1880. Kilsyth is to the north-east of Kirkintilloch and has to the north, the River Carron, the south, the Kelvin, and just beyond that, the Forth and Clyde Canal. Much work involving the town's churches went on during the Volunteer days – the Free Church opened in 1871, Parish Church altered and restored in 1892, United Presbyterian built in 1893. There were collieries and ironstone quarries in the area

14th One company formed at Alva on 17 October 1868 with James Porteous as captain, Donald

McFadyen, lieutenant and Thomas Donaldson, ensign. Included in the 1st Clackmannanshire Admin Battalion and provided 'F' Company of the new 1st Clackmannan and Kinross RVC in 1880. The making of blankets, serges, shawls, tartans and tweeds brought prosperity to the town during the Volunteer days, the hills above the town yielding copper, lead and some silver.

SUFFOLK

Three admin battalions were formed, of which the 3rd was broken up in 1877. The 1st and 2nd were, in 1880, consolidated as the new 6th and 1st Corps. Formed in November 1860 with headquarters at Halesworth, the 3rd Admin Battalion included the 4th, 7th, 9th, 14th, 15th and 17th Corps. Its headquarters were transferred to Lowestoft in 1865. There was also a 1st Sub-division, which became the 1st Corps in 1860.

1st (1859–80) Formed at Ipswich on 11 October 1859 and known as the 1st Sub-division until January 1860. Its first officers were Captain Robert Ramsey, Lieutenant Henry Haward and Ensign Sterling Westhorp. Joined the 2nd Admin Battalion and became 'A'. 'B' and 'C' Companies of the new 1st Corps in 1880. Ransome's employed many in their production of agricultural tools, their lawnmowers still produced today.

1st (1880–1908) Woodbridge was the headquarters of the 2nd Admin Battalion, formed on 24 October 1860 and including the 1st, 2nd, 3rd, 5th, 8th, 12th and 21st Corps. The 7th and 9th were added in 1877. The battalion was consolidated in 1880 as the new 1st Corps with eight companies:

'A', 'B' and 'C' Ipswich (late 1st Corps)
'D' Framlingham (late 2nd Corps)
'E' Woodbridge (late 3rd Corps)
'F' Halesworth (late 7th Corps)
'G' Saxmundham (late 8th Corps)
'H' Leiston (late 9th Corps)

Under General Order 181 of December 1887 the 1st Corps became 1st Volunteer Battalion Suffolk Regiment, a new company being added in 1900. The Queen Elizabeth's School, Ipswich, Cadet Corps was formed and affiliated in 1889, disappearing from the *Army List* by the end of 1891, but reappearing again in 1900. Framlingham College also formed a cadet corps in 1901. Transfer to the Territorial Force in 1908 was as 4th Battalion Suffolk Regiment, both Queen Elizabeth's School and Framlingham College at the same time joining the OTC. Uniform: green/black.

2nd Formed at Framlingham on 1 March 1860 with Edwin Blomfield as captain, John Pierson, lieutenant and Nathaniel G Barthropp, ensign. Joined the 2nd Admin Battalion and became 'D' Company of the new 1st Corps in 1880. Albert Memorial College, just outside of town, was built in 1865, Framlingham Station opened by the East Suffolk Railway in June 1859.

3rd Formed at Woodbridge on 26 January 1860 with Francis Capper Brooke, late of the Grenadier Guards, as captain, F W B Lord Rendlesham, lieutenant and Arthur George Brooke, ensign. Joined the 2nd Admin Battalion and became 'E' Company of the new 1st Corps in 1880. Eight miles north-east of Ipswich, the railway reached Woodbridge in June 1859. The Church of St Mary the Virgin underwent its Victorian restoration during 1874–75.

4th Formed at Bungay on 1 February 1860 with John Margitson as captain, William Mann, lieutenant and Phillip Salter Millard, ensign. Joined the 3rd Admin Battalion, transferring to the 1st Norfolk Admin Battalion in 1877, and became 'F' Company of the new 2nd Norfolk RVC in 1880. Bungay lies on the River Waveney in the eastern part of the county.

5th Formed at Wickham Market on 16 February 1860 with Andrew Arcdeckne as lieutenant and William George Murial, ensign. Joined the 2nd Admin Battalion and was disbanded in 1875. The town is five miles north of Woodbridge.

6th (1860–80) Formed at Stowmarket on 13 February 1860 with Walter Robert Tyrell, late of the Royal Horse Guards, as captain, H Aston Oakes, lieutenant and Thomas Mingaye Golding, ensign. Joined the 1st Admin Battalion and became 'A' Company of the new 6th Corps in 1880. Situated on the River Gipping, twelve miles north-west of Ipswich, Stowmarket carried on a considerable trade in corn, malt, coal, slate and timber. The town's cathedral-like church of St Peter and St Mary was restored in 1865.

6th (1880–1908) The 1st Admin Battalion was formed on 30 July 1860 and is first shown with headquarters at Stowmarket. From August 1961 the *Army List* gave the battalion's location as being at Bury St Edmunds, and from April 1864 as Sudbury. Included in the battalion were the 6th, 10th, 11th, 12th, 13th, 16th, 18th, 19th and 20th Suffolk Corps, the 9th Cambridgeshire being added in July 1862. When consolidation came in 1880, 1st Admin would be the only battalion in the land to retain the number of its senior company, the new 6th Suffolk RVC following on directly after the new 1st. The 6th had eight companies:

'A' Stowmarket (late 6th Corps)
'B' and 'C' Eye (late 10th Corps)
'D' Sudbury (late 11th Corps)
'E' and 'F' Bury St Edmunds (late 13th Corps)
'G' Hadleigh (late 16th Corps)
'H' Newmarket (late 20th Corps)

Re-designated as 2nd Volunteer Battalion Suffolk Regiment under General Order 181 of December 1887, headquarters transferring to Bury St Edmunds in 1899. There was a reduction in establishment to seven companies in 1889, but this was brought back to eight in 1900. A cadet corps at King Edward's School, Bury St Edmunds, was raised and affiliated in 1900 and transfer to the Territorial Force in 1908 was as 5th Battalion Suffolk Regiment. King Edward School at the same time joined the OTC. Uniform: grey/scarlet.

7th Formed at Halesworth on 28 February 1860 with Thomas Rank as captain, Edward Deck, lieutenant and Fairly B Strathern, ensign. Joined the 3rd Admin Battalion, transferring to the 2nd in 1877, and became 'F' Company of the new 1st Corps in 1880. St Mary's Church in Halesworth underwent three separate restorations during the Volunteer period, 1863, 1868 and 1889. The Town Hall was built in 1886, the Court House in 1891. Breweries, a malthouse and a carriage works provided employment in the town.

8th Formed at Saxmundham on 29 February 1860 with William B Long as captain, George Waller Bates, lieutenant and Ellis Wade, ensign. Joined the 2nd Admin Battalion and became 'G' Company of the new 1st Corps in 1880. Saxmundham Station was opened by the old East Suffolk Railway Company in June 1859.

9th Formed as two companies with headquarters at Aldeburgh on 9 March 1860 with Captain Arthur Thelluson in command. Joined the 2nd Admin Battalion. Much of the corps was recruited just to the south-east in the Leiston area and in the early part of 1861 the 9th was divided: the Aldeburgh portion being made independent as 21st Corps, while the Leiston personnel remained as 9th. At the same time, the new arrangement saw the corps placed into 3rd Admin Battalion, but a return was made to the 2nd in 1877. Became 'H' Company of the new 1st Corps in 1880. The Volunteer Drill Hall at Leiston was built in 1862.

10th Formed at Eye on 6th March 1860 with Phillip H Michell, late of the 47th Regiment of Foot, as captain, Sir Edward C Kerrison, lieutenant and the Hon John Major H Major, ensign. Joined the 1st Admin Battalion and became 'B' and 'C' Companies of the new 6th Corps in 1880. At Eye, twenty miles north of Ipswich, there were breweries and a small iron foundry giving employment.

11th Formed at Sudbury on 14th April 1860 with W J W Poley as lieutenant and Robert F Stedman, ensign. Joined the 1st Admin Battalion and became 'D' Company of the new 6th Corps in 1880. The original Sudbury Station, opened by the Colchester, Stour Valley, Sudbury & Halstead Railway Company in 1849, was replaced when the line was extended to Haverhill in August 1865.

12th Formed at Bosmere, one mile south-east of Needham Market, on 1 June 1860 with John Hayward as lieutenant and John K Sedgwick, ensign. Joined the 1st Admin Battalion, transferring to 2nd in June 1861. Moved to Needham Market in the same year and disbanded in 1866.

13th Formed as two companies at Bury St Edmunds on 11 May 1860 with Fuller M Wilson and John S Phillips as company commanders. Joined the 1st Admin Battalion and became 'E' and 'F' Companies of the new 6th Corps in 1880. In the town was the Depot of the 12th (later Suffolk) Regiment.

14th Formed at Beccles on 1 May 1860 with George Wilson as captain, William M Crowfoot, lieutenant and James Read, ensign. Joined the 3rd Admin Battalion, transferring to the 1st Norfolk Admin Battalion in 1877, and became 'G' Company of the new 2nd Norfolk RVC in 1880. The town had a coach-building works and brickfields.

15th Formed at Wrentham on 9 June 1860 with John F Vincent as lieutenant and Samuel A Goodwin, ensign. Joined the 3rd Admin Battalion and was disbanded in 1865. Wrentham (actually in Norfolk) lies six miles north-east of Thetford.

16th Formed at Hadleigh, ten miles west of Ipswich, on 2 July 1860 with John F Robinson as lieutenant and George Freeman, ensign. Joined the 1st Admin Battalion and became 'G' Company of the new 6th Corps in 1880.

17th Formed at Lowestoft on 11 September 1860 with Edward Leathes as captain, Thomas Lucas, lieutenant and Robert Johnson, ensign. Joined the 3rd Admin Battalion, transferring to the 1st Norfolk Admin Battalion in 1877, and became 'H' and 'I' Companies of the new 2nd Norfolk RVC in 1880. A thriving seaport, Lowestoft had a large fishing industry, ship and boat-building yards and a coachworks.

18th Formed at Wickhambrook on 22 October 1860 with William G Strutter as lieutenant and Joseph R Bromley, ensign. Joined the 1st Admin Battalion and was disbanded in 1870. Wickhambrook village is to the south-west of Bury St Edmunds.

19th Formed at Brandon on 23 April 1861 with Charles A D Tyssen as captain, John Gates, lieutenant and John Wood, ensign. Joined the 1st Admin Battalion and was disbanded in 1863. Brandon is on the western edge of Thetford Forest Park to the north-east of Mildenhall.

20th Formed at Mildenhall on 23 May 1861 with William Payne as captain, James Read jun, lieutenant and Frederick H Harris, ensign. Joined the 1st Admin Battalion, absorbing the 9th Cambridgeshire RVC in 1862, and moved to Newmarket in 1871. Became 'H' Company of the new 6th Corps in 1880.

21st Formed at Aldeburgh from part of the 9th Corps, the 21st was first seen in the *Army List* for June 1861, Lieutenant Newson Garrett in command. Joined the 2nd Admin Battalion and became the 3rd Suffolk Artillery Volunteer Corps in 1864. Aldeburgh is on the coast to the north-east of Woodbridge.

SURREY

Four admin battalions were formed which, in 1880, provided the new 3rd, 4th, 5th and 6th Corps. There were also three numbered sub-divisions, 1st, 2nd and 3rd, and these became the 9th, 14th and 15th Corps.

1st (South London) Formed as the South London RVC at Camberwell on 14 June 1859. Subsequent headquarters were listed as Camberwell Green, then Peckham (Hanover Park), Flodden Road from 1865 – a good number of early recruits to the corps were drawn from the Sports Club, Hanover Park. Absorbed the 3rd Corps, also at Camberwell, as No. 2 Company by February 1860, its title from then on appearing in the *Army List* as 1st Surrey (South London) RVC. The establishment soon rose to eight companies, the men recruited in the main throughout Camberwell, Clapham and Peckham, with Lieutenant Colonel Commandant John Boucher, late of the 5th Dragoon Guards, in command. A cadet corps was formed at Dulwich College in 1878. Became a volunteer battalion of the East Surrey Regiment in 1881, but although ranked as 1st, there was no change in title. Transfer to the Territorial Force in 1908 was as 21st Battalion London Regiment, Dulwich College at the same time joining the OTC. Uniform: green/scarlet.

According to Mr J W Reddyhoff, writing in the *Bulletin* of the Military Historical Society in November 1997, the Macdonald Freemason Lodge No. 1216 was formed from within the battalion on 13 March 1868.

2nd Formed as one company at Croydon on 16 June 1859, followed by a second in March 1860. James Hunter Campbell, formerly of the Bengal Artillery, and Adam Stewart were the company commanders. Headquarters were in the old Croydon Barracks. Included in the 1st Admin Battalion from September 1860 but in March 1867, after new personnel had been recruited from around the Crystal Palace, Norwood and Caterham areas, the establishment was brought up to six companies and the 2nd Corps was made independent. The Whitgift School Cadet Corps was formed and affiliated in 1874. Re-designated as 1st Volunteer Battalion Queen's (Royal West Surrey Regiment) in March 1883, there would be ten companies in 1900, reducing to nine in 1903 – seven at Croydon, one each at Crystal Palace and Caterham. Transfer to the Territorial Force in 1908 was as 4th Battalion Queen's, the Whitgift School cadets at the same time joining the OTC. Uniform: green/scarlet.

3rd (1859–60) Formed at Camberwell on 26 August 1859 and absorbed into the 1st Corps as its No. 2 Company by February 1860.

3rd (1880–1908) Headquarters of the 1st Admin Battalion, formed in September 1860, were at Croydon and to it were added the 2nd, 4th, 8th, 11th, 20th, 21st, 25th and 26th Corps. Headquarters transferred to Wimbledon in 1862, Southwark in 1868 and Thornton Road,

Clapham Park in 1869. The battalion was consolidated in 1880 as the new 3rd Corps with seven companies:

'A', B' and 'C' Brixton (late 4th Corps)
'D' Carshalton (late 8th Corps)
'E' and 'F' Wimbledon (late 11th Corps)
'G' Epsom (late 25th Corps)

There was also a half-company at Brixton. Headquarters were moved back to Wimbledon in 1884, this time to St George's Road. Two new companies were added in 1886 and in December of the following year 3rd Surrey was re-designated as 2nd Volunteer Battalion East Surrey Regiment. Another two companies joined in 1900 and by 1904, after several reorganizations, company locations stood at: 'A' and 'B' Streatham; 'C' and 'D' Sutton; 'E', 'F' and 'G' Wimbledon; 'H' Epsom; 'I' Wimbledon and 'K' Epsom. A cadet corps at Epsom College was formed and affiliated in 1890. Transfer to the Territorial Force in 1908 was as 5th Battalion East Surrey Regiment, Epsom College at the same time joining the OTC. Uniform: green/green, changing to scarlet/white in 1897.

4th (1859–80) Formed as one company at Brixton on 10 September 1859, increasing to two in February 1860 with Captain Commandant Thomas Eman, late of the 2nd Regiment of Foot, in command. Joined the 1st Admin Battalion and became 'A' to 'C' Companies of the new 3rd Corps in 1880. Brixton lies east of Clapham, north of Streatham and three miles south of St Paul's Cathedral.

4th (1880–1908) The 3rd Admin Battalion was formed with headquarters at Dorking in September 1860 and included the 5th, 13th, 14th, 17th, 18th, 22nd and 24th Corps. In 1880 the battalion was consolidated as the new 4th Corps with six companies:

'A' and 'B' Reigate (late 5th Corps)
'C' and 'D' Guildford (late 13th Corps)
'E' Farnham (late 18th Corps)
'F' Guildford (late 24th Corps)

There was also a half-company at Godstone provided by the 17th Corps. Headquarters transferred to Reigate in 1881 and in 1883, under General Order 37 of March, 4th Surrey RVC became 2nd Volunteer Battalion Queen's (Royal West Surrey Regiment). Headquarters moved again, this time to Guildford, in 1891. Three cadet companies were associated with the battalion: Charterhouse School Cadet Corps, formed in 1873; Cranleigh School, 1900, and Reigate Grammar School in 1907. Transfer to the Territorial Force in 1908 was as 5th Battalion Queen's, Charterhouse, Cranleigh and Reigate Schools at the same time joining the OTC. Uniform: green/scarlet.

5th (1859–80) Formed at Reigate on 12 September 1859 with the Hon William J Monson as captain, Francis Henry Beaumont, lieutenant and Henry Lainson, ensign. Joined the 3rd Admin Battalion and became 'A' and 'B' Companies of the new 4th Corps in 1880. Six miles east of Dorking, the Public Hall was built in High Street, Reigate in 1861, Municipal Offices, Castleford Road, in 1901.

5th (1880–1908) Headquarters of the 2nd Admin Battalion, formed in September 1860, were at Walton-on-Thames and to it were attached the 6th, 9th, 11th, 12th, 15th and 16th Corps. The battalion moved to Kingston-upon-Thames in 1864 and in 1880 was consolidated as the new 5th Corps with eight companies:

'A' Esher (late 6th Corps)
'B' and 'C' Richmond (late 9th Corps)
'D', 'E', 'F' and 'G' Kingston-upon-Thames (late 12th Corps)
'H' Chertsey (late 15th Corps)

Re-designated as 3rd Volunteer Battalion East Surrey Regiment in December 1887. Two new companies, one at Egham, one at Richmond, were added in 1900. Also in that year Richmond County School Cadet Corps was formed and affiliated, as was Beaumont College at Old Windsor in 1906. In South Africa during the Boer War, Lieutenant S F Brooks died from enteric fever at Newcastle on 9 June 1900. Brooks was educated at Harrow School and commissioned in March 1897. Transfer to the Territorial Force in 1908 was as 6th Battalion East Surrey Regiment, Beaumont College at the same time joining the OTC. Uniform: green/scarlet.

6th (1859–80) Formed at Esher on 29 October 1859 with Sir Henry Fletcher, late of the Grenadier Guards, as captain, John N Higginbothom, lieutenant and Robert H Few, ensign. Joined the 2nd Admin Battalion and became 'A' Company of the new 5th Corps in 1880. Queen Victoria presented a drinking-fountain to the town in 1877. Sandown Park Racecourse is close by.

6th (1880–1908) The 4th Admin Battalion was formed with headquarters at Bermondsey in October 1868 and into it were placed the 10th and 23rd Corps. Headquarters transferred to Rotherhithe in 1869 and consolidation as the new 6th Corps took place in 1880. There were eight companies: 'A' and 'B' at Bermondsey, formed from the 10th Corps; 'C' to 'H' at Rotherhithe, from the 23rd. The corps was re-designated as 3rd Volunteer Battalion Queen's (Royal West Surrey Regiment) in March 1883 and headquarters moved to Bermondsey in 1884. A cadet corps was formed in Bermondsey in 1885, but this disappeared from the *Army List* after ten years. Another was raised; this time at Streatham Grammar School, in 1899, and transfer to the Territorial Force in 1908 was as 22nd Battalion London Regiment. The Streatham Grammar School Cadets, although the Army Council did approve its transfer to the OTC, was, however, disbanded. Uniform: scarlet/blue.

7th The first company of the 7th Corps was raised at Southwark on 30 November 1859, five others following by February 1860, Major Commandant Francis Marcus Beresford taking command. In 1880 the 26th Corps of four companies at Lavender Hill, Clapham was amalgamated with the 7th to form a new battalion of ten companies with headquarters at Upper Kennington Lane, Southwark. The corps was designated as 4th Volunteer Battalion East Surrey Regiment in December 1887, headquarters transferring to Clapham Junction in 1902. A cyclist company was added there in 1900 and transfer to the Territorial Force in 1908 was as 23rd Battalion London Regiment. Uniform: green/scarlet, changing to scarlet/white in 1889.

8th (1859–80) Formed as one company at Epsom on 21 December 1859 with James Hastie as captain, John Holman Hay, lieutenant and Edward James Rickards, ensign. Joined the 1st Admin Battalion, moving headquarters to Carshalton in 1862. Became 'D' Company of the new 3rd Corps in 1880. The Volunteers at Epsom would have seen the building of the mental hospitals after the London County Council bought the Horton Estate in the 1890s.

8th (1880–1908) Formed as the 19th Corps at Lambeth on 13 March 1860 and soon comprised eight companies with Major Commandant William Roupell in command. Headquarters are given as 71 New Street, Kennington Park from 1869. Renumbered as 8th in 1880 and designated 4th Volunteer Battalion Queen's (Royal West Surrey Regiment) in March 1883. The establishment was increased to ten companies in 1890 and a cyclist company was added in 1901. The Mayall College Herne Hill Cadet Corps was formed and affiliated in 1888, but this transferred to the 22nd Middlesex RVC in 1891. Another cadet corps with headquarters at Red Cross Hill in Southwark was added in 1889 and this became the 1st Cadet Battalion Queen's in 1890. Transfer to the Territorial Force in 1908 was as 24th Battalion London Regiment. Uniform: green/scarlet.

9th Formed at Richmond on 2 September 1859 and known as the 1st Sub-division until December. Comprised two companies by February 1860, Captains Morgan Yeatman and Octavius Ommanney being appointed as company commanders. Joined the 2nd Admin Battalion and became 'B' and 'C' Companies of the new 5th Corps in 1880. On The Green, Richmond's Public Library was opened in 1880, its Town Hall in 1893, and Frank Matcham's Theatre (also on The Green) in 1899.

10th Formed as two companies at Bermondsey on 7 February 1860 with Marcus Sharpe and Benjamin Glover as company commanders. Joined the 4th Admin Battalion in October 1868 and became 'A' and 'B' Companies of the new 6th Corps in 1880. At the south end of Tower Bridge there is a bronze statue to Colonel Samuel Bourne Bevington, who was commissioned ensign in the 10th Corps on 9 March 1861. He went on to command the 3rd Volunteer Battalion Queen's Royal West Surrey Regiment (1884–99), and would become Bermondsey's first Mayor in 1900.

11th Formed at Wimbledon on 11 February 1860 with James Oliphant as captain, Timothy Richards, lieutenant and John S Oliphant, ensign. Joined the 2nd Admin Battalion, transferring to the 1st in July 1862, and became 'E' and 'F' Companies of the new 3rd Corps in 1880. Wimbledon's Christ Church on Copse Hill dates from 1860; St John's at Spencer Hill was completed in 1875, and All Saints' in 1893.

12th Formed at Kingston-upon-Thames on 16 February 1860 with William Marshall Cochrane as captain, Frederick M Arnold, lieutenant and Edward William Browne, ensign. Comprised four companies by the end of 1861. Joined the 2nd Admin Battalion and became 'D' to 'G' Companies of the new 5th Corps in 1880. Headquarters were in Orchard Road. Hidden behind the Market Place, All Saints' Church underwent two major Victorian restorations. The Volunteers would have also witnessed the building of the Surrey County Hall in Penrhyn Road during 1892–93.

13th Formed at Guildford on 18 February 1860 with William Henry Gill, late of the Rifle Brigade, as captain and William M Molyneux, ensign. The lieutenant of the original company was Ross Lewis Mangles, who had won the Victoria Cross on 30 July 1857 during the Indian Mutiny. He was later Member of Parliament for Guildford. Joined the 3rd Admin Battalion and became 'C' and 'D' Companies of the new 4th Corps in 1880. A large Victorian employer at Guildford was the Friary Brewery, its red-brick tower of the 1860s still to be seen in Commercial Road.

14th Formed at Dorking on 9 September 1859 with Henry Walker Kerrich as lieutenant and Robert Barclay, ensign. Known as 2nd the Sub-division until March 1860. Joined the 3rd Admin Battalion and was disbanded in 1877. Dorking's St Martin's Church was completed in the same year that the 14th Corps was disbanded.

15th Formed at Chertsey on 25 February 1860 with Robert Hay Murray as lieutenant and Francis L Dowling, ensign. Known as the 3rd Sub-division until March. Joined the 2nd Admin Battalion and became 'H' Company of the new 5th Corps in 1880. A new Chertsey Station was opened across the road from the original by the London and South Western Railway Company in October 1866.

16th Formed at Egham on 2 March 1860 with W Edgell as lieutenant and Lionel Booth, ensign. Joined the 2nd Admin Battalion and was disbanded in 1868. Egham is just to the west of Staines, Middlesex, which is reached by an ancient stone bridge across the Thames.

17th Formed at Godstone on 23 February 1860 with Charles Hampden Turner as lieutenant and Granville Levison Gower, ensign. Joined the 3rd Admin Battalion and provided a half-company of the new 4th Corps in 1880. On the main Eastbourne road, Godstone's St Nicholas's Church was greatly restored by Sir George Gilbert Scott in 1872–73.

18th Formed at Farnham on 6 March 1860 with Owen F L Ward, late of the 11th Regiment of Foot, as captain, William J Hollest, lieutenant and George Trimmer, ensign. Joined the 3rd Admin Battalion and became 'E' Company of the new 4th Corps in 1880. The Farnham Volunteers would have seen the opening in 1876 of St James's Church in East Street.

19th See 8th Corps (1880–1908).

20th Formed at Lower Norwood on 27 April 1860 with former captain in the Royal Madras Engineers, John Ouchteriony, as commanding officer; William E Franks, lieutenant and William Ruston, ensign. Joined the 1st Admin Battalion and was disbanded in 1863.

21st Formed at Battersea on 3 May 1860 with John B Burnley as captain, Alexander Webster, lieutenant and George Finch, ensign. Joined the 1st Admin Battalion in 1863 and was disbanded in 1866.

22nd Formed at Albury on 16 January 1861 with William John Evelyn as captain, Thomas Lyon Thurlow, lieutenant and Edward Jekyll, ensign. Joined the 3rd Admin Battalion and was disbanded in 1875. Albury, in the Tillingbourne valley, is five miles south-east of Guildford.

23rd Formed at Rotherhithe on 1 February 1861 with James Payne as captain, Frederick Wood, lieutenant and James John Stoke, ensign. Increased to six companies from two in 1868, joined the 4th Admin Battalion and became 'C' to 'H' Companies of the new 6th Corps in 1880.

24th (1861–62) Formed by cartoonist George Cruikshank in Southwark on 9 March 1861, the membership being made up entirely from total abstainers. Cruikshank, who became captain commandant, called his corps 'Havelock's Own' after hero of the Indian Mutiny and noted leader in the Temperance Movement, General Sir Henry Havelock (1795–1857). Headquarters were at St George's Road, Southwark, but were moved to 39 Bridge House, Newington Causeway by October 1861. According to one source relations, both internal and with the authorities – there were unwelcome moves afoot to merge the 24th with the 7th Surrey – were not entirely harmonious and subsequently the corps was disbanded in March 1862.

24th (1862–80) Formed at Guildford as the 25th Corps on 31 January 1862 and renumbered 24th by April of the same year. Captain Frederick George Thynne took command. Joined the 3rd Admin Battalion and became 'F' Company of the new 4th Corps in 1880.

25th Formed at Epsom on 1 March 1862. Joined the 1st Admin Battalion and became 'G' Company of the new 3rd Corps in 1880.

26th Formed at Shaftesbury Park, Lavender Hill, Clapham, on 28 April 1875. Joined the 1st Admin Battalion and, with an establishment of four companies, was amalgamated with the 7th Corps in 1880.

1st Cadet Battalion Queen's (Royal West Surrey Regiment) Raised at the Red

Cross Hall, Southwark in January 1889 as a cadet corps affiliated to the 4th Volunteer Battalion Queen's in June 1889. The idea for this corps was first put forward in January 1889 – Captain Salmond of the 3rd Battalion Derbyshire Regiment being asked to take charge of formation. On the following 30 May, at Red Cross Hall, Lord Wolseley made a memorable speech which did much to encourage sufficient boys to come forward to make up two companies. A third followed in 1890, then a fourth, which subsequently led the War Office to grant permission to form the cadets into a battalion. This, the 1st Cadet Battalion, Queen's (Royal West Surrey Regiment), was to be the first independent battalion of its kind in London. There would be six companies by 1891 – this was to make the battalion the strongest in England – and by 1904 the establishment stood at eight: 'A' and 'B' at Southwark; 'C' at the Passmore Edward's Settlement, St Pancras, and the Marlborough Road Board School in Chelsea; 'D' at the Haileybury Club, Stepney; 'E', St Andrew's Institute, Westminster; 'F', St Peter's Institute, Pimlico; 'G, Bethnal Green and 'H' at the Eton Mission in Hackney. In 1904 battalion headquarters transferred to Union Street, Southwark. Uniform: scarlet/blue.

2nd Cadet Battalion Queen's (Royal West Surrey Regiment) (1890–94) See 1st Cadet Battalion King's Royal Rifle Corps below.

2nd Cadet Battalion Queen's (Royal West Surrey Regiment) (1901–1908) Raised at Peckham in October 1901 from boys of 1st Peckham Lads' Brigade, which had been formed in 1894. Headquarters were at 53 Copeland Road, Peckham and the establishment six companies.

1st Cadet Battalion East Surrey Regiment Formed with headquarters at 71 Upper Kennington Lane, London in 1890 with four companies. Disbanded in 1896

1st Cadet Battalion King's Royal Rifle Corps Formed as 2nd Cadet Battalion Queen's (Royal West Surrey Regiment) of four companies in November 1890. Headquarters were originally at the Lambeth Polytechnic, moving later to Kirkdale in Clapham, then to Brockwell Hall, Herne Hill. Increased to six companies in 1891 and in 1894 was re-designated as 1st Cadet Battalion KRRC. Headquarters at the same time moving to Finsbury Square EC London. Uniform: green/scarlet.

SUSSEX

Not all Sussex RVC were included in the county's admin battalions, some being placed with Cinque Ports. Of the three Sussex battalions that were formed, only the 1st would survive to produce a consolidated corps (the new 2nd) in 1880.The 2nd Admin Battalion, which was formed with headquarters at Petworth in April 1860, include at various times the 2nd, 5th, 6th, 7th, 8th, 13th 14th and 18th Corps. Headquarters were transferred to Horsham in 1869 and the battalion was merged with 1st Admin in 1874. Brighton was the headquarters of the 3rd Battalion, formed in April 1860 with 1st, 2nd, 4th, 5th, 16th and 19th Corps and broken up in 1863. There was also a 1st Sub-division, which became the 7th Corps.

1st Formed as two companies at Brighton on 23 November 1859 with R Moorsom, late of the Scots Fusilier Guards, and John Stuart Roupell as company commanders. Joined the 3rd Admin Battalion but, having reached a strength of six companies, was withdrawn in 1863. Two new companies were added in 1886 and in the following year 1st Sussex RVC became 1st Volunteer Battalion Royal Sussex Regiment. A ninth company was added in 1900, the Brighton College

Cadet Corps being affiliated in the same year. Christ's Hospital Cadet Corps joined in 1904, Cottesmore School (re-designated Brighton and Preparatory Schools in 1907) in 1905. Transfer to the Territorial Force was to see the 1st Volunteer Battalion convert to artillery; but this was unpopular and the officers, having refused to comply, were then placed onto the unattached list. Brighton College and Christ's Hospital joined the OTC. Uniform: scarlet/blue. *Note*: The 1st VB eventually, in 1912, became 6th (Cyclist) Battalion Royal Sussex Regiment. The Brighton Volunteer would have seen the finish, at the Metropole Hotel in 1896, of the first ever London to Brighton car run and in the same year, the destruction in a storm of the old Chain Pier.

2nd (1859–80) Formed as two companies at Cuckfield on 2 December 1859 with George Meek and Warden Sergisen as company commanders. Joined the 3rd Admin Battalion, transferring to the 1st Cinque Ports Admin in 1863, 2nd Sussex Admin in 1870 and finally, 1st Admin Battalion in 1874. Became 'A' and 'B' Companies of the new 2nd Corps in 1880. Cuckfield is fourteen miles north of Brighton.

2nd (1880–1908) The 1st Admin Battalion was formed with headquarters at Chichester in April 1860 and included the 8th, 9th, 10th, 11th, 12th and 15th Corps. Headquarters were transferred to Worthing in 1866 and the 2nd, 5th, 6th, 7th, 13th and 18th Corps were added from 2nd Admin Battalion in 1874. The battalion was consolidated in 1880 as the new 2nd Corps with eleven companies:

'A' and 'B' Cuckfield (late 2nd Corps)
'C' East Grinstead (late 5th Corps)
'D' Petworth (late 6th Corps)
'E' Horsham (late 7th Corps)
'F' Arundel (late 9th Corps)
'G' Chichester (late 10th Corps)
'H' Worthing (late 11th Corps)
'I' Westbourne (late 12th Corps)
'K' Hurstpierpoint (late 13th Corps)
'L' Henfield (late 18th Corps)

The 2nd Sussex RVC was designated 2nd Volunteer Battalion Royal Sussex Regiment in 1887 and increased to twelve companies in 1900. The St John's College, Hurstpierpoint Cadet Corps was affiliated in 1887; Lancing College at Shoreham in 1900; Ardingly College, Hayward's Heath in 1902. Volunteers served in South Africa during the Boer War, some eighty or more going out under Major, the Duke of Norfolk; Captain Sir Walter George Barttelot; Lieutenants S W P Beale and B I D'Olier. Action was seen at Welkom Farm, the Zand River, Doornkop, Johannesburg, Pretoria, and Diamond Hill. Sir Walter Barttelot was killed while leading his men at Retief's Nek on 23 July 1900, one other man, a private, losing his life during the same action. Transfer to the Territorial Force in 1908 was as 4th Battalion Royal Sussex Regiment. All three schools at the same time joined the OTC. Uniform: scarlet/blue.

3rd None recorded.

4th Formed as one company at Lewes on 25 January 1860 with Bernard Husey-Hunt as captain, Inigo Gell, lieutenant and William Beard, ensign. The corps was with the 3rd Admin Battalion until 1863 when transferred to 1st Cinque Ports Admin. Became 'D' Company of the new 1st Cinque Ports Corps in 1880. The Lewes Volunteer would have seen the restoration of St Michael's Church in 1885, St Anne's in 1889, and the opening of the Town Hall and Corn Exchange in 1893.

5th Formed as one company at East Grinstead on 9 February 1860 with Alfred Robert Margary, late of the 54th Regiment, as captain, Arthur Charles Ramsden, lieutenant and William Alston Head, ensign. Joined the 3rd Admin Battalion, transferring to 2nd Admin, then to 1st Admin Battalion in 1874. Became 'C' Company of the new 2nd Corps in 1880. The Victorian restoration of St Swithin's Church was carried out at East Grinstead in 1882, the Literary and Scientific Institute opened six years after that.

6th Formed as one company at Petworth on 8 February 1860 with Walter B Barttelot, late of the 1st Dragoons, as captain, the Hon Percy S Wynham, lieutenant and Viscount Turnour, ensign. Joined the 2nd Admin Battalion, transferring to 1st Admin in 1874, and became 'D' Company of the new 2nd Corps in 1880. Petworth is to the north-east of Chichester, the old Mid Sussex Railway reaching the town just months before the 6th Corps was formed.

7th Formed at Horsham on 29 November 1859 and known as 1st Sub-division until February 1860. The officers then being Captain Manton Pipon, Lieutenant Sir John H Pelly and Ensign Henry Padwick jun. Joined the 2nd Admin Battalion, transferring to 1st Admin in 1874, and became 'E' Company of the new 2nd Corps in 1880. Taking place in Horsham during the Volunteer period was the restoration of St Mary's Church in 1865.

8th Formed as one company at Storrington on 16 February 1860 with Sir Charles Goring as captain, Brian Barttelot, lieutenant and George Curling Joad, ensign. Joined the 1st Admin Battalion, transferring to 2nd Admin by the beginning of 1861, then back with 1st Admin Battalion in 1874. Disbanded in 1876. Storrington is nine miles north-east of Arundel.

9th Formed as one company at Arundel on 28 February 1860 with Henry Granville, Duke of Norfolk, as captain, Thomas Evans, lieutenant and Reginald A Warren, ensign. Joined the 1st Admin Battalion and became 'F' Company of the new 2nd Corps in 1880. Arundel Station, on the London, Brighton & South coast Railway, was renamed Ford Station in August 1863.

10th Formed as one company at Chichester on 1 March 1860 with George G Nicholls, formerly a lieutenant colonel in the 90th Regiment of Foot, as captain, William L Reid, lieutenant and James Powell jun, ensign. Joined the 1st Admin Battalion and became 'G' Company of the new 2nd Corps in 1880. The Chichester Volunteer would have seen the collapse of Chichester Cathedral's central tower during a storm in February 1861.

11th Formed as one company at Worthing on 10 March 1860 with Thomas Galsford as captain, Henry P Crofts, lieutenant and Edward Martin, ensign. Joined the 1st Admin Battalion and became 'H' Company of the new 2nd Corps in 1880. To the west of Brighton, Worthing's Pier was reopened after being extended in 1889.

12th Formed at Westbourne on with Lieutenant J H Osmond commissioned on 23 April 1860. Joined the 1st Admin Battalion and became 'I' Company of the new 2nd Corps in 1880. Westbourne lies seven miles west of Chichester, its St John's Church being restored in 1863.

13th Formed as one company at Hurstpierpoint on 14 March 1860 with William John Campion as captain, Henry Lane, lieutenant and Charles Gordon, ensign. Joined the 2nd Admin Battalion, transferring to 1st Admin in 1874. Became 'K' Company of the new 2nd Corps in 1880. Headquarters was in High Street, Hurstpierpoint, the premises still in use by the Army Cadet Force.

14th Formed at Crawley on 14 March 1860 with John J Broadwood as lieutenant and John

Lemon jun, ensign. Joined the 2nd Admin Battalion and was disbanded in 1863. Crawley is just under eight miles north-east of Horsham.

15th Formed at Bognor on 9 April 1860 with Augustine Fitzgerald as lieutenant and O'Bryen Lomax, ensign. Joined the 1st Admin Battalion and was disbanded in 1865.

16th Formed at Battle on 19 May 1860 with Boyce H Combe as captain, William E M Watts, lieutenant and Julian A Worge, ensign. Joined the 3rd Admin Battalion, transferring to 1st Cinque Ports Admin Battalion in 1861. Absorbed into the 1st Cinque Ports RVC in 1876. Battle is six miles north-west of Hastings.

17th Formed at Etchingham on 4 June 1860 with Francis Reeves as lieutenant and James Brooker, ensign. Formed part of 5th Kent Admin Battalion for periodMay to November 1861, then to 1st Cinque Ports Admin. Absorbed into 1st Cinque Ports RVC in 1876. Etchingham is fourteen miles north-west of Hastings.

18th Formed at Henfield on 14 June 1860 with Percy Burrell as lieutenant and Walter W Burrell, ensign. Joined the 2nd Admin Battalion, transferring to 1st Admin in 1874, and became 'L' Company of the new 2nd Corps in 1880. Henfield Station, on the old London, Brighton & South Coast Railway, was opened in July 1861.

19th Formed at Eastbourne on 6 October 1860 with Freeman F Thomas as lieutenant and John Francis Gottwaltz, ensign. Joined the 3rd Admin Battalion, transferring to 1st Cinque Ports Admin in 1861. Disbanded 1868. Two years prior to the disbandment of the 19th Corps, Eastbourne Station was replaced by a new one further to the east.

20th (1861) A 20th Corps is shown in the *Army List* with headquarters at Billingshurst for January 1861, but was removed in December 1861 having had no officers appointed.

20th (1870–76) Formed at Uckfield on 27 October 1870. Joined the 1st Cinque Ports Admin Battalion and was absorbed into the 1st Cinque Ports RVC in 1876.

SUTHERLAND

All corps joined the 1st Admin Battalion, which provided the new 1st Corps in 1880.

1st (1859–80) General Grierson records that the first meeting leading to the formation of the 1st Sutherland RVC at Golspie took place at the Golspie Inn on 6 June 1859. Acceptance of its services as one company were received on 17 October, Captain Charles Samuel Weston being appointed as commanding officer with a commission dated 2 December. In January 1861 the 1st Corps grew to four companies as it took in the 2nd Corps at Dornoch, 3rd at Brora and a hitherto unnumbered corps at Rogart which had been raised after a meeting held there on 13 October 1860. Upon the formation of the 1st Sutherland Admin Battalion in January 1864, the four companies separated, taking on their former numbers, Rogart becoming 4th. The 1st Corps, in June 1880, became 'A' Company of the new 1st Corps.

1st (Sutherland Highland) (1880–1908) The 1st Admin Battalion, formed with headquarters at Golspie on 4 January 1864, included the 1st to 4th Sutherland, 1st Orkney and

Shetland, 1st, 2nd and 3rd Caithness RVC. A 4th Caithness was added upon its formation in September 1867 and the 5th Sutherland in 1868. The battalion, which was commanded by the Duke of Sutherland, was also known as 'The Sutherland Highland Rifle Volunteers' and was consolidated in June 1880 as the new 1st (Sutherland Highland) Corps. There were ten companies:

'A' Golspie (late 1st Sutherland)
'B' Dornoch (late 2nd Sutherland)
'C' Brora (late 3rd Sutherland)
'D' Rogart (late (4th Sutherland)
'E' Bonar Bridge (late 5th Sutherland)
'F' Lerwick (late 1st Orkney and Shetland)
'G' Thurso (late 1st Caithness)
'H' Wick (late 2nd Caithness)
'I' Halkirk (late 3rd Caithness)
'K' Watten (late 4th Caithness)

Became a volunteer battalion (without change in title) of the Seaforth Highlanders in 1881. 'F' Company was disbanded in 1884, a replacement being formed at the same time at Lairg. 'L' Company was added at Wick in 1890 and 'M' at Reay in 1901. Transfer to the Territorial Force in 1908 was as 5th Battalion Seaforth Highlanders. Uniform: scarlet/yellow with kilts.

2nd Formed at Dornoch on 2 December 1859 with Captain William Sutherland Frazer in command. Merged with the 1st Corps as its No. 2 Company in January 1861, but made independent again at the beginning of 1864. Became 'B' Company of the new 1st Corps in 1880. On the Dornoch Firth, the town's church has long been the burial place of the Sutherland family.

3rd Formed at Brora with Charles Hood as captain, George Lawson, lieutenant and John Dudgeon, ensign. All three held commissions dated 30 January 1860. Merged with the 1st Corps as its No. 3 Company in January 1861, but made independent again in January 1864. Became 'C' Company of the new 1st Corps in 1880. At Brora, just under five miles north-east of Golspie, there were collieries, brickworks and a long-established distillery.

4th Formed at Rogart on 25 December 1860 with John Hall as captain, Robert Barclay Sangster, lieutenant and George Barclay, ensign, but before receiving a number was merged into the 1st Corps as its No. 4 Company. Made independent as 4th Corps in January 1864 and became 'D' Company of the new 1st Corps in 1880. Cassell's for 1897 notes that at Rogart, seven miles west of Golspie on the road to Lairg, most on the inhabitants were agricultural labourers, a few being employed in a woollen factory.

5th Formed at Bonar Bridge with Dugald Gilchrist as captain and Alex S Black, lieutenant, both with commissions dated 6 August 1868. Ensign John Mackenzie made up the establishment in the following month. Became 'E' Company of the new 1st Corps in 1880. Bonar Bridge is on the Dornoch Firth to the south of Lairg.

TOWER HAMLETS

Tower Hamlets, London's 'East End', comprised the several areas ('hamlets') about and within the Tower of London. Twenty-one in all, these were recorded in 1720 as: Hackney, Norton Folgate, Shoreditch, Spitalfields, Whitechapel, Trinity Minories, East Smithfield, Tower Liberty Within,

Tower Liberty Without, St Katharine's, Wapping, Ratcliffe, Shadwell, Limehouse, Poplar, Blackwall, Bromley, Bow, Old Ford, Mile End and Bethnal Green. There was one admin battalion formed, which, in 1880, provided the new 2nd Corps.

1st (1860) A 1st Corps appeared in the *Army List* for April 1860. Dalston was given as its headquarters and provisions were made for four companies. No officers appear to have been gazetted and the corps disappeared before the end of the year.

1st (Tower Hamlets Rifle Volunteer Brigade) (1868–1908) Formed as the 2nd Corps and soon comprised seven companies located: No. 1 Hackney, No. 2 Dalston, No. 3 Bow, Nos 4, 5 and 6 at Poplar and Limehouse, No. 7 Clapton. James Scott Walker, who was appointed as lieutenant colonel in command, held a commission dated 6 April 1860. The original headquarters were at Arnold House, Richmond Road, Dalston, but were transferred by the end of 1860 to Pembroke Hall, Lamb Lane in South Hackney. One of the original officers was Captain Joseph D'Aguilar Samuda, the Jewish Thames shipbuilder. The 2nd Corps was amalgamated with the 4th Corps in 1868 under the title of 1st Tower Hamlets, The Tower Hamlets Rifle Volunteer Brigade. Headquarters were placed at Robert Street, Hoxton and the establishment of the new brigade was set at fifteen companies – seven from the 2nd Corps, eight from the 4th. With effect from 1 January 1874 the 1st Corps was amalgamated with the 6th of twelve companies at Dalston. Now with a combined strength of twenty-seven companies, it was ordered by the War Office that a reduction should be made to sixteen. The reorganization went as follows:

'A' Company from 'A', 'L', 'M' and 'N' Companies of the 1st Corps
'B' Company from 'A' and 'L' of 6th Corps
'C' Company from 'B' of 1st Corps
'D' Company from 'B' of 6th Corps
'E' Company from 'C' and 'D' of 1st Corps
'F' Company from 'C' and 'H' 6th Corps
'G' Company from 'E' of 1st Corps
'H' Company from 'D' of 6th Corps
'J' Company from 'F', 'I' and 'K' of 1st Corps
'K' Company from 'E' of 6th Corps
'L' Company from 'G' of 1st Corps
'M' Company from 'F' and 'G' of 6th Corps
'N' Company from 'H' and 'J' of 1st Corps
'O' Company from 'J' of 6th Corps
'P' Company from 'O' of 1st Corps
'Q' Company from 'K' of 6th Corps

Headquarters of the new and enlarged 1st Corps were transferred to those of the 6th Corps at Shaftesbury Street, Dalston. There would be further reorganizations when, in 1874, the War Office directed this time that the brigade should reduced its companies from sixteen to twelve. Regimental Orders of 28 November 1874 showed how this was achieved:

'A' Company to be formed by 'A' and 'P'
'B' Company to be formed by 'B'
'C' Company to be formed by 'O' and 'Q'
'D' Company to be formed by 'E' and 'C'
'E' Company to be formed by 'J'
'F' Company to be formed by 'F'

'G' Company to be formed by 'G'
'H' Company to be formed by 'H'
'J' Company to be formed by 'N'
'K' Company to be formed by 'K' and 'D'
'L' Company to be formed by 'L'
'M' Company to be formed by 'M'

Appeared in the *Army List* as one of the volunteer battalions allotted to the Rifle Brigade from 1881. There would be no change in title until May 1904 when, having been transferred, 1st Tower Hamlets became 4th Volunteer Battalion Royal Fusiliers. A cadet corps was formed in 1885, but this disappeared from the *Army List* during 1891. The Tower Hamlets Brigade had formed a Machine Gun Battery in 1886 and it was this, under the command of Captain E V Welby, that formed the nucleus of the machine gun section of the City Imperial Volunteers in South Africa. Welby was mentioned in dispatches, his sergeant, W J Park, received the Distinguished Conduct Medal. Transfer to the Territorial Force in 1908 was as 4th Battalion London Regiment. Uniform: scarlet/blue.

2nd (1860–68) See 1st Corps (1868–1908).

2nd (1880–1908) The 1st Admin Battalion was formed in May 1861 and to it were added the 3rd, 7th, 9th, 10th, 11th and 12th Corps. The battalion's first headquarters were those of the 3rd Corps at Truman's Brewery in Spitalfields, but after consolidation as the new 2nd Corps in 1880, a transfer was made to Whitechapel Road. The new 2nd Corps comprised eleven companies:

'A', 'B', 'C' and 'D' Stepney (late 3rd Corps)
'E', 'F', 'G' and 'H' Mile End (late 7th Corps)
'I', 'K' and 'L' Finsbury (late 10th Corps)

From 1881 the 2nd Tower Hamlets RVC is shown as being one of the volunteer battalions allotted to the Rifle Brigade, but there would be no change in title. Headquarters moved to Bow in 1894 and transfer to the Territorial Force in 1908 was as part of 17th Battalion London Regiment. Uniform: grey/scarlet.

3rd Formed at Truman's Brewery, Spitalfields with Sir T F Buxton Bt as captain, Charles Buxton, lieutenant and Thomas King, ensign. All three held commissions dated 4 May 1860. There would be three companies by June 1861 and four by 1863. Joined the 1st Admin Battalion. Subsequent headquarters were shown in the *Army List* as Great Garden Street, Whitechapel, from 1865; Granby Street in Bethnal Green, from 1870, and Quaker Street, Stepney from 1873. As part of the 1st Admin Battalion, 3rd Tower Hamlets RVC became 'A' to 'D' Companies of the new 2nd Corps in 1880.

4th Formed at St Leonard's, Shoreditch with five companies, increasing to eight by 1868. Captain Henry A Bale was the first commanding officer, his commission being dated 14 June 1860. Headquarters were transferred to Robert Street, Hoxton in 1864, the corps being amalgamated with 2nd Tower Hamlets RVC in 1868. St Leonard's parish included Hoxton and Haggerston, the Church, from which it takes its name, is in Shoreditch High Street.

5th Formed at Dalston with James McClissock as captain, Alexander Beath, lieutenant and James T Morland, ensign. All three held commissions dated August 1860. Headquarters were transferred to Kingsland in 1861 and the corps was disbanded in 1862. Dalston and Kingsland are twin localities located on the western side of Hackney, the area expanding rapidly after Dalston Junction station was opened in 1865.

6th (North East London Rifles) Formed at Dalston and comprised eight companies by the beginning of 1861, Lieutenant Colonel George Henry Money was appointed as commanding officer his, and all other original officers holding commissions dated 25 September 1860. No doubt much of this corps was found by those Volunteers intended for the original 1st Corps. During 1861 headquarters transferred from Rosemary Street to Shaftesbury Street in Hoxton and in 1865 the corps became known as the 'North East London Rifles'. Increased to ten companies, then to twelve in February 1866, and when amalgamated with the 1st Corps in January 1874 provided its 'B', 'D', 'F', 'H', 'K', 'M', 'O' and 'Q' Companies. A cadet corps was formed during the early years of the 6th Corps and was present at the Cadet Review held at the Crystal Palace on 11 September 1862. No mention of the unit, however, was made in the *Army List*.

7th Formed at Mile End with George E Ludbrook as captain, John B Jenkins, lieutenant and Thomas J Ludbrook, ensign. All three held commissions dated 13 September 1860. Joined the 1st Admin Battalion and became 'E' to 'H' Companies of the new 2nd Corps in 1880. The names of two men that helped others are linked with Victorian Mile End. William Booth began his work with the Salvation Army there in 1868, and in 1870 Dr Barnardo established his first home for orphans near Ben Johnson Road.

8th Formed with headquarters at the West India Dock, Poplar with Charles H Wigram as captain, Thomas H Sheppy, lieutenant and James G Clark, ensign commissioned on 7 November 1860. Robert G Tatham was appointed surgeon to the corps at the same time. Absorbed into the 26th Middlesex RVC in 1868. From the seventeenth century Poplar had provided homes for dock workers employed on the river front from Limehouse to Blackwall. The area also included the Isle of Dogs.

9th Formed with headquarters at London Dock House with Thomas Chandler as captain, John B Fisher, lieutenant and Samuel J Ball, ensign. All three held commissions dated 23 November 1860. Joined the 1st Admin Battalion and was absorbed into the 26th Middlesex RVC in 1864.

10th Formed as two companies at Goodman's Fields with Captain George S Davies and Captain Joseph Hobbs commissioned as company commanders on 13 December 1860. Joined the 1st Admin Battalion, moving to Mile End Gate in 1861; Great Garden Street, Whitechapel in 1865; Chapel Street, Shoreditch in 1872 and Finsbury in 1874. Later increased to three companies and in 1880 became 'I', 'K' and 'L' Companies of the new 2nd Corps.

11th An item in *The Times* for 5 December 1860 reported that at a meeting held at Zetland Hall in Mansell Street, Goodman's Fields the previous evening, it was decided to form a corps of Rifle Volunteers from London's Jewish population. Two companies were formed quite quickly, one commanded by Captain Barnett Lazarus, the other by Captain David Barnett. Both held commissions dated 21 February 1861. Headquarters are given in the *Army List* as Goodman's Fields and by June 1861 the 11th Tower Hamlets RVC is shown as being part of the 1st Admin Battalion. Regarding the disbandment of the corps in 1864, Mr Harold Pollins writes in the *Bulletin* of the Military Historical Society for February 1998 that although the 11th had got off to a good start (it numbered 180 within three months of its formation) little interest had been shown from the Jewish community as a whole – their financial support was essential in as much as at the time funds were not provided by the government. More important, noted Mr Pollins, was talk of lax discipline and a general dissatisfaction among all ranks. Subsequently, all but one of the original officers resigned and, although others took their place, the 11th Tower Hamlets RVC was disbanded and removed from the *Army List* in August 1864.

12th Formed as two companies at Stoke Newington with Captain Alfred Heales and Captain Richard W Merington as company commanders. All six officers held commissions dated 24 April 1861 and they were joined by Samuel Elwin Brand, who was appointed as surgeon in May. Joined the 1st Admin Battalion in 1863 and was absorbed into the 1st London RVC in 1870.

1st (Duke of Norfolk's Own) Cadet Battalion, The Rifle Brigade Formed in the Tower Hamlets area on 28 May 1904 with headquarters at Mile End. There were four companies, all being disbanded in 1906.

WARWICKSHIRE

All corps outside Birmingham joined the 1st Admin Battalion, which provided the new 2nd Corps in 1880.

1st (Birmingham) Formed in Birmingham on 4 November 1859 and amalgamated with the 3rd and 6th Corps, also in Birmingham, in March 1860. Lieutenant Colonel John W Sanders, late of the 41st Bengal Native Infantry was in command. The corps comprised twelve companies recruited from various sources. There was one formed by workers from several newspapers, one made up of gunmakers, another of Scots resident in the city. In 1883 1st Warwickshire RVC became 1st Volunteer Battalion Royal Warwickshire Regiment. Four new companies were added in 1891, the battalion then being divided into two: 'A' to 'H' Companies (1st Battalion), 'I' to 'Q' (2nd Battalion). A cyclist section was formed in 1894, this being increased to a full company in 1900. At Birmingham University in the same year, 'U' Company was formed from staff and students and this, in 1908, became part of the Senior Division OTC. At the same time the remaining companies joined the Territorial Force as 5th and 6th Battalions Royal Warwickshire Regiment. Uniform: green/scarlet.

A cadet corps was formed in 1864 which, according to the published history of the corps, was raised by 'The Grammar School'. No mention of this unit, however, was made in the *Army List* after 1866. Another cadet corps appeared in 1883, this disappearing by the end of the following year having had no officers appointed to it. Next, in 1904, came the company formed at Solihull Grammar School; then in 1907, that raised by King Edward's School. Both schools became part of the OTC in 1908.

Mr J W Reddyhoff, writing in the *Bulletin* of the Military Historical Society in November 1997, notes that the Freemason's Leigh Lodge of Rifle Volunteers No. 1189 (later No. 887) was formed from within the battalion on 1 November 1861.

2nd (1859–80) Formed as one company at Coventry with Captain John William Hartopp, late of the 17th Light Dragoons (Lancers), and Lieutenant Josiah Yeomans Robins commissioned on 8 November 1859. Richard Caldicott jun joined them as ensign on 2 January 1860. Absorbed the 6th and 7th Corps, also at Coventry, in 1862 and became 'A' to 'D' Companies of the new 2nd Corps in 1880. Many from Coventry were employed in the manufacture of bicycles, the Coventry Machinists Company producing the first English-made bicycle in 1870. The city was also well known for its art metal works, one of which was the Albert Memorial in London.

2nd (1880–1908) The 1st Admin Battalion was formed with headquarters at Coventry in May 1860 and consolidated in 1880 as the new 2nd Corps. There were twelve companies:

'A', 'B', 'C' and 'D' Coventry (late 2nd corps)

'E' and 'F' Rugby (late 3rd Corps)
'G' Warwick (late 4th Corps)
'H' Stratford-on-Avon (late 5th Corps)
'I' Nuneaton (late 8th Corps)
'K' Saltley College (late 9th Corps)
'L' and 'M' Leamington (late 10th Corps)

Re-designated 2nd Volunteer Battalion Royal Warwickshire Regiment in 1883 and increased to thirteen companies in 1900. There was a reduction, however, to eleven by the end of the following year. The King's Grammar School, Warwick provided a cadet corps in 1885, as did Leamington College in 1900 and King's County School, Warwick in 1905. King's Grammar, which was renamed Warwick School in 1894, was not seen in the *Army List* after 1906, the Leamington cadets disappearing after a few months having had no officers appointed to it. Transfer to the Territorial Force in 1908 was as 7th Battalion Royal Warwickshire Regiment. Rugby and King's County Schools at the same time joined the OTC. Uniform: scarlet/blue.

3rd (1859–60) Formed at Birmingham on 8 November 1859 and amalgamated with the 1st Corps in March 1860.

3rd (1861–80) Formed as the 4th Corps at Rugby with James Atty, late major of the 2nd Warwick Militia and 52nd Regiment of Foot, as captain, George Charles Benn, lieutenant and T Mave Wratislaw, ensign. All three held commissions dated 26 November 1859. Renumbered as 3rd in May 1861 and absorbed the 12th Corps, also at Rugby, as its No. 2 Company in 1868. Much of the corps was recruited from within Rugby School which, in 1873, provided a cadet corps. Became 'E' and F' Companies of the new 2nd Corps in 1880. Those at Rugby School would have taken part in its tercentenary celebrations in 1867. Outside in the town itself, St Andrew's Church was completely rebuilt in 1879.

4th (1859–61) See 3rd Corps (1861–80).

4th (1861–80) Formed as the 5th Corps at Warwick with John Machen, late captain with the South Devon Militia, as captain, Richard Child Heath, lieutenant and Eugene Muntz, ensign. All three held commissions dated 13 February 1860. Renumbered 4th in 1861 and became 'G' Company of the new 2nd Corps in 1880. Opened in Warwick during the Volunteer period was the Prison in 1866 and the Public Library six years after that.

5th (1860–61) See 4th Corps (1861–80).

5th (1861–80) Formed as the 7th Corps at Stratford-on-Avon with Henry Perrott, late of the 59th Regiment of Foot, commissioned as captain on 9 February 1860. Edward Flower joined as lieutenant and William Henry Hunt, ensign in the same month. Renumbered 5th in 1861 and became 'H' Company of the new 2nd Corps in 1880. Just a year after the formation of the 7th Corps, the house ('New Place') where Shakespeare spent his last years was purchased by public subscription. The Shakespeare Memorial Statue, presented by Lord Gower was unveiled in 1888.

6th (1860) Formed at Birmingham on 8 February 1860 and amalgamated with the 1st Corps in March 1860.

6th (1861–62) Formed as the 8th Corps at Coventry with Captain Josiah Y Robins and Lieutenant James S Whittern commissioned on 15 June 1860. Alexander Rotherham joined them as ensign in July. Renumbered 6th in 1861 and absorbed into the 2nd Corps in 1862.

7th (1860–61) See 5th Corps (1861–80).

7th (1861–62) Formed as the 9th Corps at Coventry with Richard Caldicott as captain, Thomas Darlington, lieutenant and David Hitchin, ensign. All three held commissions dated 31 October 1860. Renumbered 7th in 1861 and absorbed into the 2nd Corps in 1862.

8th (1860–61) See 6th Corps (1861–62).

8th (1861–80) Formed as the 10th Corps at Nuneaton with Henry Dewes as captain, Craddock Towie, lieutenant and Thomas J Craddock, ensign. All three held commissions dated 1 December 1860; John B Nason was appointed as surgeon at the same time. Renumbered 8th in 1861 and became 'I' Company of the new 2nd Corps in 1880. At Nuneaton, nine miles north of Coventry, many were employed in the manufacture of bricks, tiles and drain-pipes.

9th (1860–61) See 7th Corps (1861–62).

9th (1861–80) Formed at the Saltley Training College with Captain Henry Harvey Chattock and Lieutenant Henry Howell commissioned on 29 June 1861. Became 'K' Company of the new 2nd Corps in 1880. Located at Saltley were extensive works manufacturing railway carriages and wagons. Also found there were the Corporation Gas Works and the Birmingham Reformatory for Boys.

10th (1860–61) See 8th Corps (1861–80).

10th (1861–80) Formed at Leamington with James Laurie Brown as lieutenant and Phillip Lant Parsons, ensign. Both held commissions dated 15 July 1861. Absorbed the 11th Corps, also at Leamington, as No. 2 Company in 1862 and became 'L' and 'M' Companies of the new 2nd Corps in 1880. Close to Warwick in the valley of the Leam, Leamington's Theatre Royal was opened in 1882, its new Town Hall and Municipal Offices in 1884.

11th Formed at Leamington on 3 April 1862 with John Machen as captain, Nathaniel Merridew, lieutenant and William R. Magrath, ensign. Absorbed into the 10th Corps as its No. 2 Company in 1862.

12th Formed at Rugby on 22 May 1868 with James S Phillpotts as captain, Francis E Kitchener, lieutenant and Henry L Warner, ensign. Absorbed into the 3rd Corps as its No. 2 Company in 1868.

1st Cadet Battalion Royal Warwickshire Regiment Formed as four companies at Birmingham in June 1886 and disbanded in 1893.

WESTMORLAND

All corps joined 1st Admin Battalion, which in 1880 became the new 1st Corps.

1st (1860–80) Formed as one company and a sub-division at Kirkby Lonsdale with Captain William Moore, who received his commissioned dated 29 February 1860, Lieutenants George Washington Ireland and Francis Fenwick Pearson, and Ensigns Daniel Harrison and John Preston. Also appointed were Thomas Harper Whitaker as surgeon, and the Revd Edward Pigot, who became chaplain. Became 'A' Company of the new 1st Corps in 1880. Known to the Volunteers, and perhaps they to him, would have been the Victorian author John Ruskin (1819–1900), who said that Kirkby Lonsdale was his favourite town. On the River Lune, Kirkby Lonsdale is eleven miles south-east of Kendal. An ancient stone bridge of three arches ('Devil's Bridge') crosses the river just below the town, and St Mary's Church underwent major restoration in 1868. The view from its churchyard, said Ruskin, is the finest in England.

1st (1880–1908) The 1st Admin Battalion was formed at Kirkby Lonsdale in May 1860, headquarters moving to Kendal in 1861, and was consolidated as the new 1st Corps of nine companies in 1880:

'A' Kirkby Lonsdale (late 1st Corps)
'B' Appleby (late 2nd Corps)
'C' to 'E' Kendal (late 3rd Corps)
'F' Stavely (newly formed)
'G' Windermere (late 4th Corps)
'H' Ambleside (late 5th Corps)
'J' Grasmere (late 6th Corps)

Re-designation as 2nd (Westmoreland) Volunteer Battalion Border Regiment was notified in General Order 181 of December 1887. The Sedbergh School Cadet Corps was formed and affiliated in 1901 and the Kirkby Lonsdale Cadet Company in April 1902. Transfer to the Territorial Force in 1908 was as four companies of 4th Battalion Border Regiment. Sedbergh School at the same time joined the OTC. Uniform: scarlet/green, changing to scarlet/white in 1888.

2nd (1860) No location is given for the 2nd Corps, which first appeared in the *Army List* for April 1860 with John Whitwell commissioned as captain on 6 March 1860. Captain Whitwell is later joined by Lieutenant Harry Arnold, Ensign Cartmell Harrison, chaplain, the Revd Frederick T Raikes, and surgeon Robert Walker, all having been gazetted on 27 March. In September the five officers are now shown as a second company to the 3rd Corps at Kendal.

2nd (1878–80) Formed as one company at Appleby on 7 August 1878 and became 'B' Company of the new 1st Corps in 1880. Bounded by the River Eden, Appleby is thirteen miles south-east of Penrith.

3rd A two-company corps at Kendal appears in the *Army List* for the first time with a single officer, Captain William Wilson, having a commission dated 28 February 1860. George W Ireland and David Harrison are later shown as lieutenant and ensign respectively. The remaining officers required to complete the establishment are shown by September 1860 and were in fact those previously listed as forming the 2nd Corps. Later increased to three companies and became 'C' to 'E' Companies of the new 1st Corps in 1880. Kendal lies on the River Kent to the south-east of Lake Windermere, its main industries being listed in the 1890s as the manufacture of carpets, railway rugs, horse cloths and coarse blankets. There were also iron foundries and businesses producing snuff, tobacco, paper, boots and shoes. There was a military prison in the town.

4th Formed as one company at Windermere with Captain George J M Ridehaigh commissioned on 29 February 1860. He was later joined by Edward W Yeeles as lieutenant and Thomas G Postlethwaite, ensign. Became 'G' Company of the new 1st Corps in 1880. On the eastern shore of Lake Windermere, the town's St Martin's Church underwent lengthy restoration between 1871 and 1873.

5th Formed as one company at Ambleside with John R Peddar commissioned as captain on 28 February 1860. He was later joined by Lieutenant Robert Jefferson and Ensign John Bolton, who were both gazetted on 30 March. Became 'H' Company of the new 1st Corps in 1880. Ambleside lies at the head of Lake Windermere twelve miles north-west of Kendal.

6th The first officer recorded as belonging to the 6th Corps at Grasmere was Captain Augustus Ruxton, who is shown with a commission dated 17 April 1860. Provisions are made in the *Army List* for one company and a sub-division. By August, however, Ruxton has been removed and his place taken by Captain Jasper Selwyn, who has been joined by Lieutenant J Bousfield and Ensign Joseph F Green. The remaining two officers required to comply with a one-and-a-half-company establishment were not to appear and by the end of 1861 the 6th Westmorland Corps is shown as a single company. Became 'J' Company of the new 1st Corps in 1880. The Volunteers at Grasmere would have known much about William Wordsworth, who mentions the village's St Oswald's Church in his 'Excursion'. His grave lies in the churchyard. Grasmere is four miles north-west of Ambleside on the road to Keswick.

WIGTOWNSHIRE

All corps joined the Galloway Admin Battalion, which in 1880 became the Galloway RVC.

1st Formed as a sub-division at Wigtown with Lieutenant Robert V Agnew and Ensign William J McHaffle holding commissions dated 24 February 1860. Absorbed into the 3rd Corps as a section in 1874. The chief industry at Wigtown was fishing.

2nd Formed as one company at Stranraer with David Guthrie as captain, Alexander Ingram, lieutenant and John McBride, ensign. All three held commissions dated 16 March 1860 and they were joined on 22 March by Ebenezer Fleming, who had been appointed as surgeon. Became 'C' Company of the Galloway RVC in 1880. The Volunteers used the old Town Hall in George Street as an armoury and Drill Hall after 1874. Stranraer is located at the head of Loch Ryan.

3rd Formed as one company at Newton Stewart, the first officers appointed being Lieutenant Henry Stuart and Ensign Edward J S Blair. Their commissions were dated 22 March 1860 and they were soon joined by James S More MD as surgeon. Absorbed the 1st Corps in 1874 and became 'D' Company of the Galloway RVC in 1880. The town is eight miles north of Wigtown, the old Portpatrick Railway Company reaching there in 1861.

4th Formed as a sub-division at Whithorn, eleven miles south of Wigtown, with Lieutenant Hugh Dun Stewart and Ensign James Drew commissioned on 11 April 1860. Through lack of interest, the corps was disbanded in 1874.

5th Formed as a sub-division at Drumore with Lieutenant James Watson, ensign John Anderson and Surgeon George Crawford commissioned on 23 November 1860. The corps was disbanded in 1866. At the village, which is eighteen miles south-east of Stranraer, a certain amount of trade was carried on from its harbour.

WILTSHIRE

The Wiltshire RVC were placed into two administrative battalions, these forming the new 1st and 2nd Corps in 1880.

1st (1859–80) It was at a meeting held at Salisbury's White Hart Hotel in May 1859, that the decision to form a body of Riflemen, to be called the Salisbury Rifle Corps, was taken. On 28 May the *Salisbury and Winchester Journal* gave notice that the names of those wishing to enrol were being taken; the paper also pointing out that all members would be expected to pay a sum not exceeding £3/10/0 for uniform. Subsequently, John Henry Jacob Esq. was appointed as captain commandant with commission dated 10 August 1859. The War Office had sanctioned one company and a sub-division, the latter having its headquarters near Downton, and in August 1860 was increased to the strength of a full company with Captain Beverley Robinson in command. Drills were carried out in the Market Hall, Salisbury. The rifle range used by the corps was some distance from the city on the London Road. As part of the 1st Admin Battalion, 1st Wiltshire RVC became 'A' and 'B' Companies of the new 1st Corps in 1880. The Corn Exchange was opened in Salisbury in the same year as the 1st Corps was formed, the Blackmore Museum five years later. The manufacture of carpets and rugs began there in 1889, the town also giving employment in its tanneries, breweries and flour mills.

1st (1880–1908) The first Admin Battalion of Wiltshire Rifle Volunteers was formed with headquarters at Salisbury on 8 March 1861. In command was Lieutenant General P Buckley, MP for Salisbury, ex-Guards officer and veteran of Waterloo. Headquarters moved to Warminster in 1879 and consolidation in 1880 was as the new 1st Corps with eight companies:

'A' and 'B' Salisbury (late 1st Corps)
'C' and 'D' Trowbridge (late 2nd Corps)
'E' Bradford-on-Avon (late 9th Corps)
'F' Warminster (late 10th Corps)
'G' Westbury (late 13th Corps)
'H' Wilton (late 14th Corps)

Became a volunteer battalion (without change in title) of the Wiltshire Regiment in 1881. A new company ('I') was formed from around the Tisbury and Mere areas in 1892 and 'K' (Cyclist) was raised at Bradford-on-Avon in 1900. A cadet corps was formed at Salisbury and affiliated to the corps in 1890, but this had disappeared from the *Army List* by the end of 1897. Transfer to the Territorial Force in 1908 was as headquarters and five companies of the 4th Wiltshire Regiment. Uniform: green/black.

2nd (1859–80) Formed at Trowbridge with Mr Thomas Clark of Bellefield receiving his commission as captain on 16 February 1860. The 2nd Wiltshire RVC had received notification of its acceptance of service during the first week of December 1859. Captain Clark's brother, William Perkins Clark, became lieutenant and John Graham Foley, ensign. On 14 February 1861, Mr W Stancomb was commissioned as captain of a second company at Rood Ashton. Stancomb soon resigned, however, the Rood Ashton contingent being dispersed and a new No. 2 Company raised in its place at Trowbridge. As part of the 1st Admin Battalion, 2nd Wiltshire RVC in 1880 became 'C' and 'D' Companies of the new 1st Corps. The Trowbridge companies were chiefly made up of mill hands employed in the woollen industry. The Kennet and Avon Canal passed close to the town.

2nd (1880–1908) The 2nd Admin Battalion was formed with headquarters at Swindon in March 1861. Headquarters moved to Chippenham in 1864, a cadet corps was formed and affiliated at Marlborough College in 1870, and consolidation in 1880 was as the new 2nd Corps with twelve companies:

'A' Malmesbury (late 3rd Corps)
'B' Chippenham (late 4th Corps)
'C' and 'D' Devizes (late 5th Corps)
'E' Market Lavington (late 7th Corps)
'F' and 'G' Swindon (late 11th Corps)
'H' Melksham (late 12th Corps)
'I' Wootton Bassett (late 15th Corps)
'K' Swindon (late 16th Corps)
'L' Marlborough (late 17th Corps)
'M' Highworth (late 18th Corps)
There was also a sub-division at Calne.

Reduced to eleven companies in 1882 and designated 2nd Volunteer Battalion Wiltshire Regiment under General Order 181 of December 1887. Transfer to the Territorial Force in 1908 was as three companies of 4th Battalion Wiltshire Regiment. Marlborough College at the same time became a contingent of the OTC. Uniform: green/black.

3rd (1859–80) Formed at Malmesbury on 28 January 1860 with William T Keene as captain, Charles Richard Luce, lieutenant and John Alex Handy, ensign. Joined the 2nd Admin Battalion and became 'A' Company of the new 2nd Corps in 1880. Malmesbury is nine miles north of Chippenham, its station opened by the Malmesbury Railway Company in December 1877.

4th Formed at Chippenham on 16 February 1860 with Captain Daniel Hugh Clutterbuck in command. Joined the 2nd Admin Battalion and became 'B' Company of the new 2nd Corps in 1880. A thirsty Volunteer in 1879 may well have been the first to take refreshment from the town fountain opened that year, which, some forty-two years later, was used to inscribe the names of those that did not return from the Great War. In the town much was sent out, and brought in, via the great Wilts and Berks Canal wharf, which once stood in Timber Street, where the bus station is now situated. Chippenham brewed beer, made farm machinery and cheese; a firm called Hathaway made churns here, and another by the name of Rowland Brotherhood produced railway wagons. Nestlé made condensed milk and the Westinghouse Brake and Signal Co. Ltd made all things for the railway.

5th Formed at Devizes on 3 March 1860 with Captain J H Grubb as captain, Robert A Cochrane, lieutenant and John E Hayward, ensign. Joined the 2nd Admin Battalion and became 'C' and 'D' Companies of the new 2nd Corps in 1880. At Devizes, agricultural steam engines were manufactures, the corn market there being well known all over the West of England. The Wadworth Brewery of 1885 can still be seen in Market Place.

6th Robert Dwarris Gibney, in his history of the 1st Wiltshire Volunteers, records how the 6th Corps at Maiden Bradley was raised from among the tenants of the Duke of Somerset and was composed of men of a 'good position socially, and, as a rule, of means'. The duke's eldest son, Edward Adolphus Frederick, Lord Seymour, was commissioned as captain commandant on 2 April 1860. He soon resigned, however, and was replaced in July 1861 by his brother Lord Edward Percy St Maur. It was at a meeting held at the Somerset Arms that the decision to form a corps in Maiden Bradley (to be called 'The Maiden Bradley Irregulars') was adopted. As previously mentioned, the recruits came entirely from the Duke of Somerset's Estate at Maiden Bradley. There were also members from his properties at Witham Friary, five miles distant, and seven miles off at Silton in Dorsetshire. In December 1865 Captain Lord Edward St Maur was killed by a wounded bear while hunting in India, his command later being taken by Lieutenant H B Festing. The 6th Corps formed part of the 1st Admin Battalion and absorbed the 1st Wiltshire Mounted RVC in July 1861. This had been associated with the 6th Corps since its formation. It was also located at Maiden Bradley and is referred to by Gibney in a manner that suggests at times both formations were one and the same. It would seem that after the death in September 1869 of Earl Seymour, interest in the 6th Corps fell off. Captain Festing later resigned his command, the accounts wound up, and an application for disbandment tendered. The corps was last seen in the *Army List* for January 1873.

7th Formed at Market Lavington on 2 March 1860 with Simon W Taylor as captain, Charles Hitchcock. lieutenant and John B Wheeler, ensign. Joined the 2nd Admin Battalion and became 'E' Company of the new 2nd Corps in 1880. At Market Lavington, five miles south of Devizes, the Working Man's Hall was opened in 1865.

8th Formed at Mere, four miles north of Gillingham, with Captain William Chafyn Grove in command, the company's letter of acceptance of service being received on 16 April 1860. The Groves of Zeals House, whose estates included the town of Mere, were prominent in the raising of the corps and were responsible for the provision of its uniforms and equipment. Indeed, the 8th Wiltshire was recruited almost entirely from workers on the Grove lands, or its tenants. Captain Grove's commission was dated 1 May 1860 and the 8th Corps was included in the 1st Admin Battalion. Robert Dwarris Gibney, in his history of the 1st Wiltshire Rifle Volunteers, tells how interest in the corps began to fall off, the death of its founder and commander, William Grove, doing much to hasten its disbandment in 1875.

9th Formed at Bradford-on-Avon after a public meeting held on 19 December 1859, the 9th Wiltshire had its first drill at Mr Spackman's Dye Works on 24 January 1860. The officers, Captain Henry S Pickwick, Lieutenant Burton W Foster and Ensign Alfred Bevan, were not commissioned until 17 May 1860, this day coinciding with the first parade held by the company in uniform. As part of 1st Admin Battalion, the 9th Wiltshire RVC became 'E' Company of the new 1st Corps in 1880.

10th The public meeting that led to the formation of the 10th Corps took place at Warminster Town Hall on 10 December 1859. Subsequently the services of the corps as one company were accepted, and in due course the Marquis of Bath took command with a commission dated 5 March 1860. William Davis, late of the 8th Light Dragoons, became lieutenant, Mr John Scott, ensign. Drills were usually held in the Corn Market, at other times on the town's cricket field, the first to be held in the blue-grey uniform of the corps taking place on 30 May 1860. For musketry the first range used was at Knapper's Hole on Parsonage Farm, but in 1861 better facilities were found about a mile outside of Warminster at Mancomb. The armoury was at the Town Hall to begin with, but this was later moved: first to a room at the Market, then to premises on the High Street. On 16 May 1860 the ladies of Warminster presented the corps with a silver bugle and a complete set of drums and fifes. In March of the same year a sub-division was authorized at Codford, John Ravenhill and Herbert Ingram being gazetted lieutenant and ensign on 31 May. As part of the 1st Admin Battalion, the 10th became 'F' Company of the new 1st Corps in 1880. Always popular in Warminster, the corps were known locally as the 'Jolly Tenth'.

11th Formed as two companies at Swindon on 31 March 1860 with William F Gooch as captain, John S Fisher, lieutenant and William Batt, ensign. Joined the 2nd Admin Battalion and became 'F' and 'G' Companies of the new 2nd Corps in 1880. Few in Swindon could say they did not work for the Great Western, its locomotive and carriage works by the 1890s employing some 9,000.

12th Formed at Melksham on 1 March 1860 and joined the 2nd Admin Battalion. Became 'H' Company of the new 2nd Corps in 1880. Opened in the town, five miles north-east of Trowbridge, was the Cottage Hospital in 1868.

13th Formed at Westbury, four miles north-west of Wells, on 12 March 1860 with Ralph L Lopes as captain, Augustus Yockney, lieutenant and Justly William Awdry, ensign. Joined the 1st Admin Battalion and became 'G' Company of the new 1st Corps in 1880. Many from the town worked in the production of cloth, the old Laverton's Cloth Mills still there in Edward Street.

14th Formed at Wilton, chiefly from tenants of the Earl of Pembroke, with Charles Penruddocke of Compton Park in command. His captain's commission being dated 24 April 1860. George Lapworth was appointed his lieutenant, J Woodcock his ensign, both with commissions dated 1 May 1860. The company's drills were, among other places, often held in the Riding School at Wilton. Musketry was carried out at a local area known as the 'Punch Bowl'. A feature of the company's badge was a representation of the shrine of St Edith of Wilton taken from the town seal. As part of the 1st Admin Battalion, the 14th became 'H' Company of the new 1st Corps in 1880.

15th Formed at Wootton Bassett, six miles west of Swindon, on 18 June 1860, with Richard Bradford as lieutenant and Walter F Pratt, late of the 7th Lancashire Militia, ensign. Joined the 2nd Admin Battalion and became 'I' Company of the new 2nd Corps in 1880.

16th Formed at Old Swindon on 13 July 1860 with James E G Bradford as lieutenant and Edwin R Ing, ensign. Joined the 2nd Admin Battalion and became 'K' Company of the new 2nd Corps in 1880. Old Swindon, as opposed to Swindon, because it was there before the railway came to the town and gave employment to thousands.

17th Formed at Marlborough – many of the members were from Marlborough College – on 27 July 1860 with Thomas B Merriman as captain, Francis E Thompson, lieutenant and Henry J Hillier, ensign. Joined the 2nd Admin Battalion and became 'L' Company of the new 2nd Corps in 1880. Opened in 1872, on the London Road, was the Severnake Hospital, the new chapel up at the college being completed in 1886. Rope and sacking was made in the town, there was also brewing, malting and tanning.

18th Formed at Highworth, six miles north-east of Swindon, on 24 November 1860 with William H Hitchcock as captain, Jeffery G Grimwood, lieutenant and Henry C Crowdy, ensign. Joined the 2nd Admin Battalion and became 'M' Company of the new 2nd Corps in 1880. Highworth Station, on the Great Western, was opened in May 1883.

WORCESTERSHIRE

Two admin battalions were formed, which became the new 1st and 2nd Corps in 1880.

1st (1859–80) Formed as one company at Wolverley with Frederick Winn Knight as captain, Alfred John Hancocks, lieutenant and Augustus Talbot Hancocks, ensign. All three held commissions dated 1 November 1859. Joined the 1st Admin Battalion and became 'A' Company of the new 1st Corps in 1880. Wolverley is just under three miles north of Kidderminster.

1st (1880–1908) The 1st Admin Battalion was formed with headquarters at Hagley on 24 April 1860 and to it were added the 1st to 9th, 16th and 20th Corps. Consolidated in 1880 as the new 1st

Corps with eleven companies:

'A' Wolverley (late 1st Corps)
'B' Tenbury (late 2nd Corps)
'C' Kidderminster (late 3rd Corps)
'D' Kidderminster (late 4th Corps)
'E' Bewdley (late 5th Corps)
'F' Halesowen (late 6th Corps)
'G' Dudley (late 7th Corps)
'H' Stourport (late 8th Corps)
'I' Stourbridge (late 9th Corps)
'K' Oldbury (late 16th Corps)
'L' Kidderminster (late 20th Corps)

In 1882 a new company was added at Dudley and in the following year the corps was designated as 1st Volunteer Battalion Worcestershire Regiment. Headquarters were transferred to Stourbridge between 1885 and 1886, then to Kidderminster in 1891, 'A' Company moving to Dudley sometime before 1908. Transfer to the Territorial Force in 1908 was as 7th Battalion Worcestershire Regiment. Uniform: green/green, changing to green/black in 1904.

2nd (1859–80) Formed as one company at Tenbury with Anthony Charles Lowe as captain, William Norris, lieutenant and William McLaughin, ensign. All three held commissions dated 18 November 1859. Joined the 1st Admin Battalion and became 'B' Company of the new 1st Corps in 1880. Twenty-two miles north-west of Worcester, the five-arched bridge that crosses the Teme at Tenbury takes you from Worcestershire into Shropshire.

2nd (1880–1908) Worcester was the headquarters of the 2nd Admin Battalion, which was formed on 17 August 1860 with the 10th to 15th, 17th, 18th, 19th and 21st Corps. The battalion was consolidated in 1880 as the new 2nd Corps with eight companies:

'A' Worcester (late 13th Corps)
'B' Worcester (late 14th Corps)
'C' Great Malvern and Upton-on-Severn (late 11th and 19th Corps)
'D' Evesham (late 12th Corps)
'E' Droitwich (late 18th Corps)
'F' Pershore (late 10th Corps)
'G' Bromsgrove (late 21st Corps)
'H' Redditch (late 17th Corps)

The 2nd Worcestershire RVC was re-designated as 2nd Volunteer Battalion Worcestershire Regiment in 1883. A new company was sanctioned in 1900, but the battalion's establishment was back to eight companies in 1905. A cadet corps was formed and affiliated at the Victoria Institute, Worcester in 1903. Transfer to the Territorial Force in 1908 was as 8th Battalion Worcestershire Regiment. Uniform: green/green.

3rd Formed as one company with headquarters at Franche House, Kidderminster with Alfred Talbot as captain, John Dixon, lieutenant and Alfred Brinton, ensign. All three held commissions dated 17 January 1860. Joined the 1st Admin Battalion and became 'C' Company of the new 1st Corps in 1880. Volunteers at Kidderminster would have seen the opening of the Town Hall in 1877, the School of Science in 1879, the Post Office in 1884, Brinton Park pleasure grounds in

1887 and the Library in 1892. Born in the town was Sir Rowland Hill (1795–1879), who gave us the Penny Postage system. A statue in his honour was unveiled at Kidderminster in 1881. Many were employed in the production of carpets. The Volunteer Drill Hall was in Birmingham Road.

4th Formed as one company at Kidderminster with William Thomas Knapp as captain, George Adam Bird, lieutenant and Henry Goddard Mottram, ensign. All three held commissions dated 24 January 1860. Joined the 1st Admin Battalion and became 'D' Company of the new 1st Corps in 1880.

5th Formed as one company at Bewdley with William N Marcy as captain, John Bury jun, lieutenant and George Beddoe, ensign. All three held commissions dated 2 March 1860. Joined the 1st Admin Battalion and became 'E' Company of the new 1st Corps in 1880. Bewdley is on the Severn, three miles west of Kidderminster.

6th Formed as one company at Halesowen with Ferdinando D L Smith as captain and James P Hunt, lieutenant. Both held commissions dated 2 March 1860. The third officer, Ensign Jeston Homfray, was gazetted later in the month. Joined the 1st Admin Battalion and became 'F' Company of the new 1st Corps in 1880. Manufactured here were gun barrels, anchors, metal tools, perambulators and horn buttons.

7th Formed as one company at Dudley with Henry Money Wainwright as captain, Francis Sanders, lieutenant and Charles C Hewitt, ensign. All three held commissions dated 2 March 1860. Joined the 1st Admin Battalion and became 'G' Company of the new 1st Corps in 1880. There were numerous collieries and ironworks in the Dudley area. Chains, nails and bicycles were among the many products linked with the town.

8th Formed as one company at Stourport with Joshua Rogers as captain, Charles Harrison, lieutenant and Benjamin Danks, ensign. All three held commissions dated 2 March 1860. Joined the 1st Admin Battalion and became 'H' Company of the new 1st Corps in 1880. At Stourport, four miles south-west of Kidderminster, the Severn is crossed by an iron bridge opened in 1870. Carpets were made here, the not far off Wilden ironworks, owned by the father of Prime Minister Stanley Baldwin, employing many.

9th Formed as one company at Stourbridge with former 1st Dragoon Guards officer James Foster as captain, M P Grazebrook, lieutenant and Frank Evers, ensign. All three held commissions dated 2 March 1860. Joined the 1st Admin Battalion and became 'I' Company of the new 1st Corps in 1880. The town was known for its manufacture of fire-bricks, many also being employed in the production of nails, tools, chains and anvils.

10th Formed as one company at Pershore with Henry Scales Scobel as captain, Thomas Skekell, lieutenant and Edwin Bail, ensign. All three held commissions dated 13 March 1860. Joined the 2nd Admin Battalion and became 'F' Company of the new 2nd Corps in 1880. Pershore is on the Avon nine miles south-east of Worcester.

11th Formed as a sub-division at Great Malvern with Sir Henry E F Lambert commissioned as lieutenant on 9 March 1860. Former Royal Navy officer L C H Tongue became ensign on 20 April. Joined the 2nd Admin Battalion and became part of 'C' Company of the new 2nd Corps in 1880. In the days of the Volunteers, as today, mineral water was produced in the area around Malvern.

12th Formed as one company at Evesham with Benjamin Workman as captain, George Smythe, lieutenant and Thomas Nelson Foster, ensign. All three held commissions dated 13 March 1860. Joined the 2nd Admin Battalion and became 'D' Company of the new 2nd Corps in 1880. The corps also drew recruits from neighbouring Bengeworth who would have crossed the old stone bridge over the Avon to get to headquarters. Evesham is fifteen miles south-east of Worcester.

13th Formed as one company at Worcester with James A Macnaught, lieutenant and Thomas L Smith, ensign the first to be commissioned on 10 April 1860. Their captain, Royal Navy lieutenant H McLeod, was gazetted three days later. Joined the 2nd Admin Battalion and became 'A' Company of the new 2nd Corps in 1880. Worcester for some time has been well known for its manufacture of gloves, porcelain, and, of course Mr Lea and Mr Perrins's sauce, which is still made in the city.

14th Formed as one company at Worcester with John Parker commissioned as captain on 13 April 1860. His junior officers, Lieutenant John De Poise D Tyrel and Ensign Edward Green, were gazetted a week later. Joined the 2nd Admin Battalion and became 'B' Company of the new 2nd Corps in 1880.

15th Formed at Ombersley with Lieutenant Robert Bourne and Ensign Charles Gardiner commissioned on 13 April 1860. Joined the 2nd Admin Battalion and disbanded in 1868. The village is on the Severn six miles north of Worcester.

16th Formed as one company at Oldbury with Pynson W Bennett commissioned as captain on 13 April 1860. His junior officers, Lieutenant John Chambers and Ensign Arthur Wright, were gazetted in the following week. Joined the 1st Admin Battalion and became 'K' Company of the new 1st Corps in 1880. At Oldbury, five miles north-east of Halesowen, many were employed in the several iron foundries and construction of railway carriages.

17th Formed as one company at Redditch with Robert Smith Bartlett as captain, William Baulton, lieutenant and Victor Milward, ensign. All three were commissioned on 4 May 1860. Joined the 2nd Admin Battalion and became 'H' Company of the new 2nd Corps in 1880. Cassell's notes that the town was famous for its production of fishhooks and needles, a very large number of 'skilled artisans' being employed in these trades.

18th Formed as one company at Droitwich with Harry F Vernon as captain, John Blick, lieutenant and William H Clay, ensign. All three were commissioned on 15 June 1860. Samuel Roden MD joined them as surgeon in July. Joined the 2nd Admin Battalion and became 'E' Company of the new 2nd Corps in 1880. Popular in the town for centuries are the salt springs, the Royal Brine Baths easing the aches and pains, no doubt, of many of the Volunteers. Droitwich is seven miles north-east of Worcester.

19th Formed as one company at Upton-on-Severn with George Tennant as captain, John W Empson, lieutenant and Charles Brandon, ensign. All three held commissions dated 6 November 1860. Joined the 2nd Admin Battalion and became part of 'C' Company of the new 2nd Corps in 1880. At Upton, six miles north-west of Tewkesbury, the bridge that crosses the Severn was just seven years old when the 19th Corps was formed in the town. The church there was began in 1878 and opened in the following year.

20th Formed with headquarters at Greatfield House, Kidderminster with John Dixon commissioned as lieutenant on 16 November 1860. Ensign Charles J Dixon was gazetted later in the same month. Joined the 1st Admin Battalion and became 'L' Company of the new 1st Corps in 1880.

21st Formed at Bromsgrove with Captain Robert Bourne, late of the 54th Regiment of Foot, commissioned on 20 August 1861. His junior officers, Lieutenant Edward Dodd and Ensign Arthur B Shaw, were gazetted in the following October. Joined the 2nd Admin Battalion and became 'G' Company of the new 2nd Corps in 1880. Many in the town were employed at the Midland Railway's carriage works, Cassell's for 1893 also noting that the chief industry was the making of nails.

YORKSHIRE EAST RIDING

It was originally intended to group the corps formed in Hull into an admin battalion numbered as 1st. Those from outside the city to be grouped as 2nd. Both 1st and 2nd Admin Battalions did in fact exist, but by the end of 1860 the Hull companies had been merged as 1st Corps. At the same time 2nd Admin became 1st.

1st Formed at Hull on 9 November 1859 and absorbed the 2nd, 3rd, 4th, 7th and 9th Corps, also in Hull, before the end of 1860. The 'Hull Rifles', as the 1st Corps became known, now comprised eight companies with Joseph Walker Pearce appointed as lieutenant colonel on 11 August. Colonel Pearce was to hold his position for the next sixteen years, Walter Richards noting that the 1st Corps owed much to him, in particular the use of the Cyclops Foundry, in which he had an interest, for drill purposes. The 1st Corps was re-designated as 1st Volunteer Battalion East Yorkshire Regiment under General Order 63 of May 1883. The Hymers College Cadet Corps was formed and affiliated in 1900 and transfer to the Territorial Force in 1908 was as 4th Battalion East Yorkshire Regiment. Hymers College at the same time joined the OTC. Uniform: scarlet/yellow, changing to scarlet/white in 1882.

The Volunteers at Hull would have seen the building of the Town Hall in 1866, the elaborate Dock Office in 1871, Market Hall in 1887, Grand Theatre and Opera House in 1893. The building of ships, many for the Royal Navy, and fishing were the main industries in Hull.

2nd (1859–60) Formed at Hull on 24 November 1859 and absorbed into the 1st Corps in March 1860.

2nd (1880–1908) Beverley was the headquarters of the 1st Admin Battalion, which was formed in May 1860 and including all East Yorkshire corps outside of Hull. The battalion was consolidated as the new 2nd Corps in 1880 with six companies:

'A' Howden (late 3rd Corps)
'B' Bridlington (late 5th Corps)
'C' Beverley (late 6th Corps)
'D' Driffield (late 8th Corps)
'E' Market Weighton (late 9th Corps)
'F' Pocklington (late 11th Corps)

Re-designated as 2nd Volunteer Battalion East Yorkshire Regiment by General Order 63 of May 1883 and transferred to the Territorial Force in 1908 as four companies of 5th Battalion East Yorkshire Regiment. Uniform: scarlet/buff, changing to scarlet/white in 1882.

3rd (1860) Formed at Hull on 12 January 1860 and absorbed into the 1st Corps in March 1860.

3rd (1860–80) Formed at Howden, the first to be appointed to the 3rd Corps was Surgeon John Hartley, whose commission was dated 28 March 1860. Captain Eric W Clarke, Lieutenant Thomas Carter and Ensign Edwin Storry joined him in the following June. Became 'A' Company of the new 2nd Corps in 1880. The town is twenty-five miles west of Hull.

4th Formed at Hull with Charles Morgan Norwood as captain, John Joseph Thorney, lieutenant and George Hall Ringrose, ensign. All three held commissions dated 5 January 1860. John Fearne Holden was appointed surgeon. Absorbed into the 1st Corps by the end of the year.

5th Formed at Bridlington with Thomas Prickett as captain, Thomas Harland, lieutenant and Joshua Barugh, ensign. All three held commissions dated 19 January 1860. Also appointed were John Allison as surgeon, and the Revd Henry F Barnes, MA as chaplain. Became 'B' Company of the new 2nd Corps in 1880.

6th The first officers to be appointed to the 6th Corps at Beverley were Captain Harold Barkworth, Lieutenant Richard Hodgson, ensign Henry W Bainton and surgeon Robert G Boulton. All four held commissions dated 28 February 1860. Became 'C' Company of the new 2nd Corps in 1880. Cassell's for 1893 notes that the chief industry of the town was tanning; but there were also foundries, chemical works, steam mills and breweries.

7th Formed at Hull with Captain William Thomas White, Lieutenant Robert Blyth jun and Ensign Richard Glover. All three held commissions dated 3 March 1860. Henry Gibson was appointed as surgeon. Absorbed into the 1st Corps before the end of 1860.

8th Formed at Driffield with Captain D Conyers, Lieutenant Thomas Hopper and Ensign Richard Botterill commissioned on 11 May 1860. At the same time the Revd James Skinner was appointed as chaplain and Alfred Scotchburn, surgeon. Became 'D' Company of the new 2nd Corps in 1880. Volunteers attending All Saints' Church would have seen the careful restoration that took place in 1880. A new Market Hall was opened in 1888. Artificial manures and linseed cakes, notes Cassell's, were manufactured at Driffield on a large scale.

9th (1860) Formed at Hull on 12 May 1860 and absorbed into the 1st Corps by the end of the year.

9th (1860–80) Formed as a sub-division at Market Weighton with William Langdale as lieutenant, and John S W Kirkpatrick as ensign. Both officers held commissions dated 12 May 1860. Increased to a full company in June 1865 and became 'E' Company of the new 2nd Corps in 1880. The town lies ten miles west of Beverley on the main road to York.

10th Formed at Hedon with William Raines as captain, Arthur Iveson, lieutenant and Robert C Metcalfe, ensign. All three officers were commissioned on 8 November 1860. Disbanded in 1876. Six miles east of Hull, businesses making tiles and bricks around Hedon employed many.

11th Formed at Pocklington with Lord Muncaster as captain, John Vade, lieutenant and John Kilby, ensign. All three officers held commissions dated 8 August 1868. Became 'F' Company of the new 2nd Corps in 1880. Sixteen miles east-south-east of York, Pocklington produced agricultural implements, rope and twine.

YORKSHIRE NORTH RIDING

Two admin battalions were formed, which provided the new 1st and 2nd Corps in 1880.

1st (1860–80) Formed as one company at Malton with William C Copperthwaite as captain, Thomas Walker jun, lieutenant, Thomas R Etty, ensign and Richard Junes as surgeon. All four held commissions dated 18 February 1860. Joined the 2nd Admin Battalion and became 'A' Company of the new 2nd Corps in 1880. Malton is on the Derwent eighteen miles north-east of York.

1st (1880–1908) Headquarters of the 1st Admin Battalion, formed in July 1860, were at Richmond and to it were added the 2nd, 4th, 5th, 7th, 8th, 9th, 11th, 12th, 14th, 15th, 18th, 19th and 20th Corps. The battalion was consolidated in 1880 as the new 1st Corps with nine companies:

'A' Thornton Rust (late 4th Corps)
'B' Bedale (late 8th Corps)
'C' Stokesley (late 9th Corps)
'D' Catterick (late 14th Corps)
'E' Richmond (late No. 1 Company, 15th Corps)
'F' Reeth (late No. 2 Company, 15th Corps)
'G' Skelton (late 18th Corps)
'H' Northallerton (late 19th Corps)
'K' Guisborough (late 20th Corps)

Headquarters moved to Northallerton in 1883 and in the same year General Order 14 of February notified re-designation as 1st Volunteer Battalion Yorkshire Regiment. After a number of relocations, amalgamations, disbandments, and, in 1884 the formation of a new company, by 1893 company locations were: Leyburn, Bedale, Stokesley, Catterick, Richmond, Skelton, Northallerton, Thirsk, Guisborough and Wensleydale. The coming years saw further of the same, the companies by 1898 being at: Middleham, Bedale, Stokesley, Catterick, Richmond, Redcar, Skelton, Northallerton, Thirsk and Guisborough, and by 1908: Bedale, Eston, Stokesley, Catterick, Richmond, Redcar, Skelton, Northallerton, Thirsk and Guisborough. Transfer to the Territorial Force was as 4th Battalion Yorkshire Regiment. Uniform: scarlet/green, changing to scarlet/white in 1885.

Although not actually serving with the battalion at the time, mention should be made of Colonel John Gerald Wilson CB, who died in South Africa on 9 March 1902 from wounds received the previous day. Colonel Wilson had commanded the 1st Admin Battalion from 1871 to 1883 and was with the 3rd Battalion York and Lancaster Regiment when he died. Both his son and brother also lost their lives in South Africa.

2nd (1860–63) Formed as one company at Swaledale on 18 February 1860 with Sir George William Denys of Draycott Hall, Richmond as captain, Edward Leopold Denys, lieutenant and J Simm Metcalf, ensign. John George McCollah was also appointed as surgeon. Joined the 1st Admin Battalion and was disbanded in 1863. Swaledale, where there were numerous lead mines, extends from the border of Westmorland almost to Richmond.

2nd (1880–1908) The 2nd Admin Battalion was formed with headquarters at Malton in July 1860 and included the 1st, 3rd, 6th, 10th, 13th, 16th and 17th Corps. Headquarters were transferred to Scarborough in 1876 and in 1880 the battalion was consolidated as the new 2nd Corps with seven companies:

'A' Malton (late 1st Corps)
'B' and 'C' Hovingham (late 3rd Corps)
'D' and 'E' Scarborough (late 6th Corps)
'F' Helmsley-in-Ryedale (late 10th Corps)
'G' Pickering (late 16th Corps)

Under General Order 14 of February 1883 the 2nd Corps was re-designated as 2nd Volunteer Battalion Yorkshire Regiment. Transfer to the Territorial Force in 1908 was as four companies of 5th Battalion Yorkshire Regiment. Uniform: grey/scarlet, changing to scarlet/green.

3rd Formed as one company at Hovingham with William Cayley Worsley as captain, Arthur Stevens, lieutenant and George Legard, ensign. All three held commissions dated 10 February 1860. Joined the 2nd Admin Battalion and became 'B' and 'C' Companies of the new 2nd Corps in 1880. All Saints' Church at Hovingham, on the road from Helmsley to Malton, was being rebuilt as the 3rd Corps formed in 1860.

4th Formed as one company at Leyburn with Simon Thomas Scrope jun as captain, Nathaniel Surtees, lieutenant, Thomas Mitchell Fryer, ensign and Thomas E Cockcroft as surgeon. All four held commissions dated 29 February 1860. Joined the 1st Admin Battalion, absorbed the 12th Corps at Thornton Rust in 1874, and became 'A' Company of the new 1st Corps in 1880. At Leyburn, seven miles from Richmond, St Matthew's Church was opened in 1868.

5th (1860–71) Formed as one company at Forcett with John Mitchell as captain, William Swire, Lieutenant, Charles R Robinson, ensign and William Walker as surgeon. All four held commissions dated 27 February 1860. Joined the 1st Admin Battalion and was disbanded in May 1871. At Forcett, eight miles north of Richmond, the restoration of St Cuthbert's Church was just about nearing completion as the 5th Corps was being formed.

5th (1871–75) Formed at Gilling on 19 June 1871 from No. 3 Company of the 15th Corps. Joined the 1st Admin Battalion and was disbanded in 1875. Gilling is three miles north of Richmond.

6th Formed as a sub-division at Scarborough; the first officers to be commissioned were Lieutenant Tindall Hebden and Ensign Harcourt Johnstone on 28 February 1860. Also appointed was William Taylor as surgeon. Joined 2nd Admin Battalion, increased to a full company in June 1860, two in 1867, and became 'D' and 'E' Companies of the new 2nd Corps in 1880. The Scarborough Volunteers would have seen the opening in 1867 of the Grand Hotel, which was to suffer great damage during the German bombardment of the town in 1914.

7th Formed as one company at Startforth with William Sawrey Morritt as captain, Morley Headlam, lieutenant and Arthur Brown, ensign. All three held commissions dated 29 February 1860. Joined the 1st Admin Battalion, transferring to the 4th Durham Admin in November 1863. In the following month the corps moved to the 2nd Durham Admin Battalion and at the same time was re-designated as 21st Durham RVC. Startforth is fifteen miles west of Darlington and employed many in its extensive thread mills. The old bridge that crosses the Tees from the village and into Barnard Castle (Durham) was destroyed in 1881 by a great river flood.

8th Formed at Bedale with Lipton H Potts as lieutenant, Christopher Clarke, ensign and Robert Fothergill as surgeon. All three held commissions dated 19 March 1860. Joined the 1st Admin Battalion and became 'B' Company of the new 1st Corps in 1880. Bedale is seven miles south-west of Northallerton.

9th Formed as one company at Stokesley on 6 March 1860 with George Marwood as captain, James Emerson, lieutenant and John P Sowerby jun, ensign. Appointed at the same time was John H Handyside as surgeon. Joined the 1st Admin Battalion and became 'C' Company of the new 1st Corps in 1880. Stokesley, through which runs the River Levan, is ten miles south-east of Stockton-on-Tees.

10th Formed as one company at Helmsley-in-Ryedale on 9 March 1860 with the Hon William Ernest Duncombe as captain, John Bower, lieutenant and John R Phillips, ensign. Joined the 2nd Admin Battalion and became 'F' Company of the new 2nd Corps in 1880. In the market place at Helmsley there was unveiled in 1869 a marble effigy of the second Lord Feversham, father of Captain Duncombe. Helmsley is to the east of Thirsk on the road to Scarborough.

11th Formed as one company at Masham on 17 March 1860, the first officers to be commissioned being Lieutenant Thomas Smurthwaite, ensign James D R Fisher and Surgeon Midgley Cockcroft. Joined the 1st Admin Battalion, disappearing from the *Army List* in October 1866. Masham is eight miles north-west of Ripon, its station being opened by the old North Eastern Railway in 1875.

12th Formed as one company at Carperby with Christopher Other as captain, Francis Chapman, lieutenant and James C Winn, ensign. All three were commissioned on 10 March 1860. Joined the 1st Admin Battalion, moving headquarters to Thornton Rust in 1869, and was absorbed into the 4th Corps in 1874. Carperby is to the west of Leyburn, Thornton Rust to the west on the road to Hawes.

13th Formed as one company at Thirsk, the first officers to commissioned being Lieutenant Archibald Macbean, Ensign Edward D Swarbreck and Surgeon Thomas Haymes. All three were gazetted on 27 March 1860. Joined the 2nd Admin Battalion and was disbanded in 1868. Cassell's notes that a large number were employed in the town's extensive agricultural engineering works.

14th Formed as one company at Catterick with Thomas C Booth as captain, John B Booth, lieutenant and John Feyer, ensign. All three held commissions dated 19 April 1860. Joined the 1st Admin Battalion and became 'D' Company of the new 1st Corps in 1880. Catterick lies on the River Swale just over four miles south-east of Richmond, its church of St Anne's being restored in 1872.

15th Formed as one company at Richmond with Roper S D R Roper as captain, Leonard Jacques, lieutenant and William Robinson, ensign. All three held commissions dated 16 April 1860. Joined the 1st Admin Battalion and added No. 2 Company at Reeth, to the west of Richmond, on 9 March 1865; No. 3 at Gilling to the north, on 28 December, and No. 4 at Richmond in February 1868. No. 3 Company was made independent as 5th Corps in June 1871, the 15th becoming 'E' and 'F' Companies of the new 1st Corps in 1880.

16th Formed as a sub-division at Pickering Lythe with James A Legard as lieutenant and John Hill, ensign. Both held commissions dated 4 May 1860. Later increased to a full company, the senior officer then listed as John R Hill, who was gazetted as captain on 29 December 1860. Joined the 2nd Admin Battalion and became 'G' Company of the new 2nd Corps in 1880. Pickering is to the south-west of Scarborough on the road to Thirsk.

17th Formed as one company at Pickering Lythe East on 28 April 1860 with Edward S Cayley jun as captain, Escricke J Inman, lieutenant and Reginald A Cayley, ensign. Also appointed was

Archibald Meggett as surgeon. Joined the 2nd Admin Battalion, moving headquarters to Brompton, west of Pickering on the road to Scarborough, in 1861. Disbanded in 1865.

18th Formed as one company at Skelton with John T Wharton as captain, Thomas L Yeoman, lieutenant, Edward B Hamilton, ensign and Charles C E Hopkins as surgeon. All four held commissions dated 30 May 1860. Joined the 1st Admin Battalion and became 'G' Company of the new 1st Corps in 1880. Skelton is just to the south-east of Redcar.

19th Formed at Northallerton, the first officers to be appointed being Lieutenant Henry Rutson and Ensign William Fowle. Both held commissions dated 20 August 1860. Joined the 1st Admin Battalion and became 'H' Company of the new 1st Corps in 1880. Northallerton Town Hall, its lower floor forming a market place, was built in 1874.

20th (1860–61) A 20th Corps with headquarters given as Whitby appeared in the *Army List* towards the end of 1860, but disappeared from the *Army List* in April 1861 having had no officers appointed.

20th (1863–80) Formed as one company at Guisborough with William Weatherill as captain, William O Garbutt, lieutenant, William K Weatherill, ensign and George S Morris as surgeon. All four held commissions dated 3 February 1863. Joined the 1st Admin Battalion and became 'K' Company of the new 1st Corps in 1880. Guisborough is nine miles south-east of Middlesborough, Cassell's for the 1890s noting that the area was rich in ironstone, most of the inhabitants being employed in that industry.

21st Formed as two companies at Middlesbrough on 13 October 1877 with Captain Walter Johnson, late of the 2nd Dragoons, in command. Joined the 4th Durham Admin Battalion and became 'G' and 'H' Companies of the new 1st Durham RVC in 1880.

YORKSHIRE WEST RIDING

Five admin battalions were formed, which, in 1880, became the new 1st, 5th, 6th, 8th and 9th Corps. There was also a 1st Sub-division which became the 15th Corps.

1st (1859–80) The services of the 1st Corps at York were accepted on 5 September 1859, a former major of the 1st Dragoons Guards, George Briggs, being appointed as captain commandant with commission dated 10 February 1860. Four companies were soon formed, the last of which was raised by St Peter's School. Joined the 1st Admin Battalion, a No. 5 Company being raised in the early part of 1862. For details of this corps, and others in the West Riding, a reliable source comes in the form of *West York Rifle Volunteers 1859–1887* by K D Pickup. In the 1st Corps section he records how in the early days drills were held at three separate locations, St Leonard's Place, Parliament Street and Lowther Street. At a cost of £1,700, the old Sand Hill Hotel in Colliergate was purchased in 1871 and after much building work, a new Drill Hall was opened there in December 1872. Became 'A' to 'E' Companies of the new 1st Corps in 1880.

1st (1880–1908) York was the headquarters of the 1st Admin Battalion, which was formed in May 1860 and included the 1st, 16th, 17th, 27th, 31st, 33rd and 38th Corps. The battalion was consolidated in 1880 as the new 1st Corps with eleven companies:

'A', 'B', 'C', 'D' and 'E' York (late 1st Corps)
'F' Harrogate (late 16th Corps)

'G' Knaresborough (late 17th Corps)
'H' and 'J' Ripon (late 27th Corps)
'K' Tadcaster (late 31st Corps)
'L' Selby (late 38th Corps)

Under General Order 181 of December 1887 the 1st Corps was re-designated as 1st Volunteer Battalion West Yorkshire Regiment. A new company was added in 1900 and by 1908 companies were located at: York (5), Harrogate (2), Knaresborough (1), Ripon (2), Pateley Bridge (1) and Selby (1). Transfer to the Territorial Force in 1908 was as 5th Battalion West Yorkshire Regiment. Uniform: scarlet/blue, changing to scarlet/white about 1888, then scarlet/buff after 1904.

2nd (Hallamshire) According to Bartholomew's *Survey Gazetteer of the British Isles*, Hallamshire is an 'ancient lordship of the West Riding of Yorkshire'. It is mentioned in the Domesday Book and is represented by the parishes of Sheffield and Ecclesfield. It was in Sheffield on 30 September 1859 that three separate companies were formed and designated as 2nd, 3rd and 4th Yorkshire West Riding RVC, the three being amalgamated by the end of the year under the new title of 2nd Yorkshire West Riding (Hallamshire) RVC and the command of Major Wilson Overend, his commission dated 22 December 1859. At the same time as the merger took place an additional company was raised, yet another being added when No. 5 was formed from employees of the Atlas Works. The establishment of the 2nd Corps would reach seven companies by the end of1861. Re-designation as 1st (Hallamshire) Volunteer Battalion York and Lancaster Regiment was notified by General Order 14 of February 1883 and transfer to the Territorial Force in 1908 was as 4th Battalion York and Lancaster Regiment. Uniform: scarlet/white.

3rd (1859) Formed at Sheffield on 30 September 1859 and by end of year had amalgamated with the 2nd Corps as its No. 2 Company.

3rd (1859–1908) On 27 September 1859 two independent companies were formed in Bradford and designated as 5th and 6th Corps. In February of the following year, together with other Bradford companies hitherto unnumbered, the two were merged as 5th Corps. By April 1860, however, the new corps had been numbered as 3rd, its establishment being four companies with Major Commandant Samuel Cunliffe Lister in command. Absorbed the 24th Corps at Eccleshill as No. 5 Company in October 1860. Now eight companies strong, in 1887, under General Order 181 of December, the 3rd Corps was re-designated as 2nd Volunteer Battalion West Yorkshire Regiment. A cyclist company was added in 1900, the first Volunteers from the battalion in that year sailing for South Africa and active service in the Boer War. Captain J L McLaren, who was commissioned on 27 January 1897, died of phthisis on 12 March 1902 while serving with the Imperial Yeomanry. Transfer to the Territorial Force in 1908 was as 6th Battalion West Yorkshire Regiment. Uniform: scarlet/dark green, changing to scarlet/white about 1888, then scarlet/buff after 1904.

4th (1859) Formed at Sheffield on 30 September 1859 and by end of year had amalgamated with the 2nd Corps as its No. 3 Company.

4th (1860–1908) The original 7th and 8th Corps were both formed at Halifax on 13 October 1859. These were shortly followed by the 13th and 14th, also in Halifax, and on 24 February 1860 the four companies were amalgamated as 7th Corps, but renumbered, however, as 4th on 27 April. Major Commandant Edward Akroyd of Bank Field, Harley Hill, took command. A No. 5 Company was added at Sowerby in 1861 and new companies later followed at Brighouse, Hebden Bridge and Upper Shibden Hall. Reduced now to six companies, the 4th Corps was designated as

1st Volunteer Battalion Duke of Wellington's Regiment in 1883 and by 1908 located: four companies at Halifax, one each at Brighouse and Cleckheaton. Transfer to the Territorial Force in 1908 was as 4th Battalion Duke of Wellington's Regiment. Uniform: scarlet/blue, changing to scarlet/white by 1897.

Situated in the valley of the Hebble, about two miles from where it meets the Calder, Halifax's iron North Bridge was opened in 1871, its Town Hall in Crossley Street eight years before that. The Akroyd Museum and Art Gallery at Harley Hill was opened in 1886 in the former seat of Edward Akroyd, the first commanding officer.

5th (1859–60) See 3rd Corps (1860–1908).

5th (1860–80) Formed as the 9th Corps at Wakefield with J Hulme Holdsworth as captain, John Barff Charlesworth, lieutenant and George William Alder, ensign. All three held commissions dated 17 November 1859. They were later joined by Edward Waddington MD, who had been appointed as surgeon. Joined the 3rd Admin Battalion and renumbered as 5th by July 1860, the corps soon comprised three companies; the 1st being formed by tradesmen, the 2nd by clerks and the 3rd by working men. A 4th was later added and in 1880 the old 5th Corps became 'A' to 'D' Companies of the new 5th Corps. The Wakefield Volunteers would have see the building of the Industrial and Fine Art Institution, with its museum, laboratory and classrooms, in 1890, and before that the opening of the Town Hall ten years earlier with its seven statues representing the town's past main industries: mining, iron-founding, spinning, glass-blowing, agriculture, engineering and pottery.

5th (1880–1908) Formed in June 1860 with headquarters at Wakefield, the 3rd Admin Battalion included the 5th, 28th, 29th, 30th, 37th, 38th and 43rd Corps and was consolidated in 1880 as the new 5th with ten companies:

'A', 'B', 'C' and 'D' Wakefield (late 5th Corps)
'E' Goole (late 28th Corps)
'F', 'G' and 'H' Dewsbury (late 29th Corps)
'J' and 'K' Batley (late 43rd Corps)

Re-designated as 1st Volunteer Battalion King's Own Light Infantry (South Yorkshire Regiment) in February 1883, the regiment itself being re-designated King's Own Yorkshire Light Infantry in 1887. Company locations by 1908 were: Wakefield (3), Normanton (1), Goole (1), Dewsbury (2), Ossett (1) and Batley (2). Transfer to the Territorial Force in 1908 saw the Wakefield, Dewsbury, Ossett and Batley companies as 4th Battalion King's Own (Yorkshire Light Infantry), while those from Normanton and Goole provided part of the 5th. Uniform: scarlet/blue.

6th (1859–60) See 3rd (1860–1908).

6th (The Huddersfield) (1860–80) The services of a corps at Huddersfield were accepted on 3 November 1859, the number received being 10th, but this was changed to 6th Corps in July 1860. The corps, which joined the 5th Admin Battalion, soon comprised four companies with Captain Henry Frederick Beaumont in command. No. 5 was added in 1864 followed in 1868 by No. 6 at Outlane, four miles north-west of Huddersfield; No. 7 at Lindley and No. 8 at headquarters. The Lindley company was recruited mostly from the several manufacturing firms in the area. Also in 1868, 'The Huddersfield' was added to the title. Sometime during the 1870s four companies were lost, leaving the 6th to provide 'A' to 'D' Companies of the new 6th Corps in 1880. The woollen trade employed many in Huddersfield, the machinery for those mills, as well as locomotive boilers, was made in the town's several foundries. Silk spinning also went on, No. 3 Company of the corps being almost entirely recruited from workers at three firms: Leonard & Sons, Day & Sons, and E T Monk & Co.

6th (1880–1908) Formed with headquarters in Huddersfield on 18 September 1862, the 5th Admin Battalion included the 6th, 32nd, 34th, 41st and 44th Corps. The battalion was consolidated in 1880 as the new 6th Corps with ten companies:

'A', 'B', 'C' and 'D' Huddersfield (late 6th Corps)
'E' Holmfirth (late 32nd Corps)
'F', 'G', 'H' and 'J' Saddleworth (late 34th Corps)
'K' Mirfield (late 41st Corps)

Designated as 2nd Volunteer Battalion Duke of Wellington's Regiment in February 1883, headquarters at this time being at The Armoury in Ramsden Street. A new company was raised at Huddersfield in 1900 and transfer to the Territorial Force in 1908 was as part of both the 5th and 7th Battalions Duke of Wellington's Regiment. Uniform: scarlet/sky blue, changing to scarlet/white by 1887.

7th (1859–60) See 4th Corps (1860–1908).

7th (Leeds) (1860–1908) On 17 November 1859 the first company of the Leeds Rifle Volunteers was formed within the city. This was numbered as the 11th Corps, which by March 1860 consisted of five companies with Major William J Armitage in command. In May 1860 the 22nd Corps, also in Leeds, was absorbed, but this brought about no increases in establishment. By 1861, however, an additional four companies had been raised. Of these No. 6 was provided by the Monkbridge Steel Company (one of its directors, Frederick W Kitson becoming commanding officer); No. 7 by Fairbairn's Wellington Foundry (Andrew Fairbairn as captain); No. 8 from men at Messrs Greenwood & Bailey (Thomas G Greenwood as captain, George G Greenwood, ensign) and No. 9, which was recruited from Messrs Joshua Tetley's Brewery (Francis W Tetley in command). The last company to be formed was in August 1875, this brining the establishment up to ten companies, which remained the strength of the corps until 1908.

As a result of the amalgamation during the early part of 1860 between the Halifax Corps, the 7th position in the West Riding list became vacant. This was filled by the 11th Corps on 3 July 1860. In 1864 the additional title 'Leeds' was added, the next change being as 3rd Volunteer Battalion West Yorkshire Regiment in December 1887. Of the Volunteers from the battalion that saw active service in South Africa, Lieutenant Sydney Arthur Slater died from enteric fever while serving with the Imperial Yeomanry on 29 January 1901. For an action at Bultfontein in September 1900, he was awarded the DSO. There is a plaque in his honour at Giggleswick School near Settle. Transfer to the Territorial Force in 1908 was as 7th and 8th Battalions West Yorkshire Regiment. Uniform: grey/grey, changing after 1883 to green/black.

Cuthbert Brodrick's magnificent Leeds Town Hall, with its statue of the Duke of Wellington in the square outside, was less than a year old when the Volunteers first put on their uniforms. They would have dealt with the Council at the new Municipal Offices across the road, built in 1884, looked at pictures in the Art Gallery of 1888, posted letters at the new General Post Office, which first opened its doors in 1895, were entertained at the Grand Theatre and Opera House, built 1878, and put their money, perhaps, in the Yorkshire Penny Bank, which opened in 1894. Some of them may even have got themselves filmed, as the pioneer of moving pictures, French photographer Louis Aimé Augustin Le Prince (1842–90), took his camera around Leeds.

8th (1859–60) See 4th Corps (1860–1908).

8th (1880–1908) Formed with headquarters at Doncaster in August 1860, the 4th Admin Battalion included the 18th, 19th, 20th, 21st, 36th, 37th and 40th Corps. Consolidated in 1880, the battalion formed the new 8th Corps with nine companies:

'A' Pontefract (late 18th Corps)
'B' Rotherham (late 19th Corps)
'C' Doncaster (late 20th Corps)
'D' Doncaster (late 21st Corps)
'E' Rotherham (late 19th Corps)
'F' Barnsley (late 37th Corps)
'G' Wath-upon-Dearne (late 40th Corps)
'H' Barnsley (late 37th Corps)
'J' Rotherham (late 36th Corps)

Re-designated as 2nd Volunteer Battalion York and Lancaster Regiment in February 1883. A new company was added in 1884 and a cadet corps was affiliated at Rotherham in 1894. This, however, had disappeared from the *Army List* during 1899. Two new companies were added in 1900, and company locations by 1908 were: Pontefract, Rotherham (3), Doncaster (5), Barnsley (2) and Wath-upon-Dearne. Transfer to the Territorial Force in 1908 saw the Rotherham, Barnsley and Wath-upon-Dearne personnel move to the 5th Battalion York and Lancaster Regiment, while those from Doncaster and Pontefract formed part of the 5th Battalion King's Own Yorkshire Light Infantry. Uniform: scarlet/white.

9th (1859–60) See 5th Corps (1860–80).

9th (1880–1908) Formed with headquarters at Skipton-in-Craven in June 1860, the 2nd Admin Battalion included the 12th, 15th, 23rd, 25th, 26th, 35th, 42nd and 45th Corps. The battalion was consolidated as the new 9th Corps in 1880 with eight companies:

'A' Skipton-in-Craven (late 12th Corps)
'B' Settle (late 15th Corps)
'C' Burley (late 23rd Corps)
'D', 'E' and 'F' Keighley (late 35th Corps)
'G' Haworth (late 42nd Corps)
'H' Bingley (late 45th Corps)

Re-designated as 3rd Volunteer Battalion Duke of Wellington's Regiment in February 1883, new companies being added in 1884 and 1900. Transfer to the Territorial Force in 1908 was as 6th Battalion Duke of Wellington's Regiment. Uniform: scarlet/buff, changing to scarlet/white by 1887.

10th See 6th Corps (1859–80).

11th See 7th Corps (1860–1908).

12th Formed as one company at Skipton-in-Craven with Matthew Wilson as captain, George Robinson, lieutenant and Henry Alcock jun, ensign. All three held commissions dated 8 February 1860. Joined the 2nd Admin Battalion and became 'A' Company of the new 9th Corps in 1880. Matthew Wilson became the commanding officer of the 2nd Admin Battalion in August 1860. In the High Street at Skipton, in front of the Library and not far from the memorial to those who fell in the Great War, is a statue to 'Sir' Matthew Wilson, MP for Skipton. Cassell's notes that the extensive mills on the Broughton Road gave employment to some 1,200 in the 1890s.

13th See 4th Corps (1860–1908).

14th See 4th Corps (1860–1908).

15th Formed with Walter Morrison as lieutenant and John Ingleby, ensign. Their commissions were dated 17 November 1859 and the corps was known as the 1st Sub-division until March 1860. James J Luce was appointed as surgeon about the same time. Joined the 2nd Admin Battalion and became 'B' Company of the new 9th Corps in 1880. The early *Army Lists* show the 15th Corps as being at North Craven; later issues, however, give the more accurate headquarters location of Settle.

16th Formed as one company at Harrogate on 21 February 1860 with John James Harrison as captain, J Holt, lieutenant and Henry Drury, ensign. All three held commissions dated 21 February 1860. In March, William H England was appointed as surgeon. Joined the 1st Admin Battalion and became 'F' Company of the new 1st Corps in 1880. K D Pickup notes how the 16th and 17th Corps were both unofficially referred to as the 'Claro Rifles'. Harrogate, Knaresborough and Wetherby (33rd Corps) being within the Claro 'Wapentake' – a Northern and Midland term for a sub-division of a county, rather like a 'hundred' elsewhere. Harrogate's St Peter's Church was opened in 1876, the Market Hall in 1874, a statue to Queen Victoria certainly seeing Volunteers on parade when it was unveiled in Station Square in 1887.

17th Formed as one company at Knaresborough with Samuel James Brown as captain, Charles John Radcliffe, lieutenant and Ralph O Hodgson, ensign. All three held commissions dated 27 February 1860. Joined the 1st Admin Battalion and became 'G' Company of the new 1st Corps in 1880. Knaresborough, with its tall-arched railway viaduct crossing the Lydd, rebuilt its Town Hall in 1862 and restored the church of St John the Baptist, where the great Slingsby family are remembered in brass, wood and stone, in 1872. One memorial, a statue by Boehm, is in memory of Sir C Slingsby, who was drowned in 1869.

18th Formed as one company at Pontefract with Richard T Lee as captain, Charles C Templer, lieutenant and James Robson, ensign. All three held commissions dated 3 March 1860 and they were joined by Joshua H Simpson, who was appointed as surgeon, and the Revd Richard Stainforth, who was appointed as chaplain. Joined the 4th Admin Battalion and became 'A' Company of the new 8th Corps in 1880. At Pontefract the ancient church of All Saints, partially destroyed in the Civil War and where many that fell during the siege of Pontefract Castle lie, was restored in 1866. The town was once noted for its extensive gardens and nurseries and (still), its liquorice Pontefract Cake.

19th Formed as one company at Rotherham with George Wilton Chambers as captain, Arthur Hirst, lieutenant and William Hirst, ensign. All three held commissions dated 29 February 1860. Joined the 4th Admin Battalion and became 'B' and 'E' Companies of the new 8th Corps in 1880. K D Pickup, in his book *West York Rifle Volunteers 1859–1887*, shows a plan for a Drill Hall at Rotherham, the work being completed in 1873 at Wharncliffe Street. According to a letter signed by the commanding officers of the 19th and 36th Corps (the latter also at Rotherham) it would seem that both companies were using, prior to the new hall being opened, the Court House and Corn Exchange.

20th Formed at Doncaster with Archibald Sturrock as captain, James Payne, lieutenant and Richard C Hornby, ensign. All three held commissions dated 5 March 1860. Joined the 4th Admin Battalion and became 'C' Company of the new 8th Corps in 1880. K D Pickup notes how Captain Sturrock of Elmfield Park House was a railway official at Doncaster [the Great Northern Railway Company then] and that the majority of the 20th were recruited from his staff.

21st Formed at Doncaster with Henry F Pilkington as captain, William E Smith, lieutenant and John W S Collinson, ensign. All three held commissions dated 5 March 1860. Joined the 4th Admin Battalion and became 'D' Company of the new 8th Corps in 1880.

22nd Formed at Leeds on 29 February 1860 and absorbed into the 11th Corps in the following May.

23rd Formed as one company at Burley-in-Wharfedale, ten miles north of Bradford, with William Edward Foster as captain, William Macleod, lieutenant and Edward Hirst Hudson, ensign. All three held commissions dated 20 February 1860. Thomas Scott MD was appointed as surgeon. The company was requited from employees at Captain Foster's mill. Joined the 2nd Admin Battalion and became 'C' Company of the new 9th Corps in 1880. In the village the Victorian mill owners built a hall, library and reading room for their workers.

24th Formed at Eccleshill, ten miles west of Leeds, with Benjamin Farrer as lieutenant and William Yewdall, ensign. Both held commissions dated 27 February 1860. Absorbed into the 3rd Corps as its No. 5 Company in October 1860.

25th Formed as one company at Guiseley with Matthew William Thompson as captain, Henry G Baker, lieutenant and Jasper L White, ensign. All three held commissions dated 5 March 1860. Joined the 2nd Admin Battalion and was disbanded in August 1876. Standing on high ground between the Aire and the Wharfe, Guiseley's mills gave employment to many from the area.

26th Formed as one company at Ingleton with John Thomas Coates as captain and Richard Brown, lieutenant. Both held commissions dated 21 March 1860. Ensign Joseph Hunter, Chaplain Richard Denny and Surgeon Richard Elletson were included in the corps before the end of 1860. Joined the 2nd Admin Battalion and is last seen in the *Army List* for January 1874. Arthur Mee wrote of Ingleton that it was the gateway to some of the finest scenery in the north of England. High up, about ten miles from Settle, the village looks down on the River Greta, which is spanned by a seven-arched railway viaduct.

27th Formed as one company at Ripon with J Rhodes as captain, R Kearsley, lieutenant, T Wood, ensign and C Husband as surgeon. All four held commissions dated 13 April 1860. Joined the 1st Admin Battalion. A No. 2 Company was raised in 1870 and became 'H' and 'J' Companies of the new 1st Corps in 1880. K D Pickup records how the Earl de Grey and Ripon gave permission for 'Red Bank' to be used as a drill ground, Masterman Crag, adjacent, being converted to a rifle range.

28th Formed as one company at Goole with John Egremont as captain, John H Rockett, lieutenant, Robert S Best, ensign and John Stone MD as surgeon. All four held commissions dated 2 May 1860. Joined the 3rd Admin Battalion and became 'E' Company of the new 5th Corps in 1880. Goole stands where the Don meets the Ouse, an iron bridge built in 1890 crossing the former river. There are docks, from where the Aire and Calder Navigation Company operated. The smart brick and terracotta bank of Messrs Beckett and Co. was opened in 1892, in the upper portion of which were to be found the offices of many leading shipping companies. The Market Hall was destroyed by fire in 1891.

29th Formed as one company at Dewsbury with Thomas H Cook as captain, John Wormald, lieutenant, Charles E Rhodes, ensign and George Fearnley as surgeon. All four held commissions dated 3 May 1860. Joined the 3rd Admin Battalion, but on reaching the strength of six companies in 1867 was removed. The establishment was reduced to three, however, in 1873 and the 29th Corps then returned to 3rd Admin. Became 'F' to 'H' Companies of the new 5th Corps in 1880. The woollen industry was important to Dewsbury: blankets, carpets, rugs, jerseys and serges being its speciality. On the hillside to the west of the town lies the seventy-acre Crow Nest Park, opened in 1892 and the site after 1918 of the war memorial.

30th Formed as one company at Birstall in April 1860, its first officers being commissioned on 1 September 1860: Lieutenant Frederick H Knowles, ensign Arthur Knowles and Surgeon Robert Rayner. Joined the 3rd Admin Battalion and disappeared from the *Army List* in October 1873. Birstall, where Wesley's friend John Newton lies in the chapel burial ground, is seven miles south-west of Leeds. The Tudor Oakwell Hall, much loved and written about by Charlotte Brontë, is close by.

31st The 31st Corps, with headquarters at Tadcaster, first appeared in the *Army List* for July 1860. Officers were appointed – Captain Charles Shann, Lieutenant John A Bromet, surgeon Thomas S Upton – but their commissions were not issued until 16 February 1864. Joined the 1st Admin Battalion in the following September and became 'K' Company of the new 1st Corps in 1880. Witnessed by the Volunteers in 1875–77 would have been the taking- down and reconstruction on a higher level – out of the reach of flood water from the Wharfe river – of St Mary's Church. Arthur Mee noted of the town its 'sprinkling of old houses' and 'big array of brewery chimneys'.

32nd Formed as one company at Holmfirth with J Earnshaw Morehouse as captain, John Harpin, lieutenant, George H Hinchliff, ensign and Charles J Trotter as surgeon. All four held commissions dated 2 June 1860. Joined the 5th Admin Battalion and became 'E' Company of the new 6th Corps in 1880. Six miles from Huddersfield, Holmfirth stands in the valley where the Holme and Ribble meet. The Volunteer Drill Hall was built in 1891 and the town's Technical Institute two years after that.

33rd Formed as one company at Wetherby with Captain Thomas Broadbent and Lieutenant James Coates commissioned on 24 December 1860. Ensign John Hannam made up the establishment on 1 March 1861. Joined the 1st Admin Battalion and was disbanded in 1863.

34th (Saddleworth) The 34th Corps was formed as one company at Saddleworth with Francis F Whitehead as captain, Joshua Hirst, lieutenant and George F Buckley, ensign. All three held commissions dated 10 September 1860. A second company was formed in May 1861, the command of which was given to Captain James Bradbury. The Bradbury family, records K D Pickup, provided four officers to the Saddleworth Corps, one Beckett Bradbury being its first surgeon. In April 1862 'Saddleworth' became part of the 34th's full title. By 1869 the establishment stood at eight companies, these being located at Saddleworth, Delph, Lydgate, Slaithwaite, Marsden, Golcar, Woodsome and Kirkburton. Reduced to four companies, however, in 1877 and at same time included in the 5th Admin Battalion. Became 'F', 'G', 'H' and 'J' Companies of the new 6th Corps in 1880. A busy wool-manufacturing town; one large employer at Saddleworth was the Royal George Mills, one of its officials being Captain Francis F Whitehead.

35th (Airedale)   Formed as one company at Keighley with William Ferrand as captain, William L Marriner, lieutenant and Joseph Craven, ensign. All three held commissions dated 27 October 1860. Also appointed were the Revd William Busfield as chaplain and Angus Cameron, who became surgeon. Joined the 2nd Admin Battalion in 1865, 'Airedale' being added to the title in 1862. The 35th was increased to two companies in November 1861, three in 1876, and became 'D' to 'F' Companies of the new 9th Corps in 1880. The tall clock-tower of Keighley's Mechanics' Institute and Technical School (opened in 1870) gave the time to those of the town, its library books to read.

36th   Formed as one company at Rotherham with Edward Robinson as captain, Fretwell W Hoyle, lieutenant and Matthew E Chambers, ensign. All three held commissions dated 19 October 1860. Joined the 4th Admin Battalion in 1862 and became 'J' Company of the new 8th Corps in 1880.

37th   Formed as one company at Barnsley with Walter S Stanhope as captain, Robert C Clarke, lieutenant, William A Potter, ensign and John Blackburn as surgeon. All four held commissions dated 2 November 1860. Joined the 3rd Admin Battalion in March 1862, transferring to 4th Admin in April 1863. Became 'F' and 'H' Companies of the new 8th Corps in 1880. Perhaps an early drill ground for the 37th Corps was the park given to the people of Barnsley in 1861 by the widow of the railway engineer Joseph Locke. And perhaps Parkin Jeffcock, John Mammatt and Thomas Embleton, three names recorded as 'heroes' on the bronze memorial by the Doncaster road recalling a pit disaster in 1866, were known to the Volunteers.

38th   Formed as one company at Selby with Robert Parker as captain, John Marshall, lieutenant and William Liversidge, ensign. All three held commissions dated 1 January 1861. Also appointed at the same time were the Revd Francis W Harper as chaplain and Thomas W Burkitt, who became surgeon. Joined the 3rd Admin Battalion, transferring to 1st Admin in 1863, and became 'L' Company of the new 1st Corps in 1880. At Selby Abbey the big six-light window in the south transept shows various scenes from the Bible; there are also portraits of Ensign William Liversidge and his wife, who gave the glass.

39th   Formed as one company at Bingley with William Ellis as captain, John Benjamin Popplewell, lieutenant and George Henry Townend, ensign. All three held commissions dated 8 April 1861. A second company was formed in August 1869 the command of which was given to Titus Salt jun. It was no doubt due to his influence that the headquarters of the 39th Corps were moved in August 1871 to Saltaire. The industrial town with the biggest mills in Yorkshire and 800 houses for its workers which had been entirely built by the enterprise of his father, Sir Titus Salt. The corps was disbanded in April 1875.

40th   Formed at Hoyland Nether with George K Day as captain, Joshua H Dawes, lieutenant and Joshua Biram, ensign. All three held commissions dated 19 March 1863. Appointed at the same time were the Revd J Cordeaux, who became chaplain to the corps, and Robert Adamson, its surgeon. Joined the 4th Admin Battalion, moving headquarters to Wath-upon-Dearne in 1866, and became 'G' Company of the new 8th Corps in 1880. Six miles south-east of Barnsley, Hoyland Nether gave employment in its coal mines, brick and tile works. Much was the same at Wath-upon-Dearne.

41st   Formed as one company at Mirfield with Edward Day as captain, Joseph S Hurst, lieutenant and Thomas Wade, ensign. All three held commissions dated 23 November 1864. Joined the 5th Admin Battalion and became 'K' Company of the new 6th Corps in 1880. At Mirfield, on the

Calder five miles from Huddersfield, the townspeople, by public subscription, built St Mary's Church in 1871. The Masonic Hall was opened in 1887. Wool, coal, and malt kilns gave employment to the area. Blake Hall is nearby where Anne Brontë was governess.

42nd Formed as one company at Haworth with George Merrall as captain, John Sugden, lieutenant and George H Merrall, ensign. All three held commissions dated 9 April 1866. Appointed at the same time were Amos Ingham as surgeon and the Revd Joshua B Grant, who became chaplain. Joined the 2nd Admin Battalion and became 'G' Company of the new 9th Corps in 1880. The church of St Michael and All Angels, where there is a memorial tablet to the Brontë family, who came to Haworth in 1820, was built in 1880. All around there were mills much written about, of course, by the sisters.

43rd The services of the 43rd Corps at Batley were accepted on 22 June 1867, Benjamin Sherd being commissioned as captain on 16 October 1867. Joined the 3rd Admin Battalion, was later increased to two companies, and became 'J' and 'K' Companies of the new 5th Corps in 1880. Batley, a busy town of woollen mills producing much for the army, is just under two miles from Dewsbury.

44th Formed at Meltham with Captain Edward C Goody and Lieutenant Thomas J Hurst commissioned on 29 August 1868. The Revd Edward C Watson was appointed as chaplain to the corps at the same time. Joined the 5th Admin Battalion and was disbanded in 1876. Meltham, where many were employed in the mills, is five miles from Huddersfield.

45th Formed at Bingley on 30 June 1875 largely from former members of the recently disbanded 39th Corps. Joined the 2nd Admin Battalion and became 'H' Company of the new 9th Corps in 1880. On the Aire, just under six miles from Bradford and on the edge of industrial Yorkshire, Bingley's All Saints' Church was restored in 1871, Holy Trinity being opened five years earlier.

Further Research

The Army List
By far the most comprehensive record of officers that served in the Volunteer Force is the War Office *Monthly Army List*. These record every officer serving as of date of publication – although a *List* dated, eg, January 1860, will be correct up to the previous month. Here we have names, ranks, dates of commissions, which enable the researcher to compile a full record of a man's journey through the officer ranks from his entry into the Volunteer Force through to such time that he retires, resigns or dies. Later on, as Volunteer officers were required to pass as efficient in various subjects; these qualifications are also shown.

Muster Rolls
Although other ranks do not appear in the *Army List* their names were recorded in muster rolls compiled by individual volunteer corps. Here we will usually find name, rank, date of enrolment into the corps, address and occupation. Sadly, these precious references are now few and far between. Look for them in county record offices, local and regimental museums, and the National Archives, which have a good number.

Published Unit Records
If there is any printed matter connected with the Volunteer Force scarcer than the muster roll, it is the published 'Regimental History'. A dozen or so, what might be termed as 'full' records at best, these I have mentioned in my own list of sources and throughout the text. There have been, however, a good number of short booklets, or lengthy magazine articles, published over the years, which are well worth tracking down. Again, county record offices should have these to hand. But knowing what to ask for is always a problem and I recommend – what the military historian anyway has come to term as his 'bible' on such matters – Arthur S White's *A Bibliography of Regimental Histories of the British Army*. For many years out of print, but thankfully now available as a reprint from publishers Naval & Military Press, ISBN 9781843421559.

Published General Histories
I can confidently refer to my own work as 'unique' in as much as it is a complete record of every RVC that existed. But for a greatly detailed *general* account of the Volunteer Force, featuring its social and political aspects, I must recommend Ian F W Beckett's *Riflemen Form: A Study of the Rifle Volunteer Movement 1859–1908*. Again, a much welcome reprint, this time from Pen & Sword, ISBN 9781844156122.

Local Newspapers
Local newspapers are a must. Items notifying meetings to discuss the formation of volunteer corps, who joined them, where they drilled, what they wore, where they camped and what parades they took part in, were regular features.

National Archives
As previously mentioned, there are muster rolls to be seen here. Also recommended are the useful but incomplete Pay Lists for Volunteer Staff (WO 13/4622–4675), Registers of the Volunteer Officers' Decoration (WO330/3–4), and Registers for Other Ranks Volunteer Long Service Medal (WO 102/21). Those all-important *Army Lists* are available on open shelves.

Appendix A

Order of precedence of counties

1	Devonshire	34	Roxburghshire
2	Middlesex	35	Cinque Ports
3	Lancashire	36	Monmouthshire
4	Surrey	37	Cornwall
5	Pembrokeshire	38	Ross-shire
6	Derbyshire	39	Worcestershire
7	Oxfordshire	40	Inverness-shire
8	Cheshire	41	Warwickshire
9	Wiltshire	42	Lincolnshire
10	Sussex	43	Denbighshire
11	Edinburgh (City)	44	Hampshire
12	Essex	45	Somersetshire
13	Northumberland	46	Forfarshire
14	Renfrewshire	47	Cambridgeshire
15	Northamptonshire	48	Shropshire
16	Dorsetshire	49	London
17	Norfolk	50	Yorkshire (East Riding)
18	Staffordshire	51	Hertfordshire
19	Berkshire	52	Perthshire
20	Gloucestershire	53	Berwickshire
21	Brecknockshire	54	Sutherlandshire
22	Suffolk	55	Kincardineshire
23	Stirlingshire	56	Haverfordwest
24	Buckinghamshire	57	Haddingtonshire
25	Lanarkshire	58	Isle of Wight
26	Kent	59	Ayrshire
27	Glamorganshire	60	Dumfriesshire
28	Nottinghamshire	61	Elginshire
29	Merionethshire	62	Argyllshire
30	Yorkshire (West Riding)	63	Cardiganshire
31	Leicestershire	64	Durham
32	Midlothian	65	Wigtownshire
33	Aberdeenshire	66	Buteshire

67	Yorkshire (North Riding)	82	Linlithgowshire
68	Cumberland	83	Selkirkshire
69	Herefordshire	84	Banffshire
70	Dumbartonshire	85	Radnorshire
71	Huntingdonshire	86	Flintshire
72	Carnarvonshire	87	Berwick-on-Tweed
73	Montgomeryshire	88	Clackmannanshire
74	Orkney	89	Tower Hamlets
75	Carmarthenshire	90	Nairnshire
76	Caithness-shire	91	Peebleshire
77	Kircudbrightshire	92	Isle of Man
78	Westmoreland	93	Kinross-shire
79	Fifeshire	94	Anglesey
80	Bedfordshire	95	Shetland
81	Newcastle-upon-Tyne		

Appendix B

Alphabetical list of regiments with their associated Volunteer Corps

Argyll and Sutherland Highlanders: Argyllshire, Clackmannanshire, Dumbartonshire, Renfrewshire, Stirlingshire.
Bedfordshire: Hertfordshire, Bedfordshire.
Black Watch: Fifeshire, Forfarshire, Perthshire.
Border: Cumberland, Westmorland.
Buffs, East Kent: 2nd, 5th Kent.
Cameron Highlanders: Inverness-shire.
Cameronians: 1st, 2nd, 3rd, 4th, 7th Lanarkshire.
Cheshire: Cheshire.
Devonshire: Devonshire.
Dorsetshire: Dorsetshire.
Duke of Cornwall's Light Infantry: Cornwall.
Duke of Wellington's: 4th, 6th, 9th Yorkshire West Riding.
Durham Light Infantry: Durham.
East Lancashire: 2nd, 3rd Lancashire.
East Surrey: 1st, 3rd, 5th, 7th Surrey.
East Yorkshire: Yorkshire East Riding.
Essex: Essex.
Gloucestershire: Gloucestershire.
Gordon Highlanders: Aberdeenshire, Banffshire, Kincardineshire.
Hampshire: Hampshire, Isle of Wight.
Highland Light Infantry: 5th, 6th, 8th, 9th, 10th Lanarkshire.
King's Liverpool: 1st, 5th, 13th, 15th, 18th, 19th Lancashire; Isle of Man.
King's Own Royal Lancaster: 10th Lancashire.
King's Own Scottish Borderers: Roxburgh and Selkirk, Berwickshire, Dumfrieshire, Galloway.
King's Own Yorkshire Light Infantry: 5th Yorkshire West Riding.
King's Royal Rifle Corps: 1st, 2nd, 4th, 5th, 6th, 9th, 10th, 11th, 12th, 13th, 21st, 22nd, 25th, 26th, 27th Middlesex; London.
King's Shropshire Light Infantry: Shropshire, Herefordshire.
Lancashire Fusiliers: 8th, 12th, 17th Lancashire.
Leicestershire: Leicestershire.
Lincolnshire: Lincolnshire.
Manchester: 4th, 6th, 7th, 16th, 17th, 20th, 22nd Lancashire.
Middlesex: 3rd, 8th, 11th, 17th Middlesex.
Norfolk: Norfolk.
North Lancashire: 11th, 14th Lancashire.
North Staffordshire: 2nd, 5th Staffordshire.
Northamptonshire: Northamptonshire.
Northumberland Fusiliers: Northumberland, Newcastle-upon-Tyne.
Oxfordshire Light Infantry: Oxfordshire, Buckinghamshire.

Queen's Royal West Kent: 1st, 3rd, 4th Kent.
Queen's Royal West Surrey: 2nd, 4th, 6th, 8th Surrey.
Rifle Brigade: 7th, 14th, 15th, 16th, 18th, 19th, 20th, 21st, 24th, 26th Middlesex; Tower
   Hamlets.
Royal Berkshire: Berkshire.
Royal Fusiliers: 5th, 9th, 10th, 11th, 22nd, 23rd Middlesex; Tower Hamlets.
Royal Scots: Edinburgh, Midlothian, Haddingtonshire, Linlithgowshire, Berwickshire.
Royal Scots Fusiliers: Galloway, Ayrshire, Dumfrieshire, Roxburgh and Selkirk.
Royal Sussex: Sussex, Cinque Ports.
Royal Warwickshire: Warwickshire.
Royal Welsh Fusiliers: Denbighshire, Flintshire, Carnarvonshire.
Seaforth Highlanders: Elgin, Inverness, Ross-shire, Sutherlandshire.
Sherwood Foresters: Derbyshire, Nottinghamshire.
Somerset Light Infantry: Somersetshire.
South Lancashire: 9th, 21st Lancashire.
South Staffordshire: 1st, 3rd, 4th Staffordshire.
South Wales Borderers: Monmouthshire, Brecknockshire.
Suffolk: Suffolk, Cambridgeshire.
Welsh: Pembrokeshire, Glamorganshire.
West Yorkshire: 1st, 3rd, 7th Yorkshire West Riding.
Wiltshire: Wiltshire.
Worcestershire: Worcestershire.
York and Lancaster: 2nd, 8th Yorkshire West Riding.
Yorkshire: Yorkshire North Riding.

References

Awdry, Christopher. *Encyclopaedia of British Railway Companies*. Patrick Stephens Ltd, Wellingborough, 1990.

Beckett, Ian F W. *Riflemen Form*. Ogilby Trust, Aldershot, 1982.

Butt, R V J. The Directory of Railway Stations. Patrick Stephens Ltd, Sparkford, 1995.

Cassell's *Gazetteer of Great Britain and Ireland* , several editions.

Churton, E. *The Railroad Book of England 1851*. Edward Churton, London, 1851.

Cobb, Colonel M H. *The Railways of Great Britain: A Historical Atlas*, 2nd Edition. Ian Allan, Shepperton, 2006.

Dooner, Mildred G. *The 'Last Post'*. Southgate, Rochester 1903.

Grierson, Major General Sir James. *Records of the Scottish Volunteer Force*. Blackwood & Sons, 1909.

Hart, Colonel Charles J. *The History of the 1st Volunteer Battalion The Royal Warwickshire Regiment*. The Midland Counties Herald Ltd, Birmingham, 1906.

Hayhurst, T H. *A History and Some Records of the Volunteer Movement in Bury, Heywood, Rossendale and Ramsbottom in Bury*. Thomas Crompton & Co., Bury 1887.

Igglesden, Charles. *History of the East Kent Volunteers*. The Kentish Express Ltd, Ashford, 1899.

Kellerher, Jim. *The Paddington Rifles 1860–1912 in Bury*. Privately published, London 1984.

Mee, Arthur. *The King's England* series. Various volumes, Hodder and Stoughton, London, 1937–1967.

Owen, Bryn. *The History of the Welsh Militia and Volunteer Corps – Anglesey and Carnarvon*. Palace Books, Caernarfon, 1989.

Pevsner, Nikolaus (and others). *The Buildings of England* [and now Wales] series. Numerous volumes, Penguin, London, 1951–2000.

Pickup, K D. *West York Rifle Volunteers 1859–1887*. Cavendish Press, Leicester.

Richards, Walter. *His Majesty's Territorial Army*. Virtue & Co. 1910/11.

Rodney Wilde, Colonel E T. *Tower Hamlets Rifle Volunteer*s. Coningham Bros, Limehouse, 1910.

Sargeaunt, B E. *A Military History of the Isle of Man*. T Buncle & Co. Ltd, Arbroath, 1947.

Sturmey Cave, Colonel T. *A History of the First Volunteer Battalion Hampshire Regiment 1859 to 1889*. Simkin & Co., London 1905.

Winn, Christopher. *I Never Knew That About England*. Ebury Press, 2005.

Winn, Christopher. *I Never Knew That About Wales*. Ebury Press, 2005.

Winn, Christopher. *I Never Knew That About Scotland*. Ebury Press, 2007.

Winn, Christopher. *I Never Knew That About London*. Ebury Press, 2007.

Bulletin of the Military Historical Society, various issues 1948 to date.

Journal of the Society for Army Historical Research, various issues.

London Gazette 1859–1908.

Monthly Army List 1859–1908.

Territorial Year Book 1909.

Volunteer Service Gazette . Various issues.

Volunteer Service Magazine. Six Vols. May 1892 to June 1898.

Illustrated London News. Numerous issues 1859–90.

Local newspapers.

Regimental histories, magazines and journals – more than 250 consulted.